**The Soviet Government and the Jews
1948–1967**

The Soviet Government and the Jews 1948–1967

A documented study

BENJAMIN PINKUS
Ben-Gurion University of the Negev (Beer-Sheva)

General Editor
JONATHAN FRANKEL
The Hebrew University of Jerusalem

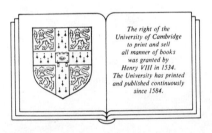

The right of the
University of Cambridge
to print and sell
all manner of books
was granted by
Henry VIII in 1534.
The University has printed
and published continuously
since 1584.

CAMBRIDGE UNIVERSITY PRESS

Cambridge
London   New York   New Rochelle   Melbourne   Sydney

Published in association with

THE HEBREW UNIVERSITY OF JERUSALEM – INSTITUTE OF CONTEMPORARY JEWRY

and

THE ISRAEL ACADEMY OF SCIENCES AND HUMANITIES

Published by the Press Syndicate of the University of Cambridge
The Pitt Building, Trumpington Street, Cambridge CB2 1RP
32 East 57th Street, New York, NY 10022, USA
296 Beaconsfield Parade, Middle Park, Melbourne 3206, Australia

First published 1984

Printed in Great Britain at
the University Press, Cambridge

Library of Congress catalogue card number: 83-18900

British Library cataloguing in publication data

The Soviet government and the Jews, 1948–1967.
1. Jews in Russia – Politics and government –
1953–   2. Jews in Russia – Persecutions
3. Soviet Union – Politics and government – 1953–
I. Pinkus, Benjamin
323.1'19'24047   DS135.R92

ISBN 0 521 24713 6

CE

Contents

v

Tables

vii

Documents

Preface

This book has been in the making for more than ten years, a relatively long period in which, even after the initial text was ready, the endless hurdles of translation, abbreviation, annotation, transliteration – in short, editing – had to be cleared. During all that time, I have been fortunate to receive help and encouragement from both individuals and institutions, here and abroad.

First, and above all, I should like to express my true thanks to my friend and colleague, Jonathan Frankel of the Hebrew University, who is general editor of a series (of which this volume is part) on the Jews in the Soviet Union projected by the Institute of Contemporary Jewry. There is no doubt that without his tireless assistance and efforts, patience and perseverance, this book would never have seen the light of day. The Institute of Contemporary Jewry, under the auspices of which this project went forward, gave it throughout both moral and material support and its successive directors during this period – Moshe Davis, Yehuda Bauer, Haim Avni, Mordechai Altshuler – together ensured that it would be seen through to completion.

It gives me much pleasure to thank Nathan Rotenstreich and Joshua Prawer, who as members of the Israel Academy of Sciences and Humanities gave their support to this project. This book is published jointly by the Academy and the Institute. Israel Getzler of the Hebrew University carefully read the manuscript and made many suggestions which proved to be of great value and for which I am very much in his debt.

It was truly a stroke of luck to find in Jerusalem a translator of the calibre of Anthony Benjamin who combines an unusual knowledge of languages with great breadth of knowledge in many areas. He prepared the initial English text, but unfortunately was no longer here in the final stages – his decision to join the Israeli Foreign Office, albeit our loss, was its gain. Norma Schneider of the Academy and Philippa Lewis (now Mrs S. Shimrat), both highly skilled editors, devoted enormous efforts to the preparation of the manuscript for publication. Elizabeth O'Beirne-Ranelagh of Cambridge University Press has been responsible for the final copy-editing and displayed quite unusual professionalism in going over this exacting text. I appreciate the work and skill which all four have invested herein and cannot find words to thank them enough.

I should like to take the opportunity to thank the following institutions and members of the Hebrew University who in various ways provided me with assistance: Geoffrey Wigoder, Aharon Kedar and Menahem Kaufman of the

Institute of Contemporary Jewry; the Centre for Research and Document-
ation of East European Jewry and its staff members, Jacob M. Kelman, Savely
Dudakov, Danuta Dvora Zeichner, Rivka Gurvich, Sima Izikas and Nina
Bibichkova; the Soviet and East European Research Centre and specifically
Edith Rogovin Frankel (the Director), Shulamit Tsur and Ginette Avram; the
University and National Library and its staff members, Avraham Wolfson,
Boris Korsch and Maya Ulanovskaya. Abroad, I mention with thanks the
Bibliothèque de Documentation Internationale Contemporaine (Paris) and,
particularly, the Director of its Slavic Division, Mme S. Kaplan; and Cam-
bridge University Press, particularly William Davies and, of course, again,
Elizabeth O'Beirne-Ranelagh. Hanna Maschler, Hava Turniansky, and
Naphtali Pratt provided me with invaluable advice on the tangled problems of
transliteration from Hebrew, Yiddish and Ukrainian respectively. Amy
Lederhendler's editorial skills and experience proved indispensable in the
proof-reading. Norma Schneider, already thanked above, went over the proofs
with the greatest care and has thus seen the manuscript over a period of years
through all the final stages on its way to becoming a book.

Finally, however banal it may sound, I do not want to overlook my wife and
three sons who found themselves perforce full partners on this long road. To
them this book is dedicated.

Sdeh Boker   B.P.
June 1983

Acknowledgements

The research for this volume was made possible by the assistance of the Memorial Foundation for Jewish Culture. It was prepared for publication with the help of the Leah Goldberg Fund for Russian Studies (The Hebrew University).

Note on transliteration and style

The system of transliteration from Yiddish is based on the YIVO system as formulated in Uriel Weinreich's dictionary; from Russian on that of the Library of Congress; and from Hebrew on that used by the *Encyclopaedia Judaica*. However, in the case of Russian and Hebrew I have introduced modifications in order to ease the way for the non-specialist reader (hence, for example, *Izvestiya* rather than *Izvestiia*; or *magid* rather than *maggid*). In the spelling of names, diacritical marks have not been used, and the system has accordingly been somewhat modified. (Hence, *Yizḥak* is used in bibliographical entries, but Yitskhak in the text.) First names have in the main been transliterated either from the Russian or the Hebrew forms. Thus, the Yiddish variant (Shloyme, not Shlomo) has generally not been used. Both variants are, of course, spelt in the same way in Hebrew and Yiddish. To have tried to divide the sheep from the goats (Yiddishists from Zionists, etc.) would have involved us in a rather arbitrary exercise given the lack of pluralist expression in the USSR. Yiddish variants are, however, given in the index. Moreover, this rule has not always been pushed to its limits (e.g. Itsik, not Yitskhak, Feffer). Finally, it should be noted that names appearing in the Documents are as a rule transliterated according to the language of the text (Russian, Polish, Hebrew, Yiddish, etc.).

Documents originally published in English have been reproduced in their original form with only minor changes in spelling made to achieve uniformity of style.

Introduction

Over two hundred thousand Jews have left the Soviet Union since 1971. Perhaps fifty thousand Germans as well as hundreds of dissidents of various national origin have also emigrated in this period. While this development is largely taken for granted today, few observers anticipated it in the late 1960s. Nonetheless, for all the element of unpredictability, the new Jewish emigration – a phenomenon which has its roots deep in Soviet history – is the culmination of a long and complex process.

This work examines the Soviet policies towards the nationality problem in general and the Jews in particular during the years 1948–67. Although emigration was not then treated by the Soviet government as a legitimate policy alternative, the period from the late Stalin years to the 1967 War in the Middle East saw the maturation of those factors which made possible the *volte-face* of March 1971. It was a time of critical historical importance in the development of Soviet Jewry.

In 1948, the State of Israel was established with the decisive support of the USSR and other countries of the Soviet bloc. At the same time, the years 1948–9 witnessed the murder (by the secret police) of the famous Yiddish actor, Shlomo Mikhoels; the closing of the Jewish Anti-Fascist Committee; the liquidation of all the institutions responsible for Yiddish culture; and the launching of the anti-cosmopolitan campaign. This dichotomy revealed as never before, and in their most extreme form, the contradictions inherent in Soviet policy towards its Jewish population.

The year 1967 was also of major significance in that it was something of a turning point. Policies sporadically introduced since Stalin's death to improve the situation of the Jewish minority at home, as well as relations with Israel, were now halted and even reversed. Henceforward, the violently anti-Israeli line which characterised Soviet foreign and information policies took forms which could be seen – and were frequently intended to be seen – as simply anti-Jewish. This development in turn encouraged a marked rise in Jewish national consciousness. The resultant pressure from above and resistance from below reinforced each other to create a syndrome which culminated in the decision to permit large-scale emigration.

Such contradiction and paradox have, in fact, always characterised the attitude of the Communist regime to Soviet Jews. Indeed, to a large extent, the latter-day problems in this field can be traced back to the 'original sin' inherent in the Marxist–Leninist ideology, and this remains true even though ideological considerations have in the main exerted a diminishing influence on Soviet policy-making since the late 1930s. The fact that Lenin, Stalin and their heirs denied the Jewish people recognition as a nationality; that they constantly declared it a relic from the historic past kept in existence by anti-Semitism alone; that they waged an unrelenting war against the Bund (more than against Zionism) because of its support for the reactionary idea of a Jewish 'nation'; that they did not revise this theory even after the October Revolution when (especially during the 1920s) they made far-reaching concessions to the non-Russian nationalities – all this inevitably exerted a profound influence on the attitude of the regime towards the Jews. As a national group, they were placed at a permanent disadvantage compared with the other major Soviet nationalities. And, as will be demonstrated in this work, even in the post-Stalin period, no really significant changes in the ideological sphere were introduced.

It is true that in its opening decades – especially in the 1920s and early 1930s – the Soviet regime developed a wide-flung network of Jewish national institutions, such as the Jewish sections of the Communist Party; the agricultural settlement societies, *Ozet* and *Komzet*; the Jewish national self-governing areas – *raiony* – and even the autonomous *oblast*, Birobidzhan. However, this constructive effort was accompanied throughout by an even more intensive campaign of destruction. The Jewish community structure (which underwent a process of rapid democratisation between February and October 1917); the entire world of Hebrew-language schools, literature and culture; and the multitude of Jewish (non-Communist) political parties and movements were all systematically undermined, outlawed and eliminated by the Bolshevik regime in its first decade of power. The synagogue has survived until the present day, but since the 1920s its numbers have been progressively reduced to the point where only a few dozen remain, their freedom ever more tightly constricted.

Furthermore, despite the large financial investments of the mid and late 1920s, the Soviet commitment to the creation of a Yiddish-based Jewish culture was never wholehearted. On the contrary, it would seem that this turn of policy was more tactical manoeuvre than strategic doctrine. Its implementation over the long run was always very much in doubt, partly because of a series of objective difficulties, but above all because of the dialectical – and fundamentally self-contradictory – nature of Soviet policy towards the nationalities in general and the Jews in particular.

The Communist regime made far-reaching, formal concessions to the non-Russian nationalities in the name of national self-determination and equality, but, at the same time, it emptied those concessions of real political substance in the name of socialist internationalism and Bolshevik centralism. Russification, condemned by the new regime as doctrinally reactionary, nonetheless retained its *de facto* legitimacy as the concrete expression of international proletarian solidarity. The Jewish people, probably more than any other national minority, found itself selected as a model to prove the thesis that non-territorial ethnic groups were pre-ordained by modern sociological trends – industrialisation, urbanisation, proletarianisation – to assimilate with the dominant (i.e. the Great Russian) nation. Thus, by the early 1930s, the debate within the Soviet leadership between those advocating Jewish assimilation and those (most notably Kalinin and Smidovich) who were for some form of Jewish national survival had been clearly settled in favour of the former school of thought.

The turn towards Russification and against the smaller nations was given official recognition at the 17th Party Congress of 1934, when Stalin made it known that in his view 'bourgeois nationalism' was a greater danger than 'Great Russian chauvinism'. Since he had long ago indicated that many of the minor Soviet nationalities (most notably the Koreans, Karelians, Greeks, and Germans) would be the first to assimilate, there was now even less reason for the state to invest substantial sums of money in their survival. From the mid-1930s, the same logic was applied to the network of Yiddish-based Soviet institutions, which were increasingly deprived of funds. Although this policy was not formulated officially, it found unmistakable expression in deeds. The chances that Stalin would permit anything to remain of Soviet Yiddish culture were further reduced during World War II, when he decided to deport a whole series of Soviet nationalities to the wastes of Central Asia – a decision which revealed as never before his contempt for the weaker national groups as well as his impatience to see them depart from the stage of history.

While Soviet nationality policies have always been marked by a high degree of theoretical dualism and practical self-contradiction, the same could not initially be said of the Communist attitude towards anti-Semitism. On the contrary, Lenin repeatedly and vociferously condemned anti-Semitism as an expression and weapon of reaction and as counter-revolution; in the 1920s, official campaigns were even launched to educate the public against it. However, even then, Stalin made covert attempts to exploit anti-Semitic motifs in his struggle for political control against Trotsky, Kamenev, Zinoviev and other leaders of Jewish origin who opposed the doctrine of 'socialism in one country'.

Surveying Soviet history as a whole, it becomes apparent that anti-Semitism, while it has different forms from those prevalent in the Tsarist period, has nevertheless remained a permanent feature of life in Russia. Nazi propaganda, which had free rein in the vast occupied areas of the Soviet Union during the war, and the crass anti-Jewish policies implemented by Stalin from 1948 to 1953 (which are traced in detail in this work), combined to reactivate those anti-Semitic energies which had largely lain dormant since the end of the Russian Civil War in 1921. The long-term result has been a permanent deterioration in the status of Soviet Jewry – a deterioration which has been increasingly institutionalised and which has produced immense bitterness among many of the Jews themselves.

The post-Stalin period has witnessed improvements in the policy towards the non-Russian nations in general, and even towards the non-territorial nationalities. For example, schools have been established in the USSR in which the language of instruction is German, Polish or Hungarian. Newspapers, theatre groups and radio broadcasts employing those languages have similarly reappeared. But these steps have been far too sporadic and piecemeal to have solved the basic cultural problems of these national groups.

As for the Jews, they came increasingly to feel trapped in a web from which there was no apparent escape. True, the post-Stalin regime made certain gestures of good will towards the Jewish population, but these (most notably perhaps the renewal of publications in Yiddish) proved to be more symbolic than substantive. Thus, the Jews were forced to conclude that, without fundamental changes in Soviet policy, their long-term situation would actually deteriorate. Such changes have not been forthcoming for a number of reasons. Any major dispensation to one national group can only provoke demands from the other Soviet nationalities for similar concessions, thereby threatening the entire system of state centralism. Moreover, in the case of the Jews, a fundamental change (e.g. the granting of Jewish education in the Russian language) would involve a far-reaching revision of Leninist doctrine. But in the nationality field, the Soviet regime has tended to change course grudgingly and with extreme reluctance. In this respect, it is noteworthy that, despite extremely heavy pressure both at home and abroad, their autonomous republics have not been returned to the Volga Germans and Crimean Tatars. And to these essentially pragmatic considerations it must be added that a considerable number of today's Soviet leaders are themselves strongly nationalistic, even anti-Semitic, and would find it psychologically repugnant to improve the situation of Soviet Jewry.

As a result, a measure of stability came to mark Soviet policies towards the Jews in the period 1953–67. For all the various initiatives and innovations, the post-Stalin leadership basically steered a course between the Scylla of late Stalinism (with its implicit threat of a new Holocaust) and the Charybdis of far-reaching liberalisation (with its threat of political and social instability). Since this policy was neither repressive enough nor generous enough to inhibit opposition, the period 1953–67 witnessed a rising level of national consciousness and activity among Soviet Jews. There was a clear feeling of spiritual malaise which, while it may have produced despair in many, drove others to seek new solutions beyond the sphere of the official ideology.

As can be seen from the documents assembled in this book, it is erroneous to argue, as many do, that the Soviet Jews' search for a national identity began only as a result of the Six-Day War. The effect of that war was rather to accelerate and accentuate processes which had long been at work.

If left to itself, the social development of Soviet Russia – modernisation, secularisation, acculturation – combined with the official ideology of Communist internationalism might well (as Lenin had always argued) have produced rapid assimilation among the Jews. To a major extent, such a development was, in fact, far advanced by the late 1930s. But other factors emerged which counterbalanced and reversed the trend towards straightforward integration. Thus World War II, which threatened to wipe out European Jewry in its entirety, had a profound emotional impact on Russian Jews. This was dramatically demonstrated when, for example, writers who were apparently totally assimilated recklessly took up themes drawn from Jewish history and the Jewish religion. When the local population in the Nazi-occupied areas demonstrated their indifference to – and even cooperated in – the destruction of the Jewish population, the deep sense of shock this produced among surviving Jews did much to encourage reassessments, new reckonings and the re-evaluation of values. Belief in the 'fraternity of the socialist peoples', so widely and deeply cherished in the twenties and thirties, was cruelly undermined.

An even greater cause of disillusionment was initiated by Stalin's policy during 1948–53, the so-called 'black years' which will be examined in detail below. That Stalin not only destroyed Soviet institutions which supported Yiddish culture but also launched a campaign against the assimilated Jewish intelligentsia (e.g. the anti-cosmopolitan campaign and the Doctors' Plot) demonstrated that the Jews were to be damned for remaining separate and damned for not. The post-Stalin leadership did put a stop to these policies of terror, but this in itself was not enough to restore faith in the justice and truth of Communist internationalism. The initial hope that far-reaching change was imminent could hardly survive the constant demonstration that anti-Jewish policies would be adopted whenever *raison d'état* so dictated. Crude attacks on Judaism, Zionism and the State of Israel became permanent features of the post-Stalin era. And, while such attacks undoubtedly intimidated many Jews, they encouraged others to abandon their Communist faith in favour of a new, or renewed, Jewish national identity.

However, an analysis which stresses anti-Semitism as the sole factor in the revival of national consciousness would be grossly one-sided. Forces of attraction exerted a powerful influence as well, e.g. the impact of Soviet Jewry's encounter with the Jewish communities in the areas annexed in 1939–40 – the three Baltic states, the eastern regions of inter-war Poland and Romania. The Jews in these areas had maintained and developed all those religious, national and political institutions which had been destroyed in the Soviet Union. And they served as living links with a past otherwise lost.

The establishment of the State of Israel, coming as it did so soon after the Holocaust, was seen by many Soviet Jews as a phenomenon almost beyond the realm of rational understanding, a phoenix risen from the ashes. The restoration of the Jewish people to its historic homeland, an event completely outside the Marxist–Leninist frame of reference (although paradoxically supported by Stalinist Russia), proved to be one more factor weakening the hold of Communist doctrine. But apart from its historical significance, the State of Israel became an active force in the life of Soviet Jewry from its inception. With the exception of the short period between 1953 and 1954, Israel and the Soviet Union maintained diplomatic relations throughout the 1948–67 period. The presence of the Israeli embassy stimulated extraordinary interest among significant sections of Soviet Jewry, an interest which the Israeli diplomatic staff strove to maintain at a high level. What is more, particularly in the 1960s, Israel became the driving force behind a worldwide effort dedicated to protesting the plight of Soviet Jewry. The knowledge that such a movement was working on their behalf in Israel, Western Europe and America gave confidence and courage to those Jews in the USSR seeking to give real expression to their rising national consciousness. Impinging upon these already active processes, the Six-Day War, as already suggested above, served as a powerful catalyst. It encouraged the older generation to make the transition from re-evaluation to active politics, and often had the traumatic effect of leading youth to make a total break with former lives by replacing their goal of integration into the USSR with exodus instead.

It is true that every individual reacts differently to the anomalous situation in which the Russian Jews have found themselves since 1953, one which permits them to be neither fully Russian nor fully Jewish, but which forces them into a situation of legalised inferiority. Nevertheless, few can escape the high internal tensions and identity crises bound to result from living in a society committed to integration by ideology and discrimination in practice.

A considerable section of Soviet Jewry (it is impossible to estimate its numerical strength) will pay any price to integrate itself into the majority ethnic group with maximum possible speed. A second group (in all probability the majority) sees no realistic way to escape the *status quo* and therefore seeks to live life as best it can under the constant pressures to which it is subjected. A third group (almost certainly many hundreds of thousands) sees emigration as an immediate alternative and is ready to join the outflow if only the Soviet authorities permit. This third group is divided into committed Zionists determined to go to Israel and those who would prefer to rebuild their lives in the developed countries, primarily English-speaking, of the West. And even this last subdivision is far from homogeneous; some of those arriving in the USA, Canada or Australia are eager to remain Jews, while others flee any association with the Jewish community, hoping to achieve the total integration denied them in the USSR.

Now, in the early 1980s, it is impossible to predict what the future holds for Soviet Jewry. Will the emigration be renewed? Might it even culminate in a policy of expulsion similar to that which was, in effect, carried out in Poland in 1968? Could there be a reversion to Stalinism, with its threat of physical destruction of Russian Jewry? Or will there be some return to the *status quo ante* associated with the 1953–67 period, when there was no terror (at least in the Stalinist sense), no significant emigration, but also no full equality for Russian Jews? And, if the latter, would such a policy of compromise and *ad hoc* adjustment prove inherently unstable as it did then?

In the material assembled here, the student can examine the forces at work in the post-war era. Essentially, the book covers two different periods: the late Stalin years, 1948–53; and the post-Stalin years, 1953–67, which divides into three sub-periods: the interregnum (1953–7), the Khrushchev period (1957–64) and the 'collective leadership', as it then was, of Brezhnev, Kosygin and Podgorny (1964–7).

The material has been arranged in an attempt to move from the general to the particular, although it has not always proved possible to maintain this policy with the degree of consistency which would have been aesthetically desirable. Thus, the first two chapters are devoted to the Soviet theory of nationality and its application to the Jews; to the legal status of Soviet Jewry; and to its demographic development. Chapters 3–6 move from theory to the harsh realities imposed by the persistence of anti-Semitism and its exploitation by the regime. The inner core, Chapters 7–12, seeks to shed light on the internal religious and cultural life of Soviet Jewry, even though here too the regime has always played a critical role. The final chapter deals with oriental Jewish communities (Georgians, Mountain Jews, Bukharans, Krymchaks), about whom relatively little has hitherto been published in English. Indeed, it should be added that this work represents the first attempt to provide the English reader with the documentary material necessary to understand Soviet policy towards the Jewish population of the USSR in a period of crucial importance.

PART I

Government ideology and the Jews

1

The Jewish national question in the Soviet Union

Do the Jews of the Soviet Union constitute a nation in the same way as the other nations living in the multi-national Soviet State? Is their political and constitutional status determined by Marxist–Leninist theory on the national question or by pragmatic political considerations alone? Does the determination of this status influence the position of the Jews in the Soviet Union and the formation of their national consciousness? And, finally, can one speak of a consistent approach in the policies of the Soviet Union towards Soviet Jewry?

These are the central questions which we shall endeavour to clarify, albeit in brief, in this chapter.

The Jewish national question in Soviet theory and constitutional documents

The Soviet theory of nationality and the Jews

There is no doubt that the Jewish problem has engaged Marxist theoreticians from the times of Marx himself, who devoted one of his early works to it, until today. As a complicated problem, an anomaly which does not easily fit into rigid theoretical frameworks, the Jewish question confronts them with a serious challenge and a perpetual torment. If Marx confines his debate on the Jewish national question to the sphere of religion and the Emancipation, and to the framework of general discussions on the question of alienation, of which he considers religion to be one of the most extreme forms,[1] Lenin and Stalin – despite their being Marx's most consistent followers in all that concerns a negative attitude towards Jewish national existence – adopt purely ethnic terminology.

Thus, faithful to his teacher Marx, Lenin declared at the outset of his career that the Jews constitute not a nation but a historical remnant that owes its existence to the persistence of anti-Semitism. He inveighed not only against Zionism but also against the Bund, which, he said, was obsessed with the reactionary Zionist concept of the Jewish 'nation'.[2] Basing himself on Kautsky, Lenin insisted that the Jews had ceased to exist as a nation because, without its own territory and common language, a nation is inconceivable.[3] The Bund therefore had no alternative, Lenin claimed with harsh irony, but to work out the concept of a special nationality of Russian Jews, whose language

(Yiddish) was 'Jargon' and whose territory, the Pale of Settlement.[4] The concept of the Jewish nation does not therefore stand up to scientific criticism and is politically reactionary.[5] The Jews, Lenin summed up, are merely a sect.[6]

In his work 'Marxism and the Jewish Question' Stalin repeated all Lenin's allegations in an even more concentrated and crude manner. In his view, the Jews are 'a nation which exists on paper only'; Zionism is a reactionary, bourgeois movement, and the Yiddish language, Jargon. Thus Russian Jewry's demand for national autonomy sounded strange, because 'autonomy is being proposed for a nation whose future is denied and whose very existence has yet to be proved'.[7]

Thus, it follows that Lenin, Stalin and the other Bolshevik leaders opposed not only the Zionist solution to the Jewish question, but also that proposed by the Bund, namely, the national–cultural autonomy programme of the Austrian social-democrats whereby the citizens of each nationality – irrespective of their place of habitation – would elect their own national council to run their cultural and educational life, while the state would maintain political and economic unity. Lenin called this solution, which had been conceived by socialist leaders, a 'bourgeois trick' intended to distract the proletariat since it would undoubtedly intensify the already considerable forces of nationalism and separatism among the several nations living in one state.

Since at this time Lenin saw the only solution to the national problem as national self-determination (and even this more in theory than in practice, because he believed that, when the time came, the various nations would choose to remain within the framework of the big state), the extra-territorial national minorities were left with no alternative but to assimilate. The general belief that socialism would devise a miraculous cure for the national contradictions inherent in the capitalist regime, and solve all the complex problems connected with the national question almost automatically, did not fade even after the October Revolution. However, as the new reality crystallised, this abstract theoretical approach could no longer be accepted. It became imperative to re-examine, this time pragmatically, the problem of meeting the growing demands of all nations within the framework of the new socialist state. The solution finally adopted was, in fact, a fairly faithful although largely unsuccessful copy of the Bundist theory. However, purely pragmatic considerations gave rise to the attempt to solve the national problem in the Soviet Union by amalgamating two contradictory theories: that of national–cultural autonomy based on the extra-territorial principle, with the Leninist–Stalinist theory of regional autonomy based on the territorial principle. This attempt concealed all those clashes, complications and inconsistencies which were to become part and parcel of Soviet policy on the national question.

The adoption of this pragmatic approach to all national minorities, including the Jews, found expression in a large number of constitutional documents,[8] as well as in the following institutions, which were established in the Soviet Union after 1918 and throughout the 1930s:

1 *Central institutions of administration*: For example, the Jewish Commissariats which operated within the framework of the People's Commissariat for Nationality Affairs

until the middle of 1923; the Jewish Sections of the Communist Party which existed until 1930; and the Organisation of Jewish Settlement (*Ozet*) which was liquidated in the middle of 1938.

2 *Local institutions of administration.* At this period these included five National Regions; about 200 Municipal National Soviets; sixty-seven Yiddish-language courts; Yiddish-language police stations; and 'Yiddish desks', whose functions were assistance to the Jewish population in its relations with the authorities.

3 *Cultural and educational institutions.* For example, the Yiddish writers' organisations, which were liquidated in 1932; four institutes of research and learning; twenty professional theatres and a large number of amateur theatrical groups, cultural clubs, museums; and about 1,400 kindergartens and schools with 160,000 pupils.[9]

However, the leaders of the *Evsektsiya*, including those from the ranks of the Bund, were well aware that the passing of the unique conjunction of circumstances – reinforced by the 12th Party Congress resolutions instituting the new policy towards the nationalities ('Ukrainisation', 'Belorussianisation') – meant that the Jewish national 'statehood', lacking as it did a firm territorial basis, could not long survive. Their acquaintance with Marxist–Leninist ideology on the national question left them no option but to understand that there was only one way in which the Jews of the Soviet Union could be removed from the category of 'unsolid', 'floating' peoples (the picturesque terms used by Stalin at the 1921 10th Party Congress), fated to disappear as soon as assimilation was intensified and to be reassigned to the more respectable classification of proper nations. They would have to be granted a territory of their own and consolidated on this territory. Hence, much effort went into various plans to establish 'a Jewish republic in the Soviet Union'.[10] But such attempts in the Crimea ended in failure due to opposition from the local Tatar and Ukrainian populations, as well as the blatant reluctance of the government to hand over the area in question for Jewish colonisation. And the Birobidzhan attempt was doomed to failure from the beginning.[11]

Even in the 1920s, two conflicting tendencies caused the Soviet leadership to be divided with regard to solving the Jewish problem: (1) the assimilationist trend, supported by Stalin and most other Communist Party leaders regardless of faction; and (2) the anti-assimilationists, with Kalinin as their most prominent spokesman. However, this second trend completely disappeared in the latter half of the 1930s with the far-reaching changes which took place in the Party and the state. And Stalin's definition – that 'a nation is a historically constituted, stable community of people, formed on the basis of a common language, territory, economic life and psychological make-up manifested in a common culture'[12] – took on its full significance.

This dogmatic and rigid definition of a nation, which disqualifies every ethnic group lacking even one of the four above-mentioned attributes, automatically excluded the Jews. Indeed, the *Large Soviet Encyclopedia* which appeared in 1952 defines 'The Jews' as 'different peoples of a common origin' who today constitute ethnic minorities at an advanced stage of assimilation (see Doc. 1). In other words, the emphasis here is on a number of Jewish minority groups rather than on one Jewish people dispersed throughout many lands.

In the post-Stalin period, and especially from the end of the 1950s, two conflicting approaches to the Jewish question began to take shape. The first and more interesting approach, which undoubtedly betokened an important change in the way the Jewish problem was being considered, was that of the Soviet ethnographer, S. Tokarev. Tokarev's definition of ethnic groups paves the way for the Jews to be included in the category of nations because (1) it was the broadest definition ever formulated in the Soviet Union; (2) he rejected the term 'characteristic feature', preferring the broader and far more flexible 'social relationships'; (3) he was one of the few, if not the only scholar who used attributes such as common origins and religion, firmly rejected by Stalin and Lenin as subjective and not materialistic, to characterise ethnic groups. Tokarev also affirmed that while territory does play an important role in the formation of every ethnic group at the outset of its development, a people may lose its common territory with further historical development and still retain its ethnic unity unimpaired. He illustrated this by giving examples of peoples who have partly lost their territorial unity, and also of those scattered throughout the world, e.g. the Armenians, Jews and Gypsies (see Doc. 3). Finally, Tokarev's argument that the ethnic community of the Jews is founded and preserved on the basis of religion further reinforced his position.

The second approach, that of the philosopher I. Tsameryan, is critical of Tokarev's stand on the Jewish question. Tsameryan felt that Tokarev's selection of the Jews to support his case on the question of common territory lacked foundation because a single Jewish nation does not exist.[13] The ethnographer V. Kozlov concurred with Tsameryan, affirming that the Jews long since ceased to be one people, with many of them having nothing left in common but the name and a number of faint notions regarding their common origin and fate (see Doc. 5). This approach is still the dominant one in the Soviet Union today.

The negative attitude towards Jewish national existence is most clearly expressed in the classifications of the ethnic groups residing in the Soviet Union. The Jews are not defined as a nation, the highest category, which is the most stable and has the most developed sense of national identity. Nor are they classified as a people (*narod*), the general term used for ethnic communities of different types. They are not even called a *narodnost*, the term used to refer to the minute groups living in Siberia and the Northern Caucasus. They are defined as a *natsionalnost* (nationality), a term of seemingly political significance, which reflects the authorities' desire to view the Jews as individuals, rather like atomised particles, and not as a united body with a feeling of national solidarity.

It is noteworthy that the Jews were even further downgraded in the Soviet hierarchy of nations after the Six-Day War. When the ethnographer Kozlov suggested his new typology of the nations living in the USSR, he began the ordering with the largest nation – the Russians – and then went on to peoples like the Ukrainians, Belorussians and Georgians, who constitute an absolute majority in the towns and villages of their republics. (In so doing, Kozlov indirectly calls into question the national sovereignty of nations like the Kazakhs, who have already lost this majority.) The Jews come only in the last category, 'ethnos', along with the Gypsies and the Assyrians (Aisors), and after national minorities like the Yukaghirs, the Ket and other minute groups.[14]

This, of course, not only contradicts the Jews' official constitutional status as a nation with its own autonomous national region, but also fails to correspond to the facts.

In sum, while the many searching debates in the Soviet Union on what constitutes a nation, which began in the 1960s and intensified after 1966, clearly pointed towards defining the Jews as a 'nation' (by eliminating the qualification of material indicators such as territory and raising the importance of national consciousness), in reality such conclusions were almost never drawn. On the contrary, it was still maintained that the Jews had not reached – and, what is more important, stood absolutely no chance of reaching – that stage of development which characterises a nation. This, so went the argument, is because of the historical circumstances which have left the Jews with a distinct structure and place in society (see Doc. 4). How far this assertion corresponds to the facts we shall see in the second section of this chapter, on the demography of Soviet Jewry.

The political and constitutional status of Soviet Jewry

The political and constitutional status of Soviet Jewry is both complicated and strange. It is our belief that it was determined on the basis of a temporary compromise between the Marxist–Leninist theory of a nation which deprives the Jews of national status and the pragmatic, circumstantial approach of the 1920s. While – ever since the establishment of an Autonomous National Area in Birobidzhan in 1928 and its up-grading to the Autonomous Jewish Region in 1934 – the Jews have in fact been recognised as a 'territorial national unit' with the corresponding political and legal status which provide for certain rights,[15] their low percentage of the Birobidzhan population has led the authorities to categorise them more and more as an 'extraterritorial national minority' (from the 1930s) or as an ethnic community on the verge of total integration with the civilisation and culture of another people (from the 1950s) (see, for example, Doc. 2). To further complicate matters, the fact that the Jews are also recognised as a religious community means that when the Soviet anti-religious policy is directed against the Jewish religion, it assumes the character of a struggle against Jewish national existence as well.

However, by far the most important edict, with regard to its effect on both the authorities and the Jews, was that of the Central Executive Committee and the Council of Peoples' Commissars on 27 December 1932, decreeing that the 'nationality' of all urban dwellers aged sixteen and over must be recorded in Paragraph 5 of his or her passport.[16]

Since the passport is of utmost importance in the Soviet Union, in the acquisition of a job or home, as well as in all the many contacts which Soviet citizens have with local government authorities, it has become a powerful means through which the authorities can control discrimination and favouritism on the basis of nationality. And since the citizen himself is not allowed to choose his nationality – apart from the one legal instance where the child of parents of different nationalities may choose the one he wishes to appear on his passport, or the illegal possibility of forgery – it is clear that this fixed legal category is of importance for the very existence of the Jews in the Soviet Union.

The retention of the paragraph on registration of nationality at the end of the 1950s and beginning of the 1960s, when there was a large-scale propaganda campaign to draw the nations closer together and integrate them, and despite the many rumours that it was to be removed shortly,[17] demonstrates that immediate practical considerations (particularly the supply of information to the security forces) outweigh not only ideological arguments but even long-term state interests.

The analysis of Soviet Government attitudes towards the Jewish question, such as that undertaken below, demonstrates that official policy not only refuses to recognise the Jews as a nation, but goes even further by fixing their political and constitutional status as a 'negative nationality', a status that holds no rights, but only restrictions.[18]

This method of viewing the Jews and fixing their political and legal status in the framework of Soviet national theory greatly serves, at least in the eyes of the leadership, the political interests of the regime. It has therefore become one of the central, dominant factors in determining the fate of Soviet Jewry for better or worse.

However, the internal contradictions inherent in this policy did much to insure that the national consciousness of Soviet Jews is, for the most part, not determined in the way that the Soviet leaders and theoreticians claim.

The national consciousness of Soviet Jewry

There is no need to emphasise the difficulties in ascertaining the degree of national consciousness among 'normal' nations, even those who have lived in their own independent state for generations. And these are nothing when compared to those involved in the case of an extra-territorial national minority lacking a clearly delineated state and territorial framework.

In order to know what national consciousness is and to permit an examination of its extent and its force, it is important first to define it; in other words, to define what a nation is. For, as we shall endeavour to show, the subjective feeling of belonging exercises a decisive and frequently even the sole influence in the maintenance of the Jewish nation.

Stalin's definition of a nation, quoted above, while it sought a purely objective basis, was obliged for political and tactical reasons to include 'psychic structure'. Since this term is understood by the majority of Soviet scholars as identical to national character or national consciousness, it contaminates Stalin's 'objective' definition with a thoroughly subjective factor. And the Marxist camp came up with an even more extremist approach, that of Otto Bauer, which, despite its claim to adherence to the historical, materialistic concept, in fact reversed it. In Bauer's 1907 definition,[19] a nation is 'a shared character which has evolved from a shared fate'. And, in Bauer's view, this common character found its expression almost exclusively in a common culture. However, the subjective approach *par excellence* found full expression in the approach of the French historian, Ernest Renan, who asserted in 1871:

A nation is a soul, a spiritual principle. Two things which are, in truth, at bottom only one, constitute this soul, this spiritual principle. One is in the past, the other in the present. The one is the possession in common of a rich legacy of memories; the other is actual consent, the desire to live together, the will to make the best use of the indivisible heritage received.[20]

This latter approach, which places the emphasis on the common consciousness of a shared past and the sense of a shared destiny, has met with the fullest and most emphatic corroboration in the historical reality of the twentieth century. In our opinion it is also the most suitable for the study of the national consciousness of Soviet Jewry.

The only numerical indicator available to those studying the national consciousness of Soviet Jewry is the declaration of nationality given during the census, because this declaration is not connected to the nationality listed in the internal passport. In the 1959 census, 2,268,000 persons declared themselves to be Jewish, while only 2,151,000 did so in 1970. Since the minimum estimate for Jews living in the Soviet Union in 1959 was about 2,500,000 and the maximum estimate about 3,500,000, one can assume that between 11% and 35% chose to conceal their Jewishness. Even if we conclude that a certain percentage refrained from declaring their Jewishness out of fear after having concealed it for a long time, and not because they lack national feeling, the fact remains that a substantial number seem to have turned their backs on their nationality because they are in an advanced stage of assimilation.

However, even though there had been no Jewish schools in the Soviet Union for more than thirty years, no Jewish culture and no secular Jewish organisations, and that contact with world Jewry had been very limited, this percentage is little higher than that of assimilated Jews in the West European and American Diasporas. Moreover, one can maintain with a great degree of certainty that at least a portion of those who did not declare themselves to be Jewish in the latest censuses are now returning to the fold and will continue to do so in the future. Of course there is always the possibility that some or even many of those who declared themselves to be Jewish did not do so specifically for reasons of national identity and would, if given the choice, decide to remove themselves from the Jewish national framework.

The central question here is how to analyse national consciousness among Soviet Jews in numerical terms, using contact with the past as expressed in terms of interest in it or the study of it, the desire to become familiar with Jewish culture, the feeling of identification with world Jewry and the sense of a shared fate, and to examine the factors influencing the formation and growth of such consciousness. As there is no possibility of carrying out sociological research on this subject in the Soviet Union itself, and as research of this kind has not yet been carried out in Israel, we must forego a statistical examination and content ourselves with an investigation of the general processes involved and the factors affecting them, as well as with giving examples of how Jewish national consciousness finds expression in the Soviet Union.

Assimilation and factors tending to strengthen or weaken Jewish national consciousness

The dominant factor in the assimilation of Soviet Jewry is increased Russification and the stifling of Jewish culture. Soviet scholars consider adoption of the culture (i.e. principally of the language) of the people in whose midst they live as one of the most important indicators for measuring assimilation. Although they generally refrain from analysing the Jewish question, they constantly use the Jews as an example to prove that national minorities in the Soviet Union are indeed in the process of assimilation through the adoption of the Russian language. And the figures from the 1926, 1939 and 1959 censuses do show a staggering rise in the percentage of Jews who declared Russian as their language. In 1926 approximately 25% of all Soviet Jews declared Russian as their language;[21] this figure rose to 54.6% in 1939 and to a record figure of 76.4% in 1959[22] with yet a further rise in 1970. However, there are a number of well-known cases where either whole peoples or large sectors of them have adopted another language without thereby losing their national identity. It can be assumed that many Soviet Jews totally acculturated to the Russian language and culture have remained committed to belonging to the Jewish nation.

The second factor which facilitates assimilation is intermarriage. As with language, Soviet scholars also consider intermarriage to be one of the main ways of accelerating the inter-ethnic integration of the nations. There is no doubt that the percentage of intermarriage among Soviet Jewry rose constantly in the 1920s (it was 11.1% in the Ukraine in 1927 and reached as high as 21% in the Russian Republic in 1926);[23] however, from the partial data available on the years 1958–65, it is evident that it was then 10.3% in the Ukraine,[24] and only 8.3% in Moldavia.[25] Even if we accept the probably justified claim that the percentage of mixed marriages between Jews and non-Jews is much higher in the RSFSR and some other republics, it would seem that, in comparison with the twenties and thirties, the rate of mixed marriages in the Soviet Union as a whole is not increasing much. But, while we lack sufficient data to make any conclusive statements, we know from partial statistical data published in the Soviet Union, and also from new immigrants to Israel in recent years, that a certain percentage of the offspring of mixed marriages do not completely lose the national identity of their Jewish father or mother.

There is a third and possibly decisive factor, one which assists assimilation in that it brings the Jew to the brink of despair and to the belief that maintaining his Judaism will forever prevent a solution to his personal problems. This is the state policy of discrimination against the Jews which induces the urge to escape by adopting Russian nationality through inter-marriage or any other way possible.

However, it should be pointed out here that there are also factors which work in the opposite direction, that of national awakening and the reinforce-ment of Jewish national consciousness. These are quite complex and their effect on different individuals varies greatly. The first of these is the feeling of rebelliousness against the injustice and deprivation perpetrated, in the past and the present, against Jews as individuals and as an ethnic group. Popular anti-Semitism, which is encouraged and supported by the authorities, further strengthens this feeling. Since the opportunities for assimilation are, as we have seen, restricted, such feelings of discrimination may be naturally chan-nelled into the search for national identity, which then comes to be viewed as the highest value.

Although in our opinion this essentially negative factor plays the most powerful and decisive role because it is the driving force behind the whole complex process of national awakening, there are also positive factors at work here which influence many individuals. The outstanding feature is the awakened identification with the Jewish people in general and with the State of Israel in particular – the pride of belonging to a people with a glorious past, a unique and specific culture, and a lofty humanistic vision. Here, it should be noted that the current rise of national feeling among most peoples of the Soviet Union has had a direct bearing on the Jewish national awakening.

We have so far analysed the central factors contributing to the continuation of Jewish national existence or, contrarily, to assimilation. However, the prime question – how this national consciousness finds expression – has yet to be answered.

The expression of Jewish national consciousness in the Soviet Union

Opportunities for free national expression, in the full sense of the word, are limited in the Soviet Union, even for those nations living within stable and fixed federal-territorial frameworks. And the limitations are infinitely greater for the extra-territorial national minorities. Therefore, since the Jews are at the very bottom of the ladder in terms of constitutional and *de facto* status, their opportunities to give public expression to national sentiment are few and far between. Working within the framework of what is legally permitted, they can, first, voice this identification through literature and art, albeit in a veiled manner. Their second possibility, no less restricted considering the small number of those who avail themselves of this option, consists of participation in the life of the synagogue. Third, they can take part in the few events in memory of the Holocaust victims organised by the authorities or on independent Jewish initiative. Forbidden activities, which involve great risk and brutal repression on the part of the authorities, are very restricted and were barely discernible and hardly influential before 1967.[26]

From the point of view of national consciousness, as it came to be expressed publicly during the period under question, Soviet Jewry can be divided into three main groups, each of which represents a significant percentage of the Jewish population; precise figures cannot be given because the necessary statistical data are lacking, and also because of the frequent internal changes within the groups themselves.

The assimilated group. Even if we discount all those who have long since totally assimilated, who have lost their Jewish identity and severed all contact with their national Jewish past,[27] we must still conclude that the overwhelming majority of the Jewish population in the Soviet Union has assimilated to a great extent. Like assimilated Jews in other countries, those in the Soviet Union are characterised by the strong desire to lose their Jewish national identity, insofar as they ever possessed any; to absorb Russian (and sometimes Ukrainian or Belorussian) culture; in short, to become swallowed up so completely that not the least reminder of their national origins remains. And if, all the same, they still remain Jews, then it is most certainly not their 'fault'.

It is simply because the government, with its stricture that nationality must be registered in the internal passport, does not allow them any other choice, or because the people among whom they live will not accept them into the general society.

The man who for many years typified the aspirations and outlook of this group was the writer and journalist, Ilya Erenburg,[28] who embarked on his path of assimilation in his earliest years. Russian literature, art and history became an integral part of his personality, while Jewish culture, which he knew only superficially, was foreign to him. Not only did he lack Jewish national consciousness in the above-mentioned sense, but he regularly and firmly rejected it. Erenburg's understanding of the national phenomenon, based as it was upon a strange blend of nihilistic and alienated sentiment with regard to Jewish national culture and boundless admiration for the culture of the host nation, was characteristic of assimilated Jews the world over. For Erenburg, if the phenomenon of inherited Jewish character existed at all, it would have found expression in the independent artistic creation of the Jews. But, considering that Heine was a German and not a Jewish poet; Max Jacob, French; Tuwim, Polish; Modigliani, Italian, and Erenburg himself, a Russian writer, how could they express Jewish national character? 'Obscurantists', he says, 'have maintained that the Jews live a separate life of their own, that they do not share the joys and sorrows of the peoples among whom they live; ... obscurantists have affirmed that the Jews of various countries are a unit, held together by some mysterious ties' (see Doc. 7).

According to Erenburg, however, if there is any bond between a Tunisian and an American Jew, then it is by no means of a mystical nature: it is the result of anti-Semitism. Thus the central point in his philosophy, which took shape early in his life and was reinforced during and after World War II, is that anti-Semitism has provided the fundamental *raison d'être* for the Jews.[29] For many years Erenburg continued to believe that anti-Semitism would disappear under socialism, thereby providing an automatic solution to the Jewish question. However, in the last years of his life he was forced to admit, in his memoirs, that the roots of anti-Semitism were so deep and strong that it would not be easy to eradicate them even under socialist regimes.

The national-Communist group. It seems that this group, which aspired to establish a Jewish national life based on Yiddish culture within the framework of the Soviet regime, was significant in the 1920s and the beginning of the 1930s. But, by the end of the 1930s, the far-reaching changes in demographic, economic and social patterns, together with changes in government policy towards the continued existence of Jewish culture in the Soviet Union, caused many of this group to make the transition to the assimilated category. The massive destruction of the Jews in Belorussia and the Ukraine during World War II proved a decisive turning point in further increasing the relative weight of the assimilated group, since it was these areas which had always provided the national-Communist group with its main base, culturally and politically, actually and potentially.[30] The liquidation of Jewish culture during 1948–9 only served to strengthen this process.

Even with the limited renewal of cultural activity in Yiddish after 1959, the chances that Yiddish culture will be revived in the future are practically nil. For if any opportunity is granted for creating a Jewish culture to express the national consciousness of Soviet Jewry, it will be in the Russian language, unless, of course, the Soviet government changes its attitude to Hebrew. Nonetheless, despite the restrictions and the serious difficulties facing those active in Yiddish culture, and despite the constantly declining percentage of those who know this language, it would be wrong to ignore the fact that Yiddish literature, Yiddish plays and other performances have a considerable anti-assimilationist influence, since any form of Yiddish culture contributes to the preservation of Jewish national consciousness in the Soviet Union.

However, the sad fact is that the most outstanding representatives of Yiddish culture in the Soviet Union were killed during Stalin's last years,[31] and those survivors who managed to return from the concentration camps were broken and discouraged. Thus, the Communist vision of creating a Yiddish-language Jewish culture in the Soviet Union, unrivalled throughout the world, has been dashed to pieces. Today the leading representative of the national-Communist orientation is Aron Vergelis, editor of the only Yiddish journal in the Soviet Union and something of a semi-official spokesman for Soviet Jewry.[32]

The national-Zionist group. While it is difficult to ascertain the size and constitution of this group, one thing is certain: in recent years, mainly after the Six-Day War, there occurred a national awakening which has come to be expressed in thoroughly Zionist terms.

Of course, there have been covert Zionists in the USSR from the inception of the Soviet regime and especially since World War II ended and the State of Israel was established (see Doc. 6). However, the numbers and ways in which this Zionism found expression have changed; there is a significant difference between the Zionism of the 1940s and 1950s and that of the late 1960s and 1970s. Perhaps the best way to describe the national-Zionist group is by pointing out that it differs essentially from the assimilationists and the Communists in that it no longer believes that the Jewish national problem can find a solution within the Soviet Union. Therefore, should such a solution even be proposed, the Zionists would firmly reject it. It also differs from the other two in that its adherents reject both the Russian and Yiddish languages, arguing that neither one allows them to express their national culture or their attachment to the Jewish people. Perhaps most important in terms of Jewish national consciousness is that this group differs from the other two in that it possesses a much stronger sense of identity with the Jewish people throughout the world, and, above all, with the State of Israel.[33]

One can sum up by saying that if no essential change takes place in the Soviet government policy towards the Jewish question in the USSR, as that policy has been formed over the last twenty years, a two-way process will occur in Soviet Jewry. First, factors such as the broad popular anti-Semitism encouraged by the authorities; the tendency among the Jews to rebel against what is seen as injustice; the feeling of solidarity with the Jewish people and the State of Israel; and the rise in national sentiment among all peoples of the Soviet Union will encourage continued Jewish national existence and

increased national consciousness. Secondly, an intensified policy of Russification; an increase in the rate of intermarriage; and the advantages of
adopting Russian nationality will further the process of assimilation. And this
latter trend would be still further reinforced if the requirement to register
nationality were waived.

Demographic and professional trends

The influence of official policies on Soviet Jewry has much less impact on its
general demographic development, which is determined by a complex of
sociological factors, than it has on the higher education and professional
distribution of the Soviet population (where it is, to a great extent, of decisive
importance).

It is true that the many difficulties encountered in making a quantitative
analysis of the Jewish question in the Soviet Union are less serious in the
sphere of demography. This is because, here, the paucity of statistics relating
to the national question, and particularly to the national minorities, does not
exist thanks to the publication of population censuses and other statistical
data. But much material is lacking nevertheless, and this makes it difficult to
draw complete and final conclusions.

Our intention here is to concentrate on the development of the Jewish
population between 1939 and 1970 and on its composition from the standpoint
of community affiliation, domicile, sex and age, as well as to analyse the state
of its educational and professional distribution.

Composition of the Jewish population

The main source of demographic data for the Soviet Union is the population
censuses held in 1920, 1923, 1926, 1939, 1959 and 1970. However, since the
first two were incomplete, more or less comprehensive details of the national
composition of the Soviet Union were only published with the 1926 census and
thereafter.[34] Each census included a question on the citizen's nationality. But,
because the questioners were forbidden to ask for documents to authenticate
the citizens' declaratory answers, it may be assumed that a certain percentage
of the Jews, as well as citizens of other nationalities, preferred for various
reasons to conceal their true nationality. Hence, as we shall see immediately
below, one must add a certain, albeit inaccurate, number of Jews to the figures
given in the census.

The number of Jews and their distribution by republics

In 1926, 2,680,823 persons declared themselves to be Jewish; according to the
Soviet economist, Yury Larin, about 300,000 (i.e. 11% of all Soviet Jews)
concealed their Jewishness by declaring themselves to belong to other
nationalities.[35] In 1939, 3,020,000 persons declared themselves to be Jewish;
according to the Jewish demographer, J. Lestchinsky, between 250,000 and
300,000 Jews (i.e. 8–10%) concealed their origins.[36]

The first important demographic change (outside natural growth rate) in the number of Jews in the Soviet Union came in 1939–40, when the USSR annexed territories formerly belonging to Poland, Lithuania, Latvia, Estonia and Romania (Bessarabia and Bukovina). J. Lestchinsky estimates that this increased the number of Jews included in the Soviet Union by about 1,880,000: 1,300,000 from Poland, 330,000 from Romania, 150,000 from Lithuania and 100,000 from Latvia and Estonia.[37] Therefore, there were more than five million Jews residing in the USSR prior to the outbreak of war between Germany and the Soviet Union in June 1941. A second drastic change in demography was caused by the war itself, and by the extermination of the Jews by the Nazis. According to Y. Tenenbaum's calculations, about four million Jews resided in the areas of the Soviet Union overrun by the Nazis, and about a million and a half succeeded in escaping. Thus, there were about 2.5 million Jews in the free part of the Soviet Union.[38] However, the Soviet Jewish demographer, Y. Kantor, states that there were no more than two million Jews in the free territories of the Soviet Union.[39] I would estimate that the losses suffered by the Jewish population totalled between 12.5% and 15% of all Soviet war deaths (2.5–3 million out of the twenty million lost).[40]

According to the first post-war census, held in 1959, there were 2,268,000 Jews in the Soviet Union, constituting 1.1% of the total population of the state. This compares with 1.8% in the 1939 census and 2.5% according to the estimate of 1940.[41] However, in my opinion one must add another 15% to account for those Jews who concealed their nationality, thereby arriving at a figure of 2,608,050 (2,268,000 plus 340,050) for the Jewish population of the Soviet Union in 1959.[42]

This is very close to the figure reached by calculating the estimated natural growth rate. For if the natural growth rate was about 1% per annum and the number of Jews in 1946 was approximately 2.5 million, then the Jewish population should have been 2,850,000 in 1959. However, if one subtracts the refugees who returned to Poland after the war (170,000) and those who returned between 1957 and 1959 (30,000), i.e. 205,000 persons, the Jewish population was 2,645,000 in 1959.

According to an official Soviet estimate, the Jewish population numbered 2.4 million at the beginning of 1965.[43] Since the annual growth of the general population between 1959 and 1970[44] averaged 1%, in theory the figure for this population should have been 2,506,000 (2,268,000 plus 248,000, minus the 10,000 who emigrated to Israel during this period).[45] But, according to the figures published in the 1970 census, only 2,151,000 persons declared themselves to be Jewish.

How is this difference of 350,000 to be explained? There are several reasons. (1) It may be assumed with a fair degree of certainty that the Jewish national awakening did not lead to a decrease in the number of 'missing' Jews, and that their number actually increased because of the extreme anti-Israel and anti-Zionist propaganda campaign which deterred many Jews from declaring themselves as such at the time of the census. (2) The results at the time of the 1970 census reveal a demographic trend of ageing in the population as a whole, and this must have been true for the Jewish population as well (while the percentage of persons over fifty years old was only 18.6% of the total

Table 1. *Jewish population in the USSR, 1939–70*

		1939			1959			1970		
		Number	%	% of total Jewish pop.	Number	%	% of total Jewish pop.	Number	%	% of total Jewish pop.
USSR	Total	170,467,000	100.0	100.00	208,826,650	100.00	100.00	241,720,134	100.00	100.00
	Jews	3,020,000	1.77		2,267,814	1.09		2,150,707	0.90	
RSFSR	Total	108,800,000	100.00	31.39	117,534,305	100.00	38.60	130,079,210	100.00	37.56
	Jews	948,000	0.87		875,307	0.74		807,915	0.62	
Ukrainian SSR	Total	30,960,000	100.00	50.76	41,869,046	100.00	37.05	47,126,517	100.00	36.13
	Jews	1,533,000	4.95		840,311	2.00		777,126	1.65	
Belorussian SSR	Total	5,568,000	100.00	12.42	8,055,714	100.00	6.61	9,002,338	100.00	6.88
	Jews	375,000	6.73		150,084	1.86		148,011	1.64	
Moldavian SSR	Total				2,884,477	100.00	4.19	3,568,873	100.00	4.55
	Jews				95,107	3.30		98,072	2.75	
Uzbek SSR	Total	6,282,400	100.00	1.69	8,119,103	100.00	4.16	11,799,429	100.00	4.78
	Jews	51,000	0.81		94,344	1.16		102,855	0.87	
Georgian SSR	Total	3,542,300	100.00	1.40	4,044,045	100.00	2.28	4,686,358	100.00	2.57
	Jews	42,500	1.20		51,582	1.28		55,382	1.18	
Azerbaidzhan SSR	Total	3,209,700	100.00	1.36	3,697,717	100.00	1.77	5,117,081	100.00	1.91
	Jews	41,000	1.28		40,204	1.09		41,288	0.81	
Latvian SSR	Total				2,093,458	100.00	1.61	2,364,127	100.00	1.70
	Jews				36,592	1.75		36,680	1.55	
Kazakh SSR	Total	6,146,000	100.00	0.63	9,294,741	100.00	1.24	13,008,726	100.00	1.29
	Jews	19,000	0.31		28,048	0.30		27,689	0.21	

Lithuanian SSR	Total			2,711,445	100.00		3,128,236	100.00	
	Jews			24,672	0.91	1.09	23,564	0.75	1.10
Tadzhik SSR	Total	1,485,100	100.00	1,980,547	100.00		2,899,602	100.00	
	Jews	5,000	0.34	12,415	0.63	0.55	14,615	0.50	0.68
			0.17						
Kirgiz SSR	Total	1,459,300	100.00	2,065,837	100.00		2,932,805	100.00	
	Jews	2,000	0.14	8,610	0.41	0.38	7,680	0.26	0.36
			0.07						
Estonian SSR	Total			1,196,791	100.00		1,356,079	100.00	
	Jews			5,436	0.46	0.24	5,288	0.39	0.24
Turkmen SSR	Total	1,252,000	100.00	1,516,375	100.00		2,158,880	100.00	
	Jews	3,000	0.24	4,078	0.27	0.18	3,494	0.16	0.16
			0.10						
Armenian SSR	Total	1,281,599	100.00	1,763,048	100.00		2,491,873	100.00	
	Jews	500	0.04	1,024	0.06	0.05	1,048	0.04	0.05
			0.02						

Sources: L. Zinger, *Dos banayte folk*, Appendix II; M. Altshuler (ed.), *Ha-yehudim ba-mifkad ha-okhlusin bi-vrit ha-moazot, 1959* (*The Jews in the Soviet Union Census, 1959*), Jerusalem, n.p., 1963, Table 1, pp. 10–11; *Itogi vsesoyuznoi perepisi naseleniya 1970 goda*; *Bakinsky rabochy*, 21 May 1971; *Kazakhstanskaya pravda*, 9 June 1971; *Sovetskaya Kirgiziya*, 5 May 1971.

Table 2. *Distribution of Jewish population by mother tongue, 1959–70*

	1959			1970		
	Population	Yiddish and Jewish dialects	%	Population	Yiddish and Jewish dialects	%
USSR	2,267,814	487,786	21.5	2,151,707	413,096	19.2
RSFSR	875,307	117,559	13.4	807,915	94,971	11.8
Ukrainian SSR	840,311	142,241	16.9	777,126	102,190	13.1
Belorussian SSR	150,084	32,910	21.9	148,011	26,391	17.8
Moldavian SSR	95,107	47,584	50.0	98,072	43,800	44.7
Uzbek SSR	94,344	46,944	49.7	102,855	38,625	37.5
Georgian SSR	51,582	37,270	72.3	55,382	44,841	81.0
Azerbaidzhan SSR	40,204	14,146	35.2	41,288	17,067	41.3
Latvian SSR	36,592	17,541	47.9	36,680	16,946	46.2
Kazakh SSR	28,048	6,475	23.1	27,689	6,322	22.8
Lithuanian SSR	24,672	17,025	69.0	23,564	14,587	61.9
Tadzhik SSR	12,415	2,879	23.2	14,615	2,914	19.9
Kirgiz SSR	8,610	2,613	30.3	7,680	2,048	26.7
Estonian SSR	5,436	1,350	24.8	5,288	1,140	21.5
Turkmen SSR	4,078	1,174	28.8	3,494	1,052	30.1
Armenian SSR	1,024	72	7.0	1,048	222	21.2

Sources: as Table 1.
Note: Discrepancies in totals are due to figures being rounded.

population in 1959, it was 20.6% in 1970). (3) A further demographic trend with important repercussions for the drop in the number of Soviet Jews was the low natural growth rate of the urban population. Since it seems that the percentage of Soviet Jews residing in towns had reached 96% in 1970, it would be reasonable to assume that their average natural growth rate was far lower than 1%, and perhaps even close to nil. (4) There might have been falsifications in local census results, although it is difficult to believe that this would happen at the central level, especially as the official line is to prove that the number of Jews in the Soviet Union is larger than it really is.

The distribution of the Jewish population by republics, as a result of the war, post-war migratory processes, and various other internal demographic trends, is shown below.

The Russian Republic. In the Russian Federal Republic, the largest republic in size and population, there were 948,000 Jews in 1939, constituting 31.4% of the Jewish population of the Soviet Union and 0.9% of the population of the republic. In 1959 there were 875,000 Jews residing in the Russian Republic, i.e. only a slight drop compared with the 1939 figures, in contrast to the vast drop in Jewish population in the Ukrainian and Belorussian Republics during the same period. The reasons behind this are the extermination of the Jewish population of the Ukraine and Belorussia and the flight of Jews from these republics to the Russian Republic before the German invasion. Although the number of Jews in the Russian Republic dropped to 808,000, i.e. only 0.6% of the total population of the republic, in 1970, in relation to Jewish centres in the whole Soviet Union, the Russian Republic continues to take first place with 37.6%.

The Ukrainian Republic. In 1939 there were 1,533,000 Jews in the Ukraine, constituting 50.8% of all Soviet Jews and 4.9% of the total population of the Ukraine. As a result of the war and migratory processes, there were 840,000 Jews living in the Ukrainian Republic in 1959, i.e. a drop to second place after the RSFSR in concentration of Jews. There was a further drop in 1970, when the number of Jews living in the Ukraine fell to 777,000 or 36.1% of all Soviet Jewry and 1.6% of the population of the republic.

The Belorussian Republic. The greatest drop in the Jewish population during 1939–70 took place in Belorussia. According to the 1939 census, 375,000 Jews lived in Belorussia, constituting 12.4% of all Soviet Jews and 6.7% of the republic's population. However, according to the 1959 census, their number had dropped to 150,000 or 6.6% of the total Jewish population and 1.9% of the population of the republic. The 1970 figures show only a small overall drop in Jewish population in this republic when compared with those for 1959. In fact, the number of Jews in Belorussia as a percentage of the total Jewish population increased from 6.6% to 6.9% during this period.

The Baltic republics and Moldavia. All four of these republics were annexed by the Soviet Union in 1939–40, and in all four the process of Jewish assimilation was less marked than in the European republics of the Soviet Union. A comparison of 1959 and 1970 census results shows that the number of Jews in Latvia, Lithuania, Estonia and Moldavia did not suffer a decrease, but actually increased by 3% (from 161,807 Jews to 164,000). It may be assumed that the reason for this, apart from the existence of a developed Jewish awareness and of relatively limited assimilatory trends, is the internal migration of Soviet Jews to these republics, especially to Moldavia.

Republics of the southern and eastern borders. In 1939, there were 164,000 Jews in the five Central Asian and the three Caucasian republics, or only 5% of the total Jewish population. The relatively high natural growth rate of the Georgian, Mountain and Bukharan Jews, and the migration to the Central Asian republics (especially Uzbekistan) during the war, led to an increase in Jewish population here (to 240,000 in 1959 and 254,000 in 1970, i.e. an increase from 5% of all Soviet Jews to 10.9% in 1959 and 12% in 1970).

The distribution of Soviet Jewry among the various republics has thus been significantly transformed by the considerable dispersion of the Jews which took place between 1939 and 1970.

Distribution of Soviet Jewry according to sex, age and domicile

Before the outbreak of World War II, there were 1,102 Jewish women to every 1,000 Jewish men in the Soviet Union, as compared with 1,087 women to every 1,000 men in the total population.[46]

That the heavy losses in the ranks of the army and the civilian population during the war seriously upset the balance between the male and female population of the state was very clearly reflected in the 1959 census, despite the fact that fourteen years had passed since the end of the war. In 1959, there were 1,220 females to every 1,000 males, i.e. the number of females increased to 133 more per 1,000 males between 1939 and 1959. In the Jewish population there were 1,200 women to every 1,000 men, an increase of 98 per 1,000 males. This difference in the male–female ratio between the total population and the Jewish population was mainly due to more men than women surviving the Jewish Holocaust, and not to less Jews having actively participated in the war against Germany.

The age divisions among Jews in 1939 were: 0–14 years 29.1%; 15–49 years 55.3%; over 50 years 15.6%. The age composition of the Jewish population was higher than that of the total population in the over-fifty group (13.4%). According to the 1959 census, the age divisions of the Soviet population were: 0–15 years 30.4%; 16–49 years 51%; over 50 years 13.6%. We have no comparable figures for the Jewish population, but the percentage of Jews in the over-fifty age group is without doubt much higher than it was in 1939 because of the low natural growth rate and the longer life span among Jews. It would be reasonable to assume that this trend was continued in 1970, since the over-fifty age group increased to 20.6% of the total population of the Soviet Union.

The urban and rural Jewish population

The process of urbanisation of the Jewish population began before the October Revolution and accelerated dramatically at the end of the 1920s, with the intensified industrialisation of the Soviet Union. According to the 1939 census, 87% of all Soviet Jews were town-dwellers. The largest centres of the rural Jewish population were in the Ukraine, where 222,474 lived in rural areas, i.e. 14.6% of the total Jewish population of the Ukraine. In the Russian Republic 97,768 Jews resided in rural areas, i.e. 10.4% of the Jewish population, and in Belorussia 45,694 Jews resided in rural areas, i.e. 12.1% of the total Jewish population of Belorussia. There was also a large concentration of Jews in rural areas in Georgia (18.6% of the total Jewish population in that republic).

In addition to the processes of urbanisation, which were particularly strong in the Jewish population from the 1930s, the increase in the urban Jewish population was influenced by the destruction of Jewish agricultural colonies in the Ukraine, Belorussia and the Crimea during the war. Apparently, the few surviving Jews from these areas did not return to their former places of residence after the war; their property had been appropriated by their non-Jewish neighbours, and it would have been virtually impossible to recover it. Hence, we are witness to a situation unprecedented in the Soviet Union with regard to its other nationalities: according to the 1959 census, only 4.7% of the Jews resided in rural areas. Moreover, some of them lived outside towns because of housing difficulties, but should really be considered part of the urban population with regard to employment.

The distribution of the rural population by republics in 1959 was: in the Russian Republic 45,079; the Ukraine 30,280; Georgia 7,752; Belorussia 5,590; Uzbekistan 4,421; plus small numbers in each of the other republics. It may be assumed that the percentage of the Jewish population in rural areas declined further in the 1970 census, and probably did not exceed 4%.[47]

It is important to point out that, according to the 1959 census, there were large concentrations of Jews in the main cities of the Soviet Union: in Moscow 239,246 Jews, i.e. 3.7% of the city's population (251,000 or 3.56% in 1970); Leningrad, 168,646 or 5.1% of the city's population (162,600 or 4.12% in 1970); Kiev, 153,466 or 13.9% (152,000 or 9.31% in 1970); Odessa, about 100,000 or about 16%; Tashkent, 50,445 or 5.5% (55,800 or 4.03% in 1970).[48] These figures show that all the objective conditions exist for the development of Jewish cultural and educational institutions in the large cities of the Soviet Union. The fact that these had disappeared entirely from the Soviet scene by the end of the 1940s (the schools by the end of the 1930s) proves that their liquidation was the result of an arbitrary decision by the authorities, who clearly intended to hasten the assimilation of Jews to Russian culture. Therefore, the claim of A. Arsenyev, Deputy Minister of Education of the RSFSR, that the parents of Jewish children have the legal right to teach their children the two Jewish languages (see Doc. 15) is completely without foundation.

The Jews in higher education and the professions

Beginning in the second half of the 1950s, partial statistics started to appear on the place of the various nationalities, including the Jews, in higher education and in a number of professions. These figures enable us to examine, at least in part, Soviet Jewry's position in the Soviet national economy, as well as the extent to which anti-Jewish discrimination exists in university entrance and appointments to various institutions.

Higher education

There were 563,000 students in the Soviet Union in 1935, including 74,900 Jews who constituted 13.3% of all students; Ukrainian students, who were in second place after the Russians, numbered only 80,600 (14.1%).[49] The first post-war figures for the number of Jewish students in the Soviet Union was for the academic year 1960–1,[50] when 2,395,545 students attended institutes of higher education, including 77,177 Jews (i.e. 3.2% of all students; see Table 3). The Ukrainian students in the same year numbered 343,600, i.e. 14.3%. While it is true that the number of Jewish students increased to 110,000 in the year 1967–8, it dropped to 2.5% of all students.[51] These figures teach us, first of all, that the Jews occupied so significant a place among the students of the USSR because they came mainly from an urban background (between 4% and 5% in the middle 1930s), when the majority of the nationalities were rural in population and their educational development was still in its infancy. The small increase in the number of Jewish students from 1935 to 1960 (2,277 students in twenty-five years) was due to war-time losses; competition from

Table 3. *Jews in higher and secondary specialist education, 1960–71*

Academic years	Students at higher education establishments			Students of secondary specialist education		
	Total	Jews	%	Total	Jews	%
1960/1	2,395,545	77,177	3.2	2,369,745	44,116	1.9
1962/3	2,943,700	79,300	2.7	2,667,700	47,200	1.8
1963/4	3,260,700	82,600	2.5	2,982,800	51,300	1.7
1965/6	3,860,500	94,600	2.4	3,659,300	52,000	1.4
1966/7	4,123,200	106,300	2.6	3,993,900	51,600	1.3
1967/8	4,310,900	110,000	2.6	4,186,600	46,700	1.1
1968/9	4,469,700	111,900	2.5	4,261,500	43,100	1.0
1969/70	4,549,600	110,100	2.4	4,301,700	41,000	0.9
1970/1	4,580,600	105,800	2.3	4,388,000	40,000	0.9

Sources: Narodnoe khozyaistvo SSSR, v 1963g, p. 579; *v 1964g*, p. 691; *v 1965g*, p. 701; *v 1967g*, p. 803; *v 1968g*, p. 694; *v 1969g*, p. 690; *Srednee spetsialnoe obrazovanie v SSSR* (Secondary Specialist Education in the USSR), Moscow, Gosstatizdat, 1962, p. 72; *Vysshee obrazovanie v SSSR*, p. 85; *Narodnoe obrazovanie, nauka i kultura v SSSR* (People's Education, Science and Culture in the USSR), Moscow, Statistika, 1971, p. 196.

the urban populations of other nationalities, which had increased greatly in size and were now far better educated than before; and probably also the official discrimination which, to judge by many reports, was exercised in the acceptance of Jews to institutes of higher education. The further drop in Jewish students between 1960 and 1967 (from 3.2% to 2.6%) was caused by the persistent effect of these same factors.

The official Soviet claim that the percentage of Jewish students is very high in comparison to all the other nationalities is only partially true.[52] If the calculation were based on the urban population and not on the population as a whole, the picture would change. For example, if it had been confined to that stratum of the urban population which constitutes the primary reservoir of recruitment for higher education, the 1967 figures would show that the Jews constituted 2.16%, whereas they constituted only 1.1% of the total population. The figures quoted by us cannot, of course, reveal accurately such localised anti-Jewish discrimination as the non-admission of Jews to certain universities or to certain faculties within given universities.

Employed personnel with secondary specialist and higher education

The number of Jews with secondary specialist and higher education was 368,900 in 1957, out of a total of 6,821,600 people employed in this category, i.e. 5.4% (see Table 4); while the number of Jews with higher education in that same year was 260,900 or 9.3% of the total in that category.

By 1964, a marked increase had occurred in the number of Jews in the work force who had secondary specialist and higher education. However, while

Table 4. *Distribution of employed personnel with higher and secondary specialist education, 1957–64*

	Total number employed	Number of Jews	%	Total number employed with higher education	Number of Jews	%	Total number employed with secondary specialist education	Number of Jews	%
1957	6,821,600	368,900,	5.4	2,805,500	260,900	9.3	4,016,100	108,000	2.7
1963	9,955,800	457,400	4.6	4,049,700	310,600	7.7	5,906,100	146,800	2.5
1964	11,249,700	482,400	4.3	4,547,600	322,700	7.1	6,702,100	159,700	2.4

Sources: Narodnoe khozyaistvo SSSR, v 1963g, p. 493; v 1964g, p. 567; v 1965g, p. 582.

their number now reached 482,400, their percentage of the total number in this category dropped to 4.3%. A similar drop occurred in the percentage of those with higher education (from 9.3% in 1957 to 7.1% in 1964). The main reason for this decline was the constant and quite speedy rise of personnel with higher education from among the other Soviet nationalities. Nonetheless, there can be no doubt that even then the Jews continued to occupy a significant place among those in the work force with higher education.

Scientists and academics

Scientists and academics are grouped together in the USSR under the general category of 'scientific workers', meaning all those employed at the academic level at universities, research institutes, academies of science and all their affiliated institutions. The number of Jewish 'scientific workers' in 1950 was 25,125 out of a total of 162,508, i.e. 15.5%. As a result of the policy of anti-Jewish discrimination in the Stalin era, this number dropped to 24,620 or 11.04% by 1955. After this date, the number of Jewish 'scientific workers' rose by an average of approximately 3,000 per annum, until their number reached 58,952 in 1967. However, as in the case of students and employed personnel with higher education, while they increased in number, the percentage of Jewish 'scientific workers' fell from 11.04% to 7.65% during the same period (see Table 5). Although the percentage of Jewish 'scientific workers' is still very high in comparison with other nationalities, there can be no doubt that the drop is due to both 'objective' and 'subjective' factors. The former includes such factors as the constant increase in the number of scientists and academics of Russian and other nationalities, and the latter, the calculated government policy aimed at restricting as far as possible the number of Jewish 'scientific workers'. It is important to note here that, despite anti-Jewish discrimination as regards promotion, and anti-Jewish restrictions at scientific institutions dealing with secret or especially sensitive fields of research, in 1967 the Jews still occupied a prominent place in the academies and research institutes, especially in the natural sciences, as a result of the ever-growing requirements of the Soviet national economy.

The Jews in the professions

Data on specific professions according to national distribution are published very rarely, and we have only found figures from 1939 and 1966. According to the Soviet demographer, L. Zinger, the situation of the Jews in various professions at the beginning of 1939[53] was as follows: 21,000 Jewish doctors (16% of all doctors); 17,000 artists and theatre workers (11% of the total number in this category); 20,000 engineers, technicians and architects (10% of the total); 46,000 teachers (5% of all teachers); 60,000 technicians (7% of all technicians); and 125,000 accountants (8% of all accountants). According to the official Soviet figures published in 1966,[54] Jewish doctors comprised 14.7% of all doctors at this period, i.e. a drop of only 1% compared to 1939, and a large increase in the overall number, i.e. about 54,000 out of a total of 365,000. This indicates that medicine remained a highly important profession

Table 5. *Jewish 'scientific workers' (scientists and academics), 1950–70*

Year	Total number	Number of Jews	Percentage of Jews
1950	162,508	25,125	15.46
1955	222,893	24,620	11.04
1958	284,038	28,966	10.20
1959	310,022	30,633	9.88
1960	354,158	33,529	9.47
1961	404,126	36,173	8.95
1962	524,500	n.a.	n.a.
1963	565,958	48,012	8.48
1964	611,964	50,915	8.32
1965	664,584	53,067	7.98
1966	712,419	56,070	7.87
1967	770,013	58,952	7.65
1968	822,910	60,995	7.41
1969	883,420	63,661	7.21
1970	927,709	64,392	6.94

Sources: M. Kammari, 'Oktyabrskaya revolutsiya i izmenenie natsionalnykh otnoshenii v SSSR' (The October Revolution and the Change in National Relations in the USSR), *Voprosy filosofii*, 1957, no. 5, p. 57; *Narodnoe khozyaistvo SSSR v 1961g* (People's Economy of the USSR in 1961), Moscow, Statistika, 1962, p. 704; *Narodnoe khozyaistvo SSSR v 1962g*, Moscow, Statistika, 1963, p. 584; *Narodnoe khozyaistvo SSSR v 1959g*, Moscow, Gosstatizdat, 1960, p. 757; *Narodnoe khozyaistvo SSSR v 1960g*, Moscow, Gosstatizdat, 1961, p. 785; *Narodnoe khozyaistvo SSSR, v 1968g*, p. 696; *v 1969g*, p. 696; N. De Witt, *Education and Professional Employment in the USSR*, p. 421; *Narodnoe obrazovanie, nauka i kultura v SSSR* (People's Education, Science and Culture in the USSR), Moscow, Statistika, 1971, p. 270.

for the Jews in the USSR. Likewise, the Jews constituted 8.5% of all writers and journalists; 10.4% of all lawyers; and 7.7% of actors and artists. These figures indicate the important role played by Jews in the scientific and cultural spheres. It should be stressed that this contribution was not only quantitative but also qualitative. Many observers, who have analysed the vacillating and selective policies of the Soviet leaders in granting emigration visas to Israel, emphasise that one of the important factors in their thinking has been fear of the damage which a mass exodus of highly trained forces could cause the Soviet economy.[55]

Documents to Chapter 1

Soviet national theory

Document 1* Soviet definition of the Jewish people (1952)

The Jews: The name given to different peoples, having a common origin in the ancient Hebrews – a people that inhabited Palestine from the middle of the second millennium B.C. till the 1st–2nd centuries A.D. The Jews do not comprise a nation since they do not represent a historically formed, settled community of people which has grown up on the basis of a common language, a common territory, a common economic life, a common culture.[56] Their economic, political and cultural life they share in common with the peoples around them. As a result, from the ethnographical point of view the Jews approximate to those peoples in whose midst they live (although not to the same degree everywhere).

Document 2† Marxism–Leninism and Soviet Jews (1960)[57]

Consequently, ethnic groups, which do not have a *special, permanent national territory* where they may abide as *compact masses for an extended time,* cannot be transformed and are not transformed into separate *nations,* but ordinarily merge in the end with those nations among whom they live.

Among such ethnic groups are included the Jews in a number of countries – in the USA, Russia, France, Holland, Poland, etc. In such lands as the USA or Poland and the USSR, where the basic mass of the Jewish people resides, they, as is well known, have not been formed and are not being formed into a separate nation, but on the contrary, they live among other nations and have more or less been assimilated, merged with them, acquired their language, culture; they live with them in a common economic, political and cultural life, having preserved only certain features of their historical origin, ethnic aspect and mentality which are determined by their special situation, occupations, their relations and connections with those nations among whom they live. [...]

---

* *Source: Bolshaya sovetskaya entsiklopediya* (Large Soviet Encyclopaedia), 2nd edition, Moscow, Gosudarstvennoe nauchnoe izdatelstvo, 1952, vol. 15, p. 377.
† *Source*: M. Kammari, 'This Is Our Jewish Policy', *Jewish Observer and Middle East Review*, 19 February 1960, pp. 13–15.

I, for instance, am by origin a Finn, my native language is Finnish, but now I have been speaking and thinking for fifty years, if not more, *in Russian*, since I live and work among Russians, and not among Finns. But in my passport I indicate that I am a Finn, to show national *origin* and in part national adherence, insofar as I do not consider myself to have completely and perfectly adopted Russian culture.

But my children do not know a word of Finnish, since their mother was a Russian and I also speak Russian with the children at home. Therefore, the children in their passports write – Russian.

In our country, the Jews and other assimilating groups, of whom we have very many (Armenians, Georgians, Tatars and others living in Russian cities), act in just the same way. These processes are natural, conform to natural laws, and are completely voluntary.

Here administrative measures could not change anything, even if such measures were attempted. But in a socialist society, where the principles of Leninist national policy are strictly carried out, any measures of compulsion in this sphere are impossible.

And the Jews themselves here determine their national adherence, and I know that some write that they are Russian and others write that they are Jews. Their position in society is not affected at all by this. This is of importance only for statistics, the calculation of the national composition of the population and how this composition is changing.

As to Birobidzhan, this Jewish Autonomous Region was formed in order to present to the Jews living in the USSR, if they want to consolidate into a separate nation, the possibility of doing so. This, as is known, is a spacious and naturally rich region.

If the Jews had the wish and aim to consolidate themselves into a nation, they could have done so. But only an insignificant part of the Jews living in the USSR went there. The majority preferred to remain where they lived, in large cultural centres, where there were far more conditions for cultural growth than in even the richest of yet undeveloped regions.

Here of importance was the habit of living in *cities*, the attachment which people feel to the place where they were born and spent their childhood. To resettle in a distant region is something which by no means all, but only *a few* young, adventurous spirits with an inclination toward travel decided to do.

To conduct a campaign for resettlement, to exert any pressure on the will of the people in favour of resettlement – all this was excluded in principle by Leninist national policy.

Document 3* Tokarev's new definition (1964)

Common territory is of course very important; it is an indispensable condition for the formation of an ethnic community (no single nation could have been formed without territorial contact of all its parts one with another); but in the ultimate history of a people the territorial community may weaken or even disappear, without in any way destroying or even always weakening the ethnic

* *Source*: S. A. Tokarev, 'Problemy tipov etnicheskikh obshchnostei' (Problems of Types of Ethnic Communities), *Voprosy filosofii*, 1964, no. 11, pp. 43–4, 45–6, 49.

unity of a given people in the process. For example, the Mordvinians, Bashkirs, Yakuts and Uzbeks have long had no continuous ethnic territory, and individual sections of these peoples have almost no mutual contacts, but this in no way destroys their ethnic unity; and one hardly need mention the Armenians, Jews and Gypsies who have settled throughout the world without losing their ethnic unity (although with some individual groups of Jews it has of course weakened).

A common origin, which is most clearly apparent (though not always) in the identity of an anthropological type, only in rare cases indicates an ethnic determinant (for example, the negroes of the USA). [...]

Finally, a common religion (denomination) does not necessarily denote an ethnic community; generally, a common religion either bears a derivative and non-independent stamp, being dependent on a political situation (as was the case in ancient eastern societies), or bears no relation at all to ethnic demarcations: 'the world religions' are spread abroad without relation to ethnic, linguistic or other boundaries. Only in a few special cases does an ethnic community arise or maintain itself on the basis of a religious community or in connection with one – this is the case with the Jews, Karaites,[58] Yezidis, Parsees, Sikhs, Maronites, Dungan, Gagauz, Bosniitsi and others.

It follows that a purely formal, and for the present rather preliminary definition of the concept 'ethnic community' might read thus: an ethnic community is a community of people which is founded on one or several of the following types of social relations: common origin, language, territory, state allegiance, economic ties, cultural way of life, and religion (if this latter is preserved).* [...]

The significance of the religious (denominational) indicator in the formation of ethnic communities at first increases with the process of historical development, but later decreases. Primitive society did not know the division of human groups according to religion. In class, slave-owning and feudal societies with their complex shuffling of ethnic and state organisations, there were frequently cases when groups of the population, isolated by their religion, broke away and preserved their isolation for a long time. In these cases religion served of course not as a set of principles but as a banner, an ideology, an outward sign of ethnic unity: for example, the previously mentioned Jews, Karaites, Parsees and others. Many of these groups continue to exist in the era of capitalism, but their isolation and exclusiveness are weakening, while no similar new groups are coming into being; it is true, that in the capitalist era new sects arose, but not one of these formed the basis of an ethnic community.

Document 4† Dzhunusov's[59] view (1966)

Several nationalities consisting of a purely urban or purely rural population do not have the possibility of employing the Soviet economic system as a

---

* I have intentionally not included in this list 'common psychic composition', or 'national character' – concepts requiring special examination, and contributing nothing to the problem posed above, except to cloud the issue.

† *Source*: M. S. Dzhunusov, 'Natsiya kak sotsialno-etnicheskaya obshchnost lyudei' (The Nation as a Socio-Ethnic Community of People), *Voprosy istorii*, 1966, no. 4, p. 28.

material base for developing into a nation. Living in small groups in various republics and provinces, they cannot achieve widely developed intra-national economic relations. For example, of 2.3 million Jews in the Soviet Union, 2.2 million (i.e. 96%) reside in cities.* By virtue of a historical formation resulting in its present dispersion and social composition the Jewish nationality cannot develop into a nation. These factors also influence the bilinguality of the Jewish population. Socialism, which opened up new vistas for the free development of all national cultures and languages, including the Jewish language and culture, did not slow down the transition of the Jewish population to the use of Russian, which had become plain even before the October Revolution. If in 1926 more than seven-tenths of the Jewish population declared Yiddish to be their mother tongue, in 1959 only a quarter of the Jewish population consider it to be their mother tongue. Several nationalities, by virtue of their small numbers, are unable to make wide use of the socialist disposition of productive forces for the fullest development of intra-national economic ties.

Document 5† Kozlov's view (1967)

One and the same group of people may simultaneously constitute an industrial organisation, a class, a political party, a religious organisation, a racial group, a nation and a state. This group of people is connected in a particular way with each one of the above-mentioned groups, and in one set of circumstances will act as an inseparable part of one community, while in another set of circumstances it will act as an inseparable part of another community. To single out from this complexity ethnic ties and distinguishing marks belonging to the ethnic community alone is not so easy. [...]

Among the circumstances that complicate this work, terminological difficulties represent a considerable factor. This concerns not only particular 'specific' concepts such as 'tribe' or 'nation', but also their general 'generic' meaning. In the present article we give a certain preference to the term 'ethnic community' and not to the essentially identical term 'people' as we consider it less open to criticism as regards terminology.[...]

As far as religion is concerned, then of course belonging to a particular religion or religious community may in a number of cases coincide with the ethnic community; religious consciousness, as the history of medieval Europe and the histories of the Middle Eastern countries demonstrate, sometimes displaces ethnic consciousness. No religion, however, can of itself establish or maintain an ethnic community, but can only aid it. To demonstrate the strength of religious ties S. A. Tokarev adduced by way of example the case of the Jews, 'who have settled throughout the world without losing their ethnic unity', but this is hardly convincing.[60] There is no doubt that Judaism, as the clearest expression of a 'national' religion, played, and in many countries still plays, a very prominent part in the life of the Jews, being reflected in their

---

* *Itogi vsesoyuznoi perepisi naseleniya 1959 goda*, pp. 184, 190.
† *Source*: V. I. Kozlov, 'O ponyatii etnicheskoi obshchnosti' (On the Concept of the Ethnic Community), *Sovetskaya etnografiya*, 1967, no. 2, pp. 102, 110–11.

self-awareness and in a number of factors in their culture and way of life. However, the ancient Hebrew people was formed on the whole over a period of several centuries, before the formation of the Jewish religion, while the ethnic separation of the Jews, who first settled in the countries of Europe, can be explained not only on religious, but also on socio-economic grounds. Judaism was unable to maintain the ethnic unity of the Jews. By the Middle Ages they had divided into two basic groups: the Sefaradim, speaking Ladino, and the Ashkenazim, speaking Yiddish. Subsequently, the ethnic dissociation of groups of Jews living in various countries of the world was further intensified, and in some of these groups (above all in the Jewish population of the USSR) Judaism has already lost its significance as an ethnic determinant. The Jews have long ceased to be a single people; many groups no longer have anything in common apart from the same name and few, frequently very confused, ideas about their common origin and historical fate. In this respect S. A. Tokarev's other examples are also unconvincing.

Jewish national identity

Document 6* An unofficial voice[61] (November 1953)

The greatest event in the history of our people has taken place: the State of Israel has been reborn. And this great miracle has displayed new wonders from day to day: the people of Israel exhibit magnificent heroism in their fight with the hordes that hate them and that attack the new state in order to erase it from the face of the earth.

The Jewish writers and the rest of those active in Jewish culture (I mean the best amongst them, those who work under coercion), well knowing the vacillations of the Party heads, have found it necessary to conceal the exultation of their hearts. An exception was the poet David Hofshteyn.[62] Even if he had wanted to conceal the meditations of his heart on that event, he would not have succeeded. From the depths of his heart he cried with joy. The historic event – the declaration of the State of Israel by the provisional government established there – found Hofshteyn in a health resort in Kislovodsk. The first thing he did was to send a telegram to the Vice-President of the Ukrainian Academy of Sciences, Academician Belitser[63] (a well-wisher of the Jewish Cultural Institute attached to the Academy and a friend of the Institute's director, the philologist, Spivak[64]), with a suggestion for founding a faculty of the Hebrew language in the section for Jewish culture.

After the news of the rebirth of the State of Israel, Hofshteyn suddenly found Kislovodsk constricting. 'I am cured now', he announced and hastened home with the intention of awakening and arousing the people. The inspired Jew and excellent poet, Hofshteyn, was the first victim in the family of Jewish writers and cultural workers to be caught up by the intrigues and falsehoods.[65]

* *Source*: Yehudi Sovieti Almoni (Anonymous Soviet Jew), *El aḥai bi-medinat yisrael* (To My Brothers in the State of Israel), Jerusalem, Kiryat Sefer, 1957, pp. 142–3.

Document 7* Erenburg's conception of Jewish consciousness (1948)[66]

I have received a letter from one Alexander R. in Munich. He writes:

'It may surprise you that I am writing to you, but I have read some of your books and I turn to you as a writer to help me solve what is to me a difficult problem. I am a German Jew, a medical student, and of course, an anti-Fascist. In 1938 I managed to get away to France. When the Nazis invaded France, I went into hiding, then fought for two years in the ranks of the Maquis, in the Gabriel Peri partisan detachment. I returned to Munich after the victory. I confess I was naive – I thought that Fascism had been wiped out. Now I am daily subject to insults. When Hitler was in power, I believed it was a temporary eclipse, I regarded anti-Semitism as one of the features of the "brown plague". But why must I still read disgusting inscriptions on walls? Why must I listen to fellow-students telling me, "Get out of here, go to Palestine"? Why was my friend not given a professorship, but was frankly told: "There's no room for Jews here"? You cannot imagine how intolerable are these insults to one's dignity. I long for a most simple thing, for the right to live without a brand of shame. The Nazis made us wear a yellow patch on our breasts. Now everything is more subtle, but it is the same nevertheless. Under the protection of the Americans the same Nazis are entrenched in all responsible positions. You probably know this, and I am not writing to complain or inform.

'I should like to know what is the attitude taken in the Soviet Union to the State of Israel. Can we see in it a solution to the so-called Jewish question? To me, these are not abstract reflections, but a matter of life. In your novel *The Storm* I read gruesome descriptions of the murder of Jews at Auschwitz and other places. My entire family perished at the hands of the Nazis. What is to be done to prevent a repetition of those horrors? Yesterday I heard a colleague of mine say loudly: "The Jews ought to be finished off." I have never been a Zionist, but I am beginning to believe in the idea of a Jewish state. I am expecting an answer from you – for you are a writer of the country in which I believe with all my heart.'...

I think the question posed by my unknown correspondent is of interest not only to him, and not even only to Jews, but to all people of intelligence and conscience. I have therefore decided to answer, not in a private letter, but in a newspaper article.

Alexander R. wants to know what is the attitude taken in the Soviet Union to the State of Israel. This question can be answered briefly: the Soviet government was the first to recognise the new state, it protested energetically against the aggressors, and when the armies of Israel fought to defend their land from the Arab Legionnaires commanded by British officers, the sympathies of our people were all for the wronged, not for the wrong-doers. This is as natural as the fact that the Soviet people sympathise with the patriots of Vietnam and not with the French suppressors, with the patriots of Indonesia and not with the Dutch punitive forces.

* *Source:* I. Erenburg, 'Po povodu odnogo pisma' (Concerning a Certain Letter), *Pravda*, 21 September 1948.

However, Alexander R.'s first question may be answered at greater length. The representatives of the Soviet Union in the United Nations have said that our people understand the feelings of the Jews who have experienced the greatest tragedy and have at last obtained the right to exist on their own land. Wishing the toilers of Israel success, Soviet people do not close their eyes to the trials in store for all honest people in the young state. In addition to the invasion of Anglo-Arab hordes, Israel is exposed to another invasion – not so conspicuous, but no less dangerous – namely, the invasion of Anglo-American capital. To the imperialists Palestine is, first and foremost, oil. The competition between marauders – Standard Oil on the one hand and the Anglo-Iranian Petroleum Company and Shell on the other – intrudes in the life of the still frail state. Israel is threatened not only by King Abdullah's cutthroats, but by the interests of the Palestine Potash Company, the question of the Kirkuk–Haifa pipeline, American designs for concessions and military bases. The State of Israel is not headed by representatives of the working people. We have all seen how the bourgeoisie of European countries, with their great traditions and older state systems, have sold out the national interests for the sake of dollars. Is there any reason why Soviet people should expect the bourgeoisie of Israel to have more scruples or display greater foresight than the bourgeoisie of France or Italy? Hardly. We trust the people. But the fact that the people in Israel are fighting, and that they are fighting bravely, does not mean that the people there are in power. [...]

Obscurantists have since long ago invented fables designed to represent the Jews as some peculiar creatures different from the people around them. Obscurantists have maintained that the Jews live a separate life of their own, that they do not share the joys and sorrows of the peoples among whom they live; obscurantists have asserted that Jews have no sense of native land, that they are eternal wanderers; obscurantists have affirmed that the Jews of various countries are a unit, held together by some mysterious ties. All these inventions found their extreme expression in Hitler's foul book *Mein Kampf* and were repeated by the SS men who buried old Jews alive and flung Jewish infants down steep banks and into furnaces.

Yes, the Jews kept to themselves and lived their own separate life when they were compelled to do so. The ghetto was not invented by Jewish mystics, but by Catholic fanatics. In those times, when the eyes of people were blinded by the mist of religion, there were fanatics among the Jews just as there were fanatics among Catholics, Protestants, Orthodox Christians and Moslems. But as soon as the gates of the ghetto opened, as soon as the mist of the night of the Middle Ages began to lift, the Jews of various countries joined the general life of the nations.

Yes, many Jews left their native lands and emigrated to America. But they emigrated not because they did not love their native land, but because violence and insults deprived them of that beloved land. And, were the Jews alone in seeking salvation in other countries? That was also what Italians did, what Irishmen did, what Slavs from the countries oppressed by Turks and Germans did, what Armenians and Russian non-conformists did. Jewish toilers, like all others, are strongly attached to the land where they were born and where they grew up.

Jews live in different countries. Many of them live in lands in which their ancestors lived since time immemorial. The first Jewish memorials in Tunis, Georgia, Italy date back to ancient times. Obscurantists say that there exists some mystical bond between all the Jews of the world. However, there is very little in common between a Tunisian Jew and a Jew living in Chicago who speaks American and thinks American. If there is a bond between them, it is anything but mystical; it is a bond created by anti-Semitism. If tomorrow a maniac appeared who proclaimed that all red-headed or snub-nosed people must be hounded and wiped out, we should see a natural solidarity of all red-headed or all snub-nosed people. The appalling atrocities of the German Fascists, their proclaimed policy of wholesale extermination of Jews, a policy which they put into effect in many countries, racial propaganda, insults followed by the furnaces of Maidanek – all that gave rise to a sense of a deep bond among the Jews of various countries. It was the solidarity of offended and indignant people.

The splendid Polish poet Julian Tuwim[67] wrote an article during the war entitled: 'We Polish Jews'. He wrote of his patriotism: 'I am a Pole, because I was told this in Polish in my father's home; a Pole because I was fed on the Polish language from infancy, because my mother taught me Polish verse and Polish songs, because, when I was young, when I was shaken by the first tremor of poetry, it burst forth in Polish words. I am a Pole, because it was in Polish that I confessed the anxieties of my first love, and in Polish that I murmured of its happiness. I am a Pole also because I am fonder of the birch and the willow than of the palm and the cypress, and Mickiewicz and Chopin mean more to me than Shakespeare and Beethoven – for reasons which I cannot explain. I am a Pole because I was born and grew up in Poland, because I was happy and unhappy in Poland, because it is to Poland that I want to return from my exile, even if I were assured heavenly bliss elsewhere. I am a Pole because I want Polish soil, and none other, to swallow me up when I am dead.' Julian Tuwim then went on to explain what bound him to the Jews: 'Blood exists in two forms: the blood that flows in the veins and the blood that flows out of the veins. The study of the first belongs to the realm of physiology. Those who, beside physiological characteristics, attribute to blood some other properties, some mysterious force, those, as we now see, reduce cities to ashes, massacre people, and, as we shall soon see, lead their own nation to ruin. The other blood is the one which the ringleader of international Fascism is extracting from the veins of humanity in order to prove the triumph of his blood over my blood. It is the blood of millions innocently slain, the blood of Jews, and not "Jewish blood". Why do I say, "We Jews"? Because of blood.'

Of course, there are nationalists and mystics among the Jews. They produced the programme of Zionism. But it is not they who have settled Palestine with Jews. Jews went to Palestine because of the ideologists of misanthropy, the votaries of racism, the anti-Semites who drove people from their homes and made them migrate to distant lands in search – not of happiness so much as of the right to their human dignity. We all remember the epic of the 'Exodus', the ship which carried to Palestine refugees from Western Germany – people who by chance had escaped the furnaces of Auschwitz and Maidanek and then found themselves fired on by British soldiers. The State of

Israel is something like that ship – an ark, a raft, holding people overtaken by the bloody flood of racism and Fascism. [...]

Let my correspondent, Alexander R., ponder over the events of the past decade, and he will realise that there is only one way to solve the 'Jewish question'. It is to abolish the 'Jewish question'.

We sympathise with the struggle of the toilers of Israel, they have the sympathies not only of the Soviet Jews, but of all Soviet people – there are no admirers of Glubb Pasha in our country. But every Soviet citizen is aware that a state is judged not only by its national character, but by its social system as well. A citizen of socialist society regards the people of any bourgeois country, and that means also the people of the State of Israel, as wanderers in a dark forest who have not yet found their way out. [...]

A citizen of socialist society can never envy the fate of people who carry the yoke of capitalist exploitation.

The future of the Jewish toilers of all countries is bound up with the future of socialism. Soviet Jews, along with all Soviet people, are working to build up their socialist homeland. They are not looking to the Near East – they are looking towards the future. And I believe that the working people of the State of Israel, who do not share the mysticism of the Zionists, are now looking northward, to the Soviet Union, which is marching in the van of mankind towards a better future.

Document 8*   I. Erenburg on being a Jew

In September 1948, at the editor's request, I wrote an article for *Pravda* on the 'Jewish Question', on Palestine and anti-Semitism.[68] [...]

A newspaper article is not a testament, there is much one cannot say in it. Now, as I near the end of my memoirs, I should like to state my beliefs on what is often called the 'Jewish Question'.

As a child I heard talk of the Dreyfus affair and Jewish pogroms. I knew that Lev Tolstoy, Chekhov and Gorky were repelled by the way the Russians were set against the Jews. Some years later, I read in the illegal newspaper an article about this by Lenin. My father said that anti-Semitism was a survival and outcome of fanaticism and ignorance, and I shared that view.

As the reader knows, I was born in Kiev, my mother tongue is Russian. I know neither Yiddish nor Hebrew. I have never prayed in a synagogue, nor yet in an Orthodox or Catholic church. I have admired and still admire certain works of art which for the believer have a religious connotation but for me connote human thoughts and feelings: the Book of Job, the Song of Songs, Ecclesiastes, the Gospels, including the Apocrypha, the Apocalypse, Chartres Cathedral, the Acropolis, Andrei Rublev's icons, Fra Angelico's paintings, the Hindu goddesses at Ellora and the frescoes in the ancient Buddhist monastery of Ajanta. These things mean to me not dead religious canons but living art. I spent my childhood and early youth in Moscow and my comrades were Russians. When I worked in the illegal organisation we called each other by aliases, and I was not interested to know whether any of my comrades were

* *Source*: I. Erenburg, 'Lyudi, gody, zhizn' (People, Years, Life), *Novy mir*, 1965, no. 2, pp. 51–5.

Jews. Then I found myself in Paris. I met two wonderful people: one of them, Apollinaire, was of Polish origin, the other, Max Jacob, was a Jew, but for me, they were both Frenchmen. I was very devoted to the Italian Modigliani; he once told me that he was a Jew, but for me he was forever associated with the anxiety of the pre-war years and with the art of the Italian Renaissance; certainly not with Yahveh.

I love Spain, Italy and France, but all my years are inseparable from Russian life. I have never concealed my origin. There were times when I did not give it a thought, and others when I said wherever I could: 'I am a Jew', for to my mind solidarity with the persecuted is the first principle of humanitarianism.

I saw Chaplin's films and it never entered my head to ask if he was a Jew; it was the Nazis who said he was. They drew up black lists: the composer Milhaud, the philosopher Bergson were said to be Jews, and so were people whom I had met without ever thinking about their origin, like Julien Benda, Anna Seghers and authors whom I had read, such as Kafka.

Is there a special innate Jewish national character? Anti-Semites and Jewish nationalists say there is. It is possible that centuries of persecution and humiliation sharpened their irony and fostered in them romantic hopes of a better future. National character manifests itself most vividly in artistic creation. Heine's poetry is full of romantic irony, but is it to be explained by the poet's origins or by his epoch? When I consider the works of my contemporaries – Modigliani, Kafka, Soutine – what I see first and foremost is the spirit of tragedy reflecting reality and mingling memories with foreboding or foresight. Mathematics is one of the manifestations of human intelligence least affected by climate, language or traditions. Yet in the early thirties there were scholars in Germany who dismissed Einstein's Theory of Relativity as a 'Jewish spoof'.

In the old days anti-Semitism was bound up with religion, with the idea of redemption: 'the Jews crucified Christ'. Then the power of the priests gradually waned. Many people began to realise that Christ was only one of those Jewish rebels who opposed the orthodox priests for their collaboration with the Roman occupation. The French Revolution declared equal rights for the Jews. Various states, one after the other, abrogated the proscriptions that had been in force for centuries. The Jews began to live the life of the peoples to whose land their ancestors had come.

At the end of the last century the Dreyfus affair demonstrated that anti-Semitism, though it had lain dormant, was still alive. For several years the eyes of millions of people were focused on Dreyfus, who was no more than an insignificant, conscientious French officer, trained to discipline. When Zola took up the defence of the wrongly condemned man he was supported by Tolstoy, Verhaeren, Mark Twain, Jaurès, Anatole France, Maeterlinck, R. C. K. Ensor, Monet, Jules Renard, Signac, Péguy, Octave Mirbeau, Mallarmé and Charles-Louis Philippe. And who were those who sided with the accusers? The nationalist writers Barrès, Maurras and Déroulède. The anti-Dreyfusards were not only anti-Semites but enemies of progress and chauvinists to a man; in their newspapers and pamphlets they called Zola 'a dirty little Italian'. [...]

In Montparnasse during the late twenties I met a Jewish writer from Poland, Warszawski, and some of his friends. They told me many amusing stories about the superstitions and the cunning of the old type small-town Jew. I read a collection of Hasidic legends which I found pleasingly poetic. It gave me the idea of writing a satirical novel. Its hero is a Gomel tailor, Lazik Roitshvanets, a poor fellow whom fate tosses from one country to another. I described our NEP men and provincial dogmatists, Polish cavalry captains, German petty bourgeois, French aesthetes and English hypocrites. Finally, in despair, Lazik decides to go to Palestine, but the so-called Promised Land turns out to be like any other: the rich have a good life, the poor a wretched one. Lazik tries to organise a 'Return-to-the-Homeland Association', on the grounds that he was not born under a palm tree but in his beloved Gomel. He is killed by Jewish fanatics. Western critics called my hero 'the Jewish Schweik'. (This book is not included in my collected works, not because I think badly of it or repudiate it, but because, after the Nazi atrocities, I think it premature to republish some of its comical passages.)

Hitler's coming to power stunned me: a civilised country was thrown back into the black night of obscurantism. The *Kristallnacht* (as the Nazis called the night of the 1938 mass pogroms) was for me one of the hateful manifestations of Fascism. The Nazis burnt books by Jewish authors and also the works of Engels, Lenin, Gorky, Romain Rolland, Zola, Barbusse and Heinrich Mann. They killed German Communists of 'Aryan' descent. In Spain I came face to face with the savage reality of Fascism.

During the Nazi invasion of our country I witnessed many atrocities. The Nazis killed Russian children, they burnt down villages in the Ukraine and in Belorussia. I was writing about this daily in the newspapers. Others also wrote about it. The Nazi leaflets claimed that they were wiping out only the Jews and it was imperative to nail this lie.

At the end of the war, Vasily Grossman[69] and I began to collect material relating to the mass extermination of Jews in those parts of the country overrun by the Nazis: letters written on the eve of death, diaries kept by a painter in Riga, a girl student in Kharkov, by old men and by children. This compilation of human documents was to be called *The Black Book*. While it showed up the hideous deeds of the Nazis, it also brought out the bright virtues of courage, solidarity and love. The type was set up, the book reached proof stage, and we were told that it would be published in 1948.[70]

The Zionist theories based on ancient history have never had any appeal for me. The State of Israel, however, exists. In the days when Arab culture flourished the Jews did not know persecutions like those of the Inquisition, and in the various Muslim kingdoms of Andalusia such men lived and worked as the philosopher Maimonides[71] and the poet Yehudah Ha-levi.[72] I like to believe that the Jews of Israel, who know from personal experiences the meaning of injustice, will find a way of making peace with the Arabs. It is clear to everyone that the millions of Jews living in the various countries of Europe and America cannot find room in Israel and, besides, they are too closely associated with the peoples among whom they live to want to emigrate. The negroes of Alabama and Mississippi do not dream of migrating to one of the sovereign states of Black Africa, they only demand equal rights and fight racial prejudice ...

Document 9* Aron Vergelis[73] (1961)

With anti-Soviet propaganda dinning it into his head that neither the Jews nor their problems have changed in the Soviet Union, the foreign visitor will sometimes say: 'I want to see a "real" Jew! Perhaps we ought to visit a synagogue? Or maybe a market?'

This makes us feel awkward. What we would like to do with such a visitor is to take him by the hand and lead him to where ordinary Soviet people live and work, relax and bring up their children. We would like to show him the new life of the Jew in the Soviet Union, his ideals and how he pictures his future.

In Western papers one often reads that, in the Soviet Union, Jews are 'kept down', that the Jewish religion is 'stifled'. It is, in fact, very easy to refute those slanders.

The Jewish Soviet citizen of today looks understandingly upon the religious feelings of his old folk, who are accustomed to go to the synagogue. But that road is not his road.

His spiritual world is the opera *Eugene Onegin* and the Jewish folk-song. He will gladly go to an anniversary celebration of Shalom Aleikhem or Osher Shvartsman, which fills to capacity any of Moscow's largest halls, and he is captivated by the latest works of Sholokhov or the Kazakh writer Auezov.

Jewish reactionaries always direct attention towards the synagogues and rabbis, trying to suggest that the 'religious problem' is the chief 'national problem' of Soviet Jews. Today, however, the problems of the Jews in the Soviet Union – like those of the other Soviet peoples – centre around their active participation in the building of Communism.

Document 10† The economic trials: Soviet Jews deny anti-Semitism (1963)

It is known that in recent months the bourgeois Western press has again set up an outcry about so-called anti-Semitism in the USSR. This time the 'reason' given was the fact that among the persons punished under the laws of the Soviet Union for crimes they had committed, termed 'economic' crimes in the Western press, have been some people of Jewish nationality.

Comrade N. S. Khrushchev, in his answer to the British philosopher, Bertrand Russell,[74] demonstrated convincingly that this was a gross invention, as well as vicious slander against the Soviet people and our country. There is not nor has there ever been a policy of anti-Semitism in the Soviet Union, since the very nature of our multi-national socialist state precludes the possibility of such a policy.

The vicious anti-Soviet fuss in the bourgeois press has aroused angry rebuttals from the Soviet people. The editors have received many letters from

* *Source*: A. Vergelis, 'Jews in the Soviet Union', *Soviet Weekly*, 13 April 1961.
† *Source*: 'O rodine i o sebe' (About the Homeland and About Ourselves), *Izvestiya*, 31 May 1963.

readers of various occupations and ages, both Communists and non-Party
people.

What has stirred them to write to the newspaper is well expressed by
L. Tseitlin, an officer in the Soviet Armed Forces: 'I read with great interest
the meaningful, highly convincing and truthful letter from Nikita Sergeevich
Khrushchev. This letter certainly leaves nothing to be said. Nevertheless, I
have deemed it my civic duty, the duty of a Soviet man, a Communist and a
Jew by nationality, to appeal through your newspaper to the people in the
West who might be led astray by bourgeois propaganda. I can state with full
conviction that in the Soviet Union there is absolutely no soil for anti-
Semitism or an unjust attitude toward any other nationality.'

This thought runs like a red thread through all the letters. [...]

The efforts of the bourgeois press to single out and isolate Soviet citizens of
Jewish nationality arouses the justifiable indignation of the Jews. N. Pernitsky
writes from Odessa: 'In this country there can be no privileges for citizens of
any nationality who have committed crimes.' Ts. Rakhlis, a jurist, and
V. Letnev, a retired officer who lives in Kharkov, express themselves still more
sharply: 'The demand for an "amnesty" for criminals of Jewish nationality is
profoundly offensive to us Jews who are citizens of the Soviet Union, since it
calls for absurd exceptions to be made and violates the principles by which our
country and people live. The currency dealers, speculators and embezzlers of
public property are criminals, and they should not be allowed to escape the
punishment they deserve, no matter who they are.'

A. Pukhovitsky, an investigator from Leningrad, explains to people in the
West who are unaware of it that the nationality of a criminal is never under
any circumstances taken into account in instituting criminal proceedings or
determining sentences. On the contrary, if we discovered among us a court
official or a prosecutor who violated this rule, a criminal charge would
immediately be brought against him under Article 74 of the Russian Republic
Criminal Code or the corresponding articles of the criminal codes of the other
Union republics.

Document 11* Grossman[75] on Jewish suffering

It is interesting that this variety of fair and dark faces, blue and black eyes is
particularly noticeable in the patriarchal, isolated Armenian villages, where
the variety cannot be attributed to recent events. Long centuries have polished
the glass that reflects the faces of contemporary Armenians.

But surely the same may be said not only of the Armenians but also of the
Russians, and particularly of the Jews. Of course, it may. Are Russian faces all
of one kind? Does not one find alongside the blue-eyed and grey-eyed, the
snub-nosed and flaxen-haired, some Russians with hooked noses, 'Gypsies',
as they are called, with dark southern eyes and tar-black curls? And the next
face you notice may have broad Mongolian cheekbones, a Mongolian slant to
the eyes and a flattened nose? And what about the Jews! Black-haired,

* *Source*: V. Grossman, 'Good Luck To You!', *Soviet Literature*, 1969, no. 6, pp. 45, 47–9, 59, 68,
   76–77.

hook-nosed, snub-nosed, dark-skinned, blue-eyed, blond – Asian, African, Spanish, German, Slav faces.

The longer the history of a people, the more wars, captivity, invasions, migrations it has seen, the greater the variety of faces. This facial diversity is the reflection of centuries, millennia of nights spent by the conquerors in the homes of the conquered.[...]

I asked Martirosyan about Mandelstam's stay in Armenia. I knew some endearing facts about the life the poet had led in Armenia and I had read his Armenian cycle of poems. I remembered his expression about 'fabulous Armenian Christianity'.

But Martirosyan could not remember Mandelstam at all. At my request he made a point of ringing certain poets of the older generation; they did not know that Mandelstam had ever been to Armenia. Martirosyan said he vaguely remembered a very thin individual with a big nose, obviously very poor. Martirosyan had twice given him supper and wine; after having something to drink, this long-nosed fellow had recited some verses. It must have been Mandelstam. [...]

I was invited to a wedding. Martirosyan's nephew was getting married. He was a driver and his bride was a sales-girl at a village shop. It would be a long journey, to the Talin district, on the southern slope of Aragats. I had doubts about going. The evening before I had felt very ill and, like a swimmer who is not sure of his strength, I hesitated to go far from the home shore. But when the telephone rang in the morning and Martirosyan said that an Erevan delegation – he, Violetta Minasovna and Gortenzia – had already arrived at the hotel and was waiting for me in the hall, I took the plunge. [...]

Almost nothing was said in the speeches about the young couple and their future happiness. People spoke of good and evil, of honest hard work, of their people's bitter fate, of their past and their hopes for the future, of the fertile lands of Turkish Armenia that had been soaked in innocent blood, of the Armenian people who are scattered all over the world, of their faith that honest toil and kindness are stronger than any falsehood.

In what reverent silence these speeches were listened to; no one made a sound, no one ate or drank. Everyone listened breathlessly.

Then a thin grey-haired peasant in an old soldier's tunic began to speak. I have seen few faces as severe as that dark, stony visage.

'He's a carpenter at the collective farm. He's addressing you.'

The silence in the barn was marvellous. Dozens of eyes were fixed on me. I could not understand what was being said, but for some reason the expression in all those eyes that were regarding me with gentle attention moved me deeply. Martirosyan translated the carpenter's speech. He was talking about the Jews. He said that as a prisoner in Germany he had seen the Gestapo picking out the Jewish prisoners. He told me how some Jewish friends of his were murdered. He spoke of his sympathy and love for the Jewish women and children who had died in the gas chambers of Auschwitz. He said he had read my war-time articles in which I described Armenians, and he had thought that these descriptions must have been written by someone whose people had endured many cruel sufferings. He would like a son of the long-suffering Armenian people to write about the Jews. And it was to this that he drank his glass of vodka.

I bow my head in the deepest respect to the Armenian peasants who in a mountain village during a wedding celebration spoke in public of the torments of the Jewish people in the days when Fascism was rampant, of the death camps where the Nazis murdered Jewish women and children, and I bow in respect to all those who listened in solemn and sorrowful silence to these words. Their faces, their eyes told me much. I bow in gratitude for those sad words about the people who died in ditches, in gas chambers and mass graves, and on behalf of the living in whose faces those misanthropic words of contempt and hate have been thrown: 'It's a pity Hitler didn't finish you all off.'

Till the end of my days I shall remember the speeches of the peasants that I heard in that village club.

2

Official Soviet statements on the Jewish question

We define official statements as the pronouncements of Soviet government and Party leaders on subjects concerning the Jewish people in general and the Jews of the Soviet Union in particular. In all cases where an official Soviet version of the declaration cited exists it is given in full. Where no such text exists, we have been compelled to use what we deem the most reliable version published outside the Soviet Union. Some reports, which seem unreliable, have not been included here.

It should be pointed out that, in the Soviet Union, official approaches are expressed not only in the public statements of the country's leaders but also indirectly, for instance in the leading article of a central newspaper or in the commentaries of other communications media. From this point of view, every Soviet report is official. However, there are of course important differences between statements coming from the Party leader or important office-holders in the government and ordinary articles, even those appearing in the most important newspaper.

The official statements brought together in the documents to this chapter do not comprise all such documents included in this book. However, there are few such statements given elsewhere, and these relate directly to the specific subject matter of the chapters to which they are appended and in which they are analysed. Our main aim here is to consider the importance of each individual document given and the general background to its publication.

The Stalin period

The first thing which becomes apparent when reading the documents to this chapter is that, for the years 1948–53, not even one official statement on the question of the Jews of the USSR was issued by Soviet leaders or their spokesmen. Nothing at all was said of the situation, the yearnings or the aspirations of Soviet Jews in any of the many saliently pro-Israeli statements made by Soviet representatives in the United Nations Organisation in 1948 and early 1949 (see Chapter 6).

In fact, Stalin's last brief statement on the Jews was made in 1941,[1] ten years after his previous pronouncement on the question of anti-Semitism (see Chapter 3). And, from 1941 until his death on 5 March 1953, he refrained from making even the slightest direct or indirect allusion to the Jewish problem. There are, however, more than a few reliable testimonies (cited in the course of this work) of Stalin's off-the-record statements, most of them negative, on various questions relating to the Jewish people.

The first document of this chapter (Doc. 12) is the statement of Soviet Foreign Minister Andrei Vyshinsky at the UN General Assembly on 16 April 1953, made in reaction to Israeli demands for a discussion on the Soviet anti-Jewish policy which was given particularly extreme expression in the January 1953 announcement on the Doctors' Plot.

The Khrushchev period

In September 1955, the pro-Communist Yiddish newspaper *Morgn frayheyt* (published in New York) reported a statement by the Director of the Information Department in the Soviet Foreign Ministry, L. Ilyichev, then visiting New York, to the effect that the poet Perets Markish, who had been secretly executed on 12 August 1952 (see Chapter 5), was alive in Moscow, and that he, Ilyichev, had personally met him in the editorial offices of *Pravda*.[2] As far as we know, this was the first official statement in the post-Stalin period in response to enquiries from Communists and pro-Communist Jewish circles in the West.

It is important to stress that no specific mention was made at the 20th Congress of the Soviet Communist Party in February 1956 of Stalin's anti-Jewish policy – a policy which had resulted in the total liquidation of Jewish culture, the extermination of the elite among Yiddish writers and artists, and inestimable suffering to all Soviet Jews – and this despite Khrushchev's having made the gravest accusations against Stalin's 'personality cult' in his secret speech, in which he even mentioned the Doctors' Plot.[3]

The first time the question of the Jews of the Soviet Union was discussed at length was in early May 1956, during a meeting between the most prominent leaders of the Soviet Union (including Khrushchev, Kaganovich, Pervukhin and Shepilov) and the heads of the French Socialist Party, or SFIO (led by Commin, the Secretary-General, and also including Marceau-Pivert, Deixonne, Verdier, Lamine-Gueye, Brutelle and Philip) (see Doc. 13). There is no doubt as to the document's reliability, for it is a stenographic record made by the delegation's interpreter, Pierre Lochak, who participated in all the discussions and transcribed exactly what was said. Among the various issues discussed at the second session, the question of the Jews of the Soviet Union occupied a central place. The initiative for this discussion came from the French delegation, which had been requested by Jewish circles in France to clarify the policy of the new Soviet leadership on this question.

The position of Kaganovich, the most prominent Soviet leader of Jewish origin at the time these sessions took place, is of interest. He kept mostly silent throughout the discussion on the situation of Soviet Jews. Apparently, the last time Kaganovich spoke on a Jewish topic was in an interview he granted the Jewish journalist, Dr Henry Shoshkes, in August 1956.[4] At that time, his basic approach was that the Jews did not need an autonomous Jewish culture. However, he did agree that if the Jews in fact demanded the maintenance of a Jewish culture, such a demand would be satisfied. He himself, he quickly added, did not believe that such a demand would be raised, even by a minority of the Jews.

The question of the liquidation of Jewish culture in the Soviet Union was at the centre of the statements made by Soviet officials in 1956. This was a direct result of unrelenting pressure by Jewish and non-Jewish Communist and pro-Communist circles in the West, who on various occasions demanded a clear and unevasive reply on the fate of Jewish culture in the Soviet Union. Of particularly strong influence was the appeal made by the editorial staff of the Warsaw Yiddish-language newspaper *Folks-shtime* (see Doc. 74) to the Soviet leaders, to transfer consideration of this question from a closed, internal discussion to an open public debate. The position of official Soviet represent-atives, as expressed in Furtseva's remarks in an interview with Tabitha Petran and those of Ilyichev (see Docs. 14 and 16), was defensive. Responsibility for past deeds was placed on the 'Beria gang', while the claim was that the Jews currently enjoyed rights equal to those of all the other peoples of the Soviet Union.

Of particular interest in this context is the letter from the Soviet Deputy Minister of Education Arsenyev to Professor Katsh (Doc. 15). Arsenyev clearly aimed to mislead the Western public by making legalistic claims which were totally insubstantial insofar as they concerned the Jews. A similar purpose was behind the letter sent to progressive Jewish circles in Australia,[5] which contained the customary claims that there was no Jewish problem in the Soviet Union, that the Jews enjoyed all rights, and that they were not in the least interested in maintaining an autonomous national culture but preferred to assimilate into the national cultures in which they lived.

In the years 1955–7, Khrushchev met with various Western journalists and public figures who raised questions related to several aspects of the life of Soviet Jewry.[6] Particularly revealing is the interview Khrushchev granted Henry Shapiro, the veteran American correspondent in Moscow. The inter-view took place when the brief 'liberal' honeymoon was on the wane, and Khrushchev came out with a harsh attack on liberal literary and artistic circles in the Soviet Union. He even went so far as to employ an extreme anti-Jewish term from the period of the anti-cosmopolitan campaign, 'types without ethnic roots and ties', in order to cast these circles in a negative light.[7] Of course, the Jews occupied quite a prominent place in Soviet liberal circles (it is sufficient to mention such names as Ilya Erenburg, Venyamin Kaverin and Margarita Aliger, among many others).

One of the most important pronouncements on the question of the Jews of the Soviet Union is found in Khrushchev's interview with Serge Groussard, correspondent of the French newspaper *Le Figaro* (Doc. 17). Here, it would seem, Khrushchev expressed his true, private view in the most overt manner. It is therefore no accident that, of the entire section dealing with the Jewish issue, only a few sentences noting that there had been pogroms against the Jews in the Tsarist period appeared in the Soviet press.[8]

At a reception during approximately the same period for guests and the diplomatic corps, Khrushchev turned to Yosef Avidar, Israeli Ambassador to the Soviet Union, and his wife, and declared: 'Here I see the Ambassador of Israel and his wife asking themselves what Khrushchev is going to say. Well, during the Queen of Belgium's visit she asked Voroshilov what the special attitude of the ruling power was towards the Jews of the Soviet Union, and Voroshilov answered that look, his wife is Jewish.' It was indeed a special attitude, Khrushchev added, since half the members of the Party Presidium had Jewish wives.[9]

Following the first steps made to renew it (see Chapter 7), the question of Jewish culture in the Soviet Union was discussed at length in a meeting between the Deputy Minister of Culture of the Soviet Union and a Jewish Communist delegation from France headed by M. Vilner, editor of the Yiddish-language newspaper *Naye prese* (Doc. 18).

The year 1959, which saw many Soviet leaders visiting abroad, brought forth important statements on issues relating to the Jews of the Soviet Union. During his January 1959 visit to the United States, Anastas Mikoyan, First Deputy of the Prime Minister of the Soviet Union and something of a roving ambassador of Khrushchev,[10] was compelled to reply to trenchant questions asked by American journalists (Docs. 19–20). As anticipated, the replies were standard and revolved around the old arguments. The only new subject was the question of Birobidzhan and the rumours then rife that Soviet authorities were about to exile some Jews to this region. During his visit to the United States in July, Frol Kozlov, another First Deputy of the Prime Minister of the Soviet Union, who also had to face American journalists, vehemently denied the existence of discrimination against Soviet Jews. He also said that there was no truth to reports that synagogues were being closed down (Doc. 21).

During the 1959 visits of Mikoyan and Kozlov, there was extensive activity on the part of Jewish organisations in the United States with regard to Soviet Jewry. This engendered the idea of a meeting between a representative Jewish delegation, to be headed by Dr Nahum Goldman (Chairman of the Jewish Agency and of the World Jewish Congress), and Khrushchev, which would take place during the latter's imminent visit to the United States.[11] But the meeting was never held. In reply to a question at a press conference, Khrushchev contented himself with the assertion that the Jews occupied a distinguished place in the team responsible for launching the Soviet lunar satellite (Doc. 23).

At the session of the Supreme Soviet in January 1960, Khrushchev made a harsh attack on anti-Semitism in West Germany and on the failure of German history books to mention Nazi crimes against the Jewish people.[12] He did not, however, mention Soviet literature's silence on the Jewish Holocaust (see Chapter 12).

Emigration from the Soviet Union apparently was raised for the first time in May 1956, in the talks between Soviet leaders and the heads of the French Socialist Party. The question was brought up again in 1958, in Khrushchev's interview with Serge Groussard. But it was only in 1959, in the wake of heavy Arab pressure on the Soviet Union and an extensive diplomatic campaign,[13] that the Soviet communications media began to deny that there was Jewish emigration to Israel from the Soviet Union.[14] In his letter to Imam Ahmad of Yemen, Khrushchev stated that the talk about emigration was nothing but false imperialist propaganda (Doc. 22). Despite this assertion, Khrushchev did state, during a July 1960 press conference in Vienna, that while the Soviet

Union did not oppose the reunification of certain individuals, no problem existed, because there were in fact no candidates for such emigration (Doc. 24).

From discussions in the international forum, renewed from time to time on the initiative of Israeli or Western representatives, we have chosen to cite the 1962 UN General Assembly debate between the Australian and Soviet representatives, in which the latter denied the existence of discrimination against Jews in the Soviet Union (Doc. 25).

The February 1963 correspondence between Bertrand Russell and Khrushchev on the economic trials (Doc. 26) is of great importance[15] because it demonstrates, *inter alia*, that pressure by influential Western circles did produce results. This was due to the Soviet leadership's sensitivity to relations with the West during this period.

In the final document from the Khrushchev period, his speech at a March 1963 conference of intellectuals (Doc. 27), Khrushchev's views on the Jewish question found extremely clear expression.[16]

The collective-leadership period (October 1964 – June 1967)

In contrast to the Khrushchev period, there were few statements on or about Jews in the Soviet Union during the three years of the new leadership, and all of these were made by Prime Minister of the Soviet Union Aleksei Kosygin. As far as is known, Communist Party Leader Leonid Brezhnev did not refer to the Jewish question in any of his various appearances inside or outside the USSR. It is of interest that Kosygin saw fit to include, in his speech in honour of the twenty-fifth anniversary of Latvia's incorporation into the USSR, the assertion that anti-Semitism is an alien phenomenon that is contrary to the Communist world-view (Doc. 28). This declaration was by no means random; it may have been meant as a hint that the new leadership intended to alter – at least in certain restricted spheres – the ruling power's policy towards the Jews of the Soviet Union. Kosygin made a similar statement in 1966.

Of great significance was Kosygin's appearance in Paris on 3 December 1966, and his reply to UPI correspondent Eli Maissy on the reunification of families, in other words, on the possibility of emigration to Israel from the Soviet Union. Kosygin's reply, which was published in Soviet newspapers (Doc. 29), served as a kind of authorisation when Jews applied to obtain exit permits for emigration to Israel.

The Six-Day War and the severance of relations with Israel by the Soviet Union and the other East European countries (except Romania) ended the partial amelioration in Soviet–Israeli relations and also in the situation of Soviet Jews.[17] Kosygin's angry reply to N. Silberberg during a June 1967 press conference in New York (Doc. 30) patently demonstrates this fact. His reply to the *Jewish Chronicle* correspondent, and his caustic claim that there was not and never had been anti-Semitism in the Soviet Union, were a long way even from statements made by the Soviet leaders in the Khrushchev period, when they were prepared to admit that there were still some isolated vestiges of anti-Semitism as a heritage of the past.

Documents to Chapter 2

Document 12* Vyshinsky at the United Nations (1953)[18]

Mr Vyshinsky said that the statements of the representative of Israel with reference to the Soviet Union and the policy of its government were merely a mixture of insinuation and slander designed to poison the atmosphere. Decent people did not indulge in debates with slanderers and those remarks, not being worthy of an answer, would be passed over by the Soviet Union in silence.

Document 13† Meeting between representatives of the French Socialist Party and Soviet leaders (1956)[19]

Second session: Saturday 5 May, 10 a.m.

Khrushchev: Please sit down. If you are thirsty, help yourself to the mineral water in these bottles. Our mineral water is not called *Vichy* (*smiles*). Who is going to begin today? Deixonne? Very well, please begin.

Deixonne: We know your position on religion – a private matter for the state. But it isn't a private matter for the Communist Party, which is a powerful and governing Party.

On 1 November 1954, your Central Committee reacted against unwarranted meddling in the life of the churches and against harassments.[20] Have these decisions had any results? Can the churches today educate priests, or have premises at their disposal? Can the Protestants publish the Bible? In short, what right do believers have to practise their religion without suffering any physical or moral pressure?

Mikoyan: The decisions of the Central Committee are respected. There has been no protest.

Khrushchev: Mikoyan is well qualified to speak about the churches. In his youth he wanted to be a priest, but he did not succeed. He was even at a religious seminary. But he became a Bolshevik.

Mikoyan: The Party takes no administrative measures. It acts on conviction.

---

* *Source: United Nations General Assembly. Seventh Session. Official Records. First Committee, 603rd Meeting,* 16 April 1953, New York, p. 645 (A/C.1/SR.603).

† *Source:* 'Les Entretiens entre Moscou et les Socialistes français' (Meeting Between Moscow and the French Socialist Party), *Les Réalités,* 1957, no. 136, pp. 64–7, 101–4.

Thanks to scientific education there has been a rise in general education which is able to restrain the influence of religion.

Marxist philosophy and religion are incompatible. But we respect the peoples who are believers. All the religions have academies and seminaries for the training of priests. The Protestants and others may publish the Bible.[21]

The Orthodox religion had to suffer from the Revolution. The Tsar was the representative of the church and of power. He oppressed the other religions. Now there is equality of churches. By reason of its amalgamation with the state at the time of the Tsars, the church was looked upon favourably at the beginning of the Revolution. It was on the side of the White Guards. At that time, we did not spare the priests. With victory and the stabilisation of the regime, the clergy turned to the people. During the war of 1941–5, the churches were patriotic. This normalised our relations. From that moment the population in its entirety treated the church better. Our church heads travel abroad; they have exchanges with their co-religionists abroad. They do not involve themselves in affairs of state and we don't involve ourselves in their affairs. Many priests preach socialism as a variant of Christianity. We don't oppose that.

Khrushchev: Mikoyan is Orthodox.

Mikoyan: No, no! That's incorrect. Christian, perhaps, but not Orthodox.

Khrushchev: Our patriarch is an erudite man. He is intelligent. He's a nice man.[...]

Deixonne: Does a certain amount of anti-Semitism exist among your people? If so, what are you doing about it?

Mikoyan: Perhaps there are some survivals from the capitalist era. On the whole, our people is internationalist. Among the Jews, if you look hard, you will perhaps find Zionist tendencies. In Georgia there are some remnants of nationalism. In so short a space of time it has been difficult to eliminate prejudices.

Deixonne: Why is Zionism prosecuted in the USSR? What is the legal basis for the anti-Zionist trials?

Mikoyan: We do not prosecute for Zionism alone. There are no Zionist trials. If the Zionists are American spies or spies for other anti-Soviet states, they can be prosecuted on this score. Likewise, they may be prosecuted and punished for sabotage, but not for Zionist activity.

Deixonne: However, you remember the Doctors' Trial?[22]

Mikoyan: There was no trial, only a preliminary investigation. Moreover, it wasn't directed against Jews alone. The doctors were, for the most part, Russians. They were accused of activities harmful to the state. The preliminary investigation was staged at all points by Beria[23] and his gang. All the doctors were rehabilitated after the investigation was reviewed.

Khrushchev: The majority were Russians and Ukrainians, such as Vinogradov, Vasilenko, Egorov; all honest people who have been rehabilitated.

The affair was given a Zionist, Jewish colouring. That was one of Beria's machinations. They were accused of spying for the Americans insofar as they were Zionists, after having first been accused of medical sabotage against Zhdanov and others. It was utter nonsense. It wasn't even a Jew who had tended Zhdanov, but the doctor Egorov.

Deixonne: Can a Jew visit Israel or emigrate there?

Khrushchev: Let me tell you the truth, we are not fond of these journeys.

Shepilov: The question does not arise in any case.

Khrushchev: Anyhow, we don't favour them. We're against them because Israel is under the thumb of the American reactionaries. Consequently, it's easy to channel every kind of espionage and provocation through Israel. It's the remnants of the Cold War which command our particular attitude towards Israel. We hope that it's only temporary and that this attitude will disappear.

Deixonne: What are the cultural freedoms of the Jews in the USSR? Is there a Jewish theatre? Can Yiddish writers publish their works?

Mikoyan: Every nationality has these rights in our country. It's a question of practical necessities. The Jews speak Russian, Ukrainian, etc., according to their place of residence in our country.

Khrushchev: If you go to Sverdlovsk, go and see Colonel-General Kreizer.[24] He's my friend, he's an army commander. He's Jewish. We also have Jewish ministers, for example, Raizer,[25] Minister of Construction. Likewise we have Vannikov[26] and Lifshits[27] among our ministers; they are both Jewish.

On the subject of the nationalities question, let me point out to you the case of Moldavia. The intellectuals in this republic don't willingly send their children to Moldavian schools. They prefer the Russian school. Similarly, in the Ukraine, the people prefer the Russian school. The Ukrainian writers aren't happy. This can be explained by motivations of a practical nature and by the interests of the populations themselves. Children are sent preferably to the Russian school because, from the Moldavian school, it's more difficult to pass on afterwards to a higher school other than in Moldavia, whereas with a certificate in Russian studies, all the schools of higher education in the Soviet Union are open to them.

As far as the Jews are concerned, if one created Jewish schools, there would be very few who would favour going there. The Jews are dispersed over the whole Union. One would never be able to create a university in the Jewish language. There wouldn't be a sufficient contingent of students. On the other hand, with Yiddish or Hebrew, there exists no opening into the Soviet administration and institutions. If one compelled the Jews to go to a Jewish school, there would certainly be a revolt. It would be considered a sort of ghetto. The Yiddish theatre has declined for want of spectators, despite donations and subscriptions. However, the theatre is open to the Jews. Thus, at Lvov there is a Russian theatre, but the majority, if not all, of the actors are Jewish.[28] [...]

Verdier: You spoke of the *détente* as necessary. We welcome it everywhere. It is jeopardised in the Middle East because of the Israel–Arab conflict. How do you intend collaborating in the *détente* in this region? Will you participate in an embargo on arms, in a settlement of the problem of the Arab refugees, in the establishment of peace along Israel's frontiers?

Khrushchev: The question is a complex one. In the conflict between Arabs and

Israelis there is something larger than the conflict proper. It's the conflict between Great Britain and the USA, and also France to a small extent.

There is a Ukrainian saying that runs: 'When two masters fight, it's the peasant that catches the blows.'

We discussed it a great deal in Great Britain. We have published declarations regarding the solution.[29] But we haven't arrived at a solution. Great Britain abides by the Baghdad Pact[30] in order to dominate the petroleum countries. These countries are adjacent to the USSR or neighbours of the USSR. We consider this pact as directed against us. This is why it is difficult to reach an understanding on an embargo. We replied to a journalist in London:[31] in order to reach an understanding between states or at the UN on the question of an embargo, we are ready to negotiate. But no one except us will agree to it because it will mean the liquidation of the Baghdad Pact, since it would be necessary to cease arming the countries which adhere to the pact. Now, Great Britain wants to arm these countries, except for Egypt.

They would like us not to sell arms to Egypt. But our Czech friends are selling them with our approval, because this sale of arms is against the Baghdad Pact. We have an interest in that.

Mikoyan: If the pact were abandoned, the question would be solved.

Khrushchev: We want disarmament and are ready to broach the subject. But no one else does. The French also want disarmament, I should add.

Commin: Pineau is against the Baghdad Pact in its military form. If one obtained a modification of the spirit of the pact in order to give it a predominantly economic aspect, would the USSR agree to an embargo?

Khrushchev (sceptically and evasively): And if this pact began to produce chickens? There are no kolkhozes down there, but they like chickens. [...]

Kaganovich:[32] There is no room for humanism so long as the final victory of the Revolution is not assured. The dictatorship of the proletariat has as its task precisely the consolidation and completion of the Revolution. Capitalism, through private ownership of the means of production, excludes humanism. It is anti-humanist. Only after its violent destruction and only when the roots of counter-revolution have been torn up will humanism be possible.

Khrushchev: Philip talks of humanism. But we in Russia were faced with an uneducated, illiterate people. However, the Bolshevik Party too fought battles like yours.

You had your Dreyfus affair;[33] we too had one. In our country, there was the Beilis affair in 1909.[34] Perhaps you don't know about it.

Beilis was a quiet Jew from the Ukraine. The anti-Semitic reactionaries accused him of ritual murder. They mounted a campaign to convince people that he had sacrificed a Russian child in order to use the blood of an unbeliever for making Jewish Passover bread, supposedly according to the rites of his religion. There was a trial which excited worldwide interest. The whole of public opinion in Russia was deeply stirred. The Bolshevik Party took an active part in this battle. We mobilised the working class against anti-Semitism, which was one of the weapons of the Tsarist government.

Brutelle: But that's not the point. Philip had not been talking about that in connection with the Dreyfus affair.

Kaganovich: The Dreyfus affair was not a question of justice and humanism. It was a manifestation of French imperialism. Jaurès sensed it well. This was to his credit. In connection with the Dreyfus affair, he drew the working class into the struggle against the imperialism of your monopolistic bourgeoisie.

Brutelle: But, again, that's not the point. What Philip is saying is much more and it's more important. [...]

Khrushchev: I would like to return to the nationalities question, and to tell you that our Revolution has solved it in our country.

Our indigenous populations have their own republics. There are so many of them that I can no longer even remember how many. In each one there is an autonomous government. Formerly backward and illiterate, these peoples now have their own lists of appointments of engineers and academicians. All these peoples live fraternally united, without racial hatred.

There exist in our country anti-Semitic feelings. These are survivals of a reactionary past. It is a problem which is complicated by the situation of the Jews and their connections with other peoples. At the beginning of the Revolution there were many Jews in the management of the Party and state. They were better educated, perhaps more revolutionary than the average Russian. Afterwards, we created new cadres ...

Pervukhin: ... our own intelligentsia.

Khrushchev: If now the Jews wanted to occupy the top jobs in our republics, they would obviously be looked upon unfavourably by the indigenous peoples. The latter would ill receive these claims, especially at a time when they consider themselves no less intelligent and no less able than the Jews. Or, for example, in the Ukraine, if a Jew is appointed to an important job and if he surrounds himself with Jewish fellow-workers, it is understandable that there may be jealousy and hostility towards the Jews.

But we are not anti-Semitic. Take Kaganovich. He occupies very high posts. He is Jewish. Then you have Mitin;[35] he is also Jewish. And Lidiya Faktor, our excellent interpreter who translates our conversations so well, is Jewish. I myself have a half-Jewish grandson. We are struggling against anti-Semitism.[36]

Document 14* Interview with Ekaterina Furtseva[37] (1956)

She [Furtseva] emphasised that the cult [of personality] had hindered progress in every sphere of activity, every field including the nationalities question. But she denied emphatically that there had never been any suppression of Jewish culture or repression of the Jewish people. She acknowledged that she had not read the article in the Polish Yiddish-language *Folks-shtime*,[38] detailing the shutting down of Jewish cultural institutions in the Soviet Union, the arrest and execution of Jewish leaders, and therefore could not express a positive opinion concerning these allegations. But she declared flatly that if there had been any drive against the Jewish people or Jewish

* *Source*: T. Petran, 'Why Khrushchev Spoke', *National Guardian*, 25 June 1956.

culture, 'we would have published it ourselves and would not need to have it published in the Polish press'.

Some mistakes might have occurred, but Jewish culture in the Soviet Union has been developing freely she said, pointing to many Jewish people prominent in science and the arts. She added that some 80% of the musicians who played at the Tito reception at the Kremlin were Jewish.

She said that some years back talk of anti-Semitism here was stirred up as a result of a misinterpretation of certain government actions. The Government had found in some of its departments a heavy concentration of Jewish people, upwards of 50% of the staff. Steps were taken to transfer them to other enterprises, giving them equally good positions and without jeopardising their rights. All of this was in accordance with Lenin's principles on the national problem, she said. But, she said, these steps were misinterpreted and added: 'It is impossible to speak of anti-Semitism in our country.'

Document 15* Arsenyev's letter[39] (1956)

Ministry of Education of the RSFSR

Moscow, Chistye Prudy, 6

Prof. A. Katsh[40]

Permit me to answer your question about what kind of facilities there are for persons of the Jewish nationality to study their mother tongue in the USSR.

Under Soviet law every parent has the right to send his child to a class where all subjects are taught in his mother tongue. To organise such a class in any school only ten parents are needed who wish their children to receive instruction in their mother tongue. This right also applies in full measure to persons of Jewish nationality.

Moreover, in schools where the studies are carried out in the language of the Union Autonomous Republic (Russian, Ukrainian, Tatar, Bashkir, etc.), if the parents so wish, supplementary studies of other languages or national literature, history and music can be arranged, with the teachers being paid from the school funds, again if there are ten people wanting to study these subjects.

Respectfully,

Deputy Minister of Education of the RSFSR

24 August 1956   A. Arsenyev

Document 16† Interview with L. F. Ilyichev on anti-Semitism (1956)

A Soviet spokesman told the correspondent that the tragic fate of the Jewish writers in the latter years of the Stalin regime was not the result of an isolated anti-Semitic drive, but rather a part of an anti-intellectual campaign which

---

* *Source*: A. Katsch, 'The Soviet Anomaly', *Jewish Spectator*, March 1972.

† *Source*: T. Petran, 'Interview with a Soviet Spokesman on Anti-Semitism', *National Guardian*, 3 September 1956.

brought a similar fate to many nationalities – Russian, Ukrainian, Georgian, Belorussian and Armenian.

The spokesman was L. F. Ilyichev, press chief of the Soviet Foreign Ministry.[41] Asked about the article in *Folks-shtime*, a Yiddish-language Communist publication in Poland, which last April reported the death and disappearance of many leading Soviet Jewish writers and artists, and the dissolution of the Jewish Anti-Fascist Committee, Ilyichev characterised the article as 'slanderous and anti-Soviet'.[42] He said it was his personal opinion that the authors of the article 'had picked up facts and distorted them according to a certain tendency'. It was, he said, 'an intermixture of certain real facts and certain fantasies. The authors used the real facts to make the fantasies look true.'

The 'true facts', he said, 'concern those Jewish writers who were charged and condemned unjustifiably. But the conclusions this article draws as to the persecution of the Jewish people and their culture is a slanderous one. Any objective-minded person can see that it is impossible to speak of discrimination in the USSR. According to our Constitution, any national discrimination is criminal, and it is condemned by public opinion. There are many different nationalities, including Jewish, represented in Soviet art, literature, science, and we are all proud of them.'

Ilyichev said that the 'good names' of the Jewish writers unjustly condemned have been restored and that their works are now being widely republished throughout the USSR. He then noted the fate of writers of many nationalities.[43] [...]

Ilyichev said that case reviews were still going on [...][44] Statements were made only in the case of the leaders of the Polish Communist Party,[45] who were victims of the 1938 purges, and of the early Hungarian CP leader Bela Kun.[46] The reason, he said, was that these cases involved political parties and foreign ones at that.[47] [...]

Ilyichev said firmly that there are not now, and never have been in the USSR, any quotas or discrimination directed against the Jews or any nationality. Admission to higher educational institutions is decided by competitive exams (industrial workers and men released from the armed forces get some preference). There are so many more applicants than there are places open, he said, that some who are not admitted might complain of discrimination. But he knew of no such complaints, he said, and if there were any, they had no basis. Applicants must state their nationality, he said, but in a multinational State like the USSR, where all nationalities are equal, this is not discrimination.

Asked about a *New York Times* report of 10 June[48] that Soviet CP First Secretary, Nikita Khrushchev, had told a French Socialist delegation that the USSR restricts the number of Jews in professional positions, Ilyichev said: 'This dispatch for the most part does not correspond with reality.' What Khrushchev said, he explained, was that after the Revolution some of the USSR's national republics did not have their own national trained core of key people, that these cadres at the time were largely Russian. But now the Revolution was almost forty years old, new national cadres had been created and the people of these republics were demanding a place for them.

'It is quite understandable,' Ilyichev said, 'that any people should want to create their own cadres and prefer their leading ones to be of their own nationality. But this doesn't mean that able Jewish people are not and will not be promoted. There are hundreds of thousands of them holding positions in our public life. In the Jewish Autonomous Region of Birobidzhan, created by the Soviet government in response to the requests of representatives of the Jewish people, all leading positions could have been occupied by Jews, but they did not want to hold all such positions, and some are held by Russians since there are also Russians living there. Many Jewish people did not want to go to Birobidzhan and remained in Russia, the Ukraine, etc., where they are represented in the leading cadres.'

Ilyichev conceded that there had been violations of official policy against discrimination in the past. He said that 'perhaps at certain offices and enterprises certain directors had followed a policy contrary to our government policy'. He said the government had been making a great effort to move people into productive enterprises and from the cities into agriculture. In this process 'certain cases may have occurred when people were moved according to nationality, that is, heads of offices may have violated government policy. Later some directors were removed because of mistakes. It would be difficult to say they were removed for anti-Semitism, but these things are interconnected. Cases of discrimination would be a matter for the trade unions. Such cases would be investigated and condemned by them.'

He was asked to explain how his statement could be reconciled with that of CP Central Committee Secretary, Ekaterina Furtseva, to the *Guardian*. She had said that in the past in departments where there was a heavy concentration of Jews, steps were taken to transfer them to equally good positions in other enterprises. Ilyichev secured from Mme Furtseva this explanation:

In her interview with the *Guardian*, she meant that 'if at some time there had taken place changes in office personnel, these changes were dictated by the economic needs of the country and under no circumstances were aimed at any discrimination of persons of any nationality. If a chief of an office or department found that in his office there existed over-saturation of a certain group of specialists, then proceeding from the economic needs of the country and with no reference to nationality, some of the specialists were given other posts in industry, agriculture and other branches. Never at any time during the Soviet power were there any quotas for Jews or persons of some other nationality, and there are not now.'

Ilyichev also revealed that the Soviet government is discussing the resettling in their old homelands of the national groups uprooted or dispersed during and after the war. These include the Crimean Tatars who were held guilty as a national group of the treachery committed by some during the war.

Document 17* Serge Groussard's interview with Khrushchev (1958)

I [Groussard][49] have met several travellers, Russians and foreigners, who, travelling across your country to Vladivostok, passed through Birobidzhan. Some of them stayed there. Not one of them saw rabbis or Hebrew schools; not

---

* *Source*: S. Groussard, 'Le Monde: Propos libres avec N. Khrouchtchev' (The World: Table-Talk with N. Khrushchev), *Le Figaro*, 9 April 1958.

the least trace of newspapers or even signs in Hebrew or Yiddish. Their surprise was so much the greater since, according to official statistics of the Soviet government, of the hundred thousand and more inhabitants of Birobidzhan more than a third are Jewish. All the travellers, moreover, came across numerous Jews many of whom spoke Yiddish.

Numerous wrinkles radiate like crow's feet from the corners of Mr Khrushchev's eyes; wrinkles of good humour, since they spread diagonally and fold every time Mr Khrushchev smiles, as at the moment when the statesman catches his breath before replying to my question:

'The policy adopted by the Soviet government towards the nationalities is both just and generous. The USSR was the first state in the world to have decided to aid the Jews not as individuals but as a people.

'For this we chose a sparsely populated region in Siberia, north of Manchuria – Birobidzhan. We placed it at the disposal of the Jews and accorded it a special status. It was a remarkable gift. There is no land more fertile than that in Birobidzhan. The climate there is temperate; cultivation of the soil is a pleasure. There is water and sun. There are vast forests, fertile lands, minerals in abundance, rivers swarming with fish. Well, then! What happened? The Jews left *en masse* for Birobidzhan. They were enthusiastic, excited. They hastened from every corner of the Soviet Union and, I might add, from all the countries of Europe from which they had managed to come, wresting themselves free from persecutions. And then? And then, very few remained. Recently, the coming and going has been continuing but one must admit that return journeys take away more and more.

'How many Jews remain in this beautiful region? In the absence of any documents before me, I would not be able to give you a precise figure. In actual fact, there must still be quite a large number there. Look, in 1955, I myself passed through Birobidzhan. And, contrary to your informants, I noticed many signs in Yiddish there, in the stations and in the streets around the stations. This being granted, if one looks at the balance sheet, it is only right to conclude that Jewish colonisation in Birobidzhan has resulted in failure. They alight there burning with enthusiasm, then, one by one, they return.

'How can one explain this disagreeable phenomenon? In my opinion, by historical conditions. The Jews have always preferred the trades of craftsmen: they are tailors, they work glass or precious stones, they are businessmen, pharmacists, frequently carpenters. But, if you take building or metallurgy – mass professions – you might not, to my knowledge, come across a single Jew there. They do not like collective work, group discipline. They have always preferred to be dispersed. They are individualists.

'Let us leave aside the new State of Israel. The Jews, for centuries, have been unable to make up their minds to live amongst themselves and to derive a living and stability from themselves alone, apart from other collectives. A second characteristic is that the Jews are essentially intellectuals. They never consider themselves sufficiently well-educated. As soon as they are in a position to, they want to go to university, whatever the sacrifices that have to be made for this end. You asked me why there are no Hebrew schools in Birobidzhan or elsewhere? Because it is impossible to get the Jews to attend

Jewish schools. And finally, their interests are too diverse and often too opposed for them to be able to satisfy them in a region where they would all be together, face to face. Non-Jews are not responsible for this. A genuine Jewish cultural community is no more realisable than a political community. The Jews are interested in everything, study everything deeply, discuss everything and finish by having profound cultural differences.

'There are in the USSR nationalities with smaller populations than that of the Jews or whose trump cards were less strong from the beginning. But these non-Jewish nationalities are capable of organising themselves on a communal basis. For this reason it is possible for them to forge national institutions which will last. I could quote you many examples. One cannot struggle against the creative will nor against the negative will. That is why I am sceptical as far as the permanence of Jewish collectives is concerned.'

[Groussard:] 'On the subject of Jews, I consider, however, that the Israeli experiment is a success.'

'We Communists feel very sorry for the Jews who emigrated to Israel. The letters which we receive from them in fact move us by their number and their sadness. Over there there is a housing shortage, there is a lack of success in accustoming people to agricultural work. Exiles arriving from so many different backgrounds experience difficulties of mutual understanding. What are all those Jews there going to do? They were conscious of the return to the land of their fathers' fathers; this is not sufficient for living side by side nor for forging a true nation.

'Israel has not adopted auspicious positions for the Jewish people. The USSR voted for Israel at the United Nations. She supported this state at its birth – in an extremely effective way. Israel has shown herself ungrateful and unfortunate in her choices. This nation plays the game of the imperialists and the enemies of socialist countries. All we buy from Israel are a few oranges. And we can make do without them.

'Finally, it is the Israeli imperialists who relate shocking tales about Birobidzhan. In the same way it is the capitalists who try to spread vile rumours about the rights of the nationalities in the Soviet Union, where all peoples can develop fully in the freedom of socialism. All this is nothing but anti-Soviet propaganda. Any discussion on this topic is pointless.'[50]

Document 18* M. Vilner's meeting with the Soviet Deputy Minister of Culture (1958)

At the outset Danilov[51] told us, in a lengthy and friendly conversation, about the vigorous participation of Soviet citizens of Jewish nationality in all branches of cultural and artistic creative activity in the Soviet Union.

'They occupy an honourable and meritorious place in Soviet culture', he remarked. 'For that we are grateful to the Soviet Jews, we admire those among them who are distinguishing themselves, and we evaluate this as a most important fact and as an absolutely positive achievement for the Jews themselves.' [...]

* *Source*: M. Vilner, 'Tog-bukh fun a rayze in ratnfarband' (Diary of a Journey to the Soviet Union), *Naye prese*, 27 April 1958.

One after the other, we then submit our opinions, how we view the matter, where, to our mind, two phenomena must be kept apart: on the one hand the natural process, which is indisputable; and on the other forcible administrative measures, which derive from underrating real needs. We recall the wrongs and deviations which were committed in the years 1948–52 and which were publicly revealed by the Soviet regime itself with exemplary courage. Did the Moscow Yiddish Art Theatre[52] disappear merely because the public had ceased to patronise it and because some of its artists began to leave it, or because, at the same time, unjustified administrative measures were adopted? In the latter case, there was, to our mind, in addition to the natural process, also a deviation. Are there, indeed, no more cultural needs in Yiddish today? And if these do exist, it would be only right and proper to restore those institutions which were closed down arbitrarily at a certain period.

Danilov suggests that we deal separately – in the course of the conversation – with the problem of the theatre, of dramatic activity, and with the problem of publications, of the written word. First he wants to inform us of the present situation, adding at the same time that, in his opinion, the matter is now in a stage of development: 'in a stage of evolution'. [...]

'We have a great number of soloists and artistic ensembles who give performances and concerts in the Yiddish language. Their appearances are organised by "Estrada", an institution that embraces all the stage activities of variety and "revue" artists and that functions under the auspices of the Ministry of Culture.

'They perform with success in cultural clubs, in large factories, in kolkhozes and in halls of various towns. In the majority of cases, these are single concerts, but often they also occupy the halls for a certain period of time, giving several repeat performances of the same programme.

'Among the soloists, I would like to mention particularly Zinovy Shulman,[53] who sings old folklore songs as well as contemporary songs in Yiddish and Russian. A young, very interesting artist is Gorovets,[54] who most successfully performs the item *Freylekhs*. The singer, Gordon, has a classical repertoire. Shaul Lyubimov[55] is a great favourite with the public. Lifshits[56] won first prize in a competition of "Estrada" artists. I would also like to make special mention of Vagi and Golubyova. The latter resides in Leningrad.

'One could also mention Anna Guzik[57] and Sidi Tal[58] from Chernovtsy, successful evenings of readings by Rakitin from the works of Shalom Aleikhem in Yiddish, and by Kaminka[59] from Shalom Aleikhem's writings mainly in Russian translation. All these concerts and performances are announced by posters and are also listed in the monthly programmes of forthcoming events.

'Thus, about three thousand such performances and concerts in Yiddish took place in 1957 all over the Soviet Union and were attended by nearly three million spectators.'

'We see now', explains Danilov, 'that this is an important matter which is undergoing a process of development, which it is worth while pondering over, which has to be solved and towards which we must adopt a respectful attitude.'

After a brief exchange of views on the conditions under which Mikhoels's Moscow Yiddish Art Theatre disappeared and on the reasons involved,

Danilov goes over to the question of Yiddish literature: 'Jews who read Yiddish are becoming fewer and fewer. Practically no one among the youth can read in that language. However, there exists an excellent Yiddish literature – authors who continue to write in Yiddish – and a keen interest to read it. Therefore, we are encouraging as many translations into Russian as possible.' [...][60]

Inter alia, he enumerates a series of books by Leon Feuchtwanger which were published in up to half-a-million copies. To our remark that Feuchtwanger doesn't write in Yiddish, Danilov apologises and explains that it is Feuchtwanger's Jewish themes that led him to this association of ideas.

For a long time we discuss with him the problem of publications in Yiddish. Only in Birobidzhan is there a Yiddish newspaper: the *Birobidzhaner shtern* (Birobidzhan Star), which comes out three times a week.[61]

'The opinions on this subject are divided', says Danilov. 'In discussing this with various people, you will have the opportunity to convince yourselves that the majority of those interested in this question believe that there is no more need for it [i.e. Yiddish publications]. The matter is therefore rather complicated.

'I must add straight away that this is not because of the small circulation. Wherever it is necessary, we are ready to meet every expenditure, because – as far as cultural purposes are concerned – we tend to overlook the expense involved and do not seek profits. The matter is under discussion, and we are giving it the utmost attention.'

Our conversation took up quite some time and it became rather late. We warmly thanked the Minister of Culture for his attention and courteous reception.

Document 19* Mikoyan in the United States (1959) (I): press conference at UN

Saul Carson (of the Jewish Telegraphic Agency): Mr Mikoyan, during your current trip in the United States, you have dissociated yourself from the late Mr Beria. [...] Mr Beria was apparently largely responsible for the liquidation of Jewish culture, particularly Yiddish culture, in the Soviet Union. As a member of the government, do you contemplate any steps in the near future to re-institute the free exercise of the Yiddish theatre, press and other Jewish cultural activities in the Soviet Union?

Mikoyan: In my country, all peoples enjoy freedom for the development of their culture. They can have their theatres and their literature, and that includes the Jews. However, the Jewish population has merged with the Russians in Russian culture so fully that Jews participate in general culture and literature, on the Russian stage and in Russian literature. There are many Jewish writers who consider themselves Russian and prefer to write Russian. We cannot interfere in that matter. This is a matter for the Jewish intelligentsia. We do create all conditions in which Jewish and Russian literatures and the literatures of all other Soviet peoples should have full opportunities for their

* *Source*: 'Text of News Conference Held by Mikoyan at Headquarters of United Nations', *The New York Times*, 16 January 1959.

development, writing and creation. There is no Jewish problem in the Soviet Union at all. This problem is created by those who wish to impede good relations. [...]

Walter Kirschenbaum (of Radio Station WMCA, New York): In a reply, Mr Minister, a few moments ago, to another question, you said that the Jews enjoy liberties in the Soviet Union. Yesterday an organisation, the Jewish Labour Committee, left a memorandum at the United Nations mission in which they said that they had documented evidence that Jewish culture had been liquidated, that Jewish writers had been killed, that a woman by the name of Lina Shtern,[62] a noted Soviet educator, had been given life imprisonment around July 1952. I should like to know, sir, does this mean that the Soviet Union recognises such liquidation of cultures or would you permit Yiddish theatres, press and literature to exist.

Mikoyan: [...] You call them a labour committee. I do not hear anything that smacks of labour in what they have to say. In my country, all peoples enjoy freedom and the development of culture, and that includes the Jews. I have many friends who are Jews. Many of our most prominent leaders, in fact, have married Jewish girls, and they have excellent relations. I would say, let others have relations that are as good.

Document 20* Mikoyan in the United States (1959) (II): statement on rumoured exiling of Jews to Birobidzhan

Anastas I. Mikoyan told a group of the American Jewish Committee yesterday that reports of an intended large-scale movement of Russian Jews to Birobidzhan in Siberia were untrue.

This was made known by former Senator Herbert H. Lehman after he and the other Jewish leaders had held a luncheon-conference with the Soviet First Deputy Premier and Soviet Ambassador Mikhail A. Menshikov. Their meeting in the Carlyle Hotel at 35 East Sixty-sixth Street lasted one hour and forty-five minutes.

Mr Lehman later told reporters that he was authorised to issue the following statement on behalf of Mr Mikoyan:

'The reported plans for the re-creation of a Jewish state in Birobidzhan and the transfer of the Jewish population in Russia to that area is without foundation.'

Mr Lehman said that he was 'gratified' with the statement. But Irving M. Engel, the agency's president, remarked: 'We are gratified but the answer does not necessarily satisfy us; there is a difference between being satisfied and gratified.'

Jacob Blaustein, honorary president, described the session as 'amiable but serious'. Without giving details, Mr Lehman reported that in addition to the Birobidzhan issue other Jewish problems in the Soviet Union were discussed.

This was the first meeting in the United States of ranking Soviet officials with a Jewish group for dealing with these problems. American Jewish organisations have frequently charged suppression of Jewish communal, cultural and religious life in the Soviet Union.

* *Source*: I. Spiegel, 'Mikoyan Denies Exiling of Jews', *The New York Times*, 16 January 1959.

Last week the American Jewish Committee, the fifty-two-year-old human relations agency, learned from its Paris office that a large-scale movement of Soviet Jews to Birobidzhan might be proposed to the Soviet Communist Party's Congress, opening 27 January in Moscow. On Wednesday Mr Lehman arranged for the meeting with the Soviet officials.

Earlier in the luncheon meeting, the Jewish leaders presented a statement to Mr Mikoyan noting that the reports of a possible movement of Soviet Jews to Birobidzhan 'have not been refuted by any responsible Soviet source'. It added:

'Today Jews constitute only one-fifth[63] of the population of this so-called "Autonomous Jewish Region" in which almost all expressions of Jewish cultural life, such as schools, theatres and publishing houses, have been suppressed.

'The renewal of the scheme would, therefore, be completely devoid of any incentive for Jews to accept voluntarily the enormous sacrifices and burdens involved.'

Document 21* F. Kozlov on Jews (during visit to United States, 1959)

In response to one question, Mr Kozlov[64] again denied there was any discrimination against the Jews in the Soviet Union. He made an unexplained reference to a claim somewhere that a synagogue in Kiev had been closed, denied it and then declared: 'Just recently I visited Kiev and I saw the Jews there leading a happy life in their usual daily pursuits and bathing in the Dnieper and they looked no worse than you.' [...]

A spokesman for the Soviet Exhibition at the Coliseum denied last night any slight to the Jewish Press and said a ticket had been sent to an Israeli wire-service representative at the United Nations.

Document 22† Exchange of letters between Imam Ahmad and N. S. Khrushchev (1959)

The Imam Ahmad's letter

From the Imam Ahmad, upholder of the religion of Allah, King of the Mutawakkili Kingdom of Yemen, to Our Friend the Honourable Nikita Khrushchev, Prime Minister of the Soviet Union:

To you best friendly wishes and greetings resting on feelings of personal friendship and traditional relations prevailing between our two countries and our two noble peoples. We thank you for your great interest in our health and for your queries about the state of our health which you directed through your ambassador in Rome.

Recently, while we were in the course of medical treatment in Italy, reports reached us the great importance of which compels us to write to you while we are still under doctors' supervision.

* *Source*: H. Schwartz, 'Kozlov, at Close of Tour, Predicts a Socialist US', *The New York Times*, 13 July 1959.

† *Source*: *Al-Ahram*, 13 July 1959.

These reports state that your honourable government and a number of other friendly governments, your allies, intend to open the gates of emigration to Israel to the Jews, something which constitutes an immense danger to the Arab nation, considering the Zionist aims, which are known to you, of expansion and imperialism against the Arab countries and against their natural rights and their most cherished aspirations. Even though we know with certainty that you oppose the expansionist and imperialist principles of Zionism and that you are vigilant in your friendship with the Arab lands and support their interests, and because of the wonder these worrying reports arouse in us, we saw fit to write you about this in order to be certain from your own lips that these reports are not correct. We are convinced that your friendly policy towards the Arab countries – in which all the countries allied to you and attached to us in relations of true friendship and cooperation are partners – will not change, to the satisfaction of world Zionism and at the price of the life, the security and the stability of our nation.

Be certain that the cause of these questions is our concern for your valuable friendship and the friendship of all within the framework of our positive neutral policy, which we have chosen for our country and our Arab nation.

We know that opening the gates of occupied Palestine to Zionist immigration will shock the Arab world and will cause it doubt and anxiety, whatever the form and nature of this immigration. We anticipate a reply which will allay our fears following your efforts and the contacts made with allies and friends. We once again send you best wishes, and feelings of friendship for your great country and your noble nation, and may God preserve you.

Khrushchev's reply

To His Majesty the Imam Ahmad the First, King of the Mutawakkili Kingdom of Yemen.

Our Honourable Good Friend:

It was with great regret that I learned that the state of your health and your illness have compelled you to depart the borders of your homeland for treatment in Italy. The Ambassador of the Soviet Union in Italy, S. Koziri, has personally been charged with conveying to Your Majesty cordial greetings in the name of the Soviet Government and on behalf of K. Voroshilov, President of the Supreme Soviet of the USSR. He will express to you our sincere wishes for your speedy recovery.

We were moved to the depths of our heart by the letter in which you expressed your hope for the development of the friendly relations prevailing between the two governments and the two nations – the Soviet Union and the Mutawakkili Kingdom of Yemen: this letter you sent us in spite of your illness. I am happy to inform Your Majesty that the government of the Soviet Union greatly appreciates the excellent role you have played in preserving and strengthening the relations of friendship and cooperation, which have not at all been marred and which continue to prevail in full happiness between our countries, and we likewise appreciate the central part played by Crown Prince Muhammad al-Badr in this matter.

The success of the development of these traditional friendly relations is subject to the principle of full equality of rights and mutual respect for national sovereignty and national honour and non-interference in internal affairs, and to economic cooperation.

The government of the Soviet Union has several times declared, and it now once again declares, that in the future it will continue with the same policy of friendship and fruitful peaceful cooperation. We are very gratified that you on your part understand these principles and support them with parallel efforts.

The good relations prevailing between the Soviet Union and Yemen express the friendly relations and the salutary policy which the Soviet Union implements in its relations with all the countries of the East, countries fighting against imperialism and for their national independence and their state sovereignty [...]

It is known that the imperialist forces have no interest in the development of friendly relations between our countries. The ruling circles within these forces waste hundreds of millions of dollars on destructive activity against the socialist states and also against the independent states in the East in order to foul the good relations prevailing between our countries. They feed armies of experts with distorted information and they prepare false documents in order to create problems among the peace-loving states.

I should like to inform you from the depths of my heart that the rumours which imperialist circles and their supporters are spreading abroad about groups of Jewish emigrants in the Soviet Union who are now prepared to go to Israel are totally devoid of any element of truth and have been deliberately invented in order to create difficulties for the Soviet Union's relations with the Arab countries.

As you must certainly remember, the official authorities in the Soviet Union published an appropriate denial of this matter. In full sincerity, I am informing you that there is no reason to think that there is a group of Jews in the Soviet Union wishing to depart for Israel, because the quality of the Soviet state and the living conditions in it are not to be compared with what exists in Israel. The Russian proverb says, 'He who lives in comfort does not look for another kind of life.' Of course, we believe it is not uncommon for a number of Jews to submit a request for an exit permit from Israel to the Soviet Union, but not the opposite.

Concerning the rumours about emigration of Jews to Israel from the countries friendly to us, the authorities have clarified the matter with the governments concerned; and notwithstanding that entry to or exit from them is the affair of the independent countries themselves, we saw fit, based on Your Majesty's wish, to unofficially inform the governments of the friendly states of the apprehensions you expressed in your letter.

Finally, we wish to convey to Your Majesty that we are convinced that the relations of trust and mutual understanding which have been established in recent years between the leaders of Yemen and the Soviet Union will flourish successfully.

We once more wish you speedy recovery and many years of life in good health and prosperity for Yemen.

Document 23* N. S. Khrushchev answers question on the Jews in the Soviet Union (1959)

The New York Times text

Q.

There is great interest here, Mr Khrushchev, in the situation as regards the Jewish minority within the Soviet Union. Can you clarify for us yourself what the status of those people are as regards equality of opportunity?

A.

I think one of the facts which characterise the position of the Jewish people in our country is the fact that among the persons who took foremost part in the launching of the rocket to the moon the representatives of the Jewish people hold a place of honour. In general, the national problem does not exist in our country. The question of a man's religion is not asked in our country. It is a matter for the conscience of the person concerned. We look upon a person as a person. In our country Russians, Jews, Ukrainians, Turkmen, Uzbeks, Belorussians, Georgians, Armenians – if I started to enumerate all the nationalities in our country I am afraid the question period would be taken up by that enumeration. They all live in peace and close friendship in our country, and we are very proud of the fact that the national problem does not exist in our country, that all the many nationalities inhabiting the Soviet Union are together marching toward one common aim.

Pravda's text

Q.

There is great interest in the USA in the situation of various nationalities in the USSR, including the Jewish population. Could you tell us a few words on the subject?

A.

In the Soviet Union the national question, in your sense of the word, does not exist. All nationalities live in friendship, all of them enjoy equal rights. In our country the attitude to individuals is neither based on their nationality nor their religion. It is a matter for the conscience of the person concerned. First and foremost, we look upon a person as a person. In our country all nationalities: Russians, Ukrainians, Turkmen, Uzbeks, Kazakhs, Belorussians, Georgians, Armenians, Kalmyks and Jews – if I started to enumerate all the nationalities in our country I am afraid the period allotted to the press conference would be taken up by the enumeration – they all live in peace and understanding. We are proud of the fact that a state as multi-national as the Soviet Union is strong and progresses successfully. All the peoples in our country live in mutual trust and march together towards a common aim – Communism. The position of the Jewish population in particular is characterised, not least by the following: among those who created the necessary conditions for a successful launching of the rocket to the moon, a notable place was occupied by the Jews as well.

Sources: 'Texts of Khrushchev Speech at National Press Club and Questions and Answers', *The New York Times*, 17 September 1959.

'Otvet N. S. Khrushcheva na voprosy amerikanskikh zhurnalistov' (Khrushchev's Answers to Questions of American Journalists), *Pravda*, 18 September 1959.

Document 24* Khrushchev on Jewish emigration to Israel (1960)

A question of an Israeli agency correspondent: Is the Soviet government prepared to consent that, within the framework of reunion of families, permission be given to persons of Jewish origin in the Soviet Union to emigrate to Israel?

N. S. Khrushchev: We do not object to the reunion of some persons, if they want it. But the words 'reunion of families' is quite a relative concept. One can probably read many advertisements in Vienna newspapers even today: how a rich widow is looking for a husband or a rich old man for a young wife. But, seriously speaking, there are no files at our Ministry of the Interior with applications from persons of Jewish nationality or other nationalities who wish to emigrate to Israel. On the contrary, we have many letters from Jews in Israel, applying to us with the request to permit them to return from Israel to their homeland, the Soviet Union.

Document 25† Soviet anti-Jewish discrimination denied at United Nations (1962)

Mrs Nikolaeva (Union of Soviet Socialist Republics) said that she had been astonished to hear the Australian representative[65] make an undeserved attack on her country. There was not a shred of truth in his charges, which were intended not to seek out areas of discrimination but merely to blacken the name of the USSR. There was in the USSR no discrimination against Jews or any other nationality or group, and no fact to prove the contrary could possibly be presented. Charges of anti-Semitism in the USSR stemmed either from ignorance or from a rabid hatred of Communism. It was a historical fact that the USSR had at the very outset abolished the oppression of national minorities and taken drastic measures to root out all forms of discrimination.

The real facts of the situation concerning Jews in the Soviet Union were the following. Although Jews represented only 1.1% of the population, they accounted for about 10% of the country's professionals, scientists and artists; in 1961 over 7,000 Jews had been elected as deputies to local organs of authority; they were well represented, too, in the highest organs of Soviet power; they had, and availed themselves of, full opportunities in every sphere of the country's life.

In answer to the malicious charges of certain Jewish newspapers in the United States, a number of prominent Jewish citizens of the USSR had written an open letter which appeared in the New York Jewish daily newspaper *Morgn frayheyt* of 6 May 1962.[66] The views stated in that letter certainly carried more weight than the words of those who had a vested interest in attacking the USSR.

---

* *Source*: 'Press-konferentsiya Predsedatelya Soveta Ministrov SSSR N. S. Khrushchev v Vene 8 iyulya 1960g' (The Chairman of the Council of Ministers, N. S. Khrushchev's Press Conference in Vienna, 8 July 1960), *Pravda*, 9 July 1960.
† *Source*: *Official Summary Report of Debate at Third Committee of the United Nations General Assembly 17th Session*, 1 November 1962, pp. 186–7.

Document 26* N. S. Khrushchev's reply to B. Russell (1963)

N. S. Khrushchev, Chairman of the USSR Council of Ministers, has received a letter from the well-known English philosopher Bertrand Russell.

Bertrand Russell's letter and Comrade N. S. Khrushchev's reply are printed below.

To Chairman Nikita Khrushchev
Moscow
USSR
Dear Premier Khrushchev,

I am deeply disturbed by the executions of Jews that have been taking place in the Soviet Union and by the official encouragement of anti-Semitism that apparently exists.[67]

I am writing about this in a private capacity; you know, of course, that I am a friend of your country and that I am sympathetic to your personal efforts directed at peaceful coexistence, efforts that I publicly support. I call on you to proclaim an amnesty, on the basis of humanitarian considerations and of our common interests, which lie in peaceful relations between East and West.

                            Respectfully, sincerely yours,
2 February 1963   Bertrand Russell

To Mr Bertrand Russell
London

Esteemed Mr Bertrand Russell,

I have received your letter expressing your concern at the fact that, among persons recently punished on the basis of the laws of the Soviet Union for crimes called in the Western press 'economic crimes', there have been people of the Jewish nationality. Some people in the West call this a manifestation of anti-Semitism. I must frankly say that I have been surprised by this conclusion. It is the result of a profound misconception.

In the past few months the Western bourgeois press has again been clamouring about so-called anti-Semitism in the USSR. I declare with full responsibility: this is a crude fabrication, a malicious slander against the Soviet people and our country. Even the bourgeois press admits that, among those sentenced in the USSR for so-called 'economic crimes', there are persons of the most diverse nationalities. And this is indeed so. Persons engaged in acquiring public wealth and living idly at the expense of other people's labour are sentenced in our country strictly in accordance with the laws covering the cases that confront us. Every person who has committed a particular crime is punished according to the nature of the crime, and the nationality of the criminal has, of course, no bearing.

What are such persons punished for in the USSR? First of all, for malicious speculation, for pilfering people's property. Soviet laws do indeed provide severe punishment for such crimes as threaten the economic foundations of

* *Source*: 'Obmen pismami mezhdu B. Rasselom i N. S. Khrushchevym' (Exchange of Letters Between B. Russell and N. S. Khrushchev), *Pravda*, 1 March 1963.

our system. These laws, reflecting the will of the Soviet people, have been in existence for a long time, from the very first years of the Soviet State, and the whole population knows them well and approves of them. They express the morality of the new, socialist society.

Every state has its own legislation. Our Soviet State too has its laws, which are based on socialist morality. What is often considered a virtue in bourgeois society is rejected by our morality and punished by our laws. In bourgeois society, for instance, it is customary not to care where capital comes from or how it has been accumulated. This is the private affair of the person who amassed it. But this capital is made through the exploitation and robbery of millions of people, and at times directly by murder and other crimes. In such a society a man with capital is held in esteem, no matter how he made his capital. The principle there is: anyone who is not caught is not a thief. But even when such a thief is caught red-handed, he is rarely imprisoned. Most often, the case never comes to trial, because a man with capital has his own people among those who are called upon to enforce the law.

I have no doubt that you are well acquainted with instances of this sort, born of the pursuit of profit and the cynical power of money.

In brief, the capitalist world has its laws, against which the people of our country fought until they won and established new laws in accordance with the interests of the working people. Our morality and our laws are based on different principles. The morality of our society is the morality of people of labour. 'He who does not work shall not eat' – that is our morality. Our state and our society with the help of laws protect honest toilers from parasites and loafers who flout the morality of socialist society and want to live by robbing others, or who through dishonest machinations acquire valuables which they did nothing to create. Such people are prosecuted in accordance with the law and with the principles of morality based on labour. I am convinced that this is the only fair morality and the most just one.

The robber, the exploiter, also thinks he works, but his 'labour' is directed toward better enjoying the fruit of other people's labour. We, however, recognise and respect labour that creates wealth for the people, in other words, useful labour. As for the 'labour', if it may be so called, of speculators, thieves, currency operators, bribe-takers, etc., this is social parasitism, an activity harmful to the surrounding milieu, to society.

The capitalist world naturally does not want to understand us and does not share our philosophy and our morality. The philosophy and morality of socialist society do not fit into the conceptions and norms to which bourgeois society is accustomed. We are not surprised at this, because our system, the socialist system, is the antipode of and is opposed to the capitalist system, its morality and its laws which permit some to live at the expense of others' labour and to lead a parasitic life; which permit the strong to rob the weak.

It is well known that bourgeois propaganda often uses slander and falsifi-cations to discredit our socialist system and our morality. When people want to discredit our system and its laws, they often use the device of maliciously ascribing to it features allegedly directed against one particular nationality – the Jewish one. But this can be easily disproved by facts.

It does not require much work to satisfy oneself, even from the trial materials published in the newspapers, that among the persons punished by our courts for so-called 'economic crimes', including those who have been sentenced to the supreme measure of punishment, there are Russians as well as Jews, Georgians as well as Ukrainians, Belorussians and people of other nationalities. In brief, these decisions of the courts are directed not against persons of any particular nationality but against the crimes and those who commit them, regardless of their nationality. Which nation will have more or less of a particular type of criminal at any one time is not a national question but a social one.[...]

The attempts of reactionary propaganda to impute to our state a policy of anti-Semitism or of its encouragement are not a new phenomenon. In the past, too, our class enemies have more than once resorted to such slander against our reality, against our system. There has not been and there is no policy of anti-Semitism in the Soviet Union, because the very character of our multi-national socialist state excludes the possibility of such a policy. Our constitution proclaims the equality of rights of citizens of the USSR irrespective of their nationality or race and declares that 'any advocacy of racial or national exclusiveness or hatred and contempt is punishable by law'.

The motto of our society is: 'Man is a friend, comrade and brother to man.' We have educated and we are educating Soviet people in the spirit of friendship and the brotherhood of all peoples, in the spirit of intolerance towards national or racial animosity. You may be assured that we shall continue to do this with all our energy and consistency.

Respectfully,

21 February 1963   N. Khrushchev

Document 27* Khrushchev denies Russian anti-Semitism at a meeting of Party and government leaders with writers and artists (1963)

Letters are being received in the Party Central Committee expressing concern over the fact that some works give a distorted view of the position of Jews in our country. The bourgeois press, as you know from the exchange of letters between the English philosopher Russell and myself,[68] is even conducting a slanderous campaign against us.

At our meeting in December we already touched upon this question in connection with the poet Evtushenko's 'Babi Yar'.[69] Circumstances require us to return to this question.

Why is this poem criticised? For the fact that its author did not succeed in truthfully showing and condemning the Fascist, specifically Fascist, criminals for the mass murders they committed in Babi Yar. The poem presents the matter as though only the Jewish population fell victim to Fascist crimes, whereas many Russians, Ukrainians and Soviet people of other nationalities died there at the hands of the Hitlerite executioners. It is evident from this poem that its author did not manifest political maturity and showed ignorance of the historical facts.

* *Source*: 'Vysokaya ideinost i khudozhestvennoe masterstvo – velikaya sila sovetskoi literatury i iskusstva' (High Ideological Content and Artistic Mastery Are the Great Force of Soviet Literature and Art), *Pravda*, 10 March 1963.

Who needed to present matters as though the people of Jewish nationality in our country are mistreated by someone, and why did they need to present them thus? This is untrue. From the days of the October Revolution the Jews in our country have had equality with all other peoples of the USSR in all respects. We do not have a Jewish question, and those who dream it up are singing a foreign tune.

As for the Russian working class, also before the Revolution it was the resolute foe of any national oppression, including anti-Semitism.

In pre-Revolutionary times I lived among the miners. The workers stigmatised those who participated in the Jewish pogroms. The inspirers of the pogroms were the autocratic government, the capitalists, the landholders and the bourgeoisie. They needed the pogroms as a means of diverting the working people from revolutionary struggle. The organisers of the pogroms were the police, the *gendarmerie*, the Black Hundreds who recruited hoodlums from the dregs of society, from declassed elements. In the cities many janitors were their agents.

For example, the famous Bolshevik revolutionary, Comrade Bauman, who was not a Jew, was killed in Moscow by a janitor under orders from the *gendarmerie*.

Gorky's wonderful novel, *Mother*, superbly showed the internationalism of the working class of Russia. Representatives of various nationalities were in the ranks of the revolutionary workers. It is enough to recall the Russian worker, Pavel Vlasov, and the Ukrainian, Andrei Nakhodka.

I spent my childhood and youth in Yuzovka where many Jews lived at the time. For a while I worked in a factory as apprentice to the fitter, Yakov Isaakovich Kutikov. He was a skilled worker. There were other Jews too among the workers of the factory. I remember that a Jew worked as a foundryman pouring copper, and this was then considered a very high skill. I often saw this foundryman; he was evidently a religious man and did not work on Saturdays, but since all the Ukrainians, Russians and others worked on Saturdays, he used to come to the foundry and spend the whole day there, although he did not take part in the work.

Russians, Ukrainians, Jews, Poles, Latvians, Estonians and others worked at the factory. Sometimes no one even knew the nationality of one or another worker. Relations were comradely among the workers of all nationalities.

This is class unity, proletarian internationalism.

When I was in the United States of America and was riding in a car in Los Angeles, a man sat down in the car and introduced himself as the deputy mayor of the city. He spoke Russian, not very pure Russian but quite fluent. I looked at him and asked:

'How do you know Russian?'

'I lived in Rostov; my father was a merchant of the second guild.'

Such persons lived in Petersburg and wherever they wished.

The Jew, Kutikov, with whom I worked at the factory, could not live wherever he chose in Tsarist times, you see, but such a Jew as the father of the deputy mayor of Los Angeles could live where he wished.

That was how the Tsarist government viewed the national question: it too treated it from a class point of view. Therefore Jews who were big merchants, capitalists, had the right to live anywhere,[70] but the Jewish poor shared the same lot as the Russian, Ukrainian and other workers; they had to work, to live in hovels and carry the burden of forced labour, like all the peoples of Tsarist Russia.

Different people also behaved differently in the period of the Patriotic War against the Fascist invaders. In those days, no little heroism was displayed, including heroism by Jews. Those of them who distinguished themselves were awarded the title Hero of the Soviet Union. Many were awarded orders and medals. Let me mention, by way of example, Hero of the Soviet Union, General Kreizer. He was deputy commander of the Second Guards Army during the great battle on the Volga; he took part in the fighting for liberation of the Donets Basin and the Crimea. General Kreizer is now in command of troops in the Far East.

There were also instances of treason on the part of people of various nationalities. I can cite the following fact. When Paulus's grouping was surrounded and then crushed, the 64th Army, commanded by General Shumilov, took part in capturing Paulus's headquarters, and General Z. T. Serdyuk[71] was a member of the Military Council. He telephoned and said that among the prisoners taken at Paulus's headquarters was Kogan,[72] formerly an instructor of the Kiev City Komsomol Committee. I asked:

'How could he get there? Aren't you mistaken?'

'No, I'm not mistaken', said Comrade Serdyuk. 'This Kogan was interpreter at Paulus's headquarters.'

A mechanised brigade commanded by Colonel Burmakov took part in capturing Paulus. The commissar of this brigade was Comrade Vinokur, a Jew by nationality. I knew Vinokur back in 1931, when I had worked as secretary of the Bauman Borough Party Committee in Moscow and he had been secretary of the Party cell at the butter and milk plant.

And so it turns out that while one Jew serves as interpreter at Paulus's headquarters, another in the ranks of our troops takes part in capturing Paulus and his interpreter.

People's acts are judged not from a national but from a class standpoint.

It is not in the interests of our cause to dig up out of the rubbish heaps of the past examples of discord among the working people of various nationalities. It is not they who bear the responsibility for inflaming national hatred and national oppression. This was the work of the exploiting classes. And as for the traitors to the interests of the Revolution – the hirelings of Tsarism, the landowners and the bourgeoisie recruited them everywhere and found venal souls among people of various nationalities.

It is absurd to attribute to the Russian people the blame for the dirty provocations of the Black Hundreds, and it would be equally absurd to blame the whole Jewish people for the nationalism and Zionism of the Bund, for the provocations of Azef[73] and Zhitomirsky ('Ottsov'),[74] for the various Jewish organisations connected at one time with the 'Zubatovites'[75] and the Tsarist *okhrana*.

Our Leninist Party consistently pursues a policy of friendship among all peoples, rears the Soviet people in the spirit of internationalism, of intolerance toward any and all manifestations of racial discrimination, of national hostility. Our art proclaims the lofty and noble ideals of internationalism, of the fraternity of peoples.[...]

The poet Evgeny Evtushenko travelled in West Germany and France quite recently. He has just returned from Paris, where he spoke before many thousands of workers, students and friends of the Soviet Union.[...]

The poet gave the members of his audience a strange account of the attitude in our country to his poem 'Babi Yar', informing them that his poem was accepted by the people and criticised by dogmatists. But it is widely known that Communists criticised Comrade Evtushenko's poem. How can one forget this and not draw conclusions for oneself?[76]

Document 28* Kosygin's speech in Riga (1965)[77]

The bonds among the Soviet socialist republics have been expanding more and more. In each of the fraternal republics multi-national production collectives are organised, mutual cultural influences are strengthened, common spiritual features are formed. We move towards the final goal of the Communists, to the fusion of nations into one family through the fullest development of the national culture of every people, every nationality.

Lenin bequeathed us a nationalities policy which is based on the principles of proletarian internationalism, on the absolute equality of all races and nations, on the strict voluntariness of their union. The capitalist system cannot exist without national differences.

National vestiges in any form, whether it be a manifestation of nationalism, great-power chauvinism, racialism, or anti-Semitism, are phenomena absolutely alien and contradictory to our world view.

The Communist Party of the Soviet Union adheres unswervingly to Lenin's national policy, discarding all that interferes with its realisation. We always remember Lenin's words that 'only the greatest attention to the interests of various nations ... creates that confidence (particularly of workers and peasants speaking different languages) without which both peaceful relations among peoples and the successful development of all that is valuable in modern civilisation are absolutely impossible'.

Document 29† Kosygin on reunion of families and national equality (1966)[78]

R. Eli Maissy (UPI, USA): The calamities of the war separated many Jewish families; some members of these families are in the USSR while some are abroad. Can you give these families hope for reunion, as was done for many Greek and Armenian families?

A. N. Kosygin: Some persons raise this question from time to time. Some even allege that anti-Semitism exists in the Soviet Union. There is nothing of the kind in our country and cannot be. It is the fruit of the imagination of those who are trying to present this question in a certain way, resorting to quite

* Source: 'Prazdnik v stolitse Latvii' (Celebrations in the Capital of Latvia), Pravda, 19 July 1965.
† Source: 'Zhit v mire, razvivat sotrudnichestvo' (To Live in Peace, To Develop Cooperation), Pravda, 5 December 1966.

cheap means and working on a public that is attuned, as it were, in a certain manner. The posing of this question, of course, cannot be taken seriously.

As for reuniting families, if some families want to meet or want to leave the Soviet Union, the road is open to them, and no problem exists here.

If the nationalities question in our country is discussed, it must be noted that no other country in the world can say it has solved the question as successfully as it has been solved in the Soviet Union. The nationalities question in the Soviet Union is not acute, because no nationality in our country is subjected to any discrimination whatever; each feels like part of a family of equal peoples. I emphasise that all the nationalities, absolutely all the nations, in our country are equal. I think someday we shall arrange a press conference in which representatives of all the nationalities of the Soviet Union – and there are a great many in our country – will take part, and they will tell you in no uncertain terms what the nationalities question is and how it has been solved in our multi-national state. Then, many people who evidently either do not understand or want to distort our policy on the nationalities question will understand the real state of affairs. In our country, each nationality feels it is the complete master of the situation. This accords with our Leninist policy, which we have steadfastly implemented and shall continue to implement. Everything I have said applies wholly and completely to citizens of the Jewish nationality as well.

Document 30* Kosygin's press conference in New York (1967)[79]

Q. This is by Mr Nathan Silberberg of the *Jewish Chronicle*. Could you comment upon reports of a new wave of anti-Semitism in the Soviet Union as a result of the Arab–Israeli war?

A. Well, I can only surmise that that is an invention trumped up by the author of the question himself. There has never been and there is no anti-Semitism in the Soviet Union and so there can be no question, either, of any new wave because there hasn't been an old one. The Jews in the Soviet Union enjoy all the rights of all the ... on an equal basis with all the other citizens of the Soviet Union. Many of them occupy very high, responsible posts. One of my deputies, a deputy prime minister of the Soviet Union, is a Jew, and there are many Jews among the scientists and statesmen and men in other positions in the Soviet Union. There is no anti-Semitism in the Soviet Union, and I think that allegations to that effect are designed to create certain difficulties and to depict in a false light the situation in our country.

Q. In the light of your own direct talks with President Johnson, do you favour direct talks with the Israeli leaders and those of Arab states?

A. That is a question which the Arab states should decide upon and reply.

Q. Will the meeting between you and President Johnson bring about any changes in the relationship between the Soviet Union and the Arab world?

A. No. We maintain very good relations with the Arab world and indeed we did not discuss – in the talks we had with President Johnson – we did not discuss our relations with the Arab states. That is – that is the concern only of

* Source: *The New York Times*, 26 June 1967.

the Soviet Union and the Arab nations themselves. We have, as I say, very good relations, and the Arab states enjoy great trust and confidence in the Soviet Union, just as the Soviet Union enjoys the confidence of the Arab nations, and we intend to go on strengthening those relationships.

Jews as victims of Soviet policy

3

Anti-Semitism in the Soviet Union

Anti-Semitism – age-old and many-faceted – is one of the most complex phenomena of historical and sociological research. It is therefore not at all surprising that it has been defined and redefined so many times in recent years alone. Its complexity stems, of course, from the fact that it is engendered by a wide range of causes – religious, national, ideological, economic, social and psychological – which work side by side and in various combinations. But this is not all, since at different historical periods now one factor exerted a decisive influence, now another.[1]

Lenin and the Bolsheviks were hostile to anti-Semitism even before the October Revolution,[2] and immediately after their October 1917 victory, they took a firm line of opposition to it. A special order of the Soviet of Peoples' Commissars, issued on 27 July 1918, sharply condemned anti-Semitism and outlawed the organisers of pogroms.[3] In the same year, Lenin recorded a special speech to be used in combating anti-Semitism among the people;[4] extensive propaganda activity was also conducted and a voluminous propaganda literature published to this same end.[5] However, it must be emphasised that none of the criminal codes approved from 1922 onwards in any of the Soviet republics contained a specific paragraph prohibiting anti-Semitism or prescribing punishments for its practice; there was only a general paragraph forbidding propaganda aimed at inciting enmity among the peoples living within the USSR's borders.[6]

The Stalin era

The official Soviet policy attacking anti-Semitism led, if not to its complete elimination, at least to a reduction in its most serious manifestations. In the latter half of the 1920s, however, a wave of mass anti-Semitism began to swell once again, engulfing practically all classes of the population, including the workers and the Soviet intelligentsia. This new wave resulted from economic and social factors such as the flow of the Jews from the Pale of Settlement to Central Russia and the big cities, and especially the occupation of important posts in the administration and the economy by Jews. Stalin, then engaged in a fierce struggle with the 'United Opposition' whose leaders were almost all of Jewish birth,[7] did not flinch from employing the well-tested anti-Semitic weapon of identifying this opposition with the Jews.[8] All the same, Stalin was not yet the omnipotent ruler of the Soviet Union; nor was it the appropriate moment for playing such a dangerous game. The Party leaders quickly understood the grave dangers which could result for the Soviet regime if they fanned the flames of such deep-rooted prejudices or even adopted a complacent attitude towards mass anti-Semitism. And, indeed, by 1927 a decision was taken to launch an all-out struggle against anti-Semitism, which was once again threatening to raise its head.

At this time, after a lapse of several years, numerous books and articles again began to appear explaining the dangers that the spread of anti-Semitism would bring in its wake.[9] Plays and films were shown, meetings and conventions held, and even exemplary trials condemning anti-Semitism publicised. At the 16th Party Congress in 1930, anti-Semitism was declared an evil that had to be countered in the same way as nationalism.[10] Stalin's January 1931 reply to a question of the American Jewish Telegraphic Agency representative – 'anti-Semitism, as an extreme form of racial chauvinism, is the most dangerous survival of cannibalism'[11] – would have fitted well in this campaign had it been published not only abroad but in the Soviet Union as well. However, the fact that this statement was not published in the USSR until November 1936 is certainly significant.[12]

Just as complex social and economic processes in the second half of the 1920s had led to a rise in overt anti-Semitism, far-reaching changes in the structure of Soviet society brought about a drop in the early 1930s. It would, however, be a mistake to think, just because from 1932 onwards the mass media almost completely stopped reporting its existence, that anti-Semitism had in fact vanished from the Soviet scene. As relations between the Soviet Union and Nazi Germany deteriorated in the second half of the 1930s, articles condemning anti-Semitism once again began to appear in the press, with the emphasis now placed on anti-Semitism in Nazi Germany.[13]

Although mass anti-Semitism did not make itself strongly felt again until World War II, the problem was evident before this. Especially disturbing was the fact that this time the government, under Stalin's leadership, chose to exploit the anti-Semitic sentiments still common in the Soviet Union for its own ends. This turning point found expression in a number of areas. For example, there was an underlying feeling in the Soviet Union that the arrests and trials of 1936–8 were mainly directed against the Jews.[14] The first to point to this and to warn against the use of anti-Semitism in the show trials was Trotsky. However, his words fell on deaf ears, and they made no impression at all in the West, not even in the Jewish press.[15] It is possible that among the results Stalin hoped to achieve from the purges was a considerable reduction in the number of Jews at the highest levels of government institutions.[16]

No less serious was the blow dealt to Jewish culture during 1937–8, when Jewish schools, cultural institutions and organisations began to be closed, and Jewish cultural leaders arrested and executed. This policy was further accentuated when the Molotov–Ribbentrop Pact was signed in 1939. The pact was followed by the extradition to the Nazis of a number of refugees including many Jews, who had fled from Germany; by a policy of censorship and silence on the fate of Jews under Nazi rule; and by a stance of official indifference to anti-Semitic actions by the population of the territories recently annexed by the Soviet Union.

World War II gave rise to a new wave of popular anti-Semitism in the Soviet Union, which spread from the areas conquered by the Germans to the ranks of the partisans, the Red Army and the rear. There were a number of interlocking factors responsible for this development which involved wide and varied circles of the population during the war. First, of course, anti-Semitism, like other prejudices, easily becomes intensified at moments of crisis and there has been no national crisis in Russian history more serious than that of World War II. More specifically, in searching for 'those responsible' for all the disasters that befell the Soviet Union at the outbreak of the war, many felt it psychologically necessary to find a scapegoat, and the Jews were natural candidates for this role. For their part, the various branches of the Nazi propaganda machine made enormous efforts to depict the Jews as the embodiment of all that was negative in the Soviet regime, thus planting the seeds of the poison more deeply and spreading them more widely.

Again, the official information policies intended to arouse patriotic national feelings in both the Russian and non-Russian peoples in order to intensify the war effort produced various side effects, one of which was to awaken latent or semi-latent anti-Semitism.[17] And, finally, the annexation of the new territories to the Soviet Union brought with it a multi-national population of some twenty-five millions, most of whom were infected to one degree or another with anti-Semitic sentiments acquired or reinforced in the pre-war period, when semi-Fascist regimes dominated Eastern Europe.

Official Soviet policy almost totally ignored this rising wave. Still more disturbing was the intentional silence on and minimisation of the Nazi extermination of the Jews.[18] Stalin himself mentioned Nazi Germany's anti-Jewish policy once only during the war years, and that was at the beginning of the war.[19] This was due to two main factors, closely and organically related: (1) a complex of political, social and psychological considerations led the Soviet leadership to conclude that reasons of state forbade any attempt to combat popular anti-Semitism; and (2) these same anti-Semitic sentiments were undoubtedly characteristic of many of the leaders themselves – of Stalin, above all.[20] Indeed, a number of personal testimonies recently published in the West clearly prove this. At a December 1941 meeting of Stalin, Sikorski, Anders and Kot, to discuss the possibility of establishing a Polish army in the Soviet Union, there was unanimous agreement that the Jews are miserable and cowardly fighters;[21] Stalin also made cutting remarks about the Jews in his conversations with President Roosevelt at Yalta.[22]

Not only did the end of the war fail to put an end to the anti-Semitic feelings then current in the Soviet Union, but it even brought about their intensification, especially in those areas which had been occupied by the Nazis. New factors now emerged to reinforce pre-existing ones. It must be pointed out here that the local population which had cooperated with the Nazis feared that the Jews returning from the forests and other places of concealment would denounce them to the authorities. There was also apprehension that Jews returning to their former homes would demand the return of their property. And, again, those who occupied the various posts which Jews had held before the outbreak of the war – especially at institutions of higher education, art and science – were similarly afraid of being replaced.

The authorities were aware of the danger inherent in this situation. The regime feared that any identification with the return of the Jews would lose them support among the population, and that this would strengthen the anti-Soviet nationalist movements, particularly in the Ukraine and Lithuania, which were exploiting the weapon of anti-Semitism for their own ends.[23] However, it could not ignore the inherent explosiveness of a policy which tolerated the most vehement displays of anti-Semitism, especially since it could hardly compete successfully with the nationalist movements in this sphere.

Thus, official policy on the Jewish minority, as it began to be implemented from 1946 onwards, emerged as a rather complex compromise. A limited and discrete struggle was launched against the most extreme manifestations of anti-Semitism, and the Jews were granted permission to return to their former homes in the liberated areas, although propaganda activity was conducted to persuade them to remain where they had lived during the war. Likewise, the Jews were generally, although not always, re-admitted to economic, educational and art institutions. But, they were not recruited to important political and security posts in the Party or the government. And, further, they were provided with strictly limited opportunities for reconstructing Jewish cultural life.

However, even at this stage there were increasing signs that Stalin had decided to follow a much more extreme anti-Jewish line. This found its most glaring expression in the systematic removal of Jews from positions which they still occupied in the government apparatus, especially from institutions in any way connected with the conduct of Soviet foreign policy, for example the Foreign Ministry, the Ministry of Foreign Trade and the army and security services. Various steps were also taken to restrict the activity of the Jewish Anti-Fascist Committee, the only Jewish representative body established during the war. The struggle against 'Jewish nationalism' assumed a far more destructive character than that then being waged against the nationalism of other peoples, because of the lowly ideological status of the Jewish minority and the tenuous state of Jewish culture in the Soviet Union after World War II. The press and other mass media began to hint that the Jews constituted a foreign element who possessed dual loyalties and were capable of betraying the socialist motherland in times of crisis. Finally, the brutal murder of Mikhoels, head of the Jewish Anti-Fascist Committee and director of the Moscow State Yiddish Theatre, on 13 January 1948, made it plain to all those who had looked forward to a revival of 'Jewish statehood' in the Soviet Union that their expectations were nothing but vain hopes and that it was necessary to prepare for the worst.

The official anti-Jewish policy reached its most severe stage between November 1948, when the Jewish Anti-Fascist Committee was disbanded and almost all its members arrested, and March 1953, when only his death put a stop to Stalin's plans for a great show trial against the Jewish doctors and the mass exile of the Jews to Siberia. Various aspects of this period are discussed in detail below. Here we shall refer to only one aspect which may perhaps have been less drastic than others but which faithfully reflects the spirit of the times, namely the disastrous influence of anti-Semitic publications in the Soviet press.

An examination of a large number of articles published during 1948–53, both 'serious' and 'humorous' (prominent examples of which are given in the documents to this chapter), reveals a completely distorted and falsified picture of the Jew. Before the eyes of the general public, including the Soviet intelligentsia, a most dangerous stereotype emerged, with the Jew portrayed to the reader as a generally corrupt person who regularly evades military service, even at the most difficult time in the history of the Soviet Union (although sent to the front he, miraculously, always reaches the rear); he is not attached to any place (being an eternal wanderer incapable of attachment to a particular spot); he is unable and even unwilling to work, his ambition being rather to make an easy living (a parasite by nature). As soon as he has settled into a job, he peoples the establishment with members of his family or acquaintances (family and community nepotism); his certificates are acquired through false claims or sharp practices; his promotion at work is also the direct result of fraudulence and swindles. Thus portrayed as exploiter, swindler and operator, the Jew (whose origins are revealed by unmistakable innuendo rather than by direct reference) inevitably arouses loathing and revulsion, jealousy and anger.

From here it is only one step to the most dangerous outright hatred. The extent to which this propaganda was accepted, not only by the ordinary people but also by representatives of the more cultured classes, can be judged from the testimonies which have reached us.[24] There are many reasons why broad circles of the population were ready to absorb anti-Semitism from above. We have already pointed out that the anti-Semitic tradition in Russia, the Ukraine, Lithuania and other nations was reinforced during the war by venomous Nazi propaganda. The disastrous economic situation, housing shortage, difficult working conditions and fierce competition for promotion at work, at a time when expectations of better things had been cruelly disappointed, were all weighty factors which contributed to the growing hatred for foreigners, for strangers, and for all those whose situation was seen, whether rightly or wrongly, as superior. If we add to this the existence of a totalitarian regime which was deliberately creating an almost hysterical atmosphere of anti-intellectualism and extreme xenophobia, the circumstances were right for the Jew to become the ideal object of hatred.

We are obliged to ask, without being able to give an unequivocal reply, to what extent official anti-Semitism was a direct result of 'objective needs', if it can be so expressed, or whether this policy arose, instead, from the strong personal anti-Jewish feelings of various Soviet leaders, especially of Stalin himself. There is no doubt that, despite the 'need' to find a scapegoat for the failures and the desire to assuage resentment by channelling it in a direction as far as possible removed from those really responsible, the government was strong enough to have coped without as drastic, extreme and potentially explosive a weapon as anti-Semitism. Because the government chose not to forego anti-Semitism, one cannot escape the conclusion that the subjective factor was of significance and ultimately, perhaps, decisive.

If Stalin was in fact anti-Semitic, as this analysis implies, it is important to examine from when and why. In our opinion, it is possible to examine his attitude towards the Jews by making use of the three clinical charts of anti-Semitic behaviour suggested by the scholar Rudolphe Loewenstein: (1) an attitude of lurking suspicion, of wariness, which when reinforced can become a feeling of loathing; (2) Judeophobia which finds expression in a kind of mingled hatred and fear, loathing and contempt; (3) the anti-Semitism of hallucination and madness, or the 'paranoic' anti-Semitism of people who believe in an international Jewish 'plot' aimed at enslaving and destroying the Aryan world.[25] Not everyone who has been aroused to anti-Jewish sentiments need pass through all three stages. It is reasonable to assume that, under normal circumstances, the majority of Judeophobes remain at one of the first two stages. In certain cases, however, the direct 'leap' to the paranoic stage is also possible. But, as regards Stalin, this 'theory of stages' seems to hold good.

After the October Revolution, Stalin had close dealings with a large number of Jews in his various Party and government appointments. By the second half of the 1920s, the conflict which broke out between him and Trotsky in 1918[26] had brought him up against the most prominent Party leaders of Jewish birth grouped in the 'United Opposition'. During this fierce and cruel struggle for control of the state, did Stalin recall Aleksinsky's old joke from the pre-war years that an anti-Jewish pogrom within the Party would solve the problems of the Bolsheviks by decimating the Menshevik faction? What is known (and this has already been pointed out) is that he used anti-Semitism in the factional struggle.

The evidence of Svetlana Allilueva[27] and of Khrushchev (Docs. 33–4) is very important in that it helps us to understand how the change from latent and perhaps even subconscious suspicion to blind hatred took place in Stalin.[28] However, it appears that the decisive stage of transition from mere hatred of the Jews to paranoic anti-Semitism began only in 1948, when Stalin, who possessed extreme Russificatory tendencies, began to imagine that an international Jewish plot was being concocted against the Soviet Union.[29]

Needless to say, Stalin was careful not to give public expression to his feelings even during 1949–53, the worst period of anti-Semitic policies. His anti-Semitic position was, however, well known in restricted circles of the Soviet leadership, and rumours about it began to filter out to the general public both within the Soviet Union and beyond its borders (see, for example, Doc. 31). Judging by the countless brutal acts perpetrated by Stalin over so long a period of time, it seems improbable that anything could have deterred him from implementing his plan to exile Soviet Jews to the distant areas of Siberia. Only his death saved them from this fate.[30]

The period of transition (1953–5)

In the period between Stalin's death and Khrushchev's consolidation of power, there were changes of great importance regarding the government's use of anti-Semitism in pursuance of its aims. These changes found expression in a number of spheres: the release of the arrested doctors and cancellation of the trial which was to have been held in the middle of March 1953; a start made on the release of surviving prisoners from the concentration camps; the at least partial and gradual return of Jews to posts from which they had been removed during the anti-cosmopolitan campaign; a general relaxation in the use of terror (which inspired hopes for a renewal of Jewish culture); the consequent resumption of contacts with relatives abroad; the renewal of diplomatic relations with Israel (which had earlier been severed by Stalin); the virtually complete cessation of articles and radio broadcasts with a definite anti-Semitic bias; an improvement in the status of the Jewish religion; a resumption (however limited) in the publication of concrete information on Soviet Jewry (for example, the number of writers of Jewish birth who took part in the 2nd Writers' Congress in 1954, and the number of Jewish scientific workers).

No matter what significance we attribute to these changes, we must not forget that there was no change whatsoever in basic Soviet policy regarding the granting of national rights to the Jewish nationality equal to those of other Soviet minorities. However, it seems that the terror campaigns against Jews in Czechoslovakia and Romania were now initiated independently by the leaderships of these states and were not necessarily carried out under instruction from the Soviet policy-makers.

In order to understand how this limited and partial reversal occurred and the extent to which it sprang from general political changes rather than from a new look at the Jewish question, we must examine the position of Stalin's closest advisers, who were locked in a struggle for power after his death. True, it seems that the number of reliable facts and pieces of evidence on this question stand in inverse proportion to the quantity of speculations published in the West. All that is attempted here, therefore, is a very cautious and limited examination of the motives that could have influenced these leaders in their attitude to the Jews.

We have no doubt whatever that, in the last years of his life and even as early as the beginning of the 1930s, the final decision on any important question lay exclusively with Stalin himself. This does not, however, mean that a number of his closest advisers had no hand in the decision-making process. But it is important to point out that this influence was steadily reduced after World War II and could be exerted only 'indirectly'; for example, by intrigue behind the scenes, by the falsification of documents, and by exploiting Stalin's various weaknesses. The Communist Party leaders closest to Stalin in the years 1946–53 were Zhdanov, Malenkov, Beria, Molotov, Kaganovich and Khrushchev. After them came Voroshilov, Mikoyan and Bulganin.

While it is difficult to imagine that Kaganovich could have had any interest in supporting a policy directed against the Jews, it seems that he did little to oppose the policy.[31] Molotov and Voroshilov, who had Jewish wives (Molotov's wife, Polina Zhemchuzhina, was even arrested and exiled for a number of years), were known for their outright opposition to nationalism and were far from harbouring anti-Semitic feelings.[32] As regards Zhdanov's position on the Jewish question, there are conflicting opinions. That he had close family and political ties with Shcherbakov, who is thought to be one of the driving forces behind war-time anti-Semitism, is well known, as is the fact that he was one of the instigators and perpetrators of the campaigns against nationalism. But he was also an energetic and consistent supporter of the Jewish-born leaders in the majority of the People's Democracies.[33] However, since Zhdanov died in August 1948, and all his associates were liquidated in the notorious 'Leningrad affair' of 1949, he could hardly have influenced the final phases of Stalin's policy towards the Jews.

Malenkov and Beria, the two Soviet leaders who exerted the greatest influence on Stalin, were also among those who implemented the new policy after his death. When, after the war, Malenkov was involved in a fierce and tortuous struggle with his rival Zhdanov for seniority in the Party leadership,[34] neither he nor Zhdanov hesitated to use an anti-Jewish policy. And it is a fact that the most extreme anti-Semitic policy in the whole history of the Soviet Union was carried out during 1949–53, precisely when Malenkov attained the summit of his career. Moreover, there is evidence that Malenkov made anti-Semitic pronouncements.[35] And yet, after Stalin's death, he was one of the principal leaders behind the changes indicated above. It seems that as long as Stalin was in power and conducted an anti-Semitic policy, Malenkov's personal interests merged with his anti-Jewish feelings, and that in the subsequent period, this personal prejudice ceased to influence his public stance.

The most complex and least verifiable case was that of Beria. Discounting the rumours that he was of Jewish extraction, it still remains possible to pin-point a few facts which may cast light on his true attitude to the Jewish question. Firstly, there is no doubt that Beria was, after 1941, involved directly in Stalin's 'Jewish' policy. He was among those who raised the idea of establishing the Jewish Anti-Fascist Committee with the aim of recruiting the support of world Jewry. He initially intended to place two leaders of the Polish Bund, Erlich and Alter, at the head of this committee, but was forced, presumably on Stalin's orders, to put them on trial and execute them that same year. He also stood at the head of the internal security forces at the time of Mikhoels's murder and was certainly involved in that affair. Lastly, he was responsible for the purge of Jews from the Ministry of the Interior, which he headed (one of the exceptions was, it seems, General L. Eitingen who was dismissed later when Beria was no longer the all-powerful ruler of this ministry). On the other hand, the view is maintained that Beria, who for many years headed the Georgian Communist Party and whose word was law in that republic even in later years, was one of the protectors of Georgian Jewry.[36] However we may assess Beria's attitude towards the Jews during the Stalin era, there is one thing that is not in doubt; it was during the four months (March–June 1953) when Beria enjoyed decisive influence in determining policy that a new policy on the national question, which *inter alia* benefited the Jews, was first adopted.

In conclusion, it seems clear that, in contrast to the preceding period, the years 1953–5 saw objective rather than subjective factors exerting the dominant influence in forming official policy on the Jewish question. It was that which made possible those important (albeit limited) changes in the situation of Soviet Jewry outlined above.

The Khrushchev era

Khrushchev's full control (which was never to equal that of Stalin) over the Communist Party leadership and the Soviet government began only in June 1957 with the elimination of the 'Anti-Party' group. However, his say in all important decisions was of predominant influence as early as 1955.

It is true that the new political constellation in the Soviet Union which came into being in February 1956 in the wake of the 20th Party Congress left the totalitarian regime intact. But the partial liberalisation in a number of spheres – especially in the cessation of mass terror which had previously paralysed any possibility of free, independent expression – could not but give rise to internal changes within Soviet Jewry. We shall deal with these changes elsewhere; what interests us here is how this liberalisation affected the continued existence of anti-Semitism at the level of official policy, and also the attitude towards the Jews held by various strata of the population.

The official policy and its motives

As can readily be seen from the documents presented in Chapter 2 and elsewhere, the question of anti-Semitism occupied Khrushchev and all the other Communist Party leaders. Interestingly, a large number of the leaders' official statements were for foreign consumption only and were never published in the Soviet Union itself. This demonstrates quite clearly that the few and isolated voices within the USSR – predominantly from within the ranks of the liberal intelligentsia – which were raised against anti-Jewish discrimination failed to exercise a significant influence on the Soviet leadership. However, the constant external pressure exerted after 1956, by Communist and left-wing circles as well as by 'bourgeois' leaders and intellectuals in both Eastern and Western Europe, did have some effect on Khrushchev and his advisers. While it did not lead to any essential changes in the anti-Jewish policy itself, it at least forced them to try and show the world that a phenomenon as disgraceful as anti-Semitism could not exist in the socialist Soviet Union. These attempts at whitewash were, however, unsuccessful. This is because the reality of Soviet discrimination was much more conspicuous at this time than it was in the era of Stalinist secrecy.

We shall not detail the ways in which the official anti-Semitic policy of 1956–64 came to be expressed as this is discussed elsewhere in the book; here we shall confine ourselves to noting the areas where anti-Semitism found its clearest expression.

From 1957 onwards, increasing numbers of *feuilletons* again began to appear in the Soviet press. Depicting the notorious Jewish stereotypes familiar from the Stalin era (including the army dodger), the Jews were described in these articles as narrow-minded, hypocritical, devoid of all moral inhibitions and ready to perform any act of fraud in order to reap such material benefits as better housing, more comfortable and better paid work or diplomas. Propaganda of this type was also carried from time to time by some of the other mass media. Moreover, anti-Jewish caricatures appeared on the notice boards of a number of factories and other places of work; glaringly anti-Semitic remarks appeared in *belles-lettres*, mainly Russian and Ukrainian; and the late 1950s and early 1960s saw an increase in the publication of anti-Jewish material in the guise of anti-religious or anti-Zionist propaganda.

A policy of deliberate discrimination, which had already been rationalised in political or economic terms, was now applied with growing frequency in the spheres of government, higher education and employment. The near total silence which continued to be maintained on the Jewish Holocaust found extreme expression in the Babi Yar affair, when both local and central authorities consistently and angrily objected to the erection of a monument there in memory of the Jewish victims. The economic trials, which reached their peak in 1961–3, were characterised by an unmistakably anti-Jewish orientation. And, where Jews were insulted or even beaten by anti-Semites, or where synagogues and Jewish cemeteries were vandalised, these actions were met by silence and handled with extreme leniency by the authorities.

In contrast to the taciturn and cautious Stalin, the impulsive and quick-tempered Khrushchev, who enjoyed talking to journalists and meeting with delegations of all kinds, would frequently express opinions on the Jewish question. A brief review of his pronouncements may shed some light on the complicated and very important question: what were the factors and motives behind Soviet policy on the Jewish national minority in the post-Stalin period?

Between 1938, the year Khrushchev reached the exalted position of First Secretary of the Ukrainian Communist Party, and 1955, when his position as Soviet leader was already secure, not one statement on the Jewish question was attributed to him in the newspapers. While it does not appear that this was due to any particular over-cautiousness on Khrushchev's part, it does seem that this factor must be considered. True, it was general policy during that period to refrain from mentioning the Jewish problem except in those few cases where it was necessary to reply to questions put by foreign visitors. However, even in his secret speech at the 20th Party Congress, in which he dwelt at length on Stalin's terrible crimes against the leadership of the Party and the various nationalities, Khrushchev said not a word about the liquidation of Jewish culture and cultural leaders. And when he mentioned the 'Doctors' Plot', he saw fit to completely ignore its anti-Semitic orientation, although it had been plain to all.[37]

On his visit to Poland in March 1956, for the funeral of Bolesław Bierut, Khrushchev told the Central Committee of the United Workers' Party: 'I believe that in Poland, too, you are suffering from an abnormal composition of the leading cadres, as we once suffered from it ... The percentage of high Jewish officials is now nil in my country, two or three per thousand ...' And, looking hard at the chairman of the meeting, Roman Zambrowski, who was born Zukerman, he concluded: 'Yes, you have many leaders with names ending in "ski" but an Abramovich remains an Abramovich. And you have too many Abramoviches in your leading cadres.'[38]

On a second visit to Poland in October 1956, when he tried to prevent the Polish leadership from handing over power to Gomulka, Khrushchev exclaimed immediately upon emerging from the airplane: 'Zhidam budete pomogat?' (Are you going to help the Yids?) He was even more explicit in his talks with the Polish leadership a few hours later: 'The Red Army shed its blood to liberate Poland and you want to deliver your country into the hands of the capitalists who are in league with the Zionists and the Americans.'[39] Although this time Khrushchev replaced the word 'Yid' by 'Zionist', the substance of his statement remained unchanged.

Khrushchev likewise revealed much of his personal attitude in his meetings of 1956–8 with the French socialist delegation, the Canadian Communist delegation and the French journalist, Serge Groussard (Docs. 13, 96 and 17, respectively). His remarks at these three meetings revealed a strong tendency to explain the behaviour of Jews in terms of simple stereotypes and half-truths, for example:

After the liberation of Chernovtsy, the streets remained very dirty. When the Jews were asked why they had not been cleaned, they replied that the non-Jews whose work it was had fled the city. [The hint here is perfectly clear: the Jews are parasites who live at other people's expense.]

Thousands of tourists travelled abroad every year from the Soviet Union, and yet it turned out that only three failed to return from the trip. All three were Jews. [Implying that the Jews are not loyal to their native land and are prepared to abandon it at any time.]

A Jew, appointed to an important post, immediately surrounds himself with assistants of Jewish birth. [In other words, ethnic nepotism is a characteristic feature of the Jews.]

The Soviet government placed an extensive area ideal for colonisation at the disposal of the Jews. The Jews received it with great enthusiasm, but this quickly subsided and they left Birobidzhan *en masse*. [The conclusion here being that the Jews have no staying power.]

The Jews are extreme individualists who prefer artisan and intellectual professions to work in big industrial enterprises. [In other words, they are unwilling to submit to collective work, group discipline and community life.]

Given the opportunity to establish their own schools, the Jews prefer to send their children to non-Jewish schools. [They therefore lack the characteristics essential to sustain an independent national life.]

Stalin was right when he refused to hand over the Crimea for Jewish settlement because there was a real danger that the region would become a stronghold (*place d'armes*) in a war against the Soviet Union. [He thus assumed that the Jews are an unreliable element from the point of view of national security.]

Of course, to be labelled an anti-Semite is embarrassing for a Soviet leader. Even Stalin had been aware of this. Khrushchev therefore needed convincing arguments to demonstrate that he could not be thus accused. Consequently, he eagerly pointed out that many of his colleagues in the government were Jewish (Kaganovich, Vannikov, Mitin); that the Jewish general, Yakov Kreizer, was his close friend; and, furthermore, that since his eldest son was married to a Jewess, his own grandson was half-Jewish. Nonetheless, evidence of Khrushchev's deep-rooted prejudices is found not only in the reports brought to the West by returning delegations but in official government statements made during this period.

Thus, in conversation with the American journalist Henry Shapiro,[40] Khrushchev resurrected from oblivion the concept of rootless cosmopolitanism which had been utilised in the Stalin era to symbolise the regime's campaign to annihilate the assimilated Jewish intelligentsia. In his speech of 8 March 1963, delivered in the presence of leading Soviet writers and artists as well as most of the Communist Party leaders, Khrushchev made his favourite comparison, between 'good' and 'bad' Jews (Doc. 27). However, a careful reading of the text leaves the impression that he used this comparison only to highlight the horrifying act of treason allegedly perpetrated by Kogan, a Jewish member of the Kiev Komsomol whom the Germans appointed interpreter in Von Paulus's headquarters. It is difficult to believe that Khrushchev was not acquainted with the facts before he made this speech. Therefore, his decision to make these charges leads to the inevitable conclusion that he was motivated more by anti-Jewish sentiments than by interests of state. And, in fact, this incident was immediately exploited by writers from the anti-Semitic camp, above all by P. Gavrutto in *Tuchi nad gorodom* (Storm Clouds Over the Town), published in 1963 (see Doc. 45).

This book contains one of the most extreme anti-Jewish descriptions in Soviet literature up to that time. It depicts the traitor, the Judas Kogan, as having delivered one thousand of his comrades from the Kiev underground forces into the hands of the Nazis. The fictitious nature of this entire incident was demonstrated in August 1966 by Ariadna Gromova (Doc. 46), whose detailed investigations led her to conclude that Kogan was not listed among those who betrayed the Kiev underground forces, and that the same Kogan recalled by Khrushchev and Gavrutto fought in the ranks of the Red Army against the Germans and could not possibly have been Von Paulus's interpreter at the Stalingrad front.

Khrushchev's fierce attack on the poet, Evgeny Evtushenko, after the 1961 publication of the poem 'Babi Yar', and the vicious attacks on Evtushenko by writers and critics openly inspired by Khrushchev, reinforce the impression that Khrushchev was hostile towards the Jews.

It seems to us that Ilya Erenburg gave the best explanation of the background to Khrushchev's anti-Semitism when he told the journalist, A. Werth, that: '[Khrushchev] had lived too long in my – though not his – native Ukraine, and had been infected with the kind of visceral anti-Semitism that is still very far from having been stamped out there.'[41] Besides the decisive effect that his long years in the Ukraine undoubtedly had on him, Khrushchev's attitude was also influenced by his personal relations with Jews like the Kaganovich brothers and Mekhlis, and by his period in Moscow under the shadow of Stalin.

Whatever the reasons for Khrushchev's prejudices, it is clear that his Judeophobia differed greatly from Stalin's paranoiac anti-Semitism in the last years of his life. It also differed from ideological anti-Semitism, with all its intellectual and pseudo-scientific claims to rationality. We would even venture to say that it was not the political anti-Semitism understood as a utilitarian or manipulative instrument of policy, although it is certain that such considerations played some role in his thinking. Khrushchev's anti-Semitism was basically what is known as popular anti-Semitism, that rooted in age-old traditions of prejudice and in stereotyped images of the Jew which arouse suspicion, jealousy and hostility.

Khrushchev's personal prejudices[42] and his use of them to promote political objectives were mitigated by a few factors which limited the impact of anti-Semitism during his leadership. One must point first to the rise in the influence of Marxist–Leninist ideology, which is fundamentally opposed to every kind of racial or national discrimination. The use of terror was also radically reduced in scope during the Khrushchev era, and the legal apparatus charged with protecting individual rights, including national rights, was granted a measure of real influence. Further, the authorities were far more hesitant than in the Stalin era to use so explosive a weapon as anti-Semitism lest they lose control of it. Also influential here was internal pressure from liberal circles (to be discussed below) against this embarrassing phenomenon. Finally, and probably most weighty, was the constant external pressure which, together with the authorities' desire to preserve their socialist image, ensured that anti-Semitism was confined within the bounds described above.

Popular anti-Semitism

By popular anti-Semitism we mean the existence of prejudices and a hostile attitude towards Jews living in their midst held by broad strata of the population. In examining whether there was popular anti-Semitism in the USSR during the 1950s and 1960s, as there undoubtedly was earlier, we find few objective observers who would claim that it had completely disappeared from the Soviet scene.[43] Even Soviet leaders admitted that there were still some anti-Semitic survivals in the USSR (see, for example, Doc. 13). However, since no sociological studies on anti-Semitism have been made in the USSR, and since it is doubtful whether any such studies will be made in the near future,[44] it is difficult to assess the extent of this phenomenon, its social distribution, its geographical location or the modifications it may have undergone as a result of psychological, social, economic and other factors. Moreover, since no serious, comprehensive study of Soviet anti-Semitism has been made outside the USSR,[45] we are forced to rely on partial sources; for example, Soviet literature, news items quoted by Western newsmen, members of delegations, students and tourists, and the testimony of recent immigrants to the West from the USSR.

The most common form of popular anti-Semitism discerned – the prevalence of which is confirmed by many sources – was the insult, often accompanied by violence, in shared living quarters,[46] places of work and study, and especially in public streets, parks, public transport. In most of these cases the Jews were accused of taking the best jobs and living off the fat of the Russian land while dreaming of Israel. Frequently they were charged with arrogance and contempt for the local population. Less often, the threatening abuse, 'It's a pity Hitler didn't finish you all off', was heard.[47] The insults repeatedly heard, primarily from hooligans and drunkards (although not from them alone), included 'filthy Jew' (*zhid*), 'Jew-face' (*zhidovskaya morda*), as well as various Jewish names in pejorative form (e.g. Abrasha and Sarechka).

A far more serious, though less common, form of anti-Semitism involved acts of vandalism against synagogues and cemeteries. There were also cases of the blood libel reminiscent of the situation in Tsarist Russia at the end of the nineteenth and beginning of the twentieth centuries (Docs. 53–4).[48] Such cases – where Jews were accused of drinking Christian or Muslim blood – occurred in Dagestan,[49] Uzbekistan and Lithuania.[50] The affair in Dagestan appears to have been the most serious, since the accusation received official approval through publication in a Communist Party newspaper.

Among the most serious cases of popular anti-Semitism reported in the West was the Malakhovka affair (Docs. 51–2). It began on 4 October 1959, when a body calling itself 'Beat the Jews and save Russia', after the slogan of the Black Hundreds, posted venomous anti-Semitic leaflets on apartment blocks and public buildings, and it culminated in acts of arson against the synagogue and the home of the Jewish cemetery warden, whose wife died as a result. As was usual in such cases, the authorities first attempted to deny the very existence of the affair.[51] However, in the end they were forced to admit that the synagogue had been set alight, and the culprits were reportedly caught and punished.[52] In May 1962, a synagogue was set alight in Tskhakaya, in Georgia. There were no casualties in that case, and the local authorities seem to have made no effort to catch and punish those responsible.[53]

The roots of popular anti-Semitism differ little from those which give rise to the anti-Semitism of Soviet leaders. However, it is more elemental, more irrational, and it finds expression in momentary, spontaneous outbursts as opposed to the calculations of political utility which play a significant role in official anti-Semitism. It is characteristic of popular anti-Semitism in the USSR that its intensity and outward manifestation are subject to decisive influence by the regime.

The Babi Yar affair – the liberal intelligentsia and anti-Semitism

The phenomenon of primitive popular anti-Semitism described above was in no way limited to the workers and peasants. There are many facts and testimonies which prove conclusively that the Soviet intelligentsia, in the broad sense of this term (i.e. the 'white collar' workers, including the bureaucracy and technocracy), was also contaminated by such prejudice. Moreover, it can be maintained with some certainty that the Jews, most of whom belong to this stratum of the population, engendered feelings of jealousy and anger among many of its members, and that these sentiments often developed into covert or overt hostility. But while popular anti-Semitism tends to express itself in particularly primitive and crude ways, among the intelligentsia it is generally more 'refined'.

However, there is also a far narrower definition of the term 'intelligentsia' – one which has been in use since the nineteenth century and which does not include all those with higher education, but only those among them committed to independent and critical thought – that minority group which considers itself the conscience of Russia; which sees protest against all social or national discrimination and injustice as its role and mission; which in Tsarist times inspired an outcry against the pogroms and blood libels in Russia and in the whole world.

'Equality for the Jews', wrote Maksim Gorky, 'is one of the more wonderful achievements of the Revolution. By recognising the Jew as the equal of the Russian we have removed the mark of shame, the blood and the filth from our conscience.'[54] To Gorky's distress the Revolution did not bring with it the immediate disappearance of anti-Semitism which he had expected, and he did not spare harsh words in its condemnation: 'When one reads all this stupid filth, put into the heads of Russian nincompoops by senseless and vile evil forces, one becomes so ashamed for Russia, the country of Lev Tolstoy, of the most humane and human literature in the world.'[55] The best representatives of the Soviet intelligentsia – writers, academics and scientists such as Gorky, Mayakovsky, Serafimovich, D. Bedny, Gusev-Orenburgsky, as well as such political leaders as Kalinin, Bonch-Bruevich, Semashko and Lunacharsky – attacked the anti-Semitism which emerged during the period of the New Economic Policy in strong and angry terms.

Unfortunately, this intelligentsia was ground down under the wheels of the Stalinist terror, its voice being silenced for a very long period. Only with Stalin's death, and especially after 1956, were isolated and rather weak echoes raised once more against anti-Semitism in the Soviet Union.

The Babi Yar affair,[56] with all the tense arguments which it aroused, seems to us to symbolise more than any other episode in the Soviet Union the struggle of the liberal Soviet intelligentsia against both official and popular anti-Semitism in the Khrushchev era.[57]

The question of why no memorial had been erected at the valley of death in Babi Yar was first asked on 10 October 1959 by the Kiev-born writer, Viktor Nekrasov (see Doc. 160). True, Nekrasov spoke of 'Soviet people', not mentioning the Jews explicitly; however, his condemnation of the Kiev City Council's plan for erecting a football stadium and park at Babi Yar instead of a memorial to the Nazi victims was very influential and made a far-reaching impact on the Soviet public. On 22 December 1959, a letter requesting the authorities to make a park at Babi Yar with a memorial in it 'dedicated to the victims of Fascism', signed by citizens living in the vicinity of Babi Yar, was published in *Literaturnaya gazeta*.[58] On 3 March 1960, in reply to this request, the deputy chairman of the Kiev City Council Executive announced that, in accordance with the December 1959 decision of the Ukrainian government, a park would be laid out at Babi Yar with a memorial at its centre dedicated 'to the memory of those citizens tortured to death by the Nazis in 1941' (see Doc. 161).[59]

The first person to extend the canvas by describing the question of the memorial at Babi Yar in sharper terms was the young poet Evgeny Evtushenko, who condemned the phenomenon of anti-Semitism that gave rise to atrocities such as those of Babi Yar. His poem 'Babi Yar' (Doc. 39) was written following a visit to the valley of death, and was published in *Literaturnaya gazeta* on 19 September 1961. Its main importance lies in Evtushenko's having placed the question of anti-Semitism in Soviet socialist society squarely and dramatically on the agenda, despite, or perhaps because of, the constantly reiterated official argument that it had disappeared completely. Moreover, Evtushenko hinted very openly at the events at Malakhovka, where the rioters had dared to revive the slogan 'Beat the Jews and save Russia'.

It is also important because Evtushenko, again in opposition to the official claim, spoke of the Jewish people as a single national unit with a continuous history of torments, tears and blood from the time of the Exodus from Egypt to the present day. Further, he tried to destroy yet another taboo in his poem: the 'conspiracy of silence' around the subject of the Holocaust, woven by the authorities and subordinate officials to present the extermination of the Jewish people as part of the general Fascist anti-Soviet policy.

Alongside this positive evaluation of his poem, one must point out that Evtushenko's explanation of anti-Semitism followed the basic lines laid down by orthodox Communism, which has never succeeded in penetrating to the roots of this complex phenomenon. His words on the 'internationalism of the Russian people' also grate on the ear when uttered in the context of the Babi Yar affair; they certainly pale in comparison with Gorky's dirge for a Russia consumed by hatred for her Jews.

As was to be expected, Evtushenko's poem invoked the wrath of the authorities as well as that of the Russian nationalist and conservative circles. This anger found vehement expression in A. Markov's poem, 'My Reply' (Doc. 40), which was printed in the 24 September 1961 issue of the Russian Republic Writers' Union journal. In addition to the usual arguments and the spirit of Great Russian nationalism embodied in his poem, Markov attempted to revive the long-neglected Zhdanovite term, 'cosmopolitan', which had caused the Jewish intelligentsia in the Soviet Union so much suffering. The literary critic, D. Starikov, was far more fundamental and comprehensive in his criticism of 'Babi Yar' in 'About a Certain Poem' (Doc. 41), published in the same paper.

It must be admitted that the experienced Starikov built his argument in a very sophisticated manner. He made effective use of the fact that Soviet Jewish writers, including Erenburg – whether because of their fundamentally ass-imilated world outlook or due to exigencies imposed by the Soviet reality – had continued to express their 'internationalism' and refrained from voicing their personal, Jewish grief and mourning while millions of their kinfolk were being cruelly and systematically exterminated. Accordingly, Starikov quoted from Erenbrug's poems and articles to prove how much more of an 'inter-nationalist' Erenburg was than Evtushenko. Erenburg was indeed left speech-less. He could only complain (Doc. 42) that Starikov had quoted from his poems and articles arbitrarily and to suit his own position. Starikov insisted that any return to the subject of anti-Semitism in the Soviet Union in the year 1961 was tantamount to a betrayal of Communist internationalism. He was especially incensed by Evtushenko's use of the term 'the Jewish people', viewing this as the expression of a petty-bourgeois approach. Further, he did not hesitate to accuse Evtushenko of inflaming national and racial feelings.

The attacks on Evtushenko continued until the 22nd Congress of the Communist Party and even at the Congress itself.[60] However, from late in 1961 the attacks ceased (they did not recur during 1962) and Evtushenko was able to read his poem 'Babi Yar' at gatherings and poetry-readings, where it was always received enthusiastically. His firmest support came from Dmitry Shostakovich, one of Russia's greatest composers and a leading representative of the liberal intelligentsia, who decided to include the words of 'Babi Yar' in his 13th Symphony, which was performed for the first time at the end of 1962.[61] During the same period, apparently under pressure from the authorities, Evtushenko agreed to make two changes in the text of his poem: he noted that besides the Jews, Russians and Ukrainians were also among the Nazi victims, and he added an entire line stating that Russian workers in the Tsarist era actively opposed the pogroms.[62] These changes led to renewed performances of Shostakovich's symphony, which had been suspended, in turn provoking renewed criticism, especially of Evtushenko's text.[63]

There is no doubt that in this affair the liberal intelligentsia won wide support in student circles at a number of universities and that this was a very encouraging sign. However, it was beyond the power of the intelligentsia to change official policy or to limit popular anti-Semitism to any great extent.

The post-Khrushchev period

After nine years of Khrushchev's rule and decisive influence in determining policy, it is legitimate to question the extent to which his removal from leadership on 15 October 1964 occasioned changes in official policy on the Jewish question. And, if there were any changes, were they tentative, or were they fundamental and far-reaching, constituting a turning point?

A cautious and accurate examination of Soviet policy during 1964–7, under the new leadership, demonstrates that there are absolutely no grounds for concluding that a fundamental change had occurred. However, it should not be concluded that there were no changes whatsoever in the post-Khrushchev period. In order to establish what they were, why they came about and the direction they took, the period needs to be divided into one ending in May 1967 and one beginning with the Six-Day War in June of that year.

October 1964 – May 1967

This period greatly resembles the 1953–5 period in the Soviet Union. Once again, a 'period of transition' and a leadership struggle led the governing circle to avoid extremist policies which could arouse internal ferment or external criticism. Once again, the new leadership, which had been totally associated with the previous regime, could not altogether deny its past, but was nonetheless eager to demonstrate its intention of rectifying past mistakes and distortions. In both cases, rival groups within the new leadership, vying with each other for superiority in the power struggle, prevented the formulation of clear-cut policies on complex issues such as the Jewish question.

How, then, did the changes in the official policy on the Jewish question make themselves felt? And to what extent did they help reduce anti-Semitism?

One important departure was evident in Soviet Premier Aleksei Kosygin's statement of July 1965, wherein he declared that anti-Semitism, like all other forms of nationalism and racialism, was alien to the Communist world-view (Doc. 28). True, Khrushchev did occasionally refer to anti-Semitism, but he concentrated on the argument that the phenomenon did not and, what is more, could not exist in the Soviet Union. In September 1965, after a long interval, a significant leading article appeared in *Pravda*, the central organ of the Communist Party (Doc. 37), emphasising Lenin's resolute words against anti-Semitism. No less important was the publication in September 1966 of the comprehensive and penetrating article by the Soviet philosopher I. Kon, in the literary journal, *Novy mir* (Doc. 38). Although Kon's article analysed various US studies on anti-Black and anti-Jewish prejudices, it also hinted quite clearly that it was essential to combat the danger of anti-Semitism in the USSR itself. A few months later, Vergelis, the quasi-official spokesman of the Soviet government on the Jewish question, admitted during a visit to London that anti-Semitism was still common in certain strata of the population, and that it would be necessary to combat it for a long time.[64]

An examination of anti-Jewish *feuilletons* in the years 1965–6[65] shows that their number dropped sharply in comparison with previous years, and that out-and-out anti-Semitic stereotypes disappeared almost completely from these *feuilletons* during this period.

Performances of Shostakovich's 13th Symphony ('Babi Yar') were renewed after an interval of two and a half years. In addition, the publication of a number of books on the Holocaust, containing harrowing sections on the Nazi extermination of the Jews – for example, Masha Rolnikaite's diary in 1965[66] and Kuznetsov's *Babi Yar* in 1966[67] – made a significant breach in the wall of silence surrounding the Jewish Holocaust. In this connection, we should also mention Ariadna Gromova's article on Kogan (Doc. 46), published in *Literaturnaya gazeta*, the newspaper of the Writers' Union. In her vigorous effort to refute the allegations of Khrushchev and Gavrutto by presenting the real facts about the 'Jewish traitor Kogan who was said to have handed his comrades in the resistance over to the Nazis', Gromova accomplished far more than a correction of the terrible injustice to Kogan himself. Her article struck a telling blow at perhaps the most heinous anti-Jewish claim: that Jews had systematically chosen to collaborate with the Nazis (an accusation directed most frequently at the Zionists, the Bund or other such non-Communist Jewish organisations).

During this period, the situation of the Jewish religion in the Soviet Union improved somewhat, most noticeably in the relaxation of the hostile propaganda campaigns (see also Chapter 8). There was also a drop in the number of economic trials involving Jews and, most important, the crude manner in which these trials were used for anti-Jewish propaganda ceased. Finally, relations between the Soviet Union and Israel took on an unusual degree of cordiality, especially in 1965.

However, notwithstanding these improvements – which we have tried to show were mainly the result of objective factors – there were also powerful factors which continued to work with unabated force against any fundamental revision of long-established policies. Thus, as long as Soviet ideology with regard to the nationalities in general was left inviolate, there could be no radical change in the status of the Jewish national minority. And the Soviet leadership perceived the tangled web of internal and external interests as leaving them with no alternative but to perpetuate the *status quo*. This reluctance to make any fundamental and far-reaching changes was compounded by the fact that the leaders who took power in October 1964 do not seem to have disagreed fundamantally with Khrushchev's attitude to the Jews.

Thus, there was no real change during 1964–7 in the government's policy on Jewish culture and education in the Soviet Union; there was still discrimination in the admission of Jews to governmental posts and to higher education; and even the use of anti-Jewish propaganda to promote government aims did not entirely disappear.

From June 1967

Since this work draws a line at the end of 1967, we shall limit ourselves to a brief survey of the changes in Soviet policy which resulted from the Six-Day War.

The reaction of Soviet Jewry to the Israeli victory of 1967 was very similar to its 1948 response to the War of Independence and the establishment of the State of Israel. Now, as then, there was grave concern for the fate of the Jewish population of Israel. In both cases, there were many manifestations of a strong desire to come to the help of the beleaguered State of Israel. And as in 1948, so in 1967 Soviet Jews were buoyed up with pride at Israel's stunning victory and at the fact that Jews could be such excellent soldiers.

Despite the fact that the USSR adopted diametrically opposed positions towards Israel and the Arabs in the two wars, there is no doubt that the reaction of the regime to both the 1948 and 1967 Jewish national awakening was essentially similar. The Soviet authorities were angered and concerned by the strange, almost incomprehensible phenomenon that Jews, who were Soviet citizens and completely integrated in Russian culture, could have strong feelings for a state so far away, so unknown to them and so much part of the 'capitalist' and 'imperialist' camps. And, as in 1948, the authorities opted for a brutal response aimed at suppressing this awakening as quickly as possible.

But here the similarity ended. While Stalin reacted by ordering the physical destruction of the most prominent figures in the sphere of Jewish culture and of all those who expressed (or were suspected of expressing) sympathy for Israel, Brezhnev, Kosygin and Podgorny were compelled to 'make do' with a virulent and wide-ranging propaganda campaign against Israel, Zionism and world Jewry. Jewish national activists were thus able to redouble their efforts, for the most part ignoring the threats of arrest and the sporadic acts of hooliganism to which they were subjected.

The torrent of abuse and unbridled incitement by the authorities, despite their unconvincing efforts to distinguish between 'good Soviet Jews' and 'Nazi' Zionists, led to a new wave of popular anti-Semitism, which, in turn, was exploited by the government in its struggle against the liberal intelligentsia. The dissident movement was presented to the general public as a Jewish phenomenon bent on undermining the foundations of the Soviet State.

From an examination of the documents presented in this book and of other relevant material we can state that, from the end of World War II to the end of 1967, official anti-Semitism existed in the Soviet Union. Indeed, at various times and levels, it exemplified all three categories of Judeophobia, including the paranoiac anti-Semitism described earlier in the chapter.

It is possible to distinguish two periods of extreme official anti-Semitism: one (and by far the more ferocious) occurred during the Stalin era (1948–53), and the other during Khrushchev's ascendancy (1959–63). There were, likewise, two periods in which a more moderate official policy prevailed (from 1953–5 and 1965–6). However, it would almost certainly be too bold to formulate a general rule that anti-Semitism is moderated during short periods of transition and intensified with the consolidation of new leadership in power.

Popular anti-Semitism also existed throughout almost the entire period under discussion. This form of the phenomenon was closely bound up with official anti-Semitism, nourished by it and to a large extent dependent on it. Popular anti-Semitism manifested itself variously, according to the prevailing influences, in passive dislike for Jews, in public insult and minor acts of violence, in blood libels, and in the most serious acts of vandalism and murder.

Active opposition to anti-Semitism in the USSR was expressed mainly by select members of the liberal intelligentsia. Even among them, however, this opposition was often seen not as an end in itself but as symbolic of their struggle to reform the regime.

Finally, the evidence suggests beyond any doubt that there is a correlation between the level of anti-Semitism in the Soviet Union and Soviet foreign policy, especially as regards Israel and the Middle East.

Documents to Chapter 3

General

Document 31* Milovan Djilas[68] on Stalinist anti-Semitism (1952)

I was a guest of Stalin's at a dinner in January 1948. Other Soviet leaders were also present. The atmosphere was different from former occasions – restrained on both sides, with many hidden unspoken thoughts and seemingly accidental sparks in the words uttered. Stalin asked me: 'Why don't you have more Jews in your CC apart from Pijade?'[69] I explained to him the development of the movement in our country and other things. A sarcastically pleased smile passed over Stalin's face, and he called me, sympathetically (and through me other Yugoslav Communists), an anti-Semite. I conversed a great deal in the USSR on this anti-Semitic theme. A man of the apparatus of the CC of the Communist Party of the Soviet Union boasted to me how Zhdanov had cleared all Jews out of the CC apparatus. The Deputy Chief of the General Staff of the Soviet Army, Antonov,[70] was accidentally discovered to be a Jew. Thus his illustrious career came to an end. The struggle against the 'rootless cosmopolitans' in the USSR is in fact a concealed form of the struggle against Jewish intellectuals. During the war, anti-Semitism was more or less openly expressed in the army. There was a great deal of talk in 1948 in Moscow concerning the Hungarian CC (which, as is known, consisted mostly of Jews). Jews had also been allocated the main role in the Moscow trials. There are no more Jews in the public life of the USSR. They are citizens of a lower, the lowest, order. This same policy is now being applied in Eastern Europe against that handful of martyred people who survived Fascist extermination. And this was, is, and will be done regardless of whether the Jews are bourgeois or socialist.

The Prague trial irrefutably exposes this very matter. It exposes reality itself – as always with Stalin – in a concealed form: a conscious, organised anti-Semitic course. Here anti-Semitism is concealed behind the struggle against Zionism, Americanism, etc., even behind the struggle against anti-Semitism! – absolutely in the style of Stalinist absurdity. This is absurdity for honest, unchained and democratically thinking minds, but normality in that world of state capitalist, bureaucratic despotism, which has succeeded in

* *Source*: Milovan Djilas, 'Antisemitizam' (Anti-Semitism), *Borba*, 14 December 1952.

bringing society under its control more deeply and more comprehensively than any other despotism in the past, not only thanks to modern means of enslavement, but above all to its very nature – because of its monopolistic role in the economy.

Anti-Semitism has already become routine in Eastern Europe. It is assuming monstrous forms which would be grotesque if they were not bloody and anti-social. The Hungarian leadership is most anti-Semitic in its propaganda today for the simple reason that it is composed of Jews. This leadership desires to prove in this way how it has freed itself from the 'Jewish cosmopolitan mentality' and how it is faithful, to the very end, to Stalin and his Great Russian 'socialist' imperialism. It strives not only to flatter Stalin, but attempts to guess the hidden, secret desires of the master. This is no wonder: men have been found among the Hungarian people who hate the leadership both as Moscow's flunkies and, in accordance with tradition, as Jews. The former ill of capitalism, which was once presented to the Hungarian peasant and ruined artisan in the form of the Jew-usurer, has now become a 'socialist' ill, again in the form of a Jew but this time a bureaucrat.

This is most convenient for the Soviet government for all sorts of reasons. And Stalin laughs satanically at Rakosi[71] and Gerö, together with the rest of the 'Jewish' brethren, as they weave the rope which they will find around their own neck one day with their anti-Semitic propaganda. Ilya Erenburg can sing songs to Great Russian imperialism at peace congresses. Those inside the Kremlin know all they need to know about him. I heard Stalin say that he considered Erenburg a hypocrite, and he said that during the war, when Erenburg was at the peak of his anti-German glory. His spirit is too worldly to be their own. They still need him because of French and other cosmopolitan intellectuals. But these are already his last songs, his swan-song in that they are the last. But they are, in fact, the hoarse barking of a dog that has served its time and begs the last morsels from his master in this way.

History teaches us that a regime was always reactionary when it began to become anti-Semitic, and that pogroms against the Jews were always a sure sign of the most sinister social reaction. Of course history does not repeat itself, but it does not end either. Great Russian bureaucratic state capitalism has had to become not only nationalist, but racial too. This is unavoidable, because how else will it justify the struggle for world hegemony and the oppression of other nations except by stressing its 'exceptional qualities'? And it must inevitably become – and already is – anti-Semitic also.[72]

Document 32* Evtushenko's memoirs of the Stalin era (1963)[73]

Unfortunately it was people such as he who sometimes made 'literary policy', infecting it with evil-smelling things like anti-Semitism. It must be said that anti-Semitism is not in the least natural to the Russian people, any more than it is to any other people. It is always grafted on. In Russia anti-Semitism was artificially stirred up under the Tsars. It was just as artificially stirred up at various times under Stalin. But to me, both as a Russian and as a man to

* *Source*: E. Evtushenko, *Avtobiografiya* (Autobiography), London, Flegon Press, 1964, pp. 88–9.

whom Lenin's teaching is dearer than anything in the world, anti-Semitism has always been doubly repulsive. The poet, K, to whom an accident of fate had bound me in an undiscriminating schoolboy friendship, was, to put it mildly, not without this failing. He attempted to convince me that the whole history of opportunism, starting with the Bund and going on to Trotsky,[74] had a specifically Jewish basis. I argued with him until I was hoarse. He reproached me for my 'political short-sightedness'.

After one such argument, he stayed the night. Next morning I was awakened by his shouts of joy. Dressed in nothing but his shorts, he was dancing a sort of African war dance, waving a newspaper which announced the discovery of the Doctors' Plot[75] and the arrest of the plotters.

'See? What did I tell you? Jews, the whole lot of them!'

I must admit that I believed the report. It depressed me unutterably, but without converting me to anti-Semitism, and I found K's happiness unpleasant to watch.

That same day, K and I went to see an old film about the Revolution. There was a scene in it of an anti-Jewish pogrom in Odessa. When the shopkeepers and common criminals moved across the screen shouting, 'Kill the Jews – save Russia!', and carrying cobblestones sticky with the blood and hair of Jewish children in their hands, I leaned towards my poet friend and asked: 'Do you really want to be like them?'

He drew sharply away from me and said in a hard cold voice: 'We are dialectical materialists. Not everything from the past should be discarded, Zhenya.'

His eyes flashed hatred.

His Komsomol badge shone on the lapel of his coat.

I looked at him in horror; I couldn't understand what sort of a man this was, sitting next to me.

He was only twenty-four. He had not been brought up under Tsarist tyranny, but under the Soviet regime based on the principles of internationalism. On the wall above his desk hung portraits of Lenin and Mayakovsky.[76] How could he unite in himself two such mutually exclusive notions as Communism and anti-Semitism?

Now that ten years have gone by, I realise that Stalin's greatest crime was not the arrests and the shootings he ordered. His greatest crime was the corruption of the human spirit. Of course Stalin never himself preached anti-Semitism as a theory, but the theory was inherent in his practice. Neither did Stalin in theory preach careerism, servility, spying, cruelty, bigotry or hypocrisy. But these too were implicit in Stalin's practice. This is why some people, such as the poet K, began to think and act in an anti-Communist way though they regarded themselves as the most orthodox of Communists.

I came to realise that those who speak in the name of Communism but in reality pervert its meaning are among its most dangerous enemies, perhaps even more dangerous than its enemies in the West.

From that day on, the poet K became for me the enemy of Communism, and therefore my own enemy as well. (In this the attitude of some dogmatists I have met differs from mine – they regard their own enemies as the enemies of Communism.)

I realised that a struggle lay ahead, a struggle to the death with those who preach Communism in theory and discredit it in practice. I foresaw that the struggle would be long and difficult. Whenever people who regard Communism as their own private monopoly are accused of perverting Lenin's ideas, they turn and accuse their attackers of the same thing.

Thus, the poet K often reproached me for my loss of revolutionary vigilance. He never suspected that revolutionary vigilance had become my spiritual motto – as applied, among other things, to such people as himself.

It was with the vigilance of a revolutionary that I watched the erection in Moscow of blocks of tall apartment houses destined for the bureaucratic elite, while thousands of Muscovites lived in tiny, wretched, overcrowded rooms.

It was with the vigilance of a revolutionary that I read the barely disguised anti-Semitic articles in the press.

With revolutionary vigilance I noted such facts as, on the one hand, the privileged position of certain officials who, besides their salaries, received supplementary sums of sometimes double their salaries (the so-called 'blue envelopes') and, on the other, the underprivileged position of those in the low-paid professions.[...]

Readers were beginning to respond a little to my poems.

'This is all very well,' said Slutsky[77] one day after I had read him a whole pile of poems about love, 'but to be a poet in our time, it's not enough only to be a poet.'

I don't think I quite understood him then.

Document 33* Khrushchev on Stalin[78]

Once the Ukraine had been liberated, a paper was drafted by members of the Lozovsky committee. It was addressed to Stalin and contained a proposal that the Crimea be made a Jewish Soviet Republic within the Soviet Union after the deportation from the Crimea of the Crimean Tartars. Stalin saw behind this proposal the hand of American Zionists operating through the *Sovinformbureau*. The committee members, he declared, were agents of American Zionism. They were trying to set up a Jewish state in the Crimea in order to wrest the Crimea away from the Soviet Union and to establish an outpost of American imperialism on our shores which would be a direct threat to the security of the Soviet Union. Stalin let his imagination run wild in this direction. He was struck with maniacal vengeance. Lozovsky[79] and Mikhoels[80] were arrested. Soon Zhemchuzhina herself was arrested. The investigation of the group took a long time, but in the end almost all of them came to a tragic end. Lozovsky was shot. Zhemchuzhina was exiled. I thought at first she had been shot, too, because nothing of what had happened was reported to anyone except Stalin, and Stalin himself decided whom to execute and whom to spare.

I remember Molotov calling to ask my advice about this whole affair. Apparently Zhemchuzhina had pulled him into it. Molotov never did agree with Stalin about the necessity for arresting Zhemchuzhina. When the

* Source: *Khrushchev Remembers*, Boston, Little, Brown, 1970, pp. 260–3.

question of removing her from the staff of the Central Committee came up at a Central Committee plenum and everyone else voted aye, Molotov abstained. He didn't vote nay, but he still abstained. Stalin blew up at this, and the incident left its imprint on Stalin's attitude toward Molotov. He started kicking Molotov around viciously. Kaganovich's maliciousness was a particularly good barometer of Molotov's precarious position. Incited by Stalin, Kaganovich played the part of a vicious cur who was unleashed to tear limb from limb any member of the Politbureau toward whom he sensed Stalin's coolness, and Kaganovich was turned loose on Molotov. [...]

A question of substance: was it necessary to create a Jewish Union or Autonomous Republic within the Russian Federation or within the Ukraine? I don't think it was. A Jewish Autonomous Region had already been created which still nominally exists, so it was hardly necessary to set one up in the Crimea. But this question was never discussed in substance. We had been conditioned to accept Stalin's reasoning, and we gave in to his absolute authority. He contended that if a Jewish Republic were created in the Crimea, then Zionism, which is rampant in America, would gain a foothold in our country. That was all there was to it. He had made up his mind, and he had people arrested, arbitrarily and without any regard for legal norms, regardless of the important and positive role which the accused had played during the war in helping to bring to light the atrocities committed by the Germans. Theirs had been constructive work, but now it counted for nothing. They were deprived of their liberty and in many cases their lives. I consider the whole affair to have been a disgrace. Stalin could have simply rejected their suggestion and rebuked them. But no, he had to destroy all those who actively supported the proposal. It was only by some miracle that Zhemchuzhina stayed alive and got off with a long term exile. More typical was the cruel punishment of Mikhoels, the greatest actor of the Yiddish theatre, a man of culture. They killed him like beasts. They killed him secretly. Then his murderers were rewarded and their victim was buried with honours. The mind reels at the thought! It was announced that Mikhoels had fallen in front of a truck. Actually he was thrown in front of a truck. This was done very cleverly and efficiently. And who did it? Stalin did it, or at least it was done on his instructions. [...]

I've tried to give Stalin his due and to acknowledge his merits, but there was no excuse for what, to my mind, was a major defect in his character – his hostile attitude toward the Jewish people. As a leader and a theoretician he took care never to hint at his anti-Semitism in his written works or in his speeches. And God forbid that anyone should quote publicly from any private conversations in which he made remarks that smelled sharply of anti-Semitism. When he happened to talk about a Jew, Stalin often imitated in a well-known, exaggerated accent the way Jews talk. This is the same way that thick-headed, backward people who despise Jews talk when they mock the negative Jewish traits. Stalin also liked to put on this accent, and he was pretty good at it.

I remember when I was working in Moscow, some kind of trouble at the Thirtieth Aviation Factory was reported to Stalin through Party channels and by State Security. During a meeting with Stalin, while we were sitting around exchanging opinions, Stalin turned to me and said, 'The good workers at the factory should be given clubs so they can beat the hell out of those Jews at the end of the working day.' When he said this, I wasn't alone. Molotov, Beria, and Malenkov were there. (However, Kaganovich was not there. Stalin never permitted anti-Semitic remarks in Kaganovich's presence.) I thought to myself, 'What is he saying? How can he say that?'

As we left the room, Beria asked me ironically, 'Well, have you received your orders?'

'Yes', I said, 'I've received them. My father was illiterate, but he never took part in a pogrom. It was considered a disgrace. And now this directive is given to me as a Secretary of the Central Committee of the Communist Party of the USSR.'

Even though Stalin had given me a direct order, I knew that if something like what he suggested were done and if it were to become public knowledge, a commission would no doubt be appointed and the culprits would be severely punished. Stalin would have stopped at nothing to punish anti-Semitism publicly. Orders or no orders, he would have strangled anyone whose actions would have discredited his name, especially with something as indefensible and shameful as anti-Semitism. there were many conversations like the one about the Thirtieth Aviation Factory, and we became accustomed to them. We listened to what Stalin told us and then put it out of our heads right away.

Document 34* Khrushchev on the Polish Leadership (1948–51)

Therefore the only way I could keep up with what was going on in Poland was to be present when the Polish comrades reported to Stalin, keep my ears open, and draw my own conclusions. From what I picked up in this way, I realised that pressures were building up inside the Polish leadership – pressures caused by conflicts over personnel policies which could blow the lid off the leadership any time.

You see, Zionism and anti-Semitism are blood brothers. Both are reactionary and inimical to the interests of the working class. It sometimes happens that people of non-Jewish nationality trip up on this slippery ground and slide either toward favouring the Zionists, who are reactionaries, or toward becoming anti-Semites, who are equally reactionary. Let's look at two of the men who contributed to the troubles in the Polish leadership: Berman[81] and Minc,[82] both of whom happened to be Jews.

Berman had great influence on Bierut.[83] Anything he wanted to do he could do through Bierut without stepping forward himself. I doubt that Bierut made a single political move without consulting Berman. However, Berman's attitude toward native Polish cadres was incorrect, and it resulted in certain difficulties for the Polish United Workers' Party.† Minc did a fine job as Chairman of the State Planning Commission, and he too was one of Bierut's key advisors and suporters. But, like Berman, Minc demonstrated certain peculiarities for which he later had to be censured by the Party. I would have to say that Bierut may have relied on both these men more than he should have.

Comrade Cyrankiewicz[84] was in an ambiguous, and certainly unenviable,

* *Source*: *Khrushchev Remembers. The Last Testament*, Boston, Little, Brown, 1974, pp. 179–82.
† 'Native Polish cadres' – as opposed to Jews.

position. He had been a representative of the more numerous Polish Socialist Party before its amalgamation with the Workers' Party.* Therefore he continued to be regarded by the other Polish comrades with a certain degree of suspicion.

Keep in mind that the two parties merged not because they held identical political convictions but because they had to make a political deal in order to bring about the socialist reconstruction of Poland. For a long time after the amalgamation, the Communists didn't entirely trust Cyrankiewicz. They used to say such things as, 'God knows who that man really is and what he's really thinking. He's a very mysterious type.'

There were all sorts of rumours about him, some of which I heard from Gomulka.[85] For instance, I was told Cyrankiewicz liked to drive his own car, without a chauffeur. He really knew how to drive fast, too. His driving habits touched off all sorts of talk. People started saying he was on bad terms with his wife and went off in his car to see other women. It's probably a good thing Stalin was dead by the time we picked up these stories, because if he'd heard them it would have meant a bad end for Comrade Cyrankiewicz.

However, Stalin was still very much alive when the rumour reached us that Cyrankiewicz was not a Pole at all, but the son of a Jewish merchant, and that Cyrankiewicz was a modified Jewish name. This rumour was meant to show that Cyrankiewicz didn't genuinely belong to the Polish leadership. Comrade Cyrankiewicz is an intelligent man; he knew exactly what was being said about him behind his back and what it meant. All the suspicions and rumours had an impact on his personality. At meetings he kept quiet, speaking only when his opinion was asked, and always addressing himself only to the matter under discussion. It was sometimes hard to know exactly where he stood on the more controversial problems.

Zambrowski[86] was different.† Everyone knew where he stood. He was the head of the Personnel Section of the Central Committee, and he was accused of having pro-Zionist sympathies. Because he was a Communist and a veteran of underground Party activity during the Hitlerite occupation, he couldn't be called a Zionist himself. But because he was a Jew and because more Jews than Poles got promoted to key economic and poltical posts, Zambrowski was accused of showing patronage toward other Jewish comrades.

Of course, promoting *only* Jews would have been a stupid thing to do even if he had been a Zionist in disguise; it would have exposed him to all kinds of charges. Zambrowski was not a stupid man. Personally, I don't think he was a Zionist either. But he did get a reputation for cold-shouldering the Polish cadres in a Polish state and promoting Jewish cadres when there was no objective grounds for choosing them over Poles. Naturally, this irritated the Polish comrades.

I'd be the first to admit that among Poles there were some very strong manifestations of anti-Semitic feeling; we've even had cases here in our own country in which Jews were denounced for Zionism without just cause. But Zambrowski deserved some criticism. The unfair promotion of Jews over Poles

* The amalgamation of the Polish Socialist Party with the Workers' (Communist) Party took place in December 1948; the result was the Polish United Workers' Party, headed by Bierut.
† Roman Zambrowski, like Berman, had reentered Poland with the Red Army towards the end of the war.

represented an absolutely unacceptable case of political myopia on the part of the Polish leadership, and there was more than one example of this myopia.

Gomulka understood how mistaken – indeed, how harmful – it was to let this virus grow unchecked in the Polish leadership.* Not only was he a Pole; he was a more mature politician than some of his comrades. He was also more straightforward in expressing himself; I would even say he was abrasive. He started objecting vociferously to Bierut about the personnel policies of Berman, Minc, and most of all, Zambrowski. Bierut, who was deeply under the influence of Berman and Minc, did not accept Gomulka's objections.

The virus spread and, after a while, came to Stalin's attention. You might have thought Stalin would have taken Gomulka's side in the dispute with Berman and Minc, since they were Jews.† But there were two factors that led Stalin to oppose Gomulka. First, Bierut supported Berman and Minc, and Stalin had more confidence in Bierut than Gomulka. Second, as far as Stalin was concerned, the conflict in the Polish leadership had nothing to do with the Jewish question. If Gomulka's opponents had accused him of being anti-Semitic, Stalin probably would have taken Gomulka's side. Instead, however, the Polish comrades accused Gomulka of being *pro-Yugoslav*. They didn't make these charges publicly, but they made sure they reached Stalin's ears. [. . .]

For a while Gomulka was left hanging. Even though he'd already made up his mind, Stalin pretended not to be involved in the conflict dividing the Polish leadership. Stalin always knew how to wait; he knew how to wear a mask of impenetrability. For a certain period, even though I saw Stalin in the presence of the Polish comrades, I didn't realise a cloud had gathered over Gomulka's head.

Then one day, when I was at Stalin's he received a phone call. He listened impassively, hung up, and came back to the table where I was sitting. As was his habit, he didn't sit down but paced around the room.

'That was Bierut calling', he said. 'They've arrested Gomulka. I'm not sure it was the right thing to do. I wonder whether they have sufficient grounds to arrest him.'

Stalin knew very well there were absolutely no grounds at all for arresting Gomulka, any more than there were grounds for arresting Spychalski, Kliszko, Loga-Sowinski, or any other comrades who were arrested at the same time.‡

Document 35§ An official attack on anti-Semitism (1955)

Our cadres must carefully study the theory and policy of the Communist Party of the Soviet Union on the national question in order to fight more successfully for the rapid eradication of national prejudices. National prejudice is a particularly tenacious trace left by capitalism in people's minds.[. . .]

Fighting against bourgeois nationalism in all its manifestations, the Com-

* The 'virus' of a Jewish take-over.

† On Stalin's personal anti-Semitism, see, for example, Doc. 33.

‡ Zenon Kliszko and Ignacy Loga-Sowinski, along with Spychalski, were closely associated with Gomulka. They were all removed from the leadership in late 1949 and arrested in July 1951.

§ *Source*: S. Kazakov, 'Chto chitat ob internatsionalnom vospitanii trudyashchiskogo naroda' (What to Read Concerning Internationalist Indoctrination of the Working People), *Partiinaya zhizn*, 1955, no. 12, pp. 71–8.

munist Party directs the attention of the working people to the particular harm of anti-Semitism. In his speech on 'Anti-Jewish Pogroms',* Lenin exposed the criminal policy of the capitalists, who deliberately incited hostility towards the Jews in order to divert the attention of the working people from their real enemy, capitalism. 'Shame on accursed Tsarism, which has been torturing and persecuting the Jews', said Lenin. 'Shame on those who sow hatred towards Jews, who sow hatred towards other nations.'† The Communist Party has always waged a merciless struggle against anti-Semitism as a phenomenon profoundly hostile to the Soviet system.[...]

Ordzhonikidze[87] dedicated deeply felt words to the memory of the twenty-six Baku commissars,[88] among whom were representatives of many of the Transcaucasian nationalities. Ordzhonikidze saw the fact that they gave their lives for the common cause of all the working people as a symbol of the international brotherhood of the working class. 'Just as the common grave of Stepan and Alesha knows neither Armenian nor Georgian nor Tatar nor Jew, so the Baku proletariat knows no national friction', wrote Ordzhonikidze. 'May the grave of Stepan, Alesha, Vani and Meshadi-bek be a reproach and a curse to those who for even a second betray the great cause of national peace and solidarity of the working people in the Transcaucasus!'‡ [...]

The social roots of bourgeois nationalism have been cut out in our country and the triumph of the ideology of friendship between peoples has been assured. But the Party teaches that even when the enemy is routed, the remnants of his ideology do not disappear by themselves, but a constant offensive must be conducted against them. The traces of capitalism in people's minds 'are far more tenacious in the sphere of the national question than in any other; they are more tenacious because they are able to disguise themselves well in national costume'.§ Accordingly, the struggle against them must be waged with particular persistence and consistency.

The propagation of proletarian internationalism and the education of the working people in the spirit of friendship among peoples are among the most important tasks facing Party organisations in their ideological work.

Document 36 Public attacks on anti-Semitism

*Evtushenko argues with Khrushchev (1962)[89]***

Evtushenko: First of all I want to thank the leaders of the Party and the government for kindly making it possible for me to speak here. Permit me to begin my speech with a verse which I wrote not so long ago which I consider very timely.[90]

Comrade Khrushchev: Comrade Evtushenko, this poem has no place here.

Evtushenko: Respected Nikita Sergeevich, I especially selected this poem and with the following purpose in mind. We all know that no one has done more

* V. I. Lenin, *Sobranie sochinenii* (Collected Works), Moscow, vol. 29, pp. 227–8.
† *Ibid.*, p. 228.
‡ G. K. Ordzhonikidze, *Izbrannye statyi i rechi 1918–1937* (Selected Articles and Speeches 1918–1937), Moscow, Gospolitizdat, 1945, p. 84.
§ I. V. Stalin, *Sochineniya* (Works), Moscow, vol. 13, p. 361.
** *Source: Commentary*, December 1963, pp. 433–7.

than you in the liquidation of the negative consequences of the Stalin cult of personality and we are all very grateful to you for this. However, one problem yet remains which is also a negative consequence of those times, but which today has not yet been resolved. This is the problem of anti-Semitism.

Comrade Khrushchev: That is not a problem.

Evtushenko: It is a problem, Nikita Sergeevich. It cannot be denied and it cannot be suppressed. It is necessary to come to grips with it time and again. It has a place. I myself was a witness to such things. Moreover, it came from people who occupy official posts, and thus it assumed an official character. We cannot go forward to Communism with such a heavy load as Judeophobia. And here there can be neither silence nor denial. The problem must be resolved and we hope that it will be resolved. The whole progressive world is watching us and the resolution of this problem will even more greatly enhance the authority of our country. By resolution of the problem I mean the cessation of anti-Semitism [*illegible*], along with instituting criminal proceedings against the anti-Semites. This positive measure will give many people of Jewish nationality the opportunity to take heart and will lead us to even greater success in all areas of Communist construction.

A speech by Mikhail Romm*

In our country, however, certain methods were imposed against which it is necessary to fight. I'm ready to fight against my own shortcomings still remaining from the past. Precisely because of that, before we take up traditions and innovations I should like to clarify the problem of certain traditions which were imposed in our country. There are good ones and there are very bad ones; for example, the one of playing the Overture of Tchaikovsky's *Symphony 1812* twice a year.

Comrades, as I understand it, this Overture expresses a very clear political idea – the idea of the triumph of orthodox religion and autocracy over revolution. It's a bad piece of music written by Tchaikovsky on command. It's a thing Petr Ilyich was himself ashamed of at the end of his life. I'm not a specialist in the history of music, but I am convinced that this Overture was composed for passing reasons, with the very clear aim of pleasing the Church and the monarchy.

Why should the Soviet power humiliate the *Marseillaise*, the marvellous hymn of the French Revolution, by drowning it out with the noise of church bells? Why should it celebrate the triumph of Tsarist ideology, the ideology of the 'Black Hundreds'?[91]

But to play this Overture has become a tradition. After the October Revolution, this Overture was played for the first time during those years when the expression 'cosmopolitan without a fatherland' was invented to replace that other expression 'dirty Jew'.

Among other things, and in certain instances, the latter expression was even printed. On the cover of the magazine *Krokodil* a cartoon appeared during those years presenting a 'cosmopolitan without a fatherland' of clearly Jewish

* *Source*: *Commentary*, December 1963, pp. 433–7.

type, holding a book in his hands on which one could read in big characters the word *zhid*. Not 'André Gide' but simply *zhid*.[92]

Neither the cartoonist nor any of those responsible for this scoundrel's joke has been condemned by us. We have preferred to keep quiet, to forget all this, as one could forget that dozens of our best theatre and movie people were declared 'cosmopolitans without a fatherland': for instance, Comrades Yutkevich,[93] Leonid Trauberg,[94] Sutýrki,[95] Kovarsky,[96] Bleiman,[97] and others present here. They have been authorised to work again, some in the Party, some in their particular union. But is it really possible to heal the wounds, to forget what one has suffered for many years, when you were trampled on and covered with mud?

And those who directed this shameful campaign with joy and pleasure, who racked their brains to invent other things and to drag other people into the mire, have they been made to pay for what they did? People don't even reproach them, holding that this would show lack of tact!

The magazine *Oktyabr*, edited by Kochetov,[98] has recently become interested in motion pictures. From January to November it published articles smearing all the progress achieved by Soviet films, expressing suspicion towards the critics of the great artists of the older generation and even the new one. These articles were inspired by the same persons who led the campaign of denunciation of 'cosmopolitans without a fatherland'. It seems to me, however, that we should not forget all that happened.[...]

It is very important to unmask Stalin and Stalinism, but the heritage left by Stalinism is not less important. And it is not less important to look around at what surrounds us and to formulate a judgement on events that occur in the social life of art.

Our meetings are conducted in a calm, tranquil, academic tone. In the meantime a very energetic group of rather bad writers hits out viciously in the magazine *Oktyabr* against the new literature and nobody answers them in this arena. On the other hand, the very moment Evtushenko published his poem 'Babi Yar', this group printed a reply in the journal *Literatura i zhizn*.

Not long ago I happened to be in Italy and America, and I should like to say that what was considered to be a scandal in the West was not Evtushenko's poem, but the response to it. The local journalists asked me, 'What do you think of the new wave of anti-Semitism in the USSR?'

I asked with perplexity what they were talking about. They mentioned Starikov's article and Markov's poem [Docs. 40–1].

That issue of the journal *Literatura i zhizn* was shameful, as are the latest issues of the magazine *Oktyabr*.

Since the articles in *Oktyabr* are aimed at me,[99] it is difficult and embarrassing for me to reply. Difficult but necessary.

Document 37* Pravda warns against anti-Semitism (1965)

The Soviet Union – the expanses of our motherland have spread from the Baltic and the Carpathians to the Pacific, from distant northern islands to the

* *Source*: 'Leninskaya druzhba narodov' (Leninist Friendship of Peoples), *Pravda*, 5 September 1965.

sunny oases of Central Asia and the Transcaucasus. And in our great land lives a friendly family of Soviet peoples – more than one hundred nationalities and peoples! – united by the common goal of building a Communist society.[...]

V. I. Lenin, the great creator of the Communist Party and founder of the Soviet State, bade our Party hold sacred the friendship of peoples of the USSR. He wrathfully assailed any manifestations of nationalism, and in particular demanded an unceasing 'struggle against anti-Semitism, that abominable inflation of racial peculiarity and national hostility'[100] created by the exploiting classes.

Document 38* On the roots of ethnic prejudice (1966)[101]

A preconceived notion of people's qualities and appearances, in other words a notion not founded on a fresh, direct evaluation of every phenomenon, but deduced from standardised judgments and expectations, is called a stereotype by psychologists. [...]

There are societies known to us where ethnic prejudice has been an officially accepted social norm – for example anti-Semitism in Fascist Germany – but this did not prevent it from remaining a prejudice, although the Fascists did not consider it as such. [...]

One and the same standard accusation is always brought against any national minority, any group that arouses prejudice: 'these people' display too great a degree of group solidarity, they always support one another, so one must be wary of them. This is said of any national minority. Is there a real basis to such an accusation? [...]

Not for nothing did a writer once say that if tomorrow one were to begin persecuting red-haired people, then the next day all red-haired people would begin to console and support one another. [...]

Not for nothing, as history testifies, do problems bound up with national minorities become especially aggravated at times when a society is going through a crisis. [...]

Today anti-Semitism is in the main bound up with anti-intellectualism.

The Babi Yar affair

Document 39 Evtushenko's 'Babi Yar'[102]

The poem†

> There are no memorials over Babi Yar –
> The steep slope is the only gravestone.
> I am afraid.
> Today I am as old in years as the Jewish people.
> It seems to me now that I am a Jew.

* *Source*: I. Kon, 'Psikhologiya predrassudkov' (The Psychology of Prejudice), *Novy mir*, 1966, no. 9, pp. 188, 190, 193–4, 200, 204–5.
† *Source*: E. Evtushenko, 'Babi yar', *Literaturnaya gazeta*, 19 September 1961.

Now I am roaming over ancient Egypt,
And now, crucified on the cross, I die.
And to this very day I bear the marks of the nails.
It seems to me that I am Dreyfus.
The worthy citizenry denounces me and judges me.
I am behind prison bars.
I am trapped, hunted, spat upon, reviled.
And good ladies in dresses flounced with Brussels lace,
Shrieking, poke umbrellas in my face.
It seems to me that I am a boy in Belostok.
Blood flows and spreads across the floor
Reeking of onion and vodka.
The leading lights of the saloon bar
Are on the rampage.
Kicked aside by a boot, I am helpless:
I plead with the pogrom thugs.
To roars of 'Beat the Yids, and save Russia',
A shopkeeper is beating up my mother.
O my Russian people!
I know that you are really international.
But those with unclean hands
Have often loudly taken in vain
Your most pure name.
I know how good is my native land
And how vile it is that, without a quiver in their veins,
The anti-Semites styled themselves with pomp
'The Union of the Russian People.'
It seems to me that I am Anne Frank
As frail as a twig in April.
And I am full of love
And I have no need of empty phrases.
I want us to look at each other,
How little we can see or smell.
Neither the leaves on the trees nor the sky.
But we can do a lot,
We can tenderly embrace in a dark room.
Someone is coming? Don't be afraid –
It is the noise of spring itself.
Come to me, give me your lips,
Someone is forcing the door
 – No, it is the breaking up of the ice.
Wild grasses rustle over Babi Yar.
The trees look down sternly, like judges.
Everything here shrieks silently.
And taking off my cap,
I feel how gradually I am turning grey.
And I myself am nothing but a silent shriek
Over the thousands of thousands buried in this place.
I am every old man who was ever shot here.
I am every boy who was ever shot here.
No part of me will ever forget any of this.
Let the 'Internationale' ring out
When the last anti-Semite on earth is buried.

There is no Jewish blood in mine,
But I am hated by every anti-Semite as a Jew,
And for this reason,
I am a true Russian.

On writing 'Babi Yar'*

This man, for instance, disapproved of my poem 'Babi Yar'. Yet I could not have written 'Snot-nosed Fascism' if I hadn't first written 'Babi Yar'. Both these poems are facets of the same struggle – the struggle for the future.

I had long wanted to write a poem on anti-Semitism. But only after I had been in Kiev and had seen Babi Yar with my own eyes did the poetic form come to me. I wrote the poem in only a few hours after my return to Moscow. That evening I gave a talk on Cuba at the Polytechnical Institute. After my talk I read 'Babi Yar' for the first time. Ordinarily I recite my poems by heart but this time I was so agitated that I had to have the text in front of me. When I finished there was dead silence. I stood fidgeting with the paper, afraid to look up. When I did I saw that the entire audience had risen to their feet; then applause exploded and went on for a good ten minutes. People leaped onto the stage and embraced me. My eyes were full of tears. Afterward a white-haired man leaning on a stick came up to me.

'I've been a Party member since 1905. Would you like me to recommend you for membership?'

Only the day before I had read a review of my poem 'Consider Me a Communist'. The reviewer said that if he were at a meeting when the question of admitting me to the Party were put to the vote, he would be opposed. The article was actually entitled 'I Am Opposed'.

Now the white-haired old man went on: 'What you've said about Cuba and what you've written about Babi Yar are one and the same. Both are the Revolution. The Revolution we once made, and which was afterward so betrayed, yet which still lives and will live on. I spent fifteen years in one of Stalin's concentration camps, but I am happy that our cause, I mean the cause of the Bolsheviks, is still alive.'

At this I burst into tears, though I am not usually that emotional.

I took the poem to the office of the *Literaturnaya gazeta* and read it to a friend of mine who was on the editorial staff. He rushed off next door, brought several colleagues, and made me read the poem again. Then he said: 'Would you let me make a copy? I'd like to have one, and the others asked for copies too.'

'What do you mean, copies? I've brought it for you to publish.'

They looked at each other in silence. It hadn't even occurred to them to think of such a thing. Then one of the editors said with a bitter laugh: 'He's still sitting in all of us, that damned Stalin.' And he wrote on the typescript the words, 'For publication'.

'Don't leave yet', my friend said. 'The editor-in-chief hasn't seen it and there might be some questions.'

For two hours I sat fidgeting. Every other minute people from various

* *Source*: E. Evtushenko, *Avtobiografiya* (Autobiography), London, Flegon Press, 1964, pp. 136–8.

departments dropped in and said reassuring words in uncertain voices. Some typists gave me some chocolates.

An old compositor came in.

'You're Evtushenko? I want to shake you by the hand, son. I've just set your poem "Babi Yar". It hit the nail right on the head. All our people in the press-room have read it, and they want you to know how much they like it.'

The old man's hand dived into the pocket of his overalls and came up with a bottle of vodka and a pickled cucumber. 'That's from the printers to cheer you up – and don't worry – I'll keep you company. Your health. That's better! You know, when I was young, I was in a workers' brigade. We used to stand by the Jews whenever there was a pogrom. No decent man could be an anti-Semite.'

The old man went on talking and gradually the weight was lifted off my chest.

At last I was called in to see the editor-in-chief.[103] He was a middle-aged man; from under his bushy eyebrows his eyes gave me a sly, peasant look. They were eyes that had seen plenty; they looked understanding.

'It's a good poem', he said with deliberation, weighing me.

I knew from experience that if the editor-in-chief began with those words, the poem would be turned down.

'What it says is right', he went on with equal deliberation. By now I was sure.

'We're going to publish it', said the editor-in-chief.

The slyness went from his eyes and they looked hard.

'I'm a Communist', he said. 'You understand? So I can't refuse to publish your poem. Of course, anything may happen. I hope you're prepared.'

'I am', I said. [...]

I went down to the press-room. The printers shook hands with me. The foreman gave a signal and the press started rolling. Suddenly there was a creaking and rumbling and it stopped. I had been so wound up that the interruption petrified me. The old compositor patted my shoulder. 'It's all right. Just be patient for another minute.'

The press started rolling again and the first copies fell at my feet.

The foreman put a batch in my arms. 'You'd better hang on to them. By tomorrow they'll be collectors' items.' We all hugged each other. I felt all of us had written it. My friend and I got into my battered old car. Miraculously, we discovered a bottle of Beaujolais on the seat. My friend went back to his office and brought down a pair of long editorial scissors. We got the cork out, finished the bottle in the car, and drove home. It was one in the morning.

Next morning every copy of *Literaturnaya gazeta* was sold out at every news-stand in a matter of minutes. By that afternoon I was getting batches of telegrams from strangers congratulating me. But the rejoicing was not universal. Two days later the journal *Literatura i zhizn* published an answering poem by Aleksei Markov [Doc. 40] in which I was described as a 'pigmy who had forgotten the people he belonged to' and in another two days a long article in the same paper [Doc. 41] accused me of trying to wreck Lenin's international policy by stirring up hatred among national groups.

A more monstrous and grotesque charge it would be hard to imagine. But the author's chauvinism was ill disguised and there was public indignation. I was showered with letters from all over the country. One morning I was visited by two young men about seven feet tall with badges inscribed 'Master of Sports'. They said they had been sent by the Komsomol organisation of the Institute to act as my bodyguards.

'To guard me?' I asked in surprise. 'Who are you to guard me from?'

The young men looked embarrassed; they told me that while, of course, my poem had been very well received by the public, we had not achieved Communism yet and there were still some bastards around. They faithfully kept at my heels for several days. I learned that they themselves were no great lovers of poetry, but had been chosen for their other qualities: one was a boxer, the other a wrestler. It was very funny and I was very touched.

I was not of course in any danger. Out of some twenty thousand letters written to me about 'Babi Yar', only thirty or forty were abusive and they were all unsigned and in obviously disguised handwriting. In our country it is the bastards who are in danger. It was not I but Markov who had something to fear. He cancelled his public appearances because the organisers of the meeting hinted that his face might be pushed in.

The Western press made a sensation of the attacks on 'Babi Yar', claiming that they proved the existence of anti-Semitism in the Soviet Union, and some of these papers dishonestly distorted the meaning of my poem to suit their own ends. But as far as I was concerned, the two attacks on me in *Literatura i zhizn* were less significant than the reaction of the wide and varied public – workers, collective farmers, intellectuals, and students – who supported me at that difficult moment. When I gave a reading in Mayakovsky Square just before leaving for Cuba, ten thousand people came to give me a marvellous send-off, and the support of the people will always mean more to me than anything else.

Document 40* Markov's reply to Evtushenko[104]

What kind of real Russian are you,
When your own people you forgot.
A Soul as narrow as breeches
And as empty as a stair-well.
You forgot how, with the rusty swastika
Almost the whole planet was braided.
How state after state
Was erased both from the map and the earth.
The Auschwitzes shrieked with groans
And obelisks of smoke
Drifted across black skies,
Higher and higher into the abyss of darkness.
The world shuddered with Babi Yar,
But this was but the first ravine [*yar*],
It would have flared up in fire
Enveloping the terrestrial globe.
And then it was that – by name
To mention them in a row on stone –
Oh! how many millions fell
Of Russia's cropped-haired children.

* *Source*: A. Markov, 'Moi otvet' (My Reply), *Literatura i zhizn*, 24 September 1961.

Winds will not blow away their names,
Nor with the pigmy's spittle defile them.
No, birth-certificates we did not demand,
Shielding the wide-eyed children.
Or was it not Russia, which with herself
Shielded that embrasure?!
But enough of turning graves,
It hurts them, it's more than they can bear.
As long as grave-yards are trampled,
Be it by one cosmopolitan[105] –
I'll say: I am a Russian, O my people!
And in my heart the ashes beat.

Document 41* Starikov[106] attacks Evtushenko

This will deal with the poetic creation of E. Evtushenko, entitled 'Babi Yar' and published in *Literaturnaya gazeta*, 19 September 1961. I cannot speak for others, but for myself, I cannot be bothered with, let us say, its rhythm, or grieve on the not-too-high qualities of the author's style. BABI YAR. Does today's young reader and listener of E. Evtushenko know what this is? Haven't middle-aged and old men forgotten all about it? And has the author himself thought about it properly?

This is the third night in a row that I have been re-reading war-time reports – books by Mikhail Sholokhov, Ilya Erenburg, Leonid Leonov, Aleksandr Fadeev. A colossal, inexpressible grief rises from these historical pages – a grief such as it really was. The grief of millions and millions of innocent men.

A crowd of 1,500 old men, women and children is driven along the road. Pits have already been dug for them three kilometres out of town. They are forced to undress. They are driven into the pits, five at a time, and shot with automatic weapons. Towards the close of day, they began covering the pits. Half-dead men stir under the thin layer of earth. The earth moves – the earth groans – [...]

Where did this happen – in the Smolensk ravines and pits, in Babi Yar near Kiev, or near Piryatina in the Poltava country; in the Pripolye ravine on the road to Obukhov or in the Zmievsk gully in Rostov; in the anti-tank ditch behind the glass factory a kilometre away from Mineralnye Vody or in the Drobitsk ravine behind the tractor factory in Kharkov?

'"Ravine" [*yar*] was once a good word, a word which meant grass, a river, sand, big daisies on which young girls made wild guesses at love. Now the word "ravine" has become terrible. One sees dead men suddenly stepping out of the ravine ... No, there is no living being who will forget this!' [...]

No, not many documents, not many names, not many phantoms – these are but a thousandth, a millionth part of what the name Babi Yar evokes! Where can one take words to relate all this?

'No memorials'? – 'The only gravestone'? – 'Wild grasses rustle'? – 'The trees look down sternly'? – 'Everything here shrieks silently'? – And more. 'I am afraid; I feel ... I am turning grey; and I myself am nothing but a silent shriek.

* *Source*: D. Starikov, 'Ob odnom stikhotvorenii' (About a Certain Poem), *Literatura i zhizn*, 27 September 1961.

No part of me will ever forget any of this!' Thus E. Evtushenko speaks of Babi Yar.

No, these are not my words. Much closer to me today are the verses Ilya Erenburg wrote in 1944 and which are also called 'Babi Yar':[107]

> I lived in towns once
> And the living were then dear to me
> And now on the dull wastelands
> It is graves I have to unearth.
> Every ravine is now known to me
> And every ravine is now my home.
> The hands of this beloved woman
> I had once kissed,
> Though when among the living,
> This woman I did not even know.

I agree that these are sick verses, as painful as a big open wound:

> Blow out the lights. Lower the flags!
> We came to you. No, not we – the ravines.

Horrifying. Yes, but with this spectacle in mind, I cannot discourse on how terrified I am, how I remove my hat and how my hair turns white.

No. I do not want to speak of verses. I do not want to compare verses. Neither does this article deal with different talents, and definitely not with different levels of talent. It deals with literature and life. Or, rather, literature and death. And also, with the man of letters' attitude to the life and death of millions.

Why did Ilya Erenburg write verses on Babi Yar in 1944?

What a ridiculous and absurd question! Why do people cry or laugh? Why does the heart beat and why does it hurt? Unsimulated pain and the just wrath of the writer echo in the fighters' souls, kindle their hate for the enemy. Then firmer becomes the hand and the more vigilant the eye in the gun-sights ...

Why, then, has E. Evtushenko returned to this subject now, in 1961?

Has he remembered Babi Yar to put the world on its guard against Fascism? Or have the hysterical howls of the West German revanchist curs prevented him from keeping silent? Or has he wanted to remind some of his contemporaries of the heroism, exploits, glory and great sacrifices of the fathers?

Nothing of the kind! Standing above the steep precipice of Babi Yar, the only inspiration the young Soviet writer found were verses on anti-Semitism! And thinking today of those who perished: – 'every old man shot here', 'Every child shot here' – the only fact he recalled was that these were Jews. This to him seemed the most significant, the most important, the most vital point.

Three days ago, I talked to a Soviet writer, no longer young, a Jew according to his passport. Among other things, he told me that immediately after the war, while serving with our occupation forces in Germany, he had been approached by an officer of one of the allied commands with a request to participate, as the Soviet representative, in a memorial service for Jews exterminated by the Fascists. He told me that Jewish officers from the American, British and French forces of the local garrison had already given their agreement to take part in this service. 'I understand that you, being a Communist, are a non-believer, but of course you cannot refuse to take part at this solemn memorial. After all, you are also a Jew.' The Soviet man retorted: 'I do not doubt the good intentions of the officers, but the prayers they are organising are blasphemy towards all those men of different nationalities who fell in the fight against Hitlerism. We are internationalists.'

Yes, the Fascist invaders shot tens of thousands of people – Jews by nationality – in Babi Yar near Kiev. 'It is in the murder of old Jewish women and infants that the baseness of Hitlerite Germany has most clearly been reflected. But don't the Fascists do the same with Russians and Ukrainians, Poles and Yugoslavians?', wrote Ilya Erenburg in 1944. 'Why did the Germans kill the Jews?', he wrote in 1943, of the tragedy of Piryatin. 'This is an idle question. They killed hundreds of Ukrainians in this very same Piryatin. They killed 200 Belorussians in the village of Klubovka. They kill Frenchmen in Grenoble and Greeks in Crete. They must kill the defenceless, for such is the meaning of their existence.' 'They say: "We are against Jews". This is a lie. In Yugoslavia, the Serbs were declared as "the inferior race" by the Germans. In Poland, they turned the Poles into slaves. They hate all the nations...' These are excerpts from an article written by Ilya Erenburg in 1941.

I seek in his war-time articles words on the anti-Semitism of the Fascists, so as to understand fully why he failed to underline in his tragic verses on Babi Yar that those who perished there were specifically Jews. And I find the explanation not only in the *sincerity* and *depth* of the writer's feelings, which absolutely exclude the classification of the dead by origin, not only in the natural *internationalism* of his world out-look at that time, but also in his understanding of 'the nature of Fascism' and 'the nature of the Hitlerite army'. [...]

The writer must know all this, regardless of the intentions he had on turning to the present subject. He has no right to evade the concrete historical content and the meaning of what is known as 'Babi Yar' when embarking on the fight against anti-Semitism – this century-long infamy, which the Hitlerites picked up from the garbage dumps of history and hoisted on their flag-staff.

To see in the tragedy of Babi Yar but one of history's manifestations of anti-Semitism?! The fate of those who perished there howls out against this – a fate linked by thousands of visible and invisible threads to that of all the other people who fell in those terrible years, both those who endured all this and those who conquered.

Life's logic is inexorable. One can be deceived by it, but one cannot deceive it. We have to close our eyes but for an instant, we have to turn aside but for a moment from this Babi Yar as it actually was, from all the ravines, pits and gullies it recalls, from all the clouds of black ash which the winds of the years have not as yet dispersed, and we, in Evtushenko's tracks, step on a highly deceptive path. Beware! The putrid swampy quagmire is avid and inexorable. How many has it already sucked in! We cannot close our eyes. We cannot turn aside. For then, the first and already fatal step is made.

Today I am as old in years as the Jewish people.
It seems to me now that I am a Jew.
Now I am roaming over ancient Egypt,

And now, crucified on the cross, I die.
And to this very day I bear the marks of the nails.

Oh! Isn't this daring, isn't this noble! But shouldn't one, among other things, ponder what is uppermost in this declaration: offensive condescension – 'not such as they' ('there is no Jewish blood in mine', says Evtushenko) – the *sancta simplicitas* of ignorance, or, finally, political tactlessness?

The Fascists adored drawing the genealogical tree. Aren't we offered some 'racism in reverse' here instead? What are the real historical ties between the closest descendants of the dear milkman Tevye, who were brutally killed in Babi Yar, and the ancient Jews whose legends have come down to us in the Old Testament? Both the former and the latter are 'Semites'? True, such an approach to the national question would have earned the most glowing gratitude of the 'Aryans' – 'The Jews crucified our Christ', howled the pogrom-makers in the old days. Must this narrow-minded abomination be indispensably replaced by another: 'Christ, they say, was a Jew!'?

Can't we do without such 'scientific' polemics?

But what is the real value of these exclamations, as ignorant as they are thoughtless, on the 'Jewish people' as such, 'in general'? I can obtain a better idea about this from those of our countrymen, albeit small in number who, harkening to the mystical 'call of the blood' (which in some wondrous way coincided with the sweet call of the sirens of nationalist bourgeois propaganda), believed that one could be a 'Jew in general' and departed for Israel. The fact that they decided to exchange their *Soviet motherland* for the alleged 'motherland of all Jews' is the affair of their own civic and human conscience! But why doesn't the tragedy of the majority of those who left the Soviet Union and resettled in Israel bother the writer who, without a moment's hesitation, launched a dashing and spectacular raid on ancient, modern and recent history all at once?

Evtushenko feels himself happily free to kindle, whether deliberately or not, the dying embers of nationalist prejudices. This is *freedom* from truthfulness, from responsibility for one's words. This is extraordinary *ease* in thinking. Babi Yar evoked in him the strangest 'historical' associations, which he hurried to share with the readers of *Literaturnaya gazeta*.

Strange? No, insulting even. Why, in point of fact, he insulted the memory of the Soviet people who perished. He also insulted the Soviet Jews. But this was not enough for him.

O my Russian people!
I know that you are really international.
But those with unclean hands
Have often loudly taken in vain
Your most pure name.
I know how good is my native land
And how vile it is that, without a quiver in their veins,
The anti-Semites styled themselves with pomp
'The Union of the Russian People.'

Exactly two years have elapsed since Evtushenko published a similarly direct address, though this time to 'Russia', to the 'Russian people', in one of the journals. He had then acquainted the readers with his native people:

though beaten with ramrods till they bled, no matter how intimidated, 'threatened with the devil knows what',

> Just as before
> Their suffering sad eyes ...
> Remained kind. [...]

What then, is such forgetfulness if not 'an outrage'?

'The Union of the Archangel Michael' – 'Multipede, intoxicated, belching lupine groans, distorted like twisted old trees, bedraggled and colourless human-like sweat-cloths and anathemas'; thus wrote Konstantin Fedin on the pogrom-makers in *Brothers*. But what does the Russian people who organised the labour detachments against the Black Hundreds and the Archangelites have to do here? Or the people, who through the mouths of Lev Tolstoy and Chekhov, Korolenko and Gorky and through that of Vladimir Ilyich, pronounced its glowing, momentous and most resounding word against anti-Semitism? A people who united all the peoples of our boundless land into a single and powerful Union of Soviet Socialist Republics. The friendship of our people is now stronger and more monolithic than it ever was. Why then does the editorial board of the All-Union Writers' paper allow Evtushenko to offend the triumph of Lenin's national policy with such comparisons and 'reminiscences', which cannot be considered other than provocative? In whose name does Evtushenko exert himself at present in his efforts to shout down the triumphant din of our working life and the polyphony of complex international affairs which is accompanied by the dull subterranean tremors of new nuclear tests? [...]

The intentions E. Evtushenko had in writing about Babi Yar do not and cannot interest me. As is known, the road to hell is paved with good intentions. One can also in all probability assume bad intentions, all those long-standing intentions of his to shock the 'audience', to hook it on any possible bait. But that is not important. What is important is that the intolerable falsity, with which his 'Babi Yar' is permeated, represents an obvious departure from Communist ideology to ideological positions of bourgeois stamp. This much is indisputable.[108]

Document 42* Erenburg disassociates himself from Starikov

Being abroad, I somewhat belatedly received the issue of *Literatura i zhizn* of 27 September 1961, which contained D. Starikov's article 'About a Certain Poem'. I deem it necessary to declare that D. Starikov quotes from my articles and poems arbitrarily, breaking them off in such a way as to have them correspond to his thoughts and contradict mine.

Respectfully yours,
Ilya Erenburg

Document 43† On Shostakovich's Thirteenth Symphony

It is quite natural that the Thirteenth Symphony recently completed by the composer, and which by the way has no subtitle but which deals with our

---

* *Source*: I. Erenburg, 'Pismo v redaktsiyu' (Letter to the Editor), *Literaturnaya gazeta*, 14 October 1961.

† *Source*: A. Ladygina, 'Slushaya trinadtsatuyu simfoniyu' (Listening to the Thirteenth Symphony), *Sovetskaya Belorussiya*, 2 April 1963.

present-day life, was awaited with particular interest. This interest was heightened by the fact that D. Shostakovich[109] has composed no ordinary symphony but a symphony for a solo singer, bass chorus and orchestra, using the texts of E. Evtushenko's poems.

The first performance of the symphony took place in Minsk. The State Symphony Orchestra of the BSSR, an augmented chorus of basses of the State Academic Choir of the BSSR and of the Belorussian Radio and Television Chorus, and the soloist, Besedin, who is a prize-winner of the All-Union Competition for Vocalists (from Moscow), carefully brought the meaning of the symphony to their listeners. The conductor, V. Kataev, who during his comparatively short stay in our city has succeeded in winning the sympathy and liking of the Minsk population, demonstrated his strong will, a fine artistic temperament, and professional skill. D. Shostakovich was present at the first performance of his symphony. [...]

Nevertheless, the ideological meaning of the Thirteenth Symphony contains essential flaws. The social command remained unfulfilled. The sense of timing which has always been inherent in D. Shostakovich, the feeling of high responsibility in face of the tasks being solved in our country, failed him this time. Moreover, as luck would have it, his symphony was performed precisely during those days when all the country was excitedly discussing the materials of the December and March meetings of the Party and government leaders with representatives of Soviet art [Doc. 27]. And it testifies to the author's misunderstanding of the Party's demands regarding art.

Some sceptic or other, one of those who do not wish to understand the life-enhancing significance of the transformations taking place in the Soviet Union (it must be owned that such fault-finders are still encountered), called D. Shostakovich's new composition 'The Composer's Symphony of Civic Courage'. A loud claim isn't it? But let us consider whether it is so.

What does the first part of the 'Babi Yar' Symphony testify to? To civic courage or to the loss of civic tact? Oh no, civic courage has nothing to do with it. This part of the symphony makes an attempt to revive artificially the so-called Jewish problem, to raise problems that were the result of the old class society and which have long since been solved and have gradually died a natural death in Soviet society. This poem of E. Evtushenko has already been criticised for the absence of historical truth in it. It may be added that it is also deeply erroneous because it rejects the question of class inequality which had existed for centuries within the Jewish people itself and replaces it with the rather dubious issue of 'national unity'. It is indisputable that Fascism's crimes against the Jews were monstrous. But, if the composer needed material disclosing the atrocities of Fascism in World War II, is this the only place to look for it? Is Fascism really terrifying first and foremost for its anti-Semitism?

The objective laws of the genre in which D. Shostakovich's composition is written should not be forgotten either. A poem is one matter. Any poet can be criticised for a greater or lesser degree of verisimilitude. But, no matter how significant his ideological faults in one poem, he cannot seriously be accused of flagrant violation of the truth of life on the basis of that single work alone. A symphony is quite a different matter. The peculiarities of this genre are such that they inevitably objectify the content, established as a basis for the symphony by the composer, and impart to it an epoch-making significance and scale.

Document 44* Kuznetsov's[110] *Babi Yar*

Even after these experiences D. M. Pronicheva came very close to death on many more occasions. She hid in the ruins of Kiev, in Darnitsa, and then went from village to village under the name of Nadya Savchenko. Some people took care of her children, whom she sought for a long time and found at the very end of the war. In 1946, she acted as a witness for the prosecution at the Kiev trial of Nazi war criminals in the Ukraine. But, because of the outburst of anti-Semitism which followed soon after, she began to conceal her escape from Babi Yar and that she was Jewish. Once again it was her surname, 'Pronicheva', that saved her.

She went back to the Kiev Puppet Theatre, where she works to this day as an actress and puppet-handler. I had tremendous difficulty in persuading her to tell the story of how she, alone of all the seventy thousand Jews executed in September 1941, managed to escape: she did not believe that it could ever be published or that it would serve any good purpose. It took her several days to tell her story, which was interrupted by a number of heart spasms. This took place in an old, decrepit room in the very same house on Vorovsky Street which she had left to go to Babi Yar. It was not until 1968 that D. M. Pronicheva succeeded in persuading the authorities to let her have a small flat in a new building, and she sent me a letter saying that after this book had appeared another inhabitant of Kiev came to see her and told her that he too had escaped from the *Yar*. Only a small boy at the time, he had scrambled out as Motya had done and had been hidden by a Ukrainian family, whose name he had adopted so that he was shown as a Ukrainian on his identity card. He had never told anyone that he escaped from Babi Yar. To judge from the details he gave, his story was true. But he simply sat for a while, told his tale, and then went off without giving his name. [...]

Babi Yar no longer exists. In the opinion of certain politicians it never did exist. The ravine has been filled in and a main road passes over it.

As soon as the war ended, people – of whom Ilya Erenburg was one of the first – started saying that a memorial should be erected at Babi Yar. But the Central Committee of the Ukrainian Communist Party, then headed by Nikita Khrushchev, considered that the people who had been executed in Babi Yar did not deserve a memorial. More than once I heard Communists in Kiev saying this sort of thing: 'What Babi Yar are you talking about? Where they shot the Yids? And who says we have to put a memorial up to some lousy Yids?'

In fact, with the spread of government-inspired anti-Semitism between 1948 and 1953, the question of erecting a monument was dropped. After Stalin's death, people again cautiously started propagating the view that Babi Yar was not just a Jewish grave, and that there were three or four times as many people in it of Russian and other nationalities. Arguments like this

* *Source*: A. Anatoli (Kuznetsov), *Babi Yar*, Frankfurt am Main, Posev, 1970, pp. 118–19, 478–9, 482 (in Russian).

always seemed to me quite ridiculous: were they trying to say that only if the proportion reached a certain figure would it be worth while erecting a memorial? How could you possibly work it out in percentages? It is PEOPLE who lie buried in Babi Yar.

But the Ukrainian Central Committee, headed in 1957 by Nikolai Podgorny, apparently worked out the percentages, found them unconvincing and arrived at a Solomon-like solution – to put a stop once and for all to talk about Babi Yar, to destroy it and to forget all about it. That marked the beginning of the second attempt to erase Babi Yar from history.

To fill in such an enormous ravine was a gigantic task. But it was possible, given the vast scale of construction work in the USSR. The engineers hit on a very clever solution – to fill the ravine not by tipping but by washing earth into it using pumping machinery.

They built a dam across the end of Babi Yar and proceeded to pump pulp – a mixture of water and mud – into it through pipes from neighbouring brick-work quarries. The ravine was turned into a lake, the idea being that the mud would separate and settle, while the water would flow away through channels in the dam.

I used to go along there and study the lake of mud which was swallowing up the ashes, bones and remains of the gravestones with amazement. The water in the lake was evil-smelling, green and stagnant, and the noise of the pulp pouring out of the pipes went on day and night. That lasted for several years. Each year, the dam was strengthened and increased in height, until by 1961, it was the height of a six-storey building.

On Monday, 13 March 1961, it collapsed. [...]

And, finally, the Jewish cemetery was destroyed. The bulldozers were led into that vast cemetery and proceeded to sweep away the graves and the gravestones, digging out bones and zinc coffins as they went. Where the cemetery had once been they started to build a new television centre, equipped in accordance with the very latest developments in science and technology – which only goes to confirm once again that science is no obstacle to barbarism.

In the very centre of all this building work, over the places now filled in where the executions had taken place, they started to mark out a new stadium and a vast amusement park. I spent the summer of 1965 writing this book by night and walking round watching the bulldozers at work during the day. They worked slowly and inefficiently, and it took time for the newly shifted soil to settle down.

On the twenty-fifth anniversary of the first executions, 29 September 1966 to be precise, people from all parts of Kiev made their way to Babi Yar. They say it was a very impressive scene. Without any previous planning, a spontaneous public meeting took place at which Dina Pronicheva spoke along with the writer, Viktor Nekrasov, and the young Ukrainian publicist, Ivan Dzyuba – and once again there was talk of erecting a memorial.

When they heard of the meeting some cameramen from the Kiev news-film studios rushed down and filmed it. This resulted in a great row in the studio, the director being sacked and the film confiscated by the secret police.

The Kogan affair

Document 45* The Kogan incident (I): Gavrutto's[111] account (1965)

'We should do better, but we cannot make it', said Ilya. 'The Fascists have worn us out. Every day new shootings, new hangings. The people are being jeered at terribly. True, at first, when Girsky's detachment was active here, they seemed to restrain themselves, but now that this detachment has been done away with, they have become violent, the rats.'

'But what about the detachment?' asked Andrei Kirillovich. 'Why were they defeated?'

'Who knows?' answered Ilya. 'We know nothing about it.'

'Surely it couldn't have been done without treachery?' the host enquired again.

'I don't know. That's also possible', said Ilya.

Andrei Kirillovich tore off a piece of newspaper, rolled a cigarette, began smoking.

'There must have been', he said firmly. 'There are still unstable elements among us, unfortunately. And what hurts most is that betrayal happens where you least expect it. For instance, in the Kiev area an unbelievable thing happened.'

Ilya was silent. His host also stopped speaking.

'And do you know who betrayed you? Is it known yet or is it still a mystery?' asked Kulik, breaking the silence that had set in.

Andrei Kirillovich heaved a deep sigh.

'A foul deed, you know, cannot long remain secret. The whole of Kiev already knows of the betrayal. This foul crime was committed by a former Komsomol worker of the city, left behind for underground activities in the Kiev area, a certain Kogan[112] by name.'

Ilya and Pasechnik looked at each other in perplexity.

'I don't understand anything!' Kulik jumped from his chair and began pacing the room nervously. 'The Hitlerites hate the Jews, destroy them. They make no exceptions for either children or old people. No, I don't believe it! A Jew could not do such a thing ...'

'As you like, my friend. But it is a fact. By his betrayal the scoundrel served the Hitlerites so well that they made an exception of him. They did not even shoot him like they usually do with almost every Jew they arrest. He was well informed, he was useful to the Germans. They appointed him interpreter to the well-known German General, Paulus. There Kogan has been quietly occupied till now.'[113]

Ilya clenched his teeth.

'Scoundrel! Traitor. He should be strangled.'

'We shall punish him, my son, we shall most definitely punish him.'

'It should be done before all the people', Pasechnik implored. 'The rat should be brought back to Kiev and executed there.'

Andrei Kirillovich smiled kindly at Pasechnik.

* *Source*: P. Gavrutto, *Tuchi nad gorodom* (Storm Clouds Over the Town), Moscow, Moskovsky Rabochy, 2nd edition, 1965, pp. 175–6, 269–70.

'It will be done', he assured Evgeny. 'True, it will take a long time, but we are sure to catch him.' [...]

Those who had betrayed our mother country and had been active in aiding the German invaders, Vasily Grigorenko among them, were caught and severely punished. The same fate overtook the foul traitor, the Judas, Kogan, who had betrayed to the Germans all the Kiev underground.[114] For almost two years the fallen man served Field-Marshal Paulus, cleaned his boots, helped to interrogate the Soviet prisoners-of-war and even shot at his own compatriots.

But at last Paulus's army of three hundred thousand men was defeated, the Field-Marshal himself was taken prisoner, and together with him Kogan raised his arms in defeat.

Document 46* The Kogan incident (II): Gromova's account[115]

I have read P. Gavrutto's book *Storm Clouds Over the Town* (Moskovsky Rabochy, 1965) which deals with the activities of the Kherson underground during the Great Patriotic War. Both the epilogue and the editorial comment say that the book is strictly documentary. 'There are no fictitious characters or incidents in the book. Everything related in the book really happened.' And yet Gavrutto's book has grave errors and misrepresentations.

The book is being published for the second time in a mass edition (it was published in 1963 by Molodaya Gvardiya). I ask the editorial board of *Literaturnaya gazeta* to publish my letter hoping that it will help to establish at least part of the truth. [...] The sensational communications of P. Gavrutto are no laughing matter at all.

A certain Pilipenko, an inhabitant of Kiev, tells the members of the Kherson underground who come to him that the Kiev underground was betrayed to the Gestapo by one man. 'The whole of Kiev already knows of the betrayal. This foul crime was committed by a former Komsomol worker of the city, left behind for underground activities in the Kiev area, a certain Kogan by name.' The people from Kherson are naturally surprised: how could it happen that the Germans spared a Jew? And Pilipenko confirms: yes, they spared him and even appreciated him highly. 'He was well informed, he was useful to the Germans. They appointed him interpreter to the well-known German General, Paulus. There Kogan has been quietly occupied till now.' And in the epilogue, the author, speaking for himself, says: 'The same fate [i.e. punishment for treason, A. G.] overtook the foul traitor, the Judas, Kogan, who had betrayed to the Germans all the Kiev underground. For almost two years the fallen man served Field-Marshal Paulus, cleaned his boots, helped to interrogate Soviet prisoners-of-war and even shot at his own compatriots. But at last Paulus's army of three hundred thousand men was defeated, the Field-Marshal himself was taken prisoner, and together with him Kogan raised his arms in defeat ...'

The whole story is told in this latest edition of the book (in the 1963 edition, the 'traitor Kogan' was just mentioned in passing).

Let us have the exact facts.

* *Source*: A. Gromova, 'V interesakh istiny' (In the Interest of Truth), *Literaturnaya gazeta*, 9 August 1966.

In fact no one person betrayed 'all the Kiev underground'. In spite of very severe setbacks, the Kiev underground never stopped its activities. Many of its heroes are still alive and live even now in Kiev. Traitors really did cause great harm to the Kiev underground, but the names of the traitors are known (though 'the whole of Kiev' could not, of course, have known them at the time of occupation), and Kogan's name is not among them. The name of Paulus's interpreter is no secret either. And it goes without saying that the interpreter of the Fascist Field-Marshal was not and could not have been a Jew. And the Gestapo could not 'send' such a person to work with the Field-Marshal (especially if 'he was well-informed'!).

And, finally, how could one and the same person be in different places at the same time? P. Gavrutto insists that Kogan served Paulus for 'almost two years'. It is known that Kiev was occupied in September 1941, and that Paulus became a prisoner-of-war in January 1943. A little more than a year passed between the two events. But the point is, when could Kogan have been in occupied Kiev and have betrayed 'all the underground'? That is evidently senseless.

We see, however, that such a contradiction does not worry either the author or the editor, V. Stepanov. And an absurd fabrication is spread abroad and is completely ruining the life of a real man, M. G. Kogan, who was never in occupied Kiev, who left the city with the Soviet army and who never even set eyes on Field-Marshal Paulus.

Gavrutto's book is not just a failure; it is harmful, as it misleads the readers and misinforms them.

Document 47* The Kogan incident (III) : a reply to Gromova

Esteemed Comrades!

I read with great interest the article, 'In the Interest of Truth' by Ariadna Gromova, which appeared in *Literaturnaya gazeta* of 9 August 1966. In this article, which sharply criticises P. Gavrutto's documentary novel, *Storm Clouds Over the Town* (Moskovsky Rabochy, 1965), one passage puzzled me and I wish to share my bewilderment with you.

The article discusses the case of M. G. Kogan, who, in A. Gromova's opinion, was slandered in P. Gavrutto's book where he is described as having betrayed the Kiev underground to the Fascists and as having served the Germans in the capacity of Field-Marshal Paulus's interpreter.

It is quite possible that A. Gromova is right (I have no intention of judging; it is a matter for the appropriate organs). To be sure, she had grounds for maintaining that M. G. Kogan did not betray the Kiev underground and did not serve as Paulus's interpreter.

But one thing appeared to me to be incorrect: why did A. Gromova never mention the fact that M. G. Kogan was court-martialled at the time for cooperation with the Germans (true, it was not in Kiev) and served a ten-year sentence? As it happens, M. G. Kogan himself (he lives here in Brovary) does not conceal his past guilt. Besides, the impression may arise among the

* *Source*: E. Fedyai, 'Pismo v redaktsiyu. Ne vsya istina' (Letter to the Editor. Not the Whole Truth), *Literaturnaya gazeta*, 19 November 1966.

readers of A. Gromova's article that the man in question is in fact completely unsullied. It seems to me, that in the interests of truth one ought to recall the fact that at the time, M. G. Kogan served a deservedly severe punishment.

As regards P. Gavrutto's book in general, it clearly has its faults and inaccuracies, but it is hardly worth writing off the story *Storm Clouds Over the Town* for this reason and declaring it 'harmful' – which is in fact what A. Gromova does.

E. Fedyai, Editor of local newspaper.   *Brovary, Kiev Province*

Document 48* The Kogan incident (IV): Kogan's own account

To the Secretariat of the Soviet Writers' Union
On 18 September 1941, I was one of the last to leave Kiev with a weapon in my hands. I was in the famous encirclement at the village of Borshchi, Baryshevka Region, where, from 20 to 26 September, we repulsed an attack of superior German forces. On 26 September, pinned down in marshland, we found ourselves prisoners-of-war. I twice escaped from the prisoner-of-war camp. In Poltava, in February 1942, I was betrayed to the Germans by Tamara Verakso, a ballerina of the opera theatre. Interrogated for over three months, I was subjected to terrible torture, but did not breathe a word about where I had worked or what I knew. I pretended to be an Armenian – a certain Kasparyan. I was freed with the help of the SD [Sicherheitsdienst] interpreter, Irina Mamodzhanova-Arekelyan, who confirmed that I knew the Armenian language and proved through external marks that I was Armenian.

She acquainted me with Abramyanov, Saakadze, Gelovani, Mamodzhanov and Dr Ivanov (a Georgian), all of whom had been in captivity and had left and opened a restaurant and shop in Poltava. They bought me a Ukrainian–German passport in the name of Moguch (Mikhail) Kasparyan, with my photograph. Subsequently Irina Mamodzhanova stole lists of all the Gestapo agents from the Germans and passed them on to our organs when Poltava was liberated. Wanting to leave occupied territory, Abramyanov helped me find work as a driver of a ZIS-5 vehicle in a unit which was supposed to be leaving Poltava in the direction of Krasnodar. When we reached Kharkov, our company remained there for three days, after which we learnt that this unit was being sent to Stalingrad by the local civilian commandant's office. We arrived in Stalingrad on 1 November 1942. On 10 November, the interpreter of the quartermaster was killed. Because I know a few languages, Major Speidel summoned me and appointed me interpreter until a proper interpreter was sent from Kharkov. On 19 November, our forces surrounded Stalingrad, and I remained translator until 22 January. On that day, I left the Germans and made off in the direction of Voroponovo. I spent the night in an abandoned dug-out, and on the following day, 23 January, I met up with our forces and immediately asked to be sent to the Special Section to hand over important information. On 24 January, I was brought to the Special Section of the 64th Army. On 24 January, I wrote affidavits on the path I had travelled

* *Source*: This document was brought to the West by an emigrant from the Soviet Union.

across occupied territory and gave depositions on *Abwehr* agents to be found in Stalingrad (as far as I know, these depositions were not filed). On the evening of 26 January, I was brought to Lieutenant-General Comrade M. S. Shumilov, commander of the 64th Army. I discussed with him the position in beleaguered Stalingrad.

On 28 January, I wrote down further depositions in my own handwriting on *Germans who knew me* (these depositions were filed). I left for Krasnoarmeisk, where German prisoners-of-war were being held, to look for Major Speidel (the commandant) and others. I took part in Major-General Comrade Abramov's interrogation of the commandant of the Novo-Alekseevka prisoner-of-war camp and other Germans, who were cross-examined by the workers of Colonel Gizha's Special Section: Major Fanshtein, Captain Vladimirsky, First Lieutenant Nevzorov.

On 7 February, I was told that I was under arrest, and the interrogations began. The investigation was conducted with provocations and beatings. I could have signed that I was Hitler, but investigator Goikhman was satisfied with my 'confessions' that I was a traitor to the Fatherland, a turncoat who ought to be shot.

The investigation was conducted at the place where I had been an interpreter for two months and twelve days, at the place where 90% of the 365,000 inhabitants of Stalingrad lived, in Dar-Gora. And yet not a single deposition was filed against me, despite the fact that the local residents were questioned about me. I was taken and shown in all the places where our liberated prisoners-of-war were being checked up on. For a few days I was assigned to take the soup round to the cells and dug-outs where detainees were being held. There I saw Andrei Repekh, Bychok, Bespalov and others (I do not recall their names). I saw A. G. Lepilin in the corridor of the Special Section. I went with Major Fanshtein and the German, Schmucker, to Dar-Gora. They could have had exhaustive details about my every move on each day.

However, I was sentenced in accordance with Paragraph 58, Article 1a to ten years only for having worked under the Germans, without taking into consideration the fact that I went to work in order to make my way back to the front. After all, I could have gone quietly to the West, moved in with people in any village, and, finally, found work in any part of the German rear, risking nothing.

In 1957, after I lodged a complaint, a verification was carried out which demonstrated that there was no incriminating material in my case.

Lepilin had testified that I was supposed to have tried to enlist him into the Gestapo, and that he had warned his fellow workers to beware of me. According to the fresh tracks of the investigation, he had not testified to anything in February 1943, and now had 'had second thoughts'.

If, however, one is to take his declaration on trust, then his wife and daughter – Aleksandrovna and the nurse Nadezhda Silina – did not confirm it. If anyone was to be forewarned then, first and foremost, it was his family. During my seventy-three days' work as an interpreter I did not take part in consultations at the commandant's (Karl, a German interpreter, worked with him); I did not translate during meetings; and only twice, on my own initiative, did I take part in cross-examinations. Once, Nadezhda Silina had to be helped out as she had been arrested for cutting a telephone cable. She was released and I took her home. The second occasion was when a certain citizen (I do not remember his name, his brick house was in Dar-Gora, not far from the mill which operated under the Germans) was denounced for keeping a rifle in his house. He admitted that the rifle was hidden in the attic, but I did not translate this and warned him not to confess. He was released.

I was often at Lepilin's house, exchanging views with his daughter on events at the fronts, holding patriotic conversations, which she even confirmed in her depositions. On the twenty-fifth anniversary of the October Revolution (1942), we met in Lepilin's house. Bespalov was also there. We drank to the victory of the Soviet forces.

I helped A. G. Lepilin to get wheat from the grain elevator, though it seems that he denies this. I gave him the German password. I myself went with him to the grain elevator and to former chemist shops in search of medicines.

I warned Bespalov and Lepilin when the Germans decided to throw the sick in their beds out of the former bath-house building and into the cold outside, and use it as a military hospital. This is precisely what the Germans did, but Bespalov and Lepilin had organised people and accommodated the patients in nearby dug-outs and houses.

While I was still working as a driver at the Aerodrome in Poltava, I would listen to the German's radio whenever he had gone out, while the mistress of the house or her seventeen/eighteen year-old daughter kept look-out, and afterwards I would tell the news to them and to the tailor, his daughter and her children who had come from Zhitomir (her husband was a commissar). I was often at this family's place, and we had frank discussions. When I arrived at the Special Section of the 64th Army, my passport was taken away and an intelligence officer was to be sent to Poltava on my passport. I then gave the address of the tailor's family, and the intelligence officer had to present himself in my name.

At the aerodrome I had cut the cable linking it with 6th Army Head-quarters. I made statements on all these points during the investigation, but the investigator repeated one and the same thing again and again: 'That you did good, you were obliged to do as a Soviet citizen, and that does not interest us; however, we shall sentence you for having worked under the Germans.'

At the present moment an appeal on my case has been lodged with the USSR Procuracy by the advocate, Comrade N. K. Borovik. There has still been no reply to this complaint. I have, however, told you everything about myself as it happened, in order to turn to the question which is the reason for my addressing this letter to the USSR Writers' Union.

The writer, P. P. Gavrutto, has written a book, *Storm Clouds Over the Town*, devoted to the Kherson underground fighters. In his book, the author interpolates, on pages 175–6, facts about the betrayal of more than 1,000 members of the Party-Komsomol underground in Kiev, left behind for underground work, by an employee of the Komsomol City Committee, a certain Kogan. For such services to the Germans he was not, despite his being a Jew, executed but sent to work as Paulus's interpreter. In the epilogue, on pages 269–70, the author writes that Kogan, who worked for about two years with Paulus, personally took part in the shooting of his compatriots.

The publishers, Moskovsky Rabochy, who brought out the book in 1965, write in a note about the author that there are no fictional characters or events in the book, that everything recorded was as it happened.

In accordance with my declarations, the KGB of the Ukrainian SSR and the USSR Procuracy have conducted a verification. Not a single fact was confirmed. I lodged a complaint with the People's Court of the Bauman Region.

The Court sat on 19 April and 7 May, but no decision was reached, insofar as Gavrutto had written his customary libel to the KGB. A review of the case may last a month or two. On account of this book I was dismissed from work on 4 February. My wife – B. B. Vinokur – informs me that after four years' work in a school she too is being relieved of her work in the new school year. I have a family of five.

I am asking the USSR Writers' Union to help me remove this base libel, the work of the writer Gavrutto in his book *Storm Clouds Over the Town*, and also to assist me in terminating the case for which I was sentenced in 1943 by the Military Tribunal of the 64th Army to ten years in a corrective labour camp in accordance with Article 58, Paragraph 1a.

M. G. Kogan

Document 49* On the embezzlement of state property (February 1953)[116]

Before me lies a pile of documents. Dry numerical calculations, bills, analyses cover each piece of paper. And when all this has been examined, the following questions arise involuntarily in one's mind: 'Is it possible to build a house out of shoe polish? or out of soda? Can one eat one's fill on nails?'

And it turns out, that all this is possible. For this, all one has to do is to go to Zhmerinka and win the confidence of Pinya Paltinovich Mirochnik. What a magician he is! A magician who knows no equal. The star of the State Circus, Kio, with his mysterious chest in which the circus's resident invisible lady vanishes, is nothing in comparison with Pinya! But, forgotten by the State Circus, Pinya Paltinovich Mirochnik is forced to remain at the tedious post of head of an industrial combine of the Zhmerinka District Union of Consumers. And he has to do without any applause or enthusiastic notices.

Remembering that in his time Kio used to appear with seventy-five assistants, Pinya Paltinovich has also surrounded himself with reliable assistants, though, to give him his due, he did not manage to reach the figure of seventy-five. Not far short, but he didn't quite manage it. Pinya Paltinovich appointed David Ostrovsky as head of the chemical shop of his industrial combine. David's son became, correspondingly, an agent of the supplies section. Rakhil Palatnik occupied the desk of the chief book-keeper. Accordingly, her son-in-law, Shaya Pudel, became her deputy. Roza Gurvich was made economic planner, and her husband was put in charge of the supplies

* *Source*: V. Ardamatsky, 'Pinya iz Zhmerinki' (Pinya from Zhmerinka), *Krokodil*, 1953, no. 8, p. 13.

section. Zyama Milzon, Pinya's brother-in-law, was given a position in a utensils shop. Yasha Dainich, Bunya Tsitman, Shunya Mironchik, Munya Uchitel, Benya Rabinovich, Isaak Paltin and others were appointed to other positions.

It is not difficult to imagine what conjuring tricks could be demonstrated with such a disposition of forces. Especially if one takes into consideration that the Zhmerinka District Procurator, Comrade Lanovenchik, was so carried away by the continued spectacle of these manifestations that he completely forgot his most immediate duties.

Pinya Paltinovich did not become a magician all at once. At first he was far from successful in all his undertakings. For instance, in 1936 he was expelled from the Party for performing a religious rite, as well as for a number of frauds. By 1941 he had become more experienced, and he managed, though being in the best of health (as he has been since), to fall ill precisely at the end of June 1941. His illness made it possible for him to leave in a direction quite the opposite of the front lines. After the war, Pinya made his home in Zhmerinka. In 1946, he joined the Party once more, cleverly concealing the fact that he, quite by chance, had already been a Party member.

Pinya Paltinovich has a family of six, not counting his wife's two brothers who live abroad, which is quite silly of them when they have a brother-in-law such as Pinya. Pinya's family lives in a richly furnished four-room flat. Not one of his five dependants does any work anywhere, though the doctor has not forbidden them to work. Every year, Pinya's wife takes her offspring to salubrious health resorts. And, indeed, why should they work when Pinya can afford to keep the house in grand style? Truly, when you know the size of his wage-packet, this becomes somewhat difficult to understand, but, then, if everybody could understand the magician's tricks, there would be no magicians.

I have no wish to describe in detail the tricks of Pinya Paltinovich and his devoted assistants because, as the readers have probably guessed, all these tricks are simply sharp practices. These tricks are accurately noted down in detail in statements, reports, certificates and other documents. Everything is described there. They tell how David Ostrovsky and Munya Uchitel agreed to write off 56,800 tins of shoe polish as scrap and how those very tins, ceasing to be scrap, filled with shoe polish, appeared in the hands of profiteers. Oh, but how wonderfully noble David Ostrovsky's conduct was during that commercial transaction! It turns out that he sold the tins which had been written off for waste to Benya Rabinovich, purveyor to the District Consumers' Union, for 30 rubles in cash and handed all that money in to the cashier of the industrial combine. What honesty! And what sleight-of-hand at the same time!

At the market in Zhmerinka (and not only in Zhmerinka) it's always possible to buy a little packet of drinking soda from someone for 3 rubles. The state price for that packet is exactly 45 kopeks ... The soda is packed and released for sale by the industrial schemer Pinya Paltinovich; and in what quantities! In 1952 alone he released almost a hundred thousand packages! It emerges from the documents that all this soda has been sold through the District Consumers' Union in Zhmerinka. But then how did it fall into the hands of the profiteers not only of Zhmerinka District but also of many other districts of Vinnitsa Province? And can it be that inhabitants of Zhmerinka developed such a liking for Pinya's soda that they were devouring it in tablespoonfuls from morning till evening!? Is it possible that the population of the entire district is constantly suffering from heartburn? Of course not; the soda business was the result of another trick. The former director of the inter-district base, Oknyansky, and his deputy, Dartman, could have explained it. But, as they are not interested in explaining it, all that is left for us is to have a look at the fenced-off private residence that Dartman bought for 56 thousand rubles. As his wages were in the region of 910 rubles a month, it could not have been easy for him to put such a sum aside. He probably went hungry, poor soul!

And if one happens to be passing through Zhitomir, one can also have a look at the house which Oknyansky, since fired from the Zhmerinka trade base, acquired for 50 thousand rubles. His position is much more difficult than that of Dartman, who is already working as deputy director of the Zhmerinka food combine, whereas Oknyansky, poor thing, has been unemployed for over a year. He probably exists on bread and water.

Indeed, the rogues in Zhmerinka have a free and easy life. They romp under the very nose of the District Procurator! Let us take for instance the case of the metal that was delivered to make nails for construction work. But who the devil cares about construction if the private shoemakers moan and groan and are ready and willing to pay any price for shoe nails. The industrial schemer, Pinya Mirochnik, pours tons of shoe nails on to the market. By the way, the Zhmerinka procurator has become somewhat pinned down by these shoe nails and has even opened a special case on them. But he has not handed the case over to the courts. He is said to be studying the documents. For a whole year already. The procurator in Zhmerinka is a very serious man, indeed; only it's a pity that he is no danger to the local rogues.

The hand of the Zhmerinka conjurers are soiled with just about everything. With shoe polish, blueing, halva, sunflower-seed oil, honey and treacle. The rogues became brazen-faced. Not long ago Dodik Ostrovsky declared: 'Give me the money and I will get you a moving excavator in a jiffy.' Luckily Pinya does not need a moving excavator, so one may rest assured that he will not give Dodik the money.

Comrades from the Vinnitsa Province Consumers' Union! Our last lines are addressed to you. We have read some of your resolutions concerning the activity of Pinya Paltinovich's gang. To tell you the truth, we became tired of reading your decisions scattered there: 'to reprimand', 'to point out', 'to suggest', etc. Doesn't it seem to you, comrades, that you overestimate the educational significance of these resolutions of yours? And, anyway, whom are you trying to re-educate? With such touching forbearance, too? Would it not be better to hand this affair over to the procurator's office of Vinnitsa Province at long last? They ought to know there how to treat swindlers.

Document 50* A literary imposter (1958)

They have long been known in fiction. In the story of the young Kuprin,[117] they were called 'shooters'. Idlers by conviction, cringers by their way of life and

* *Source*: M. Lanskoi, 'Potomki Ostapa Bendera' (The Descendants of Ostap Bender), *Literaturnaya gazeta*, 7 October 1958.

extortionists by profession, the 'shooters' earned their living by begging for money. This was a subtly worked out and confirmed system of blackmail, based on two factors: the unlimited impudence of the petitioner and the defenceless trust of the victim.

'Always reckon on psychology', says Kuprin's anonymous hero. 'For instance, I present myself to an engineer. I immediately pretend to be a building technician – high boots, and a wooden metre-rule sticks out of my pocket; with a merchant I am a former salesman; with an editor – a writer...'

The revolutionary hurricane, shattering the base of social parasitism, swept away these 'shooters' at the same time. Their puny offspring crawled out to the surface in the twenties. Giving themselves a shake they adapted themselves to the new conditions and again made an appearance in great literature. The reader has already guessed that we are speaking of 'the sons of Lieutenant Schmidt', immortalised by Ilf and Petrov.[118]

This was in the past. In the subsequent course of events, all kinds of corporations of professional swindlers were completely crushed. But individuals remained, and they will not vanish as long as there exists a psychological base for their activity: personal impudence and someone else's credulity.

Several years ago, a certain young man started visiting some of the great scholars of Leningrad. A plush hat, horn-rimmed glasses and the pleasant manners of a well-bred young man were all in his favour. He modestly introduced himself: 'Agapov, Vladimir Georgievich; from the City Executive Committee.' Then everything went off as in a bad sketch – smoothly and revoltingly. Smiling pleasantly, the scholar invites the guest into his study. 'Please, come in, glad to meet you. What can I do for you?'

Agapov slowly takes out from his portfolio a list of names printed on good-quality paper and hands it to the kind host. There has been a decision of the Executive Committee. With the approach of a significant date, funds are collected for a, so to speak, collective investment.

The scholar puts on another pair of glasses and glances through the list. All the names are familiar: academicians, distinguished public figures... In a separate column the sums are stated: three thousand – four – five... Their own signatures.

The owner of the study raises his eyes at his guest. For a second they look at each other. An idea flashes across the mind of the old scholar: 'Perhaps I should ask him for an identification card?' But he is immediately embarrassed and feels guilty. [...]

I remember these swindlers in an unusual situation. A visitor came to the reception room of one of the secretaries of the Leningrad branch of the Writers' Union. I was, by chance, the third person present. It was rare luck: the ball came to the player.

The visitor takes a pile of papers out of his portfolio and spreads them on the table. I glance at one of the pages and see the name: Flaksman A. M. The same! This was our first meeting, but by a stroke of fate his whole life-story was known to me. All of it! I very much want to mention, there and then, other names, under which he faced trial: Palatner, Kvitko, Kharik... But I am silent and listen to the conversation.

'It will be the first "Anthology of Jewish Poetry of the Middle Ages" in history', reports Flaksman in the insinuating voice of a commercial traveller. 'How much work it has cost me! Did you ever suspect that *The Lay of Igor's Campaign*[119] influenced the creative work of the Jewish poets of that time? Of course not! Nobody suspected it. I discovered it! Well, I shall leave you these poems. If you read them, it will make everything clear to you. I'll drop in at your home sometime.'

'No need to leave anything and no need to call. I don't understand; what do you want from the Writers' Union?'

'What? The Anthology was already included in the plan of the State Publishing House, and suddenly it was cancelled. They don't want to make an agreement with me. Translators are needed, money is needed. I've already spent thirty thousand rubles of my own. You have to influence the State Publishing House.'

The 'publishing plan' is extracted from the portfolio. The 'Anthology of Jewish Poetry of the Middle Ages' really features in it. I look and cannot believe my eyes. No, everything is right; a certified copy, signatures, seals...

'I negotiated on the translations with the best poets.'

On the table there is a list of well-known literary names.

'The Anthology is supported by not just anybody. After my report at the Academy of Sciences... Here, please.'

Letters, references, applications; the signatures of the greatest Orientalists and Arabists; round seals and rectangular stamps. The Institute of Oriental Studies of the Academy of Sciences of the USSR, the Institute of World Literature, the Academy of Sciences of the Tadzhik SSR.

With difficulty I tear myself away from these papers. In order to be free of the threatening fascination of the seals and stamps, I mentally turn the film of his life.

The year is 1925. Flaksman is fourteen years old. His first 'try of the pen' and his first arrest. Being a minor he is immediately released.

1929. Signs of maturity. He steals a Party membership card and is imprisoned for six months.

1930. His first tour. He leaves for the village of Aleshino in the Proskurov District, and, presenting himself as the representative of the Central Executive Committee, inspects rural institutions, the Komsomol organisation and schools. There he steals dies of seals for future operations; he is caught and is non-existent for three years.

1933. Flaksman in Uzbekistan. He steals forms, produces documents and introduces himself as a writer, a Komsomol and Party member. Buys up commodities in short supply and speculates. Is sentenced to five years.

1939. Transforming the year of his imprisonment into a university semester, he appears in Dnepropetrovsk with a candidate's degree in philological sciences. Thus, without having finished secondary school, he enters the local Pedagogic Institute on false documents as an assistant professor of a department.

1941. When arrested, he is found with more than forty forms containing the stamps of government institutions. Five more years of corrective labour are added to his 'service record'.

1947. Makeevka. For misappropriation of authority and illegal wearing of decorations – five years. After a year, he escapes and presents himself in Nikopol in the guise of a councillor of justice. On his chest are fourteen ribbons of war decorations and medals. He modestly pretends to be a deputy public prosecutor. He receives complaints, gives jobs, frowns at everybody approaching him. The frightened workmen give him leather free of charge. The shoemakers make him boots free of charge.

1948. The People's Court of Dnepropetrovsk makes a preliminary summing-up of his wild activities and sentences him to ten years' imprisonment.

1953. An amnesty is proclaimed. Our hero is free. For some time he dashes about the country. He is seen in the town of Stalino. Then he appears in Mytishchy. Here he pays a visit to the City Military Commissariat and applies for a certificate of: a supply officer. In place of a 'lost' one. The good souls of the City Military Commissariat reprove him for his absent-mindedness and issue him a temporary officer's certificate.

The end of 1954. The newly made lieutenant-colonel rushes to the shores of the Neva. A new city – new possibilities. But his first step is unlucky. Applying to the City Military Commissariat of the Petrograd District, Flaksman asks to be issued another duplicate of the certificate, because the one he received in Mytishchy he also lost. The calculation is simple: two documents are better than one. This time it does not work. The City Military Commissariat sends enquiries to a dozen military districts and organisations, referred to by Flaksman as places of his military exploits. And from everywhere comes stereotyped replies: 'No such person exists'. Even the Mytishchy gapers suddenly wake up and ask for a 'thorough check-up on Flaksman'. How he managed to register in Leningrad and to reside there for three years already without work is a murky affair requiring special investigation.

1956. Flaksman begins his most solid and well-calculated swindle. There is an inflated boom in anthologies, which has continued until this day. Who gave him this idea and from whom he swiped the initial material it is hard to say. Another thing is important. Dozens of naive people are found, who allow this boor and rogue who cares nothing for poetry or prose to speculate with their names.

Pursuing one aim, to snatch money and to acquire influential acquintances, he penetrates the homes of Moscow and Leningrad writers and scholars. Presenting himself as an old poet, literary critic, with two candidate's degrees in science, he collects distinguished companions for the philological business.

I cannot but bring another quotation from Kuprin's story: 'scum, these "shooters", they are worse than convicts. For a ruble they will sell and betray each other, play a dirty trick, denounce, gossip.'

There is this base trait in Flaksman's biography. Slandering honest people, he has brought much sorrow to families who trusted him.

And now it is September 1958. He sits before me and is engaged in a highly scientific conversation. I can stand it no longer, and ask him.

'Where do you work?'

For the first time, he looks at me steadily. The intuition of an old swindler apparently warns him that the question is not accidental. But how much he even outwardly resembles the manager of the 'Arbat Office for the Preparation of Horns and Hoofs'! Ostap Bender should have looked exactly like that, growing dull with advancing age. Deep wrinkles on the cheeks only stress the 'medal features' of the face. Reddish hair slightly covers the high bald head, and only in the eyes the same, undulled, refined impudence. He smiles in a condescending manner.

'Me? I am the head of a combined geological expedition of the Academy of Sciences.'

'And what have you got to do with philology?'

The smile becomes compassionate:

'I somehow have a candidate's degree in philological and geological sciences.'

'Both?'

'Of course! Who doesn't know that?'

'And you defended the dissertations?'

'A strange question. At Moscow University. In the year 1947. There were two opponents: Spivakovsky and Vorobyevsky.'

'Show me the document confirming that you are the head of the expedition.'

He was prepared for anything but this. In proper literary and educated circles nobody had yet dared such rudeness. His face begins to resemble that of Panikovsky, caught with a goose under his arm.

'What kind of talk is this?'

'Very simple. We want to make sure that you are who you claim to be.'

'I don't carry documents with me. You can telephone.'

'Where?'

'Not here. My expedition is in Moscow, with the Academy of Sciences. I have three detachments. One is in Kazan, one in Balashikha...'

By habit, he lies without faltering, but his voice is already different. This is the gurgling of a sinking person. He collects his papers and portfolio and promises to bring all the documents in three days and then to continue the conversation about the Anthology. Maintaining a proud bearing, he leaves the Writers' House.

I don't think that he will come again to us, to the Leningrad Branch of the Writers' Union. But, how many more institutions and organisations there are in our big country! How many kind, sympathetic and exceptionally credulous people!

This *feuilleton* is written for all of them as a lesson.[120]

The Malakhovka affair

Document 51* The Malakhovka leaflets (1959)[121]

I

Throw the Jews out of commerce, where they damage socialist property and the people's wealth. They are an obstacle to the development of commerce.

---

* *Source*: 'The Malakhovka Affair', *Jews in Eastern Europe*, November 1959, pp. 9–10.

They cause much damage to the state and to the working people, and amass profits for themselves.

Catch hold of them and pluck out their sinful deeds. Teach them how to live – they, whom we rescued from death by giving them our soil – a people as hated as they are. They, who in their impudence seized the main jobs, and, with their connections, drew each other in, until they turned their rescuers into their dependants. 'Equality of Rights' they imposed upon the inexperienced Russian people. This they could not fob off on the German people, who rounded them up and threw them out of its land. Had this not happened it is doubtful if the German people would have been capable of living as it lives today. This applies also to the Czech and Polish peoples who now have very few of that Jewish nation which is sold on money and capable of anything for the sake of gain.

II

As you enter the stores and shops of the Second Jerusalem (Malakhovka) you will everywhere see the fat countenances with their impudence who look with contempt upon every Russian; and where is all this taking place? Upon our Russian soil the Jew reached these heights; he besmirches the Russian people with curse-words, 'Idiot', 'Vanka'. And we suffer this. How long is this to continue? We rescued them from the Germans who dealt more wisely with them. We gave them shelter and they become so impudent. The Russian people do not understand just who is in their country. The people are complaining theoretically, but the day of action is not far off. To speak frankly, the Bolsheviks acted overhastily in granting equality to this nation. They [this nation] can be pushed under and will crawl up, like an excrescence it will befoul the clean and pure soul of the Russian people, and this is what actually happened. Our people are not as they used to be. They have been infected by the Jews with bureaucracy, with an appetite for comfort, with lack of politeness, have ceased to be a people with a large and open heart as is typical of the Russian soul and which nowadays can only be found in the countryside.

Document 52*   A Soviet comment on the Malakhovka incident (1959)

From a *Jewish Telegraphic Agency* report.
Rome, 12 January (JTA)

A member of the Soviet five-man Committee for Religious Affairs – the highest authority within the Soviet Union on religious problems – admitted, during an exclusive interview with a Jewish Telegraphic Agency correspondent visiting Moscow, to the 4 October Malakhovka incident.

Committee member Voshchikov presented the first official Soviet version of the case. He said that somebody had set fire to the synagogue's upper floor and to the building which is adjacent to the Jewish cemetery where the bodies are

* *Source*: 'Malakhovka – A Soviet Admission', *Jews in Eastern Europe*, February 1960, pp. 15–16.

washed and prepared for burial. Mr Voshchikov claimed that the guardian's wife was caught by flames inside the building while trying to escape and died of suffocation because of the smoke. He estimated the entire damage caused by the fire at 200 rubles (about $20).

The member of the Committee, which is directly appointed by the Soviet cabinet, told the JTA correspondent that religious services in the synagogue were not interrupted for a single day. He stated that those responsible for starting the fire have already been found and that a judicial investigation is currently being carried out.

Mr Voshchikov, who defined the incident as 'an episode of hooliganism committed by an isolated group and not an organised action', said that he did not know the names, the number or the ages of those responsible.

He claimed that 'there were persons with anti-Semitic feelings in the Soviet Union just like there were persons with anti-Protestant feelings in Italy'. Mr Voshchikov said that the Soviet authorities do not encourage such feelings and that when they are too strongly manifested they are prosecuted and punished according to the Soviet Law for the Protection of Nationalities.[122]

Blood libels in the Soviet Union

Document 53 Anti-religious propaganda

*The evils of Judaism (1960)**

I have recently read and believed an article about a Jewish synagogue which was published in the newspaper *Kommunist*. There are many religions in the world: Jewish, Muslim, Christian. They are all alike in their aim to keep their believers in the darkness of ignorance. They use fraudulent and ignoble means.

The Jews claim that their religion is the genuine religion, and say: 'We shall go to Paradise; Muslims will go to Hell, their religion being false.' The Jews behaved very badly. For instance, they believed, in accordance with their religion, that the drinking of Muslim blood once a year would be counted as a good deed. Many Jews consequently buy 5–10 grams of Muslim blood which they mix with water in a large barrel and sell as water which has had contact with Muslim blood.

The laws of the Jewish religion prohibit Jews from eating the flesh of cattle which has not been slaughtered by their rabbis (*mulla*). There are many other remnants of Jewish and Muslim rituals. 'Oppose those who observe the commands of the Lord.'

The Jews had been the enemies of the Muslims who, subsequently, became the enemies of the Jews. The believers of all religions only observe the laws of their own faith, which they consider as the genuine faith and thus oppose every other religion. There are also great differences among the religions. Why? If God created the world and human beings, why has he had to establish different religions for them?

* *Source*: D. Magmudov, 'Allaysyz da yol erkin!' (Without God the Road Is Also Clear!); *Kommunist* (Buinaksk), 9 August 1960.

The Muslims recognise no other faith than their own. They claim that the Muslim religion is the genuine religion among all religions in the world. Other religions are lies. Both Muslims and Jews have synagogues. They pray every day and are thus idle for a great deal of time. They furthermore claim that it is forbidden to work on Fridays.

The believers in the Muslim faith consequently have two rest days a week. 'We pray five times a day', they say, and consequently they waste five or six hours.

All religions in the world are lies. Our way is clear and without God. God will not do us good for a deceitful attitude towards him. We will build our life with our own forces, by ourselves.

A refutation (1960)*

In the article, 'Allaysyz da yol erkin' [Without God the Road Is Also Clear!], by Daya Magmudov, which was published in *Kommunist*, on 9 August 1960, the author and the literary contributor, Comrade Kh. Ataev, were guilty of allowing a gross political error.

The author asserts that the Jews allegedly had a religious ritual in accordance with which they used Muslim blood once a year. This most outrageous and infamous fabrication of the priesthood was designed to kindle hatred towards Jews and has long been refuted by the most prominent scholars and lawyers of the world.

Marxism–Leninism has given a precise explanation of the origin of such preposterous religious perversions.

Document 54† Pogroms in Uzbekistan (1961–2) (I): a Western report

Reports received by *B'nai B'rith* tell of scores of Jews being assaulted and injured in the streets and in their homes during wild scenes of mob violence. The riots in Margelan took place in 1961, erupting two days after *Rosh Hashanah*, the Jewish New Year. They broke out in Tashkent shortly after Passover, 1962.

Local authorities – police and public prosecutors – remained passive or sided with the attackers when Jewish homes were broken into and furniture and personal belongings were looted or destroyed.

Mr Katz[123] said that his organisation, *B'nai B'rith*, had withheld disclosure of the riots until it was able to authenticate information filtering out of the USSR for almost a year. Nothing of the outrages was reported in the provincial or major Soviet press, and no punishment or reprimand had been meted out publicly to the instigators of the violence or the police officials and local prosecutors who abetted them.

Blood libels were first used by the Romans against Christian martyrs. But in the early Middle Ages they gained great currency as a means of spreading virulent anti-Semitism, Mr Katz explained. During the era of Tsarist tyranny

* *Source*: 'Iyuzeltiv' (Correction), *Kommunist* (Buinaksk), 11 August 1960.
† *Source*: '"Blood Libel" – Anti-Jewish Outbreaks in Uzbekistan', *Jews in Eastern Europe*, May 1963, pp. 34–6.

they were widely circulated in Russia, with official connivance, to provoke anti-Jewish pogroms. The superstition then was that Jews were required to use Christian blood for religious purposes. In the pogroms in Uzbekistan, where Muslims are the dominant religious group, the libel referred to the use of Muslim blood.

The violence in Margelan, a city of more than 50,000, continued for almost a week. The details were as follows: On 14 September 1961, an inflamed group led by a man named Abdusatarov seized a Jewish woman, Mazol Yusupova, and accused her of having kidnapped and slain Abdusatarov's two-year-old son as part of a 'ritual murder'. The terrorised woman was taken by force to the local militia where, in the presence of police officials, she was formally charged with abduction and murder.

On instructions of a Captain Akhmedov, a militia officer, members of the militia, accompanied by the rowdies, conducted a search of Mrs Yusupova's home, damaging the furniture and other possessions in her house and yard, and confiscating foods and cooking vessels presumably for further investigation to see if traces of human blood would be found in them. Similar searches were conducted in dozens of Jewish homes in the area.

News of the alleged kidnapping (although without mention of the religious ritual aspect) was broadcast that day over the local radio. It was also communicated to the Muslim community in the local mosque. The following morning police also arrested Dzhuru Israelov, Mrs Yusupova's ninety-year-old father.

As word spread through the city that Jews had been arrested for kidnapping and murdering a Muslim child for Jewish ritual purposes, mob fury broke out in waves of violent assaults against Jews in the streets and in their homes.

Given no protection by the local authorities, the Jews of Margelan hastily organised their own guard to protect the Jewish quarter. This led to clashes between them and gangs of Uzbeks roaming the streets. Finally, the authorities felt compelled to post police guards to restore order in the city. The riots lasted until 20 September – six days in all.

On 7 October, the first official explanation of the abduction appeared in *Margelan Khakikati*, the local Uzbek newspaper. This reported that the missing boy had been kidnapped by an Uzbek woman named Usmanova who lived in a nearby village. Her motive had been to hide from her husband the fact that she had undergone an abortion. The couple had separated during her pregnancy. When they were reunited several years later, she feared disclosure of the abortion. On a visit to Margelan she abducted Abdusatarov's child and presented him to her husband as their son.

Beyond these bare facts, the news story reported nothing. No mention was made of the riots and no effort was made to dispel the crude blood libel that had ignited them.

The Jews who had been assaulted by the mobs or maltreated by the police brought suit against Abdusatarov. The trial opened on 14 November in the neighbouring city of Gorchakovo. The court found that the prosecutor had ignored the role of the militia in the affair and had minimised the extent of the destruction in Jewish homes.

The judge ruled that the searches and arrests were illegal. He halted the trial and directed the prosecutor to correct his file of evidence for submission at another trial. In the fourteen months since, there has been no word of a second trial, Mr Katz said. On the other hand, he added, it is known that the police who were involved in the anti-Jewish riots have retained their posts, and that the Jews of Margelan live in an atmosphere of fear and insecurity.

Mr Katz then reported the following details of the blood libel in Tashkent which, he said, occurred on 9 May 1962:

An Uzbek Moslem named Azizov (address: 22 Zagorskaya) led a band of ruffians who broke into the home of Abigai Bangieva, a seventy-year-old woman who operates a small shop. The attackers accused Mrs Bangieva of having taken blood from the ear of Azizov's young daughter 'for use in a Passover ritual'.

On the basis of this charge, the local prosecutor ordered her arrest. Her home was searched and ransacked by the police, and she was held in prison. She was not released until three weeks later, but at the time of speaking, Mr Katz said, the legal complaint against her had not been dismissed.

Following the arrest, inflammatory rumours swept the city, which has a Jewish population of 50,000. One report said that Azizov's wife, a member of the local Soviet, had loudly demanded the expulsion of all Jews from the city. Another quoted the prosecutor as asserting, in private conversation, that Jews customarily use Muslim blood for religious purposes. These wild stories led to assaults on Jews and created panic in the Jewish quarter of Tashkent.

It was later discovered that the blood libel had originated with a minor mishap on 30 April. Azizov's young daughter, leaving Mrs Bangieva's shop, had slipped and fallen, suffering a slight cut on her ear. The Jewish community had since lived in apprehension.

The *B'nai B'rith* leader said that there was no evidence that the central Soviet authorities encourage the blood libels or the violence that flows from them and might well have been embarrassed by the mob action. But the 'crucial point', he said, is that 'neither the pogromists nor the local police and prosecutors who abetted them have ever been punished or reprimanded'.

He also criticised the 'complete absence of publicity in the Soviet press'. 'If top-level Soviet officialdom was truly committed to eradicating grass-roots anti-Semitism, these riots could have served as the basis for an educational and legal campaign against anti-Jewish prejudice', he said.

In August 1961, a blood libel was perpetrated in Buinaksk, a town in the Dagestan Autonomous Republic – across the Caspian Sea from Uzbekistan. The local Communist Party newspaper published a story that Jews mix Muslim blood with water and drink it for ritual purposes. The article was also broadcast over the local radio. The Party newspaper repudiated the article as 'a political error' two days after its publication [Doc. 53]

Document 55* Pogroms in Uzbekistan (1961–2) (II): a Soviet reply

There have been no clashes whatsoever between Uzbeks and Jews, either in Tashkent or in Margelan over religious issues. This isn't just my statement. It

* Source: *Soviet Weekly*, 7 February 1963.

has been stressed by the heads of the Jewish community and the Muslim clergy of Tashkent.

In a joint statement, replying to *B'nai B'rith*'s imaginative piece of fiction on 29 January, they declared: 'The people of all nations and nationalities inhabit Uzbekistan and live in friendship and peace, whether they pursue a religious faith or not; and this is also true of the Muslims and Jews.'

What was the origin of the story? There appear to be two possible original reports which may have led to it. In one city there was a case of a child being abducted. The kidnapper was brought to trial and punished in the usual way. The second case was of an ordinary brawl involving an Uzbek and three Bukharan Jews. Such a thing could have happened anywhere and has nothing whatever to do with national enmity. These cases were reported in the press and perhaps gave someone the bright idea of 'improving' them!

Hundreds of thousands of Jewish families took refuge in Uzbekistan during the Second World War. They received a fraternal welcome there, and many of them chose to settle in Uzbekistan for good after the war. There are 93,344 Jews in Uzbekistan today – about 2% of the republic's total population. And here is another figure which the papers publishing the 'riot' story might like to consider: of the 48,282 people with college diplomas working today in Uzbekistan's economy, 8,161 are Jewish. That is – 20% of the republic's 'specialists' are Jewish, while only 2% of the overall population is Jewish. Fine evidence of 'anti-Semitism'!

The Jews in Uzbekistan take an active part in all spheres of life. Quite a few hold responsible government positions, as do Jews all over the Soviet Union. To name but a few: Vladimir Vengersky, member of the Uzbek Supreme Soviet, is a departmental deputy chief of the Central Committee of the Uzbek Communist Party. Benjamin Pinsky is a member of the State Planning Committee of the republic. Alexander Rozenfeld is deputy chairman of the Uzbek government's board of statistics. Bentsion Gartsman is deputy chief of the government's main cattle purveying and fattening department. Volf Dudler is secretary of the Kirov District Executive Committee of Tashkent. The list goes on and on.

Religious communities in Uzbekistan live 'in an atmosphere of insecurity and apprehension', the Western newspapers claimed. That is a lie. Pious Jews, like the Muslims, perform their religious rites freely, abide by their customs and religious canons. Each community lives its own way, has its own life, stresses the joint statement made by the Jewish and Muslim leaders.

Contacting a number of religious Jewish communities of Uzbekistan, I was told that services were continuing normally in the two synagogues in Tashkent (one headed by Rabbi Ikhil Yadgarov, and the other by Rabbi Solomon Kogan). In Samarkand (Rabbi Mani Animov), in Andizhan (Nish Sulaimanov), in Kokand (Rabbi Sholom Fuzainov), in Bukhara (Mukhaelov) and other cities, the rabbis were indeed surprised by my sudden interest in this question.

'The things people will say!' was the astonished comment of Yehuda-Leyb Levin, Chief Rabbi of Moscow,[124] when he was shown the 'news' from Washington. 'Anybody who knows anything at all about life in the Soviet Union', he said, 'must know that anti-Semitism is something alien to Soviet people. If an anti-Semite should turn up anywhere, he would be drowned in general contempt.'

'The Muslims of the Soviet Union', declared Imam Akmedzhan Mustafir of the Moscow Mosque, 'harbour fraternal feelings for all the nationalities of the USSR, regardless of their religions. If there had been any clashes in Tashkent and Margelan on the basis of national enmity I would have undoubtedly been informed of them at once. But it is simply comical to talk of such "clashes", for there is no reason whatever for any enmity between Muslims and Jews. They live in peace and friendship.'

Vladimir Shvartser,[125] director of a Jewish theatre company, now in Moscow, which recently played in Tashkent, tells me that the company gave a number of performances of *Tevye the Milkman* there.

'The Jews of Tashkent filled the house every time', he said.

The Jewish singer, Nehamah Lifshits, had appeared in the theatre about a week earlier. Her concerts, too, had been widely billed and had a great success.

Could people who lived in fear, as *B'nai B'rith* claim the Uzbek Jews do, go to theatres and concerts in such numbers?

4

The campaigns against 'Jewish nationalism' and 'cosmopolitanism'

Attacks on nationalism

The basic contradictions inherent in the Soviet solution to the national problem have always necessitated a constant struggle against any sort of 'nationalist' deviation. However, the campaigns against nationalism have varied radically over time in content and aim. For a long time, Soviet leaders and theoreticians differentiated (and, in theory, still differentiate today) between 'Great Russian nationalism'[1] and 'local nationalism'.[2] Their concern with this problem notwithstanding, the authorities began to wage the struggle against the former deviation with any degree of vigour only in the 1920s. It slackened off in the first half of the 1930s, coming to a complete halt in the second half of that decade. However, the struggle against local nationalism – which came to be designated by the even stronger term 'bourgeois nationalism' – has been carried out intermittently from 1917 until the present day.[3]

Jewish Communist leaders, who had headed the *Evsektsiya* for many years, were among those purged from the national cadres in the 1930s. But this campaign of liquidation, which objectively speaking dealt a fatal blow to Jewish national existence, was not directed against them as Jews; in this case, the policy aimed to liquidate the leading cadres of all non-Russian nationalities (the Jews included). As will be seen below, the period after World War II differed in this respect, since the campaign against nationalist deviations and all foreign influence then began to assume a thoroughly anti-Jewish character.

The years 1946–8

The war period brought with it a relative relaxation in the bitter struggle against nationalist deviation which had been waged by the authorities in the second half of the 1930s. Springing from the need to unite all the peoples in the desperate struggle against Germany, this relaxation enabled the intelligentsia of the Soviet nationalities to give far freer expression to their true national aspirations and feelings. However, as early as 1944, it was possible to detect the first signs of an impending change for the worse, and of a resumption of the struggle against nationalist deviations.

Indeed, in August 1944, the Central Committee of the Communist Party decided that it was necessary to improve ideological activity in the Tatar Autonomous Republic and to eliminate what were described as serious errors of a nationalist character by historians and writers.[4] In March 1945, the Kazakh historians were accused of nationalism on account of the book, *A History of the Kazakh People*, which had been highly praised when it was published in 1943.[5] In May 1945, the attacks on bourgeois nationalism, which had been aimed at historians, writers, philosophers and artists in particular, were extended to the European republics which had been liberated from German occupation.[6] The fiercest campaign, that conducted in the Ukrainian Republic, began in June 1946.[7] And in 1947–8, the fight against bourgeois nationalism was extended in both scope and vigour.[8]

These attacks, which recurred in various forms, were directed against the following 'deviations'. (1) Idealisation of the national past, as expressed in the glorification of selected historical epochs and heroes (for example, the Tatar, Idegei; the Kazakh, Kenesary Kasymov; Shamil among the peoples of the Northern Caucasus). (2) Underestimation of the national fraternity between Russians and non-Russians, or even emphasis on the enmity between them (for example, the 'incorrect' description of the War of 1812 in the play *Kakhim Turya*, which ranged Russian and Bashkir fighters against one another). (3) Devaluation of the great influence of Russian culture on other nations; failure to appreciate the progressive aspect of the Tsarist conquests – or, in Soviet terminology, the union of the non-Russian nations with Russia – which brought with them the abolition of feudalism (many Soviet historians had seen the Tsarist conquest as an absolute evil or, at best, as less of an evil than the possible conquest by another neighbouring power. Even at this period, both concepts began to be questioned, although it was only after 1950 that the new line, which viewed the Russian conquest as an absolute good, was adopted). (4) Neglect of the decisive role played by Russia in saving Europe from the Tatar yoke. (5) Underemphasis of the hostility displayed by such states as Turkey and Iran towards the peoples of the Caucasus and Central Asia. (6) Acceptance of the 'single stream' theory, which leads to disregard of the class war within nations.

As the increasingly fierce struggle against nationalist deviation involved the major nationalities of the Soviet Union, it could hardly by-pass Soviet Jews. The signal for beginning the attack on Jewish nationalism came in A. Zhdanov's speech of August 1946 and the subsequent resolutions of the CPSU Central Committee. The article that set the campaign in motion appeared in the 24 September 1946 issue of *Eynikeyt*, the organ of the Jewish Anti-Fascist Committee, under the heading, 'A Battle Programme for the Ideological Front'.

This lead article emphasised that the historic resolutions of the Central Committee were of immediate concern to Jewish theatre and literature. A number of important writers, poets and playwrights, such as Sh. Halkin, E. Fininberg, A. Sutskever and M. Pinchevsky, were accused of producing apolitical works devoid of ideas and nationalistic in character. On 10 October, *Eynikeyt* published a severe critique of S. Verite's book, *When the Earth Burnt*, in which the author was accused of being too preoccupied with Jewish history and of slandering Soviet man and Soviet reality.[9] Two days later, an article by the veteran literary critic Y. Dobrushin appeared, in which Dobrushin appealed to Jewish writers to refrain from confining themselves to a limited national framework and to describe instead the general social processes of the whole of Soviet society in their works.[10] On 14 December 1946, *Eynikeyt* called upon the writers and theatre and literary critics to write in the spirit of A. Zhdanov's speech.[11] This article also included the first attack on the writer, Itsik Kipnis, albeit on the relatively minor charge of expressing 'small town' (*shtetl*) attitudes.

In April 1947, the campaign against Jewish nationalism was resumed with an attack on variety artists, who were accused of continuing to provide their audiences with entertainment that was apolitical in nature and devoid of ideas, and for romanticising the old Jewish way of life.[12]

In July and August 1947, the attacks on Kipnis were stepped up, and a major campaign was conducted against him on the pages of the Jewish and Ukrainian press and at writers' conventions; this resulted in his being expelled from the Writers' Union and later being arrested. The occasion for the attacks was a story called *Without Giving It a Thought*, which Kipnis wrote after the war and which was published in full only in Poland.[13]

The signal for the continuation of the campaign against Kipnis was given in a lead article in *Eynikeyt*, ominously entitled 'Nationalism in the Guise of Friendship Between Peoples'.[14] 'Only a nationalist', it was stated, 'is capable of placing Soviet awards and medals, which symbolise the honour, greatness and courage of Soviet people, side by side with ... the Star of David. Jewish fighters would of course reject this award of Kipnis.' Two days later, the writer Leyb Kvitko, who had been elected Chairman of the Jewish Section of the Soviet Writers' Union at the end of 1946, joined in the attacks.[15] 'Kipnis was forewarned', wrote Kvitko. 'A series of critical remarks were addressed to him, but unfortunately he paid no attention to them. He allowed himself to ignore our criticism and went even further astray.'[16] On 15 September 1947, at a session of the Ukrainian Writers' Union convened to discuss the resolutions of the Central Committee on the journals *Leningrad* and *Zvezda*, A. Korneichuk, chairman of the Union, used his opening speech to attack Itsik Kipnis for his bourgeois nationalist deviation. 'In the story he sent to the Zionist newspaper in Poland', said Korneichuk, 'Kipnis slandered Soviet man when he expressed his wish to see the Star of David – the Zionist symbol – worn next to the Soviet Star on the breast of the Soviet soldier.'[17]

The strongest attack on Kipnis in the Ukrainian press came from the Yiddish writers, H. Polyanker and M. Talalaevsky, who wrote: 'It would not hurt Kipnis to know that the five-pointed Soviet Star has long since overshadowed the six-pointed Star of David, as well as Petlyura's Trident, and all the eagles and various other nationalistic emblems.'[18] On 17 October, at a meeting of Kiev writers, which Kipnis attended, he was again attacked by Polyanker[19] and on 28 October, Kipnis was accused of nationalist recidivism.[20]

There can be no doubt that the high point in the campaign against Jewish nationalism in Yiddish literature was reached in 1948, by Haim Loytsker's article in *Der shtern* (Doc. 56). Written in a thoroughly Zhdanovite spirit, this attack surpassed everything else written in this vein in the Soviet press. The main deviations enumerated in this article, as well as in many others which appeared during 1946–8,[21] were: an apologetic and uncritical approach to the national heritage; idealisation of the past, as expressed in the blurring of the class differences which existed among the Jewish as every other nation; an over-emphasis on Jewish national sentiments; exaggerated use of the word 'Jew' (*Yid*) in its various combinations;[22] a demonstrative and totally unnecessary use of Hebraisms;[23] the employment of national-historical and legendary-Biblical motifs (known in Soviet terminology as 'archaisms');[24] nationalistic egocentrism (for example, only the evacuation of the Jews is mentioned, when other nations shared this traumatic experience); an even more dangerous plunge into nationalism by the constant use of themes drawn from the Holocaust and Jewish martyrology; and, finally, nationalism of a Zionist stamp, for example, that of the writer Itsik Kipnis.[25]

Athough some of this criticism was similar to that levelled against historians and writers of the other nations, there also existed essential differences. First of all, it is almost inconceivable that a critic of Ukrainian, Belorussian or Uzbek 'nationalism' would attack a writer or historian on the grounds that he had made too frequent use of the words 'a Ukrainian', 'a Belorussian' or 'an Uzbek'. Secondly, even at the height of the campaign against bourgeois nationalism, the other nations were not required to sever themselves from their historical and cultural past in so drastic and unequivocal a manner. Thirdly, we have found no evidence that writers of other nationalities were criticised for mentioning their martyrdom under the Nazi occupation. Finally, in this period it was not common to link internal bourgeois nationalism (i.e. within the borders of the Soviet Union) with an external national movement; this was only done in the case of the Jews. And, far more serious, was the colossal difference in the consequences of the campaign against nationalism: the Jewish culture was the only national culture in the Soviet Union to be liquidated as a result of this campaign. This liquidation, which began at the end of 1948, was completely accomplished by the end of 1949.[26]

The years 1949–53

Since the leading Jewish writers, literary critics and theatre workers had been arrested at the end of 1948 and the beginning of 1949 – which meant in fact that the wheel of liquidation directed at the nationally oriented Communist Jewish intelligentsia had come full circle – the bulk of the campaign against nationalism was redirected against the assimilated Jewish intelligentsia. The last cases of public attacks known to us from the first half of 1949 – on Jewish personalities and on institutions then in the process of liquidation – were those directed against: David Bergelson, one of the best-known Yiddish writers who was, it seems, already under arrest at this time;[27] the critic Model who wrote in praise of the Jewish playwright Goldfaden; the stage director Golovchiner, who produced 'harmful and anti-patriotic plays' at the Yiddish Theatre in Minsk (as a result of which the theatre was closed);[28] and the journal *Der shtern*, which appeared in Kiev, and had been closed down at the end of 1948 (Doc. 57).

Attacks were even launched against a number of writers, literary critics, composers and artists who were accused of nationalist and Zionist deviations although they had never taken the remotest interest in Judaism. For example, in the Ukraine the poets Leonid Pervomaisky and Savva Golovanivsky (Doc. 59) and the composer D. Klebanov (Doc. 60), who composed a symphony on the subject of Babi Yar, were sharply castigated for nationalism and Zionism. Among those in the Russian Republic who came under fire most frequently were the poet Pavel Antokolsky (Doc. 62) and the writer Aleksandr Isbakh (Doc. 61). Nor did the literary critics responsible for the literature section of the *Large Soviet Encyclopaedia* escape a fierce attack for having dared to include 'all Jewish literature regardless of where and under what political regime it was written'. Even more serious was the fact that the entry on 'Jewish literature' was allotted as much space as the total space allotted to Uzbek, Kirgiz and Georgian literature together (Doc. 58). Jewish nationalism, Zionism and conspiratorial ties with world Jewry were the main charges against the Jewish artists and writers tried in July 1952 as well as in the public attacks of 1952 and January–March 1953 in the Soviet press (Doc. 63; see also Chapter 5).

The post-Stalin period

In the period after 1953, the struggle against the ideological deviations of Soviet Jewry took the form of fierce campaigns against the Jewish religion and Zionism, while the attacks on Jewish bourgeois nationalism almost completely ceased. There was one very simple reason for this: until 1959, hardly a word of Yiddish was published in the Soviet Union,[29] and the sole expression of Jewish culture during this period was that provided by a handful of singers who made sporadic appearances in a number of Soviet cities. And, without any Jewish cultural activity, there could hardly be charges of bourgeois nationalism, of deviation from the official line on the national problem. However, the basis for charges of bourgeois nationalism was re-established with the publication of the first Yiddish books in 1959, the growing repertory of the variety theatre and, above all, with the publication abroad (chiefly in the People's Democracies and the Communist Jewish press in the West) of works by Soviet Yiddish writers. And indeed, the severe charges levelled against the poet Meir Kharats in 1960, in Bloshtein's and Malamud's article 'An Alien Voice', clearly demonstrated this tendency (Doc. 64).

What is interesting is that one can draw a parallel between this attack on Kharats and the accusations against Itsik Kipnis in 1947–8. In both cases, the writers were accused of publishing their works abroad (despite the absurdity of this charge in view of the circumstance that no Yiddish journal yet existed in the Soviet Union of 1960). In both cases, the writers were accused of slandering Soviet reality. And, as in the case of Itsik Kipnis, Kharats too was threatened with disaster if he persisted in his nationalist deviation. Nonetheless, an important change had occurred within the Soviet regime since Stalin's death: in 1960 these ominous threats were no longer carried out.

The anti-cosmopolitan campaign

Despite the great similarity between the campaign against bourgeois nationalism and that against cosmopolitanism, there were also a number of

essential and very important differences. Most of those attacked for cosmopolitanism were members of the intelligentsia, active in the central area of the
state, the Russian Republic, and not in the national republics. Further, the
most serious charge during the attacks on bourgeois nationalism was an
'excess of local patriotism', whereas the main charge in the anti-cosmopolitan
campaign was 'a lack' or 'underestimation' of 'national sentiments'. Finally,
the aims of the authorities were different in each of the campaigns. The aim of
the campaign against bourgeois nationalism was to liquidate, or at least to
neutralise (through pressure, intimidation, dismissals), the upsurge of
national feelings which had begun during the war, whereas that of the
anti-cosmopolitan campaign was to eliminate foreign influences, which had
been granted freer play during the war, and to bring about a total divorce of
the Soviet Union and her East European satellites from the 'capitalist West'.

How, when, and why the anti-cosmopolitan campaign developed into an
outright anti-Jewish campaign, or, in other words, why this ideological
campaign should have been transformed into a violent struggle against the
assimilated Jewish intelligentsia, are the central questions we shall consider
below.

The years 1945–8

The war brought millions of Soviet soldiers and officers into contact with a new
world, a world known to them hitherto only from Soviet propaganda, for the
first time in their lives. This – together with the closer bonds now established
between Soviet and Western scientists and artists, the upsurge of nationalism
within the USSR, and the rapid post-war deterioration of relations
between the Soviet and Western camps – led Stalin to embark upon a drastic
change of policy in the realm of ideology as well as national policy.

After World War II, Soviet patriotism,[30] which had come to be identified
more and more with Russian nationalism since the second half of the 1930s,[31]
became one of the central topics for discussion in all the Soviet media.
Interesting in this respect is an article which appeared in June 1945,[32] in which
the author stated that 'Communism and a consistent, active and altruistic love
of one's homeland are one and the same thing', whereas: 'cosmopolitanism is
an ideology alien to the workers. Communism has nothing in common with
cosmopolitanism, that ideology which is characteristic of representatives of
banking firms and international suppliers of weapons and their agents.
Indeed, these circles operate according to the Roman saying *ubi bene, ibi patria.*'

In his election speech to the Supreme Soviet on 9 February 1946, Stalin
warned Soviet citizens that there would be wars as long as capitalism existed,
and that the Soviet Union must be ready for her hour of trial.[33] The meaning of
his words was clear: tension at home and abroad was to increase, and the two
hostile camps faced each other once again.

A. Zhdanov gave a theoretical basis for this re-orientation in his speech at
the plenary session of the CPSU Central Committee in August 1946,[34] at which
the following resolutions were adopted: on 14 August: 'On the journals *Zvezda*
and *Leningrad*'; on 26 August: 'On the repertoire of the drama and the means
for improving it'; and on 4 September: 'On the film *A Great Life*'.[35] The tenor of

these resolutions was to glorify the Soviet regime (a hundred times better than any bourgeois regime, according to Zhdanov), at the same time stressing the superiority of the Russian people in all fields of science and culture. They attacked the 'decadent West' and especially the USA; the 'blind imitation' of and kowtowing to foreign culture; and the absence of ideas, the apoliticism, individualism and pessimism in literature and art. Finally, the resolutions called for the utmost vigilance in the face of the enemy. True, the chief victims of Zhdanov's attack and of the Central Committee resolutions – the satirist M. Zoshchenko and the poetess A. Akhmatova – were both non-Jews. But there were also many of Jewish origin among those selected for criticism, for example, the writers and playwrights Yagdfeld, Shtein, Varshavsky, Slonimsky, Khazin, Romm and Rybak. Nonetheless, it should be emphasised that there was no anti-Jewish tone, either explicit or implicit, in these attacks.

As the campaign to strengthen Soviet patriotism gained momentum during the year 1947, the struggle against subservience to the West went beyond the realms of literature and art. A leading article in the theoretical journal of the Communist Party stressed 'that traces of subservience to bourgeois Western culture have likewise found expression in underestimation of the independence of Soviet scholarship and in the readiness of some of its representatives to bow and scrape to bourgeois Western scholarship'.[36] This point was underlined still more vigorously in Zhdanov's speech on Soviet philosophy, occasioned by the debate on G. Aleksandrov's book, *A History of West European Philosophy*.[37]

Of particular relevance to our subject is the speech of the chairman of the Soviet Writers' Union, A. Fadeev, at the 11th Plenary Session of the Union.[38] Fadeev's attacks focused on a book by the veteran Jewish literary scholar, Y. Nusinov, *Pushkin and World Literature*, which had appeared in 1941. 'In this book', declared Fadeev,

there isn't a single word to the effect that the national war of 1812 took place [...] the fundamental idea of the book is that Pushkin's genius does not express the uniqueness of the historical development of the Russian nation, as a Marxist ought to have shown, but that Pushkin's greatness consists in his being European, in his finding his own answers, as it were, to all the questions posed by Western Europe.

And, Fadeev adds: 'Out of common courtesy to all things foreign Nusinov had to place himself at Shakespeare's disposal in order to defend him against Tolstoy.'[39]

Although this vehement attack contained no allusion to the Jewishness of Nusinov ('the untiring defender of Western culture and disparager of great Russian culture'), Fadeev's choice of Nusinov was significant, for the latter was widely known, *inter alia*, as one of the most important scholars of Yiddish literature in the USSR. And Fadeev's resort to the ominous and contemptuous term, 'passportless wanderer in humanity' (used here for the first time since the war),[40] was the first portent of the anti-Jewish turn which the anti-cosmopolitan campaign was to take in the years 1948–9. At the same time, an equally serious attack was directed at B. Eikhenbaum for his essay on Tolstoy's book, *Anna Karenina*. 'Does one require a more glaring example', it was rhetorically asked, 'of lack of pride in the literature of our mother country, a better example of obsequiousness, of the lack of common respect for all things Russian which are so dear to us?'[41] The note sounded here by Vyshinsky would soon become central to the attacks on 'Jewish cosmopolitans'.

In September 1947, at the inaugural conference of the Cominform, Zhdanov stated categorically that the world was divided into two hostile camps.[42] He launched a strong attack on the American quest for world dominance, stating that the very concept of a world order was now seen as intended to weaken the progressive camp, and the Soviet Union therefore consistently supported the principle of national sovereignty. In his speech on the thirtieth anniversary of the October Revolution,[43] V. Molotov sounded a call to condemn unsparingly all manifestations of subservience to the West and its capitalist culture.

A number of writers and critics of Jewish birth – later to be among the chief victims of the anti-cosmopolitan campaign – immediately came forward in defence of the new anti-Western line.[44] The position adopted by Ilya Erenburg at the end of 1947 was exceptional. While he could not completely disregard the new anti-Western policy, and therefore had to pay it lip-service by maintaining that the Russians were masters as well as pupils in the realm of culture and science, he firmly rejected the charge that to admire Western culture was to bow down to the West. 'It is impossible', he wrote, 'to toady to Shakespeare or Rembrandt, because prostration before them cannot humiliate the worshipper.'[45]

In January 1948, the newspapers and journals continued to use the terms 'obsequiousness' and 'bowing and scraping' in their attacks on literary critics and scholars, to whose number the historians were now added.[46] At the end of February, there appeared for the first time a strongly worded article bearing a title which, in many variations, was to recur in the newspaper columns almost daily for a whole year: 'The Cosmopolitans in Literary Research'.[47]

In June, articles by Paperny[48] and Miller-Budnitskaya (Doc. 65) brought about a new stage in the anti-cosmopolitan campaign. For it was in Paperny's article on Vissarion Belinsky, one of the literary critics of the nineteenth century most acceptable to the Soviet Union, that we first find the term '*rootless* cosmopolitans'. Paperny seized on Belinksy's concept of cosmopolitanism: 'The cosmopolitan is a false, senseless, strange and incomprehensible phenomenon, a manifestation in which there is something insipid and vague. He is a corrupt, unfeeling creature, totally unworthy of being called by the holy name of man.'[49] His article also contained the first attack on Lev Subotsky, then secretary to the board of the Writers' Union, who was later to become one of the main targets of the campaign. Finally, Paperny stressed the anti-national character of cosmopolitanism, harmful not only to the Russian nation but to all the nations in the Soviet Union. This rather ecumenical approach was probably one of the reasons why Paperny was himself later attacked and accused of cosmopolitanism. Miller-Budnitskaya, in her article, linked American cosmopolitanism (presented in the degenerate and rotten image of Hollywood) with the German–Jewish writer Leon Feuchtwanger, whom she compared to the first Jewish cosmopolitan – Josephus Flavius (see Doc. 65).

This direct assault on cosmopolitanism in various fields of literature and scholarship, e.g. biology, philosophy, history and philology, continued in the second half of 1948. And, although no specific mention or even allusion to their Jewishness had yet been made, the number of Jews among those attacked increased. The expressions of contempt used to denote the cosmopolitans became ever harsher in this period.[50] This intensification of the ideological offensive was, in all probability, a direct result of the deteriorating relations with the Western powers as well as of the expulsion of Yugoslavia from the Cominform.

Special meetings and congresses in the various fields of literature and scholarship were now called to condemn kowtowing to the West. The most important of these gatherings were: the meeting of the Ukrainian Writers' Union in July 1948;[51] the plenary sessions of the All-Soviet Academy for Agricultural Sciences on 5–9 August, at which Lysenko attacked the theories of Morgan, Weismann, Mendel and their Soviet supporters; the sessions of the presidium of the Academy of Sciences on 24–9 August, 1948;[52] and, above all, the 12th Plenary Session of the board of the All-Soviet Writers' Union which took place in December 1948 and which in fact prepared the ground for the real anti-cosmopolitan campaign of January–March 1949. The chief victims at the last-mentioned session were the theatre and literary critics, Yuzovsky, Borshchagovsky, Malyugin, Kholodov and Altman, who were labelled here for the first time 'a hostile group of theatre critics'.[53]

As we have seen, the anti-cosmopolitan campaign had been pursued vigorously in the years 1947–8, but it was only in 1949 that it assumed its extraordinary dimensions and, particularly, its outspoken anti-Jewish tendency.

The years 1949–53

The main ingredients to be employed in the all-out campaign against cosmopolitanism had already been tested in 1948. But the decision to launch a campaign of such unusual scope, design and severity (even by Soviet standards) must have been taken at the highest level only at the beginning of January 1949.[54] The opening signal was given in a leading article in *Pravda* on 28 January 1949 (Doc. 66). A second leading article, similar in content, appeared in the organ of the Central Committee's Department of Propaganda and Agitation, *Kultura i zhizn*, on 30 January.[55] The two articles, written in the most virulent terms, set out to unmask an 'anti-patriotic group of theatre critics'. The issue was no longer one of individuals, each responsible for his own mistakes; rather, it had become a question of an organised and long-standing group, which – even after the important resolutions adopted by the Central Committee between 1946 and 1948 – had persisted in its anti-patriotic collective endeavour to create a kind of literary underground.

It goes without saying that, at this particular period, the accusation of organisation for purposes opposed to the accepted political line was serious beyond measure. 'This group, hostile to Soviet culture', as the articles put it, 'set itself the aim of vilifying the outstanding events of our literature and the best in Soviet dramaturgy.' The 'group', or 'tribe', of anti-patriotic critics included Yuzovsky, Gurvich, Kron, Kholodov, Borshchagovsky,

Table 6. The anti-cosmopolitanism campaign in the Soviet press, 1948–53. * Number of articles by years and months

	1948													1949													1950	1951	1952	1953	Total
	1	2	3	4	5	6	7	8	9	10	11	12	Total	1	2	3	4	5	6	7	8	9	10	11	12	Total					
DAILY PRESS (including newspapers appearing up to twice a week)																															
1. *Literaturnaya gazeta*	2	1				1	2	1	1	1			9		14	12										26					35
2. *Pravda*														1	4	1										6	1				7
3. *Izvestiya*															6	3										9					9
4. *Vechernyaya Moskva*															8	7		1								16					16
5. *Komsomolskaya pravda*															2	7										9					9
6. *Pravda Ukrainy*															1	5		2								8			1		9
7. *Pravda vostoka*																												1			1
8. *Uchitelskaya gazeta*																1										1					1
9. *Novoe vremya*																													1		1
TOTAL (daily newspapers)	2	1	0	0	0	1	2	1	1	1	0	0	9	1	35	36	0	3	0	0	0	0	0	0	0	0	75	1	1	2	0	88

JOURNALS

No.	Journal	Total
10.	Novy mir	11
11.	Znamya	5
12.	Oktyabr	14
13.	Zvezda	12
14.	Bolshevik	7
15.	Voprosy istorii	10
16.	Voprosy filosofii	6
17.	Vestnik akademii nauk	5
18.	Sovetskoe gosudarstvo i pravo	4
19.	Vestnik drevnei istorii	5
20.	Voprosy ekonomiki	1
21.	Sovetskaya musika	4
	TOTAL (Journals)	84
	TOTAL (Inclusive)	172

* Only articles in which Jews are among those attacked are included. Those articles which were reprinted in a number of newspapers are included only once.

Varshavsky, Malyugin and Boyadzhiev, most of them Jews, and all of them occupying important posts in publishing houses, cultural institutions and literary journals. The discriminatory tendency of these articles emerged first and foremost in the use of collective names, a notorious device in anti-Semitic literature at different periods: 'The Gurviches and the Yuzovskys.' Again, the rhetorical question posed by the article in *Pravda* – 'What notion could Gurvich possibly have of the national character of Soviet Russian man?' – emphasised the alienation of Jews from Russian culture. And the negative traits of the critics under attack – hypocrisy, deceit, Jesuitry, contempt for the most lofty Russian national sentiments – were stressed throughout.

The campaign against the cosmopolitans which followed in the wake of these articles was given the widest dimensions by the Soviet mass media: the radio, press, literature, cinema, theatre, scientific and popular lectures, wall notices at places of work. We have examined in some detail the only statistical data available, that on the press. Our investigation was based on twenty-one complete sets, for the years 1948–53, of the fifty-six newspapers and journals at our disposal. Of these, nine were central and republic newspapers and twelve were journals representing various areas of literature, art and the sciences.[56] An analysis of these papers shows that only twenty-three articles attacking subservience to the West and cosmopolitanism appeared throughout the whole of 1948, while the number of such articles reached a peak in the early months of 1949: February (49) and March (58) (see Table 6).[57] There was a sharp decline in April, it seems as a result of instructions from above to moderate the campaign in both quantity and content.[58]

The newspapers, *Literaturnaya gazeta* (twenty-six articles in twenty-four editions in February and March) and *Vechernyaya Moskva* (fifteen articles in February and March), played a leading role in this campaign. Central organs like *Pravda* and *Izvestiya* confined themselves to setting the tone and pace for the other newspapers. It is of interest that during the years 1948–9 no anti-cosmopolitan attacks appeared in the newspaper of the Uzbek Communist Party, *Pravda vostoka* (see below). In fact, this paper confined itself to printing articles which had appeared in the central press, 'contributing' nothing of its own – in contrast to the situation, for instance, in the Ukraine.

A considerable number of the articles in newspapers and journals comprised reports of important meetings of Party cells at scientific and higher educational establishments, special gatherings of writers' and artists' organisations, sessions of the academies of science and the arts, and various reactions of the 'Soviet public'. While not all the hundreds, and perhaps thousands, of meetings called during this period to condemn cosmopolitanism came to the notice of the public, the many reports in the press and on the radio created an atmosphere of unceasing incitement and mutual distrust among the intellectual stratum of the Soviet Union, some of whom saw this as an ideal moment to settle private accounts.

Among those Party members and government leaders who were active in this campaign were Khrushchev in the Ukraine, Gusarev in Belorussia, Pelshe in Latvia, and the ministers Bolshakov and Shcherbina; Zhdanov had died in August 1948. Among the most active campaigners in cultural circles were the following: A. Fadeev, A. Sofronov, K. Simonov, N. Gribachev, S.

Markov, A. Surkov and N. Pogodin in the Russian Republic, all leading members of the All-Soviet Writers' Union; A. Korneichuk and L. Dmyterko in the Ukraine; K. Krapiva and P. Brovka in Belorussia; theatre and literary critics V. Ermilov, M. Shkerin, E. Kovalchik, A. Markov, A. Dementyev, V. Ozerov, L. Khinkulov, V. Kirpotin (the last two of whom were denounced later); artists T. V. Khrenikov, A. Gerasimov, M. Kovalek; and scholars G. Aleksandrov (who was denounced in 1947), M. Iovchuk, V. Keldysh (who would later be attacked), S. Artomonov, B. Grekov, A. Udaltsev, V. Chkhikvadze and Y. Korovin.

As to the role played by Jews in this campaign, as we have already pointed out, there were some who joined it in the very beginning. However, as the campaign became manifestly more anti-Jewish, and many Jews became victims of the campaign (Paperny and Shtein, for example, who were referred to above), their number declined. This was also because the authorities probably decided that there was no further place for them in a campaign which aimed more and more at suggesting that Jews were to be found only on the other side of the fence. It is also likely that Jews themselves were repelled by this distasteful activity, although the influence of this factor should not be exaggerated. Among those who continued to take an active part in the anti-cosmopolitan campaign were the philosopher and member of the Academy of Sciences Mark Mitin, the journalist David Zaslavsky and the orientalist V. Lutsky. A number of Jewish writers, scientists and artists were occasionally forced to participate in various meetings to condemn cosmopolitanism, but their role was mainly limited to self-criticism.

The attacks, which, as we have seen, began in the fields of theatre and literary criticism, were extended to almost all areas of the arts and learning in February and March 1949, when new cosmopolitans were uncovered every day. Those whose names were published in the press undoubtedly represent only a fraction of those denounced, but included in this small percentage were some of the Soviet Union's greatest writers, artists and scholars. An analysis of Table 7 shows that the overall percentage of Jews in this elite group was more than 70%;[59] in sectors such as economics and sport it was more than 85%. An examination of the data by specialty demonstrates that there was not one intellectual pursuit, be it literature, art, the humanities, the social or natural sciences, in which Jews did not come under attack.[60] It seems that the only case in which non-Jews exceeded Jews was linguistics, and this may be due to the fierce internal struggles among various schools in this sphere. Those opposed to the prevailing school were now accused of cosmopolitanism.[61]

In general, the Jews accused of cosmopolitanism were attacked for longer periods and with greater virulence than their non-Jewish counterparts.[62] And over 80% of those attacked more than three times were Jews, a considerable number of whom were being arraigned almost daily during the period January–March 1949, and thenceforth at less frequent intervals.[63]

No less important, of course, was the question of the sanctions imposed on those accused of cosmopolitanism. There is no doubt that, in the campaign of incitement, a great many Jews suffered out of all proportion to the real significance of their positions and status. But complete data on this have not yet been published and it is doubtful if they ever will be.

Table 7. *The targets of the anti-cosmopolitan attacks in the years 1948–53**

Sector or speciality	Jews	Non-Jews	Total	Percentage of Jews among those attacked	Those attacked more than three times			
					Jews	Non-Jews	Total	% of Jews
Literature and Art								
1. Literary and art critics (theatre, painting, sculpture)	103	52	155	66.4	33	9	42	78.6
2. Writers, poets, playwrights	33	9	42	78.6	2	—	2	100.0
3. Musicians (instrumentalists, conductors, composers)	35	11	46	76.1	9	2	11	81.8
4. Film and theatre directors	8	2	10	80.0	3	—	3	100.0
5. Artists, sculptors	3	5	8†	37.5	—	—	—	—
TOTAL (literature and art)	182	79	261	69.7	47	11	58	81.0
The Sciences								
6. Education, psychology	8	7	15	53.3	—	—	—	—
7. Philology	3	4	7	42.9	—	—	—	—
8. History	32	9	41	78.0	6	—	6	100.0
9. Philosophy	11	3	14	78.6	2	1	3	66.7
10. Economics	12	2	14	85.7	2	—	2	100.0
11. Law	16	5	21	76.2	2	—	2	100.0
12. Architecture	5	2	7	71.4	2	—	2	100.0
13. Natural sciences (mathematics, physics)	8	2	10†	80.0	—	—	—	—
14. Sport (sports journalists)	7	1	8‡	87.5	—	—	—	—
TOTAL (the sciences)	102	35	137	74.5	12	1	13	92.3
INCLUSIVE TOTAL	284	114	398	71.4	59	12	71	83.1

* This table is based on data drawn from fifty-six Soviet newspapers and journals from the years 1948–53. Not included are former Soviet leaders such as Trotsky, Bukharin, etc., or foreigners who were attacked, e.g. Sartre, Gide, Feuchtwanger, Stravinsky. See B. Pinkus (ed.), *Evrei i evreisky narod 1948–1953*, vol. 2.

† The list is probably incomplete as not all the newspapers in this sphere were at our disposal.

‡ This is probably only a partial list, since the sports newspapers were not at our disposal.

The 200 articles dealing with cosmopolitanism which were read in the course of this research[64] lead to the conclusion that the mildest sanction, which nobody accused of cosmopolitanism could expect to escape, was the warning (*vygovor*) or severe warning (*strogy vygovor*) issued by his place of work or by the organisation to which he belonged. A stronger measure was the removal of the 'cosmopolitans' from their posts, for example: committee chairmanships (Kron from the Theatre Committee); editorial boards (Adelgeim from the senior editorship of the journal, *Vitchyzna*; Kedrov from the journal, *Voprosy filosofii*); or from the directorship of academic institutes (Traynin from his post as head of the Law Institute and Subotsky from the secretaryship of the Writers' Union).

More serious still was expulsion from professional organisations, which was frequently followed by dismissal from work. There was a repeated demand that the following theatre and literary critics be expelled from the Writers' Union: Yuzovsky, Gurvich, Boyadzhiev, Borshchagovsky, Altman, Varshavsky, Kholodov, Malyugin, Subotsky, Levin, Danin and Yakovlev. But it is not clear how many of them were actually removed. Among the composers and musicologists who found themselves threatened with expulsion from their union were: Vainkop, Mazel, Zhitomirsky, Ginzburg, Shneerson, Shlifshtein, Ogolovets, Belza, Pekelis and Lobanova. And the following were expelled from their respective unions: the well-known film director, S. Yutkevich, and cinema critics Oten, Volkenshtein, Manevich and Lebedev.

Even higher on the scale of intimidation was dismissal from places of work – a step which threatened the economic survival of the families of those accused. With regard to writers or art and literary critics, such expulsion and dismissal meant also that their books and articles could no longer be published.[65] In some cases, the news of positions and jobs lost was actually published in the press, as, for example, in the cases of Professor Goldenrikht, the writer Antokolsky and the literary critics Yuzovsky, Levin and Broverman.[66]

One of the most severe measures, which often resulted in arrest, was the removal of the accused from the ranks of the Communist Party. The theatre and literary critics whose expulsion from the Party was announced in the press were Yakovlev (Kholtsman), Altman, Kovarsky, Levin, Beskin and Danin. As regards arrest, it is reasonable to assume that more Jews were arrested for cosmopolitanism than for bourgeois nationalism, but the term 'mass arrest' was – proportionately speaking – more applicable to the latter category. This provides additional evidence that the prime object of Stalin's anti-Jewish policy in the years 1948–53 was the liquidation of Jewish culture, whereas in the case of the assimilated Jewish intelligentsia, at least until the beginning of 1953, the authorities were content to apply pressure and intimidation only.[67]

It is beyond the scope of this chapter to describe the flood of venom in all the mass media which poured forth against the cosmopolitans at this period. Selected examples are given in the documents, and we shall restrict ourselves here to noting some of its most characteristic features. First of all, the terms of contempt widely used to describe the cosmopolitans were mostly drawn from the classic anti-Semitic arsenal. Accordingly, they were persons without identity, nameless, without roots, bowing and scraping to all things foreign and passportless wanderers. There was also the use of collective names: the Gurviches, the Levins, the Yagols, the Tsimbals, etc. Again, increasing prominence was given to Jewish names; when the surname had a Russian or Ukrainian ring, the first name and patronymic were added.

Finally, in the latter half of February 1949, the press began to disclose pseudonyms.[68] Thus, the public suddenly discovered that Yakovlev was none other than Kholtsman; Melnikov turned out to be Melman; Kholodov was Meerovich; and Burlachenko, Berdichevsky. At the beginning of March, each new edition uncovered pseudonyms in almost all spheres of literature and art. However, in the beginning of April 1949, this exposure of pseudonyms stopped completely for almost two years, and, in 1951, we came across only one case of a pseudonym being disclosed in the Soviet press.[69]

The accusations levelled against the cosmopolitans were many and various, but all revolved around kowtowing to imperialism and detachment from – or even hatred for – the Russian people. Among their main themes were: *Doing outrage to the Russian nation* – the critic Altman hates all things Russian; *Foul defamation of Russian man* – the poet Golovanivsky's poem 'Abraham' insinuates that the Russians and Ukrainians turned their backs on the Jews when they were being led off to their death by the Germans; *Insult to the memory of outstanding Russian writers* – the critic Levin went so far as to rank together Abram Gurvich (sic!) and Vissarion Belinksy, while the critic B. Byalik once asserted that the poet Mayakovsky was influenced by the poet H. N. Bialik. The comparison of Mayakovsky, the Soviet poet of the Revolution, with the reactionary and mystical Jewish poet Bialik was said to be a flagrant insult to the memory of a great patriot. With this line constantly repeated in the press, it was only natural that an extreme anti-Jewish atmosphere often prevailed at conventions and meetings called to denounce cosmopolitanism.[70]

Most scholars dealing with this period do not query the anti-Jewish tendencies of the anti-cosmopolitan campaign,[71] but there are some who think otherwise.[72] In their view, the fact that many non-Jews were among those denounced and that Jews participated in the attacks on cosmopolitanism tends to disprove the claim that the campaign was anti-Jewish in character. It is also argued that the anti-nationalist campaign dealt a severe blow to many other nationalities besides the Jews. We have tried to show that the first supposition does not stand up well in the light of statistical analysis; now let us examine the second argument.

It is important to note that there is a distinction between the campaign directed against bourgeois nationalism and that against cosmopolitanism despite the similarities between them.[73] It is also necessary to examine the situation in the European republics of the Soviet Union – the Ukraine, Belorussia and the Baltic states – as distinct from that in the Central Asian and Caucasian republics.

The leadership at the republic level was, of course, obliged to introduce the anti-cosmopolitan policy into all the republics; but when it came to its implementation quite important differences developed between one republic and the next. There is no doubt that (the RSFSR apart) the Ukrainian Republic took the lead with regard to the momentum and vehemence of the attacks on cosmopolitanism, while the campaign was conducted with little enthusiasm, and even in low key, in the republics of Central Asia and the Caucasus.

No less important, however, was the question of *who* was attacked in the anti-cosmopolitan campaign. For example, the victims of the attacks in the Ukraine and Belorussia were almost all Jews, while their percentage among those attacked was low in the republics of Central Asia. The reason for this contrast does not lie in the small number of Jews who lived in these latter areas or in the fact that they held relatively few key posts in literature, art and the sciences; a very significant variable here was the degree of indigenous anti-Semitism and the desire to exploit it for various purposes.

Thus, while in Central Asia and to a certain extent in the Caucasus (chiefly in Azerbaidzhan) the anti-cosmopolitan campaign was almost identical to the campaign against bourgeois nationalism – with the usual attacks on pan-Islamism, pan-Turkism and pan-Iranism[74] and the incessant calls for fraternity with the 'Great Russian brother' – in the European republics (particularly in the Ukraine) the campaign was utilised for other purposes by some of the local intelligentsia, apparently with the support of the authorities. Most important here was the attempt to break the stranglehold of Russification, without attacking Great Russian chauvinism head on, by using the golden opportunity presented by the campaign against 'cosmopolitans', whose attitude to Ukrainian or Belorussian culture was nihilistic and disparaging. And, under the circumstances then prevailing, it was obviously far safer to attack 'cosmopolitans' who were Jewish rather than Russian in origin. Moreover, it was possible to exploit the anti-cosmopolitan campaign to settle personal accounts with the Jews who held important posts in all spheres of culture and learning in these republics.[75]

If we accept the view that the anti-cosmopolitan campaign became an out-and-out anti-Jewish campaign, the question arises, why? One of the principal reasons was the suspicion shared by Stalin and evidently by a sizeable section of the Soviet leadership that the Jews were not completely loyal to their socialist motherland and could not be relied upon fully in the event of a war with the United States. This distrust apparently induced Stalin to decide that it was necessary to fight not only 'Jewish nationalism' – those circles associated with Yiddish culture – but also 'cosmopolitanism' – the assimilated Jewish intelligentsia. In accordance with this inner logic, the sharp transition, at the end of 1948, from the first campaign to the second was natural enough, as was the apparently paradoxical fact that some persons were accused of both nationalism and cosmopolitanism consecutively or almost consecutively.

A more general but probably even more weighty consideration was the popularity which the regime could hope to gain by unleashing a thinly veiled campaign against the Jews, hated as they were by large sections of both the Russian and the non-Russian populations.

Finally, it seems that the anti-Jewish policy manifested in the anti-cosmopolitan campaign was further influenced by the internal struggles within the Party leadership, although even today it is difficult to pinpoint the particular group that supported it, or to what extent.[76]

The post-Stalin period

The anti-cosmopolitan campaign, which lasted in a subdued form until the second half of 1952, with occasional intensification (as in 1951),[77] flared up again on 13 January 1953, when it took on a most extreme anti-Jewish character following the announcement of the so-called 'Doctors' Plot'.

It was only Stalin's death on 5 March 1953 which put an abrupt end to the anti-cosmopolitan campaign, though its effects were to be felt for a long time afterwards. Not only in the years 1954–5,[78] which represented a definite transition period from one leadership to another, but even after the 20th Congress in 1956 writers were claiming at official conferences that the anti-cosmopolitan campaign had been necessary and beneficial.[79] On the other hand, even some writers who had participated in the campaign in Stalin's time admitted that it had been misused and had done great harm to Soviet literature. Such confessions, however, usually carried the added proviso that the danger of kowtowing to Western culture existed and had to be combated.[80] And, at the time when the struggle against liberal tendencies in Soviet literature was renewed in 1957, Khrushchev did not refrain from resorting once again to the notorious terminology used during the unbridled anti-cosmopolitan campaign.[81]

The deep shock which that campaign had caused a large section of the Soviet intelligentsia found expression in official publications,[82] in *samizdat* and in books published abroad[83] during the late 1950s and the 1960s. It was widely felt that, although the campaign had not been renewed in the post-Stalin period, the danger of its recurrence had not altogether passed. Moreover, some ingredients employed in the campaign were used later in the public attacks against nationalism which continued into the post-Stalin era, and, as regards the Jews, in the agitation against the Jewish religion and Zionism.

Documents to Chapter 4

The campaign against Jewish bourgeois nationalism

Document 56* Loytsker[84] attacks Jewish nationalism (1948)

The errors and distortions that our Party has exposed in the field of literature have been deeply analysed and strongly condemned in the decree of the CC of the All-Russian Communist Party (Bolsheviks) of 14 August 1946, and in Comrade A. Zhdanov's speech on the subject of the journals *Zvezda* and *Leningrad*.[85] In this historical decree stress was laid on the fact that literature and art cannot be apolitical; that 'they must abide by that which constitutes the living foundations of the Soviet order – by its policies'; that 'the strength of Soviet literature, the most progressive literature in the world, consists in its being a literature which does not have, and cannot have, interests other than the interests of the people and the interests of the state'.

In the Ukraine, deviations and errors of a bourgeois nationalist character have been exposed in the fields of history and literary history. In the decree of the CC of the All-Russian Communist Party (Bolsheviks) of 24 August 1946, it was stated that, in the *Study of the History of Ukrainian Literature*, the authors 'distorted the Marxist–Leninist understanding of the history of Ukrainian literature and exhibited it in a bourgeois nationalist spirit'; that 'smuggled into the work is the theory of the classlessness and the non-bourgeois character of the Ukrainian people in the past' – which is the essence of the bourgeois nationalist conception of M. Hrushevsky's 'school'; that 'in the *Study*, the history of Ukrainian literature was not described in its mutual connection with other kindred literatures, especially Russian literature', etc.

The Party has strongly condemned all these mistakes and has announced a series of measures to stamp out bourgeois nationalism in all its manifest forms.

The decree of the CC of the All-Russian Communist Party (Bolsheviks) on the journal *Vitchyzna* also exposed the bourgeois nationalist distortions and the narrow nationalism which had appeared in a series of critical articles and artistic works. The plenum of the Union of Soviet Writers of the Ukraine, which took place in September 1947, revealed serious and profound ideological, fundamentally bourgeois nationalist deviations in a number of Ukrainian writers: Rylsky,[86] Yanovsky,[87] Senchenko,[88] Kipnis[89] and others.

* *Source*: Haim Loytsker, 'Far ideyisher reynkayt fun undzer literatur' (For the Ideological Purity of Our Literature), *Der shtern*, 1948, no. 2, pp. 105–12.

All this is a serious warning, compelling us also to examine the situation within Yiddish literature. Let us make it very clear, therefore, that the 'theory' of the 'exclusiveness' and the non-bourgeois character of the Jewish people, and so forth, has been circulating among some intellectuals. Hence I intend to touch upon a few questions – signals which warn us that in Soviet Yiddish literature, too, the elements of bourgeois nationalism and narrow nationalism have not been avoided.

First of all, let us take a glance at the recent past. The position of the Jewish masses – enclosed, cut off and isolated in the narrow, crooked lanes of the *shtetl* (a characteristic feature of the Tsarist era), subject to the endless persecutions which were borne for many centuries by 'the most oppressed and persecuted nation, the Jewish nation'* – has left deep traces in Yiddish literature. The religious, patriarchal way of life laid its heavy stamp upon the whole subsistence of the Jewish masses and confirmed them in both their homogeneity and their distinctiveness. This was widely reflected in the classical literature.

To go by its subject matter, the pre-October Yiddish literature was narrowly national in essence, with certain exceptions in radical and socialist Yiddish poetry. Actually, there is no harm in this or that national literature describing its national environment. In fact, the artist ought to describe what is close and familiar to him. General human culture is enriched first of all by every artist bringing out the characteristically national.

Of course, this culture must be progressive, because 'we take from every national culture only its democratic and its socialist elements'.† And it does not mean at all that the artist, the writer, should sever himself from the general environment, as did the Bund[90] which in its time adopted policies of this type, even demanding special Jewish hospitals because – thus they argued from a position of extreme narrow nationalism – 'the sick would feel bad among Polish workers'.‡

The ways of life in the Jewish environment were not static. With the development of capitalism in Russia, and under the influence of the revolutionary movement, these ways of life became somewhat more secular, more universal, but Yiddish literature hardly reflected this process. In the years of reaction, following the failure of the 1905 Revolution, the nationalist tendencies in literature even grew stronger. Consequently, the decadent, devotional breast-beating and 'pouring forth the soul' of the Eynhorns,[91] with their evocation of a life centred around the synagogue; of the Nombergs,[92] the Vayters[93] and the others, with their searching for some chimera of a national ideal, became indeed false and anti-artistic. It became reactionary, undemocratic, alien to the masses.

The specifically Jewish way of life, which had become before October more sharply distinguished from the life of the surrounding peoples, disappeared as a result of the Great Socialist October Revolution; the Chinese Wall, which had fenced off the Jews from other peoples, was torn down. The Jewish people

* Lenin, *Works* (Russian), 3rd edition, vol. 18, p. 138.
† Lenin, *Works* (Russian), vol. 17, p. 137.
‡ Stalin, *Works* (Russian), vol. 2, p. 341.

received equal and full rights, Jews penetrated all the professions that had been inaccessible to them earlier, especially heavy industry.

In the course of time the new existence refashioned the Jew to a considerable extent and sharply altered his psychology. The process of this profound change has been reflected to a large extent in our Soviet Yiddish literature. The inertia of the narrow nationalism preserved in the old literature, however, can still influence a number of Soviet Yiddish writers, and – what is especially lamentable – even some from the younger generation.

[...] The works of the Soviet Yiddish writers abound with the word 'Jew' in its various forms, not only when the action concerns national characteristics but everywhere, even when a person is simply being referred to as a human being. We are so used to this phenomenon in Yiddish literature that it does not grate harshly on our ears. But just try to translate the phrases in question into Russian or Ukrainian, replacing 'Jew' [Yid] by 'Ukrainian', 'Russian', and you will see clearly what sort of a ring it has.[94] [...]

[...] We come across a reference, for example, to Ezekiel in the poem of H. Osherovich,[95] 'In Ponar'.* The prophet Ezekiel comes to Ponar from Babi Yar, 'from Auschwitz, Treblinka and Maidanek' as a spirit hovering over all the valleys of the dead bones, of those tortured to death by the Fascists.

Written in an emphatic and passionate prophetic style, this poem can make rather a strong impression. The national reference here, however, is ideologically false, because the structure of the ideas – 'Ezekiel from the valley of the bones' – remains within the framework of the Old Testament;[96] the object is simply expanded to include not only the valley 'by the river Chebar in the land of the Chaldees' but also Ponar by the river Viliya and other death-camps. The Soviet perspective is entirely lacking.

The little book of poems by the poet H. Osherovich is so filled with 'Jewishness' [*Yidishkeyt*] of every kind that the result is a bright bouquet of narrow nationalism which spills over here and there into bourgeois nationalism. In the poem 'Samson' a national-liberation epic is treated correctly. It is an interesting and powerful poem, full of earth-bound human passions and healthy protest against foreign oppression. But, in the poem 'Itsik Even', what does the parallel with Job say to our contemporary Soviet readers? It is true that the philosophy of optimisim is expressed in the legend of Job. There, however, the optimism is passive and has nothing at all to do with Soviet optimism, which is based on active deeds.

At the centre of H. Osherovich's book stands the poem 'Jews' (a title which is in no way appropriate for this particular work, but the Jews have to be brought in somehow!), a painfully unpleasant and gruesome picture of how a great many Jews were murdered 'In the old, cold synagogue'. In the general picture of death in the poem there is a specific sub-motif: Tsirl has been made

* H. Osherovich, *Fun klem aroys* (Out of the Straits), p. 61.

for as long as fifteen years as the result of what happened to her family:

> In a black night,
> In a night of the new moon
> Only *of hate for Jews**
> All were slaughtered

That is to say, Tsirl's family was not killed by the Fascist murderers recently, but fifteen years ago and as the result of 'hate for Jews'.

This incidental episode with its stress on hatred of the Jews transfers the ideological centre of the poem from its anti-Fascist direction to the idea of eternal Jewish martyrdom – and the poem acquires an expressly nationalistic purpose which is further strengthened as a result of its 'local colour' – the whole clerical inventory of the synagogue, which has for *us* an enormous 'self-recognition value': the men's courtyard entrance, the wash-stand, the Holy Ark, the curtain over the Ark, the dais, etc. Another poem has some learned Hebraisms which are far removed from reality as we live it and from our Soviet Yiddish: *sekilah* [death by stoning], *hereg* [slaughter], *shemirah* [keeping watch, observance], *metame* [defile], *metaher* [purify], *eglah arufah* [the decapitated heifer], *bi-nshika* [with a kiss], *dafn* [passages of the Talmud], *gezar zavaah* [last will], *erev-rav* [rabble], etc.

And to make it more nationalistic there are, of course, the three dozen appearances of the word 'Jew' in its various forms, the majority of which could easily have been replaced by other, more expressive, terms. For by so doing, the author would have avoided the cheap self-exposure and superficial display that we perceive in the repetitions of and variations on the word 'Jew', the aim of which is to excite 'national' feeling ...

Osherovich turns the word 'Jewish' into a common adjective, through which, together with other artistic means, he expresses the nationalist essence of the poem in question. There are such adjectives as 'Jewish pain', 'Jewish confidence', 'a Jewish nook', etc. Thus H. Osherovich drives his muse into a narrow, crowded 'Jewish nook', and he observes the world from a low spire in this nook. How 'broad' the world appears from such a nationalist observation-point can easily be imagined!

[...] Ayzik Platner[97] also appeals to the national historical memory in some sections of his book *With Love and Faith* (*Mit Libe un Gloybn*).

The story of the two sisters (the poem 'Two Sisters' (*Tsvey Shvester*)), who fled the ghetto and found refuge with their former nurse Mikhalina, evokes for the poet an association with the old and remote Jewish legend of Naomi and Ruth. The fact is that this association is not fully justified, for the one is basically a peaceful idyll, and in the other a terrible tragedy takes place; but the point is that Platner had to find a way to pay tribute to his Jewish *idée fixe*.

Platner's second poem, 'The Bridge' (*Di Brik*), is also crammed with traditional Jewish content and Biblical-Hebraic form. Here too we have an allusion to the bones from the valley: 'The bones will no more rise up from the valley, only once was the prophecy valid.' The figure of the first Jew, whom the

* Here and elsewhere my emphasis [H.L.].

author meets after the terrible events, is presented in various mystic ways and legendary forms:

'Has not a [holy] messenger (meshulah) come again?'
'From a great distance (merhakim), disguised in a tunic.'
'It must be a Jew from the ten dead men (asarah harugim)?'

We need living figures, realistic figures, not shadows and ghosts! There is also a recollection of Moses's bush (sne) – which burns and is not consumed – as a negative comparison: 'No burning bush appeared to him . . .' Thus we have in its own right an expressly religious, mystical association, that leads straight to God.

The various Old Testament associations pursue the poet and tie up not only with the description of exceptional situations – martyrdom, heroism – but also with ordinary ways of life. For example, the following idyllic way of life is depicted:

I recall the Sabbath evening in Tevet,
My father's hut floats in the snow.
My father is Noah, the room is the ark (tevah),
The snow has been blowing for forty days.

We come across religious associations and images also in Platner's 'Ballad of a Tailor' (Balade vegn a Shnayder): 'He knew well what was written in the sidur [Jewish daily prayer book], whether for rain (geshem) or for dew (tal) he prayed with devotion (kavanah).' The Germans killed the tailor, and a neighbour adopted his only surviving grandchild. This is internationalist in motif, only what is the point of the religious lining? It is not simply that the words express religious concepts which make them unsuitable for Soviet literature. They are organically alien as well, because they render this literature inaccessible to the broad masses; they are anti-democratic, strange to the mass reader. This is true even when they are entirely secular in content and significance.

One example of such Hebraisms is found in a poem 'Kishinev' by Motl Saktsier:[98]

Every day the capital city (ir ha-birah) is born anew,
Every day the coldness (kerirah) gives off more steam.

The final phrase of this little poem sounds like bitter irony against the background of such erudite Hebraisms:

Once again we talk to each other
in simple Yiddish (mame-loshen).

No, this is a long way from 'simple Yiddish'.

[. . .] We also meet with nationalist egocentrism in the book Song of Courage (Gezang vegn Mut) by Grubian.[99] First of all the question of the term 'Jew' arises once again. There is, of course, no harm in a Jewish poet writing only about the mass return of the Jews to their homes. For we know that Ukrainian, White Russian and other farmers deserted entire villages, their ancient homes, and only returned to the ruins after the Soviet lands had been liberated.

Let us grant, then, that the Jewish writer knows the life of the Jewish masses better, but why does he have to harp unceasingly on: (a) '*Jews* return here little by little'; (b) 'Arrived, said the *Jew*, arrived'; (c) '*Jews* are travelling to Odessa', etc. This kind of generalised designation adds nothing to the description at all, but, on the contrary, makes it the poorer, as already pointed out.

The poet Grubian derives great pleasure from:

> The ear that hears, how in *Jewish* homes
> It seethes with life, and music plays.

The fact that some Jewish homes survived the particularly ferocious destruction unleashed by the Fascist bandits is, of course, a legitimate source of satisfaction.

From this enjoyment, however, Grubian passes on to further specific Jewish characteristics: 'How tasty a *Jewish loaf* with caraway seeds can be.' What is the meaning of 'Jewish bread'? Kosher bread? Bread from which the priest's portion has been separated?[100] Or, for example, 'We take courage *in the Jewish manner*.' What kind of special Jewish courage is this, courage in the Jewish manner?!

Thus, in Grubian's work moral and psychological categories are Judaised. So, too, does Grubian Judaise the physiological and anatomical, almost the racial characteristics of a soldier:

> I tramped on, and the gun
> I clasped in my *bony Jewish* hands (?!)

All right then, Grubian relishes the fact that 'one sees a Jew – one sees a Jew and speaks to him in Yiddish' – but with Grubian Jewish extrovertness goes so far that even the sun (incapable of speech anyway!) also speaks Yiddish. And not just any Yiddish, but:

> And the sun upon the little honey flowers
> for the bees
> tells such stories
> *in a good, quiet Yiddish* (!?)

But to express his whole nationalist 'feeling' ordinary Yiddish is not enough for Grubian. It turns out that he can do this only in the Holy Tongue:

> I hear the roar of a thousand bombers
> I sit and I murmur '*I am the man*' [*ani ha-gever*][101]

That is to say, he seizes the holy Jewish God right by his beard. And he gives him what for! What will the Soviet reader make of this murmuring? What kind of artistic function does the 'I am the man' fulfil here? Or is this murmuring of 'I am the man', when he hears the roaring of bombers, an allusion of the poet to 'courage in the Jewish manner'?

[...] We have demonstrated here that the works of three Soviet Yiddish poets which appeared in 1947 were characterised by a totally nationalist outlook. We want also to point out some other, more random errors of narrow nationalism, nationalist egocentrism and bourgeois nationalism scattered over a number of recent works of some other Soviet Yiddish writers.

When A. Velednitsky[102] saw the mountain Ararat for the first time, it became 'dear and familiar' to the poet because:

> My people know it,
> The Bible mentions it

Believe me, to recognise the world and objects of nature through the prism of the Bible is unworthy of a writer and sets the reader a bad example.

The only productive historical and legendary associations are those which teach a profound idea, a philosophical generalisation, etc. In addition to classical literature, mythology and the heroic epos also serve as a source for such associations. Such, for example, is the myth of Antaeus applied with such brilliance by Comrade Stalin in his closing words at the plenum of the CC of the All-Russian Communist Party (Bolsheviks) of 3–5 March 1937. Associations with some of the biblical legends can sometimes also be apt, but healthy, secular, heroic legends and not themes such as the tale of Noah's ark, which is of no interest whatsoever to us; in our opinion, the evoking of such associations merely creates a nationalist after-taste and nothing else.

In his story, 'Velvl from Kurenets', H. Dobin[103] relates how a partisan fighter is killed in battle.* When the author introduces Haim, one of the partisans, into the action, he describes him as 'just another Jew'; the name 'Haim' is not enough for the writer in fixing his national origins. This Haim can find no other expression for his feelings than: 'Velvl, say the mourner's prayer, "God, full of mercy" (*El male raḥamim*), for Aksenov. He was a good lad ...' The writer could not have thought up a greater profanement of Aksenov's memory nor a greater falsification of the episodic figure of Haim in this story!

We have another false moment in this story. The brigade commander arrives at Velvl's, and when the latter begins to plead with him to take him on a fighting mission, the commander replies: 'It was the same story with Levin the shoemaker ...'. Both cobblers in the partisan detachment – and both doing everything to get into the fighting – just happen to be Jews! Is this true to life? What is more important, is it an artistic truth?!

Though it is quite widely known, we must now pause especially over the remnant of genuine bourgeois nationalism in I. Kipnis's story, 'Without Giving It a Thought' (*On khokhmes, on khezhboynes*), printed in the Lodz paper, *Naye lebn* (New Life). In this story the writer dreams that our soldiers should wear the Star of David on their breasts together with their Soviet medals. This is to spite the Fascists who, he writes, exploited the Star of David as a mark of shame for their victims, the Jews, during their rule. Kipnis wanted to transform the symbol of death into a symbol of life. In so doing, he ignored the fact that the Star of David has long been an emblem of politically belligerent Zionism, a movement which is hostile to us because it is bourgeois and anti-Soviet in essence.

Moreover, in this story Kipnis is very worried lest the children, whom a peasant woman has saved 'without giving it a thought', merely following her

---

* H. Dobin, *Af der vaysrusisher erd* (On White Russia's Land), Moscow, 1947.

Soviet humanist feelings, might, heaven forbid, lose their Jewish appearance. It's really a matter of life and death for him that all Jews should speak only Yiddish ...

The most shameless thing in this outrageous story is what can be called its 'organisational aspect': the same story was first published in our Soviet *Eynikeyt*, which excluded the nationalistic parts. But, anxious at all costs to bring these very parts to the reader – albeit the foreign readers – Kipnis preserved them in a text which he sent off to Lodz. (How significant! Bourgeois nationalism always bows and scrapes before foreign bourgeois countries.) Kipnis, so it turns out, has not forgotten his former *Months and Days (Khadoshim ve-yomim)*, although many years have passed. And he has learnt nothing in all these years of Soviet rule.

Nationalist ideology is a disclosure of capitalist consciousness. On the path to Communist society we must liquidate the survivals of capitalist conscious-ness. Our Soviet Yiddish writer must describe the Soviet Jew artistically, but he must describe the new traits in him, not those which are outlived. And he must picture him not isolated from other peoples, with whom he is closely bound, and not severed from all the processes taking place in our country.

Soviet Yiddish literature has colossal achievements to its credit, especially in internationalising its typical characters and in overcoming nationalist after-effects from the pre-October culture. To outlive the remnants of narrow nationalism and nationalist egocentrism which still survive, to uproot all trace of bourgeois nationalism, to saturate the works with lofty Bolshevist ideology – that is the most urgent task of the ever developing and advancing Soviet Yiddish literature.

Document 57* Ukrainian writer criticises *Der shtern*[104] (February 1949)

The vicious methods practised by the editorial board of the Yiddish almanac, *Der shtern*, can be explained only by the neglect of Bolshevik Party principles and the dulling of vigilance. The works published in it were ideologically pernicious, permeated with national narrow-mindedness, and depicted the Soviet people in a distorted way. The editorial board of the almanac did not direct the attention of the Jewish writers to the urgent themes of today, and lagged behind the decisive offensive of Soviet literature against the survivals of bourgeois nationalism in whatever form they might appear.

Document 58† Jewish nationalism in Yiddish literary criticism (February 1949)[105]

Wherever there are no real ideological demands, where people are indifferent to politics, the wildest, most repellent expressions of cosmopolitanism are inevitable. The glossary project for the second edition of the *Large Soviet Encyclopaedia* dispatched recently for discussion can serve as an example. [...]

* *Source*: 'Za bolshevistskuyu partiinost sovetskoi kultury. Na sobranii pisatelei Kieva' (For the Bolshevik Party Spirit of Soviet Culture. At a Meeting of Kiev Writers), *Pravda Ukrainy*, 8 February 1949.

† *Source*: E. Kovalchik, 'Bezrodnye kosmopolity' (Rootless Cosmopolitans), *Literaturnaya gazeta*, 12 February 1949.

The cosmopolitan, objectivist ideas of the authors of this glossary are clearly expressed in the way in which they analyse Jewish literature and in the names they have included there. The authors added a very 'curious' note: 'This glossary includes all Jewish literature.' Modern Jewish literature occupies the same space in the glossary as Uzbek, Kazakh and Georgian literatures taken together.

The authors of the glossary scoff at the principle of Party spirit and at the feeling of Soviet patriotism. They take 'all Jewish literature' without differentiating countries or state systems, and they juggle the cosmopolitan, bourgeois nationalist idea about the alleged existence of a 'world-wide' Jewish literature, thus playing into the hands of the enemies of our mother country. In their list, Soviet writers are mentioned along with the cunning businessmen of our days in America, Palestine and other countries. This 'viewpoint' cannot be called anything but servile grovelling before inimical bourgeois nationalist theories.

Document 59* Cosmopolitanism and Jewish nationalism in the Ukraine (March 1949)[106]

Gordon also published articles on modern Ukrainian literature. In the works of front-line poets, which he reviewed in the journal, *Dnipro*, Gordon finds a great number of 'mortal sins'. However, this aesthete changes his tone altogether when speaking of the poems of S. Golovanivsky.[107] To distract attention, he criticises the 'bookish romanticism' of Golovanivsky's poems, and then hastens at the same time to assess them most highly. He calls Golovanivsky 'the son of Lermontov' in poetry, no more and no less.

What stirred the critic so deeply in Savva Golovanivsky's works? One of his poems in the collection *Knyga voiniv* [The Book of Fighters] (1943) is called *Nadia* [Hope]. It is dated 22 June 1942. But, instead of calling upon us to fight Fascism, melancholic, depressing notes are sounded here.

Golovanivsky is the author of the poem, 'Avraam' [Abraham], nationalist and openly hostile to the Soviet people. In this poem Golovanivsky casts terrible, unheard-of accusations at the Soviet people. He lies shamelessly, saying that the Soviet people, Russians and Ukrainians, turned their backs indifferently on the old Jew, Abraham, whom the Germans led off along the Kiev streets to be shot. This is a terrible defamation of the Soviet people, who defended the freedom and independence of Soviet people of all nationalities in a hard bloody struggle at the cost of heavy sacrifice and great efforts. Golovanivsky, however, throws mud in the face of the heroic Soviet people!

It often happens that our writers – poets, prose writers, playwrights – speak on problems of criticism and on the study of literature. This is perfectly reasonable, and from this point of view L. Pervomaisky's report, 'Lesya Ukrainka and our Times', delivered at the jubilee session of the Institute of Literature of the Ukrainian Academy of Sciences, should be welcomed. L. Pervomaisky[108] is a well-known poet. Readers have highly evaluated his book *Zemlya* [The Earth] and a number of his other works. But with the very first

* *Source*: L. Dmyterko, 'Sostoyanie i zadachi teatralnoi i literaturnoi kritiki na Ukraine' (The Present State and Tasks of Theatrical and Literary Criticism in the Ukraine), *Literaturnaya gazeta*, 9 March 1949.

words of his report, L. Pervomaisky repeats in full Stebun's 'theory' of individual personalities rising above the 'single stream'.

Pervomaisky cannot discard Shevchenko[109] altogether. But he cunningly endeavours to prove the impossible – that Taras Shevchenko was not a great fighter, a revolutionary democrat, but just a victim of cruel reality which prevented him, *together with thousands of his contemporaries*, from becoming a 'poet of love'. Here is what Pervomaisky writes: 'Thus the humanism of Ukrainian classical literature widens and deepens, adding to Shevchenko's promethean-ism, his angry implacability towards the enemy and his love for his people, Franko's wider understanding of the world, and the bright humanism and total humanity of Lesya Ukrainka.'

Here Pervomaisky gives a complete theory of cosmopolitanism. It turns out that Shevchenko, with his implacability towards enemies and his love of his people, was narrow-minded; Ivan Franko,[110] whose favourite allegedly was Heine, broadened his world outlook, and Lesya Ukrainka[111] brought Ukrainian literature to 'a humanism embracing all mankind'.

'Only in the works of Lesya Ukrainka, for the first time in the history of our culture does the national grow into the universally human.' Feeling he has gone too far, Pervomaisky hastens to assure us: 'Cosmopolitanism has nothing to do with it.' No, this is complete cosmopolitanism, not that of Lesya Ukrainka, however, but of Leonid Pervomaisky. [...]

But L. Pervomaisky has even worse things to say. I mean his poem from the cycle *Pid chuzhym nebom* [Under Foreign Skies]. In this poem the Romanian hamlet, Sinaya, evokes in the poet morbid associations of the Biblical Mount Sinai upon which, according to the legend, Moses proclaimed his laws three thousand years ago. And the Soviet poet allows himself this confession:

> And possibly, this wonderful vision,
> Your voice or your face,
> A distant shadow, pale and forgotten –
> Are all I have left.

Now it becomes clear why in his *Bloknot blukan* [Journey Notes], written in 1928, L. Pervomaisky assessed Zionism from a completely false position. We would not remind Pervomaisky of what he wrote long ago, if the influences of a foreign, hostile ideology had not come to be expressed in his present works. [...]

The cosmopolitan critics did not help us unmask the serious cases of Jewish bourgeois nationalism, especially in the literary almanac, *Der shtern*, the publication of which we had to stop.[112] This almanac was cut off from the Soviet people, from the working masses of the Jewish people. It cultivated nationalist moods, small-town psychology, and, in some works, even con-sidered Soviet and foreign Jews as equal.

Document 60* Jewish bourgeois nationalism and Ukrainian nationalism (March 1949)

The ignoramus, the yes-man of the bourgeois nationalists, Beregovsky,[113] insisted that the people should not try to keep their national characteristics.

* *Source*: 'Za dalneishy rastsvet ukrainskogo sovetskogo muzykalnogo iskusstva. Na sobranii kompozitorov Kieva' (For Further Flourishing of Ukrainian Soviet Music. At a Meeting of Kiev Composers), *Pravda Ukrainy*, 19 March 1949.

Using the standpoint of hostile degenerates, he declared that the Great October Socialist Revolution had done away with the ground for the further development of popular creative activity.

The group of rootless cosmopolitans echoed the views of Ukrainian bourgeois nationalists. They propagated the slanderous theory of a single national stream in the development of Ukrainian musical culture. [...]

There are serious errors in the works of some composers. Thus, for example, the composer, D. Klebanov,[114] wrote a symphony permeated by the spirit of bourgeois nationalism and cosmopolitanism, basing it on old Jewish religious songs. The rituals of ancient Palestine, 'The Lamentation of Israel', synagogue tunes – such are the sources which inspired Klebanov in the creation of this anti-patriotic symphony.

'There can be no doubt', Comrade Dovzhenko[115] concludes, 'that Ukrainian Soviet composers and musicologists – patriots of their motherland – will rout the criminal group of cosmopolitans and continue to develop our own musical art, national in form, socialist in content.'

After the report to the meeting the discussions got under way. Composers and musicologists, teachers at music academies and music critics spoke with great passion and anger of the group of rootless cosmopolitans who were hindering the growth of Ukrainian Soviet music. They exposed the foul deeds of the pygmies who grovelled to the West, their vile ways of combating the best representatives of Soviet Ukrainian musical art.

'Our people are monolithic, firmly united around the Party of Lenin and Stalin', said the head of the music section of the Ukrainian Radio Committee, Comrade Ponomarenko.[116] 'However, there are still some ugly customers who propagate the wretched ideas of cosmopolitanism which are alien to our people. In their dirty writings, the pseudo-theoreticians A. Gozenpud,[117] Geilig,[118] Khinchin[119] and Beregovsky affirmed that the Ukrainian and the fraternal Russian cultures are not original, but derived from West European culture. The double-dealer, A. Gozenpud, contended that Mussorgsky's opera, *Boris Godunov*, was a "genuinely Shakespearian work", and not an original Russian one; that there is not a single composer who could be compared to Wagner. Only a rootless cosmopolitan and loathsome mischief-maker could have written such heresy.' [...]

The utter routing of the anti-patriotic critics, sworn enemies of Ukrainian national Soviet culture, is the urgent duty, says Comrade Gordeichuk,[120] of the musical public of the Soviet Ukraine...

The poet, A. Malyshko,[121] delivered a lively speech at the meeting. With examples of the subversive 'activities' of the cosmopolitan opera and theatre critics, he demonstrated their ideological connections with bourgeois nationalism, their grovelling before the decaying culture of the West. If one tears the mask from a rootless cosmopolitan, says Comrade Malyshko, the beastly muzzle of a bourgeois nationalist will appear beneath it.

Comrade Malyshko speaks of D. Klebanov's symphony, 'Babi Yar', in which the composer slanders the Russian and Ukrainian people. In this symphony, which is full of Biblical motifs and imbued with a sense of tragic doom, Klebanov forgets about the friendship and brotherhood of the Soviet peoples and develops the idea of the complete isolation of the Soviet peoples tortured to death by the Germans at Babi Yar.

Document 61* Aleksandr Isbakh[122] as Zionist and cosmopolitan (1949)

In 1948, the publishing house, Sovetsky pisatel, in which, as is known, rootless people without kith and kin – the anti-patriotic Levins, Danins, and others were active – published a book by Aleksandr Isbakh (the pen-name of Isaak Bakhrakh), *Years of Life*. This is a series of autobiographical stories telling us about the childhood and youth of one Aleksandr Shtein, in whom we easily recognise the author himself.

What ideas does the author propagate in his little book? First of all, he sings the praises of the Jewish religion. The whole book, from the first to the last page, is permeated by religious worship. The first story is even called 'God'. With tender emotion, and on his knees, Isbakh speaks about worship at the synagogue, gives scores of names specific to the synagogue, and explains each of them at length both in the text and in numerous footnotes. We learn the most trivial details of the Jewish ritual; we can even read the text of the prayer for the dead in Isbakh's book ...[123]

But that is not the point. The main thing is that Isbakh slanders the Jewish people by saying that for all Jews, independent of their class origin or their place in society, all their happiness is in their religion. He devotes whole pages to describing the reading of the Talmud and shows how Jews gathered in the synagogue, 'relished the wisdom of generations, tried to penetrate the meaning of every word written by mysterious wise men whose names had been lost to the ages'. This is said of Jewish toilers, shoemakers, tailors, poor people mercilessly exploited in Tsarist Russia. He slanderously avers that the only consolation in the lives of these people was the synagogue. He writes:

Life, the life of today with its joys and sorrows (more sorrows than joys) continued there – beyond the synagogue walls, in their small grocers' stores, on their shoemakers' stools, at their sewing-machines, with their many children and grandchildren – their worries. Here (that is, in the synagogue) they submerged themselves in a quite different life. Here they were not unhappy, downtrodden Jews, afraid of every policeman.

Isbakh describes the life of the locksmith Duvid Bentsman, who left his profession to become a beadle at the synagogue. The author is breathless with tender feeling when he describes vividly how this locksmith found his happiness in God's fold:

In the evenings, when only the wise Talmudists remained in the synagogue, he would sit down near them. He was not quite literate and would listen carefully to their interpretations of the holy script, trying to grasp the meaning of the discussions. Dovid would understand almost everything. He saw vividly the lights of the Jerusalem festivals, the heavy massive *menorot*, the sumptuous robes of the high priests and the levites ... That was the Temple ... That was life ... He would close his eyes, and he saw the 'Holy Land', the land flowing with milk and honey ...

(The story, 'The Beginning')

Isbakh openly propagates Zionism in his filthy little book; he speaks of the Zionist organisation 'which was very influential among the Jews in our town'.

* *Source*: S. Ivanov, 'Naglye propovedi bezrodnogo kosmopolita' (Insolent Confessions of a Rootless Cosmopolitan), *Vechernyaya Moskva*, 14 March 1949.

He speaks of a Zionist group at his high school, of the 'good men and women' who sent Jews to Palestine. He even reproduces the text of the Zionist anthem (the story 'Son of Honour').

What are the character traits of the hero? Perhaps Isbakh needed all this religious ritual as a background to disclose the character of his hero more vividly? Perhaps, against this background, he depicts his hero as an opponent of the life surrounding him, as a fighter for the new, correct life? Not at all. The main characteristic of the personage is mean cowardice. He is afraid of everything. This trait follows him throughout his life, from childhood to youth (i.e., from the beginning to the end of the book).

In his childhood, he is afraid of God: 'Fear seems to have been my predominant feeling for God. *He* was almighty. *He* was all-seeing. Nothing could be concealed from Him.' (Author's emphasis.) Fear of God was combined with belief in God. The hero of the book stands untiringly through all the services at the synagogue, every *shaḥarit*, *minḥa* and *maariv* (the author explains in detail what each term means), although no one compels him to. His father is dead, and his mother is not religious at all. But 'God is almighty', Isbakh insists. And a story follows directly about 'God's omnipotence' – God helps the hero to find a lost toy. The fear of God and the belief in his 'omnipotence' never leave the hero throughout his life as described in the book. The salvoes of the *Aurora* have sounded, the October Revolution has taken place, the hero has grown up, he is already seventeen, he moves to Moscow, and here too the same old Zionist God has pride of place with him! The hero managed to make his home with a friend, to arrange his life somehow, and immediately he remembered 'the old Zionist God ... who had forgotten all the wrong I had done Him'.

But the hero of the book does not only fear God; he is a coward always and everywhere: when he sees the Whites shooting a group of Communists; and when he sees 'a tall man in an officer's trench-coat with a skull and cross-bones on his sleeve [i.e., a White Officer]; and at the front'. The hero's permanent state is 'worry and nervousness'. When Red soldiers joke cheerfully at the front line after a battle, 'I did not take part in the jokes, I thought jokes blasphemous with death around.' All the actions of the hero are dictated by the fear of death. A shell lies near him and does not explode. No one is hurt. And this is what happens to the hero: ' "The end!" flashed the thought, "and I fell back on the gun-carriage with eyes closed." '

And Isbakh's hero is not just a coward like a rabbit; he is also an inveterate and incorrigible egoist. The whole book is permeated by his ego, his self-praise. With rapture and pride he says: 'From the age of eight I was the head of the family.' How did being the head of the family express itself? By 'being responsible for the whole family before God'. No great responsibility, as we see, but the hero 'tried to do his duty properly before Him, the Almighty'. He says: 'I did not like the Zionists', and immediately makes a small correction: 'But I was a Jew and ... became a son of honour [*Bar mizvah*], entered the respectable family of the sons of Moses and earned the right from that day to put on the receptacles with the holy prayers on my forehead.' And how ecstatically the hero speaks of the beginning of his 'creative' path: 'The screen star, Maksimov, will read my poetry at concerts in the capital. I had become a real poet.' The further he goes, the more he discloses. The summer of 1921, says the hero, was 'in our town a time of an especial flourishing of literature and art'. Why? Because a Terevsat [Theatre of Revolutionary Satire] was organised in the town, and 'I' was its 'ideological leader'. 'I was always efficient', 'I was already prominent in the newspaper', 'I am the leading poet' – 'I' occurs countless times on the pages of the book.

Among all those 'I's there is one sentence in the book which answers to the truth. The author writes: 'I thought of my short life and came to the bitter conclusion that I, the head of the poets' union, knew nothing ... I occupied so many positions, and had remained an *ignoramus*.' (Our emphasis, S.I.) The hero and the author refer the words to 1921. But even now, almost thirty years later, the author and the hero have remained ignoramuses as before. Only ignoramuses and, let us add, anti-patriots, can grovel uncritically before anything foreign as the author does in his book. Only ignoramuses and anti-patriots associate the Moscow Conservatory and the Bolshoi Theatre merely with the names of foreign musicians and composers. Only an ignoramus and anti-patriot can suggest that the very day after the October Revolution, the Executive and the Party committees of a provincial centre began erecting a monument, not to the fighters of the Revolution, not to the outstanding scientists, writers, or artists of the country, but to the Swiss, Pestalozzi. In the book he is called 'the illustrious Swiss' and 'the famous pedagogue', although it is known that the pedagogic activities of Pestalozzi were permeated by virulent formalism in the education of children and were stuffed with religious propaganda.

Aleksandr Isbakh has written a loathsome book! And only the unmasked rootless cosmopolitan, F. Levin,[124] could have helped him publish it. His name adorns the book as editor.

Document 62* Antokolsky as 'Zionist' and bourgeois nationalist (March 1949)[125]

Take Antokolsky's[126] path. Along the whole length of it, even in the Soviet period, we have had more than one occasion to note traces of these influences. And Antokolsky has now become one of our best Soviet poets. And when we criticise Antokolsky for his error in the article on Blok, we are saying that he must understand fearlessly and thoroughly his own path of development; he must have an ideologically clear understanding in order to free himself of some 'remnants of the past'.

Criticism has not helped Antokolsky to be thoroughly rid of the 'remnants of the past'. The poet's verses, 'No Eternal Memory', were deeply erroneous, full of Zionism and bourgeois nationalism. In a number of his books, including the volume of his selected poems published in the 'Golden Series', Antokolsky paid tribute to all his early mistakes and carefully presented much of what he had tried to rid himself of in his subsequent work.

* *Source*: M. Lukonin, 'Problemy sovetskoi poezii' (Problems of Soviet Poetry), *Zvezda*, 1949, no. 3, p. 195.

Document 63* Rooting out bourgeois nationalists and Zionists (February 1953)

The Ukrainian newspaper, *Stalinskoe plemya*, has published a detailed article, 'Gullible People are Accomplices of the Enemy', mentioning facts which speak of gullibility in a number of Komsomol organisations, of the mood of complacency and political unconcern which prevail there.

'What besides dulled political vigilance and gullibility', says the article, 'can explain, for example, that a despicable group of Jewish bourgeois nationalists and Zionists was active in the Odessa State University? The management of the University and the Komsomol organisation admitted to being gullible and to not having appreciated the political importance of the fact in time.'

Other instances of political short-sightedness and carelessness are given in the article. Neither the department of Marxism–Leninism nor the Komsomol organisation of the Odessa Institute of Marine Engineers reacted to the incorrect behaviour of the senior teacher Frenkel in time or unmasked the pernicious effect of some of her lectures on the formation of the students' outlook.

Document 64† Kharats attacked for nationalism (1960)[127]

The Soviet writer's place is in the front ranks of the fighters for peace and for Communism. The poet's voice, his thoughts and dreams, are the voice, thoughts and dreams of the people. His poems are the people's poems! But, unhappily, into this harmonious, amicable chorus a debased, alien voice has injected a jarring note.

An alien voice – the voice of a petty bourgeois nationalist faker, that of Meir Kharats[128] – the voice of a man who aspires to be called a poet. A meeting of the Chernovtsy Writers' Union was held to evaluate his work, which has appeared in foreign newspapers in the recent past. Writers, journalists, literary critics – Ukrainians, Russians, Jews – spoke angrily of the filthy, decadent poems of M. Kharats. There can be found in them nothing of the patriotism of the Soviet man; nothing of the voice of the citizen-soldier, of the great land of socialism; not a hint of that greatness and incomparable light which illuminates every corner of our motherland.

What is it in M. Kharats's poems that so infuriated the participants at the meeting? The reactionary bourgeois press fills its pages daily and hourly with outpourings of poisonous lies and foul slanders against the Soviet Union. And it gets carried away with its prevarications concerning the persecution of the Jews in the USSR. Foreign writers raise a hysterical outcry about anti-Semitism in the Soviet Union in order to distract the attention of their readers from the revival of Fascism and anti-Semitism in the capitalist countries, especially in West Germany. The bourgeois press of Israel is no less caught up

* *Source*: 'Nastoichivo vospityvat politicheskuyu bditelnost' (Political Vigilance To Be Persistently Inculcated), *Komsomolskaya pravda*, 21 February 1953.

† *Source*: G. Bloshtein & H. Malamud, 'Chuzhyi golos' (An Alien Voice), *Radyanska Bukovyna*, 4 March 1960.

in this falsehood, for it has to use any means to extricate Ben Gurion's circle from the crisis it created by providing weapons to West Germany, to the self-same Fascist generals who murdered, destroyed and burned Jews in the ovens of Maidanek and Auschwitz. Through his poems, Meir Kharats has transformed himself, perhaps unwittingly, into an ally of these vile anti-Soviet slanderers.

A great deal was said at the writers' meeting about his poem, 'The Wanderer', which was published in a foreign Jewish periodical in 1958. Kharats depicts the Jewish people as a wanderer, allegedly persecuted everywhere, etc., etc. And he associates himself with his forlorn wanderer:

> Let us wander together, the two of us,
> In a foreign desolation,
> Without baggage,
> Without shoes and without a shirt.

This is the ancient legend of the persecuted Jew, the eternal wanderer. But where did Kharats dig him up? Where, for example, did he ever see such a Jew among the Jews of Chernovtsy? Was it among the workers of the textile factory or machine-builders, among the doctors or teachers, among the students or scientists, among the stalwarts of Communist activity? Such a Jew exists only in Kharats's dark, sick mind, misled by Biblical legends.

Soviet Jewish literature possesses many descriptions, in prose, poetry and drama, of the improved communal life of the Jewish people under the Soviet system, descriptions of the transformation of the *luftmentsh* [an idle dreamer] into a worker, an active member of society enjoying equal rights. But, lo and behold, Kharats declares: no such thing exists or ever did exist; there is only the eternal wanderer, and Kharats is his prophet.

This slander is indeed dear to the bourgeois Jewish nationalists, and Zionists, and to all the enemies of the USSR – as though the Jews had been prevented from enjoying the victories of the Revolution, in which they took an active part. In fact, Kharats has some poetic material on this theme too, in his poem, 'Before a New Song', published in the foreign press in 1957.

> Together we built here
> This house, like a song,
> But you, the original dwellers,
> Entered and locked the door.

And Kharats stands in front of the building, not knowing how to enter it. What remains for him?

> I stand under the window,
> I rattle the window.

Is this not a vicious lie? Is it not a slander of our Soviet reality, of our Soviet motherland, of the multi-faceted construction of socialism, achieved by the effort of all the peoples of the Soviet Union bound together by mutual friendship? And the keys to this great building, the keys to happiness, were received by the Jewish people, along with all the peoples of our land.

In his poem, 'Spring', Kharats describes how 'the children from seven courtyards gather in the largest courtyard of all', but they feel strange there, 'like birds from a variety of nests'. [...]

Among Kharats's works there is a poem, 'Portrait of the Artist', also published in a Jewish newspaper abroad in 1959. The hero of that poem 'very nearly closes his eyes and so moves half-blind towards his goal'. Many of the participants at the writers' meeting compared the poet himself to that 'Artist'. The trouble with Kharats is that he closes his eyes completely, wanders in the dark, blunders and loses his way with the blind wanderer's cane. How far has it brought him? 'The poet cuts himself off from life, from Soviet reality, from the collective of writers, and this has brought him to such errors.' So said some of the participants. Others suggested that 'he never was connected with our life'. And the participants quite properly put a series of questions to Kharats: In whose name does he speak? Which readers does he address? For what end does he propagandise? For what does he fight? What does he seek to attain by his slanderous poems?

There ensued a clear, principled and spirited discussion on the writer's duties and responsibilities, on his place in the struggle for peace and Communism. The meeting advanced with utmost clarity the great, unblemished Leninist principle of the friendship of peoples and the friendship of literatures. Writers, journalists and literary critics spoke of the great traditions of Pushkin and Tolstoy, Shevchenko, Mendele Moykher Sforim and Shalom Aleikhem – all of whose work served and continues to serve the interests of the people.

> Siberia, the Urals,
> Kaluga, and Tripolye,
> And wherever I am
> A flaming Komsomol am I.

This verse – read out at the meeting by the Ukrainian poet, Ivan Kutain – was from a poem by the well known Soviet Jewish poet, Itsik Fefer. It was read out to demonstrate how profoundly mistaken Kharats is, how far behind his own times.

At the same time, all the declarations at the meeting were characterised by a quite correct desire to help Kharats understand his mistakes, to overcome his nationalistic narrowness, to emerge from his dark corner and to go forward with wide open eyes onto the sun-drenched road.

The anti-cosmopolitan campaign

Document 65* Leon Feuchtwanger,[129] Josephus Flavius and cosmopolitanism (1948)

American reactionaries trade a wide variety of wares in Europe at present. But among all the out-dated rubbish these exporters try to sell in Europe there is one commodity they are especially eager to get rid of. The product is sold in very different wrappings. It has all kinds of bright labels. But under all the

---

* *Source*: R. Miller-Budnitskaya, 'Kosmopolity iz literaturnogo Gollivuda' (Cosmopolitans of the Literary Hollywood), *Novy mir*, 1948, no. 6, pp. 282–4, 293.

packing and all the labels the content is always the same. American 'philosophers', 'literary critics', and 'writers' trade cosmopolitanism.

American ideologists use every possible way to propagate the idea of cosmopolitanism, the theory of the 'united' peoples of Europe under the aegis of the United States of America. They are trying to weaken the West European intelligentsia morally. American reactionaries spare no expense to introduce the ideas of cosmopolitanism into the consciousness of the intellectuals of Western Europe. In every possible way the reactionaries are enrolling spokesmen for their ideas. They bribe and buy renegades who sell themselves openly and cynically to their bosses across the Atlantic. They employ wavering intellectuals who, by their petty-bourgeois social nature, are unstable. They deafen people with their propaganda, press their ideology on artists who only yesterday were progressive, but who, not being sufficiently consistent, do not understand that if you offer a reactionary one finger you lose your hand.

This is just what happened to that representative of the West European artistic intelligentsia, Leon Feuchtwanger. [...] Feuchtwanger had earlier demonstrated his merits to the forces of democracy and progress. Our attitude, then, to the backward, reactionary tendencies in his works, and above all to his cosmopolitan ideas, should be the more uncompromising.

'The subject which has been troubling me deeply for a very long time', said Feuchtwanger in his speech at the Congress, 'is the conflict between nationalism and cosmopolitanism. If I tried to express the subject in the form of a contemporary novel, I am afraid that personal feelings would cloud and spoil the picture. I have preferred to place the conflict in the soul of a man who, it seems to me, lived through it (one thousand, eight hundred and sixty years ago, it's true) as many people are living through it now – in the soul of the Jewish chronicler, Josephus Flavius.'[130]

Here is the clue to the historical novels of Feuchtwanger. In all of them the idea of a world state is proclaimed in different forms: the empire of Alexander the Great against the kingdoms of Asia; Rome against Judea; the Holy Roman Empire and 'God's State' of the Catholic Church against the national monarchy; Great Britain against its colonies; America against the European countries. [...]

The problem of cosmopolitanism is presented more sharply and forcefully in the first two parts of the unfinished trilogy about Josephus Flavius, in the novels *The Jewish War* and *The Sons*. In these books, Feuchtwanger depicts the war of Judea, the centre of the national liberation movement in the East, against Rome, the master of the ancient world. The victor is Rome, the stronghold of the militarist West, the destroyer and enslaver of the national cultures of the East, the bearer of a unified and standardised civilisation bent on subjugating all the peoples of the world and depriving them of individuality. But conquered Judea, having relinquished nationalism, promotes the cosmopolitan teaching of Christianity and with this doctrine conquers the world.

The bearer of cosmopolitanism in both novels is Josephus Flavius, the chronicler of the Jewish Wars. A descendant of the Maccabees and a priest at the Temple in Jerusalem, a prophet and general of the insurgent Galilee, he became a Roman citizen and a servant of the Flavii. He is three times a renegade, hated by both sides in the strife. But Feuchtwanger depicts him as a thinker of genius, misunderstood by his contemporaries – a representative of a new mankind where 'there is neither Hellene nor Hebrew'. Thus Feuchtwanger settles the dispute in favour of cosmopolitanism.

Feuchtwanger speaks as a passionate supporter of a world state. He proclaims the historical correctness of cosmopolitanism as a 'progressive' idea for all times and all peoples, and he justifies renegades renouncing their own land and people for this idea.

What does cosmopolitanism mean in our days? Yesterday this reactionary cosmopolitan idea of a world state meant the Hitlerite 'new order in Europe', trampling on the national sovereignty and independence of the European peoples. Today it is one of imperialism's disguises in its struggle for world mastery.

In Feuchtwanger's latest novel, *Arms for America*, the problem of national feeling and cosmopolitanism takes on a new form: America against Europe. Feuchtwanger combines the idea of a world state with preaching the mastery of the Anglo-Saxon peoples. His *Anglo-Saxon Trilogy*, already published in Germany in the twenties, can be regarded as the specific prologue to this novel.

Document 66* The 'anti-patriotic' theatre critics condemned (1949)[131]

More than once the Party has pointed out the deplorable and ruinous literary consequences of detachment from the life and struggle of the Soviet people, and the fruitful and inspiring effect of the great ideas of Soviet patriotism. Shameless cosmopolitanism is not only directed against the people; it is also unproductive. It is harmful, just like those parasites in the plant world that eat away at the shoots of useful cereals. It serves as a carrier of harmful bourgeois reactionary influences.

In its decrees on the struggle on the ideological front, the Party devoted special attention to Soviet criticism. The critic is the first propagandist of what is new, important and positive in literature and art. [...] A real Soviet critic, one who loves his work and is devoted to socialist art, cannot but be an ardent patriot; he cannot but take pride in a new production – even one not yet perfected – which boldly advances a new idea and creates a new portrait of Soviet man. [...]

Unfortunately, criticism, and particularly theatrical criticism, is the most backward sector of our literature. Not only that. Nests of bourgeois aestheticism, camouflaging an anti-patriotic, cosmopolitan, corrupt attitude toward Soviet art, have until recently maintained themselves in the field of theatrical criticism.

An anti-patriotic group has developed in theatrical criticism. It consists of followers of bourgeois aestheticism. They penetrate our press and operate most freely in the pages of the magazine, *Teatr*, and the newspaper, *Sovetskoe iskusstvo*. These critics have lost their sense of responsibility to the people. They represent a rootless cosmopolitanism which is deeply repulsive and inimical to

* *Source*: 'Ob odnoi antipatrioticheskoi gruppe teatralnykh kritikov' (On an Anti-Patriotic Group of Theatre Critics), *Pravda*, 28 January 1949.

Soviet man. They obstruct the development of Soviet literature; the feeling of national Soviet pride is alien to them.

Such critics attempt to discredit the progressive phenomena of our literature and art, selecting for furious attack – supposedly because of their artistic imperfections – precisely those works which are patriotic and politically purposeful. It is worth recalling that ideological opponents once made precisely such attacks upon the work of the great writer Maksim Gorky; and upon such valuable works as *Summer Love* by K. Trenev and other similar works.

The figure of the worker-revolutionary, Nil, in M. Gorky's play, *The Philistines*, is of enormous ideological and artistic significance. But the critic, Yu. Yuzovsky,[132] tries to convey to the reader, amid casuistical praise of the play, that Nil 'is an unperfected figure of Gorky's', that the author is speaking 'here as a publicist, not always concerning himself with the question of whether such intervention in the artistic texture of the play is justified'.

The 'artistic texture', the logic of the plot, which Nil's deeds allegedly violate in Gorky's remarkable work – this is the mask of a bourgeois aesthete, behind which he hides his anti-revolutionary, anti-patriotic being. Yuzovsky is trying here to disparage the courageous, noble image – as created by the great proletarian writer, M. Gorky – of one of the early revolutionary, Bolshevist workers. [...]

The articles of A. Gurvich[133] are camouflaged differently from those of Yu. Yuzovsky. Gurvich makes a malicious attempt to contrast Soviet dramaturgy with the classics; to defame Soviet dramaturgy, employing the authority of – Turgenev! [...]

What kind of an idea can Gurvich have of the national character of Soviet Russian man if he writes that the spectator sees his own reflection in 'the complacent humour and naively trustful optimism' of Pogodin's plays, which allegedly express 'the national character of the playwright's world outlook'. Again, says Gurvich, the spectator 'experiences the joy of recognition', for 'complacency, too, is not alien to the Russian people'. This is a slander on Soviet Russian man. A dirty slander. It is precisely because complacency is deeply alien to us that we cannot but denounce this attempt to slander the national Soviet character. [...]

The sting of aesthetic-formalist criticism is directed not against the really harmful and inferior works, but against the progressive and best ones, those depicting Soviet patriots. It is precisely this which confirms that aesthetic formalism merely serves as camouflage for anti-patriotic substance.

Critics of this sort felt particularly at home in the musty atmosphere of the Association of Theatrical Critics of the All-Russian Theatrical Society (the Chairman of the Bureau of the Association was G. Boyadzhiev[134]), and in the Dramaturgy Commission of the Writers' Union (where A. Kron[135] presided). [...] It was there that the theatrical critic, A. Borshchagovsky,[136] who overlooked works which distort Soviet reality, directed the entire fire of his anti-patriotic criticism against A. Sofronov's play, *Moscow Character*, and against the Maly Theatre, which produced this play. [...] It was there that the critic L. Malyugin[137] attacked such deeply patriotic productions as

B. Romashov's[138] *The Great Force*, and N. Virta's[139] *Our Daily Bread*, both of which merit wide recognition.

These critics find nothing better to do than to discredit the most progressive phenomena of our literature at a time when we face the most acute tasks of the struggle against the rootless cosmopolitanism and bourgeois influences that are alien to the people. This does outright harm to the development of Soviet literature and art and slows down its forward movement.

As we have seen, A. Gurvich, Yu. Yuzovsky and others engage in this 'work', if it may be so termed. Their empty, inflated 'authority' has not yet been properly exposed. All sorts of distortions, in the work of many critics, are nourished by the defective views of the critics Borshchagovsky, Gurvich, Yuzovsky, Varshavsky and Boyadzhiev, all of whom occupy anti-patriotic positions. [. . .]

The editors of the *Literaturnaya gazeta* adopted a most inappropriate position towards the contemporary repertoire and in particular towards the play, *Moscow Character*. In an editorial survey with the pretentious title 'Conversation on the Destinies of the Repertoire' (4 December 1948), *Literaturnaya gazeta* undertook to defend the defective report by A. Borshchagovsky at the conference on new plays, and joined him in his malevolent sallies against the Maly Theatre's policy of producing contemporary, patriotic plays. [. . .]

It is necessary to put an end firmly and once and for all to the liberal connivance of all these aesthetic nonentities, devoid of the healthy sentiment of love for the motherland and for the people, with nothing in their souls but malevolence and inflated conceit. The atmosphere of art must be purged of anti-patriotic philistines.

Document 67* The Ukrainian Writers' Board attacks cosmopolitans (March 1949)

The plenary meeting was characterised by its high ideological level and the extensive political activity of its participants.

Step by step the Soviet writers disclosed the anti-patriotic activities and the perfidious, double-dealing methods of the group of rootless cosmopolitans and their yes-men: Stebun (Katsnelson),[140] Adelgeim,[141] Sanov (Smulson),[142] A. Gozenpud, E. Starinkevich,[143] A. Katsnelson,[144] Ya. Gordon, and some others who were closely linked with the anti-patriotic group of rootless cosmopolitans, Yuzovsky, Altman, Borshchagovsky, Kholodov, and Boyadzhiev. [. . .]

The literary critic Shumylo[145] was the first to take the floor in the discussion on the report. He used many examples to demonstrate that the anti-patriotic group of cosmopolitan critics had aimed at disorganising the literary process. Especial harm had been done by the lampoonist and anti-patriotic Adelgeim. The young writer Nekrasov,[146] said Comrade Shumylo, wrote an excellent book, *In the Trenches of Stalingrad*. The heroes of this book, our simple, wonderful, heroic Soviet people, were described movingly, warmly and truthfully in the days of the greatest trials which our motherland has had to

* *Source*: 'Do kontsa razgromit kosmopolitov-antipatriotov!' (To Rout Utterly the Anti-Patriotic Cosmopolitans), *Pravda Ukrainy*, 6 March 1949.

sustain. Everybody knows how Nekrasov's patriotic book was received by the dull-witted, foul-mouthed cosmopolitans who do not know the holy feeling of patriotism. They tried to slander his book with defamatory rumours and 'closed' reviews. The enemies of Soviet literature – the cosmopolitans – took the same attitude to Gonchar's outstanding work, *Standard-Bearers*, and to the works of other gifted young writers.

'Here is one of the most active "figures" of the anti-patriotic group, Adelgeim', says Comrade Shumylo.

He headed the criticism commission. Is it not he who kept this commission knowingly in a state of lethargic slumber? Is it not this cosmopolitan who, a year ago, objected to the harmful scribble of Sanov being criticised? He made use of direct provocations, slander and intimidation to divert sharp criticism from himself and other cosmopolitans. Adelgeim does not love the literature of our people. He does not know and does not want to know the life of Soviet people.

From the audience: 'He is a passportless tramp.' (Laughter. Applause.)

The writer Kozachenko spoke about the cosmopolitans, Stebun, Sanov and some others, who resorted to any means to defame Soviet Ukrainian literature. 'According to Stebun's theory', says Comrade Kozachenko:

there seem to have been only three progressive writers in Ukrainian literature for many years before the Revolution. As if such writers as Panas Myrny, Ivan Tobilevych, Olga Kobylanska and Vasyl Stefanyk had never existed. But is that of any interest to the cosmopolitan! He only wanted to prove his slanderous 'theory' about the poverty of Ukrainian literature. All this monstrous slander Stebun presented in his book *Literary-Historical Essays*.

Stebun's 'theory' was developed in practice by Adelgeim, who made short work of Soviet poetry, and by Sanov, who specialised in defaming Soviet prose.

The poet Pidsukha sharply criticised the cosmopolitan scribble of Golovanivsky, who writes that he has wandered about the world a good deal. He was in Italy, in Turkey, in Germany, but the Soviet poet and citizen is not to be seen in his poetry, a poetry typical of cosmopolitanism. That is why, says Comrade Pidsukha, the question arises of where the poet lives and works, from where he sets out on his travels. (Laughter.) [...]

The critic Kobeletsky devoted his speech to demonstrating how the cosmopolitan Stebun tried, with Adelgeim's help, to smuggle his people into the State University. Comrade Kobeletsky spoke in detail about the anti-patriotic 'activities' in literature of the elder and younger Katsnelson brothers (I. Stebun, A. Isachenko). Comrade Kobeletsky speaks about the confusing dictionary of Ukrainian literature prepared by Khinkulov. As Khinkulov himself confessed in his preface, he composed his dictionary not on the basis of the Leninist–Stalinist concept of the literary-historical process, but on the principle 'of the choice of names and their selection'. (Laughter.)

The poet Voronko spoke about the attempts of the cosmopolitans to discredit and belittle the work of young Soviet writers. The more party-conscious such a writer was in his works, the more they attacked him so as not to admit him into – but to throw him out of – literature. He related how Adelgeim, and sometimes the poet Pervomaisky[147] as well, had tried to discredit books by young writers.

'The cosmopolitans sitting in this hall', says Comrade Voronko, 'think: "We know you, you are good-natured. You will make a fuss, then forget everything. We shall change our positions, our names, and everything will go on in the same way."' (Laughter in the hall.) 'No, it will not be so! Wherever the dirty hand of a cosmopolitan is raised against our motherland, such a hand will be cut off.' (Stormy applause.) [...]

The poet Malyshko says: 'The cosmopolitans, who are now unmasked, instigated enmity among the Soviet peoples by their black activities and called on them to follow Europe's lead. What do such Ukrainian poets as Taras Shevchenko, Ivan Franko, Lesya Ukrainka, who dearly loved the Ukraine, mean to them! These rootless cosmopolitans need decaying, bourgeois Europe, and they sing its praises in their scribbles.' [...]

The poet-academician Tychyna delivered a long, interesting speech warmly greeted by the audience. 'At our plenary meeting,' he said:

we are discussing a problem of great importance. We are talking about the doings of those who hinder the development of Soviet literature, about the behaviour of those who are slaves of bourgeois ideology and who try to poison the healthy, creative atmosphere of Soviet art. The newspapers *Pravda* and *Kultura i zhizn* and the Ukrainian Republic papers have justly called these anti-patriots cosmopolitans without kith and kin. How disturbing it is that, at the time when the Soviet Union, and the Ukraine in particular, has enormous achievements to its credit in industry, agriculture, literature, science and art, there are petty people to whom all those achievements mean absolutely nothing, people who have been active against the Soviet people.

Comrade Tychyna adduced a number of examples to show how the rootless cosmopolitans sought to defame the works of the playwrights Korneichuk, Sofronov and others. He strongly condemned the subversive activities of Stebun and Adelgeim, who slandered our wonderful Soviet literature; Gelfandbein[148] and Yukhvid,[149] who tried to do away with the Shevchenko Theatre in Kharkov; Burlachenko (Berdichevsky), who regularly made fun of the Ivan Franko Theatre and its leading actors. An illiterate yes-man of the cosmopolitan dregs, a certain tramp, Galperin, contemptuously called the Lesya Ukrainka Russian Theatre in Kiev 'a theatre of the armchair intelligentsia'. In general, the criticism of our theatres by the cosmopolitans, both in Kiev and in the outlying districts, has always been hostile. [...]

The critic Novichenko speaks about Golovanivsky's nationalist scribble. He shows how cosmopolitanism and nationalism are intermingled in Golovanivsky's poetry. Novichenko also mentions that Golovanivsky's vicious works were carefully protected by the cosmopolitan critics. In his articles, Stebun popularised Golovanivsky as a leading writer. Sanov and Adelgeim do the same. And Gordon even proclaimed Golovanivsky 'the son of Lermontov'. (Laughter.)

Comrade Novichenko speaks about Stebun's anti-patriotic activities. In the Institute of Literature of the Ukrainian Academy of Sciences, Stebun used to talk with Gozenpud, Borshchagovsky, Tamarchenko and other cosmopolitans. The aim of this group was to slander the works of Soviet writers and classics. [...]

The plenary meeting listened with indignation to the insincere speeches of Smulson and Adelgeim. The impudence of these rascals was so shameless that the participants of the meeting had to stop their speeches. Everybody present was especially indignant at the speech of the hardened double-dealer, intriguer and ideological instigator of the anti-patriotic group of cosmopolitans, Adelgeim. True to his dishonest nature as a slanderer, he tried to brush everything aside with empty prattle. His speech was interrupted by numerous exclamations: 'Speak of your intrigues, of the anti-patriotic activities of your group!' But Adelgeim struck a pose and uttered in a threatening tone: 'Don't shout!' After that, the whole audience demanded insistently and unanimously: 'Stop talking, cosmopolitan!' The cosmopolitan pygmy had to leave the platform because of the indignant exclamations of the audience.

Golovanivsky's speech was that of a double-dealer. In the report, and in the speeches of the participants of the meeting, many facts of his vicious activities were mentioned. They showed that he continues to be a bourgeois nationalist: in a number of verses – both those written in the past and in recent work (his poem 'Abraham' and others) – he has slandered the Soviet people. In his speech, Golovanivsky did not confess or condemn his anti-popular attitude. [...]

A member of the Writers' Union of the Ukraine, Comrade A. E. Korneichuk,[150] then took the floor. He was warmly greeted by the audience and made a long, interesting speech. [...]

Some rootless cosmopolitans, in making 'penitent' speeches here, try to pretend that it is all a matter of 'some isolated errors'. Nonsense! It's a question not of errors, but of systematic and organised anti-patriotic activities carried out by a group of cosmopolitans closely linked to one another in all their criminal actions.

Stebun, Adelgeim, Sanov (Smulson), Gozenpud, Starinkevich, Berdichevsky, Shelyubsky, and other passportless, homeless lackeys of the decaying culture of the bourgeois West did not commit any errors. They consciously belittled, defamed and slandered everything Soviet and vied with each other in praising the alien, harmful culture of capitalist Europe.

All progressive mankind admires the great achievements of our socialist mother country. Millions of friends in the farthest corners of the globe applaud our achievements in national economy, culture and science. Delegations now come to us from abroad to learn how to build a new life. Only the rootless cosmopolitans are indifferent to our achievements and to our life. Only these despicable dregs continue to cringe and crawl on their knees before all that's rotten abroad. They have no motherland; nothing is sacred to them; they defame and slander everything.

Ideological wreckers, the cosmopolitans deny national form in art. That is not incidental. This is a rehash of the contemporary propaganda of American imperialism, aimed at grasping foreign lands and mastering the world. Such are the roots of cosmopolitanism. This is the swamp inspiring the anti-patriotic riff-raff.

Does Mykola Platonovich Bazhan understand what an enormous error he committed when he attempted to defend the cosmopolitan Adelgeim? No, we cannot and shall not pardon the cosmopolitan rabble in their subversive activity. The Adelgeims, Stebuns, Sanovs, Gozenpuds, and all their band consciously wrecked our literature. They dared to lift their filthy hands against the great names of Shevchenko, Franko, Kotsyubynsky, Lesya Ukrainka – names sacred and dear to the hearts of our people. These paltry pygmies tried to embroil Soviet Ukrainian literature in a quarrel with the great Russian literature, its elder sister.

But the anti-patriots are unmasked. An end has been made to their subversive, wrecking activities. Our task now is to rid the literary front of the remnants of the hostile group of cosmopolitans and, having done away with them, to start working with redoubled energy, to gladden our people, our great motherland, our Bolshevik Party with new deserving works.

Comrade Korneichuk concluded his speech by saying that 'Under the leadership of the Bolshevik Party we shall fulfil all the tasks confronting us Soviet writers!' There was stormy applause in the hall.

Thirty-five persons in all took part in the discussion. The plenary meeting of the board of the Ukrainian Soviet Writers' Union adopted an explicit resolution on the report of Comrade Dmyterko. The plenary meeting also discussed questions of organisation. The plenary meeting released E. Adelgeim from the duties of editor-in-chief of the journal *Vitchyzna* and removed him from the Union board. Comrade A. T. Gonchar is approved editor-in-chief of the journal *Vitchyzna*. Comrade N. S. Rybak[151] is approved head of the editorial board of *Radyansky pysmennyk* and is appointed to the presidium of the Union board. The plenary meeting approved the editorial board of the newspaper, *Literaturna gazeta*: M. Z. Shamota (editor-in-chief), M. M. Shumylo (assistant editor); and members of the editorial board: Comrades P. M. Voronko, L. D. Dmyterko, A. E. Korneichuk, E. P. Mynko, V. A. Ruban.

With great patriotic enthusiasm, the plenary meeting approved a letter of greeting to the great Stalin, and also to the leader of the Ukrainian Bolsheviks, Comrade N. S. Khrushchev.

Document 68* An attack on 'cosmopolitan' writers (1951)

Soviet writers and those working in other fields of art despise the rootless cosmopolitans and are conducting an uncompromising struggle against them. The anti-patriotic cosmopolitans have shockingly distorted the Leninist–Stalinist understanding of internationalism. They were contemptuous of national cultures, of our great Russian culture above all. They considered internationalism to exclude national culture. The cosmopolitans persecuted many Soviet artists, praised to the skies the reactionary artists of the West and of America, and criticised the works of young Soviet writers from a bourgeois aesthetic point of view.

No one can be a real internationalist without being a patriot of one's own mother country. No one can love and respect other peoples without loving and respecting one's own people. Only a people which develops its own genuinely national art can appreciate to the full the art of other peoples. That is why genuine internationalism is born only on the basis of a flourishing national art, only when a people has something to share with other peoples. [...]

After the decision of the Central Committee of the All-Russian Communist Party (Bolshevik) on ideological problems, Soviet literature has achieved great successes. But it would be criminal to conceal the drawbacks of our post-war literature. It was pointed out in the Central Committee's decree on

* *Source*: 'Sovetskaya literatura na novom podyeme' (New Upsurge of Soviet Literature), *Bolshevik*, 1951, no. 14, pp. 4–5, 9.

the journal *Znamya* that a number of ideologically incorrect and artistically unsatisfactory works had been published in the journal (N. Melnikov's (Melman's)[152] story, 'Editorial Board'; E. Kazakevich's story, 'Two in the Steppe'; Yu. Yanovsky's short stories; some verses). The Party press pointed out some serious ideological errors in V. Kataev's novel, *For the Power of the Soviets*. Serious drawbacks are also to be found in the works of other Soviet writers.

Document 69* Cosmopolitanism and the 'Doctors' Plot'[153]

Cosmopolitanism is not just a hostile ideology. Cosmopolitanism is the savage struggle of the doomed classes against new social forces, against everything progressive. At present, cosmopolitanism serves not only as an ideological cover for the imperialist aggression of the USA. It is also used by the American intelligence service in its direct struggle against the Soviet Union and the People's Democracies.

It is not pure chance that cosmopolitans and hardened bourgeois nationalists are given the most foul and filthy tasks by the instigators of war, including murder, espionage, sabotage, wrecking, even the assassination of the best representatives of the Russian nation. New evidence of this is the unmasking, by the organs of State security of the USSR, of a terrorist group of doctor-poisoners, enemies of the people, whose aim was to shorten the lives of active figures of the USSR.

Most members of the group – Vovsi,[154] Kogan, Feldman, Grinshtein, Etinger and others – were linked with the international Jewish bourgeois nationalist 'Joint' organisation created by the American intelligence service allegedly to give practical help to Jews in other countries. In fact, this organisation has been and still is carrying out large-scale spying, terrorist and other subversive activities in a number of countries, the Soviet Union included. The latest heinous crime of the Zionist agents of American imperialism is the explosion of a bomb on the grounds of the Soviet mission in Tel Aviv, as a result of which three Soviet citizens were injured.

Document 70† Simonov's[155] retrospective analysis of the anti-cosmopolitan campaign (1956)

But this theory was not all.[156] At the plenary meeting[157] dishonest demagogic methods were used to give a semblance of reality to the 'hostile' attitude of some critics. The chief device consisted in re-directing every critical remark levelled at this or that personage in the plays to the whole of Soviet society. If the author of a critical article was ironical about the unsuccessful, lifeless image of a Party organiser in a play, he was directly accused of mocking the Party. If the author of an article said that the struggle against obsequiousness was treated in a primitive and poor way in a play, he was accused of being an obsequious

* *Source*: M. Belov, 'Kosmopolitizm na sluzhbe podzhigatelei voiny' (Cosmopolitanism Serves the Instigators of War), *Trud*, 18 February 1953.
† *Source*: K. Simonov, 'Literaturnye zametki' (Literary Notes), *Novy mir*, 1956, no. 12, pp. 249–51.

cosmopolitan himself. If the author of an article said that the characters of a play made high-flown didactic speeches about our people and mother country, he was accused of being unpatriotic.

Correct observations were also made at the plenary meeting on aestheticising elements in the articles of a number of critics and on the weakness of their positive programme in the field of drama. But these reasonable remarks were spoilt by the general tendency in a number of dishonest speeches made by people who wanted to shield drama from criticism, to conceal its obvious weaknesses, to protect the honour of their uniform which they misunderstood, sometimes even intentionally.

The very nature of this plenary meeting had a negative influence on the development of our drama. But the position was soon aggravated by the article, 'On an Anti-Patriotic Group of Theatre Critics', which appeared in *Pravda*[158] [...]

In general, it was its one-sidedness which produced the main negative significance of this article. Just as some writers whose works depict the real drawbacks, complications and shady sides of our life were unjustly accused of insufficient Soviet patriotism, the critics who pointed out the drawbacks, the weak points, the dubious aspects of our drama, were similarly reproached and accused of 'trying to discredit the progressive phenomena of our literature and art by fiercely attacking patriotic, politically oriented works under the pretext of their supposed artistic imperfection'.

At the same time, the absolutely obvious fact that most of the patriotic, politically oriented and *artistically valuable* works during the period under discussion were unanimously supported by our critics, was overlooked. The overwhelming number of contemporary critics approved and supported such poems as 'Vasily Terkin' and 'The House by the Roadside' by Tvardovsky; such books as *The Young Guard* by Fadeev, *In the Trenches of Stalingrad* by Nekrasov, *Greetings from the Front* by Ovechkin,[159] *The Storm* by Erenburg, the first volume of Bubennov's[160] *White Birch*, Kazakevich's *Star*, Azhaev's[161] *Far from Moscow*, Panova's *Companions*, and Gonchar's *Standard-Bearers*.

The view of literary criticism expressed in this article led literature away from criticising the dark sides of life and the weak points of literature. To crown it all – and this was an error which led to many misfortunes – the people who criticised the imperfections of our drama were called anti-patriots and accused of almost conscious, premeditated group activities, with the aim of harming Soviet literature.

The opinions and appraisals expressed in this article, the appearance of which had been initiated by I. V. Stalin himself – as was known well enough in literary circles – led to the gravest consequences for literature.

The leaders of the Writers' Union at that time, the author of the present lines included, and a number of writers and critics, could not muster the courage even to attempt to prove the article one-sided and wrong and to warn of its grave consequences for our drama. On the contrary, they swam with the current (my reports at the Moscow meeting of playwrights and at the meeting of active film workers included) and not only insisted that the article was right, but also aggravated its negative effect – they, too, passed many crudely unjust judgements on the work of our theatre critics. The article 'On an Anti-

Patriotic Group', and a number of other articles, had repercussions for a long time afterwards. Many writers and critics whose works and articles were not always right about everything, but who all the same were quite undeservedly accused of anti-patriotism, were for a long time practically deprived of the possibility of normal work in literature. Many other critics and writers were intimidated by what had happened. A great many articles of literary criticism which have appeared in recent times – until 1953 – lacked truly critical spirit and were permeated by a tendency to exaggerate the success of our literature, and to keep silent about its failings.

Finally, there is at present a general revival in literature and literary criticism which is connected with the Party decisions of recent years. The errors and weak points of our literature have been justly and severely criticised in full accordance with that spirit of implacability towards all the flaws of our life which our Party teaches us. Yet, despite all that, we have not yet appraised straightforwardly, without reservations, either the wrong course taken by the discussion on theatrical criticism at the 12th Plenary Meeting of the Board of the Writers' Union in 1948, or a number of articles published in our press after that.[162]

5

Jews on trial in the Soviet Union

As has long been demonstrated, one of the main characteristics of totalitarianism in the Soviet Union – especially during the Stalin era but partially still today – is its unrelenting employment of terror in various forms. The measures used to terrorise are many and diverse. They range from relatively mild pressure and intimidation to such severe actions as arrest, trial (closed or public), imprisonment, exile, or execution of the real or imaginary opponents of the regime or its current leadership.

Particularly prominent in the web of persecution which has been the lot of the Jewish population throughout the Soviet period have been trials involving various categories of Jews. The central question with regard to this particular repressive measure is to what extent it has been employed against Jews as Soviet citizens (all of whom are liable to official persecution), and to what extent, and when, the trials have been exploited for specific anti-Jewish purposes.

In searching for the answer to this question, we should divide the first fifty years of Soviet history into two periods, the first ending in the late thirties and the second beginning then, or, perhaps more convincingly, a decade later. As we are concerned here with the second period only, we shall merely outline the main features of the earlier period.

From 1917 to 1939, four types of trials were directed against Jews in the Soviet Union: (1) anti-Zionist – directed against members or sympathisers of the Zionist movements and those active in the field of Hebrew culture, throughout this entire period; (2) anti-religious – directed against rabbis, scholars, ritual slaughterers and synagogue officials, primarily in the twenties and late thirties; (3) anti-bourgeois – directed at those defined by the authorities as the Jewish bourgeoisie (Jews of 'bourgeois' origin, *Nepmen* and those engaged in illegal commerce), characteristic mainly of the years 1918–30; and (4) anti-'nationalist' trials – directed against functionaries of the by then defunct *Evsektsiya* and those active in the field of Yiddish culture, which took place in the second half of the thirties.

There is no doubt that, in all these cases, trial and punishment was a key element in the general Soviet policy to eradicate every category of real or imagined opposition. However, it is also clear that these trials were sometimes an expression of anti-Semitism and, what was more serious, of the desire to liquidate Jewish culture. While this was not on the initiative of the authorities during the twenties, it had their full support later on. As we shall see below, these tendencies reached unknown heights in the last years of Stalin's life; however, they continued, albeit with diminished severity and extremism, in the post-Stalinist period.

The Stalin period

Trials of Zionists and Jewish nationalists

The dimension of the wave of arrests, trials and mass exiles which followed the Soviet annexation of Polish, Romanian and Baltic State territories in 1939–40 are difficult to estimate. The appropriated areas contained large Jewish populations with an extensive network of Zionist, socialist, civil and religious movements and parties. Arrests in these areas were directed principally against those who were active in or sympathised with the Zionist movement and the Bund. The wave of terror crested just when a relaxation in this war to the death might have been expected – right after the outbreak of war between the Soviet Union and Germany. Thus, at the beginning of December 1941, Polish Bund leaders Henryk Erlich and Victor Alter were imprisoned. They were tried in secret, and were executed on 9 December 1941.[1]

There was another wave of arrests and trials directed mainly against Zionist activists and also against all those who endeavoured to leave the Soviet Union by illegal means, after the war ended, in 1945–6.[2] These new arrests took place against the background of a difficult and cruel battle then being waged against nationalist movements in the European republics of the Soviet Union. But the Zionists in the USSR – in contrast to national movements in the Ukraine or Lithuania which had organised themselves for armed conflict against the Soviet regime – sought to avoid head-on conflicts with the regime. Since this was known to the internal security forces which kept those suspected of Zionism under constant surveillance, the subsequent arrests of Jews must therefore be viewed as a continuation of the traditional anti-Zionist policy and an effort to prevent any activity which might indicate support for Zionism.[3]

The period from mid-1947 until October 1948 was undoubtedly the best one in the entire history of the Soviet Union for all those who felt close to the Zionist idea. The persecution of Zionists was relaxed, although it should not be inferred that the arrests and other police operations against Jews ceased altogether.

This short period of hope was brought to an abrupt end in October–November 1948,[4] when Soviet policy on the Zionist question shifted once again. Although the shift had begun earlier, it became clearly visible in November 1948, and the new repressions against all those who showed affinity for the State of Israel – who dared express publicly their joy in its establishment or their desire to aid the new state – lasted until Stalin's death in 1953.[5] Those who had any contact with Israeli diplomats were subject to particularly draconian sentences.[6] Most of the Jews imprisoned on the charge of Zionism were sentenced secretly, before the Special Boards (*Osoboe Soveshchanie*), to lengthy prison terms.[7] The authorities also took a variety of administrative actions such as dismissal from place of employment, expulsion from place of residence and internal exile, against those charged with Zionism.[8] There were also reports, though it is difficult to judge their authenticity, of arrests among Jewish officers who had served the Soviet Union in various military and civilian duties in Eastern Germany. They were now charged with expressing pro-Zionist views.[9]

Trials of Yiddish-language writers and artists

There is a parallel between the trials which took place in the thirties and those of the late forties and early fifties. If the later trials of Zionists largely resembled the anti-Zionist trials of the twenties and thirties – with the important distinction that now they also involved young Soviet Jews who had been raised under the Communist system – so, too, did the contemporary trials of the writers, artists and Yiddish culture functionaries resemble those of the writers and *Evsektsiya* functionaries who were liquidated in the second half of the thirties.[10] There was, however, one difference of the utmost significance. While the liquidation of writers and *Evsektsiya* officials might be viewed as an internal part of the purge campaign which felled many Communist leaders of other nationalities, the new attack was primarily directed at the physical liquidation of Jewish national culture.

We still lack documentary proof that the decision to liquidate Jewish culture was taken immediately after World War II, or perhaps at the outset of the campaign against Jewish nationalism, but there is no doubt that the campaign prepared the ground for the subsequent liquidation. The first sign that there was indeed a clear and ominous anti-Jewish tendency in the Soviet leadership came in January 1948, with the murder of Solomon Mikhoels, Chairman of the Jewish Anti-Fascist Committee, Director of the Jewish Theatre in Moscow and one of the most prominent figures of Soviet Jewry.

From the events of the second half of 1948, it would seem that the high-level decision to begin the implementation of a programme to liquidate Jewish (Yiddish) culture was taken in October–November of that year.[11] The arrests were made in two main waves. The most prominent representatives of Jewish literature and art in the Soviet Union were arrested[12] in the first wave, which seems to have begun at the very end of November[13] and to have continued until March 1949. The second wave, far smaller in scope and complementing the first, was carried out in the first half of 1950.[14] Between 1949 and 1953, relatives of writers and artists already tried and sentenced were arrested and exiled to Siberia and other remote places.[15] It is still difficult to compile a complete and authoritative register of all those who were arrested in this period. According to the list drawn up by the Congress for Jewish Culture in New York after the 20th Congress of the Soviet Communist Party, the 450 persons liquidated in the late 1930s and between 1948–53 included 238 writers, 106 actors, 19 musicians and 87 painters and sculptors.[16]

Referring to early 1949, another authority[17] has stated that 'within a few days 431 Jewish intellectuals were arrested and put in chains – 217 writers and poets, 108 actors, 87 artists and 19 musicians'. But these figures seem doubtful, for while Cang was writing of the forties, his list included a large number of writers and artists who had been arrested and liquidated in the thirties as well as others who died during the war period or who escaped arrest altogether.[18] What can be established with certainty is that the arrests were carried out on a mass scale and that they included most Yiddish writers as well as some journalists, actors and artists connected with Jewish culture.

The overwhelming majority of those arrested were sentenced to ten years in forced labour camps, mainly on charges of bourgeois nationalism, slandering the Soviet Union by spreading reports that anti-Semitism existed in the country and espionage on behalf of Western powers. A small number – including the most important writers and literary critics, the Director of the Yiddish Theatre in Moscow, the former Deputy Foreign Minister and distinguished scientists, all of whom were leaders of the Jewish Anti-Fascist Committee – were interrogated over a lengthy period, presumably in preparation for a large show trial.[19]

If this assumption is indeed correct, one must then ask why it was decided to replace the planned show trial with one of the most secret trials ever held in the Soviet Union. The answer, in part, lies in Stalin's caution – despite his hostility to the Jewish people – in employing anti-Semitism for political ends. He no doubt still feared the effect which a large show trial involving the leaders of Soviet Jewry might have on foreign policy. Beyond this – as we know from Khrushchev's remarks at the 20th Congress and other sources – Stalin's central aim for the period 1951–3 was to conduct a sweeping purge among the Soviet leadership. A full-scale show trial planned as the central act in such a drama required more satanic figures than the Yiddish writers, and it was to produce these that steps were taken from November 1952 to prepare the Doctors' Trial. The authorities might also have feared that the writers would not play their parts properly during the trial.

There is no doubt that the leaders of Jewish culture in the Soviet Union were tried from 11 to 18 July 1952.[20] What is still not unequivocally certain is who the defendants were and under precisely what articles of indictment they were tried. From what has been published in the West since 1956, we know that there were between twenty-four and twenty-six defendants,[21] among them the writers Perets Markish, Itsik Fefer, Leyb Kvitko, David Bergelson, David Hofshteyn and Shmuel Persov; the Director of the Jewish Theatre in Moscow, Binyamin Zuskin; the literary critic Yitskhak Nusinov; the former Deputy Foreign Minister and Chairman of the *Sovinformuro* Solomon Lozovsky; the scientist and member of the Academy of Sciences Lina Shtern; and the Director of Botkin Hospital Boris Shimelovich. The identity of the remaining thirteen or fifteen defendants has not yet been clarified.[22]

The main articles of indictment in this trial, which was held before the Military Collegium of the Supreme Court of the Soviet Union, were:

(a)   Armed insurrection with the aim of severing the Crimea from the Soviet Union and establishing there a Jewish bourgeois and Zionist republic to serve as a base for American imperialism (Article 58/11 of the Criminal Code of the RSFSR, carrying a maximum penalty of death).[23] This plan, which had been put forward by the Americans in 1943, during S. Mikhoels's and I. Fefer's visit to the United States, was to have been implemented with the aid of the Joint Distribution Committee, the Bund and Zionist organisations.

(b)   Espionage on behalf of foreign states (Article 58/vi of the Criminal Code, carrying a maximum penalty of death).

(c)   Bourgeois nationalist activity and anti-Soviet propaganda (Article 58/x of the Criminal Code, for which, in accordance with Article 58/ii, the maximum penalty in special conditions was death).

(d)   Organisation and activity forbidden by law (Article 58/xi of the Criminal Code).

After a week of deliberations, a verdict was handed down condemning twenty-three of the defendants to death; only Lina Shtern received twenty-five years' imprisonment.[24]

These same charges were to reappear in different forms in the great show trial in Czechoslovakia as well as in the preparatory stages of the Doctors' Trial. But, first, we must examine the economic trials of Jews in this period.

Economic trials of Jews

It can be established that the phenomenon of economic trials in the USSR dates from the very inception of the Soviet regime. However, the types of economic crime for which people were indicted, how they were fought and the harshness of punishment have varied in different periods. Thus, it is natural that the Jews of the Soviet Union, like citizens of other nationalities, would sometimes be involved in crimes of this type in numbers proportionately lower than their statistical weight in the population, and at other times in proportionately higher numbers. Economic, social, geographic and perhaps even psychological factors work to create these variations.

However, in a system characterised by the politicisation of every sphere of life, by highly elitist and centralised control and by the regime's almost untrammelled power to exploit any situation or phenomenon for its own aims, trials for economic crimes have assumed a totally new dimension. For, when the Soviet authorities have so desired, they have been transformed from what we have called 'ordinary' trials into political trials in the full sense of the term.

From the relatively few reports of such trials which appeared in the Soviet press during 1948–51,[25] and from the many more articles from the second half of 1952 and early 1953,[26] it is clear that many Jews were accused of the economic crimes of theft or sabotage of state property, speculation, giving and taking bribes, evasion of work and other fraudulent practices. Moreover, in those trials mentioned in the press, the number of Jews exceeded that of non-Jews. And while the 'map' of economic crime covered all the Soviet republics, a particularly high percentage of Jews were tried for such crimes in the Ukrainian Republic.

The Ukrainian Republic was also the scene of the most serious economic trial, which took place in November 1952.[27] This trial was unusual in that the defendants had not been tried by the regular People's or District Court, but by a military court,[28] as in the secret trial of the Jewish writers, which had been conducted by the Military Collegium of the Supreme Court of the Soviet Union, the highest military court. Moreover, the indictment was in accordance with Articles 54/viii and 54/ix of the Ukrainian Criminal Code, which referred to 'activity of counter-revolutionary sabotage' in the sphere of commerce and supply, carrying a maximum penalty of death. The execution of three of the five defendants in this trial was intended to serve as a severe warning for the future. And, finally, the fact that all three of those executed were Jews was also of special significance.

However, the clear tendency to exploit economic trials for political ends, by emphasising the Jewish nationality of the defendants, only emerged after the announcement of the 'Doctors' Plot' on 13 January 1953. The press began the campaign by noting the Zionist, Bundist or bourgeois-nationalist past of the accused and implicating them for having aided American and British spies to penetrate Soviet factories. The many *feuilletons* published in the Soviet press then took up and elaborated on these themes.[29] Most of the Jews involved were factory and shop managers, warehousemen, doctors and lawyers, the latter two categories being attacked with particular ferocity and their 'criminal' acts painted in especially sombre colours.

The 'Doctors' Plot'

On 27 November 1952, the curtain fell on the Czech Communist leaders, most of them of Jewish origin, who had built the terrible totalitarian regime in their country with their own hands and now fell victim to it. Eight of the eleven 'apprentices of the Zionist movement', as the prosecutor Urvalek called them, were condemned to death; the remaining three received life imprisonment.[30]

Although the Slansky trial as such had reached its conclusion in Czechoslovakia, a new stage in the ever-widening campaign was to come a- few months later in the Soviet Union when the 'Doctors' Plot' was announced. The transition from the one case to the next was prepared for by the press and the other media in the USSR, which devoted much space to the Prague trial and to denouncing the defendants.[31]

There are many links between the Slansky trial and what was to have been the Soviet Union's first great show trial since the 1930s. In fact, the Soviet security forces exploited the Prague case to test the reactions of Western circles and to examine the possible political advantages of such trials in the conditions extant in the early 1950s. One point in common was that the Soviet advisers, who had prepared the Slansky trial, were very senior employees of the State Security Service as well as associates of Ryumin, who was responsible for preparing the Doctors' Trial. Another link may be found in the savage campaign against the 'Doctor-Poisoners', where the mass media relied on 'proofs' drawn from trials held in Eastern Europe, particularly the Rajk case (Hungary, 1949) and the Slanksy affair. Moreover, there is evidence that testimony and witnesses connected with the Slansky trial were to be used in the projected show trial.[32] It is also significant that the Slansky trial was tinged with the theme of political murder at the hand of doctors, the charge which was at the centre of the 'Doctors' Plot'. And, finally, some of the Soviet doctors charged were already in prison when the Slansky trial opened.

Thus, the Prague trial must be seen as an integral part of the mounting Soviet campaign against cosmopolitanism, bourgeois nationalism and Zionism, with its accompanying terror recalling the purges of the thirties.[33] Frol Kozlov's call for vigilance (Doc. 77), published in *Kommunist* at the beginning of 1953, provided one of the signs that an extensive campaign of denunciation was about to be launched. And the fact that this article concentrated its attack on the former Bundist and Trotskyite Gurvich indicated that the campaign would have an anti-Jewish emphasis. But it was the *Tass communiqué* of 13 January 1953 (Doc. 78) – which 'revealed' that two prominent leaders of the Communist Party, Shcherbakov and Zhdanov, had been murdered; that a plot had been uncovered to assassinate Red Army commanders; and that six of the nine doctors who had just been arrested were Jews who had worked in the service of the Joint Distribution Committee – that provided the clearest indication of Stalin's plans in this direction (see, too, Doc. 89).

Stalin's central aim had already been presaged at the 19th Party Congress in October 1952, when the Politburo was reconstructed and enlarged to include twenty-five members. It was to conduct extensive purges in the Party and the state apparatus, the chief victims apparently to be the veteran leaders Beria, Molotov, Mikoyan and Voroshilov.[34] But why did these new purges not follow the pattern of the 'Leningrad Case', in which such ranking Communist leaders as Voznesensky, Kuznetsov and Rodionov had been liquidated and thousands of their assistants imprisoned in absolute secrecy? And, more important for us: why was it necessary to place the Jewish doctors at the centre of the plot, presenting them as nationalists and Zionists in the employ of American imperialism?

The answer to these questions lies in the difficulties inherent in conducting large-scale purges of world-renowned Soviet leaders by means of secret trials alone. Although this was not an impossible task for a regime of terror such as Stalin led in 1953, he apparently decided that a series of show trials in the style of the three major trials of the thirties and those of Eastern Europe in 1949–52 would pave the way for the great purge. Moreover, despite the disadvantages inherent in public trials,[35] they had significant political and psychological advantages as well. This was especially true in view of the authorities' interest in impressing the public with the extreme danger being presented by the enemy, who was ready to use any means to destroy the homeland. If, as is often argued, one of the main reasons for the 1930s show trials was the threat of imminent war, then, so it seemed to Stalin, a similar situation existed in the early fifties. Finally, there is no doubt that Stalin's decision to use the Jews was affected by his pathological suspicion and vindictiveness, which were exploited in the internal intrigues of the ruling group.[36]

His selection of the doctors as the link between the forthcoming trials was in no way accidental. For there is little doubt that doctors had indeed acted on the orders of the security services (that is, of Stalin himself) to cut short the lives of prominent Communist leaders such as Frunze and Kuibyshev.[37] Also, the charge that various political leaders and public personages (for example, the Russian writer Maksim Gorky and his son Peshkov) had fallen victim to medical murder had already been used in the 1938 trial[38] and again in the Slansky trial.[39] Even more important, these accusations had generally been accepted at face value among wide circles in the West, principally Communist and pro-Communist,[40] as well as in the Soviet Union. In this respect, Ilya Erenburg has noted that the suspicion of doctors crept into the consciousness of even quite educated persons.[41] Therefore, for precisely these reasons, the treason of the doctors in the 1930s could be linked with the supposed treason of the 1950s, especially as doctors Vinogradov, Vovsi and Kogan had also been involved as prosecution witnesses in the 'Doctors' Affair' of the thirties.[42] Finally, Stalin may have hoped to reap an additional benefit in that a group of persons who had accumulated too much secret knowledge during long years of work in the Kremlin would be incidentally liquidated.

Placing Jewish doctors at the centre of the 'plot' and the intended trial solved the problem of finding a homogeneous group around which the web of accusations – sabotage, espionage and moral corruption – could be easily woven. Since various groups of Trotskyites had already been eliminated in the thirties and the charge of Titoism was a heresy reserved for the satellite states, the Jewish doctors (to whom several non-Jewish doctors were added as camouflage) seemed eminently suited to be the scapegoats. However, the issue that seems to have clinched the choice was Stalin's apparent decision to prepare the ground for the exile, in whole or in part, of the Jewish population to an outlying region of the Soviet Union.

The propaganda campaign, which was unleashed with the 13 January announcement of the 'Doctors' Plot', grew to nightmarish proportions with the daily appearance of articles, *feuilletons* and caricatures virulently denouncing the 'Doctor-Poisoners' and their Zionist–American overseers.[43] The authorities then began to apply behind-the-scenes pressure to 'persuade' Soviet writers and scientists of Jewish origin to join in the campaign.[44] The resultant panic, in all strata of the public, was widely described in later Soviet literature.[45] But none of the descriptions of the campaign of terror against the 'Doctor-Poisoners' surpasses that of Vasily Grossman, in his book *Forever Flowing*:

It seems a dark cloud hung over Moscow, creeping into homes and schools and worming its way into human hearts ... [Doctors said] that it had become nearly impossible to carry on work in the hospitals and polyclinics. The terrifying official announcement had made patients suspicious. Many refused to be treated by Jewish doctors ... Tales were being told on streetcars, at markets, and at work – claiming that several Moscow pharmacies had been shut down because the druggists – Jews and American agents – had sold pills consisting of dried lice. Tales were told about babies and their mothers being infected with syphilis in maternity homes ... And the rumours were widely believed – not just by half-literate and half-drunk janitors, truck drivers, and stevedores, but by certain scientists, writers, engineers, and university students too.[46]

Only Stalin's death and the *communiqué* of the Ministry of the Interior on 4 April 1953 announcing the innocence of the imprisoned doctors (Doc. 79)[47] put an end to the period of dread under which the Jews of the Soviet Union had been living during the last years of Stalin's life. But it should be noted that this important announcement almost completely ignored the grave accusations which had been made against the doctors, Zionism, the Joint and other Jewish organisations. For example, a *Pravda* lead article of 6 April 1953[48] did indeed rehabilitate S. Mikhoels, but he was now merely described as a 'People's Actor of the Soviet Union', and no mention was made of the previous allegation that he was the 'contact man between the Joint in the United States and the gang of Doctor-Poisoners'. The article contented itself with the general assertion that the Doctors' Affair had fanned 'feelings of national antagonism', and this was to be characteristic of the entire period following Stalin's death.

Khrushchev's secret speech at the 20th Party Congress in 1956 (Doc. 81), in which he made a violent attack on Stalin and the security services over the Doctors' Affair, also passed over the anti-Jewish dimension in total silence. In fact, the Doctors' Affair was seldom mentioned in official publications after 1956.[49] However, an entire generation of the Soviet Jewish intelligentsia was traumatised by the 'Affair', which seems to have played a significant role in the Jewish national revival which came later.

The post-Stalin period

One of the first steps taken by the new leadership established immediately upon Stalin's death was the publication, on 27 March 1953, of the Amnesty Decree.[50] However, it applied mainly to those who had received up to five years' imprisonment; those who had been sentenced to more than five years were to have their punishment halved. This meant that the prisoners who had been sentenced to ten or fifteen years on the charge of counter-revolutionary activity did not benefit fully from the Decree. It is impossible to determine the number of Jews released from prison and forced labour camps in the wake of the amnesty; however, since some of them had been imprisoned in 1945–7 and others in 1948–9, one may assume that it was a large number because they would have served more than half of their prison terms by 1953. And those who were imprisoned in 1948–50 did not begin to be rehabilitated until 1955.

In contrast to the Stalin period, when political trials against 'nationalists' and religious and cultural leaders constituted the central phenomenon, economic trials predominated in the post-Stalin period.

The distinction between economic and political trials is not clear cut, for economic trials often had a clear political orientation, and political trials often contained articles of indictment unquestionably belonging to the economic sphere. However, despite the difficulties involved in such categorisation, it appears necessary from the point of view of both content and methodology.

Economic trials

The economic and political structure of the Soviet regime demands the strict maintenance of an unrelenting war against economic crime; however, as has already been noted, this war assumed different forms in different periods. The changes which occurred after Stalin's death affected the struggle against economic crime in that the trials against such crimes were largely stripped of the political dimension which they had in the previous period. There was also a sharp decline in the amount of publicity now given to such trials. And, of major interest for our purposes, the trials were no longer exploited for the purpose of anti-Jewish propaganda on as massive a scale as they had been.

Thus, in the three years following Stalin's death, economic trials were generally given less coverage than before in the Soviet press and, although reports stressing the defendants' Jewishness did not disappear completely,[51] the anti-Jewish orientation of these reports was reduced. But when the struggle against the Jewish religion was reactivated in 1958, the anti-Jewish content of the publicity given these trials in the Soviet press also increased. There is no doubt that the liberal legislative tendencies which found salient expression in the judicial principles of 25 December 1958 and in the criminal codes passed by the republics in the years 1959–61[52] tended to reduce the severity of punishment, but this did not mean any lessening in the degree to which the trials were exploited to stress the Jewish origin of the defendants.

The years 1961–2 saw a reversal in Soviet policy from relative liberalisation to the imposition of more severe criminal and administrative penalties. In May–June 1961 the three large European republics ratified the Anti-Parasite Law which had previously been passed in the other republics,[53] and the Presidium of the Supreme Soviet passed a series of decrees which drastically raised the penalties for economic crimes. Then, on 25 March 1961, the Supreme Soviet passed a decree stiffening the penalties for illegal commerce in foreign currency by a known criminal and for cases involving particularly large sums.[54] But it was only on 5 May of the same year that a decree was passed fixing the death penalty for economic crimes such as the large-scale theft of state and public property and the forgery and manufacture of banknotes and securities. The instances in which the death penalty could be imposed for economic crimes were further extended by the decrees of 24 May 1961, 1 July 1961 and 20 February 1962. Now those accused of large-scale dealing in foreign currency, the submission of false economic reports and bribe-taking were also liable to the death penalty.[55]

The adoption of these decrees by the Supreme Soviet, followed by the relevant amendments in the criminal codes of the republics, had one important economic aim: to reduce the corruption, private commerce and thefts of state property which had apparently reached intolerable levels in this period. And, since the Soviet leadership was not prepared to alter fundamentally the economic structure, it was compelled to take the Draconian measures which resulted in a wave of economic trials that covered the entire Soviet Union. As statistics on crime have been classified since the 1930s, we have no official data concerning the number of trials, the types of crime or the number of defendants involved. But press reports of the period – which were extensive due to the Soviet leadership's decision to accompany the trials with a wide propaganda campaign aimed at deterring potential offenders – allow us to make partial estimates.[56]

A glance at Table 8 shows that the number of trials involving Jewish defendants grew from 38 in 1961, when the new decrees on economic crime were promulgated, to 112 in 1962 and reached a peak of 145 trials in 1963. There was a slight decline to 109 trials in 1964, and a major downward shift to 36 in 1965, when the new leadership which followed Khrushchev's ouster changed policy regarding exploitation of the trials for propaganda purposes. However, while the new policy was a factor in shrinking the number of Jews charged with economic crimes, there is little doubt that the situation was also ameliorated by the decision of the collective leadership to reduce attacks against the Jewish religion and Zionism.

The precise number of Jews brought to trial cannot be determined because, although dozens of persons were tried together, the press often neglected to

Table 8. *Number of economic trials involving Jewish defendants reported in the press, 1960–7*

Republic	1960 Total	1961 Total no. of trials	1961 No. of trials with death sentences	1962 Total no. of trials	1962 No. of trials with death sentences	1963 Total no. of trials	1963 No. of trials with death sentences	1964 Total no. of trials	1964 No. of trials with death sentences	1965 total	1966 total	1967 total	Total no. of trials	No. of trials with death sentences
1. Russian	13	15	3	37	6	53	1	47	2	21	15	4	205	12
2. Ukrainian	3	4	—	21	7	38	8	24	1	3	5	4	102	16
3. Belorussian	1	3	—	5	2	7	1	6	—	5	4	3	34	3
4. Moldavian	1	5	—	13	1	9	2	9	—	1	1	2	41	3
5. Lithuanian	1	1	—	4	2	3	—	2	—	1	1	—	13	2
6. Latvian	—	4	—	4	—	5	1	2	—	—	—	—	15	1
7. Estonian	—	1	—	3	1	—	—	—	—	—	—	—	4	1
8. Georgian	1	1	1	3	1	1	—	2	—	—	—	—	8	2
9. Azerbaidzhan	1	—	—	2	—	4	1	3	—	—	—	1	11	1
10. Armenian	1	—	—	—	—	—	—	—	—	—	—	1	2	—
11. Kazakh	—	1	—	7	1	4	1	2	—	2	2	3	21	2
12. Kirgiz	—	—	—	3	1	2	1	1	—	1	—	1	8	1
13. Tadzhik	—	—	—	—	—	2	—	3	1	—	—	—	5	2
14. Uzbek	—	2	—	6	—	15	3	6	—	2	3	—	34	3
15. Turkmen	—	—	—	1	—	—	—	1	—	—	—	—	2	—
Republic unknown	—	1	—	3	—	2	—	1	—	—	—	—	7	—
TOTAL USSR	22	38	4	112	22	145	19	109	4	36	31	19	512	49

Source: The collection of documents from the Soviet press of the years 1960–7, entitled *Evrei i evreisky narod* (Jews and the Jewish People). The collection does not include all the Soviet newspapers; it is especially deficient in local papers, where there is greater reportage of trials held in the newspaper's locale. However, there is no doubt that the collection covers a high proportion of reports on the economic trials in the Soviet Union in the period under discussion.

list the names of the defendants. However, where names were given in the press, the percentage of Jews mentioned was far higher than that of non-Jews.[57] A breakdown of the trials held in 1960–7 by republic shows that, according to reports in the Soviet Press, approximately 40% of the trials involving Jews took place in the Russian Republic, where 39% of the Soviet Union's Jews lived during that period. A similar ratio was calculated for the Belorussian Republic. As opposed to this, the percentage of such trials in Moldavia, Kazakhstan, Kirgizia and Lithuania was far higher than that of the local Jewish population.

The principal articles of indictment in the 512 trials involving Jews were: self-manufacture of goods using materials stolen or illegally purchased and their sale on the black market or through State Marketing Offices; theft of state property for purposes of self-manufacture or sale;[58] commerce in gold, precious stones and foreign currency (an offence usually exacerbated by involvement with foreign tourists); bribing officials (accountants, warehousemen, departmental directors, factory managers); and falsification of documents or submission of false reports, whether for direct personal gain or to aid a factory or institution in claiming to have fulfilled its production quota.[59]

The high percentage of Jewish accountants, warehousemen and intermediaries – which was largely the result of official policy towards the Jews – may account for the high proportion of Jewish defendants. But this fact alone cannot explain why the press and the other media laid so great a stress on the Jewishness of the accused.

Since economic trials in which the death penalty was imposed received the greatest publicity, we can examine those trials in greater detail. And the data in Tables 9 and 10 reveal that the percentage of Jews sentenced to death was very high indeed. For example, to use the most complete data (and it is impossible to obtain full consistency here), of the 84 people sentenced to death for economic crimes in 1962, 45, or 54%, were Jews, while only 1.08% of the 1959 population was listed as Jewish (Table 10). In the Kirgiz Republic, where Jews constitute only 0.4% of the entire population, the percentage of Jews sentenced to death in that year was 44%, while it was over 55% in all the republics with a significant Jewish population. In the Moldavian and Georgian republics it reached the peak of 100%. Table 9 reveals that 91 of the 117 persons sentenced to death (i.e. 78%) in trials involving Jews during 1961–4 were Jews.

Again, the explanation that so high a percentage of Jews was sentenced to death because Jews headed the groups engaged in theft, speculation and the receiving of bribes may be correct. But it does not satisfactorily explain why the Soviet authorities gave so much publicity to those trials involving Jews. This is especially perplexing in view of the official claim that Jews accounted for the lowest percentage of crime in the Soviet Union both in absolute numbers and relative to other nationalities.[60] The only reasonable conclusion seems to be that there was a two-stage sorting system for defendants about to be tried for economic crimes. First, those to appear at a particular trial were hand-picked from what was often a very large group of potential defendants. The procuracy could thus prepare a list of charges which ensured in advance who would be most liable to the supreme penalty. The stage was thereby set

Table 9. *Persons sentenced to death in economic trials involving Jews, 1961–4*

Republic	1961 Jews	1961 Non-Jews	1962 Jews	1962 Non-Jews	1963 Jews	1963 Non-Jews	1964 Jews	1964 Non-Jews	Total Jews	Total Non-Jews	Total	Percentage of Jews
1. Russian	5	1	10	—	2	—	5	2	22	3	25	88
2. Ukrainian	—	—	17	—	20	5	2	—	39	5	44	89
3. Belorussian	—	—	4	2	1	—	—	—	5	2	7	71
4. Moldavian	—	—	4	—	2	—	—	—	6	—	6	100
5. Lithuanian	—	—	5	1	—	—	—	—	5	1	6	83
6. Latvian	—	—	—	—	1	1	—	—	1	1	2	50
7. Estonian	—	—	—	1	—	—	—	—	—	1	1	0
8. Georgian	1	—	1	—	—	—	—	—	2	—	2	100
9. Azerbaidzhan	—	—	—	—	1	3	—	—	1	3	4	25
10. Armenian	—	—	—	1	1	—	—	—	1	1	2	50
11. Kazakh	—	—	—	—	—	—	—	—	—	—	—	—
12. Kirgiz	—	—	4	5	—	1	—	1	4	7	11	36
13. Tadzhik	—	—	—	—	—	—	—	—	—	—	—	—
14. Uzbek	—	—	—	—	5	2	—	—	5	2	7	71
15. Turkmen	—	—	—	—	—	—	—	—	—	—	—	—
TOTAL	6	1	45	10	33	12	7	3	91	26	117	78

Source: as for Table 8.

Table 10. *Economic trials resulting in imposition of death sentences in 1962*

Republic	No. of trials	No. of death sentences imposed	No. of Jews among those sentenced to death	Percentage of Jews	Percentage of Jews in USSR, according to 1959 census
1. Russian	10	17	10	58	0.7
2. Ukrainian	10	21	17	81	2.0
3. Belorussian	2	6	4	66	1.9
4. Moldavian	2	4	4	100	3.3
5. Lithuanian	2	7	5	71	0.9
6. Latvian	—	—	—	—	—
7. Estonian	1	1	0	0	0.5
8. Georgian	1	1	1	100	1.3
9. Azerbaidzhan	5	9	0	0	1.1
10. Armenian	1	2	0	0	0.1
11. Kazakh	3	3	0	0	0.3
12. Kirgiz	1	9	4	44	0.4
13. Tadzhik	—	—	—	—	—
14. Uzbek	2	3	0	0	1.2
15. Turkmen	1	1	0	0	0.3
TOTAL USSR	41	84	45	54	1.08

Source: Based on the source for Table 8 for the trials involving Jews, and on *Jews in Eastern Europe*, 1963, vol. 2, no. 2, pp. 84–92, for the trials in which Jews were not involved. This table (like Tables 8 and 9) is drawn up from names appearing in the Soviet press. Inconsistencies are to be explained by the fact that the tables are based on a somewhat different range of Soviet newspapers, and also by the problem of identifying nationality by the use of names.

for the press and the other media. And here there can be no doubt that in the years 1961–4 the trials that involved a number of Jews were given the greatest prominence.

Thus, trials such as the Frunze trial, which dragged on for several months in 1962, became something like show trials. That trial, conducted by the Supreme Court of the Soviet Union and not by the Supreme Court of the Kirgiz Republic, as was customary in such cases, was given almost daily publicity in local and central press reports which contained additional commentaries emphasising the Jewish defendants. Among other things, this took the form of stressing Jewish names and, where the surname did not sound Jewish, publishing both the first name and patronymic.[61] These reports, as well as prosecution statements, emphasised the defendants' connections with relatives, tourists and banks in the West, allegations intended to imply the alienation and disloyalty of the Jewish defendants. In a significant portion of the economic trials (see, for example, Doc. 85) the reports implicated either the Jewish religion (most of the dark dealings were conducted in synagogue with the knowledge of the rabbi and other synagogue officials) or Zionism (Israeli tourists or the personnel of the Israeli Embassy were involved). Finally, the press reports frequently used crude stereotypes to describe the defendants, picturing the Jews as money-grubbers who hold nothing sacred and are prepared to betray even relatives and friends to gratify their greed.

Despite official Soviet denials there can be no serious doubt today that the policy of 1961–4 and, following a two-year interval, that of 1967 was indeed characterised by an anti-Jewish bias. Even Khrushchev's attempts to whitewash the situation, in his letter to Bertrand Russell (Doc. 26), do little to eradicate the evidence to the contrary, which was only highlighted by the important and essential change which characterised the publicity given to the economic trials in the years 1965–6.

One is therefore forced to the conclusion that, aware of the existence of widespread popular anti-Semitism in 1961, the authorities decided to exploit it for their own ends. The bitter war which they then launched against economic crime found the Jew – not for the first time and, apparently, not for the last – playing the role of the ideal scapegoat.

Anti-Zionist political trials

While the post-Stalin period did not witness a repetition of secret trials such as that of the Yiddish writers in 1952 or of great show trials like the Doctors' Trial planned for 1953, the ready resort to accusations of espionage and international conspiracy did recur frequently and ominously in that period.

In 1956, trials of Zionists and of Jewish religious figures (such as heads of religious congregations, synagogue officials, circumcisers and cantors) began to be held in various parts of the Soviet Union.[62] But only in isolated instances were they reported in the Soviet press, and then in only the most modest manner. The most important trial, which was briefly reported in a local journal (Docs. 86–7), was that of Pechersky, Dynkin and Kaganov, leading members of the Leningrad religious community. The defendants were accused of maintaining contact with the embassy of a capitalist state. The report did not actually specify that it was the State of Israel. It was only seven years later in 1968 – that is, after the Six-Day War when diplomatic relations between Israel and the Soviet Union were severed – that this old trial was dredged up again and it was explicitly stated that Pechersky, Kaganov and Dynkin had agreed to work on behalf of the Israeli security services and to distribute anti-Soviet literature in the Soviet Union. The indictment of the defendants in accordance with Articles 64 and 70 of the Criminal Code of the RSFSR and the harsh sentences (ranging from four to twelve years' imprisonment) were intended to deter future contacts with Israeli Embassy personnel.

It seems that there were many such trials in the fifties and sixties, but authoritative data on their extent and the number of people involved are not yet available.[63]

One trial, with extremely serious charges, which did receive publicity was held in February 1967.[64] The defendant, Dolnik, who had a Zionist past and was a regular synagogue attender, was accused of transmitting to David Gavish of the Israeli Embassy classified information of value not only to Israel but also to the security services of other countries. Dolnik was further charged with working with an accomplice to prepare false photographs in which the Nazi swastika was seen drawn on monuments in the USSR, in order to defame the Soviet Union abroad.

Documents to Chapter 5

The writers' trial

Document 71* Erenburg denies Soviet persecution of Jews[65]

Dorfson reports further that when the correspondents began to raise questions about Jewish issues – something Erenburg never in his life expected – the Soviet writer went to pieces. Asked about Perets Markish, Erenburg stammered and stuttered incoherently. Finding his tongue at last, he disclaimed knowledge of Markish or any of the other Jewish writers. Since there were few Jews remaining in the Soviet Union who read Yiddish (Dorfson quoting Erenburg) 'why waste money for such purposes?' (That is, to print Jewish books and newspapers, etc.) [...]

And now, the truth! Jacob Leon writes in *Al ha-mishmar* that the conference took place in 'an atmosphere of tenseness and hostility'. Surrounded by more than one hundred enemies, Erenburg retained his self-possession throughout. Despite the unconcealed viciousness of the questions of reporters, who tried to rattle him with anti-Soviet arguments, Erenburg's manner was calm and good-natured. He spoke quietly and with much humour. Perhaps Leon lacks Dorfson's reportorial ability, for he did not note any weakness in Erenburg's knees.

According to Dorfson, Erenburg wanted desperately to avoid all questions about Soviet Jewry. Leon, however, states plainly: 'Erenburg declared that he would very much like to talk about Soviet Jewry.'

To the question about Itsik Fefer, Erenburg replied: 'If anything happened to Fefer, I certainly would have known about it.' Asked why no Jewish delegates had participated at the last conference of Soviet writers, Erenburg said that he 'was at the conference and personally heard delegates speaking in Yiddish'. He added that he 'heard preparations are being made to issue a new Yiddish paper in the Soviet Union'. [...]

Erenburg explained that since the destruction of the big Jewish centres of the Soviet Union by the Nazis, a great part of the Jewish youth, scattered throughout the Soviet Union, has changed in character. This change, which occurred entirely by a social process without any outside force or imposition, consists of linguistic and cultural integration in the general national life. But in

* *Source*: Zalel Blitz, 'What Erenburg Really Said', *Jewish Life*, November 1950, pp. 16–17.

those places where large Jewish communities remain, as in Chernovtsy, an energetic Jewish cultural life continues. Yiddish is spoken, Yiddish theatres are thriving, etc.

As to the insinuation that the charge of cosmopolitanism is an expression of hidden anti-Semitism, Erenburg declared that such criticism has nothing whatever to do with the Jewishness of the individual concerned. 'Take me – I am an example of cosmopolitanism. I was born in the Ukraine, I speak to you in French, I represent the city of Riga in the Supreme Soviet, and at the same time I am a Jew.' [...]

Erenburg's interview was taken to confirm the 'liquidation' of the Jewish writers in Russia. It is interesting to note, however, that a journalist like Aryeh Leneman[66] of the Jewish Telegraphic Agency – also an anti-Soviet specialist – included some remarks which cast further doubt on his colleague Dorfson's veracity. On the eve of the Jewish New Year, Leneman wrote: 'In the second half of this year, it was heard in Poland that certain members of the Central Committee of the Polish Jews received letters from a number of the banished writers, with requests for food packages. And it seems that such packages were sent from Warsaw to . . . who knows where? In any case, certainly not to homes of rest or to places where one can be creative.'

Document 72* Reply to enquiry of Markish's wife (26 November 1953)[67]

Procuracy of the
Union of Soviet Socialist Republics

Chief   Kazakh SSR, Kzyl-Orda,
Military Procuracy
                                                Kazakhskaya St, 46.
Lazebnikova E. E.   26 November 1953
                                                No. 45.62556.48
Moscow, Kirov St 41.

I am to inform you that your complaint in the case of Markish Perets Davydovich, which was addressed to the Presidium of the USSR Supreme Soviet, was forwarded to the Procuracy for a decision.

Following an investigation, it has been established that Markish P. D. was sentenced by the Military Collegium of the USSR Supreme Soviet for the perpetration of grave crimes against the state.

It has also been established that the decision taken in your case was correct and there is no basis for changing or rescinding this decision.

Your complaint is considered unfounded.

Military Procurator of the
Chief Military Procuracy Sector
Captain of Law   (Kozhura)

When replying refer to our number and date.

* *Source*: E. Markish, *Le Long Retour* (plate section between pp. 192 and 193) (in Russian).

Document 73* Rehabilitation – for lack of evidence[68]

The Supreme Military Collegium
of the Supreme Court
of the USSR

Moscow, Vorovsky St 13.

CERTIFICATE
The case of the accused — has been reconsidered by the Military Division of
the Supreme Court of the USSR in — 1955.

The sentence of the Military Collegium from 11–18 July 1952, with regard to
— (accused), was changed in the light of the new circumstances revealed, and
proceedings against him have been discontinued for lack of evidence of his
crime.

> Signed:
> The Deputy Chairman,
> The Military Collegium
> of the Supreme Court
> USSR
> Colonel of Law: Borisoglebsky
> (signature)

Seal of The
Military Collegium
of the Supreme Court
USSR.

Document 74† *Folks-shtime* on the trials of the Jewish writers[69]

The historic significance of the 20th Congress of the Communist Party of the
Soviet Union[70] consists, among other things, in its having condemned decisively and irrevocably the cult of personality which for almost two decades
introduced many distortions into Party and public life in the Soviet Union.
The sores, which in the course of those years developed on the healthy body of
the first socialist land, hampered the natural evolution of its generally *healthy*
organism in many ways, and resulted in much suffering and many innocent
victims. The situation created by the personality cult led to a certain distortion
of national politics in the Soviet Union. It enabled the Beria clique to provoke
tensions among the nationalities and to bring about to a certain extent the
growth of nationalism and anti-Semitism. In this atmosphere of the personality cult, so foreign to Marxism–Leninism, it became possible, among
other things, to arrive at the fatal decision to dissolve our heroic party – which
was militantly courageous and always prepared for sacrifices – the Communist Party of Poland. It was this atmosphere, in which the Leninist
principles of socialist democracy were not observed, that made possible a

---

* *Source*: This document was brought to the West by an emigrant from the Soviet Union.
† *Source*: 'Undzer veytik un undzer treyst' (Our Pain and Our Consolation), *Folks-shtime*, 4 April
1956.

period especially painful for us Jews – a period in which the results of the Leninist national policy towards the Jewish masses were undermined.

The Leninist national policy, in its concrete approach to the Jewish population which was oppressed and persecuted under Tsarism, was always an unfailing source of inspiration for millions of ordinary Jewish people throughout the world.

Not only documents of the highest doctrinal significance, but also the daily practice of the Leninist Party and the Soviet government was directed towards the utter eradication of every sign of national discrimination. For the Jewish masses of the Soviet land all doors were opened to every type of governmental and public life, into which they brought the full passion of people who for generations had been fenced off from the world by the ghetto wall of the Pale of Settlement. With the total passion of people who defend the freedom they have achieved like the apple of their eye, Jewish workers and toilers took their place in the armed ranks of the Red Guard and the Red Army, to defend the Socialist Revolution. From their ranks emerged legendary heroes, military leaders who reached the highest ranks of the Red Army. Can we ever forget the heroic epic, which became known in the history of the Revolution as the 'Tripolye Tragedy',[71] and in which a prominent place was taken by many young Jews from the Podol Section of Kiev headed by Misha Rotmansky, whose names have become immortalised! The innumerable tribulations suffered during the excesses perpetrated by the Petlyura[72] and Bulak-Balakhovich[73] bands in the Ukraine and White Russia, and the help and defence provided by the Soviet power, tied the destiny of the Jewish masses even more closely to that of the Great October Revolution. Feelings of the purest patriotism, love and friendship for the Soviet land were born in the hearts of Soviet Jews. The words of the immortal Lenin, who spoke out in the most decisive way against every sort of expression of Great Russian chauvinism towards the previously oppressed small peoples, against every manifestation of anti-Semitism, strengthened the certainty of the Jewish masses that this most shameful plague was over and done with forever on Soviet soil.

And so it was. Subsequent years of the Revolution's development produced ever clearer and fuller manifestations of the absolute equality of the Jewish masses, of their active participation in socialist construction, of their creative activities in all fields of political, economic and cultural life in the Soviet land. *At that time the Jewish problem was completely solved.* [...]

This effort of the Soviet Jewish community, led by the Jewish Anti-Fascist Committee, was part of the grandiose effort of all the Soviet peoples who, under the leadership of the Communist Party of the Soviet Union, bore the heaviest burden of the anti-Hitler war – in order to liberate through military victory all the peoples of Europe, in order to rescue millions of Soviet Jews and hundreds of thousands of Polish Jews, in order to save the lives of the threatened Jews in Israel and later help them in their fight for their country's independence. This will ever remain the historic achievement of the Soviet Union, which the Jews of the entire world will never forget. This happened despite the destructive effects of the Beria purge and the damaging results of the personality cult.

How could it come to this: that the Jewish community leadership, which in the most critical hours for the Soviet Union succeeded in forging the unity of the Jewish resistance – a leadership made up of the best sons and daughters of the Soviet Jewish masses, the Jewish Anti-Fascist Committee – was suddenly, without a why or a wherefore, liquidated and its members sentenced to death?

Yes, we know that to put the question this way, torn out of the *entire* context of the disruptive activities of the Beria purge – and that is precisely how the Jewish enemies of the Soviet Union put the question – is tantamount to missing *the whole scope* of the phenomenon that was disclosed with such profound thoroughness by the 20th Congress of the CPSU. The Beria purge, which was able to prevail only in the atmosphere of the personality cult, took a terrible toll of victims from among all the peoples of the Soviet Union without exception; the chief sufferer was the Communist Party of the Soviet Union itself, the embodiment of the most beautiful and finest aspirations of the entire Soviet people. It goes without saying that the charge made by *Forverts* [Forward] *Tog-morgn zhurnal* [Day-Morning Journal], *Undzer vort* [Our Word], *Undzer shtime* [Our Voice] and many other similar press organs of Jewish nationalism – to the effect that *our* tragedy was the result of a supposedly exclusively anti-Jewish policy – is false and misleading. But our object in emphasising the general damage done by the personality cult is not to seek some half-comfort in the misery of others. No, our object is to point up the truth that *all the peoples of the Soviet Union, without exception, are interested in the full-scale eradication of every trace of the personality cult. And this is true, above all, of the Communist Party of the Soviet Union,* which with Leninist boldness penetrated to the very heart of that terrible phenomenon so as to eradicate it completely. That is the victory of the Communist Party, of Leninism; and in that victory lies our consolation, in that victory lies our hope and our certainty for the future.

We Communists are not used to proclaiming our feelings of sorrow and pain. In the face of defeats (and they are inevitable in the obdurate struggle we carry on), we have more than once found it necessary to grit our teeth in order to avoid providing enemies with the occasion for baleful glee. In the course of long years, the united chorus of the Jewish enemies of the Soviet Union and the Communist movement have come forward with 'questions', with 'interventions', seeking in the most varied ways to participate in our tragedy, in the disrupted creative life of David Bergelson and Der Nister, of Perets Markish and Leyb Kvitko, of David Hofshteyn and Itsik Fefer, of Binyamin Zuskin[74] and Yitskhak Nusinov,[75] of Eliyahu Spivak and Sh. Persov.[76] They sought, in a perfidious way, to persuade the Jewish masses that under the people's power, under Communism, this was an ostensibly legitimate fate for the Jewish community and cultural leaders. Their object was to subdue the warm feelings of sympathy and respect which the Jewish masses of the whole world express for the Soviet Union.

This, and only this, was their purpose – and it remains their purpose when they again raise a hue and cry against the Soviet Union, against the Communist Party, which at its 20th Congress mercilessly settled accounts with the enemies of the Soviet peoples and revived the fundamental principles of Soviet society, which are based on Leninism. What happened to the Jewish community and to cultural leaders of the Soviet Union does not truly concern these

Jewish revilers of Communism, for now as always they have battled against the progressive Jewish leaders with denials, with falsehoods and with abuse. Their only concern is that the Jewish masses should not become aware of the whole scope and depth of the historic turn made by the 20th Congress of the CPSU. Their object is to arm the cold warriors with 'Jewish arguments' against the camp of peace (indeed, *The New York Times* and similar press organs of the imperialist forces have bought the empty bargain provided by the *Forverts'* latest propaganda blast). Their sole and exclusive purpose is to dissuade the Jewish masses from their conviction that, despite the personality cult and its consequences, the Leninist teaching, the Leninist way, as laid down by the 20th Congress of the CPSU, has triumphed.

The Jewish enemies of the Soviet Union and Communism have sought over the years to stir up feelings against us Communists with the hysterical outcry: 'Why are you silent?!'

Yes, it's true, we were silent, despite the fact that we saw and painfully felt the tragic results of the Beria purge. We kept silent because we deeply believed that only the Leninist Party is capable of unravelling the tragic web, and would in the end do so; we were convinced that the Leninist Party would in the end reveal the whole truth and present it boldly and decisively for all peoples. Our faith and our conviction have been fully justified![77]

Document 75 The purge of the writers

Yiddish writers in the camps * (B. Turner)

If I am not mistaken, it was at the end of March 1949 that we, a group of slaves, men and women, were transferred from the camp at Zayarsk on the Angara River to Bratsk where 'our' headquarters were situated. Each of us had received 2.4 kilogrammes of black bread, four herrings, and 60 grams of sugar – our provisions for a four-day journey.

Not far from the water-barrel, right by the door, I noticed an old man sitting on a stool. He was a Jew. He was in such a state that he could not do any ordinary work. That was probably why he was given the job of barrack-sweep. I was awfully tired and was looking for a corner where I could rest. I could not take my eyes away from the old barrack-sweep. Our eyes met. His penetrating glance and clever face attracted me and aroused my confidence. I went up to him and asked if he could show me a place where I could rest my weary bones. The old man turned to a person who was half reclining near by. 'Comrade Fefer', he said, 'be so kind, move aside a little and let the man lie down.' The name of the half-reclining person, as well as his appearance, shook me thoroughly. In spite of his dreadful appearance I recognised him immediately. It was the well-known Jewish poet, Colonel of the Red Army, Itsik Fefer. I had met him and the famous actor, Solomon Mikhoels,[78] in the 'Grand Hotel' in Kuibyshev in 1943, before their departure to the United States as delegates of

* *Source*: Bernard Turner, 'Meyn bagegenish mit Dovid Bergelson un Itsik Fefer in Sovetishn arbet-lager Bratsk' (My Meeting with David Bergelson and Itsik Fefer in the Soviet Labour Camp of Bratsk), *Di goldene keyt* (Tel Aviv), 1956, no. 25, pp. 33–7.

the Anti-Fascist Committee.[79] The unfortunate Fefer looked haggard and dried up – skin and bones, and a bundle of nerves. He trembled all over, nervously bit his blue lips, and looked around with an unseeing stare, mumbling something to himself. My heart bled. Itsik Fefer, the prominent Jewish Soviet poet, was wallowing in dust and mud, a few paces from the 'parasha' [latrine-bucket]. He was covered with rags, his trousers were tied with a piece of string from which a military tin flask hung. His spectacles – Fefer's characteristic spectacles – were broken and bound with string.

Later I learned that the old barrack-sweep was Bergelson, the great Jewish Soviet prose writer. We were together only one week and spent much time chatting to each other. I learned from them that Perets Markish had been in the same camp for a while. He had written a great poem of sorrow and anger, 'The Third Roman Empire' (some six or seven notebooks written in small letters). But the NKVD found the manuscript in one of their searches and sent the notebooks to Moscow. Soon after that an order came from there: Markish was to be arrested and placed in solitary confinement in the camp prison. From there he managed to smuggle a letter to Bergelson saying that a new case against him was being prepared. Since then Markish had disappeared without leaving any trace.

Fefer and Bergelson told me that their arrest was the result of a long-lasting action which had started in 1944. At that time, they had learned about the anti-Semitic line of the Party and government of Soviet Russia. In 1944, the Soviet Foreign Office raised the question of the considerable shortage of diplomats, which made itself strongly felt as relations with the countries of the West had increased. In Moscow, the Higher Diplomatic School was opened, headed by Deputy Foreign Minister Dekanozov.[80] (Later he was eliminated together with his friend Beria.) A strict quota for Jewish students was introduced at the Diplomatic School. Fefer and Bergelson mentioned the subject at a closed meeting attended by Lozovsky,[81] Deputy Foreign Minister of the Soviet Union, as well as by A. Shtern[82] (former Soviet ambassador in Rome and professor at the Diplomatic School at that time), Ilya Erenburg and Solomon Mikhoels. Lozovsky approached Dekanozov on the subject, but he could not achieve anything. Later he conferred with Foreign Minister Vyshinsky, who denied the existence of any discrimination against Jews. Lazar Kaganovich refused to say anything at all on the matter.

Some time later, Bergelson told me, clear and definitive news had reached them that an ill wind was blowing from the Kremlin and that the anti-Semitic line in the internal policy of the Soviet Union was fully sanctioned by Stalin and the Politburo. In the circles of the Jewish Communists it became known that the Central Committee of the Party had decreed, in strict confidence, that all Jews, Communists included, be excluded from the Polish and Czechoslovakian national armies created by Colonel Berling and General Svoboda on Soviet soil.

The decree stated explicitly that every Jew with a typical Jewish appearance (a Jewish nose, curly hair, a Jewish accent) was to be kept out of the Polish Liberation Army as well as out of the Red Army and NKVD attached to the Polish Army. The Jews who had 'good' faces could stay in the Polish

Army, but they had to adopt purely Polish names instead of their Jewish ones, and conceal any trace of their Jewishness.

Lozovsky informed Bergelson that Wanda Wasilewska,[83] then a member of the Supreme Soviet and wife of Deputy Foreign Minister of the Soviet Union A. Korneichuk, who had access to Stalin himself, played a great part in the 'new' anti-Semitic policy. This policy was carried out with much zeal, not only in the Soviet Union but also in the countries of Eastern Europe where Communist regimes had been established. As Bergelson and Fefer told me, neither they nor other Jewish Communist writers or intellectuals could do anything about the anti-Jewish line, though it was completely contradictory to the Communist idea. They discussed the new situation in their circles. Ilya Erenburg also took part in the meetings.

At the same time, a steady stream of mass arrests got under way, mainly among Jews who were not Soviet citizens. The anti-Semitic line was already clear to everybody. And then the arrest of the members of the Jewish Anti-Fascist Committee took place. That was the beginning of a total campaign against Jews and Jewish culture in the Soviet Union. The main witness against those arrested, when they were accused of Jewish nationalism and Zionism, was Ilya Erenburg. He also played a part in the arrests of many other Jews, especially his intimates, probably with the aim of saving his own skin. Even Lozovsky, his closest friend, he handed over to the NKVD.

As Fefer himself told me, he was additionally accused of having been closely linked with Bund leaders Erlich[84] and Alter[85] when they lived in Kuibyshev, although he had been in Tashkent at the time. Besides that he was accused of collaboration with Zionists and Bundists during his visit to New York.

Both Fefer and Bergelson, as well as other Jewish Communists, were tortured in the most abominable ways in the course of interrogations. Fefer told me that he had seen Lozovsky during a confrontation in the Lubyanka. Lozovsky's arm was broken and his face was black and blue and looked like a great wound. There were rumours that Lozovsky had committed suicide in prison. But Fefer rightly pointed to the fact that suicide in the Lubyanka was impossible, as everything that could be used for suicide was taken away from the prisoners. Without any possibility of doubt, Lozovsky was tortured to death in just the same way as many others who fell victim to the cruel tortures and torments inflicted on them.

Bergelson told me that, besides everything else, they had used the notorious method of making him sit on a two-legged stool. He had to sit on it for twenty hours a day. With the least movement he would lose his equilibrium, fall from the stool and would be hurt and bruised from falling on the stone floor. But he had to sit on the stool again, and he would fall again. More than once the stool broke, then another one was brought, and so it went on for days and weeks. In the end, a new unbreakable material was found for the stools. As for the broken limbs of the human victim, the inquisitors, of course, spared them no thought. [...]

When I was parting from Bergelson and Fefer and telling them of my plans for getting out of that hell, they expressed the following request: if I happened to meet Ilya Erenburg, I should ask him, on their behalf, to lay flowers on the unknown graves of the innocent dead in whose martyrdom he had played no small part.

Six years later, in October 1955, I had the chance and satisfaction of fulfilling the last wish of Bergelson and Fefer. That was at Vienna airport. In the presence of President of the Soviet Writers' Union Nikolai Tikhonov, I repeated to Erenburg, word for word, the last request of his fellow-writers Bergelson and Fefer. Erenburg turned as white as a sheet. His lips began to quiver, and foam appeared at his mouth. A lost man, he moved away from me and soon left.

Erenburg's reply to Turner[86]*

I ask you to publish the following.

On 22 August, your newspaper published a note signed A. P., according to which I am to be blamed for the arrest of a group of Jewish writers in the Soviet Union. A. P. refers to an article of the journalist, Bernard Turner, which appeared in *Die goldene zeit*.[87]

The victims of Beria's arbitrariness included Soviet citizens of different nationalities. In 1949, several eminent Jewish writers were slandered and arrested, among them some of my close friends. It was only when Soviet courts had completely refuted the accusations levelled at them that we learnt of their tragic fate.

According to Bernard Turner, the writers who perished would have accused me of contributing to their ruin. To accuse someone on the basis of the fictitious words of people who are no longer alive and who can no longer make a denial is not a new precedent. But what is astonishing – and I cannot refrain from expressing it to you – is that *Le Monde*, which as a rule publishes serious news, thought it possible to reserve its columns for insinuations from a doubtful source.

Ilya Erenburg.

(We are happy to reproduce Mr Erenburg's letter, while remarking moreover that he defends himself rather half-heartedly against the precise 'accusations' of the Israeli journalist, Bernard Turner, which we were obliged to print. *Le Monde* is, in the present case, in company with a serious British organ, *The Spectator* of London. Mr Erenburg will pardon us if, without taking sides, we cannot attach less importance to the evidence of an Israeli journalist than to his.)[88]

Document 76† Howard Fast answers Boris Polevoi (1957)[89]

Such was Polevoi's[90] reply to a series of deeply important questions which I had directed to him. On the day I received his letter, I answered him as follows:

---

* *Source*: 'L'Antisémitisme de M. Ehrenbourg' (Mr Erenburg's Anti-Semitism), *Le Monde*, 26 September 1957.

† *Source*: H. Fast, *The Naked God: The Writer and the Communist Party*, New York, Praeger, 1957, pp. 191–5.

Dear Boris:

To hear from you was good, believe me. Your letter came today, and I read it hungrily; and I felt the warmth and happiness of hearing your voice again, for I hear it in any letter of yours. You and Isakov I treasure as friends, as Bette does; this must not change. [...]·

Why don't we hear your voice, Isakov's, and other voices in defence of the book *Not by Bread Alone?*[91] Perhaps the book is worthless; must not the writer be defended? Why will no one tell us how Itsik Fefer died? The Poles informed us that Khrushchev attempted to use anti-Semitism to sway the inner struggle in Poland. Why does no one deny this? Where is one little word of the criticism and self-criticism we have been hearing so much about? [...]

And why – why, Boris, did you tell us here in New York that the Yiddish writer, Kvitko, was alive and well and living in your apartment house as your neighbour, when he was among those executed and long since dead? Why? Why did you have to lie? Why could you not avoid the question and tell us you did not know or would not discuss it? Why did you lie in so awful and deliberate a manner?

By now you have my statement in *Mainstream*. Publish it. Publish this letter. Answer my arguments. Tell me that terror is gone. Tell me that anti-Semitism is over and done with. Demand an end to capital punishment – the old and fine dream of socialism. Tell us the truth – only that, the truth. I may have been a fool not to have known of this terror before, but I did not know. Do you want me to worship the Communist Party as an icon? Believe me, I worship something better – truth and freedom, and how can you ask that one tyranny be traded for another?

I ventured my life and fortune to speak the truth as I saw it. Will you? Print this in the *Literary Gazette*. Open the doors! Let the words fly! Only in that way can the world-hurt be healed. And let no man suffer for speaking his mind forthrightly and honestly.

And I want to remain your friend. Can I? It is up to you.

The 'Doctors' Plot'

Document 77* Kozlov's[92] warning as a prelude to the 'Doctors' Plot' (January 1953)

Comrade Stalin compares the Marxist Party with a fortress whose doors open only for the tested and the deserving. It is known how dangerous is an enemy who has managed to get into a fortress. The imperialists do their best to plant their agents, spies, murderers in the parties of the working class. Historical experience proves that beyond any possible doubt. It was so in the USSR; Trotskyites, Bukharinites and other sworn enemies of the people, capitulators and traitors were agents of the imperialist states. The same is happening in the People's Democracies; all those Rajks,[93] Kostovs,[94] Slanskys[95] are now known to have been carefully masked agents of American imperialism. In Yugoslavia

* *Source*: F. Kozlov, 'Politicheskaya bditelnost – obyazannost chlena partii' (Political Vigilance is the Duty of a Party Member), *Kommunist*, 1953, no. 1, pp. 46, 48–9, 55.

a gang of spies and murderers, agents of the Anglo-American imperialists, have made their way to the leadership of the Communist Party and have turned it into an apparatus carrying out espionage for Tito's Fascist clique. All this reinforces the idea expressed by V. I. Lenin, in his work 'Left-Wing Communism – An Infantile Disorder', that 'the bourgeoisie no doubt sends and will go on sending provocateurs into the Communist parties'.[96] [...]

Only blunted vigilance when accepting Party members can explain, for example, the fact that a man who was a member of the petty-bourgeois, nationalist, counter-revolutionary party, the Bund, who was twice expelled from our Communist Party (for his ties with Trotskyites and for giving jobs to class-alien people) managed to conceal his past and to join our Party for the third time.

Document 78* Official announcement of the 'Doctors' Plot'

Some time ago, the agencies of state security uncovered a terrorist group of doctors who had made it their aim to cut short the lives of active public figures of the Soviet Union by means of sabotaged medical treatment.

Among the participants in this terrorist group there proved to be: Prof. M. S. Vovsi,[97] therapeutist; Prof. V. N. Vinogradov, therapeutist; Prof. M. B. Kogan, therapeutist; Prof. B. B. Kogan, therapeutist; Prof. P. I. Egorov, therapeutist; Prof. A. I. Feldman, otolaryngologist; Prof. Ya. G. Etinger, therapeutist; Prof. A. M. Grinshtein, neuropathologist; G. A. Maiorov, therapeutist.

Documentary evidence, investigations, the conclusions of medical experts and the confessions of the arrested have established that the criminals, who were secret enemies of the people, sabotaged the treatment of patients and undermined their health.

Investigations established that the participants in the terrorist group, taking advantage of their position as doctors and abusing the trust of the patients deliberately and malevolently, undermined the patients' health; intentionally ignored the data produced by objective examination of the patients; made incorrect diagnoses which did not correspond to the true nature of their illnesses; and then doomed them by incorrect treatment.

The criminals confessed that they took advantage of Comrade A. A. Zhdanov's ailment by incorrectly diagnosing his illness and concealing an infarct of his myocardium and, by prescribing a regime contra-indicated for this serious ailment, killed Comrade A. A. Zhdanov. Investigation established that the criminals likewise cut short the life of Comrade A. S. Shcherbakov by incorrectly employing strong drugs in his treatment, treatment which was fatal to him, bringing about his death.

The criminal doctors sought, above all, to undermine the health of leading Soviet military personnel, to put them out of action and to thereby weaken the defence of the country. They intended to put out of action Marshal A. M. Vasilevsky, Marshal L. A. Govorov, Marshal I. S. Konev, Army General S. M. Shtemenko, Admiral G. I. Levchenko and others; but arrest disrupted their evil plans and the criminals did not succeed in attaining their aim.

* *Source*: 'Arest gruppy vrachei-vreditelei' (Arrest of Group of Saboteur Doctors), *Pravda*, 13 January 1953.

It has been established that all these homicidal doctors, who had become monsters in human form, trampling the sacred banner of science and desecrating the honour of scientists, were enrolled by foreign intelligence services as hired agents.

Most of the participants in the terrorist group (M. S. Vovsi, B. B. Kogan, A. I. Feldman, A. M. Grinshtein, Ya. G. Etinger and others) were connected with the international Jewish bourgeois nationalist organisation, 'Joint', established by American intelligence for the alleged purpose of providing material aid to Jews in other countries. In actual fact this organisation, under the direction of American intelligence, conducts extensive espionage, terrorist and other subversive work in many countries, including the Soviet Union. The prisoner Vovsi told investigators that he had received orders 'to wipe out the leading cadres of the USSR' – from the 'Joint' organisation in the USA, via a Moscow doctor, Shimelovich,[98] and the well-known Jewish bourgeois nationalist, Mikhoels.

Other participants in the terrorist group (V. N. Vinogradov, M. B. Kogan, P. I. Egorov) proved to be old agents of British intelligence.

The investigation will soon be concluded.

(Tass)

Document 79* Official announcement of the doctors' release

The USSR Ministry of Internal Affairs has carried out a thorough verification of all the preliminary investigation data and other material in the case of the group of doctors accused of sabotage, espionage and terrorist acts against active leaders of the Soviet State.

The verification has established that the accused in this case, Professors M. S. Vovsi, V. N. Vinogradov, M. B. Kogan, B. B. Kogan, P. I. Egorov, A. I. Feldman, Ya. G. Etinger, V. K. Vasilenko, A. M. Grinshtein, V. F. Zelenin, B. S. Preobrazhensky, N. A. Popova, V. V. Zakusov, N. A. Shereshevsky and Dr G. I. Maiorov, were arrested by the former USSR Ministry of State Security incorrectly, without any lawful basis.[99]

Verification has shown that the accusations against the above-named persons are false and that the documentary sources on which the investigating officials based their findings are without foundation. It was established that the testimony of the prisoners, allegedly confirming the accusations against them, was obtained by the officials of the investigatory department of the former Ministry of State Security through the use of means which are impermissible and strictly forbidden under Soviet law.

On the basis of the conclusion of an investigatory commission specially appointed by the USSR Ministry of Internal Affairs to check this case, the arrested M. S. Vovsi, V. N. Vinogradov, B. B. Kogan, P. I. Egorov, A. I. Feldman, V. K. Vasilenko, A. M. Grinshtein, V. F. Zelenin, B. S. Preobrazhensky, N. A. Popova, V. V. Zakusov, N. A. Shereshevsky and G. I. Maiorov and others accused in this case have been completely exonerated of the accusations against them of sabotage, terrorist and espionage activities

* *Source*: 'Soobshchenie Ministerstva vnutrennikh del SSSR' (*Communiqué* of USSR Ministry of Internal Affairs), *Pravda*, 4 April 1953.

and, in accordance with Article 4, Paragraph 5, of the Criminal Procedure Code of the Russian Republic, have been released from prison.[100]

The persons accused of incorrect conduct of the investigation have been arrested and brought to trial.

Document 80* Erenburg describes the effects of the Doctors' Affair

That day their daughter, Shura, ran a temperature. It happened that the pediatrician, Filimonov, was ill himself. Lena panicked; she was convinced Shura had pneumonia. She phoned Ivan and he suggested: 'Send to our own hospital for Dr Sherer.' Vera Sherer came and said that it was ordinary flu; the child had nothing on her lungs. Lena was overjoyed, but in her agitation she insisted: 'Are you sure? Her breathing is so odd.' Vera unexpectedly lost her temper: 'If you don't trust me, why did you call me in?' Lena blushed, 'Forgive me, I don't know what I'm saying. Truly, I didn't mean to hurt your feelings. This is awful!' Vera's eyes had filled with tears; she said quietly: 'It's you who must forgive me, it's my fault. My nerves are on edge. Sometimes people say such dreadful things. It's since the announcement.† It's very bad – a doctor shouldn't behave like this.' Lena blushed a still darker red. She took Vera home. From that day they became friends.

And it was also from that day that Lena despised her husband. He came home late, tired and hungry; he asked how Shura was and Lena told him of her conversation with Vera Sherer. Ivan said nothing. She insisted: 'But don't you think it's quite outrageous? What's it got to do with Sherer?' Ivan said soothingly: 'Don't get so upset. I told you to call her in myself; she's supposed to be very good. I've got nothing at all against her. Still, you've got to be careful whom you trust, no doubt about it.'

Lena left the room without a word. Everything that had been seething in her suddenly boiled up. Sobbing, she kept repeating: 'And that man's my husband.'

Months later, after the fire, listening to Dmitry praising Ivan's conduct, she could hardly keep herself from crying out: 'If you only knew how cowardly he is, how heartless.'

When the newspapers announced the rehabilitation of the Kremlin doctors, Lena rushed immediately to the hospital, asked for Vera, and threw herself into her arms.

That evening Ivan said yawning: 'Turns out they weren't guilty after all. So your Sherer needn't have upset herself.'

Document 81‡ Khrushchev on the 'Doctors' Plot', at the 20th Congress of CPSU

Let us also recall the 'affair of the doctor-plotters'.
(Animation in the hall.)

---

* *Source*: I. Erenburg, *A Change of Season*, New York, Alfred A. Knopf, 1962, pp. 23–4.
† The announcement in *Pravda* of the arrest of a group of doctors accused of conspiring to poison several Soviet leaders.
‡ *Source*: B. D. Wolfe, *Khrushchev and Stalin's Ghost*, New York, Praeger, 1957, pp. 202–4.

Actually there was no 'affair' outside of the declaration of the woman doctor, Timashuk, who was probably influenced or ordered by someone (after all, she was an unofficial collaborator of the organs of state security) to write Stalin a letter in which she declared that doctors were applying supposedly improper methods of medical treatment.

Such a letter was sufficient for Stalin to reach an immediate conclusion that there are doctor-plotters in the Soviet Union. He issued orders to arrest a group of eminent Soviet medical specialists. He personally issued advice on the conduct of the investigation and the method of interrogation of the arrested persons. He said that the academician Vinogradov should be put in chains, another one should be beaten. Present at this Congress as a delegate is the former Minister of State Security, Comrade Ignatyev. Stalin told him curtly, 'If you do not obtain confessions from the doctors we will shorten you by a head.'

(Tumult in the hall.)

Stalin personally called the investigative judge, gave him instructions, advised him on which investigative methods should be used: these methods were simple – beat, beat and, once again, beat.

Shortly after the doctors were arrested, we members of the Political Bureau received protocols containing the doctors' confessions of guilt. After distributing these protocols, Stalin told us, 'You are blind like young kittens; what will happen without me? The country will perish because you do not know how to recognise enemies.'

The case was so presented that no one could verify the facts on which the investigation was based. There was no possibility of trying to verify facts by contacting those who had made the confessions of guilt.

We felt, however, that the case of the arrested doctors was questionable. We knew some of these people personally because they had once treated us. When we examined this 'case' after Stalin's death, we found it to be fabricated from beginning to end.

This ignominious 'case' was set up by Stalin; he did not, however, have the time in which to bring it to an end (as he conceived that end), and for this reason the doctors are still alive. Now all have been rehabilitated; they are working in the same places they were working before; they treat top individuals, not excluding members of the government; they have our full confidence; and they execute their duties honestly, as they did before.

In organising the various dirty and shameful cases, a very base role was played by the rabid enemy of our Party, an agent of a foreign intelligence service – Beria, who had stolen into Stalin's confidence.[101]

Economic crimes

Document 82* Speculation in Kiev (1948)

A number of profiteers have already been sentenced to long terms of imprisonment. The former shop-manager, A. Shtulman, had tried to secrete 6,000

* *Source*: 'V prokurature g. Kieva' (At the Kiev City Procuracy), *Pravda Ukrainy*, 4 January 1948.

cigarettes for the purpose of selling them for new money. He was sentenced to ten years in prison, confiscation of property and loss of civil rights for three years after serving his term. P. Zhorin was sentenced to the same term. During a search at his house great stores of food and manufactured goods were found.[102]

Document 83* Authorisation to released prisoner (the amnesty of 1953)

USSR	Form 'A'
Ministry of Internal Affairs	Not valid as residence permit
	Not renewable if lost

7 – A Shch

UITLK MVD TASSR　　　　　　AUTHORISATION　　　　　　No. 0008329

Given to citizen Zilber Isaak Yakovlevich, born 1918, in Kazan (TASSR), citizen of the USSR; nationality Jew, sentenced by the People's Court of the Sverdlov District of Kazan on 3 August 1951, under Article 59, Section 12 of the Criminal Code of the RSFSR to deprivation of freedom for two years without loss of civil rights; without previous sentence, on having served his sentence in MVD prisons until 15 April 1953 and by decree of the Presidium of the Supreme Soviet of the USSR of 27 March 1953, on an amnesty.

By implementation of a mitigated sentence,

Released on 15 April 1953 and proceeding to his appointed place of residence, Kazan, TASSR.

(town, village, region, province)

Signature of Section head
Signature of head of finance department
Signature of released man I. Zilber

Remarks on issuing of provisions and money for the journey.

Date and signature of person responsible for issue.
Receipt of released man.

Document 84† Execution for profiteering in Leningrad (1961)

Leningradskaya pravda of 16 September carried a report on a band of crooks who had engaged for a long time in profiteering operations in gold, foreign currency and valuables.

The profiteers, B. S. Oizerman, A. G. Kaplun, V. B. Uzdin, L. I. Levit, Ya. A. Dolgopolsky, S. Ya. Shapiro, S. Z. Markovich, L. A. Trubnikov, and B. M. Khaikin, were exposed by the organs of state security, arrested and tried.

The case was heard by the Criminal Law Division of the Leningrad City Court, with S. E. Solovyev presiding. The band of profiteers was accused of

---

* *Source*: This document was brought to the West by Zilber himself when he emigrated from the Soviet Union.

† *Source*: 'Spekulyanty nakazany' (Profiteers Punished), *Leningradskaya pravda*, 17 November 1961.

having caused great damage to the state finance and credit system by their criminal activities.

All the accused were found guilty.

In accordance with the law 'on responsibility for crimes against the state', the court sentenced B. S. Oizerman, A. G. Kaplun and S. Ya. Shapiro to the maximum punishment – shooting; V. B. Uzdin and Ya. A. Dolgopolsky to twelve years' imprisonment, L. I. Levit to ten years, B. M. Khaikin to eight years, L. A. Trubnikov to six years, and S. Z. Markovich to five years and confiscation of property.[103]

Document 85* Profiteering in a synagogue (1962)

There are five of them in the dock. Who are they? A band of profiteers trading in gold and valuables, who nested snugly beneath the vaults of the Lvov synagogue. It was their criminal activities which were related on 16 February of this year in the article 'Prayer and Profiteers'. Let us name them in the order in which they appear in the indictment: M. Chernobilsky, L. Kontorovich, A. Sapozhnikov, B. Cherkas (B. Gulko was prosecuted in another case).

The judicial investigation went on for many days. The testimonies of the accused themselves and of numerous witnesses kept adding new details to the picture of the criminal activities which took place in the Lvov synagogue. For a number of years, the accused were engaged in large-scale profiteering, in buying and selling gold, foreign currency, valuables. Acquaintances and 'business relations' began under the roof of the synagogue, the leaders of which, members of the so-called 'Committee of Twenty', were A. Sapozhnikov and L. Kontorovich.

A singular 'black market' was active in the synagogue and around it. Profiteers trading in currency, among them the above-mentioned Gulko, as well as Yu. Kuris and others, used to come flocking here from other towns. There Kontorovich and Sapozhnikov made their deals. Sendersky came there, not to pray, but to get a new assignment from Kontorovich and then to start on a new trip to buy foreign currency.

Profiteers of different kinds made use of the synagogue as a screen. They pretended to go there for religious observance, but their aims were really quite different. The criminals considered prayer a convenient cover for their sharp practices.

A thirst for profit brought different people together first in the field of currency speculation, and then in the dock. Here is Kontorovich, a synagogue official and, as he says, a deeply religious person. As you see, religion never interfered with his criminal activities. The same can be said of another member of the 'Twenty', A. Sapozhnikov. Gulko's testimony was read in court, and there he tells of his criminal deals with Sapozhnikov. Among other things, Gulko says: 'Sapozhnikov spends all his time in the synagogue and moves about among the black market dealers.'

M. Chernobilsky is about half the age of Kontorovich and Sapozhnikov. He is not religious. He is the only one of the five accused who was working. He was a senior engineer of a construction-technology bureau of the Lvov Administra-

* *Source*: 'Krushenie spekulyantov' (Downfall of Profiteers), *Lvovskaya pravda*, 9 March 1962.

tion of Local Industry. The Soviet State helped Chernobilsky to get his education, gave him everything he needed for a comfortable life. But greed, an uncontrollable passion for wealth, led him into criminal ways. The engineer became a currency dealer. He built up an exciting profiteering activity, and traded not only in Lvov, but also in Moscow, in Minsk. [...]

The members of the synagogue 'Committee of Twenty', Kontorovich and Sapozhnikov and the unbeliever Chernobilsky, found a common language in criminal currency deals. Thus, for example, in 1956–9, Chernobilsky completed up to eight deals with Kontorovich, buying and selling gold and foreign currency.

The moral character of the accused is repellent. People who owe the Soviet State so much, who, like Sapozhnikov and Sendersky, received pensions from it, were undermining the economic power of the Soviet State, were seriously harming our country, our people. During their criminal activities, the band of plunderers had made criminal deals in currency amounting to a total sum of about four million rubles (in old money).

The Province Court found Chernobilsky with Kontorovich, Sapozhnikov and Cherkas guilty of regular currency deals, over a number of years, with currency dealers from Minsk and Moscow. Chernobilsky also smuggled American dollars across the state border.

The judicial investigation proved the grave crimes against the state committed by the religious official Kontorovich. Since 1947, he had been trading continuously in gold currency, diamonds and jewels for the purpose of gain. He dealt in currency with Chernobilsky, Sendersky, Gulko and others. In court, Kontorovich was hypocritical, lied and tried to deceive the court. But the accused themselves exposed him. Sapozhnikov, a member of the 'Twenty', testified in court that he dealt with Kontorovich at home after they had come to an agreement in the synagogue.

The accused Cherkas testified that he had met the currency dealer Kuris in the synagogue. There they agreed on the buying and selling of gold currency. The fact that the synagogue had become a place of criminal activities is also supported by Gulko's evidence. Most of his acquaintances in Lvov started within the walls of this 'house of God', and he carried on his currency deals with Kontorovich there. [...]

In determining the punishment, the court took into account the sincere repentance of Chernobilsky, Sapozhnikov and some others. The Lvov Province Court sentenced the dealers in currency and valuables to varying long terms of imprisonment (strict regime conditions), and to confiscation of the impounded valuables and currency. The criminals received their just deserts.[104]

Anti-Zionist trials

Document 86* Trial of Pechersky, Dynkin and Kaganov (I)

Not long ago, the Criminal Law Division of the Leningrad City Court heard the case of G. R. Pechersky,[105] E. Sh. Dynkin and N. A. Kaganov. It was

* *Source*: 'V Leningradskom gorodskom sude' (In the Leningrad City Court), *Leningradskaya pravda*, 11 November 1961.

established by the preliminary investigation and in court that the accused had had criminal connections for a number of years with some workers of the embassy of a capitalist state accredited to Moscow. The workers of the embassy had visited Leningrad many times for this special purpose.

Pechersky, Dynkin and Kaganov had regularly passed on information used abroad to harm the Soviet State. In their turn, the accused had repeatedly received from the workers of the embassy anti-Soviet literature and undertook to distribute it.

The court found Pechersky and Dynkin guilty of crimes under Articles 64, point 'a', and 70, section 1, and Kaganov under Article 70, section 1, of the Criminal Code of the RSFSR. Pechersky was sentenced to twelve years and Kaganov to seven years of imprisonment. Dynkin, who sincerely repented and condemned his own criminal activities, received a lighter sentence – four years of imprisonment.

Document 87* Trial of Pechersky, Dynkin and Kaganov (II)

The imperialist intelligence services often use the same agents for spying and for carrying out ideological sabotage. Thus, during the trial in Leningrad of the Soviet citizens Kaganov, Dynkin and Pechersky, who agreed to work for the Israeli intelligence service, it was established that they had not only collected and passed on intelligence information, but that they also spread rumours and fabrications defaming the Soviet State and social order. These people distributed anti-Soviet literature, which they received from the Israeli Embassy. The agents of the foreign intelligence service also admitted that they had intended to send the tapes (subsequently confiscated), the contents of which slandered Soviet reality, to their chiefs abroad, who were going to use them for anti-Soviet propaganda.

Subversive propaganda and misinformation are the weapons of the imperialist states. They spend huge efforts and sums on it. Soviet people must be most vigilant and resolutely unmask the lies and slanders of the bourgeois 'knights' with their poisoned weapons.

* *Source*: K. Viktorov, 'Otravlennoe oruzhie (Ob ideologicheskikh diversiyakh imperialistov)' (Poisoned Weapons (On Ideological Sabotage of the Imperialists)), *Moskovskaya pravda*, 22 November 1968.

PART III

The Zionist issue

6

The Soviet regime and Zionism

It can be stated with certainty that there is a connection between the policy of the Soviet Union towards its Jews, its attitude towards Zionism, and its foreign policies as applied to the Middle East in general, and to Israel in particular. But the assertion itself does not serve to elucidate the nature and essence of this connection. Among the complex questions which arise, and which we believe have not yet been answered satisfactorily, are the following. Is there a direct correlation – positive or negative – between the Soviet government's policy towards the Jews of the Soviet Union, Zionism and the State of Israel; or, in other words, do the events of the years 1946–67 prove that a negative attitude towards Soviet Jewry inevitably led to hostility towards Zionism and the State of Israel, or *vice versa*? Do these correlations show any consistency, or should one perhaps speak only of points of contact and confluence, a more general law being difficult to deduce? Was the Soviet government's policy on these questions determined by domestic factors or by considerations of foreign policy?

To provide exhaustive answers to these questions would demand a study of Soviet–Israeli and Soviet–Arab relations far beyond the framework of the present work. However, together with the analysis undertaken in other chapters of this book, the material presented here will permit tentative conclusions which may serve as the basis for such a study.[1]

The Stalin period

Even before the outbreak of war between the USSR and Germany in June 1941, the Soviets maintained an anti-Zionist line which reached extreme peaks at the end of the twenties and the end of the thirties. However, it was the Ribbentrop–Molotov Pact of August 1939, which led to Soviet annexation of territories with large Jewish populations, that resulted in so large a wave of mass arrests among Zionist activists that it is difficult to make an accurate estimate of the numbers involved.[2]

The years 1941–5

Following many years of virtually total severance, bilateral relations, albeit rather shaky, began to take shape during the war period between official representatives of the Soviet Union on one side and leaders of the Zionist movement and of the Jewish *yishuv* in Palestine on the other. While the first meetings (such as those with the Soviet Ambassador to the United States, Umansky, on 17 July 1941, with the Soviet Ambassador to Britain, Maisky, on 13 October 1941 and with the Soviet Ambassador in Ankara, Vinogradov, on 6 January 1942) were held on the initiative of the Zionists, the Soviets began to initiate such contacts themselves in 1943.

The meetings in question (for example, the visit to Palestine by the foreign service officials, Mikhailov and Petrenko, in August 1943 at the invitation of the 'V' League, and Ambassador Maisky's visit in October 1943 and Novikov's visit in August 1944) were all characterised by the Soviet attempt to gauge the strength of the Zionist movement and the *yishuv* and their influence on policy-makers in the West. In addition, the Soviet representatives were interested in preparing data on the *yishuv* for their country's leaders, in anticipation of political decisions to be made after the war.

For their part, representatives of the Zionist movement and the *yishuv* were interested in securing the release of members of the Zionist movement confined in forced labour camps and prisons in the Soviet Union; in obtaining permission for Jewish refugees from the annexed areas and from Nazi-occupied regions to emigrate to Palestine; and in seeing that aid from Jewish organisations reached these refugees. Also discussed were the existence of discrimination against the Hebrew language and culture in the USSR; the establishment of a Soviet representation in Palestine, following its establishment in Syria and Lebanon; the form that aid to the USSR war effort on the part of the *yishuv* and Jewish organisations should take; and the possibility of the Red Army's destroying the Nazi extermination camps in Poland.

With the exception of the subject of aid for Russia, Soviet replies to these issues were generally negative or evasive. They may be summarised as follows. People had never been arrested in the Soviet Union because of their nationality or for being Zionists, but only because of their connections with hostile political organisations abroad. All subjects in the territories annexed to the USSR had received Soviet citizenship and were satisfied with this state of affairs; there was no need for anxiety about these citizens since the USSR had already concerned itself with them. As for Hebrew culture, it was redundant because Yiddish culture already existed in the USSR and all Jews could benefit from it. Of course they were prepared to establish representation in Palestine, but the political situation had first to be clarified. And as to bombing the extermination camps, the Soviet diplomatic corps had no right to give strategic advice to the heads of the Red Army.[3] Moreover, in their talks held in this period with American and Arab personages in the Middle East, the Soviet representatives stressed that the anti-Zionist orientation of the USSR would continue.[4]

The relations between the Jewish Anti-Fascist Committee in the USSR and Palestinian Jewry give us an indication of Soviet policy towards Zionism during the war period. It is interesting to note that, although they were undoubtedly interested in improving their country's image and in strengthening pro-Soviet feelings among the Jews of the *yishuv*, the Soviet authorities seem to have done everything possible to discourage connections between the heads of the Jewish Anti-Fascist Committee and *yishuv* leaders. A striking illustration of this policy was the fact that when Solomon Mikhoels and Itsik Fefer passed through the Middle East in 1943, *en route* to the United States and Canada, they had no meetings with representatives of the *yishuv*. Similarly, despite all the efforts on the part of the 'V' League, relations between the Jewish Anti-Fascist Committee and the League were very restricted.

It can, then, be concluded that, while there was some amelioration in the situation of the Jews within the Soviet Union between June 1941 and early 1945, this was accompanied by only a minor improvement in the attitude of the USSR towards Zionism and the *yishuv*. The shift of position in both instances was due to the grave war situation, which demanded the mobilisation of all forces for the campaign against Germany and prompted the efforts to gain the support of western Jewry. Nonetheless, there is no reason to believe that any basic change in policy was contemplated on either plane.

February 1945 – May 1947

The beginning of a change for the better in the Soviet Union's attitude towards the *yishuv* can be seen in February 1945, when Stalin agreed, together with Roosevelt and Churchill, to permit the Jews to establish a national home in Palestine, where gates could be opened to Jewish immigration.[5] This new Soviet line received far more overt expression at the founding conference of the World Federation of Trade Unions, which was held in London. There, in the same month, V. Kuznetsov, head of the Soviet delegation, voted on behalf of his delegation for a resolution which determined, *inter alia*, 'that the Jewish people should be permitted to continue with the building of Palestine as a national home, as it has begun to do with great success by means of immigration, agriculture, settlement and industrial development'.[6] However, of even greater immediate significance was Soviet acquiescence in the emigration of Jews from Eastern Europe to Poland and the Western-occupied regions of Germany and Austria, though it was clear that the emigrants' ultimate destination was Palestine.[7]

However, the official anti-Zionist line continued, and was carried in the press and other information media. 'The programmes to found a Zionist-Jewish state in Palestine are supported by influential American circles', wrote the commentator K. Serezhin at the beginning of 1946.[8] Serezhin also claimed that publication of Truman's declaration concerning the proposed entry of 100,000 Jews from Europe into Palestine further complicated the political situation. The solution for the thousands of miserable refugees, he continued, was not to be found in raising Jewish immigration quotas to Palestine, but in extirpating Fascism, in liquidating racism and its consequences, and in rendering true aid to the Jewish population.[9] In the course of a far more violent anti-Zionist attack, the same author charged that: 'The leaders of Zionism have placed the interests of the Jewish people at the disposal of British imperialism ... In the hands of the reactionary leaders of the Zionist movement the *yishuv* settlements have been transformed into an instrument of racist hate, propaganda, and chauvinism.'[10]

This line was expressed most sharply and clearly by Middle East specialist V. Lutsky, in a lecture he delivered on 9 August 1946 which was subsequently published as a special pamphlet by 'Pravda', the Communist Party publishing house.[11] The Jewish population in Palestine, said Lutsky, was under the influence of the bourgeois-Zionist nationalists who exploited it for Britain's imperialist objectives. He also claimed that Palestine was over-populated, that its natural resources were non-existent and that it was one of the world's poorest countries. The pamphlet went on to state that, while Soviet Russia and the Arab nations did not accept the imperialist mandatory system, the Zionists did so willingly because they knew that they would not be able to realise their programmes without England's help. One of the chapters, headed 'Palestine, an Arab Country', charged that the Zionists in Palestine, having arrived there when it was already populated by the Arabs, were the oppressors of the Arab nation. Those same Zionists were attempting, through terror and coercion, to expel or subjugate the local population which had deep roots in Palestine. Continuing in this vein, Lutsky's attack culminated with the claim – later to become one of the main facets of Soviet propaganda – that Zionism derived the concept of the Jews as a master-race from the arsenal of Fascism.[12]

But such attacks on Zionism were not only a function of the propaganda effort to influence Arab leaders. That they reflected official and fundamental Soviet policy during the period in question is most prominently illustrated by the off-the-record remarks of Aleksei Shevtsov, First Secretary in the USSR legation in Cairo. In his sharp attack on *yishuv* leaders, Shevtsov compared Ben Gurion's speeches to those of the Fascists.[13]

The worsening attitude towards Zionism which began in 1946 was to a certain extent contiguous with the deterioriation in the situation of Soviet Jews after Zhdanov's speech and the commencement of the campaign against local nationalism. However, this was a period of probing in terms of the Soviet attitude towards the *yishuv* and the Arab world, as the USSR had still not decided which horse to back in its mounting struggle against the Western powers.

May 1947 – May 1949

This period, one of the most complex and difficult in terms of analysis, witnessed both a pro-Israel policy which found dramatic expression in many areas, contributing decisively to the achievement of Israel's independence, and also an almost parallel anti-Jewish campaign conducted under cover of the struggle against bourgeois nationalism and cosmopolitanism, which attained unheard of heights of ferocity between November 1948 and March 1949. Was there any coherent or logical link between these two policies, the one internal, the other external? Can it be determined that Soviet policy towards the Middle East as a whole and towards Palestine in particular was made up of conjunctural and *ad hoc* decisions taken below the highest level? Or would it perhaps be more correct to see in the Soviet–Israeli 'honeymoon' a kind of brief pause – dictated by major considerations of Soviet foreign policy – in what was essentially a permanent anti-Zionist and anti-Israel line? An examination of the known historical facts will help us to answer these questions.

Despite the fact that those who shaped Soviet foreign policy (above all,

Stalin) were primarily concerned with Central and Western Europe, they did not ignore the strategic and political importance of the Middle East, and sought ways to increase their influence in the region. In late April 1947, it was decided at the highest level to commit the USSR to a sharp change of direction. In Gromyko's famous speech of 14 May 1947 in the General Assembly, the USSR gave preference to 'the establishment of an independent Arab-Jewish state, federal and democratic'. But Gromyko qualified this statement with the proviso that 'should it turn out that this solution is not implementable [...] it will be necessary to examine a second proposed solution [...] namely the partition of Palestine into two independent and non-dependent states – Jewish and Arab'. Within a few months, the Soviet Union went even further.[14] In their respective speeches of 13 October and 26 November 1947, Gromyko and Tsarapkin indicated that the USSR now favoured the second of the two alternatives – partition.

It can be concluded that the following factors contributed to this decision. (1) Already during the late thirties, but still more during the war period and after the Arab League was established, the Soviet leadership found itself disappointed in the Arab tendency to support first the Fascist regimes and then imperialist Britain. Losing faith in Arab power to expel the British from the Middle East, the Soviet Union gradually concluded that the Jews might be able to accomplish this. (2) The USSR perceived American policy in this period as aiming to increase its Middle East encroachment alongside and sometimes in place of Britain,[15] thereby endangering Soviet plans for the area. (3) The serious problem posed by the hundreds of thousands of Jewish refugees in Europe would be solved if they found shelter in Palestine. (4) The USSR had the chance to win the support of world Jewry by endorsing the partition plan.

Active Soviet support for Israel in this period found expression in a number of vital areas. Beginning with Gromyko's speech given on 13 October, the USSR consistently backed Israel's position in the international sphere in general and in UN institutions in particular. This support continued in all the discussions in which Soviet representatives as well as those from the Ukraine, Belorussia and the East European states participated.[16] It reached its finale in the vote on 11 May 1949 to admit Israel as a member of the UN. Perhaps even more important was the aid given to the *yishuv* when the USSR approved Czechoslovakia's sale of arms to Israel, arms which would prove to be crucial on the battle-field.

But a rigorous examination of Soviet speeches on the Palestinian question in international forums, of Soviet press reports and of the more academic political publications reveals that this shift, so important in itself, failed to bring with it a parallel change in policy towards Zionism.[17] Even from November 1947 to July 1948 – the most relaxed period in Soviet–Israeli relations – it was never stated that Zionism was the national liberation movement of the Jewish people, despite the fact that the Soviets often used this term to describe Arab national movements. And the total disappearance of the term 'Zionism' from the Soviet lexicon in this period revealed a deep-rooted Soviet unwillingness to rehabilitate a movement which had been so consistently and continually attacked by the founders of the USSR. Had Soviet long-range interests so demanded, the USSR leadership would undoubtedly have been able to find some formula to overcome this ideological difficulty – as it did in the case of Titoism. However, no doubt it soon became clear to the Soviet leaders that the usefulness of the *yishuv* in the struggle against British imperialism and in building up the Soviet position in the Mediterranean region would be of only short duration. The entire political constellation had been radically transformed by the United States' entry into the Middle East, with its increasing influence (real or imaginary) on the State of Israel.

The first signs of an imminent change in the 'neutral' attitude towards Zionism were apparent as early as August 1948. A new pamphlet based on a lecture by Lutsky stated, *inter alia*: 'With the support of England and the United States, the bourgeois Jewish nationalists have attempted to transform Palestine into a purely Jewish state without taking into consideration the interests and rights of the local population.' He continued: 'The Soviet Union has rejected the programmes for transforming Palestine either into a Jewish state or into a purely Arab state.'[18] In early September, a Soviet commentator's review of M. Stürnsfeld's book, which was published in Stockholm, contained the following statement:

In her description of the Jewish population's struggle for the establishment of the State of Israel, the author ignores the anti-imperialist national liberation movements of the Arab peoples. At the same time, there is no distinction made in the book between the interests of the broad democratic classes of the Jewish population and the interests of the Zionist bourgeoisie and its leaders, who are closely tied to Anglo-American capital. These leaders, who have pinned their hopes on London and Washington, have caused much harm to the Jewish people. They are not a little responsible for the tragedy of Palestine.[19]

These 'new tunes' in Soviet publications of the period were most clearly expressed by Ilya Erenburg, in his long article, 'Concerning a Certain Letter', which appeared in *Pravda* of 21 September 1948 (see Doc. 7). Another Jew, Izrail Genin, was also chosen to criticise Israel.[20] But the most violent attacks on Zionism were interwoven with the campaign against cosmopolitanism and bourgeois nationalism (see Docs. 88–9 and Chapter 4).

Circles associated with the Jewish Anti-Fascist Committee were very careful that their treatment of Israel, as expressed in the newspaper *Eynikeyt*, did not deviate from the general political line prevalent from June 1947 to 18 November 1948. The one possibly autonomous gesture made by the Committee was its telegram to Dr Chaim Weizmann following the establishment of the State of Israel.[21] Few commentaries were published in *Eynikeyt*, and those that did appear were written by persons assigned to the task, such as Itsik Fefer, David Bergelson, A. Hindes and G. Mindlin,[22] whose treatment of Israel and Zionism was almost totally congruent with that in the general press. However, in certain cases the newspaper anticipated the general press, as (to take one outstanding example) when Itsik Fefer sharply attacked the Joint in February 1948.[23] Following the appearance of Ilya Erenburg's article, *Eynikeyt* published attacks on those in the West who criticised Erenburg's theses,[24] particularly those Zionists who claimed that 'Israel is allegedly the homeland of all the Jews in the world'. One of these articles stated that the Soviet Jews 'will never desire to exchange their Soviet homeland'.

In sum, the positive Soviet attitude towards the establishment of the State of Israel and towards its War of Independence ameliorated the Soviet leadership's attitude towards Zionism only insofar as, for the space of a year until August 1948, the term was ignored rather than attacked. Moreover, this amelioration did not lead to the granting of permission for Soviet Jews to emigrate to Israel. Indeed, there was instead an inverse correlation between the authorities' attitude towards Israel and that towards Soviet Jewry: the *pro-Israel* policy led to an increasingly *anti-Jewish* policy in the following stages: (1) mounting attacks on Jewish nationalism, such as the episode involving the writer Itsik Kipnis (see Chapter 4) beginning in the second half of 1947; (2) the murder of Solomon Mikhoels, Chairman of the Jewish Anti-Fascist Committee on 13 January 1948; (3) the dissolution of the Jewish Anti-Fascist Committee and of most of the Jewish cultural institutions in November 1948; (4) mass arrests of leading figures in the Yiddish cultural world at the end of 1948 and the beginning of 1949; (5) the anti-cosmopolitan campaign which assumed a clear anti-Jewish character from 28 January 1949; (6) increased discrimination against Jews in various spheres.

At first glance this inverse correlation appears inconsistent with the desire to maintain and even improve relations with Israel, which would seem to demand that the Jews of the Soviet Union be treated no worse than other national minorities there, and (additionally or alternatively) that the Jews be allowed to emigrate to Israel. After all, the fate of Soviet Jewry – which after World War II constituted one-quarter of the Jewish people – was obviously perceived as vitally important to, and by, the State of Israel and the Zionist movement. But a closer examination of the factors determining Soviet policy at home and abroad demonstrates that a *positive–negative* attitude (positive towards Israel and negative towards Soviet Jewry) or *negative–positive* (negative towards Israel, positive towards Soviet Jewry) correlation was even more 'natural' than a completely positive correlation would have been during this period.

Soviet foreign policy was then being determined by fast-changing political, strategic, considerations, and by the determination to exploit temporary international constellations. However, the dominant and finally decisive factor at the time was not Soviet foreign policy in the Middle East but the necessity to deal quickly with a severe internal problem which arose as the result of precisely this foreign policy, namely the Jewish national awakening. This sudden upsurge in national consciousness found highly unusual expression in the spontaneous mass demonstrations of Soviet Jews in honour of the representative (Golda Meyerson) of a foreign country, and one that was not even socialist.[25] It can therefore be assumed that even if Israel had changed its foreign policy to one that was actively and consistently neutral, the course of events would not have been altered. (There is, of course, a chance that if Israel had become a Communist state in the full sense of the word, that is a Soviet satellite, things might have been different.)

June 1949 – early April 1953

This period was characterised by renewed Soviet efforts to expand its sphere of influence in the Middle East, but its attempts to gain a political foothold in the

Arab world proved ineffective. This no doubt goes a long way to explain why the Soviets, in spite of their extreme anti-Jewish and anti-Zionist policy, maintained correct, if extremely cool, relations with the State of Israel throughout virtually the entire period. Thus, in UN discussions the Soviet representatives adopted a position which can best be characterised as aloofness towards the Arab–Israeli conflict.

The orientalist V. Lutsky, whose anti-Zionist and anti-Israel positions have been discussed above, was one of the first to attempt the formulation of a thereoretical basis for the transformation of Soviet policy towards Israel.[26] In a speech published in October 1949, Lutsky stressed that Israel had not fulfilled its duty to establish a democratic and independent state. He also noted that Israel's Zionist leaders had mortgaged its sovereignty by opening the gates to foreign capital, and that the country was not in a position to survive without the support of one or another imperialist state. Even worse, the leaders were prepared to join the aggressive Mediterranean bloc being established by Anglo-American imperialism and were conducting a policy hostile to the Soviet Union. Thus they had come out in opposition to the World Peace Conference, to the related peace movement and to the participation of the *Histadrut* in the World Federation of Trade Unions. Finally, Lutsky's analysis of the situation prevailing in the Middle East led him to conclude that all the objective conditions for the resurgence of the national liberation struggle had now been created in the Arab states.

A theme which Lutsky did not raise in his speech was that pan-Islamic organisations (such as that established in 1935 in Al Azhar, the religious university of Cairo)[27] and other 'reactionary' forces in the Arab states had played a delaying role in the development of the national liberation movement in the Middle East. Later, in a return to the Comintern policy of the twenties and thirties, commentators did state that the reactionary ideologies included pan-Islamism, pan-Turkism, pan-Gandhiism and Zionism.[28] But this all-embracing approach was not long-lived, and from the end of 1949 increasingly harsh attacks were levelled specifically at Zionism.[29]

In the Rajk trial of September 1949 in Hungary, it was claimed that Zionism and the American espionage services were closely connected. This led to the virulent anti-Zionist campaign being broadened to include the whole of Eastern Europe, where it reached a peak in the Slansky trial of 1952.[30] In the Soviet Union itself, articles combining criticism of Zionism and the State of Israel began to appear in 1951. Attacking Zionism as a 'reactionary national movement', they linked it with the 'Fascist methods of government and discrimination against the Arab population in Israel'.[31] But this was only a preliminary to the malicious campaign of incitement and slander which was to be unleashed against Zionism, the Joint and Israel upon the 'discovery' of the 'Doctors' Plot' in January 1953 which continued until the day Stalin died (see Chapter 5).

The press and other communications media began by characterising the Zionist movement as a ramified organisation that embraced the whole world. Then the hopelessly reactionary character of the movement was stressed, and illustrated. For example, in 1903, Herzl had offered the good offices of the Zionist movement to the Tsarist Minister of the Interior von Pleve – murderer of the workers and organiser of the pogroms – in the struggle against the revolutionary influence on Jewish youth. And the leaders of Zionism had always cooperated with reactionary rulers such as the Sultan of Turkey and the German Kaiser. Furthermore, the Zionist, Jabotinsky, who organised Jewish legions for the Allies, was connected with Petlyura. It was also well known that Zionist leaders such as Abba Eban and Reuven Shiloah had operated as agents of the English espionage services at the same time as discussions were being held with Mussolini on establishing a Jewish state under the protection of Fascist Italy. Zionist organisations and the Bund in Poland had cooperated with the Nazis during the war, after which the movement became a tool of Anglo-American imperialism. And now, as was amply demonstrated by the Rajk and Slansky trials and by the confessions of the imprisoned doctors, Zionism was involved in subversive action against the socialist regimes in Eastern Europe and against the Soviet Union itself. Organisations such as the Joint, supposedly devoted to welfare and relief, had been set up as a cover for Zionist espionage operations, and Israel – the imperialist base in the Middle East – was portrayed as the lynch-pin in this world-wide system. Finally, the media did not fail to point up the sinister connection between the Zionist movement and Jewish millionaires, such as the bankers Lehman, Warburg, Morgenthau and Blaustein.

In sum, the period from 1949 until Stalin's death in 1953 saw a direct negative correlation between anti-Jewish policies within the USSR and anti-Zionist and anti-Israel policies abroad.

The post-Stalin period

The period following Stalin's death brought political changes in the USSR which resulted in a variety of policy changes towards Soviet Jews, Zionism and Israel. Significant though some of the shifts were, however, they did not result in any fundamental lessening of hostility towards the Jews or the Zionist enterprise.

The years 1953–6

This transition period was characterised by the emergence of a new foreign policy which had an effect on Soviet–Israeli relations. There is no doubt that the decision to resume Soviet–Israeli diplomatic relations was in large part based on the internal thaw and on the desire to normalise external relations. Thus, after several months of exhausting negotiations, relations were renewed on 21 July 1953.[32] However, the primary objective of the Soviet Union in the Middle East during this period was to advance its relations with the Arab states. Hope concentrated mainly on Egypt, which the Soviets (reversing their position held at the time of the Free Officers' Revolt of 1952) assigned to a 'progressive' neutralist policy. As such, it was a country ideally suited to act as a springboard for the extension of Soviet influence to other Arab states. The new Soviet leadership, eager to increase its influence, first attempted to play a mediatory role in the Arab–Israeli conflict. But when this appeared impractical, it gradually moved towards unilateral support for the Arab states in general and for Egypt in particular.

Nonetheless, following the resumption of diplomatic relations, the USSR made some further gestures of good will towards Israel: the Israeli and Soviet legations were raised to embassy rank in August 1954; trade relations were improved by the Soviets' proposal to sell Israel 75,000 tons of crude oil and to buy citrus fruit in return[33] (bilateral trade rose from $150,000 in 1950 to $3,120,000 in 1954);[34] and a limited number of emigration permits were issued to Soviet Jews (609 persons emigrated to Israel during 1954–6).[35]

However, the pro-Arab stance of the USSR brought about a deterioration in relations – even in comparison with the Stalin period – when the Soviets used their right of veto in the Security Council for the first time in January 1954 to demonstrate their full support for the Arabs *vis-à-vis* Israel,[36] and repeated this action on 29 March 1954. But the increasingly pro-Arab orientation found its most dramatic expression in the Czechoslovak–Egyptian arms deal of September 1955, which laid the groundwork for political, military and economic cooperation between the USSR and Egypt and Syria.[37] Khrushchev described this policy in a speech delivered to the Supreme Soviet at the end of December 1955:

We understand the aspirations of the Arab peoples, who are fighting for full liberation from foreign rule. Accordingly, we cannot but condemn the actions of Israel, which from the first days of its existence has menaced its neighbours and has adopted a hostile policy towards them. It is clear that this policy does not serve Israel's interests and that those adopting it are supported by the imperialist powers (and we all know who they are). They aspire to use Israel as an instrument against the Arab peoples with the aim of ruthlessly exploiting the natural resources of this region.[38]

Paradoxically, despite these overtures to the Arab side in the Middle East conflict, there is no doubt that anti-Zionist propaganda went into clear decline in this period, both quantitatively and in terms of content.[39] This is doubtless to be explained both by the marked improvement in the situation of the Jews within the Soviet Union and by the correct, albeit highly equivocal, relations maintained with Israel. (And, yet again, behind the scenes, a number of secret anti-Zionist trials were held at this time following the expulsion of Israeli diplomats accused of maintaining contacts with Soviet Jews.)

It may be concluded that there was a positive correlation between the relatively improved Soviet relations with the State of Israel, the cessation of the campaign against Zionism and the partial amelioration in the situation of Soviet Jews during this transition period. In other words, the situation was significantly altered from that which characterised the previous period. Of interest here is that a direct correlation between the three variables (Israel, Zionism and Soviet Jewry) existed in both these periods, a negative one in the years 1949–53 and a positive one from 1953 to 1956. The inverse relationships which had prevailed during 1947–9 derived from the exceptional international conditions unique to that period.

It is more difficult to draw concrete conclusions regarding the correlation between Soviet policy towards the Arab states in these years and its attitude towards Zionism and Soviet Jewry. However, what can be stated is that the shift which had already begun to characterise Soviet–Arab relations (mainly those with Egypt and Syria) was still not broad enough to bring about a basic Soviet policy change in these two spheres. Here, in the years 1953–6, internal factors ultimately continued to predominate.

November 1956 – October 1964

A marked deterioration in Soviet–Israeli relations could already be perceived in August 1956, following the nationalisation of the Suez Canal and the consequent further rapprochement between the Soviet Union and the Arab countries. However, it was the Sinai Campaign and the subsequent efforts of the USSR to consolidate its position in the Arab states which severely exacerbated Soviet–Israeli relations. On 5 November 1956, Soviet Premier Marshal Bulganin sent a letter to Israeli Prime Minister David Ben Gurion which stated *inter alia*: 'The government of Israel is criminally and irresponsibly playing with the fate of its people. It is sowing a hatred for the State of Israel among the peoples of the East which cannot but leave its marks on the future of Israel, and calls into question the very existence of Israel as a state.'[40] On 7 November 1956, the Soviet government unilaterally cancelled the fuel agreement which had been concluded with Israel in July 1956. And on 10 November, threats were uttered about dispatching Soviet 'volunteers' if military operations were not terminated and if the invading Israeli armies did not withdraw from Egyptian territory.[41]

While the Soviet media in this period heaped fire and brimstone on the 'Anglo-French-Israeli aggression', it was Israel which came in for the most vituperative attacks.[42] During January–March 1957, official Soviet representatives and communications media constantly reiterated that the Straits of Tiran were Egyptian territorial waters. They sharply condemned the United States for supporting Israel's demand that the Gulf of Aqaba be declared international waters.[43] The return of the Soviet Ambassador, Abramov, to his post in Israel in April 1957 did not lead to a significant improvement in relations between the two countries.[44] Starting from late July 1957, and more markedly after the Moscow Youth Festival in August, the regime waged a mounting anti-Israeli and anti-Zionist campaign. The intensification of this campaign may well have resulted, at least in part, from the enthusiastic reception given to the Israeli delegation to the festival (an episode reminiscent of similar and fateful events in 1948). When the anti-Zionist agitation merged, as it often did, with the anti-religious campaigns characteristic of the Khrushchev period, the over-all result produced a clearly anti-Jewish impression.[45]

An early sign that the Soviet leadership had decided to launch an anti-Zionist campaign can be seen in the episode of Hazan, an attaché to the Israeli Embassy in Moscow who was arrested by Soviet security services in September 1957, during a visit to Odessa, and charged with distributing anti-Soviet propaganda literature.[46] The virulent attack on 'the diplomat from Lilienblum Street', published in *Pravda*[47] by the Jew and former Bundist David Zaslavsky, drove home the message that the authorities viewed any contact between Israeli diplomats and Soviet Jews as intolerable. But the most concentrated Soviet press and radio campaign in this period was that directed against the 'Zionist propaganda' which had managed to lure individual Soviet citizens to the 'Israeli paradise'. The media kept up a barrage against these emigrants, who, it was claimed, had quickly become disillusioned and were constantly writing letters requesting permission to return to their socialist homeland.[48] Khrushchev himself reiterated the claim that Soviet Jews were not interested in leaving their motherland; on the contrary, 'many of those who have left it and reached Israel are requesting permission to come back'.[49] Every rumour in the West about a mass emigration of Soviet Jews was at once angrily denied. 'The aim of these rumour-mongers', it was stated in the press, 'is to undermine the friendship between the Soviet Union and the Arab countries.'[50]

But the authorities did not leave it there. Sensing the danger of a Jewish national awakening in the Soviet Union (a danger brought home by the surprising number of young Jews who openly aspired to emigrate to Israel), they decided to engage in an active anti-Israel, anti-Zionist and anti-Jewish policy. During 1959–63, this policy reached peaks that in some ways even recalled the years 1949–53. The campaign was waged simultaneously on two fronts. The one, quiet and clandestine, involved the arrest and penal exile of Jews who had expressed any manner of sympathy for, and a desire to emigrate to, Israel; the other, loud and unrestrained, took the form of a propaganda campaign conducted in all the Soviet media. It brought with it the renewed output of anti-Zionist books and pamphlets, after a ten-year hiatus in such publications, as well as many articles in the central and local press along with coverage in the other media.

The anti-Zionist propaganda concentrated on four areas: (1) a sombre portrayal of the State of Israel as the base and bridgehead of imperialism;[51] (2) angry condemnation of Zionism; (3) attacks on Israeli diplomats and tourists who brought the 'venom' of Zionism to the Jews of the Soviet Union; and (4) the disappointment of USSR citizens who had emigrated to the 'Israeli paradise'.

The State of Israel. It was claimed that the State of Israel had, from its very inception, conducted a policy of mass expulsion of Arabs from their lands: the total driven out, it was stated, had now reached the figure of one million persons.[52] This charge, which began to appear in 1957, was repeated with greater frequency in most of the later books and articles, and was combined with a rewriting of the history of the Israeli War of Independence. In a review of Glubb Pasha's *A Soldier with the Arabs*, the Soviet critic agreed with the former Jordanian chief-of-staff that the Israeli army had numbered 120,000 men in the years 1948–9, while all the Arab armies together had only 56,000 in the war period. Moreover, according to this reviewer, the Israel Defence Forces were better trained, had better weapons (American, of course), and had American officers fighting in its ranks.[53] Since its establishment, Israel had conducted a consistent and brutal policy of blowing up Arab houses, murdering Arabs, expelling them by force of arms, and border provocations. The one objective behind all this was to expand Israel's territory at the expense of its neighbours.

As to Israel's foreign policy towards the Soviet Union and the Soviet bloc, Khrushchev declared that it showed ingratitude (see Doc. 17). Israel had marched hand in hand with the imperialist states, had contributed to the rehabilitation of the Third Reich by agreeing to accept reparations from (and forge ties with) West Germany and had acted as the instrument of imperialism on the African continent.

Israel's socialism was nothing but a propaganda myth. The gross inequality which existed in the country led to unemployment and bankruptcies, which often ended in suicide. The kibbutzim, attacked even more fiercely than the socialist parties and the *Histadrut*, were generally portrayed as labour camps in which idealistic workers were exploited by bloodsuckers from Wall Street.[54] And finally, Israel was described as the willing stooge of American capitalism, on behalf of which it plotted and conspired against the progressive governments in the Arab world.

Zionism. The attacks on Zionism became particularly violent and were reminiscent of Stalin's last years (see Doc. 17). Zionism was charged with being a nationalist bourgeois movement which fostered the reactionary theory that there existed a worldwide Jewish nation. Since the thirties, anti-Communism had become the standard around which had rallied the Zionist movement, the Jewish bourgeoisie, clericalism and world reaction. New names were now added to the long list of reactionaries (cited above in our analysis of the anti-Zionist campaign of 1949–53) with whom the Zionist movement had allegedly cooperated. These included Kerensky, Prime Minister of the Provisional Government in Russia in 1917, the White generals Denikin and Kolchak and the Fascists Mussolini, Hitler and Adolf Eichmann.[55] Zionism deliberately fanned world anti-Semitism in order, as was (allegedly) declared by the Israeli Prime Minister Ben Gurion, to increase immigration to Israel.[56] Nor were such Jewish organisations as the Joint omitted from these attacks.[57] And, of course, stress was again laid on the close connection between Zionism, Israel and the Jewish and non-Jewish capitalists throughout the world (see Doc. 91).

Attacks on Israeli diplomats and tourists. The attacks on Israeli diplomats, which began with that on Hazan in the second half of 1957, continued with minor breaks throughout the entire period. Apart from the ambassadors themselves, not one Israeli Embassy worker of any rank was overlooked, starting with the archivist and going right up to the First Secretary. Among those who came in for particularly violent denunciation were Levanon, Sharett, Prat, Halevi, Agmon, Eliav, Gat and Zimrat. The broadsides appeared in almost all the Soviet newspapers, but the trade-union organ, *Trud*,[58] and the Odessa newspaper, *Znamya kommunizma*, were particularly active in the attacks, as were a number of local newspapers.[59]

The media gave great play to the anti-Soviet activities of Israeli diplomats and tourists who distributed published material and Zionist emblems in synagogues and elsewhere. They were also accused of recruiting spies from among the Jewish population, of receiving secret documents and of coordinating provocative acts against the regime. The press even published letters, purportedly written by Jews, demanding that an immediate and permanent end be put to the criminal activities of the Israeli diplomats.

One cannot ignore the fact that the authorities were outraged by contacts between the diplomats of a foreign state and Soviet citizens, which they regarded as intervention in their internal affairs and a threat to their internal security policy. Their extreme sensitivity to this issue, no doubt, goes far to explain the severity of Soviet attacks on the Israeli Embassy.

The disappointment of the emigrants to Israel. The best known of the many letters published in the Soviet press from emigrants who had been disappointed in Israel after having gone through the Zionist 'seven circles of hell' was that of May 1959, addressed to K. Voroshilov, Chairman of the Presidium of the Supreme Soviet, in which 107 persons requested permission to return to the USSR.[60] Other letters came from emigrants who had already returned and now, contented, were warning the Jewish population against the blandishments of Zionist propaganda. Articles bearing headings such as 'Tears from Paradise', 'We Paid Dearly for Our Mistake', 'In an Alien Land', 'The Truth about the Promised Land' appeared often during these years; they described in the most sombre colours the everyday tribulations faced by new immigrants from the Soviet Union upon their arrival in Israel.

This extreme propaganda campaign was accompanied by the harassment and arrests of potential emigrants, as well as by a curtailment in the number of exit permits granted.[61] The objective was, of course, to sever all contact between Soviet Jews and Israel. While this anti-Israel policy was no doubt exploited to augment Soviet influence in the Arab countries, it would seem that this factor was only of secondary importance, although certainly more significant than during the Stalin era. The rare and minor improvements in Soviet–Israeli relations which found expression in limited areas such as tourism and cultural exchanges did not imply any basic change in the essentially anti-Israel policy of the Khrushchev period.

The partial worsening of Soviet–Egyptian relations which followed the Egypt–Syria unity pact of February 1958, and the ideological contretemps between Khrushchev and Nasser, do not seem to have led to a parallel improvement in Soviet–Israeli relations. It may therefore be concluded that the Soviet Union was convinced that rapprochement with the Arab states was paramount to Soviet needs during this period because of the immense economic, demographic and revolutionary potential of the Arabs.

The collective leadership period

Khrushchev's ouster from power in October 1964 did not lead to any fundamental shift in Soviet policy towards Israel and Zionism. This is not to say, however, that there were no minor or temporary changes in the new leadership's treatment of these questions.

The collective leadership, which had been at the centre of power under Khrushchev since the second half of the fifties, was undoubtedly interested in demonstrating its desire for change (at least of style) in internal and foreign policy alike. However, a collective leadership – which by nature is divided in its views – has to measure its steps with the utmost caution. This may help us to understand the fluctuations in policy which characterised Soviet–Israeli relations between the end of 1964 and April–May 1967.

The first sign of improvement in the Soviet attitude towards Israel and, to a lesser extent, towards Zionism was the slight reduction in the tone and in the quantity of hostile statements.[62] Thus, the most extreme anti-Israel sections were now frequently omitted when the speeches of Arab leaders were published, and reports of life in Israel tended to show less hostility than in the Khrushchev period. There was also a let-up in the attitude of the authorities towards Israeli diplomats in Moscow,[63] although the press still printed occasional attacks on individual diplomats (including Ambassador Yosef Tekoah) for meeting with and attempting to influence the Jewish population.[64]

A further improvement during this period was evidenced in the expansion of cultural relations, in the exchange of scientific delegations and in the growth of Israeli tourism to the Soviet Union. Still more important was the increase in emigration to Israel, which began in 1965 and reached some 2,000 immigrants in 1966. Of particular significance in this connection was the formal declaration of Aleksei Kosygin, Soviet Premier, in Paris in December 1966 that exit permits would be extended to all who requested them within the framework of family reunification (Doc. 29). This declaration caused a considerable stir and resulted in many Jews applying to *Ovir* in order to receive exit permits.

On the other hand, there were a number of factors (both internal and external) which acted with increasing force to curb and eventually to counteract these tendencies.[65] The internal factor which was decisive in determining Soviet anti-Israel policy was the unwillingness of the regime to alter its basic attitude towards the Jewish national minority either by expanding its cultural privileges or by allowing large-scale emigration to Israel. Indeed, the persistence of significant numbers of Jews in applying to emigrate despite all the obstacles raised in their path only served to strengthen the resolve of those in the Soviet leadership who were already opposed to any relaxation of emigration policies. The gradual shift from the relative liberalism characteristic of the domestic scene in general in 1965 to renewed repression – typified most dramatically by the Sinyavsky–Daniel trial of February 1966 – no doubt reinforced this tendency to keep a firm check on the Jewish minority too.

Although it was pure coincidence that in the same month (February 1966) there was a revolution in Syria which brought the new Ba'ath to power, this coup was of profound political significance in terms of Soviet policy towards Israel and Zionism. Without going into the complex web of factors which followed from this event to the outbreak of the Israel–Arab war in June 1967, it is important to note, if only in brief, the consequences of the Six-Day War in terms of the severe deterioration in Soviet–Israeli relations.

Immediately after the June war, the Soviet Union and all the East European countries with the solitary exception of Romania broke all diplomatic ties with Israel. Even more significant, perhaps, was the decision of the USSR to rearm Egypt and Syria, to despatch instructors to their armies, and to extend them massive economic aid. Simultaneously there began an anti-Zionist and anti-Israel propaganda campaign of such ferocity that it outdid in scope and virulence the worst excesses of the times of Stalin[66] (see Doc. 92).

Among the new themes employed was the transformation of Zionist and Israeli leaders from collaborators with reaction, Fascism and Nazism into their actual partners and even into Nazis themselves. Zionist ideology, which had already been characterised as racist, treacherous, aggressive and practising genocide, was now described as barely distinguishable from the Fascist and Nazi ideologies. The Zionist movement, which had already been portrayed as a ramified network in the service of imperialism, now became a kind of gigantic spider ensnaring every sphere of life in the entire world in its web – a picture very close to that in the *Protocols of the Elders of Zion* and Nazi anti-Jewish propaganda. And, finally, Israel was said to have already begun to carry out its plan, based on principles of *Lebensraum*, to establish an empire stretching from the Nile to the Euphrates (see Doc. 92).

In sum, the period which opened with some minor improvement in Soviet–Israeli relations underwent a reverse process which could already be discerned in 1966 and which took on enormous momentum following the war of June 1967. Thus, as in the years 1949–53, there was once again a direct correlation between the extremely negative attitude towards the State of Israel, towards Zionism and towards Soviet Jewry.

However, it should be noted in conclusion that although there has been no essential change in the Soviet attitude towards Zionism and the State of Israel since 1967, there was a highly significant shift of policy in March 1971, when the Soviet authorities permitted the mass emigration of its Jews: the years 1971–81 saw the departure of some 250,000 emigrants from the USSR. But an analysis of the reasons which produced this shift lies outside the framework of the present work.

Documents to Chapter 6

Document 88* Lutsky on Zionism as a weapon of imperialism in the Middle East (March 1949)

An augumented meeting of the Academic Council of the Pacific Institute and bureau of the Moscow group of the Oriental Institute of the USSR Academy of Sciences was held in Moscow on 4–6 April. The meeting was devoted to the struggle against manifestations of bourgeois cosmopolitanism in scientific oriental studies.

The discussion was animated, scientifically creative and politically keen. About thirty people addressed the meeting. [...]

In his introductory report E. M. Zhukov,[67] Director of the Pacific Institute and corresponding member of the USSR Academy of Sciences, examined the political essence of bourgeois cosmopolitanism and its role in the ideological preparation for a new world war carried on by the Anglo-American aggressive bloc. [...]

V. B. Lutsky[68] devoted part of his report to the tasks of the Eastern research front in the struggle against Zionism – the reactionary ideology of Jewish bourgeois nationalism. The speaker pointed out that the tasks of this struggle had always existed, but that now they had become especially urgent insofar as Zionism was one of the active weapons of American and English imperialist policy in the Middle East. Besides, at the present time, Anglo-American war-mongers are utilising Zionism as a disruptive weapon in other countries of the world. The immediate task of Soviet orientalists studying the Middle East consists in exposing and smashing the cosmopolitan ideology of a 'single Jewish nation' – an ideology duly subjected to devastating criticism by Lenin and Stalin.

Document 89† M. Mitin[69] on Zionism at the time of the 'Doctors' Plot' (February 1953)

I

The different Zionist organisations to be found in many capitalist countries represent nowadays quite a widespread international espionage network in

* *Source*: A. G., 'Ucheny sovet tikhookeanskogo instituta' (The Academic Council of the Pacific Institute), *Voprosy istorii*, 1949, no. 3, pp. 155, 158.

† *Source*: M. Mitin, 'Sionistkaya agentura amerikanskogo imperializma' (Zionist Agency of American Imperialism), *Za prochny mir, za narodnuyu demokratiyu*, 20 February 1953.

the service of the US imperialists, carrying out their criminal assignments. There is nothing fortuitous in this role of Zionism. It stems from the entire history and activity of the Zionist organisations.

Zionism made its appearance at the end of the eighties of the last century as a reactionary nationalist movement of the Jewish bourgeoisie in Austria, Russia, Germany and other countries.

In 1896 Theodor Herzl,[70] a reactionary Austrian journalist, published the booklet *The Jewish State*, and a year later the first Zionist congress took place in Basle. This was quickly followed by the establishment of a Zionist society in London and a Zionist bank, supported by Rothschild, the well-known millionaire.

A central task of the Zionist movement right from its inception was to divert the Jewish working masses in all countries from participating in the general revolutionary struggle of the proletariat. In furtherance of this aim, Zionism advanced its ultra-reactionary idea of the so-called 'Jewish community', irrespective of country, of the economic, social and cultural conditions of the Jewish people and of the classes to which they belonged. [...]

The Zionists entered into contact with monarchs and 'highly placed persons' in different countries: with Kaiser Wilhelm II,[71] with the Sultan of Turkey,[72] with the Pope, with Chamberlain,[73] and so on. There is perhaps hardly a reactionary force in the world which the Zionist leaders did not try to contact. They had dealings with Petlyura,[74] with Pilsudski[75] and with Mussolini.[76] The Zionist movement, in the person of its leaders and inspirers, was not averse to entering into contact even with Hitlerite Fascism. It is common knowledge that Jewish financiers in America, the men who subsidised the Zionists, simultaneously lavished money on Hitler before his advent to power. Incidentally, the meeting between von Papen[77] and Hitler, which took place just before Fascist rule was installed in Germany, was held on the premises of Baron Kurt von Schröder, a director of the Stein Bank (which was connected with the Zionist movement) and correspondent for the Levi, Solomon, Oppenheim and Co. firm. The big American banking firms, Dillon Read and Co., Kuhn-Loeb, Lehman Brothers and others with which the Zionist movement has always been closely connected, gave tremendous financial help to the German monopolists and facilitated Fascism's advent to power. At present, the same banking interests are again active in helping to revive predatory German imperialism.

II

For years the Zionists have been closely connected with British imperialism and with the British secret service. Their head office was located in London for a long time, and all their activity was directed by British diplomacy. The late Dr Weizmann,[78] leader of the Zionist movement and later president of Israel, was until 1946 an official of one of the British ministries. Other Zionist chieftains were direct agents of British imperialism. Eban, the Israeli representative to the UNO, and Shiloah, who heads the Israeli intelligence service, worked for the British intelligence service for years.

Since the end of World War II, the Zionist movement, headed by reactionary bourgeois elements, has come more and more under the control of the US imperialists. With branches all over Europe, the Zionist movement, which includes numerous and varied organisations, has proved for the new pretenders to world domination a highly convenient instrument for organising espionage, sabotage and subversive work directed against the Soviet Union and the countries of the Peoples' Democracies.

American capital is establishing financial and political control over the World Zionist Organisation, meeting all the expenditure incurred in maintaining its widespread espionage apparatus. In America the Zionist organisation was headed by Robert Szold,[79] businessman and brother of Harold Szold, an associate of the Lehman banking firm.

At the Rajk trial in Hungary, the accused, Tibor Szönyi, who confessed that he was a US secret agent, testified as follows: 'I know, and I understood very well while in Switzerland, that the Zionist movement as a whole maintains very close contact with the US secret service.'[80]

The trial in Czechoslovakia of the anti-state conspiracy centre headed by Slansky showed the important role the Zionists played in the organisation of the centre. The witness Orenshtein testified in court that already 'in 1947, prior to the formation of the State of Israel, a secret conference was held in Washington, attended by Truman, Acheson, Ben Gurion, Sharett and Morgenthau Jr.[81] At this conference Morgenthau, Ben Gurion and Sharett agreed that Zionist organisations would be used for espionage and other subversive activity in the Peoples' Democracies, while the US on its part would help the Israel Zionists carry out their plans.'

Thus, recognition of Israel in May 1948, by the former US President Truman, was preceded by the 'Morgenthau–Acheson' plan, by an agreement between the US rulers and Zionist leaders to the effect that the Zionists would place themselves wholly and completely in the service of US imperialism for the realisation of its aggressive designs.

III

[. . .] The criminal act of terror perpetrated by the Zionist bandits against the USSR Legation in Tel Aviv was not fortuitous.[82] It was the natural and logical result of the anti-Soviet line carried out in the past, and carried out now, by the Israeli rulers at the instigation of the US imperialists. It should be noted that the bomb thrown into the Soviet Legation, with the connivance of the police, was preceded by two attacks against the Czechoslovak Embassy in Tel Aviv on the part of Zionist bandits.

Cultivating the lowest chauvinistic instincts, the Israeli government seeks, on the one hand, to divert the attention of the working people in the country from the catastrophic state of the economy and, on the other, to fulfil the utterly provocative assignments of the war-mongers, with a view to aggravating international tension.

All the foulness and monstrosity of the crime of the Zionist Fascist gang against the Soviet Legation in Tel Aviv stands out particularly in the light of the fact that it was precisely the Soviet Union which, by smashing Hitlerite Germany, saved millions of Jews from extermination.

The wrath and burning indignation of the working people in the Soviet Union and of all progressive people in all countries were aroused by the foul crime of the terrorist group of doctor-killers,[83] exposed and rendered harmless by the security organs of the Soviet Union. Most members of this criminal gang were associated, as is known, with the international Jewish bourgeois nationalist Zionist organisation known as 'Joint' – a branch of US intelligence.

The names of the doctor-killers, who, on orders from the US and British secret services, killed Comrades A. A. Zhdanov[84] and A. S. Shcherbakov,[85] outstanding leaders of the Communist Party of the Soviet Union, will be cursed forever. Progressive mankind will never forget these black crimes of the Zionist lackeys of the imperialist secret services.

The evil crimes of the group of doctor-killers, like the activities of the Zionists – participants in the anti-state conspiracy centre in Czechoslovakia and in the act of terror against the Soviet Legation in Tel Aviv – are all links in the same chain. All are manifestations of the criminal activity of the US–British imperialists and their hangers-on, aimed at preparing a new world slaughter. This explains why the active struggle by all progressive forces in all countries against the machinations of the war-mongers, why the sharpest vigilance by the masses, are the vital tasks of the day.

Peace-loving people in all countries brand with shame the imperialist predators who commit monstrous crimes, resort to provocation after provocation and whip up war hysteria. The day will come when the war-mongers and their henchmen will be tried for all their crimes by the great court of the peoples!

Document 90* Zionist delegation at the Moscow Youth Festival (1957)

This was the first meeting in Moscow. It held no surprises for us after the long train journey. However, there is still no knowing how they will behave. We had heard many stories about the reservations, fears and cautiousness of the Jews of Moscow. Even now, we see them in large numbers in the crowds, greeting us with radiant eyes, but not daring to approach.

'Shalom aleikhem!'

Where the traffic was held up by the crowds breaking through the wall of policemen dividing the vehicles from the masses, people would come up to the slowly moving vehicles which were clearing a way for themselves through the crowds, to shake hands and exchange badges and souvenirs. How profoundly different was the firm and friendly handshake of a Russian lad who wanted our badge from the trembling handshake of a Jewish boy whose heart went out to us, hovering between hope and despair, that he might be one of us. After he had withdrawn his hand, a crumpled piece of paper was left in my palm: 'My name is — I am in class — at the — school, my address is — I want to learn Hebrew, do something for me. My mother and I want to emigrate to Israel. Goodbye dear brothers, we are proud of you.'

How much we wanted to know the story behind this crumpled scrap of

* *Source*: Natan Shaham, *Pegishot be-moskvah 1957* (Encounters in Moscow 1957), Merḥaviah, Sifriat poalim 1957, pp. 12–13, 21–2, 36–7.

paper, pleading for 'my mother and me'. And where was father? What was the meaning of 'want to emigrate to Israel'? How and when was this decision taken? And what caused it?

The vehicle drove on. From the midst of the throng we threw glances in search of our brothers, the Jews. We saw them, absorbed but not assimilated, their eyes revealing what is written in their passports: Jew. Eye meets eye and glistens with tears.

'Hurrah for the heroes of our people! Greetings from Moscow.' Another note falls to the floor of our vehicle, among the scraps of chocolate wrappings and food bags.

And there are those who do not have the courage. In the crowd I saw a man and a woman, getting on in years. Their faces were so familiar to me. They sensed my look. The woman made as if to approach, but the man seized her hand. I was holding a Hebrew–Russian calendar in my hand, for all to see. The man's eyes dwelt on it and showed the excitement within his heart. The vehicle was moving slowly. I did not take my eyes from their faces. They followed the vehicle by themselves, forty paces from it and to the side. When the vehicle stopped, they stopped. I looked at them with pity. The vehicle accelerated and for a moment they were lost, but again I spotted the man's hat in the distance. The vehicle stopped and they quickened their pace. Now they were able to come close. Once again the man took hold of the woman's arm. I could see his fingers firmly gripping her. She gave him a look, the meaning of which will for ever remain impenetrable to me. How many trials have the two of them experienced? How many horrors have hung over them? How many pogroms have raged about and weighed down upon their hunched shoulders? The man lowered his eyes. Suddenly she broke away from him and ran towards our vehicle. I did not manage to say anything to her, but pressed the calendar in to her hand while shaking hands with her. The woman began sobbing. The vehicle started and moved off. Above the radiant faces of the people hailing us with 'peace and friendship' I could see the woman crying, standing hunched next to her husband, with his hand resting on her shoulder. His gaze was fixed on me and the glass of his spectacles sparkled. A moment later they were lost to sight. [...]

There were those who spoke altogether differently. One, a tall old man approached the window of our bus and stared at us with a look of longing.

'Jewish?'

'Yes, but not Zionist', he replied in Hebrew to my Yiddish.

'Where are you from?'

'Moscow, but I'm not a Zionist. I've always been opposed to Zionism and am still opposed today. Well, how are things in Israel?'

'Fine.'

'Fine, eh? But no emigration to Israel!'

'Everybody is entitled to his own opinion.'

'Yes, that's right. But Zionism is very bad for the Jews. I fought against Zionism, I did.'

'Fine. If that's the case why are you standing at the window? Let the others approach. Look, they also want to meet us.'

'Yes, of course. Aren't you going to give me a calendar, then?'

On receiving the calendar he stuck it with trembling hand into his pocket and said, 'I'm not a Zionist, not a Zionist.'

'We heard you. Now, why don't you leave the window?'

'Can you possibly give me a badge, an Israeli flag?'

'Of course, what else?'

'A pencil. I have a little grandchild at home. He will be very pleased.'

He took the pencil, and with tears flowing down his cheeks, went his way – the opposer. [...]

I looked at the face of my companion [a Russian Jewish youth]: how much he resembled them [youngsters from the USSR and abroad dancing in Red Square]. His eyes were also sparkling. In another moment he would leave me and be swept into the circle.

Suddenly I asked him, 'In what way are you a Jew?'

He knows nothing about his people except that once they left Egypt and once they went back. The first time it was all right and the second time it was not all right. He does not know Yiddish, nor Hebrew. He knows nothing about Israel apart from what was written in *Pravda* with my corrections.

He gave me a crafty look: 'That's what's written in my passport.'

It is impossible to evince a rational answer from him. He is Jewish and that is sufficient for him. He will never marry a non-Jewish woman, he would not be able to. Why not? Because one day she would call him 'yid' and that would mean the end of their family life. He was twenty-seven, from a family of labourers.

'Did anyone bother you in your childhood?'

'Take a look at me', he said proudly. 'Did anyone bother me?'

He has a strikingly handsome face, a typical Russian face, the type to be photographed and printed on the cover of a Russian propaganda weekly.

'Were you discriminated against when you graduated from university?'

'A man of my age who has found work in his profession in Moscow itself cannot complain of discrimination.'

All the same, he is careful in what he says and keeps his goal in sight. Unlike the elderly who do not believe in their future and are satisfied with a great emotional awakening which will nourish them in their declining days, he, like many other youngsters, believes that one day the gates will open, and he is consciously preparing himself to emigrate to Israel.

Others are more richly endowed than he. Some have known suffering and discrimination; some possess a wide and varied knowledge of their people; and others are firm in their Judaism – with pride and torments they are ready to pay the price of being a Jew, day by day and hour by hour.

Document 91* The Zionist movement and imperialism

The 25th World Zionist Congress was inaugurated on 27 December 1960, in Jerusalem (Israel), after having been preceded by congresses of the Zionist parties of Israel, the USA and other capitalist countries.

* *Source*: 'Sborishche bankrotov' (A Gathering of Bankrupts), *Trud*, 6 January 1961.

In its reports on the Congress proceedings, the Western press mentions that the present Congress takes place in an atmosphere of crisis in the Zionist movement. The Israeli paper *Kol ha-am* notes: 'the source of this crisis does not lie in external circumstances, but in the very essence of Zionism itself. The idea having failed in its realisation, crisis and organisational havoc have ensued.'[86] Even Goldmann, the president of the so-called 'World Zionist Organisation', was forced to admit that 'Zionism is now undergoing the greatest moral and spiritual crisis of its existence.'[87]

What is Zionism and why is it not supported by the Jews of the world?

Zionism first appeared in the eighties of the nineteenth century as one of the forms of reactionary nationalist ideology of the strong Jewish bourgeoisie closely connected with imperialism. The Zionist organisation was officially established in 1897 in Basle (Switzerland), and proclaimed as its aim the resettlement in Palestine of all the Jews of the world. A number of similar organisations were subsequently created and Zionism gained its acceptance not only in the midst of the Jewish bourgeoisie, but also to a certain extent among the Jewish workers who were looking for the means to struggle against national and class oppression. By preaching Zionism, the Jewish bourgeoisie tried to divert the working masses from the class struggle.

The history of the Zionist movement proves that its link with imperialism is permanent and organic. For instance, on the very day following the Great October Socialist Revolution, the leaders of Zionism called on their members to oppose the Soviet regime. During the Civil War and the period of foreign intervention in Russia, the Zionists came to terms with Kolchak,[88] Denikin,[89] Petlyura and Pilsudski, despite the monstrous pogroms these counter-revolutionaries had organised in the Jewish townships of the Ukraine and Belorussia.

According to the materials of the Gruenwald–Kasztner trial[90] held in Jerusalem in 1955, the so-called international Zionist organisations supplied military equipment to the Hitlerites in 1944–45, on condition that these would be used against the Soviet Army only. And this occurred at a time when millions of innocent Jews were being bestially exterminated behind barbed-wire fences in the Nazi concentration camps.

On 14 May 1948, the State of Israel was established on a part of the territory of Palestine on the basis of the UN General Assembly's resolution. During the 1947 UN debate on the Palestine question, the Soviet Union, faithful to its policy of protecting all the oppressed peoples of the world, came out against any colonial yoke in Palestine and upheld the right of the Jewish and Arab populations of that country to an independent state existence.

However, taking advantage of the weakness of the democratic movement in Palestine and leaning on the support of the American and British imperialists, the most reactionary elements among the Zionists, Ben Gurion at their head, came to power in the new state. They turned Israel into a tool of imperialism and first and foremost of the American monopolies.

The Zionist ideology is being inculcated in Israel. The Arab minority and Jews originating from Asian and African countries are subjected to persecution and discrimination. This can be proved by an example of an appeal by the Indian Jews published in September–December 1960, and by the letters from former Soviet citizens on their sufferings in the 'land of the fathers'. Thus Zionism comes close to racism in the Israeli government's internal policy towards national minorities.

The foreign policy of the Israeli Zionists is closely linked with the aggressive line followed by the USA and other imperialist powers in the Near and Middle East. Striving to increase the manpower and military potential of the State of Israel, the Zionists use all means at their disposal to achieve mass immigration of Jews to Israel and also to solicit economic assistance from the Jewish population and governments of the USA and other Western countries.

The Israeli Zionists clamour their readiness to receive all the Jews living in different parts of the world. Particularly zealous activity was deployed in this context in the first years of the State of Israel's existence, when the Zionist propagandists succeeded, through deceit, blackmail and the exploitation of religious prejudices, to persuade a certain number of trustful people from European and African countries to depart for Israel.

Believing the fables of the Israeli propagandists on the 'life of paradise' in the 'promised land', thousands of people found themselves in unbearable conditions on Israeli soil. They have no permanent employment, cannot live like human beings. According to data provided by the Israeli Ministry of Social Security, there were 363,000 needy immigrants in the country in 1958, rising to 400,000 in 1959.

After all this, it is permissible to ask the Zionist lords: whom do they represent at the present gathering in Jerusalem? Whose interests do they defend?

Events of the last years have shown that a time is approaching when history will write off imperialism and its faithful servants. Cringing before Washington, the Zionists go out of their way to curb the present development of events. They increase their anti-Soviet propaganda, spread lies about the Soviet Union's policy. Paid propagandists dispatch to our country the Zionist Russian-language journal *Vestnik Izrailya*, diffuse slanderous information on the alleged miserable existence of Jews in the USSR.

Who will believe you, Israeli gentlemen and foreign Zionists? Here is what D. H. Khaimov, an American citizen who visited the USSR as a tourist in the summer of 1960, writes: 'I came to your country for the first time since 1913. American propaganda attempts to convince the American man in the street that there are no comfortable dwellings, shoes or foodstuffs in the Soviet Union. I was told I couldn't even take a bath in the Soviet land, as there was no sewerage system there.

'I believed this propaganda so much that I brought a few packets of sugar for my relatives, before seeing life in the Soviet Union with my own eyes. On my arrival I saw that all sorts of goods and provisions abound here. I came to the conclusion that American propaganda deceives the people...

'As to the Jewish question, I saw with my own eyes that there is no anti-Semitism here. One of my nephews is the manager of a large enterprise. My brothers are directors of important institutions. My sister's daughter is a lawyer, my brother's son, an engineer and his wife, a doctor. Forty-seven years ago not one of our family could have achieved any of these things, we were very poor and had no means for studying.'

Document 92* Soviet reaction to the Six-Day War (June 1967)

The shooting is over in Israel's 'Six-Day War' with the Arab countries. The wind has dispelled the ashes of the fires, of those cremated with napalm. An anxious and uneasy quiet has settled on the Middle East. The pain of irreplaceable losses and grief has settled upon many Arab families on the banks of the Nile and the Jordan, in the tents of the Bedouins and in the houses of the *fellaheen*.

Meanwhile in Tel Aviv the telegraph is working full blast. The teletype keeps rattling dispassionately, conveying 'victory congratulations' from New York, Johannesburg, Paris, London, Rio de Janeiro, Tokyo and many other countries and cities, large and small. The telegrams come from individual admirers and entire corporations and Zionist societies scattered over the world. The martial ardour of the Israeli aggressors is fanned by the support of the invisible but huge and mighty empire of Zionist financiers and industrialists, an empire not to be found on any map of the world, but one that exists and operates everywhere in the capitalist camp. Mankind saw Zionism in its real guise for the first time in the mid twentieth century.

'We can hate', the author of the book, *Israel – The Jewish State*, recently published in Tel Aviv, frankly confesses.

The practical application of Zionism in the affairs of the Middle East includes genocide, racism, treachery, aggression and annexation – all the characteristic attributes of Fascism.

The notorious principle of 'extension of *Lebensraum*' lay at the basis of the aggressive acts of Hitlerite Germany against the European states. The same principle has been elevated to the status of state policy by Israel. As early as 1952, Moshe Dayan declared: 'Our task consists in preparing the Israeli army for the new, approaching war to achieve our final aim – the establishment of an Israeli empire.'

The experience of history has shown that the Hitlerite Fascists and the leaders of Zionism easily found a common tongue and cooperated with one another. Highly characteristic in this respect was the so-called Kasztner case. During the years of World War II, Kasztner was the representative of the Jewish Agency in Hungary and the Chairman of the 'Committee for the Rescue of Hungarian Jews'. He came to terms with the Hitlerite Gestapo and the SS on the rescue of 1,000 of the wealthiest and hence the most useful Jews in the eyes of the Zionist leaders. At the same time, his own relatives and Zionist activists were forgotten. As for the remaining 500,000 condemned to death, these were no concern of his. The truth of these 'efforts' of Kasztner to save the Jews in Hungary came to the surface only many years later. When the matter took an ugly and very scandalous turn for the Zionist leaders, Kasztner was murdered, on their instructions, by the secret police of Israel to avoid further exposure.

During the war, the prominent representative of Zionism, Dr Nossig,[91] served as an advisor of the Gestapo implementing Hitler's cannibalistic plan for the physical annihilation of the Jews in Poland and other countries seized

* *Source*: E. Evseev, 'Lakei na pobegushkakh' (Lackeys at Beck and Call), *Komsomolskaya pravda*, 4 October 1967.

by the Fascists. He was sentenced to death and executed by the Jews themselves in 1944, shortly before the heroic insurrection in the Warsaw Ghetto. In the years of Fascism's heyday, the Zionists actively cooperated with the Nazi leaders and were their direct accomplices in a number of cases. The same thing is being repeated now, but the other way round: now it is the German revanchists and militarists who are performing services for Zionism in its practical affairs.

Even a fleeting acquaintance with the activities of the Zionist organisations in various countries of the world, the facts of the social, political and official status of the leaders of the Zionist organisations and their most active members, reveals the imperialist nature of Zionism.

As testified by a series of foreign sources, the number of Zionism's adherents in the United States of America alone comes to between twenty and twenty-five million. There are Jews and non-Jews among them. They belong to associations, organisations and societies that play the greatest role in the American economy, politics, culture and science. The Zionist lawyers comprise about 70% of all the American lawyers; the physicists, including those engaged in secret work on the preparation of weapons for mass destruction, comprise 69%, and the industrialists, more than 43%. The adherents of Zionism among American Jews own 80% of the local and international information agencies. In addition, about 56% of the big publishing houses serve the aims of the Zionists.

One cannot find a single Jewish worker, peasant or craftsman among the most authoritative and prominent figures of Zionism. Such a figure is sure to be a big businessman, a banker, a senator, or a member of the Supreme Court of the USA. Golda Meir, the leader of the Mapai party, for instance, headed the diplomatic service of Israel for many years and was at the same time a member of the Executive Committee of the World Zionist Organisation. Moshe Shapiro [sic], [92] Minister of Justice in Eshkol's government, was at the same time a member of the Executive Committee of the Jewish Agency and a member of the General Council of the World Zionist Organisation. Moshe Kol,[93] a prominent Israeli political figure, was the Minister of Development and Tourism in Eshkol's government and a member of the Executive Committee of the World Zionist Organisation. P. Lavon,[94] the former Minister of Defence of Israel, was a member of the Executive Committee of the *Histadrut* (the Israeli trade-union association), a leading figure of the Mapai party and a member of the Executive Committee of the World Zionist Organisation. Senators Javits and Ribicoff[95] of the USA, who came out in support of Israel's aggression, are dyed-in-the-wool Zionists who took part in the conference of twenty-four major American Zionist organisations, convened to adopt special programmes of anti-Soviet activity.

There is no essential difference between American and Zionist racists, since the former justify the latter, and *vice versa*. Everybody knows the tragic events in the South of the USA, the heroic struggle of the Negroes for their rights, freedom and human dignity. It is impossible to regard the statement of Sheman, representative of *B'nai B'rith* (one of the largest of the reactionary American Zionist organisations), without indignation. He approved the activities of the American racists. The Zionists do not merely share the views of the American racists on the superiority of the whites. The ideologists of Zionism claim that the Jews are allegedly 'a people chosen by God' and superior to all other peoples. Here we learn once more the inventions – by now banal and recast in the Zionist style – about the 'great' races and 'sub-races', about 'chosen' and 'unchosen' nations, myths once before buried beneath the ruins of the Third Reich.

Despite their desperate efforts, the ideologists of Zionism have simply been unable to make ends meet in their theoretical constructions of the so-called 'world nation'. The example provided by Israel's own development is highly instructive in this respect. Independently of the will of the Zionists, this small and ordinary capitalist country is undergoing the process of the formation of a bourgeois nation. A class struggle is unfolding in it with the active participation of the toiling masses of the cities and villages. 'Social harmony and class peace' is as much an illusion in Israel as it is anywhere else in the capitalist world. The policy of oppression and racial discrimination, conducted by the ruling circles of Tel Aviv, has provoked the indignation of the most varied groups within the Jewish population in Israel itself. All Asian and African Jews, for instance, are regarded as black and inferior. There is no 'clean' and 'honourable' work for them, and their situation is reminiscent of that of the Negroes in America. The 'black' Jews build the roads, dig the ditches and work on the plantations under the scorching sun. Dark-skinned Jewish women can find jobs only as day-labourers and household servants.

A source of widespread slanderous inventions about the existence of anti-Semitism in the socialist countries, a source of the most unbridled anti-Soviet and anti-Communist propaganda, is the well-known American Jewish Committee in which the dominating role is played by such prominent businessmen as the Lehman billionaires in New York.

A malodourous source of anti-Soviet propaganda is the American Jewish War Veterans Organisation,[96] the so-called New York Youth Conference for the Defence of Soviet Jews and many other Zionist organisations 'concerned about the welfare of their brothers in spirit and blood'. The Zionists quite recently held one of their large anti-Soviet demonstrations in Lafayette Park in Washington DC. Gathered there from different cities of the USA were 19,000 representatives of various Jewish nationalistic organisations for a protest meeting 'in defence of the rights of Soviet Jews'. The body which organised this provocative mob – the 'Conference of American Jews on the question of the situation of the Jews in the USSR' – unites the twenty-four main Jewish nationalistic organisations of the USA.[97]

The persistent and constant attacks of the reactionary Zionist circles upon the USSR, the accusation of anti-Semitism and the demand that Zionist organisations be given free activity in the Soviet Union under religious or other guises actually conceal the policies of the imperialist octopuses, aimed at ushering hostile propaganda into the USSR and introducing a split in the fraternal unity of the working people of all the nationalities whose only homeland is the one born fifty years ago, the great proletarian state – the Land of the Soviets.

The interests of the Zionist-minded bourgeois and of the bourgeois holding other views are so closely interwoven that it is practically impossible to separate them. It is not only the monopolies and companies run mainly by Zionist capital, but also those in which it plays no part that have their interests in the Near East. There is the Palestine Economic Agency, for instance, an undistinguished association, at first glance. It is made up of the representatives of large financial and industrial American organisations, and its function is to render generous material aid to the Jewish funds and organisations that in turn supply Israel with funds. The nature of capital is such that it cannot exist without increasing, without exploiting. The 'philanthropist' Zionists are generously supplying their confederates and spiritual brethren at the trough of power in Tel Aviv through exploitation of the working people, regardless of their nationality.

PART IV

Jews and the Jewish people in Soviet society

7

Jewish culture in the Soviet Union

An autonomous, flourishing national culture in its diverse manifestations is one of the principal characteristics of national existence, the very essence of a nation. Hence government policy towards the cultures of national minorities is immensely important in a multi-national state. Despite the extreme anti-Jewish policy of the regime in Tsarist Russia, a rich tri-lingual Jewish culture – in Hebrew, Russian and Yiddish – developed there in the second half of the nineteenth and beginning of the twentieth centuries.[1]

However, the Soviet regime, in the very first years of its existence, severed the Hebrew branch of this tri-lingual culture when it launched its relentless war on the 'clerical' Hebrew language, Hebrew cultural institutions 'connected with Zionism' and the Jewish religion.[2] The 'Russian' branch of Jewish culture began to be subjected to a similar fate in the 1920s and 1930s, as independent Jewish research institutions such as the Historical and Ethnographic Society were liquidated, the publication of Jewish research and literary collections in Russian was terminated and the newspaper *Tribuna*, the organ of *Ozet*, was closed. The axe was poised over the Yiddish branch in the second half of the thirties, and it was only the outbreak of the war and the subsequent change in policy on the whole national problem which kept it from falling on the third branch of Jewish culture. There seems little doubt that the Soviet leadership sought to 'denationalise' the Jewish minority by severing it from its historical past and, in particular, by stifling its national culture. However piecemeal its implementation, this policy, which unfolded in a number of broadly distinct stages, reached its peak in the late forties with the total liquidation of Yiddish culture.

We shall undertake to examine the main stages in Soviet policy towards Jewish culture during and after the war, as well as the desperate attempts to renew the culture liquidated by Stalin. This examination will cover the four principal spheres in which contemporary national culture normally finds expression: education; literature and journalism; art; and academic research.

Jewish education

The Yiddish school system achieved its maximum development in the USSR in the years 1931–3, when there were more than 1,100 schools throughout the Soviet Union, and some 160,000 pupils.[3]

Only partial data were published on the Jewish schools in the Soviet Union after 1935, when they began to decline in number, and the late 1930s witnessed their elimination at an even faster rate. According to official sources, the Ukraine contained only nineteen Yiddish schools before it annexed the territories of the Western Ukraïne in October 1939.[4] Other estimates give the number of pupils in such schools in the entire Soviet Union as about 75,000 – that is, only 20% of school-age Jewish children.[5] There was an increase and a certain renewal of Yiddish school activity in the regions annexed to the Soviet Union in 1939–40. The partial data in our possession indicate that there were thirty Yiddish schools in Lvov active during this period,[6] and forty-three such schools, with 6,000 pupils, in Bialystok.[7] However, the mass flight and exile of Jews from these regions in the years 1939–41 and the pressures exerted to send Jewish children to general schools caused a drastic reduction in the number of pupils attending Jewish schools.

In the years 1941–4, Yiddish schools were apparently maintained only in the Jewish Autonomous Region of Birobidzhan. However, their exact number is unknown, since the central and local press had already ceased publishing data on them.[8] After the war the number of Yiddish schools in the Soviet Union was insignificant. The small number of such schools in Birobidzhan included Jewish schools, a mixed secondary school (Yiddish–Russian) and a mixed pedagogic technical institute which was divided into Jewish and Russian departments (the former was apparently closed in 1947).[9] In Chernovtsy there were two Jewish schools in 1945 (elementary and secondary),[10] but these seem to have been closed quickly. In Vilnius and Kaunas there were a school and an orphanage where the language of study was Yiddish. The Vilnius school, established in 1945,[11] was apparently closed in early 1950.[12] The Kaunas school, in addition to its curriculum of studies, formed a choir which appeared in the city and in other places with a repertoire of songs and readings.[13]

In the new era which followed the 20th Party Congress, none of the attempts to open schools or even special courses in Yiddish came to fruition. The efforts of Jewish writers and cultural activists inside the Soviet Union and of Jewish Communists outside the country were of no avail. The question arises as to what led to the decline of the Yiddish schools even before their final liquidation and why, even in the post-Stalin period, the Soviet authorities uncompromisingly opposed any attempt to renew the Yiddish school network, especially in view of the fact that a number of extra-territorial minorities in certain Soviet Republics have their own schools.[14]

Some of the factors which encouraged the decline in Jewish school attendance may be classed as objective, but a large proportion which, at first glance, would seem to fall into this category were in fact largely engendered by political decisions taken at various levels of the Soviet governmental system. In the first place, despite the existence of the Institute for Proletarian Jewish Culture of the Academy of Sciences in the Ukraine (which was closed in 1936)[15] and of the pedagogic institutes in Vitebsk, Minsk and Odessa, Jewish institutions encountered many difficulties in their attempts to prepare teachers for the Yiddish school network. Secondly, the problems in connection with designing curricula and text-books were exacerbated when the campaign against ideological deviations, especially against the nationalist deviation, was intensified. There were, in addition, budgetary and other material difficulties due in no small part to the incessant opposition of the local authorities. Moreover, teachers in the Jewish schools were offered emoluments in the endeavour to have them transfer to Ukrainian and Russian schools. But most detrimental to the Yiddish school system was the lack of a corresponding network of institutions of higher learning.

On an entirely different level were the powerful socio-economic forces which acted to reinforce the flight from the Yiddish schools in the late 1930s. Thus, the processes of urbanisation and of migration, especially from towns in Belorussia and the Ukraine, undoubtedly accelerated the processes of assimilation.

However, these great obstacles notwithstanding, the Jewish educational system in the Soviet Union would not have suffered total liquidation had it not been for the prevailing attitude of the Soviet leadership towards Jewish national existence in the USSR. In 1930, the regime began by dismantling the *Evsektsiya*, which had played such a notable role in establishing and developing the Jewish educational network in the Yiddish language, without replacing this body with any similar institution.[16] This left Jewish educational institutions without a central directing body and, even more important, without support or protection.

The status of the Yiddish school was also severely undermined by the change in general policy towards the nationalities, which entailed the abandonment of Ukrainisation and Belorussisation. Since the Jewish school system had been raised up on the wave of this mildly devolutionary stratagem, it was bound to be cast down by its repudiation. But the severest blow to Jewish education in the Soviet Union was struck in the second half of the thirties, when the wave of purges engulfed many of the leading figures active in Jewish cultural organisations. It was these factors, together with the unrelenting pressure on Jewish parents to send their children to Russian, Ukrainian or Belorussian schools, which led to the precipitous decline in the number of Jewish schools in the late thirties and to their total disappearance during the war.

The fact that there was no renewal of the Jewish school network in the Soviet Union after the war – despite the endeavours of the Jewish Anti-Fascist Committee and the demands of many Jews whose flickering national consciousness had been rekindled by the Holocaust – demonstrates clearly that the Soviet leadership had now determined to do all within its power to accelerate the assimilation of Soviet Jewry. The official justifications for the absence of Jewish schools are unconvincing (see, for example, Doc. 15). The primary argument was that the dispersion of the Jews throughout the Soviet Union would necessitate excessive outlays on the establishment of Yiddish schools. But has the establishment of schools for German, Polish or Hungarian children, who are no less scattered than the Jews, cost any less? A second and similarly unconvincing attempt at justification was that, since the Jews were not interested in Jewish schools for their children, the Soviet leadership did not wish to force this upon them. As Khrushchev claimed during his talks with the French socialist delegation, the Jews would revolt, viewing such a measure as an attempt to enclose them in something like ghettos (Doc. 13).

The real question is, what percentage of parents would have been interested in sending their children to Yiddish schools if there had been any in the Soviet Union? To judge by past experience, the percentage would not have been high, especially if attendance in the Jewish school system did not permit its students to continue in institutions of higher education. However, it is likely that the awakening of national feelings among the Jewish population would have induced some parents to see it as their national duty to make this choice, even at the cost of certain disadvantages to their children's future careers.

Given present-day realities, it is difficult to imagine the renewal of the Yiddish school network as it existed in the twenties. Over thirty years of cultural desolation and the gradual disappearance of Yiddish speakers, and even more of Yiddish teachers, would make such an undertaking extraordinarily difficult.[17] On the other hand, a Hebrew school system would enjoy far better prospects today if the Soviet authorities would permit it. However, the attempts to open private *ulpanim* (study centres) for the study of Hebrew, which began at the end of the sixties, have generally met with harassment and ultimate suppression.

Yiddish literature and journalism

The development of a ramified system of Yiddish publishing (newspapers, *belles lettres*, text-books) in the twenties and thirties resulted primarily from the more latitudinarian nationality policies adopted by the Bolsheviks after the October Revolution. Also influential in this respect was the influx of Jewish writers, journalists and researchers into the Soviet Union, who came with the aim of establishing a vibrant Yiddish culture. Leading Yiddish-language writers and critics, both those already living in the country and newcomers from abroad, now converged upon the Yiddish periodicals and publishing houses in centres with significant Jewish populations: Kiev, Kharkov, Odessa, Moscow, Minsk, and later Birobidzhan as well.[18] But it was the *Evsektsiya*, the motivating and organising force behind Jewish cultural activity in the Soviet Union, which played a central role as supporter and protector of Yiddish literature in the USSR so long as it existed (1918–30). The physical liquidation of the former *Evsektsiya* leaders at the end of the thirties inevitably led to a sharp reduction in the amount of Yiddish publishing.

If we take 1932 – the peak year of Yiddish book-publishing in the Soviet Union, with 668 books – as a starting-point, we shall see that while 431 books could still appear in 1936, the number dropped to 356 in 1937, and to 339 in 1939.[19] There was a minor upsurge in 1940, when the USSR annexed territories containing some two million Jews.

The themes most common in Yiddish literature of the twenties and thirties were the October Revolution; the Civil War and the defeat of internal and external enemies; and the pathos of socialist construction with the joy of work and the happiness of life in the world's first socialist state. The specific Jewish background was interwoven into these themes via Jewish protagonists, portrayals of the old Jewish way of life and the struggle against phenomena which the Yiddish writers viewed as negative: the cult of a remote historical past; the *ḥeder*; the synagogue; and the Jewish political movements, especially Zionism and the Bund. In the early and mid-thirties, the salient national elements in Yiddish literature began to fade, as they were replaced by paeans and hymns to the Party and to its adored leader, Joseph Stalin. Monotony, simplicity bordering on primitivism and pathetic rhetoric gradually began to dominate Jewish literary creation in the Soviet Union.

However, the major shift in Soviet nationality policy, aimed at stimulating patriotism in the Soviet population, especially but not only among the Russians, served to open up limited new horizons for Yiddish literature as well. Characteristic of the spirit of the time are Der Nister's great work, *The Mashber Family* (volume I appeared in Moscow in 1939), and Shmuel Halkin's plays, *Bar Kokhba* (1938) and *Shulamis* (1940). The turn to the Jewish historical past of the nineteenth century in *The Mashber Family* and to ancient Palestine in Halkin's dramas foreshadowed a significant change in Jewish literature which was to occur during the war period. The new emphasis on the historical continuity of the Jewish nation was, of course, powerfully reinforced by the war experience and by the profound shock of the Holocaust, which demonstrated in the clearest manner the common destiny of all Jews, regardless of country, class or regime.

During and after the war, the Jewish Anti-Fascist Committee stood at the centre of Jewish cultural activity.[20] Together with similar anti-Fascist organisations, it was established by the authorities as part of the immense effort to mobilise all available forces for a war to the death against Germany.[21] The Committee, which commenced activity in May 1942 within the framework of the Soviet Information Bureau (*Sovinformburo*), had Solomon Lozovsky, Deputy Foreign Minister and Deputy Director of the Bureau, as its direct administrator. The Committee did not include Jewish personages and organisations in other countries, as had been proposed by Henryk Erlich and Victor Alter, fugitive leaders of the Bund in Poland, and it was strictly controlled throughout its existence. However, as the sole Jewish organisation in the country, it nonetheless played a decisive role in the development of Jewish culture. And because of the special nature of the war period, the Committee was able to do something without precedent in the Soviet period: it brought writers, artists and scholars involved in Yiddish culture together with their counterparts of Jewish origin who, because they worked in Russian and other languages, had hitherto been far removed not only from Jewish culture but from any Jewish activity whatsoever.

Although most of the Committee's operations were directed at public opinion outside the USSR, its leaders – such as Yiddish Theatre actor Solomon Mikhoels and the writers Itsik Fefer and Perets Markish – were also committed to bringing Jewish culture to the widest possible public. Thus, the Committee founded the newspaper *Eynikeyt*, its official organ until it was closed down on 20 November 1948; it concentrated Jewish writers, journalists and artists previously scattered throughout the Soviet Union in Moscow; and it renewed the operations of the 'Der emes' publishing house. While the editors of *Eynikeyt* consistently underlined the part played by Soviet Jews in the campaign against the Nazi enemy, they did not ignore those Jews who fought in the ranks of the Allied armies and the various partisan movements.

Table 11. *Yiddish books in the USSR, 1946–67*

Year	Number of books
1946	18
1947	49
1948	47
1949–58	0
1959	2
1960	3
1961–3	0
1964	2
1965	6
1966	4
1967	6

Sources: Cohen & Shmeruk (eds.), *Pirsumim yehudiim bi-vrit ha-moazot*; *Pechats SSSR v 1956–1968 godakh* (Publications in the USSR, 1956–68), Moscow, Vsesoyuznaya knizhnaya palata, 1958–69.

The newspaper dealt at length with the life of the Jewish communities on the home front and with the contribution made by Jews to science, industry and culture, laying particular stress on 'the Jewish theme'. But the paper's primary concern both during and after the war – in essays, reportage and articles – was with Jewish literary and artistic creation in the Soviet Union.

War-time difficulties limited the number of Yiddish books and pamphlets published during 1942–5 to only fifty-eight. But even in 1946, a year after the war ended, only eighteen books were published; in other words Yiddish publications showed no increase until 1947, when forty-nine Yiddish books and pamphlets were published.[22] It may be assumed that if the plan for 1948 had been realised the number of Yiddish books and pamphlets would have far exceeded the forty-seven books actually published (see Table 11 and Doc. 94). But the central publishing house, 'Der emes', was closed down in November 1948. In the same year, the Academy of Sciences in the Ukraine and the Belorussian government also ceased their Yiddish publications. Yiddish publishing in the Soviet Union was silenced from then until 1959. It should be stressed here that the circulation of those Yiddish books which were published during and after the war showed an increase rather than a decrease compared with the thirties.[23] Even more important, about 85% of the Yiddish books published between 1946 and 1948 had some specifically Jewish content.[24]

Three Yiddish-language literary-political periodicals played an important role in the dissemination of Jewish culture after the war. *Heymland*, a literary-artistic and socio-political periodical published by the Writers' Union of the USSR in Moscow in 1947–8, put out a total of seven issues. *Der shtern*, a literary periodical of the Jewish writers in the Ukraine in the same years, also published a total of seven issues. *Birobidzhan*, a literary periodical of the Jewish writers in Birobidzhan, was published in 1946–8. It is of interest that the periodicals had a far higher circulation than did the Yiddish literary monthlies at the end of the thirties.[25]

In addition to original Yiddish literature and journalism, translations from Yiddish into Russian and other languages also played a part in the dissemination of Jewish culture in the Soviet Union. The new Soviet policy in the second half of the thirties led to a notable increase in the Russian translations so that 120 appeared between 1937 and 1941, as opposed to only thirty-one between 1932 and 1936. Such translations suffered a precipitous decline during and after the war; twenty-one books appeared in 1942–5 and only fifteen in 1946–8. An inverse correlation between publication in Yiddish and translation into Russian or other languages may have been at work here; that is, as the authorities increased the output of Yiddish books, they may have decided that there was less need for translations from that language.

The major themes of *belles-lettres* during the war, and to a somewhat lesser extent during the years 1946–8 as well, were focused on a national awakening hitherto unknown in Yiddish literature in the Soviet Union. This upsurge in Jewish consciousness was the direct result of two interlocking factors: the profound shock of the Holocaust and the relatively relaxed nationality policy now being pursued by the regime. The Yiddish writers took advantage of the liberalisation in policy to give expression to their innermost feelings on such topics as Jewish heroism; the Jewish role in the victory over the Nazis; the destruction of entire Jewish communities; Jewish solidarity and Soviet patriotism; and the socialist brotherhood of nations. Traditional Jewish motifs expressing grief and deep affliction and anxiety for the future of the Jewish nation were also presented, as were works portraying symbols of the remote historical past and a rediscovery of religious and national themes which had previously been angrily rejected.

With the end of the war, and especially following the shift in Soviet policy of August 1946, Yiddish writers found themselves in a complex and dangerous situation. A retreat from their proud national position, even had they desired this, was virtually impossible. Since their stories, poems and essays had been printed in thousands of copies and their plays performed often, it is doubtful that any disavowal would have altered their fate. On the other hand, to continue developing the same themes was not only dangerous but impossible given the strict political control of literature; hence, their vexation and their search for a way out of this tragic entanglement.

The change in Soviet policy towards Jewish national aspirations in Palestine, which found expression in its UN vote of 29 November 1947, and in Soviet support for the State of Israel as soon as it was established, encouraged many Yiddish writers to hope for a parallel shift in official policy towards the Jewish minority within the USSR. But such hopes were quickly dashed. Although the decision to liquidate the vestiges of Jewish culture was apparently taken at the highest levels of government in the first half of 1948, the authorities implemented their programme cautiously, secretly and gradually.

The first and most serious stage in the liquidation of Jewish culture involved the closing down of *Eynikeyt*, the organ of the Jewish Anti-Fascist Committee, on 20 November 1948, and, shortly thereafter, of the three Yiddish periodicals in Moscow, Kiev and Birobidzhan. This was immediately followed by the dissolution of the sole Yiddish publishing house, 'Der emes', and the ban on Yiddish publishing in the Ukraine and Belorussia. During the second stage, Yiddish radio broadcasts were terminated and Yiddish theatres and their companies disbanded.

The one trace of Yiddish literature permitted during the years 1949–53 was the appearance of a small number of translations from that language into Russian and other languages.[26] Stalin's death in March 1953 did not lead to an immediate change in attitude towards Yiddish literature. The years 1954–5 saw the publication of only one Yiddish book, and that in Russian translation (see Table 12), and of two poems by Aron Vergelis translated into Russian by Evtushenko (in the literary periodical, *Novy mir*, 1955, no. 9).

The first sign of a change for the better – the result of the general political 'thaw' and also of specific pressure exerted by Communist and left-wing circles abroad – came with the rehabilitation of the poet Perets Markish on 29 December 1955 (Doc. 97). This was followed in 1956 by the rehabilitation of other writers who had been imprisoned and executed under Stalin (Docs. 99, 101 and 102). In the wake of the 20th Party Congress in February 1956, external pressure for the renewal of Jewish culture in the Soviet Union was stepped up. Encouraged by this support and by the sympathy of liberal writers within the USSR, Yiddish writers and literary critics – most of whom had only just been released from forced labour camps – appealed to the Union of Soviet Writers to support the renewal of Yiddish publishing.[27] Aleksei Surkov, then Secretary of the Union, told Haim Suler, editor of the *Morgn frayheyt* published in New York,[28] that the plans to renew Jewish culture in the Soviet Union included a new publishing house, a newspaper and literary quarterly in Yiddish, as well as a nation-wide conference of Yiddish writers and cultural activists. From the end of 1956, rumours were rife that a Yiddish weekly which would soon become a daily was about to appear.[29] A number of low-ranking official institutions competent in this area attempted to convince the Party leadership that it was indeed important to implement at least some of these plans, arguing that this would silence anti-Soviet agitators in the West.[30]

There were technical[31] reasons why Yiddish books were not published until 1959,[32] a literary periodical did not appear until 1961[33] and a daily Yiddish newspaper did not appear at all (there was, for example, a lack of matrices for typesetting Yiddish). But the primary reason was the Soviet leadership's hope that if they deferred action long enough the external and internal pressures to renew Jewish culture would decline.

From 1959 to 1964 – that is, from the publication of the first Yiddish book until Khrushchev was removed from power – only seven such books appeared in the Soviet Union (five of them *belles-lettres* and two socio-political in content).[34] It is noteworthy that no books in Yiddish appeared at all between 1961 and 1963, while in the early period of Brezhnev and Kosygin, sixteen books were published in three years.[35]

The principal forum for Yiddish literature in the USSR is *Sovetish heymland*, which began as a bi-monthly in 1961 and became a monthly in January 1965. Most of the more than one hundred Jewish writers who have been published in this periodical were over sixty years old, meaning that they had been active in

Table 12. *Book publication of Yiddish literature in translation in the USSR, 1946–67*

Year	Russian	Other languages	Total
1946			4
1947			2
1948			9
1949	1	1	2
1950			0
1951	1		1
1952	1	1	2
1953			0
1954	1		1
1955			0
1956	13		13
1957	21	3	24
1958	20	13	33
1959	19	9	28
1960	19	6	25
1961	18		18
1962	20		20
1963	21		21
1964	18		18
1965	14		14
1966	11		11
1967	6		6

Sources: Pechat SSSR v 1956[–1960] g. (Publications in the USSR, 1956[–1960]), Moscow, Vsesoyuz-naya knizhnaya palata, 1958, 1959, 1960, 1961; Pinkus, Greenbaum & Altshuler (eds.), *Pirsumim rusiim al yehudim.*

the Yiddish literary sphere since the twenties and thirties. The absence of Yiddish schools for so many decades made the rise of a new generation of Yiddish writers virtually impossible. Thus, Stalin's liquidation of the greatest Jewish writers has proved to be a fatal blow to such literary production.[36]

The major themes of Yiddish literature in the sixties were drawn from two main areas: the life of Soviet Jews within contemporary Soviet society, with the accent on the regime's prodigious achievements; and the historical past, both the pre-revolutionary period and, still more, the Holocaust years. But as Ch. Shmeruk points out: 'At present these works are neither innovating nor searching nor combatant. They do not seek new stylistic or artistic expression; nor have they anything new to say in the realm of ideas.'[37]

The years 1957–64 saw the annual appearance of about twenty translations from Yiddish literature into Russian (see Table 12), as well as a smaller number of translations from Yiddish into other languages. There was significant decline in the period 1965–7;[38] however, four of the works that were published then were Russian translations from the Hebrew of books by Israeli writers, as opposed to only one such book in the Khrushchev period.[39] Despite the bias in the selection of writers and works to appear, and the unfaithful translations, there is no doubt that the publication of Hebrew literature in the Soviet Union had a great impact on Jewish readers. Of major importance in this context was the publication of P. Shapiro's Hebrew–Russian dictionary in 1963.

However, with regard to new works in Yiddish itself, it appears that literature and journalism in that language never recovered from the blows suffered in the years 1948–52, even though the authorities partially rehabilitated them in the late fifties. The situation was not ameliorated by the continuing curb on publication in Yiddish in the sixties, despite what was permitted extra-territorial national minorities such as the Germans, Poles or Hungarians, who are also dispersed throughout and within the various republics, and who have access to numerous newspapers and books in their own languages as well as schools in their mother tongues.[40]

One of the factors disadvantageous to the restoration and development of Jewish culture in the Soviet Union is the absence of a central Jewish institution to fill the role played by the *Evsektsiya* in the twenties and by the Jewish Anti-Fascist Committee in the forties. The one Yiddish newspaper being published, *Sovetish heymland* edited by Aron Vergelis, can hardly lay serious claim to represent Soviet Jewry. And Jewish literature and journalism in Russian does nothing to fulfil the central criterion required in the USSR for the maintenance of an autonomous national culture – the possession of a language. The inevitable conclusion, therefore, is that the Soviet leadership has no intention of maintaining and developing Jewish culture in the USSR.

The Jewish national expression in Russian found in the works of writers such as Ilya Erenburg, Vasily Grossman, Pavel Antokolsky, Margarita Aliger and Lev Ozerov describes the shock of the Holocaust and the heroism displayed in the war against Nazi brutality. But, following the war, there was a great diminution of Russian works which wove the Jewish historical heritage into their fabric, a development which resulted from the lack of interest on the part of the authors, and also from the extreme sensitivity of the Soviet authorities to any concentration on Jewish topics.

Jewish art forms

The various forms of non-literary Jewish art – theatre, cinema, music and painting – achieved their maximum flowering in the twenties and thirties and enjoyed a brief resurgence during and after the war, before their virtual liquidation in 1948–9. In what follows we shall deal with the scope of this art and its Jewish content, but it can be stated immediately that from the latter point of view, Jewish art in the post-Stalin period never reached the richness of expression and high standard attained during earlier periods.

The theatre

The theatre, both professional and amateur, holds a primary place when it comes to potential influence on a broad public. In the twenties and the first half of the thirties, there were eighteen Jewish theatre companies in the Soviet

Table 13. *Appearances by professional and amateur theatre companies,* * *1948–52*

Company	Republic and city	1948	1949	1950	1951	1952
	Ukraine					
Sidi Tal Company	Chernovtsy	X	X			
Comedy Company	Vinnitsa	X				
Dramatic Company	Chernigov	X				
Theatre Company	Lvov	X				
Amateur Company	Zaporozhye	X				
Amateur Company	Ovruch	X				
Dramatic Company	Odessa	X				
Amateur Company	Krivoi Rog	X				
Amateur Company	Poltava	X				
Amateur Company	Kirovograd	X				
	Belorussia					
Amateur Company	Bobroisk	X				
	Lithuania					
Amateur Company	Kaunas	X				
Dramatic Company	Vilnius	X	X			
	Latvia					
Theatre Company	Riga	X				
Amateur Company	Riga	X				
Dramatic Company	Dvinsk	X	X	X	X	X
	Azerbaidzhan					
Dramatic Company	Baku	X	X			
TOTALS		17	4	1	1	1

*17 Companies: 9 professional; 8 amateur.

Sources: *Eynikeyt*, 1 January – 16 November 1948; *Folks-shtime*, 1948–9, 20 December 1956; *Naye prese*, 1948–9; Russian and Ukrainian newspapers, 1948–9, based on the collection of documents in Pinkus (ed.), *Evrei i evreisky narod 1948–1953*.

Union,[41] in addition to a multitude of amateur companies. In the second half of the thirties, with the persistent restrictions on Jewish culture, their number decreased to ten.[42] With the outbreak of the Soviet–German war in 1941, several theatre companies were dissolved, while others – such as those of Odessa, Kiev, Minsk and Moscow – were transferred to remote regions.[43] After the war, they began to return to their permanent sites, but some of them (especially in the Ukraine) found it most difficult to get back their buildings and to obtain budgets.

In 1946, the following Jewish theatre companies were in operation in the Soviet Union.

1. The State Yiddish Theatre in Moscow, which had about one hundred actors and administrative personnel. It was headed by Solomon Mikhoels, until he was

murdered on 13 January 1948. Its second director, the actor Binyamin Zuskin, was arrested at the end of 1948. Attached to the theatre was a drama school under Moshe Belenky which included among its faculty stage directors and experts in Yiddish literature.

2. The Shalom Aleikhem Yiddish Theatre in Chernovtsy, which was headed by Grigory Spektorov until early 1948, and by Moshe Goldblat after Spektorov's death.
3. The Yiddish Theatre in Odessa under Efraim Loyter.
4. The Belorussian Yiddish Theatre in Minsk, under the artistic direction of Viktor Golovchiner.[44]
5. The Kaganovich Yiddish Theatre in Birobidzhan, with Alex Shteyn as artistic director.
6. A Yiddish theatre company in Uzbekistan, founded in early 1945, which apparently ceased functioning immediately after the war.
7. Yiddish theatre companies in Kishinev (Moldavia) and Riga (Latvia), about which little is known except that they were apparently very short lived.

Besides the permanent theatres, a further seventeen theatrical companies, nine professional and eight amateur, operated in the Soviet Union (see Table 13). Over half of these companies – ten of the seventeen – were located in the Ukrainian Republic, primarily, no doubt, because its large Jewish population had not yet assimilated (this explanation is supported by the similar situation in the Baltic republics). The artistic standard of the permanent theatres and companies was not uniform, but the State Yiddish Theatre in Moscow under Mikhoels attained a standard comparable to that of the best Soviet theatre companies, and the theatres of the Ukraine, Belorussia and Birobidzhan also had notable achievements to their credit.

An examination of the repertoire of the theatres in the final years of their existence throws much light on the question of the extent to which Yiddish culture in the Soviet Union was Jewish not only in form, but also in content. In the years 1948–9, the five permanent and professional theatres then still active performed thirty-two plays, some of which had already been staged at the end of and immediately following the war, and others which had their premiere in 1948 (see Table 14). Thirteen of the thirty-two productions staged in this period (41%) were original plays by Soviet Yiddish writers. *Freylekhs*, by Z. Okun, a play permeated with Jewish folklore which was first performed on the stage of the State Yiddish Theatre in Moscow on 23 July 1945, was such a great success that it earned a high state prize in 1946.[45] Gershenzon's *Hershl Ostropoler*, which also leaned heavily on Jewish folklore, enjoyed great popularity and was in the repertoire of all the permanent theatre companies for a lengthy period.

More important in terms of content and literary-artistic value were Perets Markish's play *Revolt in the Ghetto* and Itsik Fefer's *The Sun Does Not Set*, both of which described the struggle of Polish and Soviet Jews against the Nazis.[46] Two plays dealt with the restoration of Jewish life in the USSR after the war, *To Life* by Fefer and *Holiday Eve* by Moshe Broderzon. There were also the comedies, *Exorcise the Devil* by Moshe Pinchevsky, *Other People* by O. Holdes and *It's Worth Living in the World* by I. Huberman.

Ten of the thirty-two productions were by the classical writers of Yiddish prose and drama: Shalom Aleikhem (who was represented by seven plays) and Avraham Goldfaden (three plays). Shalom Aleikhem's theatre pieces – even in their Soviet adaptations which had already begun in the twenties – are certainly among the finest Yiddish plays in the world. All of them are steeped in 'social background', apparently one of the reasons they were selected for performance in the Soviet Union.

Of the nine plays translated into Yiddish from Russian and other languages, only two have any Jewish content, *Zoriah Bilinkovich* by Zinger and Vitenzon and *The Sighing of the Forests* by Linkov and Brat. Both of these plays were produced only at the State Yiddish Theatre in Moscow.[47]

At the end of the war or immediately afterwards, several older plays with distinctly Jewish national character were withdrawn from the stage. Most notable among them were Shmuel Halkin's dramas, *Shpilfoygl* and *Bar Kokhba*,[48] *I Am Alive* by Moshe Pinchevsky,[49] *Revenge* by A. Levin[50] and Gordin's *Mirele Efros* (staged in the years 1944–6). Among the plays in various stages of preparation which never reached the stage because of their national content was David Bergelson's *Prince Reuveni*. Perets Markish's *King Lampeduza* and Vasily Grossman's *The Old Teacher*, prepared in 1948–9, also failed to be staged apparently because of their Jewish content (see Table 15). Other plays withdrawn before they reached the stage were apparently left unperformed for technical, not political reasons.[51] The repertoire of the seventeen Jewish theatrical companies was very similar to that of the permanent theatres in these years.

While the campaign to liquidate Jewish culture did not have an immediate effect on the existence of Yiddish theatres and companies, budgets were cut or discontinued. Thus, on 12 March 1948, the Committee for Art Affairs attached to the Council of Ministers of the Soviet Union cancelled its financial support of 646 theatres, including the State Yiddish Theatre in Moscow (Doc. 107). The subsequent cancellation of governmental subsidies to the remaining Yiddish theatres – a measure not applied to other national minorities – was the first sign of the imminent liquidation.

The official harassment began when the authorities ordered the theatres to undertake road tours which were then suddenly cancelled half-way through.[52] Then the selling of subscription tickets, which eased the financial situation of the theatres, slowed down when leading figures in the Jewish cultural sphere were arrested at the end of 1948 and rumours were spread that Yiddish theatre-goers, not to mention permanent subscribers, also faced arrest. There was a drastic drop in attendance at all the theatres not yet closed down, which led to the dismissal of many Yiddish theatre actors, musicians and workers. The data on 'full halls' published from time to time in *Eynikeyt* were certainly exaggerated;[53] the decline in Jewish attendance at the Yiddish theatres, which began in the second half of 1948, accelerated greatly in early 1949.

First to be closed, at the end of 1948, was the Yiddish Theatre in Odessa.[54] The Kaganovich Yiddish Theatre in Birobidzhan was shut down on 5 October 1949.[55] The Belorussian Yiddish Theatre of Minsk ceased operating in March 1949,[56] following sharp attacks on its director Viktor Golovchiner for staging 'nationalistic' and 'cosmopolitan' plays.[57] The Shalom Aleikhem Yiddish Theatre of the Ukraine in Chernovtsy was shut down in September 1949.[58] Last to be closed was the State Yiddish Theatre in Moscow, towards

Table 14. *Jewish plays in the USSR and their performances, 1948–9, by play, author, place and year*

	Author	Moscow	Ukraine*	Minsk	Odessa	Birobidzhan
PLAYS BY CLASSICAL YIDDISH WRITERS						
1. *200,000*	Shalom Aleikhem	1948		1948		
2. *Wandering Stars*	Shalom Aleikhem	1948	1948	1948		
3. *Tevye the Milkman*	Shalom Aleikhem	1948/9	1948		1948	1948
4. *The Bloody Jest*	Shalom Aleikhem				1948	
5. *Stempenyu's Love*	Shalom Aleikhem		1948		1948	
6. *The Enchanted Tailor*	Shalom Aleikhem		1948			
7. *Stempenyu*	Shalom Aleikhem					
8. *The Pampered Bride*	A. Goldfaden	1948/9	1948	1948	1948	
9. *The Witch*	A. Goldfaden	1948/9	1948			1948
10. *The Tenth Commandment*	A. Goldfaden		1948			
PLAYS BY SOVIET YIDDISH WRITERS						
1. *To Life*	I. Fefer	1948	1948	1948	1948	
2. *Hershl Ostropoler*	Y. Gershenzon	1948	1948	1948	1948	1948
3. *Freylekhs*	Z. Okun (Shneer)	1948/9			1948	
4. *Exorcise the Devil*	M. Pinchevsky		1948		1948	
5. *To Life, Moscow*	Y. Dobrushin				1948	
6. *The Sun Does Not Set*	I. Fefer	1948				
7. *Revolt in the Ghetto*	P. Markish	1948	1948	1948	1948	
8. *Holiday Eve*	M. Broderzon	1948	1948			
9. *Other People*	O. Holdes		1948			

	Author					
10. *He's From Birobidzhan*	B. Miler					1948
11. *With a Foreign Name*		1949				
12. *It's Worth Living in the World*	I. Huberman	1948/9	1948	1948	1948	
13. *Wedding*	Y. Dobrushin (after Perets)	1948				1948
PLAYS IN TRANSLATION						
1. *Zoriah Bilinkovich*	Zinger & Vitenzon	1948/9				
2. *The Invasion*	L. Leonov		1948		1948	
3. *Deep Roots*	Geo & Dyusi	1948/9		1948		
4. *Two Camps*	A. Yaakobson	1948/9				
5. *The Young Man*	Mdivani & Nikirov Petrov		1948		1948	
6. *The Isle of Peace*			1948			
7. *The Sighing of the Forests*	Linkov & Brat	1948/9	1948			
8. *Uncle Vanya*	Chekhov		1948			
9. *The Miser*	Molière		1948			
TOTAL 30		17	16	8	12	7
Total number of performances: 60						

* Shalom Aleikhem Theatre

Sources: As Table 13.

Table 15. *Plays prepared but not staged, 1948–9, by author, theatre and date of newspaper report*

Play	Author	Moscow	Chernovtsy	Birobidzhan	Minsk
1. *The Old Teacher*	V. Grossman	5.2.48			
2. *King Lampeduza*	P. Markish	11.3.48		27.5.48	
3. *The Sun*	Pochaev		7.10.48		
4. *Far from Moscow*	V. Azhaev		11.9.49		
5. *The Alien Shadow*	K. Simonov		11.9.49		
6. *To Life**	I. Fefer			27.5.48	
7. *The Power*	B. Romashov			1948	
8. *200,000**	Shalom Aleikhem			18.2.48	
9. *The Song of Songs**	Shalom Aleikhem			18.2.48	
10. *The Bee*	A. Voinich			1948	
11. *Life in the Citadel*	A. Yaakobson				24.2.48

* The press reports do not make it clear whether these three plays were staged for very brief periods or not at all.

Sources: Eynikeyt and the periodical *Birobidzhan* (dates given in the table).

the end of November 1949.[59] We have no precise data regarding the dates on which the companies were dissolved. All we do know is that of the seventeen companies which existed in 1948, only four remained in 1949. And in the years 1950–2, the only Yiddish dramatic company in the Soviet Union was in Dvinsk.[60]

The last performances in Yiddish known to us from the Stalin period are Anna Guzik and Amirov on 24 September 1950 in Georgia; Sidi Tal on 29 January 1951 in Uzbekistan; and a number of Yiddish singers in June 1951 in Belorussia (see Table 16). These isolated performances only highlight the Jewish cultural wasteland created in the Soviet Union by the onslaught unleashed in November 1948. As far as we have been able to ascertain, no Yiddish performances took place between 1952 and 1954.[61]

The first post-Stalin performance took place in Tashkent in February 1955 with the actor Yitskhak Rakitin reciting from the works of Shalom Aleikhem in Yiddish and Russian.[62] In August 1955, Shaul Lyubimov and Sidi Tal began to give concerts of Yiddish songs in Moscow (Doc. 112). Table 17 shows that the first Yiddish dramatic companies to be founded in the Soviet Union after a lengthy break were those in Vilnius and Dvinsk, in 1956. In 1957, five new companies were established in Lvov and Tashkent and one in the Russian Republic (in Leningrad). From 1956 to 1967, there were twenty such companies in the Soviet Union.[63] Three of the companies were given the status of permanent theatres: the Moscow company under the direction of Binyamin Shvartser; the Vilnius company; and that of Birobidzhan. The opposition of republican and local authorities, which tended to create obstacles to the establishment of Yiddish companies, seems to have required the direct intervention of the central authority. Even when new companies somehow

Table 16. *Individual appearances by Jewish artists, 1948–51, by artist, place and date of appearance*

Performer	RSFSR (Moscow / Gorky*)	Ukraine (Chernovtsy† / Kiev‡ / Odessa§ / Berdichev**)	Belorussia (Minsk)	Latvia (Riga)	Estonia (Tallin)	Uzbekistan (Tashkent)	Georgia (Tbilisi)
1. Amirov							24.9.50
2. Apelbaum	13.5.48					19.5.48	24.9.50
3. A. Guzik	28.2.49					14.5.49	
4. Halbraikh					28.2.48		
5. D. Vinogradsky		10.7.48†					
6. Vaintraub		15.1.48‡ 22.8.48† 22.7.48§					
7. S. Tal	24.2.49					16–29.1.51	
8. Tamarkin					28.2.48		
9. Yezvits							4.9.50
10. Yung	1.4.48						
11. Yampolsky		24.8.48† 22.7.48§ 22.4.48**					
12. Loyter	16.10.48*						
13. Lyubimov		13.5.48‡					
14. Furman		13.3.48§					
15. Plotkina							
16. Kaminka	13.1.48; 18.11.49						
17. Rakitin	18.11.49						
18. Shulman	5.1.48					19.5.48	
19. Shifman		13.3.48§					
20. Sharoshevsky				10.6.48			
21. Names not published			6.51				

Sources: as in Table 14 and *Zarya Vostoka; Pravda Vostoka; Sovetskaya Belorussia.*

Table 17. *Professional and amateur theatre companies, 1956-67*

Company	Republic/city	Year founded	Plays staged
RSFSR			
1. The Dramatic Company (Shvartser)	Moscow	1962	*Tevye the Milkman; Wandering Stars; 200,000* (Shalom Aleikhem); *The Spaniards* (Lermontov)
2. Music and Reading Company	Moscow	1960	
3. Musical-Dramatic Company	Leningrad	1957	*Hershl Ostropoler* (Gershenzon); *Green Fields* (P. Hirshbeyn); *The Witch* (Goldfaden); *Merry Beggars; Happy Holiday*
4. Company for the Small Stage	Leningrad	1965	
5. Amateur Company	Leningrad	1958	
6. Dramatic Company*	Birobidzhan	1965	
Lithuania			
1. Amateur Company	Vilnius	1956	*200,000* (Shalom Aleikhem); *Freylekhs* (Okun); *Green Fields* (Hirshbeyn); *Across the Ocean* (Gordin); *Wise Men of Helm* (Gershenzon); *Who Is Guilty* (Zoshchenko); *A Woman Lived in the World* (Agrinenko)
2. Artistic Company†	Vilnius	1960	
3. Children's Company	Vilnius	1958	Folk-songs; Poems by Soviet Yiddish writers; translated poems
4. Dance Company	Vilnius	1962	
5. Choir	Vilnius	1957	
6. Amateur Dramatic Company	Kaunas	1960	*We Sing around the Bonfire; The Bloody Jest* (Shalom Aleikhem); *Way to Life* (Glebov)

	Latvia		
1. Amateur Company	Dvinsk	1956	
2. Choir	Riga	1958	*Musical Ballad; Revolt in the Ghetto*
3. Dramatic Company	Riga	1958	*Human Beings; Menahem Mendl* (Shalom Aleikhem)
	Estonia		
1. Amateur Company	Tallin	1957	
	Ukraine		
1. Musical Company	Lvov	1957	
2. Sidi Tal Company	Chernovtsy	1962	*With You Always; In an Unlucky Hour* (Saktsier)
	Uzbekistan		
1. Amateur Company	Tashkent	1957	
	Moldavia		
1. Amateur Company	Kishninev	1966	

* In 1967: Dramatic Theatre.

† From 1965: Popular Jewish Theatre.

Table 18. *Appearances of performers in Yiddish, as reported in the press, 1955–67**

1955	1956	1957	1958	1959	1960	1961	1962	1963	1964	1965	1966	1967	Total
6	11	11	10	13	8	10	11	24	12	20	25	17	178

* Return performances in the same city have not been included.
Sources: the newspapers *Naye prese*; *Folks-shtime*; *Sovetish heymland*; *Jewish Chronicle*; and the collection *Evrei i evreisky narod*, 1960–7.

managed to establish themselves they still faced difficulties. Added to the problems caused by the lack of a permanent hall and of actors of high standard were those brought about by authorities who sought to restrict their activity by such means as insufficient allocations, refusal to lease them suitable halls for rehearsals and performances, and constant intervention in matters of repertoire.

The repertoire of the Yiddish theatre companies in the Soviet Union during the period 1956–67 greatly resembled that at the end of the forties. They presented abridged and adapted plays of Shalom Aleikhem (*Tevye the Milkman, Wandering Stars, 200,000, The Bloody Jest, Human Beings*); Goldfaden's *The Witch*; Gershenzon's *Hershl Ostropoler* and *The Wise Men of Helm*; and plays based on Jewish folklore (*Merry Beggars, Happy Holidays* and M. Saktsier's *In an Unlucky Hour*). There was an important innovation in the staging of the plays *Green Fields* by Perets Hirshbeyn and *Boytre* by Moshe Kulbak. Of the dramas in translation Lermontov's philosemitic *The Spaniards* deserves special note.

The standard of the companies was, by common consent of those who attended, quite low, as they comprised few professional actors. And individual performances were sometimes preceded by propaganda paeans, ordered by the authorities, to the level of Jewish cultural activity available in the Soviet Union, as proved by the staging of that particular play. However, the hackneyed repertoire, low standard of production and propaganda onslaughts notwithstanding, Jews in the large cities – among them many young people who did not even understand Yiddish – flocked to the performances.

There were forty-two Yiddish-language performers (some singers, others who gave readings) who were active throughout the Soviet Union in the years 1955–67.[64] While it is difficult to determine the number of performances held in this period, the data in Table 18 suggest that the claim of Danilov, the Soviet Deputy Minister of Culture, that 3,000 concerts were attended by some three million spectators in one year alone is highly improbable (Doc. 19). It is doubtful that the performers appeared on average more than ten times a year each, which would provide a sum total for the entire twelve-year period of less than two thousand.

The repertoire of these performances varied little from that of the drama companies; they included passages from the works of Shalom Aleikhem, Mendele, Perets, and from various Soviet authors (either written in Yiddish or translated from Russian and other languages); poems by Soviet Jewish writers such as Kvitko, Fefer, Markish and Kerler, and Jewish folk-songs. Among the singers who achieved great popularity in the fifties were Zinovy Shulman, Emil Horovets and Shaul Lyubimov; Nehamah Lifshits was the star of the sixties. Yiddish records, including concert recordings, also began to appear in the fifties.[65]

The Jewish Communist press in the West, which sought to stress any sign of Jewish cultural expression in the Soviet Union, reported that Yiddish plays in translation were being performed throughout the USSR. However, it seems that only a small number of such plays were performed on the Soviet stage between 1955 and 1967, mainly those of Shalom Aleikhem.[66] In September 1967, Perets Markish's *The Ghetto Dancer* was dramatised, with music composed by Dmitry Shostakovich.[67] In February 1968, Hirsh Osherovich's *Men and Supermen* was given its première in the City Theatre of Ponevezh.[68] Additionally, there were a number of plays on Jewish life and on what may be termed 'Jews in Soviet and world literature and culture'.[69] These included *The Diary of Anne Frank*,[70] *The Life of Janusz Korczak*,[71] Vadim Sobko's *Kiev Notebook*,[72] Blauman's *Days of the Tailors* and Karl Gutzkow's *Uriel Akosta*, which was often performed on the Yiddish stage in the pre-war period.[73]

The cinema

In contrast to the Yiddish theatre, a Jewish cinema never existed in the Soviet Union, even in the period when Yiddish culture was in full flower. It was only in 1935 that the first film on a distinctly Jewish subject was made: 'The New People in Birobidzhan', based on the screenplay 'Seekers of Happiness' by Kovach and Zelder.[74] Two more films about Jews, 'The Oppenheim Family', based on the book by Leon Feuchtwanger, and 'Professor Mamlock', based on the play by F. Wolf, were made in the thirties, when the Soviet Union still sought to stress Jewish suffering under the Nazi regime. The Holocaust, on the other hand, was never given expression in Soviet films.

Attempts to make films based on Jewish national material in the post-Stalin period failed because of the unyielding opposition of the authorities.[75] The sole film on a Jewish subject produced in the sixties was 'In the Family of Friendly Nations', an essentially propagandistic documentary.

Radio and television

During and after the war, Radio Moscow and local stations in Minsk, Odessa, Lvov, Kiev and Kishinev broadcast special programmes in Yiddish aimed at both Soviet and world Jewry. In addition to news and commentary the broadcasts also included fairly diversified literary and artistic programmes.[76] The commentaries, in which the heads of the Jewish Anti-Fascist Committee actively participated, clung to the general political line, changing as policy fluctuated. This was particularly noticeable in internal affairs with regard to the nationalities policy, and in external relations as regards the Soviet attitude towards the State of Israel.

The Yiddish broadcasts directed to American Jewry did not cease with the liquidation of the Jewish Anti-Fascist Committee and the termination of

Yiddish publication in November 1948, but continued until mid-February 1949.[77] From then until April 1956, there were no Yiddish broadcasts in the Soviet Union.[78] During the period 1956–67 there was a limited number of such broadcasts on radio and television, mainly of soloists and choirs who presented Jewish folk-songs.[79] But broadcasts of the kind and scope permitted in the 1940s have not been renewed.

Music

Jewish music in the USSR – that is, music on Jewish themes by Jewish composers – falls into three main categories. First, there was music composed especially for plays (i.e. closely linked to the Yiddish theatre), in which particularly distinguished contributions were made by Iosif Akhron, Aleksandr Krein and Lev Pulver.[80] Other composers who wrote music for the Yiddish theatre in the forties were M. Milner, Sh. Rabunsky, S. Shteinberg and Yakov Vinokur.

Then, again, there were the arrangements of Jewish folk-songs and music for poems by Soviet Yiddish authors (i.e. music closely linked to the small Yiddish stage). Particularly noteworthy here were Sh. Senderei,[81] Zinovy Kompaneets,[82] Rivka Boyarskaya,[83] L. Kogan[84] and Moshe Beregovsky.[85] Finally, in the third category, was music by Jewish composers on Jewish subjects unrelated to Yiddish literature. Notable in this area are Dmitry Klebanov, who composed a work on Babi Yar after the war,[86] and Moshe Veinberg.[87]

Painting and sculpture

In contrast to literature, journalism, theatre and even vocal music, in which Jewish national expression in the USSR is attained through the medium of Yiddish and explicit content, it is often far more difficult to determine the extent to which a particular painting or piece of sculpture is an expression of Jewish art.

Of course, theatre sets and illustrations for Yiddish literature are much more easily distinguishable in this realm. Indeed, the greatest Jewish painters and sculptors in the Soviet Union have contributed their spirit and skill in these two areas. It is sufficient to mention Marc Chagall, who until he left the USSR in 1923, designed the sets for the State Yiddish Theatre in Moscow, and the painter Y. Rabinovich, who was likewise connected with that theatre from the twenties. In the forties, décor for Jewish theatre productions was designed by A. Tishler, who did most of the stage sets for the Yiddish Theatre in Moscow; Shifrin and R. Falk, who also contributed to the State Yiddish Theatre in Moscow as well as to other theatres; and Motin, Rabichev, Kipnis and Rosenblit, who were active in the Kaganovich Theatre in Birobidzhan. The sculptor, Jacob, was yet another artist known for theatre design.

In the field of illustration – mainly for children's literature in Yiddish – the artists M. Akselrod, H. Inger, A. Rabichev, M. Gorshman and P. Polishchuk are known for their important contributions.[88] Tanhum Kaplan's work in this area in the fifties was especially distinguished.[89]

Exhibitions devoted to specifically Jewish art began to dwindle in the forties.[90] There were, however, several general exhibitions which included works by outstanding Jewish painters and sculptors who had given expression to Jewish subjects, for example Z. Asgur, Y. Itkind, N. Altman, Y. Bershatsky, I. Brodsky, M. Veinman, M. Zhitnitsky, Z. Tolkachov, A. Tishler, Sh. Yudovin, E. Neizvestny, R. Falk, V. Tsigal, B. Kratko and P. Shabtai.[91] The major Jewish themes of these artists were the Jewish village, the old Jewish way of life, portraits and statues of the great figures in Jewish literature and theatre (among them Shalom Aleikhem, Mendele and Mikhoels), the Holocaust and the extermination camps, Jewish heroism and post-war Jewish life in the Soviet Union.

Research institutes, museums and libraries

The main importance of these institutions in fostering and preserving a national culture are the educational services and the research facilities which they provide the scholar and layman alike.

Research institutes

In the twenties and the first half of the thirties, the Soviet Union had a ramified network of Jewish research institutes, the majority of which were affiliated to general Soviet academic institutions. As such, they were subject to constant government and *Evsektsiya* supervision, and few of them succeeded in preserving their organisational and ideological independence past the end of the twenties.[92]

The scientific institutes operating in the twenties fell into two categories. First, departments and commissions attached to universities or academies of science, which were restricted in their sphere of activity and terms of reference and were totally dependent upon the institution to which they were affiliated. These included the Historical-Archaeological Commission at the Ukrainian Academy of Sciences in Kiev (1919–29), which engaged in research into the history of Ukrainian Jewry; the Jewish Department for Regional Ethnographic Research at Leningrad University (1926–7); the Philological Commission attached to the Central Jewish Department of Education, Kharkov (1921–5); the Jewish Scientific Society at the Second State University in Moscow (1928–31); the Society for Research into the History and Economy of the Jewish Proletariat at the Leningrad branch of the Russian Academy of Sciences (it functioned only in 1930); the Jewish Department in the Saltykov-Shchedrin Public Library (1931–7), which engaged in research and bibliographic publications; and the Bibliographic Commission attached to the Central Jewish Department of Education, Moscow (1923).

Secondly, there were centres and institutes with a more independent status and a wider range of activity: (1) the Jewish Scientific Institute at the Belorussian Academy of Sciences, (2) the Institute for Proletarian Jewish Culture, (3) the Jewish Department of the All-Russian Society for Theatre, (4) the Mikhoels Bureau for the Yiddish Theatre, (5) the Jewish Department in the Belorussian Academy of Sciences, and (6) the Bureau for Yiddish Literature.

The Jewish Scientific Institute at the Belorussian Academy of Sciences, Minsk (1924–35),[93] comprised three principal departments: historical (headed by V. Sosis), literary (under N. Oyslender) and linguistic (under M. Viner); the Institute for Proletarian Jewish Culture, Kiev (1927–48),[94] while from 1929 to 1940 comprised historical, literary, linguistic, socio-economic, pedagogic and ethnographic departments, and had an affiliated library, bibliographic centre, press and folklore archives.

With the outbreak of the Soviet–German war, the Institute for Proletarian Jewish Culture (now retermed 'Bureau') was evacuated to Ufa together with the Ukrainian Academy of Sciences. Despite its being forced to leave its rich library and a significant part of its archival material in Kiev, the Bureau managed to preserve some especially important documents, its Jewish folklore archive and rare treasures of medieval Yiddish literature. In August 1943, the Ukrainian Academy of Sciences, and with it the Bureau, was transferred to Moscow. The Bureau's limited staff in this period included E. Spivak as director and the researchers Loytsker, Maidansky, Bergovsky and Shapiro. Its departments were therefore considerably reduced; those of history and literature were in effect abolished and most of the activity was concentrated in the folklore department.

In February 1944, a small group of survivors from the former Institute and Bureau returned to Kiev, where it was given the status of an independent institute within the framework of the Ukrainian Academy of Sciences and its staff was increased to twelve. Moreover, many senior scholars residing in Moscow and other cities were of assistance in its work.[95]

Of the six departments which had existed in the thirties, only the language, folklore and literature departments were re-established; efforts to re-activate the historical department were to no avail. However, a commission was formed in 1947 for the perpetuation of the memory of the Jewish writers who had died in the war.[96] Among the permanent workers until its closure in 1948 were E. Spivak,[97] N. Oyslender, M. Bergovsky, M. Mezheritsky, H. Loytsker, A. Velednitsky and Maidansky. The Bureau's five-year plan (1946–51) included a wide variety of ambitious research programmes on such topics as Jewish participation in the partisan movement; thirty years of Jewish folklore; and thirty years of Soviet Yiddish poetry. But in the end only a few articles were published in the Yiddish periodicals of the time.

The Jewish Department attached to the All-Russian Society for Theatre, established in 1943, was headed by Prof. Y. Nusinov. The Department enlisted the active participation of Jewish dramatists, theatre researchers and critics. Among its principal achievements were lecture series on the Yiddish theatre organised during the war and the preparation of a book on *The History of the Yiddish Theatre* (edited by Nusinov, Dobrushin, Oyslender, Lyubomirsky and Finkel).[98]

The Mikhoels Bureau for the History of the Yiddish Theatre in Moscow (1946–7) was directed by Nahum Oyslender with Israel Serebryany as secretary. The Bureau framework comprised, among other things, a Biblio-graphic Commission. It also prepared the work 'Thirty Years of the Soviet

Yiddish Theatre' in association with 'Der emes' publishing house. It was one of the first Jewish institutions to be closed down.

The Jewish Department in the Belorussian Academy of Sciences was established by government edict in 1944 to prepare studies on the history of Jewish culture in Belorussia, with emphasis on the Holocaust period. Nothing is known of the Department's actual activity: it apparently expired immediately after its establishment.[99]

The Bureau for Yiddish Literature in Lvov was more a library than actual research institute. Directed by Yakov Honikman and Binyamin Valakh, the library contained some 25,000 books, including 5,000 in Hebrew.[100]

Post-war Jewish scholarly activity in the Soviet Union was, then, extremely narrow in scope, irresolute in operation and meagre in achievement. Therefore, the Soviet authorities, although they were not anxious to see Jewish culture renewed, did not close them down immediately after the war, hoping that they would die a natural death. It was only when they saw that this was not happening that they decided, at the end of 1948, to see that this was accomplished through administrative measures.

Museums and libraries

Among the several Jewish museums founded in the Soviet Union during the twenties were the Jewish Museum in Samarkand, established at the end of 1923, which exhibited articles used in religious worship, musical instruments, photographs of monuments, coins and manuscripts; the Jewish Department at the Belorussian State Museum in Minsk (1924), which engaged mainly in collecting paintings, illustrations, antique books, and the like on Minsk and its environs; and the Mendele Museum in Odessa (1924–35), which concentrated its work in the literary, historical and political areas, and where the manuscripts, books and personal effects of the writer Mendele Moykher Seforim were exhibited in a room set aside for this purpose.

The following museums were in operation during and after the war.

1. The Historical-Ethnographic Museum of Georgian Jewry (1933–51) in Tbilisi, which was founded with the declared aim of preparing scholars who would engage in the historical and ethnographic research of Caucasian Jewry in general and of Georgian Jewry in particular. During 1938–9, the Museum prepared an exhibition on 'The Old and New Ways of Life of the Georgian Jews'. From 1940 to 1945, it published three volumes of studies and documents. The Museum ceased operation in the war years, but immediately thereafter, its staff, under Aharon Krikheli, began to collect material on the Jews of Kutaisi. In 1948, the Museum prepared and held an exhibition devoted to the culture of Soviet Jewry. It is of interest that, despite the liquidation of Jewish institutions throughout the Soviet Union, the Tbilisi Museum continued to function at least until the end of 1951, for when the American journalist Harrison Salisbury visited it on 26 May of that year, he saw an exhibition devoted to Jewish heroes of World War II.[101]

2. The Museum for Environmental Knowledge of the Jewish Autonomous Region Birobidzhan (1944–8), whose first director was G. Greenberg, comprised four departments: for the nature study of the region; for the history of the revolution; for socialist construction; and for Jewish culture. The latter, which concentrated on

Jews and human culture, Jewish culture before the October Revolution, and the Jews in the war, was closed down during the 'purge' in the region.[102]

3. The Jewish Museum in Vilnius (1945–8) contained about 3,500 books, periodicals and newspapers on the history of the Jewish theatre, Jewish social movements, and the Soviet period in Lithuania in 1918–19. It was closed down at the end of 1948.[103]

4. There were departments of Yiddish literature still functioning after the war in the libraries of Moscow, Leningrad, Kharkov, Lvov, Minsk and Kherson; however, all of them apparently ceased operations in 1948–9.

The partial renewal of Yiddish culture after Stalin's death did not lead to a corresponding resuscitation of the Jewish research institutes and museums which had been liquidated. The sole vestige of Yiddish culture today is to be found in the Jewish departments of public libraries in Moscow,[104] Vilnius,[105] Riga and Birobidzhan. It is an irony of history that the sole surviving sphere of Jewish research in the Soviet Union today is the study of the Hebrew language and of ancient and contemporary Hebrew works.[106]

Conclusion

The chances of a rooted Jewish culture ever flourishing in the Soviet Union have always been poor, for many reasons. One of the major obstacles to such a development in the Marxist–Leninist state is the ideological legacy, which refuses to recognise the Jews as a nation. Even those nationalities which possess their own republics have found it extemely difficult to develop an autonomous national culture within the Soviet framework. Thus, the task is far more complex for an extra-territorial national minority dispersed through-out various republics. And in the case of the Jews, the accelerated processes of urbanisation, demographic change and social mobility which resulted in fewer and fewer Jewish parents sending their children to Jewish schools exacerbated the situation to the point where general interest in Yiddish culture itself declined.

Nevertheless, a Jewish culture in Yiddish did manage to survive in the Soviet Union in the twenties and thirties, because the Soviet leadership opted for a highly pragmatic policy during its first decade. The administrative measures taken to liquidate Yiddish culture – after Hebrew and Russian had already been eradicated – were put into effect in the second half of the thirties. The great blow was struck during 1937 and 1938, when those central Jewish institutions still in operation were closed. Only the outbreak of the war prevented the total elimination of Jewish culture at that time.

To sum up, the fate of Jewish culture during 1939–67 may be viewed from the vantage point of four distinct periods.

The war years (1939–45). In the wake of the annexation of territories containing about two million Jews in 1939–40, the Soviet authorities were compelled to permit the existence of Jewish schools, newspapers and institutions of art in order to assert their influence upon the new population. Then the Soviet–German war brought about a relaxation in the regime's obduracy towards all the nationalities, providing a respite during which the Jews were able to resuscitate literary and cultural activity. The national awakening in the aftermath of the Holocaust also left its mark in the works of many Jewish writers.

The years 1946–8. The favourable conjunction of events which characterised the war years had not yet completely disappeared when Zhdanov made his notorious speech of August 1946, presaging coming campaigns against Jewish nationalism and cosmopolitanism. Few Yiddish schools were still in operation then, and the number of Jewish scientific institutions continued to dwindle. The only fields to undergo a resurgence were Yiddish publishing and theatre.

The years 1949–53. November 1948 until March 1953 – justly called the 'black years' or the 'years of dread and desperation', among the darkest in the entire history of Soviet Jews – was marked by the brutal persecution of the Jewish intelligentsia and the complete annihilation of those Jewish cultural institutions that had managed to survive until then.

The years 1954–67. This period, especially after the 20th Congress of the Communist Party in February 1956, was characterised by endeavours to renew Jewish culture in the Soviet Union. The external pressures exerted on the authorities during both the Khrushchev and the Brezhnev–Kosygin periods led to a restoration which nevertheless still left Yiddish culture in the USSR a mere shadow of what it was until 1935, or, indeed, even until 1948.

Documents to Chapter 7

The liquidation of Jewish culture: the Yiddish writers

Document 93* Jewish folklore of World War II (1948)

Jewish folklore of the period of the Great Patriotic War was the subject of the report by the Candidate of Philological Sciences, M. Ya. Beregovsky (Kiev).[107] The speaker concentrated mainly on folk-songs, among which the songs of the ghetto and German concentration camps occupy a specially prominent place. The most characteristic feature of the style of Jewish folk-songs of the war period is the closing of the gap between the poetics of traditional Jewish songs and modern literary forms. This is expressed both in the rhythmics of the songs and in their imagery. On the musical side, the Jewish folk-song of the war period also draws to a considerable extent on the expressive means of folk melody. In some songs of the ghetto and camps the melodies of Russian Soviet songs were used to express protest and the call for vengeance and struggle.

Document 94† Publishing plans of 'Der emes' for 1949 (August 1948)

The number of books produced by the State publishing house 'Der emes' grows every year.[108] It has increased especially in the last two years. During 1947 and the first half of 1948, a number of fundamental works of the classics of Marxism–Leninism were published: Marx and Engels, *The Manifesto of the Communist Party*; V. Lenin, *Karl Marx and Friedrich Engels*; I. Stalin, *The Foundations of Leninism, On Questions of Leninism, On the Great Patriotic War of the Soviet Union, History of the All-Union Communist Party (Bolsheviks)*. These publications are proof of the growing capability of the publishing house, its editorial and technical staff and printing-shop.

In the second half of 1948 and in 1949, the publishing house plans to produce in Yiddish the selected works of Marx and Engels in two volumes; the selected works of V. I. Lenin in two volumes (four books); and a number of works by I. V. Stalin.

* *Source*: B. Gershkovich, V. Krupyanskaya & V. Sokolova, 'Soveshchanie po voprosam sobiraniya, izucheniiya i izdaniya folklora Velikoi otechestvennoi voiny' (A Meeting to Discuss Questions of Collecting, Studying and Publishing Folklore of the Great Patriotic War), *Sovetskaya etnografiya*, 1948, no. 2, p. 213.
† *Source*: L. Strongin & M. Belenky, 'Bafridikn dem nokhfreg afn yidishn bukh' (To Satisfy the Demand for Yiddish Books), *Eynikeyt*, 10 August 1948.

In the last year and a half, many works of classical Yiddish literature have been issued by 'Der emes' publishing house. The demand for this literature is very great. Therefore, we plan to publish next year the selected works of Mendele and Perets, as well as six volumes (III–VIII) of the complete works of Shalom Aleikhem. As is known, the first volume of the complete Soviet edition of Shalom Aleikhem's works has already appeared; the second volume will soon be issued.

In 1949, the Yiddish reader will also receive the works of the classics in the Library for the Masses which the publishing house is going to produce. Besides the works of Shalom Aleikhem and Perets, the Library for the Masses of 'Der emes' publishing house also includes works by D. Bergelson and Der Nister.

One of the most important tasks of 'Der emes' publishing house is to produce the works of our Soviet Yiddish writers. Soviet Yiddish literature occupies pride of place in the plan of our publishing house. During the first half of this year, the following works have been published: D. Bergelson's *By the Dnieper*, Sh. Gordon's *The People of Birobidzhan*, Shire Gorshman's[109] *The Force of Life*, Y. Rabin's *We Live*, H. Malamud's[110] *Earth*, and H. Zilberman's[111] *How Long Ago Was It*. Y. Falikman's *The Light Comes from the East*, Note Lurye's *The Steppe Calls*, and H. Polyanker's *Shmaye The Robber*, will appear soon. This year Der Nister's *Mashber Family* (in three parts), A. Gontar's *The Great Family*, H. Riskin's book of short stories, Y. Lyumkis's[112] *Trains Go to Birobidzhan*, the book by M. Yelin and D. Galperin *In the Kaunas Ghetto*, and books of prose by Noah Lurye and M. Altman are to appear.

In the last half year, 'Der emes' publishing house has issued the following works of Soviet Yiddish writers: the collected works of D. Hofshteyn, Sh. Halkin, A. Kushnirov, L. Kvitko, and E. Fininberg, P. Markish's poem *War*, I. Fefer's *Anew*, and B. Heler's *The Road to Warsaw*. The collected works of Sh. Rosin[113] will soon appear as will a book of poems by Y. Kotlyar.[114] Collections of poems by M. Teyf,[115] Z. Telesin[116] and Y. Shternberg are now in preparation.

It is already possible for the Yiddish reader to assemble a fine library of the works of our Soviet prose writers and poets, of our classical Yiddish literature and, especially, to subscribe to the first complete Soviet collection of Shalom Aleikhem's works.

Next year, we envisage the publication of D. Bergelson's new novel *Two Worlds*; a collection of short stories by Der Nister; a new novel by P. Markish; books by H. Malamud, Z. Vendrof, I. Kipnis and others; a number of works by Soviet Yiddish poets; as well as the works of deceased and murdered prose writers such as Godiner,[117] Daniel[118] and Orland.

The historical decisions on literature and art by the Central Committee of our Party[119] have been of great help in turning the attention of our writers to the most urgent themes in our socialist life. One of the main themes of our prose writers and poets in recent years has been the part of the Jews in the heroic struggle of the Soviet people against the Fascist beast. Now socialist construction must become the dominant theme of our Yiddish literature. So far we do not have many works of high artistic value reflecting the heroism of the present-day Soviet Union, the enthusiastic drive of the masses in our country to bring about the transition from socialism to Communism, the organising role of the Leninist–Stalinist Party in our whole social life, the struggle against the survivals of capitalism in the consciousness of Soviet man, the new moral and spiritual nature of our builders of Communist society.

Our Soviet Yiddish writers, above all the prose writers, should quickly cover their debt to the reader.

In the first half of 1948, some works of criticism dealing with the history of our literature were issued by 'Der emes' publishing house. In 1949, we plan to publish a book by Y. Dobrushin on Soviet Yiddish literature, the selected works of M. Viner[120] and A. Gorshteyn, a book by M. Notovich[121] and Sh. Roytman[122] on the history of Yiddish literature, a book by U. Finkel[123] on Shalom Aleikhem, E. Lyubomirsky's[124] *The Actor Zuskin* and others. The collection *On Soviet Paths* (critical papers on the creative path of twenty-four Soviet Yiddish prose writers and poets) will soon be in print, as well as some lexicological works (E. Spivak's *Russian–Yiddish Dictionary*, E. Falkovich's[125] *Grammar*) and also *A Reader For Beginners* by Ye. Khatskels.

The plan of the publishing house for next year includes the book by Grinberg, *The Jewish Autonomous Region (Social-Economic Essays)*; Sheyman's *Communism and Religion*; Gurev's *Was There a Beginning and Will There Be an End to the World*, etc. The booklet *Body and Soul* by M. Altshuler[126] will also appear.

In recent years, 'Der emes' publishing house has started issuing a number of Yiddish books in Russian translation. This work will be continued. Two volumes of selected works by Shalom Aleikhem are soon to appear in Russian, as will *By the Dnieper* by D. Bergelson and the collection *Partisan Friendship*.

In 1949, we plan to publish in Russian Mendele's *Fishke the Lame* and *The Travels of Benjamin the Third*, the third volume of Shalom Aleikhem's selected works, one-volume selections of Y. L. Perets and D. Bergelson and also a book of children's songs by Kvitko.

The publishing plan of 1949 will require much work. It can and will be successfully fulfilled by the combined creative efforts of our writers and publishing house.

It is clear that just fulfilling the plans of publication is not much. It is important to publicise the books and bring them to the readers. Here we expect the help of the broad Soviet public, above all of our Soviet Yiddish writers and workers in the field of culture.

L. Strongin,
    Director of the State Publishing House 'Der emes',
M. Belenky,
    Editor-in-Chief of the Publishing House.

Document 95* Korneichuk criticises Yiddish writers at the 2nd Congress of Ukrainian Writers (December 1948)

A considerable number of Jewish writers, thirty-five persons, work in the Ukraine. It is a pity that the Jewish writers of the Ukraine have created few works of importance in recent years. Among those who are actively creative the gifted prose writer N. Lurye, author of the novel *The Steppe Calls*, should be

* *Source*: 'Sostoyanie i ocherednye zadachi ukrainskoi sovetskoi literatury' (The Present State and Immediate Tasks of Ukrainian Soviet Literature), *Literaturnaya gazeta*, 8 December 1948.

mentioned first. His novel presents a broad canvas of the creation and consolidation of a collective farm. Now Lurye is writing a new novel about present-day Odessa. New works have also been created by such prose writers as Y. Falikman, G. Polyanker;[127] the poets M. Talalaevsky,[128] H. Levina,[129] and others.

But in all frankness we must say that the Jewish writers in the Ukraine, among whom there are many gifted writers, especially the young who arrived after the war, would be much more successful if they did not stew in the stuffy atmosphere of their section; if they concentrated more on the central themes of our life and did not devote their works to petty subjects or harp on collisions typical of times long past which have been overcome by the Jewish people long ago. During the war, the Jewish people produced many Heroes of the Soviet Union, outstanding Stakhanovites, progressive scientists; but most Jewish writers do not see them. The Jewish writers do not develop their own criticism and self-criticism. They consider it heroic not only to keep silent about, but also to defend, those who make serious ideological mistakes in their creative activities. Such a situation cannot but hinder the creative work of the Jewish writers of the Ukraine.

Document 96* Salsberg discusses the Jewish cultural scene with Soviet leaders (August 1955)

In my first conversations with responsible, although second-rank representatives of the Party in Moscow, an effort was made to convince me that there really existed no Jewish problem in the USSR. When I insisted on an official discussion, the Party's Central Committee appointed a special commission to meet with me.

The commission gave me in substance the following answers to my questions.

The Jewish Anti-Fascist Committee was dissolved because it had ceased to fulfil the function for which it had been established. It had been created during the war for specific war needs, and after the victory over Fascism it became superfluous.

Bourgeois nationalist influences had penetrated the Anti-Fascist Committee. A Jewish member of the commission added that, shortly after Golda Meir arrived in Moscow as the first ambassador from Israel, a large crowd of Jews staged a demonstration for her in front of the Moscow synagogue. He also said that he knows that secret Zionist groups exist.

Jewish writers had been arrested. This was the work of Beria and 'regrettably innocent people died as his victims'. Writers of numerous nationalities – not only Jews – also suffered.

The Soviet government was reviewing all cases involving Beria's arrests. All those falsely arrested were being freed and rehabilitated. A number of the Jewish writers had already returned home. I was urged to be patient and assured that those still remaining in prison would shortly be released.

When I asked when and where, assuming the Anti-Fascist Committee was

* *Source*: J. R. Salsberg, 'Soviet Leaders and the Jewish Question', *Jewish Life*, February 1957, pp. 23–4, 32–3.

infected, the question of bourgeois nationalism was discussed with the committee, I received no answer. I then wanted to know why this committee, having outlived its usefulness, as they said, a new social-cultural committee along the lines existing in Poland was not organised. They replied that there was no need for such a committee.

I received no clear-cut answer to my question regarding the fate of such prominent writers as Bergelson, Fefer, Markish, Kvitko, Hofshteyn, Der Nister. One of the members of the commission repeated, however, that he knew that 'innocent people had been done away with'. (I believe that the members of the commission really didn't know the details.)

The representatives of the Central Committee were exceedingly hospitable. They arranged a number of personal meetings for me with important individuals. I had a long talk with Rabbi Shlifer and some of his congregational leaders. I also met Saul Lyubimov, a singer who had just returned from 'Beria's exile'. I attended the first of his three concerts in Moscow – the first completely Yiddish concerts for many years. Although the weather was very hot, tickets were sold out well in advance. I had a long talk with the manager of the central concert bureau. They outlined for me their plans for a series of Jewish concerts in some ten cities. They were confident that these concerts would all be sold out. I also spoke to many Jewish people in the streets, in restaurants, in stores, although not all were prepared to talk to a foreigner.

Document 97*   First Soviet announcement of Markish's[130] death and rehabilitation (December 1955)

The secretariat of the Writers' Union of the USSR has organised commissions on the literary heritage of the poet Perets Markish and the playwright Vladimir Kirshon.[131] The commissions were charged with preparing suggestions for the publication of their works. The commission on the literary heritage of P. Markish is headed by P. Chagin, and that of V. Kirshon by Yu. Libedinsky.[132]

Document 98†   Sutskever[133] on Markish's last days (1962)

In reply to my letter from Vilnius in July 1944, in which I tried to describe to him my first impressions upon returning to the liberated, ruined city, Markish wrote to me from Moscow:

'There is nothing to be said. One wants to lower one's head and smash it against a stone. To our greatest misfortune we shall perhaps have to read this "literature" till the end of our lives. It is our destiny, and nowhere shall we be free from it. I wanted to travel to Vilnius and its seems to me that to journey to those holy ashes is sacrilege.'

Markish came to Vilnius and breathed in the 'holy ashes'. The Jewish

* *Source*: 'Literaturnoe nasledie P. Markisha i V. Kirshona' (The Literary Heritage of P. Markish and V. Kirshon), *Literaturnaya gazeta*, 29 December 1955.
† *Source*: A. Sutskever, 'Perets Markish un zayn svive' (The World of Perets Markish), *Di goldene keyt*, 1962, no. 43, pp. 36–8, 40, 44–7.

partisans, the few thousand rescued Jews, received him like a brother. From this journey his poem *Milkhome* [War] was enriched with grief and heroism. He wove into it a number of interesting heroes of the Vilnius ghetto, even calling them by their real names: Hirshke Glik and Naomi — (a girl from Vilnius, a partisan, now living in Israel in Kibbutz *Loḥamei ha-getaot*).

Hundreds of verses from that poem, which Markish had read to me, were not included in the published version of *Milkhome* (Moscow, 1948). Every day the political line shifted, and fear of an unclear morrow continually compelled Markish to erase the uncertain and write in a manner that would please the rulers.

The same thing happened to almost all Yiddish writers. The more liberal breathing-spell had come to a rapid end. Whoever lived to see the years 1942–5 lived with the feeling that he had entrusted to eternity his pure, unfalsified writer's truth. Bergelson wrote his *Prints Reuveni* [Prince Reuveni] at that time and had taken upon himself the writing of a novel about Rabbi Akivah. At that time too, Halkin had begun writing a dramatic poem on a ghetto rising, where one of the heroes was also a *ḥaluz* [pioneer]. Der Nister had worked on the continuation of his epic *Di mishpokhe mashber* [The Mashber Family], and on his table lay an open copy of the *Zohar* and books of Hasidic and *Kabalah*[134] literature. [...]

However, whether it be Fefer or Markish or any of the other writers, deep in their hearts they knew that the time did not belong to them.

And just as the survivors of the ghetto did not believe that the 'campaigns' would overlook them, so the Yiddish writers in Moscow did not believe that they were more privileged than Kharik, Kulbak, Tsinberg, Litvakov and the scores of others whose bones had frozen in the Siberian *taiga*.

Some of them had at one time committed a sin, and somewhere it had been noted down. *One* had the misfortune to have been abroad, *another* had once written to a friend in America; and yet another – one is forbidden even to contemplate it – had celebrated Trotsky. [...]

Markish had written the poem ['To a Jewish Dancer'] in 1940. Because of the non-aggression pact with Germany, he had been unable to publish it earlier. Later, after the outbreak of war, one had to write mainly patriotic and war poems. Also, his rather strong national emphases did not fit into the political line. Only in 1946 did fragments of the poem appear in his book of verse translated into Russian, and a few years later – after his death – in the book *Yerushe* [Heritage], (Buenos Aires, 1959).

Listening to the vivid lyricism of the poem, I was deeply impressed, and kissing him out of genuine enthusiasm, I said to him: 'Comrade Markish, you know your uniform is lying around on the floor, evidently your Order of Lenin has also got drunk on your poetry...'

'Let it lie there. It cost me enough blood.' With these words Markish seemed to be venting his fury on someone, but I still did not know on whom. 'I'll tell you something, but no one must know about it.

'One night a loud bang on the door woke me up. Three men in red-striped caps came in and ordered me to get dressed. Esther became hysterical. The children moaned: "Daddy, where are they taking you?"

'A black car took me along Moscow's streets. I asked: "Where to?" No one answered. I already pictured to myself a cell in the Lubyanka. Suddenly the car pulled up by the editorial buildings of *Pravda*. There, I was asked to sit down in an isolated room. A guard with a bayonet remained at the door. Only towards day-time did the drunken editor of *Pravda* come bursting in and stretch out his hand to me: "Congratulations, Comrade Markish, you have been awarded the Order of Lenin ..."'

And Markish concluded:

'That night I turned grey.' [...]

I was destined to witness how even in those 'good years' they had wanted to liquidate Markish. I was at that time his temporary saviour and consider it my duty to tell of this now.

At the beginning of the summer of 1945, the secretary of the Director of the Informburo Lozovsky telephoned to ask me to come to see him.

Lozovsky received me in his office very warmly. He was seated in his grey uniform with the golden epaulettes, and above him on the wall hung an oil painting of the 'Lord of the Great Land', painted by the court artist Gerasimov. The lord and master was smiling at a child whom he held in his arms.

After a polite, familiar conversation Lozovsky told me the good news that the Lithuanian government, with his agreement, had decided to honour me with a Stalin Prize.

I felt that a net was being woven around me. No Stalin Prize winner would be allowed to leave for Poland.

'It's a great honour for me', I pretended to look pleased, 'but I don't know why I should receive it. My ghetto poems haven't appeared in book form, and I wasn't at all aware that the jury could read Yiddish – '

'That's not important', Lozovsky silenced my uneasy confusion. 'Submit the manuscripts of your poems in Yiddish; they'll be read and translated...'

When I had thanked him once again and was about to take my leave, Lozovsky stood up, rapped his desk with his finger and looked me in the eyes: 'Yes, one other thing, what is your opinion of Perets Markish? Is it true that in Poland he wrote counter-revolutionary poems? And did you know that here, in Moscow, he wrote a poem in which he slanders the Red Army?'

He took a blue sheet of paper out of a drawer and gave it to me. 'Here, read it, tell me your opinion.'

The text, written in Russian, read as follows (I quote from memory, of course):

We, the undersigned, consider it our Soviet and patriotic duty to inform you that the writer Perets Markish, after having published counter-revolutionary poems while he was abroad, has also unashamedly presumed, here in Moscow, to slander our heroic Red Army which saved mankind from destruction. The following is a quotation from a poem of his printed not long ago in the journal *Tsum zig*:

With sacks in their hands
with infants at their breasts
with broken heart and crazed look –
on the by-ways of death – day in and day out –
the homeless Jews sought a city of refuge,

a place, a night's lodging, a roof,
between forging frost and smelting fire,
desperation broke forth undammed from them
and led them like a wandering, thousand-year funeral procession.
Stopping occasionally, separately or together –
against the whistle of buckshot and the whistling rain –
extending a hand to someone who had fallen,
and burying a fallen man in passing,
and dragging oneself further with no one's help,
wandering on in a hopeless existence,
each one exhausted his vital strength,
bearing misfortune on his shoulders, just like a mountain.

Following the text in Yiddish, there was a literal translation in Russian. The passages where the Red Army was allegedly slandered were in large print.

I was interested to know who the informers were. The text was on the other side. *I* did not have the courage to turn the page over without Lozovsky's permission. I let the paper fall from my fingers and – on picking it up – chance favoured me; it lay with the other side facing upwards and I was immediately able to catch the names of the signatories. They were Shakhne Epshteyn and — (the name of the other I do not wish to divulge because he was also among the victims who were shot in August 1952).

I explained to Lozovsky that for as long as I could recall the name of Perets Markish, he had always been the symbol of Yiddish revolutionary poetry and that I saw no slander whatever of the Red Army in the fragment. The Russian Jews, persecuted and tormented by the Germans, sought 'a place, a night's lodging, a roof' in Central Asia and, with the help of the Red Army, they found such a place.

When I finished my testimony in Markish's favour, a girl came in from another room with a document in which everything I had said had been written down exactly as she had heard it with complete accuracy in her concealed room. I signed it, took my leave and left.

Document 99* First Soviet announcement of David Hofshteyn's[135] death and rehabilitation (August 1956)

Kiev. (Our correspondent.) The Presidium of the Ukrainian Writers' Union has decided to organise commissions on the literary heritage of O. Dosvitny[136] (chairman–P. Panch)[137] and D. Hofshteyn (chairman–N. Tereshchenko).[138]

Document 100† Sutskever's meeting with Hofshteyn (1962)

After the reception at the Writers' House I left with David Hofshteyn for a walk in the streets of Moscow. It was already midnight. His heavy black coat showed up his parchment-like frightened face. It was as though his face was

---

* *Source*: 'V komissiyakh po literaturnomu nasledstvu' (In the Commissions on the Literary Heritage), *Literaturnaya gazeta*, 23 August 1956.
† *Source*: A. Sutskever, 'Perets Markish un zayn svive' (The World of Perets Markish), *Di goldene keyt*, 1962, no. 43, pp. 31–3.

floating by itself in the night, without a body. A face of a sixty-year-old child, or a six-year-old-man.

He talked freely: in Kiev, his old home, he did not recognise his neighbours. The city had cold-shouldered the Jews who had returned from the Urals and Central Asia. No one in Kiev needed his Yiddish poems. He was trying his luck by writing in Russian or Ukrainian, but his manuscripts were being returned. His Yiddish poems too, he complained, were seldom printed in the only Yiddish newspaper, *Eynikeyt*.

'A poem like the one you read to me earlier, the Ukrainians certainly won't understand', I said, looking into his watery eyes.

'Fefer doesn't understand it even in Yiddish', he hinted broadly with a smile, 'and Surkov, the editor of *Literatura i iskusstvo*, doesn't print my poems in Russian. ("Never mind, don't write Russian poems, we have enough *of our own.*")'

'Comrade Hofshteyn', I was unable to control myself, and what I said to him spoilt our walk, 'what good are your Russian and Ukrainian poems to you? Think of your own verses:

On winter evenings in Russian fields,
Where can one be more alone, where can one be more alone!

'And since you are Hofshteyn, whose song has given pleasure to the Jewish youth of Poland, then forgive me for asking you a painful question; it's been gnawing at me now for a few years: why did you need to write a poem about Bohdan Khmelnytsky![139] I saw it in 1940. There was already a ghetto in Warsaw at that time.'

The head, which earlier had swum in the night like a watermelon afloat, began bobbing, sinking. I did not know how to save him. But suddenly a miracle happened. Shmuel Halkin appeared and saved us both.

The following day, at about midnight, I was already lying in bed, when someone knocked at the door of my hotel room.

'Who is it?'

'Hofshteyn.'

And before I had time to dress, he poured out his heart: 'Here's the poem. Read it again and you'll understand differently.'

The whole business was very distressing. Why did I have to hurt him? With or without Khmelnytsky – he would anyhow remain *Hofshteyn*, the finest and purest Yiddish poet in the Soviet Union. However, I had no choice and tried reading the poem, which was called, I think, 'In Memory of Bohdan Khmelnytsky'.

'Well, how do you understand the line "Your sword is outstretched to the east"?' (I quote from memory – A. S.)

'I don't see anything mysterious in it. I understand the line simply as it is written.'

'Do you know what I meant by that line', Hofshteyn said, looking around suspiciously, and leading me by the arm into the nearby wash-room where there was no danger that the telephone receiver should overhear. 'I meant in that line that Khmelnytsky had *once again* stretched forth his sword to the East, to us, Jews ...'

I was silent. What could I have replied? Only my lips quietly whispered: 'A Marrano – Hofshteyn is a Marrano.'

Document 101* The rehabilitation of Fefer[140] (May 1956)

The Commission on Literary Heritage

The secretariat of the Writers' Union of the USSR has organised commissions on the literary heritage of I. Batrak (chairman – G. Korenev), I. Bespalov[141] (chairman – I. Anisimov), Artem Vesely[142] (chairman – V. Grossman), I. Kataev[143] (chairman – N. Chukovsky) and I. Fefer (chairman – A. Prokofyev).

Document 102† The rehabilitation[144] of Bergelson and Kvitko (January 1956)

The secretariat of the board of the Writers' Union of the USSR has organised a commission on the literary heritage of D. Bergelson[145] (chairman of the commission – Vs. Ivanov), L. Kvitko[146] (chairman – L. Kassil)[147] and B. Yasensky[148] (chairman – V. Lidin).[149]

Document 103‡ The tragedy of Bergelson's last days

It was just at that time that I met David Bergelson.

I went into the Anti-Fascist Committee and saw a group of writers. They were all sitting with heads bowed and sad faces. In the middle of the group, however, stood David Bergelson holding forth in a high, grating voice:

'Comrades, I've told you already, it is a provocation. It's the enemies of our dear Soviet fatherland who have spread such a rumour. What do we Jews in Russia need our own territory for? That's a survival of the bourgeois Palestine theory. We Jews are all right in Russia, wherever we are. Tell me, comrades, what doesn't suit us here in Moscow? What do we lack?'

The audience remained seated, listening and silent. The silence, however, spoke volumes.

But Bergelson did not weary. He continued to pour forth the law.

'I'm telling you, comrades, that we must be thankful to our government that it frustrated those provocative rumours. Can you imagine what would have happened if the people of the Soviet Union had come to know that the Crimea was to be given to the Jews? It would have greased the wheels of the anti-Semitism left behind in our country by the Hitlerite occupationists. Can you imagine?'

I looked around and saw that Bergelson's speech was making the audience impatient and edgy. I understood why. But I had by no means suspected that the audience's animosity would all of a sudden turn into such undisguised anger at David Bergelson.

* *Source*: 'Literaturnaya khronika' (Literary News Items), *Literaturnaya gazeta*, 15 May 1956.
† *Source*: 'Literaturnaya khronika' (Literary News Items), *Literaturnaya gazeta*, 24 January 1956.
‡ *Source*: Yitskhak Yanasovich, *Mit yidishe shrayber in rusland* (With Yiddish Writers in Russia), Buenos Aires, Kiyyum Farlag, 1959, pp. 258–59.

Suddenly I heard someone say: 'Comrade Bergelson, we all know that our government has done the right thing. But your construing of its motives is not Soviet. Our government does not reckon with anti-Semitic feelings. Only bourgeois, reactionary governments make allowances for anti-Semitic moods.'

Having spoken these words, in which one could detect the 'yes' in the 'no', that is, the real reason why the Soviet authorities had actually cancelled the Crimean project – with these words the speaker got up and left. After him all the other writers left quickly, leaving Bergelson behind alone, a bewildered man with outstretched hands and an open mouth.

Bergelson, who suddenly caught sight of me next to him, all but seized me by the lapels and began justifying himself.

'You understand, comrade, I didn't say – I didn't mean – What I wanted to say was that – '

To this day I don't know what he meant to say. But I know that he made a terrible impression on me then. It was not merely that I had then heard him saying exactly the opposite of what he had said – according to what I was told – a week earlier. It was also his way of talking, his hackneyed phrases, his arbitrary manner of hiding behind divine judgement, his decision so clumsily to pour salt on his own and other people's wounds and, above all, his pitifulness and bewilderment when he was shown that the speech, with which he thought he had justified himself, had in fact made him a prey and perhaps, who knows, even revealed what lay concealed in the depths of his soul.

The liquidation of Jewish culture: Mikhoels and the Yiddish theatre

Document 104* Soviet artists mourn the death of Mikhoels[150] (January 1948)

The Soviet theatre has suffered a severe loss: Solomon Mikhailovich Mikhoels is dead. Death has torn from our midst a remarkable artist, actor and producer; a great public figure.

S. M. Mikhoels was an active builder of Soviet art and culture. After the great October Socialist Revolution, wide creative possibilities were open to S. M. Mikhoels. S. M. Mikhoels was the organiser of the State Yiddish Theatre and headed it for many years.

In the long gallery of figures created by S. M. Mikhoels on the stage he expressed the deep feelings of a citizen, the striking individuality of a great artist. The courageous Soviet patriots Yulis and Ovadis, the rebel Tevye full of optimistic folk wisdom, the tragedy of Lear at the moment of enlightenment; such is by no means a complete list of Mikhoels's brilliant stage creations.

In the years of the Great Patriotic War, Mikhoels created a number of plays permeated with a profound sense of Soviet patriotism: *Freylekhs*, *The Sighing of the Forests*, and others.

Mikhoels's many-sided creative activities brought him the recognition and

* *Source*: 'S. M. Mikhoels', *Pravda*, 15 January 1948.

love of Soviet audiences. The pathos of thought, the passion, the striving for broad generalisation, the constant search for something new, the great fastidiousness of his attitude to himself and to his art characterise Mikhoels's creative path. He trained a number of talented actors and producers, worked constantly and indefatigably with the playwrights, took great care of the growing young generation of actors. [...]

We have lost a great artist and public figure who devoted all his life to serving the Soviet people. Chairman of the Jewish Anti-Fascist Committee, member of the Arts Council of the Committee of Art Affairs and of the Committee for Stalin Prizes in art and literature, member of the presidium of the All-Russian Theatre Society and of the Central Committee of the Trade Union of Art Workers – this is far from a full list of the public duties of S. M. Mikhoels.

For his outstanding service to the theatre the Soviet authorities awarded S. M. Mikhoels the title of People's Artist of the USSR, Laureate of the Stalin Prize and the Order of Lenin.

The image of the outstanding Soviet artist S. M. Mikhoels will always live in our hearts.

Document 105* Markish's tribute to Mikhoels[151]

1

Your last public appearance was
Amidst debris covered with snow.
But – without words, without your voice,
Only your frozen breath.

Yet, overhead, we hear even now, as always,
The unseen eagle's wings beat in ascent –
Your people has bestowed upon you
To be its comfort, its reverberation, its reproach.

The curtain does not fall,
The lights are not extinguished in the hall.
Your sleeping lion's head shines as when alive,
And floating forms whisper the immortal word.

To bid farewell to you, we all came here
Where you – like generations' echoes of ordeal –
Carried aloft the song of Shalom Aleikhem's tear
So that it may glitter like a precious gem.

2

The crowds are streaming in. It's full of people.
Your last performance, and your last surprise.
A guard of honour descends to the bier,
Ghosts, like a magician, you have brought to life.

* *Source*: P. Markish, 'Sh. Mikhoelsn – A ner tomed baym orn' (To S. Mikhoels – An Eternal Light at the Bier), in B. Hrushovsky, Ch. Shmeruk & A. Sutskever (eds.), *A shpigl oyf a shteyn* (A Mirror on a Stone), Tel Aviv, Di Goldene Keyt–I. L. Perets Publishing House, 1964, pp. 508–12.

There is no need now for the wig,
The royal cloak is still less necessary,
To see that you are King Lear,
Who exchanged his crown for wisdom.

No make-up, not the slightest hint of hue,
The paints are weeping on your table, orphaned.
Hotsmakh, alone, falls in his full attire,
Though stars don't fall, stars only wander.

To the strains of the funeral dirge they awake.
And float through the folds of the curtain,
Without any sound, with eyes lowered in pain,
They want to carry your coffin into eternity.

3

Snow has covered the wounds on your face
That the devil of darkness should not touch you,
Your eyes, though dead, seethe with pain,
Your heart, though shattered, roars in deep anguish:

'Eternity, to your dishonoured door I come,
With bruises, the marks of murder, on my face,
Thus walks my people on five-sixth of the globe,
Scarred with marks of the axe and hatred.

'Read it well! Engrave it on your mind,
Remember it in your unapproachable indifference:
– For every wound on my murder-maimed face
A mother has escaped with her child from the hangmen.'

You're not deadened by the murderer's hand,
The snow has not concealed the least sign;
Torment in your eyes, from beneath ravaged lids,
To the sky surges up, like a mountain to heaven.

4

A crowd goes by and more crowds come on,
And one column of people joins the next:
Six millions will rise to honour you,
The murdered, the tortured – the dead,

As you have honoured them by falling down,
Alone, in dead of night, and in terrible torment,
In Minsk, amidst its ruins and its snow,
In a dark snow-drift and in a whirling snow-storm.

Though lifeless, you'd be there
To champion their woe, their peace and honour –
A blood-bedecked reproach to the whole world –
Your fragments chained by frost.

Grief flows forth. Stormily
Grief has pierced the hearts of your whole people:

Six millions will rise in their graves to honour you,
As you honoured them when you fell in the ruins of Minsk.

5

Sleep – slumber peacefully! No care will trouble you again,
It seems as if your eyes still flash in contemplation in death,
As if upon you rests the moral light of the *Ger* star,[152]
As if Reb Levi Yitskhak's[153] pipes resound through you.

Can love be smothered by sombre snow-storms?
Can wrath be entombed by snow?
Like two candles, for a blessing aglow,
Your hands shine from out of the coffin.

You loved to close your eyes in silent contemplation,
When thinking about something, to see things more clearly –
Now you shut off your agony behind them
So that it should not spill over the bier.

So much pure light around you – from mirrors,
As if you're making up for a first night.
It seems that in a moment your lips will move apart
And to the stars your blissful rise will start.

6

Your features are changing back into matter,
Already death begins its ruinous work;
Imbibe the music for the last time into your tissues,
It's your beloved – from 'Benjamin the Third'.

Amid these sounds, with tears drenched and with light,
Enter eternity in unpainted colours,
Don't be ashamed of your disfigured ancient face,
Or of your bullet-ridden regal skull.

It is your word in blood. It is the best make-up
In which you live – though dead – over the stage.
Enter eternity – your entrances are renowned,
The stars of the creation will greet you, dancing.

Somewhere, amidst the wandering, glittering light of the firmament,
A star assumes your brilliant name;
Don't feel ashamed of your abuse and your torment –
Let eternity bear the shame!

7

The curtain does not fall.
Not even now in the presence of death do your eyes close,
A whole generation will proudly bear your gift,
As you carried the people's golden heritage.

You are not leaving us.
You penetrate us still more deeply, laden with ripeness,

As, beneath the warmth of the sun,
The seed penetrates the awakened earth.

We shall no more knock at the door
Of your study, see your profile,
But without a knock we shall enter
Your heart, which is open to all,

Which belonged to everyone,
Like the sun to both the hills and the valleys –
And further – with the dream of our country
Into the heights, as upon a golden gondola.

Document 106* Erenburg's reaction to Mikhoels's death (1965)

The months of which I am about to write are probably amongst the most painful in my life. I interrupted work on this book for a long time trying to summon up the courage to embark on this chapter. I should have been glad enough to omit it altogether. But life is not like a set of galley-proofs; what you live through cannot be deleted on second thoughts. Fifteen years have passed since then. I do not want to re-open old wounds that are healing, and I shall leave out certain names as I find the role of prosecutor distasteful. In any case, there is much that I myself do not know, so I shall confine myself to a brief and unadorned account of my own experience.

I realise now that the start of the events which I intend to recount is bound up with the tragic death of Solomon Mikhoels and, before going further, I shall speak of him. I had met him a long time ago, in the twenties, but did not get to know him well at that time; it was only during the war years that I really began to understand him and grew very attached to him. There was a period when he often came to see us at the Moskva Hotel. On some days he would lustily complain about things or play the fool; on others he would sit in silence, his arms and legs hunched up. He was a great artist, and art was his natural element.

I shall always remember his King Lear. He was unrecognisable. In real life he was short and his face was by no means kingly; it was rather that of a slightly puckish intellectual with a prominent forehead and pouting lower lip. But on the stage his tall, tragic Lear was superb in its grief and wrath. Mikhoels's talent was recognised by actors of various schools of thought. I remember the admiration with which Kachalov, Meyerkhold and Pitoëff[154] spoke of him. He had never been a nationalist; his feeling for the Russian language made his friend Aleksei Tolstoi often remark: 'I can't understand why Solomon won't play in the Russian theatre.' But Mikhoels's special love was the Jewish theatre. People who did not even understand Yiddish were amongst its regular audiences, for Mikhoels and Zuskin acted so expressively that everyone was entranced by the adventures of some small-town Jewish Don Quixote or the misfortunes of Tevye the Milkman.

During the war, Mikhoels was the animating spirit of the Jewish Anti-Fascist Committee. No one at the time could spare a thought for art. In the little towns of the Ukraine and Belorussia the Nazis were murdering Shalom Aleikhem's classical characters – and girl-guides. Mikhoels and the poet Fefer

* *Source*: I. Erenburg, 'Lyudi, gody, zhizn' (People, Years, Life), *Novy mir*, 1965, no. 2, pp. 50–1.

were asked to go to America. In 1946, several Americans told me that in one town where they spoke the platform gave way under the weight of the people who rushed it in order to get closer to the Soviet emissaries. Those two raised millions of dollars for Soviet field hospitals and children's homes.

After the victory, thousands of people went to Mikhoels for help, because they saw him as the wise rabbi, the defender of the oppressed.

And then Mikhoels was killed.

At the time we were told that he had gone to Minsk with Golubov-Potapov[155] on some assignment for the committee which awarded the Stalin Prizes; he was supposed to be judging a production nominated for the award. One evening he was invited to some people and, accompanied by Golubov-Potapov, was walking along a street in the suburbs when they were either set upon and killed by bandits or, according to another account, run over by a lorry. In the spring of 1948 either version was credible, but six months later both began to be doubted. When Zuskin was arrested everybody asked themselves how Mikhoels really met his death. Not long ago a Soviet paper published in Lithuania reported that he had been killed by Beria's agents.[156] It is not for me to hazard a guess why Beria, who could quite easily have arrested Mikhoels, should have had recourse to such a criminal ruse; certainly it could not have been out of respect for public opinion; it can only have been that it was his idea of fun.

I went to the funeral service at Mikhoels's theatre. His mutilated features had been made up with grease-paint. There were speeches. I remember Fadeev's in particular. A crowd stood outside in the street and many people wept.

Document 107* Financial support is withdrawn from the State Yiddish Theatre (March 1948)

The committee for Art Affairs of the Council of Ministers of the USSR has decided, as of 15 March, to withdraw state subsidies from 646 theatres, including ten within the competence of the Union Republic. The rest will continue to receive subsidies for the time being, in curtailed amounts. In Moscow, the following theatres are to be self-supporting: Vakhtangov, Yiddish, Stanislavsky and the state mobile theatres; in Leningrad: the Comedy Theatre.

The practice of handing out complementary tickets is forbidden.

Theatres are required regularly to give parallel, guest, exchange and touring performances and also guest concerts. (Tass)

Document 108† On the State Yiddish Theatre of Moscow (*Goset*)[157]

Founded 1919 by A. M. Granovsky[158] in Petrograd. Originally called the Yiddish Chamber Theatre. Transferred 1920 to Moscow. 1925 renamed the

---

* *Source*: 'Reorganizatsiya teatralnogo dela' (Reorganisation of Theatre Affairs), *Pravda Vostoka*, 13 March 1948.
† *Source*: *Tsentralny gosudarstvenny arkhiv literatury i iskusstva SSSR. Putevoditel. Iskusstvo* (Central State Archives of Literature and Art of the USSR. Handbook. Art), Moscow, Glavnoe arkhivnoe upravlenie, 1959, p. 309. Collection 2307; storage unit 108; 1938–1950.

State Yiddish Theatre of Moscow (*Goset*). From 1929 to 1948 the theatre's artistic director was S. M. Mikhoels. Theatre liquidated 1949.

Theatre statutes (1948), orders of the theatre (1938–49), plans and accounts (1940–9).

Theatre's correspondence with the Committee for Art Affairs and with other institutions (1947–9), agreements and contracts with writers, composers, directors (1940–9).

List of personnel (1941–9), personal affairs of the artists (1942–9).

Minutes of the sessions of the liquidation commission (1949–50).

Attempts to revive Jewish culture

Document 109* Private attempt to revive Jewish cultural activity (I): reply of RSFSR Ministry of Education (October 1957)

Copy

State Emblem
Ministry of Education of the RSFSR

Moscow. Chistye Prudy, 6	Telephone: ко – 28 – 00
5 – x – 1957	Leningrad, Razezzhaya St 9/8
Reference No: 10619/12–2	To: Comrade G. Pechersky

On behalf of the Ministry of Education of the RSFSR the Chief Administration of Schools has considered your letter in which you raise questions on the opening of fee-paying courses in Leningrad for the study of the Hebrew and Yiddish languages and ancient and modern Jewish literature and history, the giving of periodic lectures on these subjects for persons being unable to attend courses regularly, and also the allocation of appropriate premises for these purposes.

We have to inform you that a decision on the above questions does not fall within the competence of the Ministry of Education of the RSFSR. In the cities the organisation of various courses, not financed by the state, and likewise the allocation of premises for these purposes is conducted by the executive committees of the local Soviets of Workers' Deputies. On the question of holding periodic lectures on the Hebrew and Yiddish languages, ancient and modern Jewish literature and history, you should, it seems, turn to the All-Union and All-Russian Society for the Dissemination of Political and Scientific Knowledge.

Deputy Head of the Chief Administration of Schools
    (signature – P. Makarov)

---

* *Source*: This document was brought to the West by an emigrant from the Soviet Union.

Document 110* Private attempt to revive Jewish cultural activity (II): a letter to the Chairman of the Leningrad City Executive Committee (1957)

To the Chairman of the Leningrad City Executive Committee of the Soviet of Workers' Deputies – Comrade N. I. Smirnov

Two months ago a group of Leningrad Jews applied to the Ministry of People's Education of the RSFSR requesting permission to open in Leningrad fee-paying courses for the adult Jewish population on the study of the history of the Jewish people, its literature and the two languages of the Jews, Hebrew and Yiddish.

This request was motivated by the fact that both wide Jewish circles have shown and still show a deep interest in their history, literature and language and also that the policy of the Soviet power in the nationalities question grants each nationality of the USSR every opportunity within the law to study its national culture in all its aspects.

In the programmatic work of the founder of the Soviet State, Vladimir Ilyich Lenin, *Critical Remarks on the National Question* (4th edn, vol. 20, p. 27) one reads that 'any citizen would be able to demand that orders prohibiting, for example, the hiring, at state expense, of special teachers of Hebrew, Jewish history, and the like, or the provision of state-owned premises for lectures for Jewish, Armenian or Romanian children, or even for one Georgian child be rescinded'.

Hence it follows that the Jewish population has the right to demand that the local authorities grant it the opportunity to study its language and history, equally with other peoples.

Vladimir Ilyich Lenin in fact writes: 'At all events, it is by no means impossible to meet, on the basis of equality, all the reasonable and just wishes of the national minorities, and nobody will say that advocacy of equality is harmful.' (*Ibid.*)

Thus it is clear from the statements of V. I. Lenin that no obstacles need hinder the opening of courses so that Jews may study their language, literature and history, or likewise the giving of lectures on these subjects in Russian, Yiddish and Hebrew, or the allocation of appropriate premises for this purpose.

As can be seen from the enclosed answer of the Ministry of People's Education of the RSFSR of 5.x.57, Reference No. 10619/12–2, the Ministry, too, voices no objection to the opening of such courses, but considers that the immediate solution of this question as well as the allocation of appropriate premises for the courses must come from the Local Executive Committee.

In accordance with the foregoing, we, the undersigned, request:

1. Permission to open in Leningrad fee-paying courses for adult Jews for the study of the history of the Jewish people, its literature and the two languages of the Jews.

2. Instructions to the corresponding organ to make available suitable premises for these courses.

As far as teaching personnel for these courses is concerned, they exist in Leningrad in sufficient numbers and with suitable qualifications.

Enclosed: The reply of the Minister of Education of the RSFSR.

1957

* *Source*: This document was brought to the West by an emigrant from the Soviet Union.

Document 111* *Sovetish heymland*: announcement of projected publication (1957)

A London *Jewish Chronicle* correspondent reported to his paper in July that he had been told by Moscow Chief Rabbi Y. L. Levin[159] that plans are in the works for publication of a Yiddish newspaper in the Soviet Union. He reported from Moscow that conferences are now being held by Soviet Jews to discuss the project. The paper is being planned to appear weekly at first and later as a daily. Rabbi Levin also told the correspondent that 10,000 copies of a *sidur* (Hebrew prayer-book) have been published in the Soviet Union and that Leningrad Jews were planning to bring out their own *sidur*.

Document 112† Announcement of Yiddish performance (1955)

Moscow State Variety Theatre

An Evening of Yiddish Songs

SAUL LYUBIMOV

Taking part in the concert:

O. Kofman   Z. Privalskaya
(violin)   (piano accompaniment)

Concert begins at 8.00 p.m.

Document 113‡ Amateur Yiddish theatre in Vilnius (1960)

What could be more cheerful and interesting than *Freylekhs* – this colourful, characteristic entertainment based on the motifs of Jewish folklore? Here, before an enchanted audience, pure love between a boy and a girl is born on stage, here it blossoms and here it is burned out by the hot wind of momentary sorrow and bitterness so inevitable in such cases. And just when it seems as if the love is coming to an end, and the audience is becoming gripped with sadness looking at the young couple, then everything on stage stops – the wedding begins! A Jewish wedding, with its customs, songs both sad and joyful, dances, unbounded joy and the traditional *batkhn*.

Batkhn – these are comedians full of folksy humour without whom such a wedding is unthinkable. One must say that this role on the stage is much more complicated than in a real wedding. *Batkhn* – there were two of them – a furrier of the 'Raudonje žvaigžde' [Red Star] Judel Kac and the tailor Mendel Kanowicz. They gave an excellent entertainment from beginning to end.

The rest of the performers in this show were not professional actors but amateurs – members of the Jewish Amateur Arts Company at the House of Culture of the Republic's Central Council of Trade Unions in Vilnius.

* *Source*: 'Report [that] Yiddish Paper to be Issued in USSR', *Jewish Life*, September 1957, p. 29.
† *Source*: *Naye prese*, 17 August 1955.
‡ *Source*: A. Prokopowicz, 'Motywy folkloru żydowskiego na scenie' (Motifs of Jewish Folklore on the Stage), *Czerwony sztandar* (Vilnius), 14 January 1960.

It is a relatively young company brought into being only two years ago. The local conductor, Szoul Blecharowicz, an elderly but energetic person and a fiery enthusiast and propagator of choir singing, helped to organise it. Around him clustered the nucleus of the future choir which is now directed by his daughter Aliza, a graduate of the choir directors' faculty of the Vilnius Conservatory. As regards the followers of dramatic art, they were led by the amateur producer Dogem. Under his leadership the members of the dramatic circle produced *200,000* by Shalom Aleikhem and *Grine Felder* [Green Fields] by [P.] Hirshbeyn.[160]

But real progress in the company's development only started when A. Lurie took over the job of producer.

About fifty people take part in *Freylekhs*. The overwhelming majority of them are workers and artisans in Vilnius enterprises: locksmiths, carpenters, spinners, glaziers, metal-workers, paper-hangers, furriers, etc., and only 10% are employees of the institution. These people are whole-heartedly devoted to art, for what else could compel them to come to the club in the evenings after working hours to rehearse for hours one fragment or another of the show. They did it three or four times a week and, before the first night, every day until late into the night.

Apart from the above-mentioned performers of the *batkhn* roles, one has to mention the photographer, Sara Strymling, and the housekeeper, Anna Pakialczyk, who distinguish themselves in their roles as two lovers, and also the painter, P. Klejn, in his role of Nikolai's soldier.

Freylekhs was performed by the company not only in Vilnius but also in Kaunas, where they were no less sincerely applauded.

The tickets for the performance were, as a rule, sold out two or three days in advance. Altogether, more than ten thousand people saw the show. It became one of the main items in the repertoire of the company.

The success of *Freylekhs* not only encouraged the members of the company but also attracted new talent. It gave the company the opportunity to prepare, for the centenary of the birth of the great Yiddish writer Shalom Aleikhem, two productions at the same time: Rubinshtein's staging of *Tevye the Milkman*, based on the work by the immortal author, and his one-act play *Mentshn* [People].

When, during the first performance of *Tevye the Milkman*, Menahem Mendel appeared on the stage – a character introduced by Rubinshtein and now already a classic – a deathly hush descended on the auditorium and this silence at first disturbed Moshe Szarfszteyn, a tailor who took upon himself the difficult task of performing this subtle role. 'Was my interpretation so unreal that the spectators remained entirely indifferent?' the worried young actor asked himself. And then the first applause broke out in the audience. Szarfszteyn was delighted. The applause was heard in quite insignificant episodes, and this indicated that his Menahem had been accepted.

The opinion of the audience and of the members of the cast was unanimous in appreciation of the performance of Rebeka Dawidson, a student at the philology faculty of the University of Vilnius, who appeared in the role of the daughter Hava. A housekeeper, Sara Beker, performed the role of Golda, wife of Tevye.

The play *Tevye the Milkman* was produced by the director A. Lurie, and the one-act play *Mentshn* was produced by his assistant, Jakub Epsztejn. This engineer, with a high position in the Republic's Ministry of Agriculture, is not only an ardent admirer of Melpomena but also her devoted servant. His production of *Mentshn* is the work of a mature master.

In this connection we shall again mention the name of Szarfszteyn, though this time it belongs to a representative of the fair sex. It has a lot in common with the performer who is already known to us. Firstly, the twenty-year-old Zina Szarfszteyn is his wife, and secondly she is a member of the company and her talent was particularly outstanding in this modest show.

And the choir? Its members take part in most of the above-mentioned plays. Who could otherwise be able to perform the solo numbers or duets of which, for example, *Freylekhs* is full? Apart from this the choir takes part in the concert programme and is always warmly applauded when it sings the humorous songs, 'Wen ikh wolt gewen der bore-olam' [If I were the Creator] or the lyrical song 'Wos dreystu sikh arum mayn fenster' [Why do you walk by my window].

In the rich repertoire of the choir there are, apart from the Jewish musical and choral items, songs of fraternal nations: Russians, Lithuanians, Poles, Belorussians, Ukrainians.

The growing Jewish amateur company is full of creative vigour. It is now preparing three plays at the same time. One of them, *Boytro the Bandit* by Moshe Kulbak,[161] tells about the social injustice within the Jewish community during Tsar Nikolai's times. The role of Boytro, a kind of Jewish Dubrowski, the people's avenger, will be performed by Marek Mozes, a structural engineer at the Vilnius factory 'Elfa'. Other dramatic pieces being prepared by the members of the company are the one-act play *Agents* by Shalom Aleikhem and the musical vaudeville *Hershl Ostropoler*, with its rich Jewish folklore.

Document 114* A Yiddish song recital in Moscow (1964)

The concerts of the popular Jewish singer Nehamah Lifshits were held in Moscow, in the Tchaikovsky Hall. The singer rendered old popular Yiddish songs and romances to the words of Soviet Yiddish poets.

Nehamah Lifshits does not just sing; she creates original dramatic and lyrical miniatures. The singer makes good use of facial expression and gestures, but her splendour lies chiefly in her wonderful voice.

The modern Yiddish song was created in our times, songs originating in folklore. The singer successfully propagates it on the concert stage. The melodies heard in the hall are deeply national, but they move everybody. All the songs rendered by Nehamah Lifshits are full of life-affirming optimism, lofty civic feeling, Soviet patriotism.

With great skill the singer rendered 'The Jewish Lullaby', the lyrical folk-song 'Katerina-moloditsa', the comic song 'Mamma, Don't Beat Me, It's Too Late'.

* *Source*: Val. Goltsev, 'Kontsert evreiskoi pesni' (Concert of Yiddish Songs), *Izvestiya*, 29 February 1964.

The song 'Fire!' sounded as a curse on Fascism. It was written in the Cracow ghetto by the carpenter Mordekhai Gebirtig[162] in July 1942. Later the author was executed by the Hitlerites. This song is a passionate hymn to man, the dauntless fighter.

Laureate of a variety artist competition, Nehamah Lifshits has given hundreds of concerts during recent years. Her appearances always attract a large and grateful audience. It is noteworthy that most listeners are not at all discouraged by not knowing the language in which she sings. Art knows no language barriers.

The performances of Nehamah Lifshits are outstanding and delightful stage events.

8

The Jewish religion in the Soviet Union

Marx's antipathy towards religion in general and towards the Jewish religion in particular was shared by Lenin and the entire Bolshevik leadership. They all viewed religion as the primary and most harmful form of alienation, the opium of the people. Nonetheless, in this as in many other areas, the Bolsheviks were compelled to take the multi-national and multi-religious reality of Russia into account after their 1917 victory. The pragmatic Soviet solution to this conundrum was the constitutional separation of religion from the state and of the schools from religion. It was established – at least in constitutional theory – that religion was the citizen's private affair and that all religions were equal before the law.

The Stalin period

The first and most important law in this sphere, that of 20 January 1918,[1] enumerated in detail the rights and obligations of the religions in the state. Its major articles proclaimed the nationalisation of church property; forbade religious congregations from maintaining educational, health and welfare institutions; prohibited religious instruction in the public schools or the establishment of any form of religious school. Finally, it declared that no religious association could enjoy the rights of a legal entity.

The second law regulating the relations between religion and state – one still in effect – was passed on 8 April 1929 in the RSFSR and later in all the other republics of the Soviet Union. Far more stringent than its predecessor, this law severely restricted the already limited legal rights of religious institutions; its clear aim was to compel religious associations to engage exclusively in prayer and personal worship. It empowered the state to dissolve a religious association and to close its house of worship.

Although formal responsibility for the execution of laws related to religion was lodged in the special departments established for this purpose in the Ministry of Justice, the Ministry of the Interior and the Council of Ministers as well as in the given local authority, it was actually the Commissariats for Nationality Affairs (until 1923) and the Nationalities Sections in the Communist Party (until 1930) which played the decisive role in everything relating to the religions of national minorities. Thus, the Jewish Commissariats and Sections in all cities and towns with large and cohesive Jewish populations became the driving force in the all-out war against the Jewish religion.

In all probability, even the Draconian measures employed in the various campaigns against the Jewish religion would not in themselves have sufficed to ensure the virtual liquidation of religious institutions in the Soviet Union. But this process was intensified by powerful economic and social factors, and above all by the far-reaching structural changes that occurred within the Soviet Jewish community at the end of the twenties when large segments of the population flowed from villages and small towns towards the large cities.

Following the brief period from 1933 to 1937, when Stalin decided on a relative relaxation in the anti-religious struggle, he reinstituted the campaign in 1938 with measures that far surpassed those employed previously. Even Rabbi Medalia, one of the senior rabbis in the Soviet Union, was accused along with several other rabbis of the gravest of crimes. The press *communiqué* issued stated that, hiding behind the mask of religion, the accused had acted on behalf of the Fascist secret services. The main charge was that they dispatched agents to disrupt socialist construction in Birobidzhan.[2] They were also accused of running underground religious schools and of illegally baking and selling *mazot*.

However, the outbreak of the Soviet–German war in June 1941 led to an almost immediate change in the official attitude towards the religions. This was due in part to the patriotic stance adopted from the first by the churches and in part to the need to unite all available forces against Germany. Also of major import here was the Soviet desire for Western support. Among the steps taken to ameliorate the situation of the Jewish religion was the appointment of Rabbi Shlifer and other rabbis in Moscow, which had been without a rabbi since the imprisonment of Rabbi Medalia. Rabbis were also appointed in other cities in which religious congregations were re-established and had their synagogues returned to them. Rabbi Shlifer, now made a member of the Jewish Anti-Fascist Committee as representative of the Jewish religious institutions, issued synagogue appeals to world Jewry[3] and, together with the well-known Rabbi Chobrutsky, issued press releases. These changes, together with the profound shock which the war had generated among the Jews of the Soviet Union, caused many Jews – among them young people and soldiers in uniform – to stream to the synagogues. But the changes did not extend to granting the requests of the Jewish communal council in Moscow for representation on the 'Council for the Affairs of Religious Cults' (established in the summer of 1944). The reason given was that the Jewish synagogues, unlike the churches and mosques, were not organised on a hierarchical basis and lacked a central body.

The positive attitude towards religion persisted in the immediate post-war years, although even then the Jewish religion was granted narrower privileges than the other major (and recognised) religions. But synagogue attendance was reduced with the intensification of the Cold War, the increasing severance of the Soviet Jewish population from world Jewry and Israel,[4] and the anti-Semitic campaign (masked as a war against nationalism and cosmopolitanism). And those who did attend were reluctant to express themselves freely there and feared any contact with Israeli Embassy personnel or with the few tourists who managed to enter the Soviet Union in this period. Renewed arrests among the rabbis and their families strengthened the atmosphere of terror and resulted in widespread paralysis of Jewish religious activity. The sole public role permitted to rabbis such as Rabbi Shlifer of Moscow and Rabbi Shekhtman of Kiev was that connected with the political Clergymen for Peace (Doc. 115). The rabbis were also used by the authorities to defend anti-Jewish Soviet policies, most notably when Rabbi Shlifer was forced to claim, following publication of the charges against the Jewish doctors in January 1953,[5] that the doctors were not being accused because of their Jewishness but because of their criminal acts.

At this point it is appropriate to ask why, despite the extremely shrill and merciless anti-Jewish policy of 1948–53, there was no propaganda campaign against the Jewish religion itself during this period. How is one to account for the fact that, as far as is known, not one book or article attacking the Jewish religion was published at a time when numerous articles condemning the Jewish cosmopolitans and nationalists were being aired daily? Why, from this point of view, does this period differ so greatly from other periods in Soviet history[6] when the Jewish and other religions constituted an important if not central target?

A combination of factors was probably involved here. First, the Soviet leadership decided to continue its liberal line on the various religions in the Soviet Union and chose not to exclude the Jewish religion from this general rule. (The one major exception, indeed, proved to be the Catholic religion, which came under heavier attack than any other religion in the USSR; but this decision derived from foreign policy considerations.)

Secondly, with the liquidation during 1948–9 of all the Jewish institutions in the Soviet Union, the Jewish religious congregations remained the one surviving form of Jewish institution; to have liquidated even those would have aggravated the authorities' embarrassing position *vis-à-vis* the outside world.[7] Besides, there were already so few synagogues functioning in the Soviet Union (about one hundred in the entire country), so few rabbis and so few worshippers that a vociferous anti-religious campaign probably appeared to the authorities as superfluous.

The fourth reason was that the remaining rabbis could be used for purposes of propaganda, especially within the various peace organisations established in the Soviet Union from 1949 onwards. And finally, it is very possible – and we have confirmation of this from later periods – that the existence of official synagogues, open to everyone, with rabbis, *gabaim* (synagogue officials) and *shamashim* (beadles), all of whom had to report to the ruling power on synagogue activity, was – from the official point of view – preferable to worship in private homes, where the possibilities for police supervision were obviously more limited.

The post-Stalin period

The first act symbolising the political thaw that followed Stalin's death may perhaps be seen in the dispatch of Rabbi Shlifer's personal greetings for the Jewish New Year to English Jewry in 1953.[8]

However, the attitude of the immediate post-Stalin leadership and of the Khrushchev regime towards religion in general and the Jewish religion in particular was complex and underwent many changes between 1954 and 1964. Various gestures, some of real significance, were made to demonstrate that church and synagogue enjoyed religious freedom in the USSR. These concessions were characteristic of the years of the post-Stalin power struggle, 1954–7. But, as opposed to the policy of relative liberalisation in many other spheres, the policies of the regime in this area aimed preponderantly (although not consistently) to counterbalance the concessions that had been granted to the religious institutions during and after the war. As a result, there was a major revival of anti-religious propaganda, with the establishment of special periodicals devoted to this theme, again in something of a return to the policies of the twenties and thirties.

At the same time, however (taking this anti-religious animus as a given), it is clear that in few if any other spheres of policy was there so sharp a break between the post-Stalin interregnum and the years of Khrushchev's personal domination.

The years 1954–8

The Central Committee's resolutions of 7 July 1954, which were made public only seven years later,[9] were to have marked the opening of an anti-religious propaganda campaign and, indeed, the press and other media immediately began to work towards that end.[10] But shortly thereafter, on 10 November 1954,[11] Khrushchev signed another Central Committee resolution criticising the press and the lecturers on religion for having gone too far in their attacks on clergymen. While this later resolution did not put an end to the anti-religious propaganda, it now became far less intensive in general (a change which was of benefit to the Jewish religion, too). Moreover, the marked relaxation of political control in the Soviet Union at this time – the end of mass terror – made it possible, for example, for the chairman of the Jewish community of Leningrad to lodge a complaint against illegal police operations in the synagogues (Doc. 121), an action inconceivable during the Stalin period.

In many ways this period may be categorised as one of the most liberal from the standpoint of the Jewish religion and its observance in Soviet history. In the first place, contacts with world Jewry began to be renewed in 1954, when Rabbi Shlifer invited the Chief Rabbi of Israel, Herzog, to visit the Soviet Union,[12] and also sent a letter of greetings to the rabbinical conference in Israel.[13] In 1956, for the first time in many years, a delegation of American rabbis visited the Soviet Union. Accompanied by Rabbi Shlifer, they visited Moscow, Leningrad, Kiev and Odessa, as well as places in Georgia, where they were enthusiastically received by thousands of worshippers. The delegation also had a meeting with Khrushchev, at which they discussed the situation of the Jewish religion in the Soviet Union.[14]

That year, Rabbi Shlifer also wrote a letter (in Hebrew) to Nahum Goldmann, President of the World Jewish Congress, which dealt with the need to establish relations between the Jews of the Soviet Union and the world Jewish community[15] even though, apparently under pressure of the authorities, Rabbi Shlifer was subsequently compelled to announce that there had been 'a misunderstanding' here.[16] In the same year, rabbis of *Agudat yisrael* and *Ha-poel ha-mizrahi* received invitations to visit the Soviet Union.[17] But the crowning point of 1956 was unquestionably Rabbi Shlifer's trip to Paris in November to attend the unveiling of a memorial to the six million Holocaust victims.[18] The Rabbi's appearance abroad in a delegation which also included General David Dragunsky, and his speech in Hebrew on the need for world peace, made a great impression on the West. This event recalled the visit to the United States and other countries in 1943 of Mikhoels and Fefer, members of the Jewish Anti-Fascist Committee.

The single most important concession made to the Jewish religion in this period was the establishment, on 6 January 1957, of the *Kol Yaakov Yeshivah* (Voice of Jacob Seminary) at the Great Synagogue in Moscow.[19] This was the first time that a Soviet government had permitted an institution of this kind to open. It started with ten pupils and grew to fifteen in 1958–9 (six from Georgia, five from Moscow, two from Tashkent and one each from Minsk and Dnepropetrovsk).[20] The age of the students ranged from twenty to fifty-four. Studies in the *Yeshivah* lasted for eight hours a day, and there were about another four hours devoted to prayer. To be accepted to the *Yeshivah* candidates had to apply to its secretary and show sufficient knowledge in Talmud, Torah (Pentateuch), Neviim (Prophets) and Shulkhan arukh (Code of Laws). Of course, the authorities, who controlled the granting of residence permits for pupils coming from outside Moscow, had the final say on who would be accepted.

During these years, the *Yeshivah* had eight teachers, of whom three were rabbis (Shimon Trebnik,[21] Haim Kats and Yaakov Kalmenson). Its study programme generally lasted from four to six years. The budget for the maintenance of the *Yeshivah* came exclusively from contributions made by the Jews of the Soviet Union.

Another important event was the publication in 1956 of Rabbi Shlifer's *Sidur ha-shalom* (Prayer Book of Peace), which was comprised of pages photocopied from old prayer-books, with a number of revisions and a 'prayer for peace' added. The *sidur* was printed in 3,000 copies.[22] In the same year, the religious community in Moscow began to publish a Hebrew calendar. Moreover, the figures, although admittedly contradictory as will be discussed further below, clearly indicate that there was a significant increase in the number of synagogues permitted to function in the USSR in the mid-1950s.

An interesting development of this period was the fact that, until his death on 31 March 1957, Rabbi Shlifer served as the unofficial Chief Rabbi of Soviet Jewry. This role found expression not only in matters of faith and ritual, but also in his involvement in the election of rabbis and *gabaim* in cities outside Moscow and in his intervention as arbitrator when disputes arose among members of the 'committees of twenty' or among synagogue directors. (The authorities often sought to ferment such disputes within synagogue administrations even though they did everything to staff them with 'loyal' persons; see Doc. 124.) Of course, Rabbi Shlifer acted with the consent of the regime and in many instances at their explicit command. His successor, Rabbi Levin, played a similar part, if somewhat less actively.

It should also be noted here that, as in the Stalin period, rabbis were required to sign declarations which they did not always agree with (Docs. 116–19). One such appeal, that of March 1955, was even directed to world Jewry, a body whose existence was vehemently denied in the Soviet Union. As regards the signatories to the declaration against the 'English–French–Israeli aggression', it is important to note that they were rabbis and *gabaim* of the Georgian and Bukharan communities: that is, the Jews who resided closest to the Muslim and Eastern peoples of the Soviet Union. And it is no coincidence that the authorities were interested in having this fiercely anti-Israel declaration signed precisely by representatives of the Oriental (non-Ashkenazi) section of Soviet Jewry.

Within the over-all context of the anti-religious revival, as we have said, the partially positive attitude of the government towards the needs of the Jewish religion remained a relatively minor theme. By 1958 there were clear signs that even the degree of balance characteristic of the years 1954–7 would not be long maintained.

Whether because of real fears that the various churches might be able to exploit the thaw and de-Stalinisation in order to win greater popular support, or whether because of Khrushchev's desire to return to a 'Leninist policy' in this sphere as well, May 1957 saw a decision to re-initiate the struggle against religion. The first and most prominent expression of this new policy was the Seminar for Propagandists against Religion held between 20 and 30 May.[23] At this conference the Jewish religion was fiercely criticised by Mitin, a Jewish member of the Academy of Sciences, who had 'specialised' in virulent attacks on Zionism and Judaism in the Stalin period (Doc. 127), and by M. Shakhnovich, Deputy Director of the Museum of Religion and Atheism in Leningrad. Anti-religious activity in general, and that directed against the Jewish religion in particular, was intensified in 1958, when eleven books devoted to propaganda against the Jewish religion were published.[24] This number was all the more remarkable since no books in this category had appeared at all for many years. The years that followed were to see even more drastic changes in this sphere.

The years 1959–64

In glaring contrast to the previous period, every sphere touching directly or indirectly on religious observance came in for extraordinarily harsh treatment during these years. The authorities launched a fierce and widely publicised propaganda campaign; closed synagogues and put their directors on trial; expropriated Jewish cemeteries; and incessantly placed obstacles in the way of *mazot*-baking and the performing of circumcisions. The period was thus one of the most difficult ever experienced by the Jewish religion under Soviet rule.

The campaign against the Jewish religion. The resolution adopted by the Central Committee of the Communist Party in November 1958 calling for a concentrated campaign against religion in the Soviet Union unleashed a wave of attacks in the press and all the other media, which accused the clergy in general of violating Soviet law in religious affairs; of exerting harmful social influence; and, in certain cases, of conducting subversive activity against the state.[25] The sharpest, most vitriolic shots were directed against the Jewish religion. The number of articles attacking it reached a peak in 1961–2 and again in 1964: there were forty in 1960, seventy-three in 1961, seventy-two in 1962, fifty-seven in 1963 and seventy-two in 1964.[26] We have no data on radio and television broadcasts devoted to the Jewish religion, but to judge by those recorded in the West, their harshness exceeded even the press articles.[27] During this period special seminars were organised for propagandists engaged in the anti-religious campaign. But what lent an especially sharp edge to the attacks on Judaism was that they almost invariably linked it to Jewish bourgeois nationalism (for example, Doc. 130).[28] And in the Soviet reality such a link could not bode well for rabbis and Jewish believers. Seminars were now organised for propagandists dealing exclusively with the Jewish religion.[29] And, finally, it should be noted that periodicals and year-books devoted entirely to anti-religious propaganda gave the Jewish religion a disproportionately large amount of space.[30]

This period saw the publication of fifty-four books against the Jewish religion in Russian alone, with editions reaching 100,000 copies, high even for the Soviet Union where many books appear in large editions. The authors who were particularly active in the production of this type of literature were Livshits, Belenky and Shakhnovich (all of whom are Jews), and the non-Jews Kychko and Mayatsky. Kychko's book *Judaism Without Embellishment* (Doc. 133), which received worldwide publicity and caused sharp reaction everywhere, did not differ in format, content or vulgar denunciation from many other books of the same kind that appeared in this period. What seems to have been the last straw, even causing agitation in Western Communist parties, were the book's many illustrations, all of them in the style of the notorious Nazi newspaper *Der Stürmer*, and the fact that it was published by no less a body than the Ukrainian Academy of Sciences. The storm of protest it aroused in the West compelled the Soviet Communist Party leadership to come out with criticism of the work. But, as Document 134 shows, this criticism was no more than lukewarm, referring only to some 'incorrect facts' and other errors, which had permitted certain places in the book to be interpreted as anti-Semitic in spirit.

The topics which constantly recur in Kychko's book and other literature dealing with this subject – sometimes in the crudest and most virulent form, sometimes rather more subtly – are divisible into three groups: (1) on the essence of Judaism; (2) on the Jewish religion as a hostile force within the Soviet Union; and (3) on the believers as agents of world imperialism and reaction.

1. The reactionary nature of Judaism, it was claimed, finds expression in its endorsement of profiteering, that is, in a fundamentally negative attitude towards work. It also encourages permanent inequality for women. It teaches not only social injustice but actual immorality, for it prohibits only those crimes committed against other Jews, while drunkenness and dissipation are in the nature of a moral imperative. The Jewish religion is based on the theory of the chosen people, a notion which resembles the Nazi master-race theory and involves hatred of other peoples and religions. Finally, it is hostile to science and progress; it reinforces superstition and lays

down extremely savage 'precepts' that endanger health (circumcision, ritual ablution, etc.).

2. The Jewish religion (so these attacks went) is the sworn enemy of the October Revolution, and its rabbis excommunicated the young Soviet State at their conference of 1918 in Odessa. It rejects Soviet patriotism and imbues the Jews of the Soviet Union with the spirit of nationalism. Graver still, the synagogues have become clandestine meeting places for subversive organisations and also hotbeds of speculation.

3. Already in the nineteenth and early twentieth centuries, the rabbis of Russia had come out against the principles of Marxism. They – the Rabbis Katznelson and Yampolsky, for example – had served as intelligence agents in the Tsarist secret police. In 1930, the rabbis of the world had joined the Vatican crusade against the Soviet Union. The synagogues in the United States and in many other countries serve the ruling classes, while in the Soviet Union itself they have become centres for the distribution of Zionist literature hostile to the Soviet Union.

The closure of synagogues. To determine the number of synagogues that were closed down in the Soviet Union during this period, we must first clarify how a synagogue is defined, how it can be established and closed down by Soviet law, and how many there were in former periods.

According to Soviet law, any citizen who has reached the age of eighteen may unite with other believers to arrange for joint worship. The religious associations established are in accordance with the number of believers, and may be of two kinds: a religious society or a religious group. If the number of believers is twenty or more, a society is formed; if less, a group. The believers who have combined in a religious union submit a request to the executive committee of the regional or city soviet for a permit to open a house of worship. But these bodies are not authorised to take a binding decision on the matter; they only add an opinion and pass on the request to a higher level executive committee until, in an autonomous republic, it reaches the Council of Ministers, while in the Union republics it is forwarded directly to the Council of Ministers of the given republic. These bodies then contact the Council for the Affairs of Religious Cults attached to the government of the Soviet Union, which takes the final decision on whether to register the applicants as a society or a group.[31] Thus even in this primary stage the believers encounter multiple administrative difficulties before they can acquire a permit to open a house of worship. The next major obstacle is the necessity of finding a vacant building or site suited to this purpose.

Jewish houses of worship in the Soviet Union are of three different kinds: permanent synagogues built especially for this purpose; small places of worship, generally located in private homes; and temporary prayer groups (*minyanim*) in private homes which function with the tacit consent of the authorities although under the potential threat of heavy penalties. Statements, which occasionally appear in Soviet sources, on the number of synagogues no doubt take only the first two types into account; even so, they often contradict each other. The Soviet Union has never published any official list of the synagogues and their locations.

In 1926, there were still 1,103 synagogues in the Soviet Union;[32] by 1954 apparently only 100 remained.[33] If this latter figure, given by Rabbi Shlifer, is accurate, there was then a definite increase in the number of synagogues between 1954 and 1959. According to a Soviet report submitted to the UN, there were as many as 450 synagogues in 1959,[34] but another Soviet statement of 1960 put their number at only 150.[35] This last figure appears more realistic and will serve as a basis for a comparison with the data for the years 1961–5. In January 1964, Radio Moscow announced that 150 synagogues were functioning in the Soviet Union, half of them in the Ukraine and Moldavia. But in that same year, P. Dogorozhny, Deputy Chairman of the Soviet Council for the Affairs of Religious Cults, stated that 100 synagogues were open in the Soviet Union.[36] The data we have for the years 1963–5 are of ninety-six[37] and ninety-seven[38] synagogues. However, according to various estimates, the number of synagogues left in the Soviet Union by the late 1960s was between sixty-two and seventy, about thirty of which were in the Caucasus and Central Asia.[39] Even if we take into account only the official data, more than fifty synagogues were closed between 1959 and 1965, principally in the Ukraine and the RSFSR (in Lvov, Zhitomir, Chernovtsy, Zhmerinka, Belaya-Tserkov, Sverdlovsk, Kazan, Pyatigorsk, Grozny and other cities). But the Soviet authorities often denied that they were conducting a plan to reduce the number of synagogues.

According to Soviet law, a synagogue (like a church, a mosque, etc.) may be closed down under the following conditions:[40] if there are not enough believers desirous of maintaining their own house of worship, that is, if the religious association dissolves; if the association has violated Soviet law on religious observance; if it has failed to observe the conditions of the contract signed between it and the state body; if it has refused to fulfil the legal directives of the state bodies; if the house of worship is too old or stands in the way of the construction plans of the city or village where it is located; if it proves necessary to expropriate the house of worship in order to use the building for alternative public purposes. It is thus clear that when the authorities decided to close down a house of worship they had no particular difficulty in finding a suitable article in the law.

The way in which they prepared the ground for the closure strongly recalled the style used in the twenties. First, the local press conducted an extensive campaign against the (allegedly) criminal and illegal activities of the synagogue leaders, who were accused of exploiting the synagogue to conduct shady business deals or of engaging in Zionist propaganda. Then, the press began to publish articles and letters 'from all sectors of the public' – including believers and former synagogue leaders – who categorically demanded that the 'nests of corruption' be liquidated and their community purged of the 'abomination of religion' (see Doc. 132). In the end, the authorities 'responded' to these pleas and closed the house of worship. Moreover, during the campaign against the synagogue, the police would often make arrests among members of the 'committee of twenty' and the synagogue staff, accusing them of grossly misusing their positions; of conducting shady business deals; or of having contacts with representatives of capitalist states (tourists or Israeli Embassy personnel; Doc. 132).

Less extreme methods of intimidating the religious leaders included frequent changes in the synagogue administration (the president and vice-president of the Jewish community, the *gabaim* and other office-holders); the recruitment of informers; and the forced entry by the police into the private homes where *minyanim* were held. While the *Kol Yaakov Yeshivah* itself was not closed, the number of its pupils declined rapidly over these years, so that by 1963 only four remained.[41] This reduction was caused by the refusal of the authorities to issue residence permits to pupils from outside Moscow.

The observance of religious precepts. The particularly difficult situation of the Jewish religion in the Khrushchev years was further exacerbated by the fact that the Soviet authorities placed major obstacles in the path of Jews seeking to observe basic religious precepts.

Sabbaths and festivals have always played a primary role in the observance of the Jewish religion, and they are of especially great importance to the Jews of the Soviet Union.

According to various testimonies, the number of synagogue worshippers on Sabbath eves and Sabbaths was quite small. Those who attended regularly were for the most part older people, joined by only a small number of young persons either from religious families or who had come to religion on their own. While we have no data on their exact number, it is clear that, relatively, there were a great many more worshippers from the non-Ashkenazi population[42] than from the Ashkenazi community. Differences also existed between the various regions of the western border republics and between the large cities in the Russian, Ukrainian and Belorussian republics.[43] It was not unusual for Jews to hold private *minyanim* in their homes, with the authorities generally turning a blind eye.

The Jewish holy days which began to attract thousands of worshippers to synagogues from the end of the fifties are principally the Day of Atonement, the New Year and the Rejoicing of the Law *(Simḥat Torah)*.[44] Most of those who came to the synagogues did so as the result not so much of religious as of national motivations, which could find no other legal outlet. The Soviet authorities used various means to discourage these mass assemblies, but they proved ineffective.

A particularly fierce struggle was conducted against Passover observance. Here, the principal issue was the right to bake *maẓot*. A partial ban on *maẓot*-baking had already been in force in the 1950s (for example, in Kiev, Odessa, Kharkov, Rostov, Kishinev and Riga), but in 1961, the ban was extended to virtually the entire country.[45] In 1962, a total ban was declared,[46] so that many Jews were compelled to bake *maẓot* clandestinely. In many cities, when the organisers were discovered, they were charged with illegally selling *maẓot* and heavy punishments were imposed. Shipments of *maẓot* from Israel, the United States and England were also subjected to frequent interference, and their recipients were compelled to return them as well as to protest to the press against these 'acts of provocation'.[47] But by 1964, apparently as a result of world protests, the authorities decided to permit religious congregations in Moscow, Leningrad and Tbilisi to bake *maẓot*.[48] According to the estimate of a Soviet Jew close to Jewish religious affairs in the USSR, in a normal year about 80 tons of *maẓot* were baked in Moscow alone, enough for 25 to 30 thousand persons.[49]

Soviet Jews also encountered great difficulties in obtaining *lulavim* and *etrogim* for *Sukot*. However, the festivals of *Ḥanukah* and *Purim* were hardly interfered with as they did not arouse great interest on the part of the Jews and were not widely celebrated in the Soviet Union in this period.

Prayers of mourning in memory of the Holocaust victims were introduced in synagogues in various Soviet cities, but no special date was yet fixed for such remembrance, nor did the ceremonies follow a strictly uniform pattern. It did, however, become a widespread custom to light six candles in memory of the six million Holocaust victims and to recite *Yizkor* and *Kadish* (prayers for the dead). Sometimes verses from Psalms were read, and also poetry by such writers as Bialik and Yitskhak Katznelson.[50]

In Riga, for example, the ceremony in memory of Holocaust victims was held on the Fast-Day of Gedaliyahu. Thousands of Jews customarily visited the cemetery on that day, and a memorial service was held in the synagogue in which the *gabaim* spoke on issues pertaining to the Holocaust, and the cantor, accompanied by a choir, chanted the requiem prayer *El male raḥamim* (God, full of Compassion). Similar memorial services were also held on 10 and 18 Kislev, the dates (according to the Jewish calendar) on which extermination operations commenced in the Riga ghetto in 1941.[51]

In Kiev, on the evening following *Kol Nidrei* and on the morning of the Day of Atonement before the Torah was taken out, it was the custom of the entire congregation to recite *Kadish* in memory of the victims of Babi Yar. From the early sixties, a memorial service was also held annually at Babi Yar itself.[52]

Throughout the entire period under discussion, the observing of religious rites and ceremonies such as ritual slaughter, ritual ablution, religious marriage and *Bar-mizvah* faced enormous obstacles. The authorities greatly hampered the few *shoḥtim* (ritual slaughterers) still to be found in a number of Soviet cities, and the local and central press occasionally published vitriolic articles attacking them. It is impossible to determine the number of Jews observing *kashrut* (the Jewish dietary laws), although its number was apparently small among the Ashkenazi Jews. (The situation was radically different among the non-Ashkenazi communities.) There were apparently very few *mikvot* (ritual baths) still functioning in the Soviet Union and these were to be found in the large cities (such as Moscow, Leningrad, Kiev and Riga), in those Caucasian cities where Georgian and Mountain Jews reside, and in Central Asian cities where the Bukharan Jews live. There also seem to have been few religious marriages or *Bar-mizvah* ceremonies.

Another serious problem was posed by the local authorities' almost systematic liquidation of Jewish cemeteries on the grounds that the sites were required for public needs. Among the burial grounds so expropriated was the Jewish Cemetery of Moscow, in 1963.[53] But the Jewish communities were usually allocated new plots of land in place of the expropriated cemeteries.[54] Gravestones were also frequently damaged or destroyed by all manner of hooligans,[55] and from the testimonies that have reached us it seems that the police did not act energetically to put an end to this.

But it was when they dealt with the rite of circumcision that the authorities reacted most harshly on both the propaganda and the police-administrative levels. Their assumption – often correct – was that the very act of circumcision was directed against the official assimilation policy; hence its great threat. The few *mohalim* (ritual circumcisers) still surviving in the Soviet Union performed their work in real danger of arrest.

Using the available sources – some official, others unofficial but reliable – we have portrayed in brief the difficult situation of the Jewish religion in the Soviet Union from 1959 to 1964. Now we must ask what caused the shift from the relatively liberal policy that preceded it to this extremely severe course of action.

First, the change clearly resulted in large part from the new policies which Khrushchev applied to all the religions in the state. He was no doubt motivated to a considerable extent by the realisation that what the official propaganda had been describing as 'the vestiges of religion' was actually a living, mass phenomenon that was probably increasing its influence even over some members of the Communist Party. And to 'eradicate this dangerous pestilence' Khrushchev was ready – even during a period when he was conducting a relatively liberal policy in many other areas – to apply an extreme line on the question of religion.

But this answer, although certainly correct, does not suffice. For it does not explain the essential difference between the overall religious policy – both propaganda and coercion – and its particular application to the Jewish religion. And there were specific reasons for this disparity.

In the second half of the fifties, the synagogue became the one legal assembly point for the Jews, including the youth, and a focal point for their rising national consciousness. It could thus be seen as a threat to basic Soviet policy, which sought the assimilation of Soviet Jewry. Again, the synagogue also became the sole permanent site where Jews could meet with their co-religionists, including, the Israeli Embassy personnel. The importance of these meetings for both sides was well understood by the authorities, who employed a wide variety of means to restrict and control them.[56] To the Soviet rulers, then, the synagogue represents an extremely dangerous phenomenon which keeps national consciousness alive, and intensifies loyalties to national or ideological foci beyond the borders of the Soviet Union.

The period of the 'collective leadership' (1965–7)

Even after Khrushchev was removed from power in October 1964, there was no decisive change in the basic Soviet policy towards the Jews which had found expression, *inter alia*, in campaigns against Judaism. But this is not to say that there was no amelioration in the official attitude towards the Jewish religion.

Whether in an effort to improve its image both within the Soviet Union itself and throughout the world, or in response to mainly external pressures, the new leadership restricted the propaganda campaign against the Jewish religion and cancelled some of the more Draconian anti-Jewish measures. The number of published articles dealing with Judaism, which had been seventy-two in 1964, dropped to thirty-seven in 1965 and to twenty-nine in 1966. But following the Six-Day War and the deterioration in Soviet–Israeli relations, the number of such articles rose sharply in 1967.[57]

A no less important change between the previous period and the years 1965–6 took place in the tone of those articles that were published: there were more 'scientific' articles and fewer *feuilletons*; the attacks on the Jewish religion became notably less vitriolic; and – most important – the personal attacks on religious figures ceased. Although there was no decline in the number of books attacking the Jewish religion, those published, like the articles, took a more 'scientific' approach and were much less venomous.[58]

This new, more lenient treatment of Judaism found expression in other areas as well. The authorities abolished the ban on the baking of *mazot*, which became more easily obtainable in many Soviet cities, even though supply still failed to meet demand.[59] It was also announced by Rabbi Levin that the Council for the Affairs of Religious Cults had authorised him to publish a new *sidur* in three volumes and in 10,000 copies. While no such *sidur* has actually appeared, the earlier (1956) *sidur* was reprinted in 3,000 copies.[60] The *yeshivah* in Moscow was promised twenty new pupils from throughout the Soviet Union, another pledge that was never fulfilled.[61] There was, however, no improvement at all either in the treatment of Jewish cemeteries or in the attitude to circumcision. And even the partial concessions granted in 1965 and 1966 began to be rescinded in 1967, when the harsh attacks again began. But now the authorities made efforts to distinguish between Zionism and the State of Israel, on the one hand, and the Jews of the Soviet Union loyal to 'their socialist homeland', on the other.

Our limited framework has not permitted a comparison between the situation of the Jewish religion and that of the other religions in the Soviet Union. Nonetheless, it is clear that, just as among equals there is always someone more equal, so, too, among the less equal there is someone even less equal. Despite the fundamentally negative attitude of the Soviet rulers towards every religious group in the USSR, they have permitted the Russian Orthodox Church – and, to a lesser degree, all other officially recognised religious communities – to exist and function within a restricted framework of laws and regulations. Apart from Christian sects such as the Uniates and Jehovah's Witnesses, which are totally prohibited and have been persecuted ruthlessly, it is the Jewish religion which has fallen prey to the most repressive acts of the Soviet leadership. The ruling power identifies Judaism with Jewish nationalism and Zionism, and, as such, holds it as fundamentally suspect.

Perhaps to an even greater degree than any other area of Soviet Jewish life, it is the future of the Jewish religion in the Soviet Union that appears to be without any hope. For without a new generation of rabbis and other religious leaders, it is impossible to imagine any amelioration in its situation or even, indeed, its survival at its current level. Nonetheless, so long as the synagogues remain open, they make an important contribution to the maintenance of a Jewish national identity, even though, paradoxically, the Jews are one of the most secularised national minorities in the Soviet Union.

Documents to Chapter 8

Soviet rabbis defend government line

Document 115* Soviet rabbi on peace: Chief Rabbi Shlifer's address at the Zagorsk Conference (May 1952)[62]

Peace unto ye, dear brethren, headed by the initiator and organiser of this conference, His Holiness Aleksis, Patriarch of Moscow and All Russia, and Metropolitan Nicholas, member of the World Peace Council.

On behalf of the Moscow Jewish Religious Community I extend cordial greetings to the delegates and guests of the Conference of all the Churches and Religious Associations of the USSR, devoted to the problem of defending peace in all the world.

Although in the Soviet Union the church is separated from the state and we ministers of religion do not engage in politics, when the 'books of life and death' are open and the enemies of peace threaten humanity with a new world war, we believers cannot remain passive and must exert maximum effort in this sacred fight for the defence of mankind from impending extermination.

For us Jewish believers the word *peace*, besides its general meaning of peace, understood as tranquillity and friendship among nations, has a profoundly religious symbolic significance, since *peace*, *Shalom*, is one of the names of our Lord God, the Ruler of the Universe, and we must fight for this sacred idea without sparing ourselves. [...]

We rabbis must bring up Jewish believers in the spirit of peace and friendship among nations and call upon all Jews who have not yet espoused the sacred cause of peace, to join the ranks of the world-wide army of peace champions.

Our religious community's participation in the fight for peace throughout the world has taken the following forms:

1. Our community took an active part in collecting signatures to the Stockholm Appeal;
2. It took an active part in collecting signatures to the World Peace Council's Appeal for a Five-Power Peace Pact;
3. It sent a delegate to the Third USSR Peace Conference;
4. It received fifteen delegates from different countries of Europe, Asia, the United States and Australia, conducted educational talks with them in the form of

* *Source*: 'Two Soviet Rabbis on Peace', *Jewish Life*, June 1953, pp. 28–9.

questions and answers, repudiating the slanderous insinuations against the Soviet Union spread in capitalist countries;

5. I personally, as the rabbi and head of my community, always dwell in my sermons on the problems of peace and defence of peace.

All the members of our community pray that peace may be granted unto the multi-million Soviet people and all peace-loving peoples.

It is a known fact that many of the major instigators of war, the atom-mongers, also pharisaically pray to God to send 'peace and well-being to humanity'.

At the same time they forge atomic bombs and use the germ weapon for the mass extermination of people in the Far East.

Bacteriological warfare is a heinous outrage, a monstrous crime against humanity!

Document 116* Soviet rabbis against nuclear war (1955)

We rabbis, leaders of the largest Jewish religious communities of the Soviet Union, welcome and fully support the Appeal of the Bureau of the World Council for Peace against preparations for nuclear war – and we call on the Jews of the world to add their voice to the voices of millions of people protesting against the menace of using atomic and hydrogen bombs.

The tragedy of the peoples who lost scores of millions of lives in the last war may be repeated on an even more terrible scale.

The possibility of a new war makes people the whole world over shudder.

Honest people everywhere are gripped with the heavy foreboding of the possibility of an atomic war, a war many times more destructive and cruel than the previous one, than all the wars in human history.

Hiroshima is child's play for the manufacturers of death. They crave more blood, more sufferings.

With what cold-blooded cruelty, with what terrifying cynicism is a handful of madmen – who have forgotten God and have become corrupted by their impunity – preparing the mass murder and the destruction of millions of human lives.

A fundamental feature of the Jewish religion is that it is life-asserting. [...]

SH.M. SHLIFER, Rabbi of Moscow; PANICH, Rabbi of Kiev;

I. DIMENT, Rabbi of Odessa; M. MASLYANSKY, Rabbi of Riga;

KH.D. ELIASHVILI, *Ḥakham* of Kutaisi; BERGER, Rabbi of Minsk;

I. RABINOVICH, Rabbi of Vilnius; VORKUL, Rabbi of Kaunas.[63]

Document 117† Bukharan Jews protest against the Sinai campaign (1956)[64]

In the name of all religious Bukharan Jews of Tashkent the Board of the Religious Community of Bukharan Jews expresses its great indignation at the actions of the government of Israel, whose armed forces have invaded the

* *Source*: 'Obrashchenie ravvinov krupneishikh evreiskikh religioznykh obshchin v Sovetskom Soyuze protiv podgotovki atomnoi voiny' (Appeal of Rabbis of the Largest Jewish Religious Communities in the Soviet Union against Nuclear War Preparations), *Izvestiya*, 18 March 1955.

† *Source*: 'Zayavlenie religioznoi obshchiny bukharskikh evreev gor. Tashkenta' (Statement of the Religious Community of Bukharan Jews of Tashkent), *Izvestiya*, 28 November 1956.

territory of Egypt and carried out an armed intervention at the instigation of the Anglo-French imperialists.

Such actions are incompatible with a religious morality that condemns aggression and unprovoked attacks on neighbouring states. They contradict the laws of the Holy Scriptures which speak of the obligation of preserving peace on earth. They contradict the principles of international law sanctioned by the Statutes of the United Nations Organisation.

Resolutely condemning the aggressive actions of the governments of England, France and Israel against Egypt, we stand firmly on the side of the just struggle of the Egyptian people in their defence of national independence.

We ask the USSR government to do everything possible to stop the fighting in Egypt and to secure the withdrawal of the armies of the interventionists.

Hands off Egypt!

> Chairmen of the Religious Community of the Bukharan
> Jews in the city of Tashkent,
> A. Yadgarov
> Rabbi M. Zargarov
> Member of the Board of the Religious Community,

Tashkent   A. Babkhanov

Document 118* Jewish religious leaders condemn the Sinai campaign (1956)

We religious Jews of the Soviet Union join our angry voice to that of all the honest peoples of the whole world protesting against the Anglo-French–Israeli aggression in Egypt, and demand the immediate withdrawal of the invading armies from the territory of Egypt.

We welcome the decision on the cessation of hostilities in Egypt, remembering that thousands of years ago on Mount Sinai the ever-new commandment, Thou shalt not kill, was proclaimed for the first time.

We remind our co-religionists in Israel that the humane essence of our religion directs us to solve disagreements between peoples in peaceful ways.

We insist that the instigators of the war against Egypt should start peace talks with the Arabs immediately and establish a just peace.

We sincerely believe that the collective conscience of mankind and common sense will triumph over the madness and chaos of war and that justice and peace will settle on the globe forever and for all peoples without distinction of religion or nationality.

Rabbis and heads of Jewish religious communities:

Shlifer, Olevsky (Moscow); Lubanov (Leningrad); Panich, Bardakh (Kiev); Diment (Odessa); Hurary, Makhnovetsky (Lvov); Kogan, Erusalimsky (Tashkent); Maslyansky, Goldberg (Riga); Frid (Minsk); Rubinshtein, Dozortsev (Baku); Vorkul (Kaunas); Kats (Tallin); Openshtein (Sverdlovsk); Aronovich (Rostov); Rozin (Dnepropetrovsk);

* *Source*: 'Zayavlenie evreiskikh religioznykh obshchin' (Statement of the Jewish Religious Communities), *Izvestiya*, 29 November 1956.

Shumyatsky, Plaks (Kursk); Landsman (Penza); Grinberg (Kishinev); Kheifin (Omsk) and others.[65]

Document 119* Georgian Jews condemn the Sinai campaign (1956)

We, religious Jews of Georgia, are indignant at the unprovoked attack of the English, French and Israeli aggressors against Egypt.

It is clear to all that the attack on Egypt, with the support of the imperialist countries, does not serve the aims of peace in the world. It destroys the well-being of peoples and implants mistrust among them. Our Jewish Scriptures stress that God declared it the sacred duty of every religious Jew to preserve peace always and everywhere, to fight for the love of mankind, just as all peace-loving peoples of the world have always striven and still strive for peace. The religious Jews of Georgia hold this covenant sacred.

The Jews of Georgia fervently support the efforts of the Soviet Government directed at eliminating the hotbed of war in the Middle East. We also firmly support the resolution of the United Nations Organisation for the immediate withdrawal of the aggressors' armies from the territory of Egypt. We sincerely believe that controversial issues can be solved only by peace talks. Therefore we are convinced that the peace-loving peoples, both of Israel and of the whole world, will do everything possible to avoid fresh bloodshed, which is the sacred aim of all religious Jews of Georgia.

> Chairman of the Tbilisi Community,
> E. Paltagashvili
> Rabbi E. Davidashvili
> Board Member,
> Sh. Tetraushvili

Document 120† A Tashkent rabbi on religious freedom in the USSR (1963)

Issue no. 12 for 1962 of our journal published an article on the angry Zionist declarations which the head of the USA Rabbinical Council, D. Hollander, made on his visit to the Soviet Union.[66]

Among the comments on this article received by the editorial board is a letter from a minister of religion, the Tashkent Rabbi Sh. Maryanovsky, which is published below.

Tashkent rabbi to American rabbi

I was deeply sorry to learn that David Hollander, head of the USA Rabbinical Council, had declared that the Jews are persecuted in the Soviet Union and that those who believe in God cannot freely practise their religious observances. I am used to a rabbi's word having weight and would be happy to excuse Hollander, to believe he has been misled or misinformed. But how can

* *Source*: 'Zayavlenie evreiskikh religioznykh obshchin Gruzii' (Statement of the Jewish Religious Communities of Georgia), *Izvestiya*, 14 December 1956.
† *Source*: 'Iz redaktsionnoi pochty' (From the Editorial Mail), *Nauka i religiya*, 1963, no. 9, p. 79.

he be excused if he made his declaration after visiting the Soviet Union? After seeing for himself that the Jews in the Soviet Union have equal rights with other peoples?

I chanced to meet the head of the American rabbis twice, once in Moscow and the other time in Tashkent. And let me say openly: something in his behaviour made me suspicious. The American guest came, without my permission, to my home when I was praying, and I asked him to leave me in peace. My premonitions have not deceived me. The American rabbi now turns white into black, supporting the deceit with his authority.

I know that Hollander was looking for people with whom he could become closely acquainted in Tashkent. But even in the synagogue the Jews kept to themselves, because they did not trust him. Too often do American 'friends' deceive our expectations. And it is not our fault that the American rabbi with his slander estranges us still more from the American 'way of life' which, like a black shadow, has settled on the land of Israel.

Hollander talks a great deal of the love of Jews for Israel. There is some truth in that. I, as a deeply religious man, would very much like to be buried in the land of my ancestors, as required by the Talmud. For me 'Israel' is a sacred word. But I can also say that I would not like to live in Israel. And the reason is because the holy land of our ancestors is desecrated by such people as Hollander, who are ready to trade on the feelings of Jews to please the millionaires.

I want to believe that there are many honest people among the American Jews who are not like Rabbi Hollander. I can say to the honest people of America: come to us, and you will see that in the Soviet Union the Jews, religious and non-religious, live the same happy life as Russians, Uzbeks, and others. Come to us, and you will know what to think of your rabbi's words.

Sh. Maryanovsky,
Tashkent   Rabbi

Leningrad Jewish religious community in correspondence with government bodies

Document 121* A complaint from Pechersky: the administrative section of the Leningrad City Militia (1954)

No. 1/14 – 101   May 1954, Leningrad

To Citizen Gdalye Ruvimovich Pechersky[67]
HERE: Razyezzhaya Street, block 9, flat 8.

I wish to inform you that your statement on the unlawful activities of members of the militia has been examined. Legal proceedings against the guilty have not been instituted, but disciplinary measures have been taken.

Director of the Militia Administration
of the City of Leningrad
(Solovyev)

* *Source*: This document was brought to the West by an emigrant from the Soviet Union.

Document 122* Certificate of synagogue registration (1954)

USSR
Commissioner of the Council
for the Affairs of Religious Cults[68]
of the Council of Ministers of the USSR
for Leningrad and Leningrad Province

6 May 1954   Leningrad, Zagorodny Prospekt, 18.
No. 54/65   Tel: 79–08

CERTIFICATE

For the registration of the executive organ and the auditing committee of a
religious society.

The present certificate is issued by the Commissioner of the Council for the
Affairs of Religious Cults of the Council of Ministers of the USSR for
Leningrad and Leningrad Province, on the basis of the registration dated 2
October 1945, of a religious society of the Jewish faith in the October District
of Leningrad, Lermontov Avenue, 2, for the registration as of today of:
An executive organ comprising citizens:

> 1. — Chairman
> 2. — Member
> 3. — Member
> 4. — Member
> 5. — Member

An auditing committee comprising citizens:

> 1. — Chairman
> 2. — Member
> 3. — Member

with the rights and obligations stipulated in the laws and resolutions of the
Government of the USSR valid with regard to religious worship. This
certificate is to be kept with the papers of the executive organ of the religious
society.

> The Commissioner of the Council for the Affairs of Religious
> Cults of the Council of Ministers of the USSR for Leningrad
> and Leningrad Province.
> (Vasilyev)

Document 123† On the baking of *maẓot*[69] in Leningrad (1955)

To the secretary of the CC CPSU, N.S. Khrushchev
From: *the Leningrad Jewish Religious*
Community, Leningrad,
Lermontov Avenue, 2

STATEMENT

The Leningrad Jewish Religious Community has received authorisation of the

---

* *Source*: This document was brought to the West by an emigrant from the Soviet Union.
† *Source*: This document was brought to the West by an emigrant from the Soviet Union.

Ministry of Provisions of the USSR for the baking of *mazot* for the Passover of 1955. The baking of the *mazot* is being carried out by the Leningrad Bread-Baking Trust at the Bakery of the Jewish synagogue.

According to Jewish religious rules, the baking of *mazot*, even when carried out in a Jewish bakery and by Jewish workers, must be presided over by a 'supervisor', whose tasks can be summarised as follows:

1. To ensure that the water necessary for the baking of *mazot* for each subsequent day be prepared prior to sunset;
2. To ensure that the workers are not permitted to eat, or bring onto the premises where the unleavened *mazot* are being baked, bakery products prepared from leavened dough;
3. To ensure that the workers wash their hands after eating leavened bakery products;
4. To ensure that the vessel in which the dough for the *mazot* is prepared be thoroughly cleansed after the preparation of each portion, thereby preventing any leavening of the dough.

Despite the repeated requests of the Leningrad Jewish Religious Community, the Leningrad Bread-Baking Trust responsible for baking the *mazot* is not allowing the presence of one Jewish worker in each shift who would, at the same time as he is working, watch over the execution of the above-mentioned rules for the preparation of *mazot*. The significance of the preparation of *mazot* is thereby lost, and this represents a snub to the religious feelings of the Jews.

The appeals of the Leningrad Jewish Community to the Leningrad City Executive Committee to regulate the matter of the baking of *mazot* have shown no results.

This obliges us to appeal to you personally.

The Leningrad Jewish Community considers that the present case constitutes an affront to the feelings of believers, which contradicts the decree of the CC CPSU of 10 November 1954.[70]

The Leningrad Jewish Community *requests* you, Comrade Khrushchev, to instruct the Leningrad Soviet organs to admit to each shift one Jewish worker who will be entrusted with the supervision of the above-mentioned rules.

Enclosed:
Letter of the Leningrad Jewish Community and the rejection of Comrade Grishmanov (Deputy Chairman of the Leningrad City Executive Committee).
– Chairman of the Managing Committee of the Leningrad Jewish Community –
– Secretary (ditto)

1 February 1955
Leningrad.

Document 124* Rejection of a complaint from Pechersky (1956)

USSR Procuracy

Procurator of the City of Leningrad

Leningrad, Belinsky St 13,   21 June 1956
tel. Zh–3–38–33   No. 3/1086 t

Pechersky, G. R.
Razyezzhaya St, block 9, flat 8.

With regard to your statement on the unseemly behaviour of the synagogue worshippers Pinkin and others, I am to inform you that your declaration has been checked several times in the 2nd dept of the LGM [Leningrad City Militia], in the Procurator's Office of the October District, and the request to institute legal proceedings has been rejected.[71]

The Procuracy of the City of Leningrad also finds no basis for the institution of legal proceedings.

Regarding the question of instituting criminal proceedings against Pinkin and others for insulting behaviour, in accordance with Art. 10 of the Criminal Code of the RSFSR, you are required to turn directly to the People's Court.

You can settle questions connected with procedural matters in synagogue work with the official of the Committee for the Affairs of Religious Cults.

Procurator of the City of Leningrad
State Councillor of Justice
3rd class   (Tsypin)

MV
20. VI

Rabbi Shlifer

Document 125† Announcement of Rabbi Shlifer's death (1957)

(Obituary) – SOLOMON MIKHAILOVICH SHLIFER

The congregation of the Chief Synagogue in Moscow announces with deep sorrow the sudden death in Moscow on 31 March 1957, in his sixty-ninth year, of Solomon Mikhailovich Shlifer, rabbi of the synagogue and Rector of the Higher Theological Seminary, and extends sincere condolences to his family.

Document 126‡ Rabbi Kiselgof's[72] funeral oration on the death of Rabbi Shlomo Shlifer (1957)

It is written in the anthology 'Song of Songs': 'I went down to the nut orchard.'[73] A fruit, upon falling to the ground, makes no sound because it is

---

* *Source*: This document was brought to the West by an emigrant from the Soviet Union.
† *Source*: *Izvestiya*, 2 April 1957.
‡ *Source*: Z. N. Kiselgof, 'Hesped al mot ha-rav de-mata r. Shlomo Shlifer zikhrono li-vrakhah' (Funeral Oration on the Death of the Local Rabbi, Shlomo Shlifer of Blessed Memory) in his *Ba-maẓar* (In the Straits), Jerusalem, Mosad ha-rav Kook, 1970, pp. 412–13.

soft, and therefore it is not heard; but when the nut falls to the ground it is heard. Likewise, when the righteous man dies it resounds throughout the world; but when the nut falls the sound issues only from its exterior, while from its interior, from its kernel, nothing is heard. And therefore, gentlemen, I say to you, as King David – may he rest in peace – said when Avner, King Saul's general, died: 'Do you know that a prince and a great man has fallen this day in Israel';[74] the rabbi of this place, Rabbi Shlomo, son of the late Rabbi Yehiel Mikhael, of blessed memory, who was one of the greatest teachers in our days and a public figure of whom it has been said: 'In his shadow we shall live among the nations', who was honoured by the government, and laboured hard and toiled to found the *Yeshivah* in our city of Moscow, and restored religion to its rightful place and laid down that twice each day there should be lessons in the Gemara for his eternal rest, apart from paragraphs of the Mishnah and *Ein Yaakov*.[75] Therefore, let all the house of Israel mourn the burning and the loss which has overtaken us with his demise.

The anti-religious struggle: General

Document 127* From a lecture to anti-religious propagandists (1957)[76]

Imperialist reaction is also armed with the Jewish religion. Its organisations abroad are as hostile to Communism as the churches of other denominations. The Jewish religion distracts believing Jews from the struggle for a better life here on earth, from the struggle for the building of Communism, and lulls them with sweet hopes of a life of paradise in the 'world to come'. In Israel where Judaism is the state religion, the bourgeoisie uses religion to arouse enmity between toilers of different nationalities. Almost no Jewish religious holiday passes without clashes between Jews and Arab Muslims.

Zionism – a variety of bourgeois nationalism and cosmopolitanism[77] – acts in league with the Jewish religion. Zionist organisations make use of Judaism as a means for the spiritual subjugation of the Jewish toilers. Zionism plays a most harmful part: it conceals class differentiation thereby weakening the class consciousness of the Jewish proletariat and the toiling poor people.

Document 128† Measures against synagogues (1959)

UNITED NATIONS, NY, 18 June. The synagogue in a Ukrainian city was reliably reported today to have been closed by Soviet authorities last month in the Kremlin's campaign against the practice of the Jewish religion.

According to these reports all the Torahs (Books of Scripture) in the synagogue, situated in Chernigov, were confiscated. A delegation of Jews set

* *Source*: M. B. Mitin 'O soderzhanii i zadachakh nauchno-ateisticheskoi propagandy v sovremennykh usloviyakh' (On the Content and Tasks of Scientific-Atheist Propaganda in Contemporary Conditions), in P. N. Fedoseev, M. M. Sheinman, N. N. Rozental, *et al.* (eds.), *Nauka i religiya* (Science and Religion), Moscow, Znanie, 1957, p. 23.
† *Source*: 'Anti-Jewish Acts in Soviet Listed', *New York Times*, 19 June 1959.

out to seek the intervention of Dr Yehudah Levin, rabbi of the Moscow congregation.[78]

This followed the arrest last fall of a number of Jews in Chernovtsy, also in the Ukraine, including synagogue officials, on the charge that they had participated in 'Zionist propaganda'. This was based on the fact that during the Passover celebration they participated in the traditional toast to 'Next year in Jerusalem.'

So far as can be determined, the measures against the practice of the Jewish religion are inspired primarily by the Kremlin's belief that Soviet Jews are under the sway of 'bourgeois Jewish nationalism', and thus are bound together. In other words, the campaign may be inspired by political motives rather than by the desire to crush the Jewish religion.

The Soviet government is against [the] practice of any form of religion, and the severity of its current measures against the Jewish religion may be inspired primarily by political motives. The campaign is centred in the Ukraine, but measures have been reported from widely scattered cities.

In Minsk, Belorussia, eight Jewish students were arrested and jailed last December for 'having organised a Zionist cell'. A number of Jews in Kishinev, capital of the Moldavian Republic, were arrested for having violated a government decree and making *mazot* (unleavened bread) at a recent celebration of the Passover.

Document 129* Soviet rejoinder on synagogue closure (1959)

A lie, even a big lie, is like a small coin. You can't live on it long. You've hardly jingled it before bankruptcy begins to set in. This is just the situation in which certain American newspapers and the Israeli radio, which were suddenly seized with sentimental feelings for the Jews in the Soviet Union, find themselves.

The American and Israeli liars could think of nothing more original than a fable about how the Soviet Union's Jews are allegedly subjected to discrimination, and that the road to science and the country's cultural life is closed to them. Proofs? If you please, these slanderers, whose writings and broadcasts poison the international atmosphere, assert that religious Jews in the Soviet Union are deprived of the opportunity to conduct religious services because someone closed the synagogue – this took place, they say, in Kiev – and is persecuting the worshippers.[79]

The fabrications about discrimination against Jews in the Soviet Union do not even deserve refutation. Moreover, those who spread this slander are not in the least motivated by concern for Soviet Jews, who enjoy the same rights in our country as the citizens of any other nationality.

The letter to *Izvestiya* that is printed below, sent to the editors by the Board of the Jewish Religious Community in Kiev, testifies to the true value of the bourgeois scribblers' scandalous concoction concerning religious freedom for Jews in the USSR:

'To the editors of *Izvestiya*: we have learned that slanderous reports alleging that the synagogue in Kiev has been closed and that Jewish believers are

* *Source*: 'Kak amerikansko-izrailskie klevetniki "zakryli" v Kieve sinagogu' (How American and Israeli Slanderers "Closed" the Synagogue in Kiev), *Izvestiya*, 24 July 1959.

deprived of the opportunity of worshipping have been spread recently in a number of newspapers in the USA and Israel and in radio broadcasts in these countries.

'Any unbiased person can visit the Kiev synagogue at 29 Shchekavitskaya Street at any time of day and convince himself with his own eyes of the falseness of these reports.

'American and Israeli tourists, who can see for themselves that the synagogue is operating completely freely, visit the Kiev synagogue almost every day. Why, when the truth is evident, do such provocational fabrications appear in the American and Israeli press?

'Only recently the Israeli Ambassador to the USSR prayed in the Kiev synagogue on the festival of Pentecost; late in June a group of Israeli engineers, Israeli representatives to the UN and many others visited our synagogue.

'The Kiev synagogue is open every day from 6 a.m. to 10 p.m., and any Jewish believer can freely satisfy his religious needs.

'At the request of the religious Jews of the city of Kiev, we ask the editors of *Izvestiya* to publish this letter in order to disprove the current invention of the bourgeois press. – S. I. Bardakh, Chairman of the Board of the Jewish Religious Community in Kiev; G. L. Yurovitsky, Deputy Chairman of the Board; M. Kh. Feldman, Z. D. Shir and Kh. L. Tversky, members of the Committee of Twenty; and K. I. Kleiner, cantor of the synagogue.'

Comment on this letter would be superfluous. The Kiev synagogue was 'closed' not by the Soviet authorities but by the bourgeois slanderers.

Document 130* Preparing anti-religious propagandists (1959)

A ten-day seminar for atheist propagandists has just ended. Two hundred and fifty people participated in it.

The propagandists heard lectures on the following subjects: Marxism–Leninism on religion; pre-Marxist atheism and its militant character; Christianity, its origin and class nature; Catholicism and Protestantism; the Russian Orthodox Church and its present state; contemporary Judaism and Jewish bourgeois nationalism; forms and methods of scientific-atheist propaganda; the attitude of the Communist Party and the Soviet government towards church and religion.

The propagandists visited the republic's Museum of History and Regional Studies where they were shown a series of documentary and scientific films.

The seminar participants discussed several problems related to the establishment of circles and seminars on scientific atheism within the network of Party education.

Document 131† Satire against a religious Jew (1960)

Who are they? (Feuilleton)

Late one night, a man alighted from a long-distance train at Kazan Station, waited for the special late-night tram and asked the driver to put him off at

* *Source*: 'Seminar propagandistov-ateistov' (Seminar for Atheist Propagandists), *Sovetskaya Moldaviya*, 8 October 1959.

† *Source*: Yu. Yakovlev & I. Noffenman, 'Kto zhe oni?' (Who Are They?), *Sovetskaya Tatariya*, 6 January 1960.

'Dostoevsky' stop. Soon, after looking around, he stopped by one of the houses. The gates were locked. Without further ado, the man climbed over the high fence. In no time at all a faint light flickered in the upper windows of the house – a candle had been lit. The big-time speculator, Bentsion Vugman, was admitted to the flat. The police had been looking for him for a long time and were to arrest him within a month in the same flat.

Who, then, harboured him?

'Mummy, please let me sleep a little longer.'

'Get up, you'll be late for school.'

'Mummy, just a little bit longer.'

'Get up, you're told, you lazy thing.'

Sobbing, the little girl jumps out of bed, puts on her dirty, patched-up dress, swallows down her breakfast and runs to the tram stop. Shivering with the cold, she wraps her wretched coat around her. She thinks of her friends who, getting up early, managed to get so many things done in the house and to learn their lessons. After all, there is a whole hour and a half before lessons begin. However, to make her way to school, on the other side of town, she had to change trams more than once.

When the little girl falls sick she misses her lessons, but on Saturday she misses them for other reasons – on this day her mother and father pray, instilling it into her and her brother that the Almighty bids them work six days and that the seventh day – Saturday to be precise – is to be devoted to God.

The little girl is jealous of many people. Especially her brother. It is good to be brilliant. Her parents say that he is a brilliant boy. They dress him far better than her because there are not enough 'holy' threads for both of them, and her father does not allow clothing to be sewn with ordinary threads.

Once the little girl overheard her father and mother talking. They were dreaming of her brother's future. 'He must definitely become a brilliant rabbi like his grandfather', her father said. 'I can't wait for the day', whispered her mother.

The parents of this little girl are God-fearing people. Her father studied in a private *ḥeder*, and has the right to be called rabbi.

Almost every evening, and on Saturday without fail, he would go to synagogue, but now that the latter has ceased to exist, he goes to a prayer-house, which, by the way, is not registered with the state organs.

There are so many 'things' to be done there. The prayers alone drain one's strength. There are many of them, and each one must, as they say, be brought to the hearts of the believers. But you know what the flock is like nowadays. You talk to them about saving their souls, and they talk to you about sputniks. [...]

This 'holy' couple do everything within their power to make sure their children grow up 'pleasing to God'. When their daughter finished primary school a new trial lay in store for her. Her father found an evening school for working youth, where there was no work on Saturday, and sent her there. 'We did it out of necessity', says the mother, 'there's nobody to leave our sick son with during the day.'

This, to put it mildly, is not true. Firstly, the boy is not confined to a sick-bed, and there is someone to give him his meals when, having run about to his heart's content in the street, he puts in an appearance in the house – a domestic worker lives with the family; secondly, the health of one child cannot be sacrificed for the sake of another. Any doctor will tell you that it is prohibited for children to study at a school where lessons finish after 11.00 p.m.

'I never heard her complain of her lot', the mother shouts pathetically.

Yes, the little girl still suffers without a murmur the oddities of her parents, who have deprived her of the joy of companionship with her contemporaries. After all, in school the pupils are for the most part young workers. Moreover, under existing circumstances there is neither a Pioneer nor a Komsomol organisation here.

'If you please, there is a document, signed by Comrade Lukoyanova, the director of the 65th School, in which she thanks us for the excellent upbringing of our daughter', says the father.[80]

Indeed, Comrade Lukoyanova unfortunately did give the girl's parents such a document a few years ago. They were standard words of gratitude rolled off on the duplicating machine.

'A quiet, gentle girl, would never say an unkind word to anyone, her marks were good, so we sent the parents a letter of gratitude', say the workers of the 65th School.

Let us be frank: the letter of gratitude clearly did not apply to the preacher.

With their son the parents behaved differently. When the boy had finished the fourth class, his father did not allow him to continue his studies. After all, in order to become a rabbi the boy had to receive a talmudic education. Already, although he is only ten, he is almost his father's equal in knowledge of religious customs, history, various biblical wisdoms. Together with his father he is an *habitué* of the prayer-house. The people we are talking of live in Kazan, in Ovrazhnaya Street.

The enlightened father of the unfortunate children is Isaak Yankelevich Zilber, a graduate of Kazan University, a teacher at School No. 13 for the working youth. His wife, Gita Benyaminovna, is a teacher at the 6th Secondary School. She was once in the Komsomol and graduated from the Kuibyshev Industrial Institute. By the way, when she is not busy praying, she is currently studying Marxism–Leninism at university evening courses(!).

So much for the *feuilleton*. But have all the *i*'s been dotted? Do the authors have the right to leave unmentioned those who willingly or unwillingly aided and abetted the Zilbers?

According to the testimony of the director of studies of the 6th Secondary School, M. M. Sutorova, G. B. Zilber is 'a good teacher' and an 'exemplary, public-spirited person'.

'Only, I don't know Gita Benyaminovna's inner world, her family, and am perhaps at fault in this', Maria Mikhailovna hastens to correct herself.

Indeed, not only the director of studies, but also the whole teaching staff of the school are greatly at fault for failing to understand, after many years of joint work, what is concealed behind the exterior of the rabbi and his wife.

The conduct of the teachers Berta Moiseevna Press and Mariya

Yakovlevna Roza, under whom Sora and Bentsion Zilber studied from the first to the fourth class, also deserves severe censure. They paid no attention to the frequent absence of the children from lessons and knew of the abnormal conditions in which they live. They knew and were silent.

M. B. Peredelkina, who replaced B. M. Press on a number of occasions, drew attention to the fact that Sora lives a long way from school, to the girl's reserved nature and to her tattered clothes, but did not concern herself with her fate any more deeply.

The teaching staff of the 1st School for the Working Youth, where Sora is presently studying, looks calmly on the fact that the girl misses her lessons on Fridays (according to religious law, a believing Jew is not allowed to work on Friday evenings).

Zilber Senior's patron is the Director of the Lenin District Department of People's Education, Comrade Shalashov. With his blessing the preacher works as a teacher.

Zilber has other well-wishers. Candidate of physical and mathematical sciences and senior research associate of the Kazan filial of the USSR Academy of Sciences, I. V. Svirsky, for example, considered it the greatest honour to help him to become acquainted with an ancient manuscript of the Pentateuch in the university's academic library. And afterwards, he even boasted to the library's workers: 'Do you know whom I brought along? That was a preacher.'

He had something to boast about.

Document 132* Chernovtsy synagogue charged with being Zionist centre (1960)

The Soviet peoples, led by the Communist Party, are engaged in the successful building of Communism, a society which will meet all the material and spiritual needs of mankind, while delivering human beings from the superstitions of the past. The great majority of the workers have already been liberated from the harmful survivals of the past and are actively participating in the building of Communism. Everywhere there are big building projects, state farms on virgin lands, factories and kolkhozes – the Soviet peoples are working with inspiration in creative work and are exerting themselves in fulfilment of the great plans of the 21st Congress of the CPSU, to bring nearer the bright day of mankind – Communism.

However, we still find, here and there, people who, under the mask of religious functionaries, for instance, do not participate in the production of material welfare, live on the account of trustful believers and are occupied in affairs far from godly.

Radyanska Bukovina has, on numerous occasions, published information on the shady affairs conducted in the synagogue at 53 Ruska Street. In our country nobody forbids believers to perform religious rituals. But the indignation of the town's population, its Jewish believers and non-believers, has been roused by the foul activities of the synagogue leaders. It is universally

* *Source*: 'Get darmoidiv i nosiiv mrakobissya' (Down With Parasites and Carriers of Obscurantism), *Radyanska Bukovyna*, 9 September 1960.

known that the leaders of what is known as the 'Committee of Twenty', Raish, Zilber and Barenboim, have on more than one occasion come to blows when dividing the takings. They attract to the synagogue even Orthodox Christian believers from the neighbouring villages, promising them happiness in life in return for their money. Money for everything. Money is everything in life for them.

The anger of all honest people has been aroused by the *feuilleton* 'Jerusalem Skull-Caps' in *Radyanska Bukovyna*.[81] Soviet people are always happy to welcome guests. A great number of tourists from all corners of the earth visit our country. When they come with good intentions we greet them with a sincere 'Welcome!' But the intentions of the official from the Israeli Embassy in Moscow, Yaakov Reuveni, were far from genuine when he went to Chernovtsy. The synagogue-goers sized him up. They not only refused the gifts brought by Reuveni – prayer shawls, prayer-books and post-cards of Israel – but even threw him out of the synagogue.

Everybody was infuriated by the activities of Raish, Zilber and Barenboim, who gave a hospitable welcome to the Israeli preacher of Zionism. Many Jewish workers, believers and non-believers, sent letters to the editorial board in which they requested the closure of the synagogue, this hotbed of religious obscurantism, this refuge of parasites.

We publish several of these letters below.

Close the hotbed of harmful ideology

We, scientists of the Chernovtsy Medical Institute, were terribly angered by the hostile propaganda activities of Yaakov Reuveni, the Israeli Embassy representative. Reuveni did not choose the synagogue in Ruska Street accidentally. This building has long ago become a place for shady affairs and the diffusion of various anti-Soviet rumours, a refuge for suspects, a place used less for the performance of religious rituals than for anything else.

In his *feuilleton* 'Jerusalem Skull-Caps', Comrade Shvartsman presents the synagogue in its true light, as a site of fights, rows, 'business meetings', speculations, diffusion of anti-Soviet propaganda and praise of imperialist Israel.

We lecturers, as men responsible for the education of youth, regard this situation as intolerable and raise our voices against the religious hypocrisy of Judaism, against the hostile and false bourgeois propaganda, and regard it as imperative to close the hotbed of harmful ideology. We are infuriated by the improper behaviour of the Israeli Embassy representative, whose activities do not conform with the performance of diplomatic functions.

Professors: Ya. D. Kirshenblat[82]
            N. B. Shchupak
            S. A. Kats[83]
            V. I. Triger
            V. L. Khenkin[84]
Reader: L. N. Zamansky
Candidate of Medical Sciences: M. I. Kleiman.

. . .

I am leaving the 'Committee of Twenty'

I sometimes went to the synagogue on Ruska Street, but was not an active parishioner. I was, nevertheless, elected to its 'Committee of Twenty'. I have never agreed with the shady affairs conducted in the synagogue. The last incident, when its leaders hospitably welcomed an Israeli diplomat who arrived in Chernovtsy with hostile intentions, literally infuriated me.

I do not wish to participate in such filthy affairs of the synagogue and have consequently decided to retire from the 'Committee of Twenty'. As a Soviet citizen, I wish to live and work honestly.

Menash Elkin
Worker of Industrial Artel 'Nove Zhytya'

The anti-religious struggle: the Kychko affair

Document 133* Kychko's[85] description of Judaism (1963)

On the 'Mishnah'

The Mishnah consists of six chapters according to thematic principles. The chapters are divided into sixty-three treatises, the treatises into sections, and the sections into separate verses or paragraphs. The most important part of the Mishnah is the *Avot* (Ethics of the Fathers), or a treatise 'concerning principles'.†[86] The biblical texts here, just as in other treatises, are written in a religio-nationalistic spirit. [...]

Quite characteristic is the interpretation of the Decalogue – the Ten Commandments of the Bible: you may not steal from or cause any other damage to your *ḥaverim* (neighbours), i.e. just the Jews. As to how this applies to *goyim*, to those of different religions, the Jews are free to take from them, because, as Judaism teaches: 'Jehovah delivered all of the wealth of non-Jews to the use of the Jews.' If the Jews did not take everything into their hands, it was because in doing so they would have been deprived of many productive forces which help the Jews profit from non-Jewish peoples without exerting any particular effort.‡ [...]

On the 'Talmud'

In humiliating working people, the Talmud at the same time glorifies persons of wealth; in downgrading agriculture, it praises trade and usury. According to the Talmud, even the prophet Moses made a fortune through trade machinations which he practised by speculating with community property.

---

* *Source*: T. Kychko, *Iudaizm bez prykras*, pp. 34, 37, 40, 61, 86–7, 91–2, 93, 96, 135, 144.
† N. Pereferkovich, *The Talmud, Mishnah and Tosefta*, vol. vi, treatise *Avot*, ch. i–v, St Petersburg, pp. 500–4.
‡ *Hoshen Mishpat*, Code of Laws, cccxxviii, i.

'Moses grew rich by selling pieces of sapphire which broke off during the cutting of the stones for the Ten Commandments',* says the Talmud.[87]

The Talmud morally corrupts people, instilling in them the spirit of commerce and extortion. An example of practitioners of extortion are the priests themselves, the teachers of the law – the rabbis, who supervise adherence to the religious prescriptions which permit common people (*am ha-arez*) 'to be cleaned like fish'.†[88] [...]

The Talmud is saturated with contempt for work and for the common people, *am ha-arez*. [...] The Talmud takes an especially negative position towards the work of peasants. [...]

Jews and money

Judaism considers a person to be moral if, not working for the good of society, he devotes all of his free time to prayer and to the performance of religious rites. For Judaism, not work but prayer is the highest manifestation of morality. Furthermore, all of Judaic ideology is impregnated with narrow practicality, with greed, with the love of money and with the spirit of egoism.

'What is the temporal basis of Judaism?' wrote K. Marx. 'Practical necessity, self-interest. What is the temporal cult of the Jew? Commerce. Who is his temporal God? Money. What was the actual basis of the Jewish religion? Practical needs, egoism. The God of practical need and self-interest is money. Money is the jealous god of Israel before whose face there must not be any other god.' [...]‡[89]

The entire Judaic cult is the translation of trade and commerce into religious language. The sale of *mazah*, the auction of chapter-readings of the Torah (*aliyah*), burial rites, circumcision, marriage and divorce – in all of these money is of prime importance, as is contempt for productive work. [...]

Jews taught 'false witness' and 'dishonesty'

The Jews like to talk a great deal about the commandment which forbids them to bear false witness. However, when the welfare of a Jew is in question, false witnessing and even false oaths are permissible. [...] While giving a false oath, it is only necessary, the 'Holy Scripture' teaches, to negate the oath in the heart and soul, and therefore the oath is meaningless. But this must be done in such a manner 'that the glory of the name of the God of Israel, and honour and worth of the Jewish religion and the people of Israel do not suffer.'§ [...]

One of the commandments of Judaism is 'thou shalt not steal'. However, as the *Hoshen mishpat* interprets, it is only from *haverim* (i.e. from your Jewish neighbours)** that you must not steal. But you can steal everything from others, because, as it is written in the 'Holy Scriptures', Jehovah handed over to the Hebrews all the wealth of non-Jews. If the Jews did not take everything

---

* Talmud, Chapter *Nashim* (Women), treatise *Nedarim*, 38a.
† *ibid.*, Chapter *Moed*, treatise *Pesahim*, 19b.
‡ K. Marx & F. Engels, *Tvory* (Works), vol. 1, Kiev, 1958, pp. 379, 381.
§ Talmud, treatise *Shevuot*, Hase 232, 14.
** See Talmud, *Hoshen mishpat*, ch. cccxxviii, para. 1.

into their own hands, it was because they did not want to lose the labour-power of non-Jewish workers. Moreover, Judaism teaches the believer that his exclusive purpose is to study the Torah, and that if the Jews always engaged themselves only in studying the Law of Moses, then God would force other people to work for them.[90]

Although the commandments of Judaism teach not to steal, nevertheless in many places in the Old Testament recommendations are made for the people to resort to common theft.

The ethics of Judaism do not condemn such disgraceful actions as hypocrisy and bribery. The well-known commentator on the Talmud, Rashi, teaches: 'Basing himself on biblical teachings, the Jew at the very outset must work with bribery in order to tempt his enemy, and in other cases he must resort to a variety of artifices.'* [...]

Synagogues and speculation

Speculation in *mazah*, pigs, thievery, deception, debauchery – these are the real characteristics of many synagogue leaders.

Shrewd operators convert the synagogues from religion into their own personal feeding-grounds; they make free with the contributions of the believers, and become wealthy from them. [...]

Passover 'harmful'

Under contemporary conditions the Passover holiday harms us in a great number of ways, by engendering disrespect for work and fostering elements of nationalism among the Jewish workers. In celebrating the Passover the believers do not go to work for several days; thus they hinder production plans and violate work discipline.

The celebration of the Passover is especially harmful because the entire Passover legend, all the prayers, orient the believing Jews towards returning to Israel which is now the centre of Judaism and Zionism. The Passover prayers urge the believing Jews: 'May God grant that we meet in Jerusalem next year.' Invitations summon the Jews to move to Israel where they – free workers of our country – will become slaves, will become cannon-fodder for Ben Gurion's clique and for his imperialistic masters. [...]

'Contempt and hatred' for others

This cruel rite [of circumcision] has been filled with a reactionary meaning by the Jewish religion. It proclaimed circumcision as a unique mark of Jewish nationalism itself; in other words, it endowed it with a clearly expressed religious-nationalistic character. It is not difficult to substantiate the latter again by texts from the Bible. Acquiring a mark of belonging to 'their own people', to the Jews, a mark which would simultaneously inoculate them with

---

* A. Alekseev, *Ocherki domashnei i obshchestvennoi zhizni evreev* (Essays on the Family and Social Life of the Jews), St Petersburg, 1896, p. 229.[91]

contempt and even hatred towards those who do not possess this mark – this is the basic meaning of the rite.

Document 134* Party criticism of Kychko's book (1964)

The CPSU Central Committee's Ideological Commission has examined the question of scientific-atheist literature.[92]

The Commission noted that central and local publishing houses have published a number of useful books and pamphlets in which various trends of religious ideology are subjected to well-reasoned criticism on the basis of the achievements of modern science and in which the experience of atheistic work in the USSR is illuminated. The publication of such books and pamphlets contributes to the formation of a materialist world-view among Soviet people.

The session of the Commission called the attention of press organs, publishing houses and scientific institutions to the need for a further rise in the ideological and scientific level of atheistic literature.

Useful publications have been issued in recent years, including the popular text-book *Conversations on Religion and Knowledge*; the course *Popular Lectures on Atheism*; the reader *About Religion*; the anthology *Thoughts About Religion*; A. Osipov's book *The Catechism Without Embellishment*; A. Chertkov's *From God to People*; P. Kurochkin's *Orthodoxy and Humanism*; and many other atheistic works. At the same time, certain poorly prepared books and pamphlets that harm our ideological and educational work have come off the presses.

In particular, the participants of the session criticised the serious mistakes made in T. Kychko's *Judaism Without Embellishment*, published late in 1963 by the Ukrainian Republic Academy of Sciences Publishing House. The book's author, as well as the author of its foreword, in striving to expose the reactionary essence of Judaism, incorrectly explain certain questions linked with the rise and development of this religion. A number of the book's erroneous statements and of its illustrations may offend the feelings of believers and might be interpreted in a spirit of anti-Semitism.

But, as is known, such a question does not and cannot arise in our country. 'From the days of the October Revolution', N. S. Khrushchev has said, 'the Jews in our country have had equality with all other peoples of the USSR in all respects. We do not have a Jewish question, and those who dream it up are singing a foreign tune.'

The mistaken tenets contained in the book contradict the Party's Leninist policy on questions of religion and nationality and only give our ideological opponents, who are trying to create a so-called 'Jewish question' at any cost, food for anti-Soviet insinuations. It is precisely for this reason that the mistaken parts of T. Kychko's book cannot but arouse objections on the part of the Soviet public.

The Ideological Commission recommended that officials of the press and publishing houses be more careful in their approach to the publication of literature on scientific atheism.

---

* *Source*: 'V ideologicheskoi komissii TSK KPSS' (In the CPSU Central Committee's Ideological Commission), *Pravda*, 4 April 1964.

Evidence of continuing Jewish religious life

Document 135* Survivors of the Hasidic movement in the Soviet Union

I met them in Moscow, too, and Kiev. They are associated with various Hasidic houses, not just the Lubavitch. And they all pray in the same synagogue, indeed in the same room, each group according to its own liturgical formulas. Standing in the prayer hall you hear the Karlin version with one ear and the Bratslaver with the other. Yet their hearts are united in true brotherhood. You find no trace of the dissensions that plague most Hasidic houses, rather an infinite and uninhibited love of Israel, a pure solidarity of spirit, and a sanctity which Hasidic leaders in Jerusalem or Williamsburg would do well to study.

How many of them are there? No more than a few thousand, scattered throughout the country, mostly in large cities. Their children grow up in a Jewish atmosphere and receive a traditional education. Some of them wear earlocks, and I saw a number of young men with beards. They gather in a private home to study Talmud. On Sabbath they attend a lecture on the Bible, and during long winter evenings they tell Hasidic wonder tales, passed on from generation to generation like an underground Oral Law.

What about observance, I asked one of them, certain he would tell me that in light of extenuating circumstances (which one need not go into) it had become necessary to adopt a more lenient attitude toward the commandments. Not at all. On the contrary, he had become stricter than ever in his observance, stricter than Jews elsewhere. His children, for instance, stayed home from school on the Sabbath, although he knew that the consequences were likely to be unpleasant. But there was no alternative, he told me. Perhaps God will take pity; if not, not. His children might suffer, but they will not have desecrated the Sabbath. I quoted him the law: preservation of life supersedes observance of the Sabbath. Not here, he replied. Once we forfeit this commandment, or another like it, the next step is to forfeit all of them. Better not begin in that direction.

* *Source*: E. Wiesel, *The Jews of Silence*, pp. 30–1.

9

Jews in Soviet government

Following the October Revolution, the Jews entered positions in the Soviet government[1] in numbers far exceeding their proportion in the country's population. But their relative role began to decline from the late twenties, in part because members of other nationalities, previously under-represented, rose to responsible positions, and in part because of specific discrimination against Jews.[2] This process accelerated in the second half of the thirties when the waves of purges that engulfed the Communist Party resulted in the veteran Bolshevik leadership being virtually wiped out: the Jews, who still constituted a disproportionately high percentage of that leadership, suffered far more than the other nationalities.[3] However, until after World War II, the decline in the Jewish role was basically a decline in influence, to be measured in relative rather than absolute numbers.

We shall examine here the process which reduced the role of the Jews in Soviet government. We shall also endeavour to determine whether the factors operative in the twenties and thirties continued to play a role, together with the new factors that emerged, in the period under discussion.

The Jews in the Communist Party and its central institutions

The Party, the sole source of rule in the Soviet Union, executes its numerous and complex functions either directly, by determining general policy and through the resolutions passed by its supreme institutions, or indirectly, through the important posts occupied by its members at every level in all governmental institutions. (An up-to-date list, called *nomenklatura*, specifies the posts to which only trusted Party members can be appointed.) Thus, theoretically, the mere fact that one is a member of the Communist Party should provide one with the opportunity to influence the selection of governmental leadership and the formation of its policies. But in practice such influence is limited to rather narrow circles of top officials.

We shall therefore discuss both the composition of the Party as a whole and also that of its leading institutions.

The national composition of the Communist Party and the proportion of Jews in it

The last complete data on the national composition of the Communist Party applied to the year 1927, when the Party contained 49,627 Jews, or 4.34% of the 1,131,250 members.[4]

We have only partial figures for later periods. Thus, for example, in 1940 the Jews constituted 13.4% of the membership in the Communist Party of the Ukraine, whereas according to the 1939 census they represented only 4.9% of the total population in that republic. As the Jews of the Ukraine constituted over half the Jewish population in the Soviet Union (50.8%),[5] and since the proportion of Jews in the Communist Parties of the RSFSR and Belorussia – the two republics with large Jewish concentrations – was not greatly different, Rigby has concluded that the Jews then constituted 4.9% of the Communist Party of the Soviet Union. But one may question the assumptions underlying this calculation. While there is no doubt that the proportion of Jews in the Communist Party in the Ukraine in 1940 is highly indicative – more useful by analogy for Belorussia, however, than for the Russian Republic – it should not be applied to the CPSU as a whole.

It is impossible to know whether the proportion in the RSFSR was higher or lower. It could be anticipated that the Jews as a major urban element in the Ukraine would there be particularly well represented in the Party. But, as against this, there was a clear migratory trend into the RSFSR during the 1930s which could have more than counterbalanced this trend. Whatever the exact figure, however, there can be no doubt that as a predominantly urban population heavily represented in the professional and educated class from which a large proportion of Party members were recruited, the Jews were able to preserve a relatively high percentage in the Party. (According to the 1939 census 87% of the Jews were town-dwellers.) This was true despite the powerful sociological and political factors which (as indicated above) were working from the late 1920s to reduce their importance.

The profound demographic changes undergone by the Soviet Jewish population in the wake of the war must have affected its proportion within the Party. During the war years the Party adopted a policy of expanding its ranks both to make up for the losses caused by the many purges and also to strengthen the morale of the army. Indeed, the Party grew by almost 50% (from 3,872,415 members and candidates in 1941 to 5,760,369 in 1945). As the majority of new members came from the army, especially from the officer corps, it could (*ceteris paribus*) be assumed that the proportion of Jews accepted into the Party from the Red Army was relatively high. This is based on the estimate that Jews constituted 2.5% to 3% of the armed forces (about half a million[6] out of a total of 15 to 20 million soldiers), even though they probably represented far less than the 1.8% of the overall population ascribed to them by the 1939 census after the exterminations in the occupied regions.[7] (The large Jewish population annexed to the USSR probably contributed rather few members to the CPSU during the very short period which lasted at the longest from September 1939 to June 1941.) Then, too, a very high proportion of the officer corps was Jewish, as they were urban and educated. Against this, however, it is also known that, from the very onset of the war, and especially from 1943, Stalin and Shcherbakov conducted a policy of deliberate discrimination against Jews which was especially marked in procedures of promotion in rank, in the award of decorations and in the assignment of posts. It is possible that similar discrimination existed in the admission of Jews into the Party, but the lack of data on the national

Table 19. *National composition of the Communist Party, 1961–5*

Nation	Population in 1959		Communists as a %		Number of Communists per 1,000 of population	
	% of general population	% of urban population	1961	1965	1961	1965
Russians	54.65	65.80	63.54	62.39	52	58
Ukrainians	17.84	14.60	14.67	15.42	36	44
Belorussians	3.79	2.60	2.98	3.28	35	44
Georgians	1.29	1.00	1.77	1.65	61	65
Armenians	1.34	1.60	1.67	1.60	55	61
Azerbaidzhans	1.41	1.00	1.10	1.21	35	44
Kazakhs	1.73	0.90	1.56	1.54	38	45
Uzbeks	2.88	1.30	1.48	1.64	23	29
Turkmen	0.48	0.30	0.28	0.28	26	29
Kirgizians	0.46	0.10	0.28	0.30	27	33
Tadzhiks	0.67	0.30	0.34	0.36	22	29
Latvians	0.67	0.70	0.35	0.38	23	29
Lithuanians	1.11	0.80	0.44	0.52	18	24
Estonians	0.47	0.50	0.25	0.29	25	31
Moldavians	1.06	0.30	0.28	0.34	12	17
Other Nationalities	10.15	8.20	9.00	8.90	39	44
Jews among them	1.10	2.20	no figures		no figures	

Sources: Rigby, *Communist Party Membership in the USSR 1917–1967*, pp. 366–88; J. A. Newth & Z. Katz, 'Proportion of Jews in the Communist Party of the Soviet Union', *Bulletin on Soviet and East European Jewish Affairs*, 1969, no. 4, pp. 37–8; *Itogi vsesoyuznoi perepisi naseleniya 1959 goda*.

composition of new Party members in the war period makes it very difficult to draw any final conclusions.

We have two classes of data on the national composition of the Communist Party from 1945 to 1969. First there is the data for the country as a whole, in which only the nationalities having Union republics appear, with all the other nationalities, including the Jews, listed under 'other nationalities' (see Table 19). Complete data do exist, however, for the years 1959–69 on the national composition (including Jews) from four republics: Belorussia, Moldavia, Uzbekistan and Georgia (Table 20). But according to the 1959 census these republics contained only 18% of the Jewish population whereas at that time 76% lived in the RSFSR and the Ukraine. We shall therefore concentrate on what we can learn from Table 19.

First, there were some nationalities with a far higher Party membership than others, for example, the Russians, Georgians and Armenians, as compared with the Uzbeks, Turkmen and Moldavians. This situation derived from numerous and complex factors, among them: (1) the historical legacy – the highly active past role of these nationalities in the Party, the results of which have carried over for many decades; (2) the disproportionate represent-

Table 20. *National composition in four republics, 1959–69*

Nation	Population – 1959		Party		Communists per 1,000 of population
	Number	%	Number	%	
Belorussia – 1962					
Belorussians	6,532,035	81.1	168,300	67.4	25
Russians	659,093	8.2	49,800	19.9	73
Poles	538,881	6.7	2,700	1.1	5
Jews	150,084	1.9	16,000	6.4	103
Others		2.1		5.2	
Moldavia – 1963					
Moldavians	1,886,566	65.4	26,201	34.6	13
Russians	292,930	10.2	23,620	30.9	73
Jews	95,107	3.3	4,742	6.3	45
Others		21.1		28.1	
Uzbekistan – 1959					
Uzbeks	5,038,273	62.1	92,878	49.5	18
Russians	1,090,728	13.5	44,132	23.5	40
Tatars	444,810	5.4	10,200	5.4	23
Jews	94,344	1.2	5,422	2.9	57
Others		17.8		18.7	
Georgia – 1969					
Georgians	2,600,588	64.3	214,217	74.1	82
Armenians	442,916	11.0	23,397	8.1	53
Russians	407,886	10.1	16,120	5.5	39
Jews	51,582	1.3	2,150	0.7	42
Others		13.3		11.6	

Sources: Rigby, *Communist Party Membership in the USSR 1917–1967*, pp. 366–88; J. A. Newth & Z. Katz, 'Proportion of Jews in the Communist Party of the Soviet Union', *Bulletin on Soviet and East European Jewish Affairs*, 1969, no. 4, pp. 37–8; *Kommunist*, 1970, no. 2, pp. 22–3; *Kommunist Belorussii*, 1962, no. 5, p. 57; *Kommunist Moldavii*, 1963, no. 9, p. 37.

ation of the bureaucracy in the Party ranks; (3) the rate of urbanisation, which also influences (and is influenced by) professional composition and educational standards; and (4) the deliberate preferences exercised in membership selection which, on the one hand, favoured not only Russians but all the other Slavic nationalities as well, and, on the other, gave preference to the local nationalities in their own republics.

The Jews certainly belong to this first category. Their Party membership was high as a result of their historical past, their place in the Soviet bureaucracy and technocracy and their having the highest proportion of urban dwellers in the Soviet Union (95%). As against this, the recruitment policy, which sought to reduce the number of Jews in the Communist Party, apparently[8] operated in the opposite direction.

The data on 'other nationalities' – which include the Jews – are also of help in determining the proportion of Jews in the Party. Since the Tatars, Germans, Poles and Jews between them constituted the majority in this category, and since the Tatars, and still more the Germans and Poles, provided relatively few Party members, we can assume that the Jews made a disproportionately high contribution to the 9% of total Party membership drawn from all these nationalities combined.

By comparing column 2 (percentage of the urban population) with columns 3 and 4 (percentage of Communists), we find a clear correlation between proportion of urban population and that of Party membership. In eight of the fifteen republics the figures were nearly identical. And since this correlation held true for the several republics for which we have data, it may, following Newth and Katz,[9] be assumed that the proportion of Jews in the Communist Party in 1961 was close to 2%, or 200,000 members and candidates.

However, if we extrapolate general conclusions directly from the specific data in Table 20, the proportion in the 1960s comes out considerably higher than 2%. Figures recently published on Lithuania also provide a figure there of over 3% of the CPSU membership in the early 1960s.[10] As against this, though, the new data from 1976 give the number of Jewish members as 294,000 or 1.9%. This percentage drop is to be explained by the rapid growth of the Party drawing on an enlarged urban population; by Jewish emigration (85,000 from 1961 to 1975); by the high age structure of the Jewish population; and, in all probability, by the various difficulties and inhibitions now facing Jewish candidates.

The only firm conclusion which we can draw from these data is that, while from 1940 to 1976 Jewish membership in the Communist Party decreased as a result of objective factors and probably of deliberate Soviet policy as well, the Jews still remained a nationality with high Party membership and continued to occupy an important place within the Party (this, too, because of objective factors noted above).

Jews in the supreme institutions of the Party

The institutions responsible for determining and implementing policy in the Soviet Union are a number of quite limited bodies comprising between 200 and 400 persons. It is, therefore, important to examine how many Jews were to be found among the select group at any given time.

During the first half of the twenties, Jews constituted between 16% and 23% of the Central Committee and between 23% and 37% of the Politburo. They had less weight in the Orgburo and the Secretariat. In the second half of the twenties, figures prominent in the first two institutions – among them Zinovyev, Kamenev and Trotsky – were removed from all their positions in the Party and, along with many other leaders of Jewish origin, dismissed or demoted. However, other Jews, some of whom had already held positions in the governmental machinery and the Party, now rose in the Party hierarchy: most notably M. Kaganovich, L. Kaganovich (Doc. 138), Lev Mekhlis (Doc. 137), M. L. Rukhimovich, A. A. Yakovlev (Epshtein) and the Generals Y. B. Gamarnik and I. E. Yakir.[11] As far as is known, with the exception of

Table 21. Jews in the Central Committee, 1939–71

	Members	Candidate members	Total	No. of Jews Members	No. of Jews Candidate members	No. of Jews Total	% of Jews
1939 – 18th Congress	71	68	139	11	3	14	10.10
1952 – 19th Congress	125	111	236	4	1	5	2.11
1956 – 20th Congress	133	122	255	3	1	4	1.57
1961 – 21st Congress	176	156	332	1	0	1	0.30
1966 – 22nd Congress	195	165	360	1	0	1	0.28
1971 – 23rd Congress	241	155	396	1	0	1	0.25

Sources: E. L. Crowley, A. J. Lebed & H. Schulz (eds.), *Party and Government Officials in the USSR*, Metuchen, New Jersey, The Scarecrow Press, 1969; *Bolshaya sovetskaya entsiklopediya* (Large Soviet Encyclopaedia), 2nd edition; *Pravda*, 9 and 10 April 1971.

Table 22. *List of Jewish members and candidate members of the Central Committee, 1939–71*

	Party Congresses					
	1939	1952	1956	1961	1966	1971
Members	11	4	3	1	1	1
N. M. Antselovich	Member till 1941 Candidate member from 1941					
V. Dymshits				/	/	/
L. M. Kaganovich	/	/	To 1957			
M. M. Kaganovich	/					
M. M. Litvinov	Member till 1941					
S. A. Lozovsky	To beginning of 1941					
Lev Mekhlis	/	Died 1953				
M. B. Mitin	/	/	/			
G. M. Shtern	To 1941					
B. L. Vannikov	/	/	/			
Y. Yaroslavsky	Died 1943					
R. S. Zemlyachka	/					
Candidate members	3	1	1			
David Raizer		/	/			
Ya. V. Smushkevich	To 1940					
G. D. Vainberg	To 1941					
P. Zhemchuzhina	To 1941					
Total number of members and candidate members	14	5	4	1	1	1

Sources: As Table 21.

L. Kaganovich and Mekhlis, all these men were liquidated during the great purges of 1936–9.

The Central Committee. As shown in Table 21, despite the great purges which swept away so many Jewish Communist leaders, Jews still occupied quite an important place on the Central Committee elected at the 18th Party Congress in 1939: fourteen members and candidates, or over 10% of the entire Central Committee, though as already noted, they probably constituted only slightly over 4% of the Party.[12] From this point of view their situation was no worse than it had been in the first half of the thirties.[13] Thus, there was apparently a balance between those expelled from the defeated factions and those loyal to Stalin who were able to rise in the Party hierarchy.

The shift towards the removal of Jews from the Central Committee began in the period of the Molotov–Ribbentrop Pact. At the 18th Party Conference in February 1941, six members, among them two Jews (Antselovich and Litvinov), were transferred from membership in the Central Committee to candidacy, and fifteen candidates, among them Vainberg and Zhemchuzhina (Molotov's wife) – both Jewish – were expelled, while there were no Jews among the seventeen new members and candidates.[14]

As a result of Stalin's extreme anti-Jewish policy between 1948 and 1952, there was a drastic decline in the number of Jews on the Central Committee: from 10.1% of the Committee in 1939 to 2.1% in 1952. And far from this process coming to a halt with Stalin's death, it was accelerated during the Khrushchev period. In 1956 there were still four Jewish members and candidates on the Central Committee (1.57%), approximately equalling their proportion in the Party. But, by 1961, only one Jew, Veniamin Dymshits (Doc. 143), remained (0.30%). As the number of Central Committee members increased, its percentage of Jews correspondingly decreased; at the 23rd Congress in 1966, it stood at 0.28%, and it reached a low point of 0.25% at the 1971 Congress.

When we examine the list (Table 22) of the Central Committee's Jewish members and candidates in 1939, and follow their fate during and after the war, we find that at least six of the fourteen were liquidated or arrested by Stalin. Two of them – Lozovsky (Doc. 142), who was executed on 12 August 1952 together with the Yiddish writers and cultural figures, and Zhemchuzhina, who was arrested in 1949 – were purged clearly because of their Jewishness.[15] The reasons why Smushkevich, Shtern and M. Kaganovich (Lazar Kaganovich's brother) were arrested are not known. Three others retained membership on the Committee for many years (from 1939 to 1956): L. Kaganovich, Vannikov (Doc. 141) and Mitin. The only prominent leaders who remained after 1946 were L. Kaganovich and Mekhlis; the others who continued to hold posts in the Party during the fifties were technocrats such as Vannikov and Raizer (Doc. 140), or merely representative figures, such as Professor Mitin.[16]

The Politburo, the Secretariat and the Orgburo. Since its inception, the Politburo has been the most influential body in the Party. Until 1927, three of its eight or nine members were Jews, whereas, in the thirty years between then until June 1957, its only Jewish member was Lazar Moiseevich Kaganovich, one of Stalin's close associates and always at his command. But, of course, it has to be remembered that this is a very restricted body (eleven members and candidates in 1939, thirty-six in 1952, seventeen in 1956).

Immediately following the Revolution, the Secretariat was headed by Yakov Sverdlov, a Jew, and Kaganovich and Yaroslavsky held important positions in the twenties and thirties. But, from the second half of the thirties until today, not one Jew has been elected to this body.

Jews occupied an important place in the Orgburo, particularly during the twenties and thirties; Kaganovich, Yaroslavsky, Gamarnik, Granik, Rukhimovich and Mekhlis were among its members. In 1939 the only Jews still to be found there were Kaganovich and Mekhlis, and by 1946 only Mekhlis remained.

The situation in the republics

We have no precise data on the proportion of Jews in the supreme Party institutions in the republics, but it is evident that the same process which operated at the centre was paralleled there. Thus, following the October Revolution, Jews occupied key Party positions in the various republics, especially in those that were underdeveloped and lacked local cadres. Fear of provincial opposition to the Bolshevik regime and of local nationalism meant that many emissaries from the centre, especially Russians and Jews, were despatched to the outlying regions. Among the many Jews who played a central role in the republics were the leaders Kaganovich, Popok, Khatayevich, Khatskevich and Dimanshteyn.

But, from the early fifties, Jews began to disappear from all key positions at the republic level – and this was true not only of first and second secretaries and of secretariat members, but also of representation at Party congresses and on the central committees. Among the few who still occupied any kind of responsible position in the Party during the period under discussion one may note Spivak, a regional secretary in the Ukraine, and Birenboim, who served as a Party regional council member in the Kiev Region. In Lithuania, where there were still several Jews on the Central Committee after the war, only one, G. Zimanas, remained throughout the period surveyed here (Elias Bilyavichus was also a Central Committee member until 1963). At the end of the fifties, the Komsomol secretary of the Vitebsk Region was Mikhelson, a Jew. In the two major cities of the RSFSR, Moscow and Leningrad, where large Jewish populations are concentrated (about 500,000 in 1965), elections to the local committees brought the following results: in Moscow, three Jewish delegates out of 178 were elected to the urban branch and in Leningrad, two (or three) out of 122, or about 2% representation, whereas Jews constitute about 5% of the total population of each city.

In the late sixties, several Jews still held various positions at the lower level of the senior administration in Party institutions, but, as one may see from the list below (which is very possibly incomplete), this was a miniscule group which only throws the remarkable decline in the number of office-holders of Jewish origin into even greater relief. According to what can be winnowed from the Soviet press, these officials were: Zevin, head of the Department for the History of the Communist Party in the secretariat of the Central Committee; Vengersky, a senior official on the Central Committee of the Uzbek Republic; and Faikin, a senior official on the Central Committee of the Kirgiz Republic.

Jews in the representative institutions of the USSR

Although, in terms of their political and practical importance, the Soviet parliamentary institutions lack decisive authority in the country's network of ruling institutions, the Supreme Soviet of the Union, the supreme soviets of

Table 23. Jews in the Supreme Soviet of the USSR, 1937–74

Supreme Soviet	Number of delegates			Jewish delegates				Jewish population	Percentage of population
	Soviet of Union	Soviet of Nationalities	Total	Soviet of Union	Soviet of Nationalities	Total	Percentage of Jewish delegates		
1937–46	569	574	1,143	32	15	47	4.10	3,020,000 (1939)	1.8
1946–50	682	657	1,339	6	7	13*	0.97		
1950–54	678	638	1,316	3	5	8*	0.60		
1954–58	708	639	1,347	3	4	7*	0.52	2,268,000 (1959)	1.1
1958–62	738	646	1,384	2	3	5	0.36		
1962–66	791	652	1,443	2	3	5	0.35		
1966–70	767	750	1,517	2	3	5	0.32	2,151,000 (1970)	0.9
1970–74	767	750	1,517	2	4	6	0.39		

* There are no official figures. The calculation was made on the basis of the delegates' names. The margin of error is minimal (see Table 24).

Sources: M. G. Kirichenko, Verkhovny Sovet SSSR (The USSR Supreme Soviet), Moscow, 1962, p. 75; Vybory v Verkhovny Sovet SSSR i v Verkhovnye Sovety soyuznykh i avtonomnykh respublik 1937–1938 (Elections to the USSR Supreme Soviet and to the Supreme Soviets of the Union and Autonomous Republics 1937–1938), Moscow, Izdatelstvo vedomostei Verkhovnogo Soveta RSFSR, 1939, p. 11; Pravda, 15 February 1946; Izvestiya, 18 March 1954; Izvestiya, 19 March 1958; Deputaty Verkhovnogo Soveta SSSR (Deputies of the USSR Supreme Soviet), Moscow, Izvestiya Sovetov Deputatov Trudyashchikhsya SSSR, Shestoi sozyv (Sixth Convocation), 1962; Sedmoi sozyv (Seventh Convocation), 1966; Vosmoi sozyv (Eighth Convocation), 1970.

the republics and the local soviets hold a prominent place, at least in terms of formal status. In what follows we shall examine the place of the Jews in these bodies.

The Jews in the Supreme Soviet of the USSR

In the 1937 elections in the USSR, the first following ratification of the new constitution (December 1936), there were 47 Jews among the 1,143 delegates elected to the Supreme Soviet. Thus, the Jews constituted 4.1% of the delegates of the two houses, whereas they then constituted only about 1.8% of the country's population. Because of the war, this convocation of the Supreme Soviet continued for nine years instead of the four fixed by the constitution.

The decisive shift in representation of Jews was already visible in the 1946 elections to the Supreme Soviet. (This shift was not discernible in the Party itself until the first post-war elections to the Central Committee were held in 1952.) As shown in Table 23, there was a precipitous decline in the number of Jewish delegates in 1946 (0.97%), as compared with 1937, whereas the Jewish population as a whole had decreased by about a third since 1939 (the post-war population was approximately 2,100,000, if we discount those Jews who concealed their national origin). A further drastic decline occurred in the last elections to the Supreme Soviet held during Stalin's life, when the anti-Jewish campaign, in the guise of a struggle against cosmopolitanism and nationalism, was at its peak. Thus, in 1950, only eight Jewish delegates were elected out of a total of 1,316 (0.60%).

The situation remained virtually static in the elections held about a year after Stalin's death, in 1954, with the second substantive change occurring in 1958 under Khrushchev, when the percentage of Jewish delegates fell to 0.36%. This situation continued until 1966 (0.35%), although according to official data Jews constituted 1.1% of the population in 1959. Thus, in contrast to the Central Committee, where Jewish 'under-representation' began only in 1961, in the most representative body in the country and one elected by the entire population the same trend began as early as 1946.

The reason for the increase by one delegate in the elections of 1970 is amply clear: to demonstrate that, at least in the Jewish Autonomous Region of Birobidzhan, there was high Jewish representation (two delegates out of the five elected by the region). It is interesting that, apart from the elections of 1946 and 1970, Birobidzhan never had more than one Jew in its five-man delegation to the Supreme Soviet.

From an analysis of the data in Table 24 together with material from additional sources, we can provide the following information on the Jewish delegates.

Length of term of office in the Supreme Soviet. The scientist Yuly Khariton was elected for the most terms – six, or twenty-four consecutive years; the writer Ilya Erenburg was elected for five terms; and Lazar Kaganovich for four terms (including the first convocation of the Supreme Soviet from 1937 to 1946). Three Jewish delegates were elected for three terms each: the engineer S. Lavochkin, Professor Mark Mitin and the Deputy Premier Veniamin

Table 24. *Jewish delegates to the Supreme Soviet, 1946–70*

Name of delegate	Place of election	Convocations of the Supreme Soviet						
		2	3	4	5	6	7	8
1. Abelman, Mikhail Iosifovich	Birobidzhan – RSFSR							—
2. Bakhmutsky, Aleksandr Naumovich	Birobidzhan – RSFSR	—						
3. Chakovsky, Aleksandr Borisovich	Mordvinian Autonomous Republic – RSFSR						—	—
4. Dymshits, Veniamin Emmanuilovich	Khabarovsk – RSFSR				—	—	—	—
5. Erenburg, Ilya Grigoryevich	Stalin Region and Daugavpils – Latvia	—	—	—	—	—	—	
6. Freidkina, Rakhil Grigoryevna	Birobidzhan – RSFSR	—						
7. Geiko, Anna Abramovna*	Kazakhstan	—	—					
8. Ginzburg, Semen Zakharovich	Borisov – Belorussia	—						
9. Gleizer, Vera Yakovlevna	Birobidzhan – RSFSR			—				
10. Glikas, Kostas Yakubovich	Šakiai Province – Lithuania							—
11. Goldenberg, Rozaliya Mikhailovna	Birobidzhan – RSFSR	—						
12. Kaganovich, Lazar Moiseevich	Tashkent Province – Uzbekistan	—	—	—				
13. Khariton, Yuly Borisovich	Gorky Province and Leningrad – RSFSR			—	—	—	—	—
14. Khersonsky, Rafail Khaimovich	Birobidzhan – RSFSR					—		
15. Kluger Anna Ilievna	Teleneshty Region – Moldavia	—	—					
16. Kochina, Shifra Markovna	Birobidzhan - RSFSR	—						
17. Kreizer, Yakov Grigoryevich	Far Eastern Territory – RSFSR					—		
18. Lavochkin, Semen Alekseevich	Bashkir Autonomous Republic – RSFSR			—	—	—		
19. Litvinov, Maksim Maksimovich	Karelo – Finnish Republic	—						
20. Lozovsky, Solomon Abramovich	Kirgizia	—						
21. Mekhlis, Lev Zakharovich	Kamenets-Podolsk – Ukraine		—					
22. Mitin, Mark Borisovich	Irkutsk Province – RSFSR	—	—	—				
23. Peller, Vladimir Izrailevich	Birobidzhan – RSFSR				—			
24. Spivak, Moisei Semenovich	Zhitomir – Ukraine	—						
25. Vailand, David Zemilovich	Latvia	—						
26. Vannikov, Boris Lvovich	Novosibirsk Province – RSFSR	—						
27. Vishchinkina, Riva Evseevna	Birobidzhan – RSFSR					—		
28. Zaltsman, Isaak Moiseevich	Chelyabinsk Province – RSFSR	—						
29. Zemlyachka, Rozaliya Samoilovna	Kursk Province – RSFSR	—						

* We are not certain that she is Jewish.
Source: As Table 23; also Soviet press and standard biographical sources.

Dymshits; and three delegates were elected twice: Geiko, Chakovsky and Kluger. The large majority (twenty delegates) were elected for only one term during the thirty-year period starting in 1937.

Geographical representation. The largest number of delegates elected in the period 1946–70 (nine out of twenty-nine or 31%) represented the RSFSR (apart from Birobidzhan); the Jewish Autonomous Region was also represented by nine delegates. The Ukraine, where 40% of all the Jews of the Soviet Union are concentrated, chose only two delegates of Jewish origin during those same twenty-four years. There was a relatively high Jewish representation in the Latvian Republic (two delegates), but in republics such as Belorussia, Georgia and Moldavia Jews received very low representation, or none at all, over this same lengthy period.

Professional composition. We have succeeded in clarifying the professions of twenty-four of the twenty-nine Jewish delegates listed in Table 24. The largest group (nine delegates) comprised government officials or Party functionaries (or both together); three of them were engineers and the rest Foreign Ministry employees or heads of various offices. The second largest group (five delegates) was composed of agricultural workers, mainly kolkhoz chairmen in Birobidzhan and Lithuania, but also some agronomists. The list also includes two writers (Erenburg and Chakovsky), two scholars (Khariton and Mitin), two engineers, one woman doctor, one teacher, one metal-worker and one general in active service (Yakov Kreizer). Finally, it should be noted that only nine of the twenty-nine Jewish delegates listed filled important posts in the Party and government.

It is worth recalling that the first two chairmen of the Supreme Central Executive Committee of the Soviets (later to be transformed into the Presidium of the Supreme Soviet) were Jews: Kamenev (from 7 November 1917 until 7 January 1918) and Sverdlov (from 18 January 1918 until his death on 16 March 1919). Jews also occupied important positions on the Presidium in the twenties and thirties. However, we know of only one instance of a Jew on the Presidium since the war (and we are not even absolutely certain as regards him); this was Natalevich, Deputy Chairman of the Presidium of the Supreme Soviet, who was relieved of this post on 16 March 1949.[17]

Jews in the supreme soviets of the republics

The only complete data published in the USSR on the supreme soviets of the Union and the autonomous republics, as well as on the local government, were for the year 1959. Partial data exist for 1963 and 1971 (on republics) and for 1965 (on the local government).[18] A study of Table 25 evinces the following as regards the proportion of Jews in the supreme soviets of the republics and the local soviets.

The supreme soviets of the Union republics. A comparison of column 3 (percentage of Jews in the supreme soviets of the republics) with column 7 (percentage of Jews in the population) shows that only in the Kazakh, Lithuanian and

Table 25. Percentage of Jews in the supreme soviets of the republics and in the local soviets, 1959

	Supreme soviets of the republics			Local soviets			Percentage of Jews in population (1959 Census)
	Number of delegates	Jewish delegates	% of Jews	Number of delegates	Jewish delegates	% of Jews	
Union republics							
RSFSR	835	1	0.12	972,004	3,471	0.36	0.70
Ukrainian	457	1	0.22	381,477	1,966	0.52	2.00
Belorussian	407	2	0.49	77,944	853	1.09	1.90
Uzbek	444	2	0.45	58,826	261	0.44	1.20
Kazakh	450	2	0.44	81,186	337	0.42	0.30
Georgian	368	0	—	49,429	62	0.15	1.30
Azerbaidzhan	325	1	0.31	33,120	100	0.30	1.10
Lithuanian	209	3	1.44	33,171	74	0.23	0.90
Moldavian	281	0	—	26,518	210	0.79	3.30
Latvian	200	0	—	20,876	88	0.42	1.70
Kirgiz	329	0	—	17,493	83	0.48	0.40
Tadzhik	300	1	0.33	14,880	50	0.34	0.60
Turkmen	282	1	0.36	14,123	38	0.27	0.30
Armenian	300	0	—	17,882	4	0.02	0.10
Estonian	125	0	—	11,731	27	0.23	0.50
Autonomous republics							
Dagestan	152	1	0.60*				2.00
Tatar	194	1	0.50*				0.40
Chuvash	140	1	0.70*				insignificant
Yakut	165	1	0.60*				insignificant

* These figures, reproduced from the source cited below, have been rounded to one decimal place.

Source: Sostav deputatov Verkhovnykh Sovetov soyuznykh, avtonomnykh respublik i mestnykh sovetov deputatov trudyashchikhsya (The Composition of the Deputies of the Supreme Soviets of the Union and Autonomous Republics and Local Soviets of Workers' Deputies), Moscow, Izvestiya, 1959. pp. 12, 13, 22, 23, 70–85.

Table 26. *Jewish delegates to the supreme soviets of the republics, 1940s–1960s*

Name	Republic	Period of office
1. Benkovich, Lev	RSFSR	1950s
2. Bilyavichyus, Elias	Lithuanian Republic	1950s and 1960s
3. Dragunsky, David	Georgian and Armenian Republics	1950s and 1960s
4. Gosdiner-Roshchinkiner	RSFSR (?)	1960s
5. Gurvich, Y. G.	Azerbaidzhan Republic	1960s
6. Khazan-Andreeva, Dora	RSFSR	1940s
7. Kreizer, Yakov	RSFSR and Ukrainian Republic	1950s and 1960s
8. Malkin, Iosif Mikhailovich	Kazakh Republic	1950s and 1960s
9. Ratner, Shakhna	RSFSR	1950s
10. Shildkrot, M. A.	RSFSR	1960s
11. Yegudin, A. A.	Ukrainian Republic	1960s
12. Zimanas, Genrik	Lithuanian Republic	1950s and 1960s

Source: As Table 23.

Turkmen republics did the representation of Jews in the supreme Soviet exceed their percentage in the population. In republics such as the Ukraine, Belorussia and the RSFSR, those with the largest proportion of Jews in the population, the absolute and relative Jewish representation would be expected to be high. For example, if representation in the Ukraine had been in proportion to population, the Jews would have had about ten delegates, whereas they never had more than one. In the Moldavian Republic, where Jews constituted 3.3% of the population, not even one delegate of Jewish origin was elected in 1959.

If we calculate the average for all fifteen republics for the year 1959, we find that the Jews had only 0.26% of all delegates to the supreme soviets, whereas they then constituted 1.1% of the population of the Soviet Union. In 1963, there was a further slight decline, to 0.23% (thirteen Jewish delegates out of a total of 5,761). This downward trend was halted in 1971, when Jews constituted nineteen delegates or 0.32% of the 5,879 elected.[19]

We can therefore conclude that the official policy of restricting the number of Jews in the supreme ruling institutions was applied even more stringently in the republics than in the central government.[20] This trend was, no doubt, the result of nationalism and of the preferential representation which is granted the dominant local nationality at the expense of outsiders, or at least of those outsiders belonging to a national group bereft of political influence.

Supreme soviets in the autonomous republics. In 1959, Jews lacked representation in fifteen of the nineteen autonomous republics. However, it must be remembered that there are only about 110,000 Jews in these republics, and that even the four where Jews were represented have a very sparse Jewish population. Jewish representation at this level (in all nineteen such republics) was therefore extremely low – only 0.15%. However, there was a definite increase in 1963, when eleven Jewish delegates were elected out of 2,892 (0.38%) in all the autonomous republics. In 1971, there were nine Jewish delegates out of 2,994, or 0.30%.[21]

The local soviets. In the majority of the republics, Jewish representation at the local level is higher than that in the supreme soviet of the republic (see Table 25, columns 3 and 6). Thus, it is three times as high in the RSFSR, 2.5 times as high in the Ukraine, and more than twice as high in Belorussia. It is significantly lower only in the Uzbek, Kazakh and Lithuanian republics. Jewish representation in the local soviets is also higher on average than their representation in the Supreme Soviet of the USSR.

Although such Soviet sources as the *communiqués* of the *Novosti* news agency and the declarations made by 'representatives' of Soviet Jewry emphasise the large number of Jewish delegates elected to local soviets, they avoid indicating their percentage among all delegates. Thus, while Table 25 does indeed show that 7,624 Jewish delegates were elected in 1959, this figure constitutes less than 0.5% of all delegates to soviets for that year, whereas the Jews then constituted 1.1% of the population. There was a further decline in Jewish representation in 1965, when 0.4% of all the delegates elected were Jewish.[22]

Names of Jewish delegates elected to the supreme soviets of the republics. As no list of these delegates has ever been published in the Soviet Union, we have given only a partial enumeration collected from diverse sources (see Table 26). Many of the delegates to the Supreme Soviet (Table 24) were also elected during various periods to the supreme Soviet of their republics, for example, Vannikov in the RSFSR and Kaganovich in the Ukraine.

In sum, given the tendency of many Jews to engage in political activity – as was clear in the twenties and thirties – and given the general tendency to appoint educated people as delegates (at least to the supreme soviets), the percentage of Jews in the soviets should have been immeasurably higher than it was. And, since their highest representation was less than 0.5% (in local government) and their lowest 0.15% (in the supreme soviets of the autonomous republics), one is drawn to the inevitable conclusion that this phenomenon represents a consistent trend deriving not only from objective factors, but also from a deliberate policy of the Soviet leadership.

Jews in the Soviet government

Although official policy is determined by the supreme institutions of the Party, there is no doubt that the government and the senior administrations of the various ministries exert a significant influence in all spheres of life, the more so since in the USSR those heading the government are also members of the top Party leadership.

Jews in the government of the Soviet Union and in the governments of the Union republics

While no study has yet been made of the extent of Jewish participation in the governments of the republics during the twenties and thirties, it is known that

Jews occupied a no less notable position in the central government than they did in the Party and the soviets. The question then is: did the same process of reduction in Jewish representation which began during or before World War II take place in the Soviet government as a whole, and if so, was its extent and degree similar to that in the Party institutions and the soviets? We shall attempt to answer these questions on the data we have managed to collect.

The Prime Minister and his deputies. None of the eight Prime Ministers who held office in the first fifty years of the Soviet regime's existence (1917–67) were Jewish. One Jew, Lazar Moiseevich Kaganovich, held the office of First Deputy Prime Minister from 1953 to 1957, until he was relieved of all his Party posts in June 1957. During the years 1939–67, the following served as deputy prime ministers: Rozaliya Samoilovna Zemlyachka (1939–43); Lev Zakharovich Mekhlis (March–May 1941); Lazar Moiseevich Kaganovich (1944–53); Veniamin Imanuelovich Dymshits (1962–). It should be noted that as regards the deputy prime ministership Jews were far better represented than many other nationalities in the USSR, including those of the Union republics. Except for the years 1957–61, we find Jews represented in this important office throughout most of the period covered.

Ministers and deputy ministers. It is far from simple to classify the posts of minister and deputy minister in the USSR, because its government is composed of various kinds of ministers with immense differences in authority. Rather than enter into this labyrinth, we shall examine this question in a purely formal manner.

As may be seen from Table 27, there is a clear watershed in the representation of Jews at this level, namely the year 1946. During 1939–46, eight Jews still served in the Council of Ministers, four of them (Ginzburg, Vannikov, Mekhlis and L. Kaganovich) throughout almost the entire period. Four Jews held the post of deputy minister.[23] In 1947, however, the number dropped precipitously to two ministers and no deputy minister. While David Raizer was appointed as a minister in 1950, he in fact replaced Lev Mekhlis, another Jewish minister (it is unclear whether this was coincidence or policy) who resigned (or was dismissed?) from his post because of illness (see Doc. 136).

We have divided the years 1954–70 into three periods that accord with the accepted periodisation of Soviet history and also mark the gradual removal of Jews from the Soviet government. In fact, during 1954–7, until Khrushchev's final victory over his rivals of the 'Anti-Party Group', Jews continued to occupy a strong position in the government: L. Kaganovich was First Deputy of the Prime Minister (as well as Minister of Railways) and Raizer was Minister for the Construction of Heavy Industry Enterprises. With the expulsions of Kaganovich in June 1957 (it is unclear whether his national origins played a part here) and Raizer (for no apparent reason), Jewish representation in the government was totally eliminated. There was no Jewish minister from 1958 to 1961, and only one deputy minister: Veniamin Dymshits, who may be seen as having enjoyed a ministerial rank because of his position on the *Gosplan* (State Planning Committee). There was no substantive change in this policy following Khrushchev's removal, when the

Table 27. *Jewish ministers and deputy ministers in the government of the USSR, 1939–70*

Name of minister/ deputy minister	Position and ministry	1939–46	1946–53	1954–7	1957–64	1965–70
Antselovich, N. M.	Minister and Deputy Minister of Timber Industry	1939–40, 1945–?				
Berman, M. D.	Minister of Communications	1937–9				
Bokserman, Yuly	Deputy Minister of Gas Industry				?	1965–70
Dymshits, V. E.	Minister (Chairman and Deputy Chairman) of State Planning Commission and of Council of National Economy		1950–1957 Deputy Minister		Minister from 1962	
Ginzburg, S. Z.	Minister of Construction	1939–46	1946–50			
Glikman, Leonid	Deputy Minister of Machine Building and Chemical Industry				?	1965–70
Kaganovich, L. M.	Minister of Railways and of Building Materials Industry			1956–7		
Kaganovich, M. M.	Minister of Defence Industry	1938–44				
Khazan-Andreeva, D. M.	Deputy Minister of Textile Industry and of Light Industry	1936–9				
Levinsky, Avram	Deputy Minister of Electrical Engineering Industry	1939–46			?	1965–70
Litvinov, M. M.	Deputy Foreign Minister	1943–6				
Lozovsky, S. A.	Deputy Foreign Minister and Chairman of Soviet Information Bureau	1939–46	1946–8			
Mekhlis, L. Z.	Minister of State Control	1940–5	1946–50			
Ogorets, Y. I.	Deputy Minister of Electrical Energy	1939–46				
Raizer, D. Ya.	Minister of Construction of Heavy Industry Enterprises		1950–3	1954–7		
Vannikov, B. L.	Minister of Armaments	1939–46				
Zhemchuzhina-Molotov, P.	Minister of Fishing Industry	1939–40				

Sources: E. L. Crowley, A. J. Lebed & H. Schulz (eds.), *Party and Government Officials in the USSR*, Metuchen, New Jersey, 1969; *Bolshaya sovetskaya entsiklopediya* (Large Soviet Encyclopedia), 2nd edition; *Pravda*, 9 and 10 April 1971; *Ezhegodnik bolshoi sovetskoi entsiklopedii* (Yearbook of the Large Soviet Encyclopaedia), 1957–70; S. Rabinovich, *Jews in the Soviet Union*, Moscow, Novosti, 1966; *Soviet Jews: Facts and Fiction*, Moscow, Novosti, 1970; *Sovetish heymland*, 1970, no. 3 (appendix).

sole remaining Jew in the government was Veniamin Dymshits, who had been elected to his post in 1962, that is, under Khrushchev. The appointment of Bokserman, Glikman and Levinsky as deputy ministers improved Jewish representation at that level, but we have not been able to discover the year or years in which they were appointed to their posts. (Iosif Ravich's status is insufficiently clear.)

Not only did the number of posts given to Jews decrease under Khrushchev, far more so than in the period that followed, but Khrushchev and his various spokesmen justified this development by claiming that preference must now be given to those nationalities previously deprived for historical and other reasons. They did not attempt to explain why this representation had to be granted primarily at the expense of the Jews.[24]

Taking only the ministerial level and ignoring that of deputy minister, we find a decline no less precipitous than in the supreme Party institutions or in the supreme and local soviets. Table 27 shows that while there had been eight Jews with ministerial rank in the years 1939–46, there was only one in the sixties. However, in terms of relative weight in the government (a limited body of fifty to seventy persons), the Jews still had a preference over other nationalities, their proportion in the government exceeding their ratio in the population (1.79% in 1962 and 1.45% in 1966).

It is interesting that of the seventeen ministries in which Jews held office in 1939–70, fourteen were clearly economic ministries (and not always of primary importance), one was a general ministry (State Control) and one, the Foreign Ministry. There were no Jews in the two most important ministries – Defence and Interior – after the end of the thirties, whereas Trotsky had headed the former until 1925 and Yagoda the latter in the thirties.

The lack of any systematic data makes it difficult to analyse the position of the Jews in the ministries of the republics. As regards ministers or deputy ministers, it emerges that there has not been a single Jew in the governments of the republics since the beginning of the sixties (whereas in the twenties and even the thirties there had been numerous ministers of Jewish origin in most of the republics).[25] In the fifties we know of A. A. Goldberg, who was Minister of Health of the Estonian Republic, and E. Bilyavichus, Minister of Fisheries in the Lithuanian Republic.[26] From the data we have been able to gather on deputy ministers, which is certainly incomplete, we can mention: Y. G. Shapiro, Deputy Minister of Light Industry in the Ukraine, who was relieved of his post in February 1949;[27] L. S. Paperno, Deputy Minister of Construction in Belorussia;[28] and I. I. Bulat, Deputy Minister of Construction in Moldavia from 1963 to 1967.[29]

Jews in the senior administration

The difficulties in finding reliable data on the proportion of Jews in the various institutions mentioned above pale to insignificance alongside the search for any data at all on the senior administration. Nevertheless, we shall attempt to provide a list of Jews who occupied important positions in that governmental sector we have defined as senior administration: the directors and deputy directors of the various government ministries, and the heads of those committees and councils which enjoyed a status equivalent to ministries.

The senior administration at the central level. Although no thorough study has yet been made of Jews in the senior administration at the central level and in the republics during the twenties and thirties, the significance of their role in this important area is well known.[30] But their situation after World War II is less clear, as is the truth about reports to the effect that all the ministries were 'purged' of senior administrators of Jewish origin during the 'Black Years' (1948–53).

There is no doubt that the final years of Stalin's life, when his anti-Jewish policy disguised as a campaign against cosmopolitanism, bourgeois nationalism and Zionism ran rampant, saw many Jews dismissed from positions in the realms of higher education, art and culture: this phenomenon has been amply documented. It is more difficult to discover how the purge affected senior administrators in central government institutions, although there is no doubt that it did strike in this sphere as well. The information available about the many open and secret trials of the early fifties, in which engineers and directors of economic enterprises were indicted, clearly shows that senior Jewish administrators fell victim to the purges. However, we have no exact information on who was expelled, from which ministries, and when.

What we do know is that all or nearly all the Jews were expelled from all branches of the Ministry of Defence (especially the counter-espionage and other clandestine services);[31] the Foreign Ministry, in which quite a large number of Jews had served as late as the forties (for example, Yakov Surits, USSR Ambassador to Brazil until 1946; Borish Shtein, member of the Soviet delegation to the UN and holder of important posts in the Ministry until 1952; Khefets, consul in San Francisco during the war); and the Ministry of Foreign Trade.

To the best of our knowledge, the only Jew who held a position of any importance in the Soviet Foreign Ministry throughout the 1960s was L. I. Mendelevich, who was a member of the Political Committee of the UN and later served as Director of the Latin American department.[32] An examination of the list of ambassadors and embassy staffs of the Soviet Union from the late fifties until 1967 has failed to turn up one Jewish name. It is also known that since the 1940s Jews have not been admitted to the special educational institutes where cadres for the Foreign Ministry are trained.

In the twenties and even in the thirties, the Ministry of the Interior – so prodigiously important in the Soviet regime – employed many Communist activists of Jewish origin; this information was often exploited by anti-Semitic propagandists within the Soviet Union and in the West. (The names of NKVD heads Yagoda, Shpigelglas, Slutsky, Rapoport, Kogan, Berman, Brodsky and many others cast dread until most of them fell victim to the regime of terror they themselves had served and fostered.) The claim that Beria recruited many Jews to key positions has received no factual confirmation. While Jews were still employed in the lower echelons of the ministry and in the services subordinate to it throughout the 1960s, it would appear that they no longer held positions at the senior administrative level.

Table 28. *Jews as senior government officials, 1950s and 1960s*

Babichkov, Abram Mikhailovich	Senior official in the Ministry of Transport
Eidelman, Moisei Ruvimovich	Departmental Director at the Central Statistics Board
Ginzburg, Semen Zakharovich	Chairman of the Board of Directors of a Construction Bank
Levitin, Mikhail Abramovich	Deputy Director of OKB (since 1967)
Maizenberg, Lev	Deputy Director of the State Prices Committee of the State Planning Commission of the USSR
Mendelevich, L. I.	Director of the Latin American Department of the Foreign Ministry
Ravich, Iosif	Director (or Deputy Minister) in the Ministry of Communications
Rimsky, Lev Abramovich	Departmental Director in the Ministry for Party and State Control
Shendler, Yu. I.	Deputy Director of a department of the State Planning Commission
Turin, Natan Markovich	Deputy Director of 'Glavspetspromstroi'
Volodarsky, Lev	Deputy Director of the Central Statistics Board

Sources: As in Table 27.

As regards senior administrators of Jewish origin in other ministries – especially in the economic ministries – and their proportion in the overall senior administration, we have only partial information. If the meagre list of names given in Table 28, which is based on the *Large Soviet Encyclopaedia* and on reports in the Soviet press during the years 1960–8, is in fact complete, it certainly demonstrates that the Jews constituted an extremely low percentage of the senior administration in the Soviet Union.

We have no data on the senior administration in two non-ministerial institutions of nonetheless great importance in the USSR: the Procuracy and the Supreme Court. That there seems to have been a few Jews who still held various positions in these two institutions in the sixties is not surprising considering the high proportion of Jewish jurists in the USSR, but even they did not occupy what we define as senior administrative positions.[33] Although there were high army officers of Jewish origin still occupying important positions in the late sixties, lack of data for comparison does not allow us to determine the extent to which the general process of reduction operated here. It is, however, clear that it was no less effective in the army than in other institutions.[34]

Senior Jewish administrators in the republics. Although the situation at this level varied from republic to republic, there seems to have been little essential difference between them and the centre. In the RSFSR, we found four Jews holding senior positions in the ministries. The most important post, that of Deputy Procurator of the RSFSR, was held by Aron Grigoryevich Kogan; the other three posts were two directorships and one deputy directorship in economic departments. Of the three Jews who held senior positions in Belorussia, the most important post was held by Petr Shvartsbund, who was Acting Chairman of the republic's *Gosplan*. In the Ukraine, with its large Jewish population, we found only two Jews in senior positions: Kucher and Polyakov. The same applies to the Latvian Republic. In Georgia, the President of the Chamber of Commerce was Rafael Eligulashvili. It would appear that some other republics also had a few Jews as department heads during this period.

The very fact that there are so few details on Jews holding senior administrative positions in the various republics that it is impossible to draw any general conclusions is perhaps the most telling statement that can be made on the position of Jews in this area.

An analysis of the statistical data cited in this chapter conclusively demonstrates that there was a relentless process of reduction in Jewish representation in Soviet government between 1939 and 1970. There seems no doubt, moreover, that this decline was not evenly spaced but was marked by periodic sweeps aimed to accelerate its progress. For there is a clear correlation between the general policy of the regime on the Jewish question at any given moment and the rate of this reduction in virtually all the ruling institutions discussed herein. The situation may be summarised as follows.

The years 1939–41. Under the influence of the change in foreign policy which came with the signing of the Ribbentrop–Molotov Pact, a policy of reducing the number of Jews in Soviet government was apparently also adopted. This trend found expression in Litvinov's dismissal from the post of Foreign Minister; in the restriction of Jewish representation on the Central Committee; and in the decline in the number of Jewish ministers. Some Jewish delegates were also expelled from the Supreme Soviet as part of this process.

The years 1941–5. There were two opposing tendencies at work, one apparently cancelling the other out to a large extent. While the anti-Jewish policy which had begun at the end of the thirties continued, the requirements of the war effort led to the reinstatement of some Jews (among them, Litvinov and Antselovich) to their former positions.

The years 1946–53. During this period there was a decisive shift in Jewish representation in all the institutions of Soviet government. It was in this period, which began with the change in internal policy in 1946 and of foreign policy in 1947, and which has justly been named the period of *Zhdanovshchina*, that the organised and systematic campaign against bourgeois nationalism, cosmopolitanism and Zionism hit hardest at the Jews of the Soviet Union.

The years 1953–6. Although witnessing major internal power struggles, these years may be seen as static from the point of view of Jewish representation:

there was only a minor decline in such representation in the institutions of Soviet power.

The years 1956–64. The years of Khrushchev's ascendancy saw a second shift – though far less dramatic than in 1946–53 – in Jewish representation. The change was especially discernible on the Central Committee, in the Politburo, in the government and, less sharply, in the Supreme Soviet.

The years 1965–70. Under the collective leadership, there was no significant change in this area (as there was none in many other areas) from the previous period. In fact, there was even a slight rise in Jewish representation in the Supreme Soviet and the government, probably the result of influence from abroad.

Our principal conclusion is that, at least as early as 1946, there was a clear and consistent policy of reducing Jewish representation in the Party and government to the lowest possible minimum. This does not in itself demonstrate that there was a kind of 'master-plan' involved. However, in view of the mechanism of elections and appointments in the Soviet Union, under which candidates must either be directly proposed by the highest authority or at least receive *post factum* approval from above, it is clear that the top leadership controls every appointment to office. And there is no doubt that national origin, a factor of decisive importance in the Soviet Union, has been taken into account when selecting candidates for office.

Finally, although it is self-evident, it should be emphasised that we in no way mean to imply that Jewish representation or Jewish representatives in Soviet government should be seen as representing the interests of the Soviet Jewish population. The opposite may indeed be the case. For, far from seeing themselves as representatives of Soviet Jewry, most of these Communist leaders would have been happy to be rid of the doubtful privilege of being considered Jews. Their relation to Jewry was confined to their having been born Jews, and they generally attempted to keep their distance from any Jewish matter, and to shun any action liable to arouse the suspicion that they had Jewish ties. It is here that the tragedy of generations of Jewish Communists lies. They devoted their entire lives to what they saw as a lofty end, assuming that its triumph would bring with it the solution to their own nationality problem. But they, too, encountered a reality that cruelly refuted this hope and this assumption.

Documents to Chapter 9

Document 136* Shift in Jewish ministers (1950)

Comrade S. Z. Ginzburg[35] was relieved of his post of Minister of the Building Materials Industry of the USSR by the Presidium of the Supreme Soviet of the USSR.

David Yakovlevich Raizer[36] was appointed Minister for the Construction of Heavy Industry Enterprises by the Presidium of the Supreme Soviet of the USSR.

Document 137† Obituary of Mekhlis (1953)

Lev Zakharovich Mekhlis, one of the outstanding figures of the Communist Party and the Soviet government, a member of the Central Committee of the Communist Party of the Soviet Union, died on 13 February 1953 after a prolonged and serious illness.

L. Z. Mekhlis devoted his whole conscious life to the Soviet people. Mekhlis was born in 1889 and started his active working life at a young age. In 1911 he was called up for military service. During World War I he served in the artillery.

In March 1918 he entered the ranks of the Communist Party. During the Civil War he performed active military work as a brigade and division commissar, as well as a commissar of the Right-Bank army group in the Ukraine.

At the conclusion of the Civil War Mekhlis was given a leading position by the Party in the People's Commissariat of Workers' and Peasants' Inspection. Afterwards he worked for five years on the staff of the Central Committee of the Party.

In 1930, as a graduate of the Institute of Red Professors, Mekhlis was assigned to work on the editorial board of *Pravda*. In carrying out responsible work for *Pravda*, he conducted an active struggle for the general line of the Party against its enemies and the enemies of the Soviet people.

From 1937 to September 1940 Mekhlis was head of the Chief Political Administration of the Red Army. He took part in the rout of the Japanese aggressors at Lake Khasan and in the district of Halhin-Gol.

* *Source*: 'Khronika' (News Items), *Izvestiya*, 30 May 1950.
† *Source*: 'Lev Zakharovich Mekhlis', *Izvestiya*, 14 February 1953.

In 1940 Mekhlis was appointed People's Commissar of State Control of the USSR. There he conducted an energetic struggle for state discipline, and against violations of Soviet legality.

From the first day of the Great Patriotic War, L. Z. Mekhlis was once again assigned by the Central Committee of the Party to work in the Soviet army. He spent the war years on the battle fronts as a member of the Military Soviets of the Army and Fronts. The Soviet government conferred the rank of General on him.

After the Great Patriotic War, Mekhlis was again appointed Minister of State Control of the USSR.

He was bedridden during his last years, suffering from a serious illness.

The Soviet government held the services of L. Z. Mekhlis to the people and motherland in high esteem. Mekhlis was awarded four Orders of Lenin; two Orders of the Red Banner; the Order of the Red Star; the Order of Kutuzov, First Class; the Order of Suvorov, First Class; and many medals. Mekhlis was a faithful son of the Party of Lenin and Stalin and was, to the end, devoted to his socialist motherland. He will always be remembered by the Soviet people for having devoted all his efforts to the building of Communism.

Document 138* Podgorny attacks Kaganovich[37] as a member of the 'Anti-Party Group' (1961)

Comrades! From the height of our achievements it is especially clear to each of us what enormous importance the decisive rout of the Anti-Party Group by the Party Central Committee had for the life of our Party and the entire country. By sweeping these despicable, bankrupt intriguers from its path our Party has indeed straightened its shoulders. It has become easier to breathe and to look ahead more alertly and clearly.

The Central Committee report states with absolute correctness that Molotov, Kaganovich, Malenkov and Voroshilov opposed the Party line of condemning the cult of personality and developing inner-Party democracy, of condemning and rectifying all the abuses of power and exposing those specifically guilty of repressions because they bear personal responsibility for many mass repressions against Party, Soviet, economic, military and Komsomol cadres.

In this connection, one cannot but tell of Kaganovich's provocational activities in the Ukraine. After becoming Secretary of the Ukrainian Communist Party Central Committee in 1947, he surrounded himself with a pack of unprincipled people and toadies, betrayed cadres devoted to the Party, and trampled upon and terrorised leading officials of the republic. Like a true sadist, Kaganovich found satisfaction in mocking activists and the intelligentsia by belittling their human dignity and threatening them with arrests and imprisonment. It is no accident that many Party, Soviet and professional workers still call the period of Kaganovich's tenure the 'black days' of the Soviet Ukraine.

* *Source*: '22-oi syezd KPSS – Rech t. N.V. Podgornogo (Pervy sekretar TSK Kompartii Ukrainy)' (22nd Congress of the CPSU – Com. N. V. Podgorny's Speech (First secretary of the CC CP of the Ukraine)), *Pravda*, 20 October 1961.

Document 139* General Kreizer's career (1962)

Kreizer, Yakov Grigoryevich.[38] Deputy of the Soviet of Nationalities of the Far East Electoral District no. 6, RSFSR.

Born in 1905, a Jew, member of the Communist Party since 1925, secondary education. Army General. Hero of the Soviet Union.

In 1920 worked as foreman in road building. From 1921 served in the Soviet Army. After graduating from military college for infantry he became section, then platoon, company, battalion, assistant regiment, deputy division and division commander. During the Great Patriotic War he was an army commander. At present he is Commander-in-Chief of the Far East Military District.

Member of the Central Auditing Committee of the CPSU.

Document 140† Obituary of Raizer (1962)

David Yakovlevich Raizer, one of the most eminent builders of our country and former USSR Minister of Metallurgical and Chemical Plant Construction, died on 24 December 1962 after a serious and prolonged illness.

All the many years of D. Ya. Raizer's activity were inseparably linked with the creation and development of domestic heavy industry.

D. Ya. Raizer was born in Kakhovka, Kherson Province, in 1904. He joined the ranks of the Communist Party in 1939. After graduating from the Odessa Polytechnic Institute, he worked continuously in the field of industrial construction, building the largest metallurgical combines and plants in the country in Magnitogorsk, Dneprodzerzhinsk and Zhdanov, and traversing the path from project superintendent to chief engineer of a trust. In 1936 he was assigned to administrative work in the People's Commissariat of Heavy Industry, and later the People's Commissariat of the Defence Industry and the People's Commissariat of the Shipbuilding Industry. Possessing great organisational abilities, D. Ya. Raizer did a lot for the construction and reconstruction of ferrous metallurgical enterprises during and after the Great Patriotic War. In 1950 D. Ya. Raizer was appointed to the post of USSR Minister, and from that time, for seven years, he headed the construction of metallurgical and chemical industry enterprises.

Until the last days of his life D. Ya. Raizer worked tirelessly on improving construction work and raising the level of the industrialisation of construction, passing on his great experience and knowledge. He won the universal respect of the builders with his outstanding abilities as a major builder and organiser and with his devotion to the Party and the people, his modesty and sensitivity

. . .

D. Ya. Raizer was elected candidate member of the Party Central Committee at the 19th and 20th Party Congresses.

* *Source: Deputaty Verkhovnogo Soveta SSSR, shestoi sozyv* (Deputies of the USSR Supreme Soviet, Sixth Convocation), Moscow, Izvestiya Sovetov Deputatov Trudyashchikhsya SSSR, 1962, p. 233.
† *Source*: 'David Yakovlevich Raizer', *Pravda*, 26 December 1962.

Document 141* Obituary of Vannikov (1962)

Boris Lvovich Vannikov, member of the Party since 1919, one of the outstanding organisers of the defence industry, winner of two State Prizes and holder of the title of Hero of Socialist Labour, who held responsible state posts for many years, died suddenly on 22 February 1962.

B. L. Vannikov was born into a worker's family in Baku in 1897. While still young, he went to work as a fitter and turner in Baku enterprises and took an active part in the underground revolutionary movement. In 1918 he volunteered for duty in the Red Army.

From 1920 to 1926, B. L. Vannikov held a responsible post in the People's Commissariat of the Workers' and Peasants' Inspection of the USSR and, at the same time, studied at the Bauman Higher Technical Training School in Moscow. During the first Five-Year Plan he was director of the Lyubertsy, Tula and Perm Machine-Building plants. His tireless work, modesty and sensitivity to people earned B. L. Vannikov the affection and respect of workers, employees, technicians and engineers at these industrial enterprises.

In 1937 B. L. Vannikov was appointed Deputy People's Commissar of the Defence Industry, and in 1939 he was appointed USSR People's Commissar of Armaments. During the Great Patriotic War B. L. Vannikov held the post of USSR People's Commissar of Munitions and, as such, he showed himself to be a major specialist and a capable organiser and manager of the armaments industry. In the years after the war, B. L. Vannikov held responsible state posts in the defence industry and in machine building.

All of Boris Lvovich's life was devoted to selfless service to the Party and the Soviet people. Wherever the Party sent him he demonstrated lively creative energy, outstanding talent as an engineer and outstanding capability as an economic organiser. Boris Lvovich did a large amount of work on the development of Soviet science and industry. He personally guided the training of wonderful cadres of scientists and commanders for industry who are now successfully performing highly important state tasks in various branches of industry and technology.

At the 18th, 19th and 20th Party Congresses, B. L. Vannikov was elected a member of the Party Central Committee. He was a delegate to the second convocation of the Supreme Soviet and to the third convocation of the Russian republic supreme soviet.

For his great services to the homeland, B. L. Vannikov received the title of Hero of Socialist Labour; a second and third gold Hammer and Sickle Medal; six Orders of Lenin; Orders of Suvorov and Kutuzov, First Class; and two State Prizes.

B. L. Vannikov held the military rank of General of the Engineer-Artillery Service.

B. L. Vannikov went into retirement four years ago for reasons of health.

The working people of our country retain a bright memory of Boris Lvovich Vannikov, a true son of the Party, who gave all his talent and energy to the cause of developing socialist industry and strengthening the might of our homeland.

* *Source*: 'Boris Lvovich Vannikov', *Pravda*, 23 February 1962.

Document 142*   Posthumous tribute to Lozovsky (1963)

Solomon Abramovich Lozovsky (Dridzo),[39] an active participant in the revolutionary and trade union movement, publicist and Soviet diplomat, was born on 29 March 1878, into a poor family in the former Ekaterinoslav Province. [...]

S. A. Lozovsky's path as a revolutionary and Communist was complicated. In 1912 he joined a group of Bolshevik appeasers; in 1917 he opposed the Party's tactics in the Revolution and in December was expelled from the Party. Later, reminiscing about this period in his life, S. A. Lozovsky wrote: 'Despite my differences and my sharp opposition to the leaders of the Party, I regarded the Bolshevik Party as my own, and I reached boiling point when representatives of other parties criticised it. As the Revolution moved ahead, the correctness of Lenin's viewpoint became manifest, and it is not surprising that already by the end of 1918 I was confronted by the question of returning to my Bolshevik fatherland.' In 1919, after a long interview with V. I. Lenin, which Lozovsky was to remember for the rest of his life, he was again received into the ranks of the Communist Party by decision of the Central Committee of the Russian Communist Party (Bolsheviks).

Lozovsky was one of the organisers of the Trade Union International, of which he became General Secretary in 1921. In this post he carried out the major task of consolidating the unity of the international workers' movement and rallying the proletarian masses for the struggle against the danger of Fascism and war. All these years he contributed to Soviet newspapers and magazines on questions of the international movement and international policy and was a member of the presidium of the USSR Communist Academy, a professor at the Moscow State University and a member of the All-Russian Central Executive Committee.

In 1937 S. A. Lozovsky was released from his work in the Trade Union International and was appointed Director of the State Literature Publishing House. From 1939 to 1946 he worked as USSR Deputy People's Commissar (later Minister) of Foreign Affairs, working simultaneously in 1941–5 as Deputy Director (and later Director) of the Soviet Information Bureau. The last years of his life were taken up with scientific work.

S. A. Lozovsky was a delegate to a number of Party Congresses and conferences. At the 15th, 16th and 17th Party Congresses, S. A. Lozovsky was elected candidate member of the All-Russian Communist Party (Bolsheviks) Central Committee and at the 18th Party Congress, Member of the All-Russian Communist Party (Bolsheviks) Central Committee.

S. A. Lozovsky died in 1952 after being arrested on a false charge.

Soviet people honour the memory of the prominent revolutionary and active builder of Communist society.

---

* *Source*: V. Ivanov & L. Terentyev, 'Zhizn revolyutsionera. K 85-letiyu so dnya rozhdeniya S. A. Lozovskogo' (The Life of a Revolutionary. On the 85th Anniversary of S. A. Lozovsky's Birth), *Izvestiya*, 29 March 1963.

Document 143* Dymshits's career (1966)

Dymshits,[40] *Veniamin Emmanuilovich*

Delegate to the Soviet of the Union from the Khabarovsk City Election District no. 105 of Khabarovsk Territory.

Born in 1910 into the family of an employee, Jew, CPSU member since 1937, higher education, graduated from the Bauman Higher Technical School in Moscow. Laureate of State Prizes.

From 1931 to 1950 worked on the construction of metallurgical works: Kuznetsk, Azovstal, Krivoi Rog, Magnitogorsk, Zaporozhye. From 1950 headed the Chief Administration for the Construction of Lead Industry Enterprises and was Deputy Minister of the Metallurgical and Chemical Plant Construction of the USSR. From 1957 he was chief engineer of the Bhilai metallurgical plant in India. From 1959 he headed the department of capital construction of the USSR State Planning Committee; was a USSR minister, First Deputy to the Chairman of the USSR State Planning Committee and Chairman of the USSR Council for National Economy. At present he is Deputy Chairman of the USSR Council of Ministers, Chairman of the State Committee of the USSR Council of Ministers for Material and Technical Supplies.

A member of the Central Committee of the CPSU.

Elected delegate to the sixth convocation of the USSR Supreme Soviet.

* *Source: Deputaty Verkhovnogo Soveta SSSR, Sedmoi sozyv* (Deputies of the USSR Supreme Soviet, Seventh Convocation), Moscow, Izvestiya Sovetov deputatov trudyashchikhsya SSSR, 1966, p. 149.

10

The Jewish Autonomous Region of Birobidzhan

The name Birobidzhan reappears in the news every few years as the result of Soviet initiatives which seem to be inspired by two very different calculations. On the one hand, Birobidzhan is called in to demonstrate that the Jewish people enjoys full equality in the USSR – for an autonomous Jewish region has existed there since 1934. And, on the other hand, it has served as a veiled threat to the Jewish people in the USSR to remind them that they can be transported to that region should the need arise. The fact that the Jewish Autonomous Region has not been abolished despite the small number of Jews residing there, and despite the fact that only vestiges of Jewish culture remain, is presumably to be explained by these same considerations.

The Stalin period

As we have seen in Chapter 1, members of the *Evsektsiya* and a part of the Jewish intelligentsia close to Jewish national affairs in the Soviet Union concluded quite early on that the only way that the Jewish problem could be solved within the framework of the Soviet regime was on a territorial basis.[1] They did not, however, envisage such a territory in the Far East on the Chinese border, but rather on the shores of the Black Sea. The idea of allocating the Birobidzhan area for Jewish settlement, with the aim of establishing a national unit there, was raised for the first time in early 1927 by the heads of the RSFSR People's Commissariat of Agriculture, with the support of the Commissariat for Defence. Mikhail Kalinin, Chairman of the Presidium of the Central Executive Committee of the USSR, became one of the most outspoken advocates of the project.

Although the Soviet leadership apparently took up this project in the hope of reconstructing Jewish life in the USSR on a new and solid basis and thereby, among other things, dealing a decisive blow to Zionist theory, there is no doubt that general considerations of state also exerted a significant influence. Above all there was the major security problem which demanded the rapid and extensive population of the huge areas on the frontiers with Japan and China. But there was also the desire to exploit the rich natural resources in the Birobidzhan region with all possible speed. And this would be accomplished more quickly with the help of immigrants who, unlike the sparse local population, could be expected to possess the necessary cultural level and technical skills. More generally, the authorities were interested in thinning out the European section of the Soviet Union through a gradual shift to the east.[2]

At first, the Birobidzhan project was received with open opposition and notable lack of enthusiasm by the important figures in Soviet institutions responsible for Jewish settlement, such as *Komzet* and *Ozet*, and with more covert opposition by other functionaries. From the year 1932, however, and especially from May 1934, when the Presidium of the Central Executive Committee of the Soviet Union decided to transform Birobidzhan from a district (*raion*) into a Jewish Autonomous Region (*oblast*), this opposition all but ceased. All those involved then threw themselves into the campaign to accelerate the flow of Jewish immigrants to Birobidzhan. However, immigration data for the years 1932–7 reveal that, for all the official enthusiasm, of the 36,000 persons who arrived in Birobidzhan – among them about a thousand immigrants from abroad[3] – less than half stayed.

The first blow to the Birobidzhan project – which in any case had enormous objective difficulties to overcome – was struck in August 1936. In the course of the great purges most of the leaders of the Jewish Autonomous Region were arrested on charges of Trotskyism, nationalism and espionage on behalf of foreign powers. The second blow came in 1938, when all the special institutions that had dealt with Jewish settlement in the USSR since the midtwenties were closed down.

Nevertheless, once the wave of purges was over, and particularly following the annexation to the Soviet Union of new territories with a large Jewish population in 1939–40, fresh hopes arose for the renewed development of the Jewish Autonomous Region. Although plans were prepared to transfer between thirty and forty thousand Jewish families to Birobidzhan, nothing came of this grandiose project. In fact, very few Jewish immigrants arrived in the region between 1939 and 1941, and immigration to Birobidzhan virtually ceased with the outbreak of the Soviet–German war, to be renewed only in 1945.

The old argument as to whether a Jewish republic should be established in Birobidzhan or in the Crimea arose again towards the end of the war. Interest in the Crimea was revived as a result of the expulsion of the Tatars from that area for alleged collaboration with the Nazis, as well as by the feeling in circles of the Jewish Anti-Fascist Committee that survivors of the Holocaust would have to be settled in a more suitable area than Birobidzhan. But the idea was hastily dropped the moment it became clear that the authorities had decided against it.[4]

The years 1946–53

At the end of 1945, when the new five-year plan for 1946–50 was in preparation, it was assumed that the Far East would absorb a significant part of the population displaced by the war. The Jewish Autonomous Region was apparently assigned a role within this framework. This becomes clear from the official resolutions of the Council of Commissars of the RSFSR on 26 January 1946, and from an edict issued by the Council of Commissars of the USSR on 27 January 1946, both of which concerned measures for strengthening the economy of the Jewish Autonomous Region. Although very little was said in these resolutions about the Jewish national aspect of Birobidzhan settlement, they were sufficient to arouse new hopes among various circles of Soviet Jewry. The parties most interested in renewing Jewish settlement in Birobidzhan were circles of the Jewish Anti-Fascist Committee who had previously supported the establishment of a Jewish autonomous republic in the Crimea but soon realised that this project would not win the support of the authorities; many Jews who had survived the Holocaust and encountered hostile treatment by the local population when they returned to their former places of residence; and, apparently, a number of Soviet leaders known for their earlier support of this programme.[5]

Added to the pressing internal factors influencing the Soviet authorities to renew immigration of Jews to Birobidzhan – for example, the disputes between the local population of the Ukraine and the returning Jews, Birobidzhan's vital need of additional population, and the desire to divert the attention of Soviet Jewry away from Zionism and Israel – were weighty external factors. There was the long-standing aspiration to prove to the whole world that the Jewish problem had found its socialist (that is to say, the best and only possible) solution in the Soviet Union. The Soviet leaders hoped, too, to capitalise on the renewal of Jewish settlement to gain extensive Jewish and general public support in the West.[6] And there also seems to have been an unsuccessful attempt to use the Birobidzhan project to solve the difficult and complex problem of the Jews from Poland who had found refuge in the Soviet Union during the war.[7]

In its first stages, from 1945 until the end of 1946, Jewish immigration to Birobidzhan was disorganised and involved only limited numbers. The systematic registration of those seeking transfer to Birobidzhan began in October 1946, after the government took over the direct organisation of mass Jewish immigration to the region in special trains (*eshelony*).[8] During 1947–8, twelve special trains carrying about 6,500 persons arrived in Birobidzhan from the cities of Vinnitsa, Kherson, Nikolaev, Dnepropetrovsk, Odessa and Samarkand.[9] All in all, until its cessation at the end of 1948, the immigration over this two-year period apparently totalled about 10,000 persons. The data cited by A. Bakhmutsky, Secretary of the Communist Party in the Birobidzhan District, according to which over 20,000 Jews immigrated over a period of eighteen months (see Doc. 144), were greatly exaggerated.[10] The new immigrants included urban and agricultural workers, as well as a high percentage of persons in the technical professions – engineers, technicians, doctors, agronomists, and teachers. In this respect, the post-war composition differed from that of the first settlers in the twenties (see Doc. 145).

The influx of immigrants, together with the change in Soviet policy on the Jewish Autonomous Region, breathed some new life into Jewish cultural activity in the region.[11] But it was not long before Jewish hopes for the establishment of a 'sovereignty' within the USSR were dashed. In the years 1948–9, the Kaganovich Yiddish Theatre, the Jewish publishing house, the periodical *Birobidzhan*, the rich library of Yiddish and Hebrew books, and the Jewish research institutions and schools were all closed down. The mass anti-Jewish purge carried out at this time in Birobidzhan – which hit especially hard at functionaries, writers and artists – dealt an even harsher blow to the 'Birobidzhan project' than the purges of the thirties.[12]

Connections between the Jewish Autonomous Region and the outside world were completely severed in the years 1949–53, and only rare reports were received in the West of what was happening there.[13] The Soviet authorities discontinued reports in any way related to the Jewish nature of the region. Their information services rested content with the image created by Communist and pro-Communist circles outside the USSR, who endeavoured to refute 'anti-Soviet propaganda' by painting the prosperity of the Jewish Autonomous Region in glowing colours and describing the contented life of the Jews living there (Doc. 144).

Immigration by means of the special trains still continued, albeit in much reduced numbers, in the first half of 1949. However, later on (principally in 1952 and early 1953), the Jewish Autonomous Region became an area of penal exile where Jews sentenced in the economic trials that were then being held were sent to do forced labour. Moreover, in the months prior to Stalin's death, rumours were rife that Birobidzhan was to absorb a considerable portion of the Jews about to be exiled from the European section of the USSR.

The post-Stalin and Khrushchev periods (1953–64)

After Stalin's death, the sole change for the better with regard to the Jewish Autonomous Region was the lifting of the veil of secrecy that had enveloped it for several years. The *New York Times* correspondent Harrison Salisbury visited the region in June 1954 and published two articles on his findings and impressions upon his return to the United States.[14] Two months later, in August 1954, the Israeli Ambassador to the Soviet Union, Dr S. Elyashiv, visited Birobidzhan.[15] And in 1955, reports from Jewish Communist sources began to appear in the press.[16] But the information provided was meagre and tendentious, and it was clear that these newspapers were attempting to conceal the depressed conditions of Jewish education and culture in the 'Jewish' national region.

Reports on Birobidzhan began to appear in the Soviet Union itself only in early 1958. In March of that year, Radio Moscow inaugurated a series of foreign-language broadcasts devoted to the Jewish Autonomous Region which were picked up in the West. The Jewish participants in these broadcasts tried to lay great stress on the Jewish nature of the region.[17] On 6 August 1958, V. Pakhman wrote a long article for the organ of the Communist Party and Council of Ministers of the RSFSR describing the happiness and well-being of the Jews living in Birobidzhan (Doc. 147). In honour of the twenty-fifth anniversary of the founding of the Jewish Autonomous Region, there appeared – albeit somewhat belatedly – a special collection in Yiddish and Russian devoted entirely to that region.[18] On the occasion of the anniversary, articles were published and radio programmes broadcast in which the region's Jewish nature was once again stressed.[19]

No report, however glowing, could alter the fact that, in 1959, the Jewish Autonomous Region was inhabited by a mere 14,269 Jews, who constituted 8.8% of the region's overall population (and only 0.7% of the entire Jewish population in the USSR).[20] There has been no other autonomous republic or even autonomous region in which the 'dominant' nationality constituted so low a percentage. Thus, for example, the South Ossetians then constituted 65%, the Adigeians 23%, and the Khakas 12% of the local population in their respective autonomous regions.

Moreover, the Jewish population in Birobidzhan was also an ageing one.[21] According to the 1970 Census, the Jewish population of Birobidzhan decreased to 11,452, that is 6.6% of the total population of the region. While the percentage of Jews in Birobidzhan that declared Yiddish as its mother tongue in 1959 (39.2%) was higher than that for the Jews of the Soviet Union as a whole (21.5%), it was among the lowest in the USSR in terms of percentage of population who spoke their own national language in their own autonomous region (South Ossetians: 98.6%; Adigeians: 99%; Khakas: 90.2%). Clearly, the lack of Yiddish schools since the end of the forties results in an increasing process of Russification.

Yiddish cultural life in the Jewish Autonomous Region was very meagre during this period. There was no permament Jewish theatre company, no museum exhibiting Jewish art, in fact, virtually no activity of any kind in this sphere. The only signs of Jewish cultural activity were the appearance of a Yiddish newspaper restricted in circulation and poor in content; the existence of Yiddish books in the library of the city of Birobidzhan (10,000 out of a total of 120,000); and a limited number of guest appearances by Yiddish artists who occasionally reached there. Furthermore, in contrast to the thirties and forties, Jewish participation in the administrative institutions of the region was quite limited.[22]

Khrushchev provided his own explanation for this situation as early as April 1958, when, in conversation with the French journalist Serge Groussard, he stated that the Jews themselves were responsible for the failure of the project because they were incapable of collective work and were not inclined to agricultural labour (Doc. 17). However, the recurrent rumours, which began in 1959, that the Soviet authorities intended to transport compulsorily masses of Jews to Birobidzhan were vehemently denied by the heads of the Soviet regime; and they did indeed turn out to be incorrect.[23]

The collective leadership (1965–7)

The new leadership brought no essential changes in policy towards the Jewish Autonomous Region. The Russification process which had been clearly visible in the previous period intensified, apparently as a result of the absence of Yiddish schools and the mortality rate of the older generation. The official claim, occasionally made, that the Yiddish schools were closed down as the result of parental pressure[24] is untenable, even though there is no doubt that many Jewish parents would prefer their children to attend Russian rather than Yiddish schools. For some reason the solutions instituted in other autonomous regions – such as study of the mother tongue in the early grades and/or the establishment of bi-lingual schools – have never been tried in Birobidzhan. The situation of the Jewish religion continued to be lamentable. And this was not only because the vast majority of the Jews of Birobidzhan swore that they were atheists (according to an official Soviet survey made in 1967 (Doc. 148)). In fact, there was only one synagogue in Birobidzhan in the 1960s, and that in a small wood cabin; there were no rabbis, and no Jewish cemetery.

The only ameliorations visible in the years 1965–7, as compared with the previous period, were the formation of a local theatre company; increased appearances by Yiddish-language readers and singers; and a greater emphasis on Jewish issues (both local and general) in the *Birobidzhaner shtern*.[25]

We have seen that in reality – if not in theory – Birobidzhan differed only slightly from many other regions of the Soviet Union. By 1967, it was clear beyond a shadow of doubt that, barring some radical change of official policy, the Jews were destined to become an ever more negligible minority in the region. Eventually, it can be assumed, the authorities will be compelled to remove the final remaining symbols of Jewish 'sovereignty' in the Soviet Union.[26]

Why did the Birobidzhan project fail while other autonomous national units in the USSR have succeeded? It would seem that Khrushchev's explanations, as cited above, are largely rendered unconvincing not only by the existence of Israel but also by the success of the Jewish settlement plans of the twenties and thirties in the Ukraine, Belorussia and the Crimea. The reasons for the failure of the Birobidzhan project must therefore be sought elsewhere.

The first seeds of this failure were already sown by the very selection of this site for Jewish settlement. The remoteness of Birobidzhan from the existing centres of Jewish life; the difficult climatic conditions of a desolate land; and the security dangers that loomed over the area for a lengthy period certainly had an adverse effect on the project. Then, the concentration of the Jewish population in the western USSR, where there were rapidly expanding economic possibilities for the individual and a highly developed cultural infrastructure (albeit primarily in Russian), deflected many Jews from volunteering to transfer to Birobidzhan.

Added to this was the lack of a consistent official policy towards the project. There is no doubt that the paucity of resources, the constant reversals of the authorities and, above all, the two great purges in the years 1936 and 1948 fatally sabotaged it in the difficult early stages of establishment and growth. And finally, the absence of any spiritual or historical attachment to Birobidzhan on the part of the Jews of the Soviet Union has to be seen as a key factor in deciding the fate of the region as a Jewish national home.

Documents to Chapter 10

Document 144* Fefer replies to Lestchinsky on Birobidzhan (1948)

For many years Jacob Lestchinsky[27] has been paraded by the Jewish press as the leading authority on economic and population problems of the Jews, and especially on Soviet Jewry. The value of this 'authoritative' work can be judged from the following article by Itsik Fefer, noted Soviet Yiddish poet and officer of the Moscow Jewish Anti-Fascist Committee, exposing a recent effort of Lestchinsky to slander Soviet policy on Birobidzhan. Last spring the Secretary of the Communist Party of Birobidzhan, A. Bakhmutsky,[28] stated that over 20,000 Jews had arrived in Birobidzhan in the previous eighteen months. And, since Fefer wrote this article, news has come of a new migration of Jews to Birobidzhan from Central Asia, where they had been evacuated during the war. – Editors [of *Jewish Life*]

There was a time when enemies of the Soviet Union wrote that Jews were being forced to go to Birobidzhan, where they would starve. But this fabrication was short-lived, for almost immediately the facts showed that the migration was entirely voluntary. As a matter of fact, when some Soviet Jewish leaders suggested the mobilisation of a hundred thousand young Jews for settlement in Birobidzhan, the government made short shrift of this idea. In a talk with Solomon Mikhoels and myself, the late Soviet President Mikhail Kalinin, a great friend of Birobidzhan, said that, like all Soviet citizens, Jews are free to decide where they should live. [...]

How could these men, who have shouted so loud and long about assimilation of Jews in the Soviet Union, give even an inkling of the rich Jewish cultural life in Birobidzhan? How could these men, who kept insisting that Jewish culture is dying in the Soviet Union, report the renaissance of all aspects of Jewish cultural life in the Soviet Union in the post-war years? Have they reported that Yiddish magazines have begun to appear in Moscow, Kiev, Birobidzhan, Minsk? Has there been even a single notice in these papers of the work of Yiddish theatres, schools, writers' organisations and scholarly institutions in the Soviet Union?[29] No such notices appear in these papers, which are not interested in the life of the Jewish masses in the Soviet Union. They are interested solely in grist for their anti-Soviet mill.

I have always known these things. But they became clear once again when I read the article on Birobidzhan by the anti-Soviet journalist, Jacob Lestchinsky, in the *Forward* of 26 June 1948.[30] Lestchinsky disapproves of an article

* *Source*: I. Fefer, 'Fact and Fancy on Birobidzhan', *Jewish Life*, January 1949, pp. 9–10.

on Birobidzhan printed in the Information Bulletin of the Soviet Embassy. He faced a serious problem. He just could not find anything to criticise. Birobidzhan exists. New mills are being built. Cities are expanding. Jewish culture is growing. Honest Jews would be happy over this and impressed by the fact that one can find such solicitude for the Jewish people in the Soviet Union. In what other country does the government assign colossal sums for Jewish theatres, libraries, newspapers and other cultural institutions, for the settlement and rehabilitation of the Jewish masses?

What then was Lestchinsky's complaint? The figures on Birobidzhan, it appears, are quite bad. The rich and colourful life of the Jewish Autonomous Region he dismisses with a cheap remark about the 'Birobidzhan Paradise'. Then he goes to town on those statistics on Birobidzhan which do not satisfy him. What troubles him? He cannot learn the precise number of Jews in Birobidzhan. In any event, he comes to the conclusion that Birobidzhan still has very few Jews. Correct. There are not enough Jews in Birobidzhan. There are not yet a hundred thousand. *If there were, Birobidzhan would already have become a Soviet Socialist Jewish Autonomous Republic.* There was a time when Lestchinsky was feeling quite well. There were few Jews in Birobidzhan. But the post-war Soviet Union has witnessed the migration of thousands of Jews to Birobidzhan. This is a fact.

Before me is a report of the Chairman of the Birobidzhan Regional Committee, Comrade Levitin.[31] According to this official report, nine migrations totalling 1,770 families arrived in Birobidzhan during 1947 alone. Of these, 830 families settled on collective farms. In the light of this report one can only be roused to anger by Lestchinsky's question, 'Why do the Jews remain in the cities and the non-Jews settle on the land?' Such unadulterated hogwash and venomous questions appear frequently in the anti-Semitic press. Lestchinsky's questions come from just these anti-Semitic arsenals. It seems that if one wants to attack the Soviet Union, even such sources and techniques are kosher. [...]

For all honest people it is quite clear that migration to Birobidzhan was previously kept down because this land was close to imperialist Japan, whose empire was continuously menacing the Soviet borders. In view of this danger, it would have been a crime to encourage immigration to Birobidzhan. It is therefore quite natural that the defeat of imperialist Japan should be followed by a growing interest in Birobidzhan. As a matter of fact, post-war immigration to Birobidzhan has exceeded all expectations. *If this immigration continues at the present rate, an autonomous Socialist Soviet Jewish Republic will be set up in the Far East in a few years.*

What will Jacob Lestchinsky do then? I am certain that even when there are many Jews in Birobidzhan, he will manage to find something to complain about. In that case he will probably pull out of the archives the first anti-Soviet slander, that Jews were forced to go to Birobidzhan.

At any rate, Lestchinsky will not be without work. Like the *Forward* [*Forverts*], he can always concoct some fantasy that he believes will lead him out of difficulties. But we can assure him that his situation will grow worse and worse, even though he may try to strengthen his position with the aid of certain renegades like Shmerke Kacherginsky.[32] This man is still alive only because the Soviet Union rescued him from the Nazis. Instead of gratitude to the great free country that saved him, Kacherginsky feeds Lestchinsky with nonsensical anti-Soviet slanders.

Document 145* Birobidzhan after the war (1948)[33]

New perspectives have opened for the region with its colossal natural resources, great land areas, increase of industrial establishments, collectives and state farms, growing production experience, developed cadres and broad network of cultural institutions. The region still has an insufficient number of immigrants. At the beginning of 1946, the executives of the Soviets of the USSR and the RSFSR proposed to take measures to consolidate and further develop the economy and culture of the Jewish Autonomous Region. These measures of the Party and the government heartened the workers of the Jewish Autonomous Region and strengthened the desire among the Jewish population to settle in the region and build a Jewish socialist state.

This decision of the Soviet government was inspiring to the Soviet Jewish population, who looked on it as further evidence that the Bolshevik Party and the government wished to strengthen the Jewish Autonomous Region. Among the settlers who came from the city of Vinnitsa the following skills and social groups are represented: 48 builders, 25 locksmiths, 18 turners, 25 chauffeurs, 20 smiths, 48 shoemakers, 37 tailors, 155 collective farmers, 5 tractor drivers and a number of engineers, technicians, doctors, teachers, agronomists, etc.

A comparison of the composition of the first settlers in the Crimea not long after the Revolution with that of the current settlers in the Jewish Autonomous Region reveals enormous differences.

Social composition	The Crimea	Jewish Autonomous Region
Workers and artisans	38.3 per cent	40.0 per cent
Farmers	7.8 per cent	29.0 per cent
Intellectuals	6.8 per cent	31.0 per cent
Traders and others	47.1 per cent	—

The present Jewish settlers are no longer largely non-productive in agriculture and industry. The percentage of intellectuals has increased many times. These intellectuals are in a position to assume leading posts in the economy and cultural institutions of the region. While merchants and other declassed elements comprised almost half of the Crimean settlers, they are totally absent in the region.

A government decision of 19 June, 1947 provided aid to settlers on the region collectives with loans for the building of homes, maintenance loans for two years and long-term credit for the purchase of cows. Every family gets financial aid for the purchase of household articles. Exemption from agricultural taxes and deliveries to the state are granted to collectives that accept a certain number of new settlers.

The Jewish Autonomous Region now has every possibility for economic and cultural development, but lacks only people to harness its natural wealth. The rich natural resources of the region and the existing and growing establish-

* *Source*: L. Zinger, 'Post-War Reconstruction', *Jewish Life*, March 1949, pp. 24–5.

ments await builders, technicians, engineers, etc. The region needs specialists in light industry. It must have people for slate and cement production, for the lime industry, for work on marble, for extracting and working on graphite and sapphires. There is need for agronomists, shepherds, gardeners, bee keepers, landscape gardeners, irrigation engineers, etc. There is urgent need of cultural and medical workers, etc.*

Document 146† American journalist visits Birobidzhan (1954)[34]

I was unable to take a single step in the streets of Birobidzhan without the company of the agents. The detail included a number of local MVD lads, youngsters from the Birobidzhan headquarters. Their role was obvious. They were to make it evident to the local residents that I was being followed and that it was more healthy not to talk to me. The lesson was easily understood by the populace. No one talked to me on the street. Several times I was spoken to while eating in the restaurant. But, conversation on a normal human level was out of the question.

Nonetheless I learned a great deal about Birobidzhan. I was the first outsider to come there in many years, probably since before World War II. Established originally as a Jewish settlement colony in an obvious move to provide a counterweight to Palestine in the early thirties it was plain that Birobidzhan had lost its significance as a Jewish centre a long time ago.

To be sure the street signs were still posted in Yiddish as well as Russian. And the name was officially the 'Jewish Autonomous Region'.

But, beyond this, as I told Lev Vingkevich,[35] a Communist of Jewish descent who is the Chairman of the executive committee of the Regional Soviet, a position roughly comparable to that of governor, I could not see that the place had any special Jewish character. I said I thought it should be called the 'Soviet Autonomous Region' because it was, outside of its special history and a certain percentage of Jews in its population, merely an ordinary Soviet administrative region. He was inclined to agree with me.

I suppose that about half the residents of this region, which has a population of about 200,000, are Jews. In the city, which has 40,000 residents, the percentage may be somewhat higher than in the country.

But no special effort was now being made to send Jews to Birobidzhan. In fact, I doubted that any had been sent since 1948, the real watershed year in Birobidzhan and Jewish history in Russia. That was the year of the 'anti-cosmopolitan' drive.

Exactly what happened in Birobidzhan that year no one would tell me. But part of the story came out. The Jewish theatre was closed and turned into a Young Communist Club.[36] I think the Jewish newspaper was suspended, but perhaps a vestigial edition remained. Now it was published three times a week in an edition of a thousand copies, but the twenty-three-year-old Jewish girl who had become editor only three weeks before admitted that circulation had been 'less' in the past.

* A. Bakhmutsky, 'Main Questions of the Present' [Kardinale tog fragn], *Eynikeyt* (Moscow), 28 August 1947.

† *Source*: H. E. Salisbury, *American in Russia*, New York, Harper and Brothers, 1955, pp. 281–4.

I think that in 1949 the regional museum was closed but I could not find anyone to admit it. It was open now and was obviously brand new. It looked to me as though, perhaps, it had been open less than a year. There wasn't a word in the museum about Jewish culture or the Jewish language or the Jewish contribution to the region. The only indication that Jews had had any part in Birobidzhan was three old copies of the Yiddish paper which I saw in one obscure cabinet along a side wall.

I embarrassed the black-eyed young Jewish woman who ran the local library by asking to see the latest books and literature in Yiddish. At first she said the Director of the Yiddish book section was away on vacation and had locked up the books before going away. Then she and an assistant hastily pawed over a huge pile of books, looking for Yiddish ones. They found Mark Twain's *Prince and the Pauper* and a few others but none, of course, dated later than 1948 when the Yiddish Publishing House in Moscow was shut. In the local bookstore I found they had a few volumes in Yiddish, two or three by Shalom Aleikhem, and copies of Stalin's *Problems of Leninism* and a *Short History of the Communist Party*, translated into Yiddish.

I bought two of the Shalom Aleikhem volumes, and apologised to the book clerk for her trouble. She had had to climb a ladder and get the books off the very topmost shelf of the section devoted to foreign-language books. She in turn apologised to me for having nothing but these dusty old copies. I assured her it made no difference whatsoever.

So, as the Deputy Mayor of Birobidzhan assured me, Jewish culture was not dead in Birobidzhan. In addition, he recalled, they had sung some Jewish songs at a festival which had been conducted recently on the occasion of the twentieth anniversary of the establishment of the region.

But what, I asked him, about the Jewish religion? Was there a synagogue?

Assuredly, he said, and he would be glad to take me to visit it. We had a little trouble finding the place because the Deputy Mayor, who until a year previous had been in charge of highway construction for the MVD, had never been there before. But, aided by the 'hotel-keeper', who said he also had not been there before but who proved astonishingly familiar with the neighbourhood, we found the plain barracks-like wooden building which served Birobidzhan as a synagogue.

But it was a little harder to find the rabbi because he was off drinking wine with some friends. But finally we located him and he proved to be a spry and egregious man of sixty-odd years named Solomon Kaplan and he was not a rabbi but a cantor. However, he said he had founded the synagogue in 1947. Before that, he said, there were only illegal congregations and he appealed to the 'hotel-keeper' for confirmation of his words. His congregation numbered about fifty persons, he said, 'all of them older than me'. He said no young people came to the synagogue and that even on the high holidays not more than sixty assembled.

It was plain enough that within a predictable number of years the Jewish congregation of Birobidzhan would simply die out. It was also my very strong suspicion that Cantor Kaplan had founded the congregation in 1947 with the blessing if not at the inspiration of the 'hotel-keeper' or his predecessor in the MVD.

Deputy Mayor Zhelenov told me repeatedly that Yiddish was still used in the schools, but when I asked the teachers and pupils in the half-dozen schools which I visited whether any language besides Russian was employed I got a uniformly negative answer.

So, I soon came to the conclusion that it was also merely a matter of time before the Jewish aspect of the region faded out completely. The name might be perpetuated for a while simply because the Foreign Office in Moscow might think that the day would again arise when it would be of some value to have a Jewish Autonomous Region for diplomatic or propaganda purposes.

But it was dead as a Jewish centre and never had had too much vitality. I knew from my visits to schools and talk with the Mayor of Yakutsk that there was a large Jewish minority there. It was easy to see that in the Jewish population transfers of 1948 and 1949 they had been sent to places like Yakutia rather than to the 'Jewish' Region.

Document 147* Birobidzhan – a Soviet view (1958)

In 1928 the Presidium of the Central Executive Committee of the USSR issued a decree about the consolidation of these lands near the Amur, for the needs of those working settlers who were of Jewish nationality. This deed on the part of the Soviet government had no precedent in history: as is known, Jews had been subject to constant persecution for thousands of years.

And it was only in the land of the Soviets, where the national problem had been solved on the basis of Marxism–Leninism, that the working Jews were granted land at all. That is why trains packed with Jewish settlers were drawn to this place.

In the thirties there appeared on the screens a cheerful film called *The Seekers of Happiness*.[37] Who among the representatives of the older generation would not remember Pinye Kopman, who went to Birobidzhan in search of gold, and dreamed of the title 'King of Braces'. Such types ran shamefully away. But the others prevailed in numbers, artisans, tailors, hairdressers, salesmen, people who in the past had never worked on the land because they had none; these came to Birobidzhan, were granted land, became members of kolkhozes and made this territory their home.

By the time six years had elapsed, the Birobidzhan Jewish National Area had been transformed into an Autonomous Region.

To defend this land, the inhabitants of the region joined with all the Soviet people in their fight against the enemy, during the years of World War II. In the local Museum of Regional Studies there are portraits of Soviet Army warriors, representatives of the Jewish Autonomous Region, who were awarded the title of Hero of the Soviet Union. One of them, Iosif Bumagin,[38] in the fight for Breslau, repeated the heroic deed of Aleksandr Matrosov. Another, David Kudryavitsky,[39] bravely fell during the forced crossing of the Dnieper. Their names will always be revered by the people. [...]

Cadres of local intellectuals have been formed in the region. Iosif Lvovich Bokor,[40] Secretary of the Birobidzhan Party Town Committee, enjoys great

* *Source*: V. Pakhman, 'Evreiskaya avtonomiya' (Jewish Autonomy), *Sovetskaya Rossiya*, 6 August 1958.

respect and authority. The editor of the local paper, Naum Abramovich Korchminsky,[41] has lived in Birobidzhan for quite a long time and he has a sound knowledge of his country. The writer Boris Izrailevich Miler[42] is known far beyond the borders of Birobidzhan. One of his books has recently been translated from Yiddish into Russian and is being published in Moscow.

We talked with Miler at the editorial office of the local paper, *Birobidzhaner shtern* [Birobidzhan Star]. The paper is issued in Yiddish, and he is one of its most active authors. Miler has travelled over the whole area, and knows many of the kolkhoz members living in the most remote villages along the Amur, their lives, joys and cares.

'I became wedded to this country', says Boris Izrailevich, 'I do not know where else I could have lived.'

At the Birobidzhan town library, named after Shalom Aleikhem, there is a large collection of literature in Yiddish. The literary works of writers are often discussed here. Not long ago, evening meetings were held for reading the works of the poet Shmuel Halkin, and those of the local poet and song-writer, Yitskhak Bronfman. Such evenings were full of activity: the readers would criticise the authors, artists would recite poetry and sing Jewish folk-songs.

Much can be told about the cultural life in the region; and about the regular and interesting radio-broadcasts in the Yiddish language by the local union. Also about the literary union set up at the editorial office of the paper; and about the literary and artistic anthology 'Birobidzhan', which will be published on the twenty-fifth anniversary of the Autonomous Region, and will be issued both in Yiddish and in Russian.

'How could one change this land for somewhere else?' say local inhabitants.

There have been such people. They did change. Some of them, under the influence of Zionist propaganda, left for Israel. What did they find there? Immigrants, especially those arriving from the Soviet Union, the Peoples' Democracies, India and some other countries, were treated by the Israeli authorities as unwelcome guests. The people were cooped up in barracks, often could not find work, dragged out a half-starved existence, and all the time were scoffed at.

I happened to visit the family of pensioner Peysakh Yakovlevich Mikhelson. He and his wife, his son Yakov, a worker of the Birobidzhan tractor-trailer plant, and his daughter Asya – all of them spoke excitedly about the tragedy in their family. In 1946, the elder daughter of the Mikhelsons, called Rakhil, married and left for Israel with her husband. How much sorrow she suffered in that foreign land! Her letters are documents of a great human misfortune.

'I curse the minute', writes Rakhil in one of her last letters, 'when I parted from you. I was young and foolish. [...] I suffer terribly here. [...]'

'Dear Asya!' she writes in another letter addressed to her sister. 'You should never do such a foolish thing as I did. You are happy with what you have. [...] The Soviet Union takes great care of you, and gives the people every opportunity for a decent life. In the Soviet Union everything is by far better.' [...]

People have grown; the region has developed beyond recognition. One cannot recognise it because the country of socialism has offered equal opportunities to people of all nationalities.

Document 148* Survey on religious faith among Birobidzhan Jews (1967)[43]

Not long ago, in order to ascertain how widespread Judaism was among the Jews of Birobidzhan, about 300 people were questioned in a survey – men and women, workers, office-workers, doctors, teachers, housewives, pensioners, all living in different parts of the city. The questionnaire was at the same time directed mainly at those people whom there was every reason to consider as believers. Only eight people however referred to themselves directly as believers. Nonetheless, we ought to increase their number a little, as we can also conditionally include among the believers those whose answers were formulated as follows: 'Who knows, perhaps, there is a God, and perhaps there isn't.'

A few people said: 'I am 99% a non-believer.' But what about the one per cent of faith? Cannot the idea of God slip through this one little chink and under favourable circumstances wholly possess a man's consciousness? For this reason we associate such people with the believers. We note that they were all born into families where the parents believed in God and, in the majority of cases, conscientiously observed the religious rites. [...]

What kind of people are the believing Jews of Birobidzhan as regards age and education? In the Jewish community here there are forty-three people. The 'youngest' is sixty-three, the oldest eighty-four. They all have elementary education. It is strange that they are poorly informed about their religious dogma, and the most 'erudite' persons in this respect among those questioned were convinced atheists – people with secondary and higher education. The source of their knowledge is study and reading.

* *Source*: A. Vinokur, 'Ugasanie drevney very' (The Dying Out of an Ancient Faith), *Nauka i religiya*, 1967, no. 1, pp. 41–3.

PART V

The Jewish experience as mirrored in Soviet publications

11

Jews in Soviet literature

There are several reasons why Soviet literature is of considerable importance for the study of politics and society in the USSR. First, it often provides information about the country which is not made available by any other Soviet sources. Even during the period of the Stalin terror, and still more during the more liberal period of the fifties and sixties, *belles lettres* were granted greater freedom than other forms of publication to describe reality. Thus, such important aspects of Soviet public life as the image of the Jews and the attitude of the general population towards Jews found broader, deeper, and often more objective expression in Soviet literature than they did anywhere else. At the same time, an examination of the literature published at any given moment makes it possible to trace the relationship of the Soviet authors of Jewish origin to their people.

The broad scope and complexity of the subject[1] and the limited space available to us here preclude a detailed analysis of the content or the literary, documentary and political importance of each work. We shall therefore have to be content with a more general analysis of the important works, paying particular attention to the authors' aims in each period. As in the other chapters, we shall deal with the differences in Soviet policy in the Stalin, the post-Stalin, and the Brezhnev–Kosygin periods.

The Stalin period

Despite the fact that over five million Jews then lived in Russia in conditions of poverty, discrimination and pogroms, the Jewish theme was accorded only minor treatment in pre-Revolutionary Russian literature. To the degree that some of the greatest Russian writers and poets – such as Pushkin, Lermontov, Gogol, Turgenev, Dostoevsky, Chekhov, Leskov, Korolenko, Kuprin, Gorky and Andreev – did refer to the Jewish issue, their treatment was episodic, superficial and fundamentally stereotypic, with the Jew generally portrayed as a repugnant and ridiculous type, or at best as a romantic and ideal character. Such portraits had little connection with reality.[2]

The Revolution and the Civil War brought about a quantitative as well as a qualitative change in this sphere, and the Jewish theme began to occupy quite a notable place in the new Soviet literature. There were far-reaching historical and political factors involved here: the Jewish national minority had moved to the centre of events, both as an active factor (its place in the Revolution, in the

Civil War and in the period of the New Economic Policy) and as a passive factor (as one of the chief victims of the anarchy, destruction and pogroms). Also important in this regard was the rise of a generation of Soviet writers and poets of Jewish origin, some of the most important of whom were I. Babel, I. Erenburg, Y. Libedinsky, I. Utkin, M. Svetlov, A. Bagritsky, M. Golodny, L. Kasil, I. Selvinsky and M. Kazakov.[3] Others who devoted considerable attention to the Jewish theme were, *inter alia*, the non-Jewish writers A. Fadeev, M. Sholokhov, N. Ostrovsky and V. Kataev.

In the thirties, following the far-reaching changes that occurred in Soviet nationalities policy and the imposition of stringent limitations on free expression, Jewish themes were given less consideration than in early Soviet literature. Moreover, even when a Jewish character did appear in a literary work of this period, everything was done to portray him as just another Soviet citizen without emphasising specific national characteristics.

Signs of a partial change began to appear in the second half of the thirties when the approaching danger of conflict between the USSR and Nazi Germany resulted in a number of works stressing the anti-Semitic policy prevailing in Germany and, hardly less so, in countries such as Poland and Romania. But following the signing of the Molotov–Ribbentrop Pact in 1939, this tendency ceased, not to reappear until the outbreak of the Soviet–German war in June 1941[4]

Indeed, it was during the war period that the most important substantive change occurred. Although many non-Jewish Russian, Ukrainian, Belorussian and other Soviet writers and poets dealt with the Jewish Holocaust and Jewish heroism in the works they wrote during and immediately after the war,[5] it was the Soviet authors of Jewish origin who – out of profound shock and a feeling of common destiny – expressed most deeply the dreadful tragedy; national-Jewish motifs made themselves felt with great force in their writings.

The years 1941–7

The gathering storm and the grave dangers implicit in it, especially for the Jews, were expressed by Ilya Erenburg as early as 1940, in a powerful poem which describes the wanderings and isolation of the tortured Rachels and Haims and Leahs.[6] Erenburg later described, in many articles and newspaper stories, the atrocities against the Jewish population and the acts of heroism of Jews who revolted against the Germans even though the odds were heavily against them.[7] In 1946–7, he wrote his great literary work, *The Storm*, in which he described the war, the Holocaust and the tragedy of Babi Yar.

Another of the writers who dealt with Jewish martyrology at the beginning of the war was Vasily Grossman. While the Jewish theme is given only minor and episodic treatment in his first book, *Immortal Is the People* (1942), which describes the panic-stricken retreat of the Red Army in the summer of 1941, he raised in the clearest manner the fateful question that hundreds of thousands of Jews had then to ask themselves: to remain or to flee? Grossman attempted to answer this question in his book *The Old Teacher*, written in 1942 and published the following year. The Jews in a small Ukrainian town are unaware of the extent of the approaching disaster. The only person who reads the situation correctly is the old teacher Rosental who wants to leave, but is too late.

Grossman was among the first to describe the relations between the Jews and the local population under the Nazi occupation. He attempted to make a clear distinction between the majority of the local population, who took no part in the destruction of the Jews, and a minority of nationalists, careerists and deserters, who collaborated with the enemy. It is in fact this theme which, in different variations, was reiterated in many of the literary works dealing with the war period. Among the very few who dared deal with the gross apathy of the local population when the Jews were led to slaughter was the Jewish–Ukrainian poet Savva Golovanivsky, in his poem 'Abraham'.[8]

As against this, while the attitude of the local population towards the Nazi extermination of the Jews was dramatically conveyed in Boris Gorbatov's interesting work *The Undefeated* (1943), the description was not free of idealisation. Gorbatov's explanation of why the Russian population saved the fleeing Jews is noteworthy: the acts of heroism performed to aid the Jews are not the result of Communist ideology; rather, 'the smell of blood / of Jews shot somewhere outside the city / imposed a duty . . . this was a duty of conscience'. However, the brotherhood of Soviet nationalities did pass the test, perhaps because of strong family ties, in A. Bezymensky's story 'Tamara Savitskaya', which was published only in Yiddish translation in 1944.[9] Powerful poetic expressions of shock at the terrible Jewish Holocaust are to be found in works by the poets (all of Jewish origin) Ilya Selvinsky,[10] Leonid Pervomaisky,[11] Pavel Antokolsky,[12] Margarita Aliger,[13] Lev Ozerov[14] and Yakov Khelemsky.[15]

Descriptions of the mass murder of Jews carried out by the Nazis and their local henchmen in the extermination camps, ghettos, villages and forests are contained in literary reportage and in the documentary collections of great historical importance which were written and prepared for publication by many Jewish writers.[16] But these writers also noted the heroic acts of Jews – solitary and in groups – in the occupied territories and in the ranks of the Red Army. They saw the description of Jewish heroism as critically important, not only for determining the historical truth, but even more because they felt obliged to stop the wave of rumours about the Jews as shirkers who skulked in the rear while the Russians and other nationalities were shedding their blood on the battlefield.[17]

What strikes us first when we come to review the works of non-Jewish Soviet writers during the war is how seldom Jewish themes were taken up.[18] However, in the years 1946–7, with the publication of works by T. Valednitskaya,[19] P. Vershigora,[20] G. Linkov,[21] V. Nekrasov,[22] I. Kozlov,[23] A. Fadeev,[24] V. Katlinksaya,[25] I. Vilde,[26] A. Fedorov,[27] F. Panferov[28] and V. Kataev,[29] something of a reverse trend could be discerned. In their descriptions of the war, these writers dealt with the Jewish Holocaust and the attitude of the local population to it. The most important book on the Holocaust itself is Tatyana Valednitskaya's *Sun From the East*. It is entirely devoted to a portrayal of the Lvov Jewish ghetto and its multi-faceted life up until the extermination of all its inhabitants, but the Jewish tragedy is presented throughout as part of the general Soviet tragedy.

The non-Jewish writers, to an even greater degree than authors of Jewish origin, stressed the fact that those who collaborated with the Nazis were a small group of traitors, army deserters and members of nationalist bourgeois organisations. The majority of the population was moved by the tragedy of its Jewish neighbours but lacked the means to save them. However, an active minority did do everything in its power to extend aid to those Jews who sought to flee (as is described in Kozlov's *In the Crimean Underground*). The Jewish opposition in the ghettos found virtually no expression in these books except for that of Valednitskaya, who described the spontaneous uprising in the Lvov ghetto by a Jewish populace lacking arms and without hope of victory. However, Jewish participation in the partisan movement and in the Red Army was fairly extensively described by these authors.

An analysis of the literary works published during and immediately after the war shows that even those Russian, Ukrainian and Belorussian writers who did touch on the Jews made almost no reference to national symbols, Jewish motifs, specific Jewish qualities or the link with the national past. This is what differentiates their work from that of the Soviet writers of Jewish origin noted earlier. It is therefore noteworthy when such elements do occur (mainly in poetry), for example, in the poems of the Russian A. Surkov,[30] the Belorussian M. Tank,[31] and the Ukrainians M. Rylsky[32] and P. Tychyna;[33] they also appear in the prose of V. Panova.[34]

As we have seen, the years 1941–7 were a period of relative freedom for literary expression, and Soviet writers, poets and dramatists exploited this opportunity to the maximum; they were finally able to express the hidden feelings, thoughts and aspirations which they had long silenced. Of course, not everything was published, even in this period. And not all the writers dared commit everything in their hearts to paper, for the great purges of the recent past, which had claimed numerous writers among their victims, still loomed before their eyes.

Signs of an imminent change in this liberal policy were already visible at the end of the war; they became even more obvious in August 1946, following Zhdanov's much publicised speech. Thus, while Jewish themes occupied an important place in the works of Soviet authors in 1946–7, those who studied the official publication policy closely were not likely to overlook the deliberate policy of silence on the Holocaust in political statements and in documentary works. Moreover, wide circles were also aware of the pressure being exerted behind the scenes by the authorities to discourage those engaged in collecting documentary material on the Holocaust and Jewish resistance. This seems to have worked, as many writers, especially those of Jewish origin, dropped Jewish subjects in general and the Holocaust in particular.[35] That the continuation of Valednitskaya's *Sun from the East* was never published – despite constant promises that it would soon appear – is perhaps the clearest external sign that the new policy went into effect as early as 1946.

The years 1948–53

During the war and the two years that followed, the Jewish theme in Soviet literature was almost entirely devoted to war events. However, beginning in

1948, some works that dealt with the pre- and post-war years began to appear. We shall discuss the treatment of the pre-war, war and post-war periods separately.

Pre-war themes. Our examination of a large number of literary periodicals and books published during 1948–53 has revealed only six works that treated the pre-war Jewish themes extensively or even episodically. Five of these are by non-Jewish writers and one by a Jew.

In terms of our analysis, there is no doubt that the most important book – and one which to a large extent marked the end of a phase in the official publication policy – was *Years of Life* by Aleksandr Isbakh (Yitskhak Bakhrakh).[36] The book is a collection of semi-autobiographical stories portraying in depth Jewish village life in the Pale of Settlement before World War I (beginning in 1911) and during and after the Revolution. In relating the history of the main protagonist, the orphan Shtein, who traverses the long road from synagogue beadle to active Communist, Isbakh succeeded in portraying the old way of life, the synagogue experience, anti-Semitism and the relations among the various strata of the Jewish population, its parties and movements. Even though the author's approach to the Jewish religion is a negative one, the very fact that he described Jewish festivals, prayers and customs – and even quoted the words of the Zionist anthem, *Ha-tikvah* – was in itself remarkable. Isbakh, apparently misled by the new Soviet policy on the establishment of the State of Israel, inferred that this would also mean a shift as regards Zionism; but a few months after his book appeared he was furiously attacked by the daily press and the periodicals (see Doc. 61).[37]

There were two works, different in nature and in the period portrayed, which contained descriptions of pogroms and other acts of violence against Jews. In the second part of his trilogy, *An Extraordinary Summer*, the veteran Russian writer K. Fedin includes a short but powerful passage describing the pogroms carried out by the Cossacks during the Civil War.[38] The novel *Beyond the Dnester* (1950), by the authoress L. Kabo, portrays life in Moldavia before the outbreak of the Soviet–German war and the Nazi occupation of the region.[39] One of its characters, the student Greenberg, is badly beaten by an anti-Semitic student; his room-mates, who witnessed but did not intervene in this act of hooliganism, decided nonetheless to teach the anti-Semite a lesson for his 'Fascist actions'. Another Jewish character, the canteen-keeper Itsik, who is a member of the cooperative, makes sure that the crops do not fall into the hands of the approaching Germans. Kabo also mentions the Nazi murder of Moldavian patriots in the Jewish cemetery in Kishinev. Her portrayal of Jewish protagonists is generally positive and sympathetic, a phenomenon particularly remarkable given the year of publication.

There were three other works which, if anything, portray Jews in a negative light. The most important of these is L. Leonov's novel, *The Russian Forest* (1953).[40] The author describes the rape of 'the Russian forest' (his symbol for the Russian people) by its enemies, among whom he gives prominent place to a Jewish timber merchant from Riga.[41] This portrayal of the Jews as hostile to the Russian people during a peak period of Stalinist anti-Semitism, and by one of the most important Soviet writers, was undoubtedly a grave act, but, as we shall see below, it was also an exceptional one.

War themes. The war continued to occupy the central place in Soviet literature during the years 1948–53, with the Jewish theme appearing in twenty-four works, only three of them by writers of Jewish origin (German, Erenburg and Grossman).

'Her Family', by Boris Polevoi (Doc. 151), describes the Jewish Holocaust in various regions under Nazi occupation; it forms part of his book *We Are Soviet People* (1948). In Polevoi's second book, *Gold*, published at the end of 1949, Goldshtein, an old Jewish doctor who is loved and admired by all, is murdered by the SS; they drag him from his home, shoot him, and then trample on him.

A story by V. Popov[42] presents a shocking description of how Jews under Nazi occupation were transported from the ghetto to their death in an industrial town in the Donbas. The bitter fate of the Jews under Nazi occupation in Lvov is portrayed in the collection of sketches, *The People of the Lvov Ghetto* (1950),[43] by the Ukrainian writer Yaroslav Galan, and V. Kataev reports on the Jews of Odessa in *For Soviet Rule* (1951).[44] However, Galan did not treat the Jewish tragedy as the result of deliberate anti-Jewish policy on the part of the Nazis. He concentrated on the general tragedy of Lvov, where Ukrainian, Jewish and Polish blood alike was shed. This reflects an important substantive change since the publication of Valednitskaya's *Sun From the East*, which also dealt with Lvov. And Kataev – a writer who had devoted so many pages to the Jewish theme in other works – allotted a very minor place to the Jewish aspect of the tragedy in Odessa. But here, we must of course recall the year in which his book was published. In his novel *To a New Shore* (1951),[45] V. Latsis depicts – briefly – the liquidation of the Jews in a Latvian village. O. Maltsev relates the murder of a Jewish bookshop owner in Yugoslavia in his novel *The Yugoslav Tragedy*.[46]

Among the Jewish writers who mention the Jewish Holocaust – also briefly – are Ilya Erenburg, in *The Ninth Wave* (Doc. 152),[47] the plot of which is a continuation of *The Storm*, and V. Grossman in *For a Just Cause*, which was sharply attacked by Soviet critics. (The second part of Grossman's book has never been published in the USSR.)[48]

As against this, Polevoi and Popov (mentioned above) devoted much space in their works to the attempts of the local population to save Jews, as did Panferov in *In the Land of the Defeated*,[49] and Panferov, Galan, Kataev, Vershigora[50] and Medvedev[51] portrayed the struggle of Jews in the underground and the partisan movements. While the hostile treatment accorded many Jews who sought to join the partisan movement and their suffering once they succeeded in joining did not find open expression in Soviet literature, this issue was indirectly reflected in V. Andreev's *The People's War*.[52] By relating how the Germans infiltrated their agents, in the guise of Jews, into the partisan ranks, Andreev revealed the kind of thinking which prompted hostility against the Jewish recruits.

Of the number of works which tell of the participation of Jews in the ranks of the Red Army, not one makes specific reference to the fact that the characters involved were Jews. The readers are left to learn this only from the names of the protagonists. For example, while Jewish participation in the Medical Corps occupies a particularly notable place in Soviet literature of this period, Olga Dzhigurda's *The Motorboat Kakhetiya*,[53] although it contains a whole gallery of Jewish characters – Doctor Izrail Grigoryevich Tsibulevsky, courageous and loyal to his patients; female doctors Mariya Isakovna Belokon and Epshtein; nurses Etya Geller, Milya Roizman and Zhenya Kogan; and the son of a Leningrad professor, Ginzburg – they are not specified as such. In contrast to the Georgians, Armenians or Russians in the book, they are described merely as Soviet citizens, without any nationality. It is significant that the only time that Dzhigurda did note the Jewish nationality of a character was in the case of a tailor from Novosibirsk, a picturesque figure from a past that no longer existed.

In A. Korovin's reportage, *Notes of a Military Surgeon*,[54] mention is made of the Shvartsgoren couple, of Dr Roitman and Raya Epshtein. And Dr Levin, the protagonist of Y. German's novel *Colonel of the Medical Service*, who tends wounded pilots devotedly while suffering from a serious illness himself, and who receives a medal for his service, is never specifically described as a Jew in the novel (even though the author was of Jewish origin).[55]

A Jewish officer is portrayed in a negative light in the widely publicised work by M. Bubennov, *The White Birch*.[56] Quartermaster Rubin is so cowardly and selfish that his commanding officer warns him that he might be obliged to transfer him to a fighting unit. Especially when contrasted to the other officers in the novel, Rubin undoubtedly constitutes one of the most negative characters in Soviet literature of the period.

The novel *Far From Moscow*, by the young writer V. Azhaev,[57] was probably the most important work in early post-war Soviet literature, and it was of particular importance from the point of view of Jewish themes as well. Set in the Far East during the war period, the plot concerns the construction of a massive oil pipeline, which will contribute to the war effort. One of the central characters on the 'economic front' is the plant's Party Secretary, Zalkind, who is seen by the narrator as reminiscent of the partisan commander of the same region, Levinson, from A. Fadeev's well-known novel *The Rout*. Of the Soviet elite, Zalkind is a man in harmony with himself and with the new Soviet life. He regards himself not only as a descendant of Ermak, but also as following Lenin's path. However, Zalkind's Jewishness finds no expression in the novel, except, perhaps, in the hint that his relatives remained 'there in Maryupol'.

A second Jewish character, the chief quartermaster Liberman, belongs to the category of 'negative characters' in Soviet literature. 'There is nothing of socialism in Liberman', remarks one of the plant's engineers. 'This is Tartuffe himself', comments someone else. For his part, Liberman argues that, 'In quartermastership it is impossible to get along without all manner of cunning and wangling.' But there are moments when even Liberman rises to the level of a 'positive character': in his concern for the plant, in his joy at its success, and in his desire 'to acquire a rifle in order to take revenge on the enemy'. Although Azhaev did not refer directly to Liberman's nationality, it is hinted at in his description of Liberman's appearance and in the references to his family, which remained behind in the occupied areas. Despite the negative aspects of Liberman's character, it can be argued that this novel continued the tradition of the twenties, wherein Jews were portrayed positively in Soviet literature.

The widespread anti-Semitism of the war period on the front and in the rear found only rare expression in the Soviet literature of this period: most notably in the novel *Burning Rivers*,[58] by the writer of Polish origin Vanda Vasilevskaya (Wanda Wasilewska). In a brief episode which occurs during a train trip, a Jewish family that requests milk for its children when food rations are being distributed is told, 'The end has come for your Jewish Kingdom.'

Post-war themes. The Jewish issue rarely found a place in literary works dealing with the post-World War II period. And when it did appear, it was mainly with reference to the revival of industry and the institutions of higher learning. In two works by V. Dobrovolsky, published in 1948 and 1950, there is a character named Dr Goldberg, who is appointed Dean of the Faculty of Physics and Mathematics because there is no one more suitable for the post.[59] An unrealistic man who is not disposed to deal with the 'little things' of everyday life, Goldberg is ready to learn and devoted to the institution in which he works. In a debate on the natural sciences, it is Goldberg who emerges as the enthusiastic supporter of the official line in that period. Although the author tells us nothing of Goldberg's past, one understands that during the war he was in the rear along with the staff of the university at which he works. Goldberg can, in the last resort, be regarded as a positive character according to the accepted criteria of Soviet literature and criticism.

One of the central characters in F. Panferov's novel *Great Art* (1949)[60] is the chief engineer and temporary factory director Altman, who is portrayed as a man who recoils from responsibility, is interested only in plans and not in human beings, and is constantly concerned for his post. Nevertheless, amongst the novel's gallery of characters, Altman does not necessarily represent the negative type. There is one episode in the novel in which a Russian who has disguised himself as a Jew then protests to those in charge that he is being persecuted because he is a Jew. The Party spokesman tells him: 'We respect the Jews as we respect the other peoples in our country.' It is difficult to determine from this whether or not Panferov was hinting that there was indeed a policy of anti-Jewish discrimination in the Soviet Union.

There is no doubt, however, that in his novel *Height*,[61] it was E. Vorobev's intention to present a completely positive character in the form of Ginsburg, a former labourer who has become chief engineer in a factory. In contrast, the Kazakh writer Mustafin has created a negative character in Gitelman, a construction foreman in Kazakhstan.[62] Portrayed as a hypocrite who works little, who likes to talk a lot and who knows 'how to arrange things', Gitelman builds himself a six-room apartment while the Director of the Trust Shcherbakov and his family live in two small rooms. In the end, however, the criticism directed against him prevails, and Gitelman reforms his behaviour. In *My Victory*, a play by V. Sobko and B. Balaban staged at the Lvov theatre, a student of Jewish origin named Mark Shtibner is a traitor who is recruited for monetary gain while in a camp, to act as a spy against the Soviet Union.[63]

But the sole work known to us of unmistakably anti-Semitic flavour in

Soviet literature of 1948–53 is V. Kochetov's novel *Zhurbiny*, which began to be published in 1952.[64] One of the most unsympathetic characters in this novel is Veniamin Semenovich, director of a cultural club and coordinator of its drama group. Kochetov portrayed him as a man who, while not without erudition, is over-ambitious, quarrelsome, contentious and boisterous – despite the fact that he 'doesn't drink vodka'. A wanderer, accustomed to a gypsy life, who continually changes women and places of work, he spent most of World War II in the rear in Kirgizia, where his main concern was how to get some sort of medal. Finally, Veniamin Semenovich reaches a nadir of selfishness when he leaves the city, abandoning his pregnant wife. In this novel, Kochetov concentrated all the stereotyped Jewish characteristics common to anti-Semitic *feuilletons*.

In his novel *The Ninth Wave* (1952), Ilya Erenburg described the popular anti-Semitism of certain circles (mainly those which collaborated with the Nazis during the occupation) (Doc. 152). He was also, as far as we know, the only author to raise in this connection the relations between the Jews of the Soviet Union and the State of Israel. When the Soviet Jewish officer Osip Alper is told by an anti-Semite to go to 'his state, Israel', the former is incapable of understanding how anyone dare suggest that he move to 'an American colony'.

The post-Stalin and Khrushchev period (1953–64)

From many points of view, the period of collective leadership and Khrushchev's ascendancy was undoubtedly more complex and diversified than the Stalin period. The relative liberalisation; the political fissures within the Communist Party and the Soviet intelligentsia; the criticism of the 'personality cult'; the greater diversity in the forms and possibilities of expression; the contradictory policies of relaxation and discrimination towards the various nationalities; and the increased external influences as the result of the breaching of the 'Iron Curtain' – all these could not but bring about changes in Soviet literature.[65]

How these changes were expressed in the presentation of Jewish subjects in Soviet literature and the extent to which this period's complexity was reflected in the treatment of the Jewish issue are among the principal questions we shall attempt to clarify.

Pre-war themes

As long as the events of the war were still in the immediate past, the interest of Soviet writers was concentrated on that period; beginning in the fifties, however, more and more works began to appear which dealt with earlier periods. The interest shown by many writers in the relatively remote events of Tsarist Russia derived from their being able to write with greater freedom about the pre-Soviet periods as much as from the past being of intrinsic interest to them. Moreover, turning to distant history enabled them to deal with current events by Aesopian analogy – something particularly important, for instance, for anyone seeking to protest against anti-Semitism in the USSR.

The old Jewish way of life in the villages of the Pale of Settlement and, less often, in larger urban centres, was portrayed in a number of works by non-Jewish Soviet writers. Thus, for example, K. Paustovsky's heart-rending story about the tragic events in the town of Kobrin during World War I shows open sympathy to the Jews (Doc. 149).[66] Anti-Semitism in the Tsarist army during the war is described in N. Brykin's story 'Changes on the Eastern Front'.[67] As usual in Soviet literature, however, hate of the Jews on the part of the Tsarist regime was treated as simply one of the means employed by the forces of reaction within the student and worker ranks.

As against this, few Soviet writers of Jewish origin dealt with the period preceding the October Revolution. One of the stories in a collection by the children's writer Y. Taits tells of life in the Pale of Settlement.[68] In *Spring*, the autobiographical book by A. Brushtein, another children's writer, the author-ess mentions the Dreyfus Affair and the Jewish revolutionaries.[69] And to the list of children's writers one must, of course, add S. Marshak, whose memoirs mention the Dreyfus Affair together with his experiences in his grandfather's house and his study of Hebrew.[70] A part of Ilya Erenburg's memoirs – one of the most important documents on the Jewish national problem in the USSR published in recent times – is devoted to life in the cities of Kiev and Moscow during Tsarist times.[71] Again, in the list of memoirs concerned with Jewish life in the Tsarist period, it is important to mention the notes of the well-known Soviet Jewish singer and musician Leonid Utesov,[72] as well as the publication in 1964 of the stories discovered among the literary remains of Isaac Babel.[73]

Jewish themes took up a very small place in works on the period of the Revolution and the Civil War. In his short story of 1963, 'Enemies',[74] Emanuel Kazakevich related how Lenin 'smuggled' the Menshevik leader Martov out of the country under the very nose of Dzerzhinsky, head of the *Cheka*. The critics excoriated this story in the name of 'historical truth', severely attacking the author for daring to portray the Bolshevik leader Lenin 'as a liberal humanist' who took account of private feelings and acted on his own respon-sibility.[75] In this story, as in his 'The Blue Notebook'[76] – which deals with Lenin and Zinovyev – Kazakevich made no mention of the fact that Martov and Zinovyev were Jews. However, it was not by chance that these two 'enemies of the revolution' re-appeared in Soviet literature after so long an absence. And even though they were portrayed negatively, this was accomp-lished without employing the notorious epithets of the Stalin period.

The participation of Jewish unit commanders and commissars in the Communist forces during the Civil War is described by the Ukrainian writer A. Rutko and the important Russian authoress V. Panova.[77] Rutko's novel, which describes the war between the Bolsheviks and the anarchist military units of Nestor Makhno, recounts the latter's limitless anti-Semitism and his order forbidding 'Christians to give refuge to Jews'. The scene in which the commander of the 'Whites' demands that the Jewish and Communist pris-oners divide off from the others – to be shot – was bound to arouse associations with the World War II period, as an identical order by the Germans appeared in many Soviet literary works.

Panova's *A Sentimental Novel* provides an extensive portrayal of the life of the Gorodnitsky family in a city of southern Russia during and after the Civil War.

The father is a well-to-do merchant who follows Jewish religious precepts and customs, whereas his two sons are loyal revolutionaries. The elder son, Ilya, is a Bolshevik, a division commissar and a member of the revolutionary court, but he is also a careerist; the younger son, Semka, a Komsomol member, is fanatic and idealistic, devoting his energy to the struggle against religion. In general, Panova's Jewish characters are objectively portrayed and faithful to the reality of the historical period described.

Yury Kolesnikov's *The Darkness Thickens Before the Dawn*, which appeared in Kishinev in 1959,[78] ranges widely over the life of Romanian Jewry during the period of rising Fascism and persecution of the Jews. The author wrote knowledgeably – apparently from personal experience – of Zionist movements such as 'Gordonia', and of the preparation for and emigration to Palestine. As is to be expected of a Soviet writer, 'Gordonia' is presented in an extremely negative light: the pioneers fall victim to the double exploitation of the owner of the estate on which they work and of their leaders, and Zionism is depicted as aspiring to extend the territory of Palestine in order to establish an expansionist Jewish state and intending to attain this goal by force of arms.

Nikolai Chukovsky's 'The Wanderer', published in 1956 (though written in 1932), and 'Varya' (1958),[79] contain two 'protagonists' whom all the signs indicate to be Jews; both are portrayed as so unsympathetic that they are bound to arouse revulsion in the reader. Mishka, in 'The Wanderer', is a money-grubber without any homeland or ideal, who deserts from the army after he has succeeded in becoming rich through underhand deals. He wanders through many lands, including Palestine, with the one aim of getting rich quickly – until he meets his death at the hands of a smuggler who robs him of his gold teeth. Leva Kravits, in 'Varya', betrays his friend and his sweetheart who are defending the city of Petrograd, killing one of them during his attempt to escape to the enemy camp.

We meet characters of Jewish origin who are even more repulsive in N. Ilyina's novel *The Return*.[80] One of the main characters, the journalist Roizman, arrives at the city of Kharbin, where he founds a newspaper and uses it for purposes of blackmail, threats and other criminal acts. A man of no principles, he has but one aspiration: to get rich quickly and reach the land of his dreams, the United States of America. In the fairly full gallery of negative characters portrayed, Roizman is one of the basest; in contrast to other White Russians, he even despises his homeland, Russia.

If there is any small doubt as to the anti-Semitic orientation of the above-mentioned authors, there can be no question of this kind regarding the trilogy entitled *The Rachinsky Sisters*, by the Ukrainian authoress Irena Vilde (Darya Drobyazko);[81] the novel *Granite Does not Melt* by the Russian writer of Armenian origin, V. Tevekelyan;[82] and the novella *In the Paths of Life* by the Ukrainian writer A. Dimarov (Doc. 150).

Virtually all the Jewish characters in Vilde's work are speculators, swindlers and thieves, but outdoing all the others is Suleiman, a character who might well have stepped straight out of the *Protocols of the Elders of Zion*. He is a swindler, a speculator, a hypocrite, an agent of the Polish police (the novel is set in a town in the Carpathians on the eve of World War II) and a sadist. In a rape scene (though the rape does not take place in the end because of his impotence) Suleiman, enraged and full of bestial hate, tears apart the book of Psalms which he has never abandoned – just as he used to tear apart baby birds in his childhood.

Tevekelyan, a former *Chekist*, writing in 1962 at the height of the anti-Jewish economic trials, portrayed the Jews Kats, Zelding, Shekhman and others as speculators who smuggled silver and gold during the Civil War. (However, as we shall see below, this author was to write an even more extreme anti-Semitic novel in 1966.)

Dimarov's novella, which is set in the period following the October Revolution with historical digressions to earlier periods, is one of the most virulent and dangerous anti-Semitic tracts ever written in the Soviet Union. It portrays the Lander family as always having been among the sworn enemies of the Ukrainian people and of having received control not only of lands and property from their Polish masters, but of the churches as well. They are even worse than the Tatars who attack, plunder and then flee, because they remain forever. Dimarov portrays Solomon Lander as having an extraordinarily developed sense of timing, always knowing how to choose the right party and abandon it at the appropriate moment. He is variously a nationalist-Bundist, a member of the Social-Democratic Party, a Trotskyite and a member of the secret service: all excellent objects for hate in Soviet terms.

Dimarov's addition of a second Jewish character, this one a positive type in the Soviet sense of the word (for it is he who exposes the traitorous 'enemy of the people' Lander), was doubtless deliberate; many anti-Jewish writers in the Soviet Union employed this device to forestall any possible accusation of anti-Semitism. Vilde uses it in the second part of her trilogy, in which she inserts the revolutionary Dubich, a positive Jewish character.

War themes

The war theme not only continued to occupy a central place in Soviet literature during the post-Stalin and Khrushchev period, but its importance actually increased both quantitatively and qualitatively. Particularly following the 20th Congress, many works began to contain criticism (though still quite modest) of the grave political and military blunders which led to the severe defeats in the first stages of the war. Jewish themes in this literature also appeared with more frequency than they had during the period 1948–53. In the incomplete material at our disposal, we found fifty works dealing – whether episodically and briefly, or more extensively – with these themes.

A large number of works contain a description of the Holocaust in the Nazi-occupied areas. The most shocking portrayals of how Jewish prisoners of war were murdered after having been sadistically abused appeared in the memoirs and documentary novels of Pilyar, Bondarets, and Larin and Nozarov.[83] The aid which captive soldiers extended to their Jewish comrades when the Germans ordered them to step forward was described by the Jewish author Mikhail Lev.[84] The extermination of the Hungarian Jews in the gas chambers was also described by an author of Jewish origin, A. Yoselevich.[85] But the most powerful and most enraging account of the death-transport of Jews, who were even compelled to dig their own graves, is to be found in a work by the Ukrainian writer M. Yatskiv; this book, with its sympathetic interest in traditional Jewish life, including rabbis and *gabaim* – an exceptional phenomenon in the Soviet literature of this period – was written in 1956–7 and published in 1960.[86]

There was a relatively large number of works dealing with relations between Jews and the local population in the Nazi-occupied territories, and these stressed the noble deeds of non-Jews who attempted to save their Jewish neighbours and friends. A story by V. Vasilevskaya[87] tells of an old Jewish doctor whose German wife leaves him, whereas his Ukrainian housekeeper, Marpa, elects of her own good will to accompany him on his final path: to Babi Yar. The writer points out that Ukrainian and Russian women frequently chose to go with their husbands to certain death. One of the more original works on relations between Jews and non-Jews is A. Batrov's story[88] about a Mexican woman who was brought to the Ukraine many years before. Although her name is Sarita, she is known by everyone as Sarah – which, of course, leads to her death. Although she might have been able to spare her life by explaining that she is not Jewish, she prefers to remain silent and be executed with her Jewish friend Fanya. In the story's moving conclusion, Sarita–Sarah's husband, old Bogdan, elects to join his wife on her final way.

The Moldavian authoress Anna Lupan describes how an attempt to save a Jew fails when someone informs the authorities that he is being hidden in a certain house; what is important in this presentation is that the captured Jew does not betray his benefactors.[89] And, as mentioned previously, there are other works that deal with the aid extended to Jews in camps and ghettos.[90] In contrast, the collaboration of the local population with the Nazis in general, and in the murder of Jews in particular, found virtually no reflection in the Soviet literature of this period.[91]

Minimal treatment was given to the armed Jewish struggle against the Nazis in the occupied territories, in the ghettos and in the partisan movement. V. Ampilov and V. Smirnov briefly relate the organisation of a partisan group in the Lida ghetto,[92] and V. Belaev,[93] in a book dealing with the Lvov ghetto, mentions the distribution there of the leaflet on the Warsaw ghetto revolt and the heroic battle of its inhabitants. The organisation of Jewish Communists in preparation for the uprising in the Minsk ghetto is described by the Belorussian writer Ilya Gursky.[94] In the two last-mentioned books, and particularly in Gursky's, there is an attempt to contrast the Jewish Communists, brave fighters loyal to the Soviet regime, with the well-to-do Jews, former members of Zionist or other nationalist parties, and religious people who collaborate with the Nazis.

Gursky has the Jewish Communist Stolarovich declare that it is necessary to fight not only against the Nazis, but also against the Zionists, who preach apathy and despair. And if Stolarovich's demand for the application of Lenin's theory on the duty of every nationality to conduct a war against its own bourgeoisie appears extremely strange in the conditions of the Nazi occupation and just before the extermination of the Jewish population, his next remarks border on anti-Zionist and anti-Semitic propaganda of the worst kind. The Zionists and Bundists, declares Stolarovich, 'like racists, incite us against other peoples'. 'While they themselves', intervenes another character, 'they, together with the Hitlerites, killed our men.'

Three works written between 1961 and 1963 portray non-Jews who, after the war has ended, recall with affliction and remorse their Jewish wives or sweethearts murdered by the Nazis.[95] The Nazi race theory is mentioned briefly in an earlier book by B. Polevoi,[96] whose works in the forties had devoted a prominent place to the Jewish tragedy. But Soviet writers of Jewish origin now rarely dealt with the anti-Jewish genocide of the Holocaust period: they were well aware that works by Jews on this subject were often not published and, if they were, that they could cause their authors great difficulties with the authorities.

Among the few works on this subject published during the post-Stalin years – aside from Ilya Erenburg's memoirs, a significant portion of which was devoted to the war and the Holocaust – there are two of particular importance: I. Selvinsky's poem 'The Terrible Day of Judgement',[97] written in symbolic language which powerfully describes the Jewish Holocaust, and the book by the Lithuanian Jewish writer Y. Meras, *Stalemate with Death*, published in Lithuanian in 1963.[98] The Jewish Holocaust, albeit in its relationship to the Soviet anti-Semitism of the Khrushchev period, was the theme of E. Evtushenko's renowned poem 'Babi Yar', discussed in Chapter 3.

The participation of Jews in the war as soldiers of the Red Army was another central subject in works dealing with Jewish themes in this period (appearing in some fifteen works out of fifty). In contrast to the years 1948–53, the soldiers and officers of Jewish origin were now portrayed more positively. Furthermore, in a majority of cases, there were clear signs that these characters were indeed Jews. We have found no essential difference between Jewish and non-Jewish writers in the presentation of this subject.

In two novels published between 1959 and 1964, K. Simonov presented Jewish characters and touched on Jewish themes. Although he treated them only episodically, Simonov raised a number of interesting and significant points which help us to understand the attitude of this important Soviet writer towards the Jews. *The Living and the Dead* contains a brief, but powerfully impressive, portrayal of an *Izvestiya* photographer, Mishka Vainshtain, who seeks to photograph destroyed German tanks and is killed *en route* to Moscow. One of the central characters in 'New Year's Eve', a chapter from his major novel *One Isn't Born a Soldier*, is Commissar Breznoi, whose papers indicate, Simonov explicitly stresses, that he is a Jew. Simonov's treatment of this point was exceptional in this period. Later in the novel there is an interesting episode concerning a Soviet German named Goffman, who fights heroically and whom everyone thinks is a Jew (that is, Simonov is saying, the identification of Jews on the basis of their surnames was quite usual in the Red Army).[99]

A novel by I. Gerasimov relates the heroic act of a Jewish soldier, a violinist by profession, who loses his life in an attempt to save his fellow-soldiers in his unit.[100] The important novel by the Soviet Jewish poet L. Pervomaisky also tells of a heroic deed, performed by a soldier named Shreibman; he destroys a German tank, but his posthumous decoration is not awarded him because someone claims that a soldier named Guluyan had performed the deed and that, in any case, the dead need no glory.[101] A. Isbakh wrote of Jewish fighters who fell on the battle fields in France and were posthumously awarded the decoration of National Hero of France.[102] The participation, dedication and loyalty of non-combatant Jews in the war effort have also been described in a number of works published in this period.[103]

Nonetheless, side by side with these positive and sympathetic presentations of Jews and the Jewish theme, there arose a grave phenomenon which had not existed even in the blackest years of the Stalin period: the publication of virulently anti-Semitic literature dealing with the Holocaust period. We have already referred in Chapter 3 to P. Gavrutto's *Clouds Over the City*, published in 1963 under the clear influence of a speech by Khrushchev. In 1964 there appeared G. Makhorkin's *And Again Life*, one of the most venomous anti-Semitic pasquinades published in the Soviet Union until then.[104]

Makhorkin portrays a Jewish family named Krauze, all of whose members seem to compete with each other in performing the basest and cruellest acts. When the Nazis arrive in the Ukrainian city where the father runs a foreign language institute, he immediately begins to work for the Gestapo as a translator (it is worth recalling here that 'the traitor Kogan' in Gavrutto's novel is a translator in the German army), and during interrogations of adults and children behaves with a bestial cruelty which surpasses that of the Germans. This, however, does not save him from death when the Germans learn that he is a Jew. His younger brother, Daniel, who begins his 'career' as an informer even before the outbreak of the war, is taken prisoner by the Germans and becomes a traitor and a *provocateur* who betrays members of the underground to the Germans. After undergoing a special course in sabotage, Daniel is sent to the Soviet Union to carry out espionage and sabotage operations. In the course of his infiltration into the USSR he kills one of the fishermen who had previously saved his life; he is finally caught by the security services and pays the penalty for his deeds.

To complete the picture Makhorkin does not forget to add that, after the war, the family's mother falsely accuses the Ukrainian Zrobeiko of having collaborated with the Nazis. Though completely innocent, Zrobeiko is tried and sent to a concentration camp. It need hardly be added that a book of this kind could only be published with the special approval of the authorities, probably at the highest levels.

Post-war themes

The decisive influence of the war was also reflected in Soviet literature devoted to the post-war period. A number of these works make retrospective mention of the Nazi atrocities against the Jews. We have already noted the works of Gor, Barsky and Voinovich; to them may be added M. Prelezhaeva's 'The Pushkin Waltz',[105] which tells of the murder of the daughter of an old Jewish watchmaker in Poland after she had spat in the face of a Nazi officer. G. Kalinovsky's tale 'Forgotten Story'[106] mentions the murder of a Jewish geologist in Belorussia, and in Y. German's novel *I Am Responsible for Everything*[107] the non-Jewish acquaintances of Dr Lurya wonder how he can enthuse over German machines and sing hymns of praise to Germany (of the post-war period, of course) when the Nazis all but exterminated his people.

In the post-1953 period, Stalin's anti-Jewish policy – which reached its peak in the anti-cosmopolitan campaign and the 'Doctors' Plot' – was treated in few works. Ilya Erenburg – who, according to the testimony of Soviet immigrants to Israel, was perhaps the only person who, even before Stalin's death, dared publicly oppose the slander of the 'Doctors' Plot' and the preparations for the exile of the Jews – published his story 'The Thaw' in 1954 (see Doc. 80). Erenburg began to write his story – which deals, *inter alia*, with the case of the doctors – immediately upon the announcement at the beginning of April 1953 of their acquittal. Again, we find clear allusions to this libel in Evtushenko's poem 'Winter Station', written in 1955 and published the following year.[108] In his two-part novel *Silence* and *The Two*,[109] Yuri Bondarev describes how the Jewish critic Laikman was attacked during the anti-cosmopolitan campaign and how the propaganda against the 'doctor-poisoners' exercised a destructive influence on the population. But the deepest and most exhaustive analysis of the grave Jewish aspects of the anti-cosmopolitan campaign is to be found in G. Nikolaeva's important book, *The Battle on the Way*.[110]

There is no doubt that, from a political point of view, any writer who raised the subject of popular anti-Semitism as a phenomenon still existing in the post-Stalin period was treading on dangerous ground. 'Apartment No. 13', by the authoress A. Valtseva (Doc. 153), is one of the few works which dealt with this issue (the title is apparently an allusion to a similarly entitled work by Korolenko written at the beginning of the century in protest against the anti-Jewish pogroms). The interesting point in Valtseva's story is that this time the anti-Semite is not, as is usually the case in Soviet literature, an enemy of the regime or a man limited in his class awareness, but an officer of over thirty years' service in the Red Army. Admittedly, her portrayal of anti-Semitism as resulting only from Nazi propaganda did nothing to clarify what other factors contributed to its persistence in the Soviet Union. However, immense importance attaches to the very fact that the issue was raised despite the official claims that anti-Semitism no longer existed in the Soviet Union. This story's publication in early 1957 can be attributed to the new freedom of action that the editors of literary periodicals allowed themselves in the period immediately following the 20th Congress.

The English–French–Israeli 'aggression' against Egypt in 1956 was given an incidental mention in a story by N. Shundruk.[111] We have found no other reference to Israel in *belles lettres* of the period, although it received considerable space in the Soviet press and political literature.

In sum, although, as we have seen, the post-Stalin and Khrushchev period did not see the publication of any major literary work either wholly or even mainly devoted to Jewish themes, there were a number of works in which they occupied a significant place. Moreover, in comparison with the years 1948–53, such themes were now often treated in a more penetrating manner, less dependent upon the official line. The publication of literary works overtly and sharply attacking Stalin's anti-Jewish policy, and especially of those stressing the existence of anti-Semitism in the Soviet Union, was of undoubted political importance. From an internal Jewish point of view, there was great interest in the publication of memoirs by Soviet writers of Jewish origin, in which their longings, feelings and world-views found at least partial expression. However, one must also recall the negative phenomena which accompanied literary publication in this period: the publication in hundreds of thousands of copies of extreme anti-Semitic works and their destructive effect in a country where popular anti-Semitism is in any case fed by mass media such as the press, radio, television and cinema (see Chapter 3).

The period of the post-Khrushchev collective leadership (1965–7)

Pre-war themes

We found some eighteen works from these few years which dealt either extensively or episodically with the Jewish issue of the pre-war period; five of the most important of these are by authors of Jewish origin. It is intersting that all these five writers devoted most of their attention to the life of Soviet Jewry in the Tsarist period, whereas their treatment of the Soviet period was partial and marginal.

The memoirs of the well-known writer and literary critic Y. Tynyanov (d. 1943), published in 1966, contain a sombre description of the poverty, oppression and fear which were the lot of Jews in small towns during the pre-revolutionary period.[112] Similarly, the veteran screenwriter E. Gabrilovich, also in his memoirs,[113] recalls the pogroms carried out during his childhood in his home town of Voronezh and the difficulties he encountered when he was about to enter secondary school. The pogroms helped to form his 'Jewish national consciousness'. He relates: 'When I wanted to go outside [during the pogroms] in order to join in the fun along with everyone else, I was told that I, too, was a Jew, and that it was therefore for me to weep, not to be merry.' In his autobiographical book *O My Youth*,[114] I. Selvinsky tells of the overt anti-Semitism of the teachers in an Odessa school. The heroes of the book, a Jewish lawyer and his son, become active Bolsheviks and make many sacrifices in the belief that only socialism is capable of eliminating national discrimination.

In his story 'Such Is Life' the Ukrainian writer of Jewish origin N. Rybak integrates an episode from his novel of 1940, *The Error of Honoré de Balzac*.[115] This is the tragic tale of a poor and good-hearted Jewish innkeeper, whose only daughter falls victim to the designs of a rich and evil man (likewise a Jew). Despite the schematic portrayal of this 'class war' among the Jews – a quite common subject in Soviet literature – Rybak's work is dramatically written.

Without doubt, in terms of its wide range and depth of understanding of the life of Soviet Jewry in the Pale of Settlement, David Halkin's 'The Tsimbalists'[116] is one of the most important works of literature on the Jewish issues written in these years, and perhaps in the entire period beginning in the forties. Against the background of the pogroms (in which the book's hero, Aharon, lost his parents) the author described very dramatically the war, the Revolution and the complex relations of love, friendship and conflict between the Jewish family, the Tsimbalists, and their non-Jewish neighbours.

A number of writers briefly raised the issue of the anti-Semitism which prevailed among the nationalist and rightist circles during the Civil War period and in Nazi Germany.[117] More significant, perhaps, is the fact that Jewish leaders of the *Komsomol* and the Communist Party were treated far more extensively in this period than in the Stalin or Khrushchev periods. S. Dongurov, in his novel *Diplomats*,[118] and V. Dmitrevsky, in his story 'Bandera rossa' (The Red Flag),[119] stress and portray sympathetically the fine Communist qualities of the veteran diplomat and long-time Foreign Minister, M. Litvinov, and of one of the *Komsomol* heads, L. Shatskin.

In contrast, the traditional 'enemies of the people', L. Trotsky and G. Zinovyev, are portrayed in an extremely negative manner in novels by V. Zakrutkin[120] and V. Kochetov,[121] both of which were published in the 'conservative' periodical *Oktyabr*. Whereas Kochetov, an experienced veteran in literary and political spheres, was fairly cautious in his allusions to Zinovyev's Jewishness, his younger literary colleague saw no need to restrain himself in this way.

Zakrutkin employed all the tried and tested methods of the notorious anti-Jewish *feuilletons* and propaganda articles in order to underline Trotsky's Jewishness. Thus, he calls him by the shameful name 'Yudushka' (i.e. Judas Iscariot) and stresses that the name of the 'Trotskyite' and White Guard member who in 1933 made an attempt on the life of the German Embassy adviser in order to bring about a war between the USSR and Germany' is *Yuda Shtern*. All Trotsky's friends and supporters in this book have Jewish names and all are described as feeble, treacherous and totally incapable of understanding Russia. Zakrutkin also notes that Hitler very much enjoyed reading Trotsky's autobiographical *My Life*, and even learned a great deal from it.

War themes

The great interest in the war shown by Soviet writers, poets and dramatists ever since its conclusion continued into the years 1965–7. Russian, Ukrainian and Belorussian writers continued to concentrate on themes centred round the Holocaust in the Nazi-occupied areas.[122] Interestingly enough, however, their works contained few Jewish characters, which was symptomatic of a process that had begun at the end of the forties, and that had not changed significantly in the post-Stalin and Khrushchev periods.

One novel, by Irzhi Marek, did, however, contain a shocking description of Jews chanting Psalms as they were being transported on their final way.[123] The mass murder of the Jews of Kiev and Kaunas was described by Golovchenko, as well as by A. Klenov, a writer of Jewish origin.[124] Ilya Konstantinovsky very skilfully conveyed the tragedy of a young Warsaw Jewess who escaped from the ghetto and found a hiding place, but who again fell into the hands of the Nazis when she was compelled to leave it.[125] Konstantinovsky, who devoted attention to the fate of the Jews in the Holocaust, points out that the poison of anti-Semitism was even to be found among the Red Army prisoners in German hands. V. Taras, too, writes about the anti-Semitism among the Soviet population in the occupied areas.[126] But such references to this sensitive subject remained rare during this period.

On the other hand, a great many literary works still stressed the unsuccessful attempts of neighbours and friends to help the Jews in distress, even at the cost of great personal sacrifice and danger.[127] G. Baklanov and N. Dubov powerfully described such attempts by imprisoned soldiers and officers[128] where the chances for success were non-existent and the risk mortally grave. Dubov is one of the few authors who was not content merely to describe the events; he also endeavoured to generalise and draw conclusions. He has one of the prisoners, who is witness to the Germans' inhumanly sadistic treatment of the Jewish prisoners, ask his friend: 'Why are the Germans so cruel to the Jews?' 'Is it only the Germans?' asks another prisoner. 'It's all the Fascists. Every man – and it doesn't matter how he disguises himself – whoever's an anti-Semite is also a Fascist.'

The terrifying spectacle of the slaughter of masses of old people, women and children is powerfully recounted in the poems 'Children in Auschwitz' by the Soviet Jewish poet Naum Korzhavin,[129] and 'The Cry of the Lake' by the young Russian poet Voznesensky.[130] It is significant that while both these poems speak of the Jewish Holocaust, the word 'Jew' is never mentioned explicitly in either.

Post-war themes

Jewish topics were discussed in few works dealing with the post-World War II period, despite the fact that the number of such works increased as the war became more distant. This was mainly due to the danger inherent in dealing with controversial current topics, and there is certainly no doubt that the Jewish issue in the Soviet Union belonged to this category.

From our point of view, I. Grekova's *During Tests* is the most important of these works, particularly because of its open references to the anti-cosmopolitan campaign and to the terrible pressure which it exerted on a Jewish general, Gindin, who was still on active service in 1952.[131] In M. Roshchin's story 'From Morning to Evening', there is an elderly Jewish agricultural worker named Raikhel, who is considered 'strange'.[132] B. Kostyu-kovsky tells of an old doctor named Rapoport, who continues to work dedicatedly even though he is already aged seventy.[133] (Soviet writers seem to assume that all the Jews in the USSR are old, as the younger generation has assimilated.) R. Zernova portrayed the wedding of the daughter of a mixed Jewish–Russian family, where the guests danced the Jewish 'Freylekhs'.[134]

The play *The Wolves in the City*, by the veteran Jewish dramatist Lev Sheinin, is of interest because of Sheinin's caustically critical treatment of the nationalities problem in general and the Jewish problem in particular.[135] One of his main protagonists is a speculator and generally shady dealer from Odessa who changes his name – from Buker (a Jewish name) to Bukashvili (Georgian) to Bukshyan (Armenian) to Bukov (Russian) – in accordance with his needs and region of operations. One first has the impression that Buker is a Jew, but, the playwright reveals, he is in fact of German–gypsy origin: 'When I fled from Krasnodar to Odessa', he tells his interrogators, 'I decided that it was more convenient to appear as a Jew than as a German; but some years later [i.e. at the end of the forties] I would perhaps have done the opposite.'

The extreme anti-Semitic story by the Armenian–Russian writer V. Tevekelyan (whom we discussed above) which appeared in 1966 was well suited in tone to the virulent propaganda against the Jewish religion which the Soviet media conducted from the end of the fifties.[136] The main character is Solomon Moiseevich Kazarnovsky, an orthodox Jew who strictly observes all the religious precepts and lives modestly as a pensioner not far from Moscow. As the head of a dangerous gang, Kazarnovsky has no qualms about ordering the murder of any gang member of whom he is suspicious; he also deals in speculation and steals icons from ancient churches, which he sells to people who live outside the USSR. A kind of satanic force (or perhaps his racial origin) drives him to increase his already vast property, even though he needs for nothing. Nor, of course, does Tevekelyan forget to relate at length how Kazarnovsky, weaver of dark intrigues, traps in his web a Russian of weak character who seeks an easy life. Many of the elements in this story recall Dimarov's no less extreme anti-Semitic work, but this time, instead of the main character being a Trotskyite and Bundist, he is, according to the requirements of the time, an orthodox Jew.

We may conclude this section by stating that the period of the new Soviet leadership saw no substantive change in subject matter as compared with the Khrushchev period. While many literary works of the time treated Jewish issues in a positive manner, the extremely anti-Semitic works also published were no less virulent than those that appeared during the Khrushchev period. However, indicative of an incipient change was the fact that writers of Jewish origin were apparently now more willing to introduce Jewish themes into their works.

The Jewish theme in *samizdat* and *tamizdat* works

Works written in the Soviet Union which are passed from hand to hand in mimeograph, photocopy or typewritten form have received the general name *samizdat*; works by writers living in the Soviet Union which are published abroad are collectively called *tamizdat*. The restricted framework of this chapter permits only a brief survey of the principal works on Jewish themes in this important literature.

Samizdat poems by authors of Jewish origin on saliently Jewish subjects began to be passed from hand to hand in restricted circles during and immediately following World War II. While the author's name sometimes appeared, more often they were anonymous.[137] This phenomenon seems to have died out completely during 1949–53, the peak years of the terror, and was only resumed after the 20th Party Congress. Due to the very nature of *samizdat*, only a small fraction of this material is known to us.[138]

We do know, however, that many such works were published in reaction to the fierce debates around Evtushenko's poem 'Babi Yar'.[139] Among the poems signed with pseudonyms, those by 'Magen' (David Markish, son of the famous Yiddish poet Perets Markish) are of a high literary standard, and excelled in profound and powerful national motifs. Two poets of the younger generation, I. Brodsky and A. Galich (Ginzburg), whose works were published both in *samizdat* and *tamizdat*, wrote very frequently on Jewish themes.[140]

In the realm of prose, Boris Pasternak's important novel *Doctor Zhivago* holds a special place – from our point of view. The author devotes many pages to his reflections on Judaism and Christianity, on the reasons for the existence of anti-Semitism and the ways to overcome it.[141] The Jewish theme found even more prominent expression in V. Grossman's novel *Forever Flowing*.[142] In a fantastic-allegorical work, *This Is Moscow Speaking*, which tells of the 'day of the open murders', the young Jewish writer Yuly Daniel (son of the well-known Yiddish writer, Meerovich) presents a Jewish character named Margolis who declares that he will fight if pogroms break out, for never again will there be a Babi Yar.[143] Daniel's close friend A. Sinyavsky, who was tried together with him in February 1966, also focuses on the issue of anti-Semitism in the Soviet Union in his discussion of the anti-cosmopolitan campaign and the 'Doctors' Plot'.[144]

Among the lesser-known writers who have dealt with the Jewish issue in the USSR in general, and with anti-Semitism in particular, are A. Remizov (in a play entitled *Is There Life on Mars?*, which he published abroad under the pseudonym I. Ivanov)[145] and Alla Korotova.[146] There is no doubt, however, that the treatment of the Jewish theme in the works of the greatest living Russian writer, A. Solzhenitsyn, is of special importance. Of course, his complex attitude towards Jews, which finds particular expression in *The First Circle* and *August 1914*, requires a precise and cautious examination, for it was highly symptomatic of how 'the other Russia' views the Jewish issue.[147]

Documents to Chapter 11

Pre-war themes

Document 149* Paustovsky:[148] Jewish sufferings in World War I (1955)

From Brest we went to the small town of Kobrin. Mr Gronsky came with us in his dilapidated and scratched old Ford. Brest was ablaze. The fortifications were being blown up. Rosy smoke was filling the sky behind us.

Near Brest we picked up two children who had lost their mother. They were standing at the edge of the road, huddled together, a little boy in a torn school greatcoat and a thin girl of about twelve. The boy pulled down the peak of his cap over his eyes to hide his tears. The girl clasped his shoulders tightly with both arms. We seated them in a cart and covered them with old greatcoats. A heavy stinging rain was falling.

Towards evening we entered the small town of Kobrin. The coal-black earth had been churned into a muddy wash by the retreating army. Crooked houses with sloping, rotten roofs sank down to their very thresholds in mud. The horses were neighing in the dark, lanterns shone dimly, the shaky wheels clanked, and rain flowed down from the roofs in noisy streams.

In Kobrin we saw the Jewish holy man known as a *zadik* being led away from the town. Gronsky told us that there are several such *zadikim* in the Western territory and Poland. They always live in the small towns. Hundreds of people from all over the country come to the *zadikim* for all kinds of worldly advice. The population of the small towns makes its living from these visitors.

Near a squat wooden house a crowd of dishevelled women were sighing. A closed carriage harnessed to four thin horses stood at the door. I had never seen such an ancient carriage. Dismounted dragoons were smoking. It seems that this was the escort which was to guard the *zadik* on his way.

Suddenly the crowd started shouting and rushed to the door. The door burst open, and a huge, tall Jew with a face overgrown with a black beard emerged carrying in his arms, like a baby, a wizened white-bearded old man wrapped in a blue quilt.

The *zadik* was hurriedly followed by old women in talmas and pale young men in caps and long frock-coats. The *zadik* was placed in the carriage, the

* *Source*: K. Paustovsky, 'Bespokoinaya yunost' (Restless Youth), *Novy mir*, 1955, no. 5, pp. 99–102.

408

old women and the young men took their seats by him, and the sergeant-major gave the command: 'Mount!' The dragoons mounted their horses, and the carriage set off in the mud, rocking and creaking. The crowd of women ran after it.

'You know', said Gronsky, 'a *zadik* never once in his life leaves his house. And he is fed with a spoon. Word of honour! So help me God!'

In Kobrin we billeted in a damp old synagogue. Only one man was sitting there in the dark and muttering something that might have been a prayer or a curse. We lit our lanterns and saw an elderly Jew with sad mocking eyes.

'Oi-oi-oi', he said, 'what joy you have brought to us poor people, my dear soldiers.'

We maintained a gloomy silence. The medical orderlies dragged in a sheet of iron. We lit a fire on it and put on a kettle to boil some tea. The children sat quietly by the fire. [...]

There was no one else in the damp and dark synagogue. The fire was dying out, and only the elderly Jew was sitting at the boy's side, muttering something between a prayer and a curse.

'Where are our men?' I asked him.

'Do I know?' he answered and sighed. 'Everybody wants some hot soup.'

He was silent for a while.

'Sir', he said to me softly and distinctly, 'I am a saddler. My name is Iosef Shifrin. I cannot tell you what lies upon my heart. Sir! We Jews know from our prophets how God can take His revenge on men. Where is He, that God? Why has He not burned in fire, torn out the eyes of those who ushered in such a misfortune?'

'What do you mean, God, God!' I replied rudely. 'You talk like a fool.'

The old man smiled sadly.

'Listen to me', he said and touched the sleeve of my greatcoat. 'Listen, you clever and educated man.'

Again he was silent for a while. The glow hung motionless on the dusty synagogue windows.

'I was sitting here and thinking. I do not know as well as you do whose fault all this is. I never even attended *ḥeder*. But I am not quite blind and I see some things. So I ask you, who will avenge? Who will settle the large account for this little human being here? Or are you all so good that you will feel pity and pardon those who bestowed upon us this lovely gift – this war. Heavens above, when will people come together and create a real life for themselves!'

He raised his hands to the synagogue ceiling and, closing his eyes and swaying, cried piercingly: 'I do not see who will avenge us! Where is the man who will wipe away the tears of the poor and give milk to the mothers that the babies should not suck an empty breast? Where is he who will sow bread upon this earth for the hungry? Where is he who will take gold from the rich and give it to the poor? Accursed be forever those who sully man's hands with blood, who rob the poor! Let them have neither children nor grandchildren! Let their seed rot and their own spittle kill them, like poison. Let the air be sulphur to them and the water boiling tar. Let a child's blood poison a piece of rich bread and let them choke on that piece and die in torment like crushed dogs.'

The old man was screaming with raised arms. He shook them, closing his fists. His voice thundered and filled the whole synagogue.

I felt terrified. I went out, leaned on the synagogue wall and started smoking. It was drizzling, and darkness was settling more and more thickly upon the ground. It was as if it were deliberately leaving me alone with my thoughts of the war. One thing was clear in my mind: we must put a stop to it – whatever the cost. We must devote all the strength and all the blood of our hearts for the final triumph of justice and peace on this poor and desecrated earth.

Document 150*   Dimarov:[149] a sinister portrait of Jews in the Ukraine (1963)

And while Vasil is ponderously meditating on the new trap which life has set for him, we must return to Lander. To GPU chief, Comrade Lander, who was deeply offended by the Chairman of the village Soviet, to his dirty plans, to his vindictive thoughts.

'They are all like that, those damned *khokhly*'.† Lander summed up his reflections. 'No matter what you do for them, you will never get their thanks.'

The Landers had early clashed head-on with the Ukrainian nation in those distant times when the Polish nobility appointed concessionaires of Orthodox churches. Isaak Lander also took up this *gesheft* [racket]. He gave a rich Polish nobleman a sackful of money and was given in exchange three churches in the Podolya region, including their priests and deacons, as well as the whole of their inventory and all their parishioners.

From that time on Isaak became a wall separating God from the faithful. If you want to baptise your child, first you must go to Isaak, and only then you may proceed to the church. If you wish to bury your dead, you must first grease Isaak's palm, and then he will issue you a permit. If it's blessing Easter food you desire, you can bless it to your heart's content, provided you first render unto Isaak that which is Isaak's; only then can you render unto God that which is God's. And so the silent poor carried their last possessions earned with their sweat and blood to Isaak, whose hand was always out-stretched. They cursed in a whisper the greedy infidel, saying that he was worse than a Tatar. A Tatar might attack you, grab whatever he can, and then go back to his Crimea. But this leech, they said, is always at work: you cannot get rid of him or wish him away with the sign of the cross!

Having saved up some cash, Lander began to size up other churches, until the Zaporozhye Cossacks caught up with him. It is clear that the neighbouring people had really taken to Isaak, for the Cossacks rejoiced over him, as over a dear brother:

'So you were caught after all, you pig's ear! What, friends and comrades, can we offer to our dear guest?'

But while the slow-witted Cossacks debated whether the infidel is to be hanged or drowned, Jehovah took pity on his faithful servant and sent a

* *Source*: A. Dimarov, 'Shlyakhamy zhyttya' (In the Paths of Life), *Dnipro*, 1963, nos. 9–10, pp. 32–3.
† [A pejorative term for Ukrainian.]

detachment of Polish noblemen. And soon the Cossacks' own long-haired heads began to sway in greasy nooses, for the greater glory of God.

Isaak's grandson, Haim Lander, wanted nothing to do with churches. The more so since there was no Polish nobility, either; its broken teeth were chattering somewhere beyond the Zbruch. Never mind, the Landers had become pretty well accustomed to their new masters, for as wise people say: whoever is God, his is the prayer; or, in whoever's cart you are riding, his song you should sing. Why fight the *goyim* when it is so much simpler and easier to bloat them with vodka and then strip them of their last possessions. And so Haim built an inn near a highway and engaged in a legal *gesheft*. Any sheep that happend to be passing by would lose some of its fleece.

In his old age, Haim was mistreated by the ungrateful Ukrainian nation. He was raided by the *haidamaki* [rebel Cossacks] who burned his inn down to the ground and even took the little sack filled with gold that he had buried in the ground. May they and their children, and their children's children, never see a penny again!

From then on the Lander family referred to the Ukrainians only as 'those damned *khokhly*'.

The Lander family, God be praised, did not die out or wither. It survived all crises and storms and spread its tenacious branches throughout the Ukrainian land. Some Landers were rich and other Landers less so, some Landers lived in Podolya and other Landers lived near Kiev. But they were all renowned for their clannishness and their traditional hatred of 'those damned *khokhly*'. Not only, they said, may one cheat a *khokhol*. Rather, it is a duty to cheat a *khokhol*, and it would be no sin to make fun of him, either.

Our Lander was born in Poltava Province into the family of a small-town trader. He was the fourteenth child, and Hersh, touched by this omen of God's infinite mercy, had him named Solomon.

Solomon's childhood was like that of all his contemporaries. In the winter, he attended a *ḥeder* where he memorised the Talmud. In the summer, together with other urchins, he visited country fairs where he accosted slow-moving peasants – 'Greasy *khokhly*, let's tease them.' He pushed around the weaker ones and was himself beaten up more than once, but the parents, blinded by their love, could not praise their offspring enough: 'If you only knew what a wonderful child! God should grant you as much money as little Solomon has wisdom in his head!'

Solomon's future was viewed differently by his two parents. The father had hopes to see his son a rich merchant, while the mother dreamed of his becoming a rabbi, or, if the worse came to the worst, a *zadik*. But Solomon had other ideas. Even as a youth he displayed not only unusual intelligence but sharp political acumen as well, and he joined the Bund. The same unfailing acumen helped him appraise correctly the situation after the Revolution, and, after breaking with the Bund and joining the Russian Social-Democratic Workers' Party, Lander began building a career for himself. He chose Lev Trotsky as his model, imitating him in all respects, down to the pettiest detail of dress, including even his mannerisms. Since, however, Russia could support on her shoulders only one Trotsky, Lander chose to be modest and to rest content with remaining, at least for the time being, a Trotsky on a district scale. His behaviour toward his subordinates was that of inaccessibility and severity; he enjoyed being feared, having it said in warning anticipation when seen on the street: 'Sssshh, Lander is coming!'

He wore a tunic of military cut, riding-breeches tucked into ever-polished chrome-leather boots, and had a ready reserve of the most revolutionary phrases, from world revolution to the immediate expropriation of all private property. He boasted of his revolutionary implacability just like a young girl with a colourful kerchief, made it a motto for his life, that fortunate mount which sooner or later would carry him to the crest of a high wave.

There was only one small flaw in his otherwise spotless character. Try as he would, he could not rid himself of a barely noticeable, tiny flaw he had inherited from his father, Hersh, and his father from grandpa Motele, which he had in turn inherited from great-grandpa, Haim – a hatred of 'those damned *khokhly*'. To him they always smelled of tar and manure, were incomprehensible and hostile; and he was even terrified of them. He himself could not point to the cause of the contempt for Ukrainians that was found in his whole family. Possibly this was the disdain a thief feels for his victim. Otherwise, how could a thief retain any self-respect? He must spit at the people, the labour of whose hands feeds him and his children, the future thieves. This hatred within him was already instinctive, stronger than himself, uncontrollable. And although he covered it up and concealed it, it would occasionally break out.

War themes

Document 151* Polevoi:[150] rescue of a Jewish woman during World War II (1948)

Her family

A small stooping woman of about sixty, but lively for her age, entered with tiny shuffling steps the miniscule room built of wooden planks. It was here, in one of the few remaining buildings in the settlement, that the Chairman had been driven out. The woman's fluffy locks, protruding from her firmly pulled-on beret, were snow-white, but her eyes, large, black, still beautiful, looked young, and their liveliness was in strange contrast to the silver of her hair.

For a moment she rested her gaze attentively on the tired face of the Chairman, and then, as though having made up her mind that he was a man of worth and that one could speak to him frankly, she asked: 'Have you ever been in Toropets? No? A great pity. If you had been in Toropets before the war, you certainly would have known my husband. I am Sara Markovna, Sara Markovna Fonshtein. The wife of Hershl Fonshtein, the best men's tailor in Toropets and the mother of three sons who are all in the Red Army now fighting the Germans. God grant all good people sons such as mine!'

* *Source*: B. Polevoi, 'My – Sovetskie lyudi' (We Are Soviet People), *Oktyabr*, 1948, no. 1, pp. 53–8.

She sat down sideways on the edge of the luxurious armchair offered her, which had somehow got into this uncomfortable little room with its dark log walls, and, as her parchment-like fingers fiddled with the fringe of her black shawl, she went on: 'No, you should not think I've come to ask for something as a mother of Red Army men. Oh no, I would never. I've come from very far away on business, on business of great importance. Are you listening to me? I spent three days coming here from Toropets, in jolting trucks along those terrible wooden roads – Hitler himself should use them to his very death! You hear me? I have come to tell you what noble people live in your District. You needn't worry, I won't keep you long ... It doesn't concern just me. God forbid, I should travel so far if it were my business only! But you are the head of the District, so you should know what worthy people you are in charge of. Do you know the Budenny collective farm, the one on the Toropets Highway? Know it? Well, why don't you answer? Say yes or no.'

'I know', the Chairman said at last in a strange muffled voice, suppressing a smile, with some effort.

For about a year, while the District was occupied by Germans, he and his unit had been partisans in the nearby forests – specifically in the forests, as the Germans had turned the region into a 'dead zone' and had burned down almost all the villages except for those on the highways. During the year spent in the forest thickets, in mud-huts, around bonfires, the Chairman had become completely unaccustomed to houses, and now could not adjust his strong, sonorous bass to the tiny dimensions of the room, and so he was afraid to speak in the presence of strangers lest he should deafen them.

'Well, you know it, that's good. Now listen to me, and listen attentively. I shall tell you something which cannot fail to impress you as the head of the District.'

Hurriedly and excitedly the old woman began to tell him of what she had seen and lived through in these parts under the German occupation.

The very first day of the war, Sara Markovna accompanied her younger son to the military office. Soon her elder son left for the front, leaving his wife Hannah in the care of the old folk. Their middle son in the regular army was already fighting somewhere in Belorussia.

When the German divisions broke through to the Nemen and Toropets was declared besieged, old Hershel found a rusty pick in the shed and joined one of the workers' battalions constructing defensive lines just outside the town.

'Don't worry, Sara. The main thing is not to panic. They won't get beyond the old border', he said when taking his leave of her.

'And if some stray detachments do break through, they will be stopped at our trenches. You know what trenches there will be!' and he solemnly shook his rusty shovel [*sic*] before his wife's tear stained face.

But the Germans broke through the old frontier. And the new defence lines in those parts did not stop them either. And soon the stream of refugees going east along the Toropets Highway, a stream of silent, broken people, trucks and horse-wagons, engulfed the family of the Toropets tailor.

Leaving everything, without even locking the apartment, Sara Markovna left her native town early one morning together with her daughter Raya and her daughter-in-law Hannah. They supported her under the arms and carried her small bundle. Those were the days when the Fascists revelled in their victories. The Berlin radio played marches all the time and broadcast reports on captured villages and towns every hour. The German pilots enjoyed swooping down onto the human rivers flowing along the large and small roads to the east, into the heart of the country. They were improving their bombing skill by aiming at refugees. Fighter planes flew low over the heads of the defenceless crowds, spraying them with fire from their machine-guns and cannon.

When leaving Toropets Hannah was killed on the bridge by a bullet from such a fighter. Her body was carried away together with others and laid to rest in the shade of a willow on the river bank.

Another day passed, and Raya was killed by a bomb from a German dive-bomber. A deep smoky shell-hole was all that remained where the girl had stood.

And Sara Markovna went on and on, went on mechanically, grief-stricken, without thinking of anything, mindful of nothing except that she should not lag behind the stream of people, that she had to move on, move east at any cost.

Someone's kind hands helped her up when she fell into the burning dust of the road. Somebody would give her a piece of bread or a potato, and, without even thanking them, she would eat it, feeling neither hunger nor the taste of the food. At night voices of strangers would call her to their fires, and she would go up to them, would warm herself at somebody else's fire, a mother of a large family, suddenly left utterly alone.

On the fourth day she fell ill. She left the road and fell into the dusty grass which smelt of tar and petrol. She was sure she would die there as she no longer had the strength to move on. Wagons rolled past her, their wheels creaking. Sad, uncomprehending eyes of children looked out from behind dusty bundles. Tired horses dropped yellow foam, wheels creaked, cattle bellowed, tormented by the heat and stifled by the dust. [...]

Still not understanding what had happened, Sara Markovna felt it was something terrible and cried out mournfully. The woman looked at her with the same dry, sad eyes as those of the refugees.

'You've come round? My dear, you'd have done better – ' The woman did not finish and stared again at the windows. The tense whining and clanging struck in waves, now so strong that the walls shook and the panes rang, now dying away in the distance. After a short silence, she added: 'The Germans, the Germans are here!'

Sara Markovna threw off the old ragged blanket with which she had been covered and jumped out of bed. But she staggered and leant against the wall.

'I'll go, I cannot stay here, I'll go', she said.

The woman gave her a severe, stern look and merely shrugged: 'Where will you go?! Lie down. What must be cannot be avoided.'

In a flash Sara Markovna remembered the terrible stories of the Germans' savage slaughters of the Jews. How, in the small town of Sebezh, the Jews were summoned into the local synagogue allegedly for registration, and then heavy logs were placed against the synagogue doors, and the old wooden building was set afire. How in the town of Nevel the Jewish families were driven on to a narrow spit of land jutting far out into the lake, and then tanks were driven along the spit, and how that day the water of the lake, always renowned for its transparency, became brown from blood.

No, she had no right to bring disaster to the family who happened to give her shelter. No, she cannot, she must not stay here.

'I'll go. Let me go', she said and stood up. 'I'm not afraid of death. I have lived my life, brought up my children. You have three, I do not want others to die because of me ...'

'And you know what she answered me, this collective farmer, Ekaterina Fedorovna Evstigneeva?' the old woman was telling the Chairman of the District Council while wiping the tears, which now and again rolled down her wrinkled cheeks, with the edge of her shawl.

'I beg you write her name in your notebook! Ekaterina Fedorovna Evstigneeva from the Budenny collective farm. You'd better hear what she said to me. She said I was an old fool. Yes, an old fool, no more, no less. That I was out of my mind if I thought that she, a collective farmer, would throw out a live human being to be torn to pieces by the beasts just to save her own skin ... she said the Soviet power had not brought me up properly if I dared think that of her.' [...]

So Sara Markovna lived through the winter without leaving the house. When there were snow-storms the Germans made the entire population clean the paths without bothering about the children who were left alone at home. The women would bring their little ones to Evstigneeva's house, where Sara Markovna took care of them until their parents returned. Little by little the women got used to her; they even became attached to her. And together with the children, in order not to mention her name, they began calling her 'mother', as if by agreement.

Then, on the gate of the fire-shed the routine announcement of the German command appeared. Jews were to be registered at the nearest commandant's office immediately. Those with whom Jews lived or who knew where they lived had to inform the commandant's office the same day. In the event of failing to comply with this order both the former and the latter would be shot.

When she learned of the order, Sara Markovna decided to go and register. This time she did not say anything to the mistress. She just put on her things and gathered her few belongings, but at the threshold she met the women returning with picks and shovels from the road.

'Where are you going?' Ekaterina Evstigneeva asked, looking her guest up and down.

Sara Markovna looked down silently. Then one of the women guessed.

'To the registration?! Dear me, it's sheer suicide!... Don't you know what they did to your people in Toropets?' [...]

Taking care of the old woman became the common cause of the collective farm, which, although formally disbanded, was in fact the more united by shared adversity. [...]

'I shall remember', answered the Chairman in his bass voice. He bent down and for a long time searched for something in the drawer of his writing-table. When he looked up, his face was a little red and moist as if he had suddenly caught a cold.

From the day the Germans burned down her house, Ekaterina Evstigneeva and her children lived at her sister's. And Sara Markovna whom everybody called 'mother' moved from house to house, living with each family in turn like a shepherd in summer.

In January, the field commandant's office got wind somehow that the peasants were hiding a Jewish woman. The Gestapo came in cars from Nelidovo itself. Detachments were stationed at all the approaches to the village. A general search began. But, while the soldiers went from house to house, two boys, Vasya and Petya, the children of the same Nikifor Churilin, led Sara Markovna through the backyards and out of the village. They led her to the next village and hid her in the house of their uncle Mikhail Churilin who also did not live in the village and also, according to the rumours, was a partisan in the woods.

Sara Markovna lived there without any special adventures, to the very moment when all at once the close shrill cannonade of a nearby tank battle was heard over the woodland stretches. And then suddenly, sweaty, flushed skiers with ear-caps pushed back and in dirty frost-covered camouflage cloaks burst into the Churilin home and in hoarse merry voices asked in the purest Russian for a drink.

That very day Sara Markovna returned to the Budenny collective farm, returned as if to her own family. Here she lived taking care of other people's children until her native town was liberated. Then she was taken to Toropets with an ambulance going the same way.

The whole village saw her off, they gave her warm clothes, baked potatoes for the journey and told her not to forget them.

Post-war themes

Document 152* Erenburg:[151] return to Kiev after the war (1952)

On a gloomy, rainy day he went to Babi Yar. He wanted to see once more the place where his mother and Alya had died. He walked along the endless Lukyanovka and thought of how old Hannah had gone along that same street with little Alya who did not understand where she was going.

For a long time he stood on the white sand of Babi Yar, remembering his mother, his daughter, thinking of Raya's fate. The thoughts took him far back, uplifted him; he saw Raya's heroic deed.

When he had been happy, he had not understood his happiness. He thought everything was good, he had a loving wife, a daughter. He had really understood the power of love only on losing Raya. Captain Chumakov's wife had died in 1944, in evacuation. A year ago he had told Osip with hesitation: 'I think I shall get married . . . ' Osip was glad. He said Chumakov had come to a great decision. It's hard to be alone. Now he will have a home, children. But Osip himself could never even imagine having a new family. In his pocket he carried a small photo of Raya in uniform. Before posting it, Raya had written:

* *Source*: I. Erenburg, 'Devyaty val' (The Ninth Wave), *Znamya*, 1952, no. 2, pp. 58–61.

'Don't think I'm like that. That's the photographer's doing. For you I'm the same as I was in Kiev ... ' He kept looking at the photo, Raya's eyes would come alive, her long lashes would flutter, she would whisper: 'You silly, you understand nothing ... ' That was true, he had not understood what love was. There was nothing to be done about it, he would never find another Raya. But he has friends, comrades, a great cause, a great country. And Raya is with him, she will never leave him alone.

In the evening he felt lonely, he wanted to sit with somebody, to talk to somebody. He remembered his promise to visit Yashchenko and decided, no, not today. He will start talking of production. And I want to have a good rest – I'll go to Lieutenant Vorobyev, he wrote that I should drop in. After all, we spent three years of the war together, we have something to reminisce about.

When thinking of Vorobyev, Osip would add 'lieutenant' without thinking, but Vorobyev had been demobilised long ago. He was working at a machine-building plant. Osip remembered the street and the house number. The only thing he had forgotten was which flat. He found the house easily. Four floors, that meant many flats. A small man with a long, thin moustache was standing at the gateway. Osip asked:

'Would you mind telling me in which flat Aleksandr Andreevich Vorobyev lives?'

The moustached man spat and answered unwillingly:

'Second doorway, to the right ... Got a cigarette?'

Osip put his hand in his pocket, took out a box. Empty.

'Sorry, not even one.'

'You never have anything for others ... Why don't you go to Palestine? You've got a state of your own now ... '

Osip did not grasp his meaning at first, he asked again, 'What?' Ugh, the rat! But the man with the moustache had disappeared.

Vorobyev was helping his daughter to solve a problem when Osip arrived. They kissed, and at once began to recall their friends. The girl looked at the guest smiling, then she said pitifully:

'Daddy, I won't solve it by myself ... '

'Now now', replied Vorobyev, 'you see who's come? Do I often have such guests?'

Osip began laughing:

'Give it to me, Mashenka, let me try ... '

He knit his brow.

'It's hard ... In the fifth form? You – mathematicians – I've got it! You have to multiply sixteen by three, yes, by three hours, then you divide by four. There are four basins – twelve buckets. Here you are ... '

He was thinking: a nice girl. Alyenka would have been in the fifth form too. Marvellous idea to have come to see Vorobyev. You feel immediately that he lives a real life, has a fine wife, Mashenka, flowers on the window-sills, interesting work.

Vorobyev's wife, a bustling plump woman, was preparing the supper and saying over and over again: 'If I'd known you were coming ... I would have treated you to dumplings ... ' Her speech was soft, with a Kiev accent, and Osip kept smiling from sheer enjoyment. They had something to eat. Vorobyev was joking: 'One has to drink a hundred grams anyhow, and a hundred more to celebrate our meeting, that's nothing ... You remember, I nearly froze to death near Kastornaya, and you poured me a full tea-glass ...'

They recalled the war years, the mound near Stalingrad, Minaev, Zarubin, Shapovalov, Lina, those still alive and those who perished, the long way to the Elbe, their joys, failures, anxious moments, hopes. Vorobyev's wife sighed as she listened. Throughout the war she had been working at a plant in Chelyabinsk, living on her husband's short letters. Now she was listening to Osip and wondering again at their good fortune: the things he had done and he had returned. [...]

He stayed with the Vorobyevs till two o'clock in the morning, then he went to the hotel. He had no relatives, he had simply not wanted to inconvenience the Vorobyevs. The night was warm, the rain had stopped. Osip was walking deep in thought, he was thinking about the sand of Babi Yar, and about the pink camel his brother had brought for Alya, and about Nastasya Ivanovna's kind smile. Then he stopped with a shudder: this is the corner where I parted from Raya. That was also in May, and I thought then, for a month – my dear Raechka! He saw her all of a sudden, her long lashes were fluttering, she whispered: 'You understand nothing ...' Now he understood all: love, motherland, life. He was standing alone at the crossing of the two empty streets. Above him a chestnut thrust its flowers like candles into the black sky. And Osip's face shone from within with a great human love.

Document 153* Valtseva:[152] grass-roots anti-Semitism (1957)

The Kovalevs invited us again to come and see them. Sergei Sergeevich was bored and had taken up drawing once more. He wanted to show us his drawings. Several times I had refused, saying that Pavel was busy. In the end, it simply became awkward to keep refusing.

'Well, let's go then, damn him', said Pavel. 'But I hope there won't be a guided tour.'

As if it depended on me.

Lida and Yakov Arkadyevich came with us. They were at our place when Kovalev came to call for us, and he invited them too.

The drawings were not numerous, and I had to admit once again that he was undoubtedly a capable artist. If the drawings had been those of a young man one could have entertained high hopes of him. But Kovalev must be about sixty, no less, though he looks younger.

Pavel started a professional conversation, began to analyse a drawing, to give advice. I was surprised to see how Kovalev was listening: attentively, without his usual arrogance. Pavel's attention, his interest flattered him.

I was showing Yakov and Lida the drawings on the walls, discussing them. I was eager to use the pointer, but I was afraid Kovalev would stand up, take it from me and 'head the excursion' himself. [...]

We sat down for tea. Vera Alekseevna is a very good housewife, and the table was spread with different cakes. But we didn't succeed in tasting them.

* *Source*: A. Valtseva, 'Kvartira no. 13' (Apartment no. 13), *Moskva*, 1957, no. 1, pp. 91–3.

While speaking to Yakov Arkadyevich, Kovalev referred to him several times as Yakov Abramovich.

'Arkadyevich', Vera Alekseevna gently corrected her husband when he made the mistake for the first time.

'Arkadyevich', I corrected him the second time.

Vera Alekseevna's face became frightened. Pavel became all tense and pale. I glanced at Kovalev. He sat with a crooked smile and reproduced his signature on the table-cloth with the blunt edge of the knife: SK – and a wavy line down.

When Kovalev said 'Abramovich' for the third time, Pavel banged his fist on the table and stood up.

'Home we go!' he said to me, Yakov and Lida, and went out first.

We went home, sat down at the table, and the men began smoking.

'I was sorry for Vera Alekseevna', said Pavel after some silence. 'Otherwise I would have given him a hiding. I was dying to. I could hardly control myself.'

Lida told us how, once in the underground, Pavel beat up one of those types. He had been pestering an old Jewess. Pavel punched him twice in the solar plexus and once on the back of the neck. The man fell, then knelt on all fours and crawled to one side, very quickly, crab-like. Then he stood up and ran away.

'All of them are cowards', said Pavel. 'This Kovalev too, I'm sure. They're brave with old people, with children, with those who are defenceless. I'd like to see him on hands and knees.'

'But, you know, that's also not the right way', I said. 'Though it helps sometimes.'

At that moment Seva appeared from behind the curtain.

'Uncle Misha says', he began, 'that if you scratch an anti-Semite, you will always find something mean beneath. Not every scoundrel is an anti-Semite, but every anti-Semite is a scoundrel!'

To my surprise Pavel did not utter his usual 'formulas'!

He must have asked himself, as I did, when it was that Mikhail Ivanovich and Seva had discussed such topics.

Yakov finished his cigarette, said goodbye and left. Lida also left soon after. I listened for the sound of the front door closing behind her, but did not catch it.

'We did not have this before the war', Pavel was saying to Seva, 'but during the war the Fascist poison seeped in – racialism – to assert oneself by humiliating others. A way as old as the world.'

He was still pale.

Somebody knocked softly at the door. Vera Alekseevna came in. She sat down at the table, leaned on it and became sunk in thought. How hard the poor woman's life is!

'Let's have some tea anyway', I said as gently as I could.

Seva began laying the table.

A few days later Nurya came running over to us. She was worried. She had heard Kovalev speaking on the phone. He had been offered a job. He was asking about the conditions and promised to come to discuss the proposal.

'Wherever he goes, it will be bad', Nurya kept repeating. 'He is a heartless official, a bureaucrat.'

'He won't go!' laughed Pavel.

'He will! He's bored. And he's as strong as a bull. He has connections. No friends (nobody goes to see them!), but connections he has!'

'Why should he work?' says Pavel. 'He is well provided for. Unless pensions are reduced.'

'Have you heard anything?' asked Nurya, anxiously.

'No, no!' Pavel calmed her. 'He won't go anywhere. He's used to different working conditions, and now they're changing. He understands that, you can be sure!'

Nurya left, though not completely reassured.

12

The Holocaust and Jewish resistance as reflected in Soviet academic literature and the press

One of the best gauges of official Soviet policy towards the Jewish question since World War II has been the portrayal of the Holocaust and Jewish resistance in the Soviet mass media. The attitude of the authorities – from the highest to the lowest levels – towards a subject as sensitive as the Holocaust undergone by Soviet and European Jewry reflects and underlines their real, and perhaps hidden, intentions and feelings towards the Jews. The attitudes expressed in these official publications in turn affected the Jewish population in the Soviet Union.

Since the manner in which the Holocaust and Jewish heroism are reflected in *belles lettres* is discussed in the previous chapter, we shall concentrate here on an analysis of the press and of historical and political literature. As in the other chapters, we shall try to examine the differences between the various historical periods and to elucidate their causes.

From the outbreak of the war until Stalin's death

Attacks on the anti-Jewish actions of Nazi Germany ceased to be published in the Soviet Union after the signing of the Molotov–Ribbentrop Pact in August 1939. Until that time, they had appeared with greater or lesser intensity depending on the fluctuations of Soviet foreign policy. Moreover, the methodical extermination of European Jewry in countries which came under German rule in 1939 and 1940 was not remarked upon in any official Soviet publication. This deliberate and systematic silence, maintained for political reasons, was unquestionably disastrous for the Jewish population, at least for that part which did not flee while there was still time because it was unaware of the Nazi atrocities,

As was to be expected, there was an immediate and profound change in this opportunistic and short-sighted policy when the Soviet–German war broke out in June 1941; but the changes, as we shall see, were only partial. For example, even then the press in the USSR published few reports on the killing of Jews in the occupied territories. And those reports that were published never undertook to stress that what the Germans were undertaking was the immediate extermination of the Jewish people. Moreover, official publications directed mainly abroad – such as the appeals of the Soviet Foreign Minister, V. Molotov, on 6 January and 27 April 1942 to governments with which the USSR maintained diplomatic relations[1] – mentioned the destruction of the

Jews only twice, in passing; the chief subject of these lengthy reports was German policy against the Russians, Ukrainians, Belorussians, Latvians, Moldavians, Estonians and other nationalities. It is true that the Soviet statement of 19 December 1942 (which was issued in the wake of a declaration on 'the issue of the German policy of exterminating the Jewish population of Europe' by the twelve countries fighting against Germany and its allies) did indeed mention that 'in proportion to its small population the Jewish minority in the Soviet Union suffered particularly heavy losses because of the bestial bloodthirstiness of the Hitlerite devils'. But even this article devoted incomparably greater space to a detailed description of Nazi policy against the Russians, Ukrainians, Belorussians.[2] Indeed, very few of the reports of the 'Special State Commission for the Determination and Study of the Hitlerite Atrocities' (established in November 1942) concerned the Jewish Holocaust.[3] Again, in a trial of Nazi war criminals in Kharkov, which was held following its liberation in December 1943, reference was made only to the extermination of 'peaceful Soviet citizens'; no mention was made of the fact that the majority of these 20,000 citizens had been Jews.[4]

As against this, we should point out that the Holocaust and Jewish resistance occupied quite an important place in Yiddish-language publications – both in books and in many articles in *Eynikeyt*, the organ of the Jewish Anti-Fascist Committee.[5]

The main reason for this dualism in official Soviet policy – concealing the Jewish Holocaust in publications in Russian and in the languages of the other nationalities, and underlining it in Yiddish-language publications – was amply clear. The leadership was afraid that Nazi propaganda stressing the absolute identification between Bolshevism and Jewry could prove effective and so undermine the Soviet attempts to unite all the nationalities in the war effort. This, however, is not the entire answer, for, as we shall immediately see, the policy of concealment in the portrayal of the Jewish Holocaust continued after the war, when the danger of Nazi propaganda had passed. Hence it is hardly possible to avoid the conclusion that anti-Semitism among the Soviet leadership played a significant part in the adoption of this policy. This anti-Semitism was both utilitarian (the desire to exploit it for political ends) and subconscious (the reluctance to recognise either Jewish heroism or suffering as worthy of attention).

The policy of concealment in the post-war portrayal of the Jewish Holocaust is exemplified in the episode of *The Black Book*. As early as June 1942 – that is, immediately upon its establishment – the Jewish Anti-Fascist Committee decided to publish material on the Nazi atrocities against the Jewish population in Nazi-occupied territories.[6] In 1943, apparently on the initiative of the writers Ilya Erenburg and Vasily Grossman, a 'literary commission' was formed to prepare a book of testimonies and documents on the Nazi extermination of the Jews.[7] But, on orders of the Deputy Director of the *Sovinformburo*, S. Lozovsky, the commission was dissolved (apparently in 1944) and the book's preparation transferred to the Jewish Anti-Fascist Committee. The Committee set up a new editorial board, whose members included the writers Ilya Erenburg, Vasily Grossman and Konstantin Simonov, the literary critic A. Efros, the jurists A. Traynin and I. Traynin, and others.

In conjunction with Jewish circles abroad it was now decided that *The Black Book* would appear simultaneously in the Soviet Union (in Russian and Yiddish), the United States (in English) and Palestine (in Hebrew). There was also an idea of forming a 'Black Book Committee', in which all the groups interested in working towards its publication would participate. In May 1946, the Presidium of the Jewish Anti-Fascist Committee announced that the Russian version of the book was ready for printing.[8] However, the authorities, apparently opposed to immediate publication, vetoed various sections of the book; finally, at the end of 1948, they broke up the type prepared for it.[9] Parts of *The Black Book* – which included letters and diaries, descriptions by writers and journalists, and documentary material placed at the disposal of the editorial board by the Soviet Governmental Commission for the Determination and Investigation of Nazi Crimes – were published at the time in English and Romanian editions.[10]

A similar fate befell *The Red Book*, which was to have portrayed the part played by Jews in the battles fought by the Red Army, as well as the history of the Jewish resistance movements in the ghettos and the partisan units. Ilya Erenburg, one of the book's principal initiators, told a correspondent of the Yiddish paper *Morgn frayheyt* that the book contained 'much material underlining the heroism and valour of the Jewish fighters [...] It appears in the Russian language since it is of major importance that the Russian reader learn the full scope of the Jewish tragedy.'[11] Non-Jews contributed a significant part of the material for the book, one of the main objectives of which was, as Erenburg's words imply, to refute the anti-Semitic claims propounded during the war that the Jews did not endeavour to resist the Nazi occupier.

The authorities' real attitude towards Erenburg's concept was sharply expressed even during the war itself. In the summer of 1944, Kondakov, an assistant of A. Shcherbakov (Chairman of the *Sovinformburo* and head of the army's Political Department), banned the text of Erenburg's appeal to American Jewry on the brutality of the Nazis. Kondakov claimed that there was no need to mention the heroic acts of Jews who were soldiers of the Red Army because 'that is arrogance'.[12] Although *The Red Book* did not appear in the Soviet Union, parts of the material assembled for it did appear in another book on Jewish fighters in partisan units, *The Brotherhood of the Partisans* (see Doc. 154). The latter, however, does not seem to have been distributed either in the Soviet Union or abroad.[13]

The period 1949–53 saw a turn for the worse in Soviet policy on the portrayal of the Holocaust in the mass media and in historical political literature. Partial concealment of the Holocaust and Jewish resistance was replaced by total silence. These subjects were not mentioned at all in the central Soviet press, nor apparently in the local papers. The policy of silence was carried so far that any mention of Jewishness was erased from the few monuments erected after the war to the memory of the Jewish victims of the Nazis.[14]

The post-Stalin and Khrushchev periods

The policy of concealment was continued in the first years after Stalin's death. A book entitled *The National Traditions of the Peoples of the USSR* was published in

1955. It contains a lengthy list of the nationalities whose members had received the award of Hero of the Soviet Union, among them such peoples as the Komi (with ten such awards), the Udmurts (with nine), the Latvians (with eight) and the Karelians (with six). But it completely ignores the role of the Jews, who had won 121 of these awards; that is to say, who occupied fifth place, following the Russians, Ukrainians, Belorussians and Tatars.[15] In so doing the authorities were following the precedent of 1952.[16] (It was only in 1965 that the names of Jewish recipients of the award Hero of the Soviet Union re-appeared.)[17]

However, in 1955 books of documents, history books, reportage and memoirs began to be published in the Soviet Union in which, whether in only a few lines or in many pages, the Holocaust and Jewish resistance did receive mention. The first such book was a collection of documents from the Nuremberg trials.[18] In 1957 the number of publications dealing with the Holocaust and Jewish resistance began to increase, particular significance attaching to the Russian translation of *The Diary of Anne Frank* (1960) with an introduction by Ilya Erenburg,[19] and the Lithuanian publication in 1963 of the diary of Masha Rolnikaite, a Jewish girl from the Vilnius ghetto (see Doc. 158).[20]

The daily and periodical press are important sources of information on the war for the Soviet public. From 1957 to 1964, a relatively large number of articles were published in which discussions on the war period included information about, and reactions to, the Holocaust and Jewish resistance. This material dealt with Jewish resistance in the extermination camps, the partisan units and the Red Army; the Jewish Holocaust and the observance of remembrance days; the conduct of trials against Nazi war criminals and their henchmen in the USSR; and the Eichmann affair.

The portrayal of Jewish resistance. The majority of books and articles dealing with the war and describing acts of heroism by Soviet soldiers and the civilian population in the struggle against the Nazi occupation are studded with Jewish names, but their nationality was seldom mentioned explicitly.[21] In those instances where Jewish nationality was mentioned, it was usually done in the context of the brotherhood of nationalities in the Soviet Union – which can withstand not only the test of peace, but also, and especially, the severe test of war. 'In a tank crew that demonstrated its supreme heroism', one of the books states, 'there were the Russian Pushkarevsky, the Ukrainian Bonderenko, the Jew Holtsman.'[22] A relatively large amount of material was published on the resourcefulness and courage of such senior Jewish officers as the Generals Kreizer, Dragunsky, Vainrub and Kremer.[23] The leaders of the underground organisations in the ghettos and in the partisan movement who fought with valour and sacrifice against the Nazis were also portrayed, but they always appeared as members of the Communist Party or the Komsomol. And in those cases – such as that of the Warsaw Ghetto – where Zionists or members of the Bund headed the uprisings, the authors passed over the fact in total silence (see Docs. 154–7).[24]

Thus, while there was now much more material on Jewish participation in the war against the Nazis than there had been during the Stalin period, the Soviet reader was still left largely unaware that Jews were being referred to.[25]

To have publicised the many acts of heroism by Jews – whom Nazi propaganda had portrayed as cowards hiding in the rear – would have been to strike a blow at anti-Semitism in the USSR. However, this was not done in the Khrushchev period, when only a few of the gravest distortions of the Stalin period were corrected.

The portrayal of the Jewish Holocaust and the perpetuation of its victims. In the period 1957–64, hundreds of books and a huge number of articles were published dealing with the war and the relations of the Nazi occupation authorities to the local population. The treatment of the Jewish Holocaust in these books and articles was far from uniform, for a number of reasons. First, the relative liberalisation that occurred in this period enabled many authors – among them Jews who had moved through all the circles of the Nazi hell – to express with greater freedom their true attitude towards issues which had troubled them for some time, but to which they had been unable to give expression. Second, the struggle which the Soviet Union was then conducting for political reasons against neo-Fascism in West Germany, Italy and other countries unquestionably influenced the authorities' attitude on issues related to Nazi war crimes; they could not, therefore, totally ignore the destruction of the Jewish population in Europe. And, third, Eichmann's capture and trial in Jerusalem had a further influence in this direction. For the Soviet authorities who, as we shall see below, had attacked the Israeli authorities for their 'moderate' and 'considerate' attitude towards Eichmann and his henchmen, 'who hold key positions in West Germany', now felt themselves compelled to conduct a show trial against the Nazi criminals and their henchmen residing in the USSR, and to flood the mass media with incriminating material against them.

As early as 1957, a book was published in Lithuania which may perhaps be seen as the beginning of the wave of Holocaust literature in which the extermination of the Jews occupied quite a central place: M. Eglinis's *The Death Fort*, which contains a shocking description of Nazi atrocities and the escape of their helpers.[26] Between the years 1959 and 1964, in the course of trials conducted against those who had assisted the Nazis, much testimony was given describing how Jews were exterminated in the cruellest and most sadistic manner.

The sufferings of Jews in the extermination camps were also portrayed in many books of the period.[27] Of particular interest is the way in which the extermination of the Jews at Babi Yar is described. For example, in *That's The Way It Was*, Bryukhanov gives an account of the murder of children, who were thrown alive into pits, but he does not say that they were Jewish children.[28] On the other hand, another book, published in 1964, states: 'People who arrived from the city of Kiev relate that the German soldiers ringed the vast pit at Babi Yar into which were hurled the bodies of tens of thousands of Jews who were murdered at Kiev at the end of September 1941.'[29]

In 1963, a collection of 153 documents was published on the crimes of the Nazis in the occupied areas. Of the forty-six documents in the section on the extermination of the Soviet population, Jews are mentioned in only four.[30] In comparison with the late Stalin period, even this represents progress. But while this and similar publications symbolised the end of the 'conspiracy of silence' regarding the Jewish Holocaust, they hardly marked a fundamental change in official Soviet policy.

The most notable proof of this was the attitude of the Soviet authorities towards the erection of monuments and towards other efforts to perpetuate the memory of the Nazis' Jewish victims. As far as we know from official Soviet publications and from personal testimonies, not one act of remembrance was organised between 1949 and 1956. It is difficult to imagine that anyone would even dare raise such a proposal to the local or central authorities during the period of anti-Jewish terror. On the contrary, we know from various evidence that inscriptions mentioning Jewish victims on the monuments that were erected during and after the war were erased during 1949–53. Hence it represented a great act of courage on the part of the former Jewish partisans who were veterans of the Kaunas ghetto when they decided to exploit the unveiling ceremony of a memorial to fallen partisans (held in the Shantsya Cemetery in Kaunas on 2 June 1957) by organising their own, separate procession.[31]

The unsuccessful struggle of a part of the Soviet intelligentsia to erect a monument at Babi Yar in memory of the many victims murdered there in 1941 may perhaps be the best demonstration of the Soviet leadership's attitude to this issue under Khrushchev (see Docs. 159–61 and Docs. 39–44). Hardly less important was the struggle of the Jews of Riga – which began in October 1962 and continued for many years before attaining some success – to erect a monument and memorial tablet to the Jews murdered at Rumbuli.[32]

Trials of Nazi war criminals and their henchmen in the USSR. It appears that the years 1954–9 saw few trials conducted against Nazi war criminals or against the Russians, Ukrainians, Belorussians, Lithuanians, Latvians and Estonians who took part in the extermination of the Jewish population and in the war against the partisan movement in the occupied areas.[33]

The twenty-four trials, in which 127 persons were tried (eight of them *in absentia*) in six republics in the years 1961–5[34] demonstrate that the decision to capture and prosecute war criminals who had been hiding for many years was taken at a high political level. In all probability Eichmann's capture and trial in Jerusalem stimulated the Soviet effort to prove that it occupied the primary place in the war against Fascism and Nazism, in contrast to the Western powers which refused to place the Nazi criminals on trial in their countries and even refused to extradite them to the Soviet Union or the other socialist states.

An additional factor which may have influenced this decision was the desire to prove to world Jewry and to the Western public in general that anti-Semitism could not exist in a state where all those who had assisted in the extermination of the Jewish population during the war were punished with the full severity of the law. (Most of those tried were condemned to death; a minority received fifteen-year prison terms, the maximum in the Soviet Union.) From the extensive coverage given these trials in the Soviet press and from the books and pamphlets published in the wake of the trials, it turns out that the extermination of Jews as Jews was explicitly cited in most of the trials, and that detailed descriptions were given of the defendants' brutal acts.[35] This

public telling and reporting of war-time atrocities against the Jews undoubtedly led to a growing awareness of the Holocaust among the Jews of the Soviet
Union; that is to say, it was one of the elements in the complex web of factors
that contributed to the awakening of Jewish nationalism.

The Eichmann affair. As we have seen above, the Eichmann affair had a major
influence on Soviet policy towards the portrayal of the Jewish Holocaust as
well as towards the treatment of local war criminals. But the handling of this
episode also throws much light on the motivation of Soviet policy in this
sphere and on the tendency to exploit this tragic event for political purposes.

The initial reaction of the Soviet media to Eichmann's capture and
imminent trial was one of sympathy for the Israeli operation (Doc. 162).[36]
However, even before the trial opened, and still more during and after it, the
Soviet tone changed completely, and Israel was attacked with increasing
sharpness.[37]

Soviet commentators began by noting that Eichmann's capture had caused
great embarrassment to the ruling circles in West Germany. Later, Washington and the Vatican were added to the list of those 'concerned' at
Eichmann's capture and at his being tried in Israel. It was also claimed that
Israel was doing everything possible to collaborate with Bonn to ensure that
the trial did not affect the Nazis ruling in West Germany, and that a German
attorney was being permitted to defend Eichmann in opposition to Israeli law
– this last to curry favour with Adenauer. The commentators also pointed out
that, in spite of its promises, Israel did not publish the material Eichmann had
recorded during his time in Israeli prison. Soviet judicial experts then argued
that Eichmann should have been tried in an international court, such as
Nuremberg, while the Soviet press harshly attacked the Zionist movement for
allegedly having collaborated with Eichmann during the war. Finally, an
unprecedentedly ferocious attack was made on David Ben Gurion, 'who is
striving to earn thirty shekels of silver for the blood of six million Jews
murdered by the Nazi executioners'.

The post-Khrushchev period

It is difficult to discover any substantial changes in the portrayal of the
Holocaust and Jewish resistance in the Soviet press and literature in the years
1965–7. There were, however, a number of events in this period which
symbolised minor concessions in Soviet policy in this sphere. In 1965, there
was a Russian translation of the diary *I Must Tell* (Doc. 158), written by
Masha Rolnikaite in the Vilnius ghetto and published in Lithuanian in 1963.
On 10 December 1965, during an appearance on Moscow television, the
author told the millions of viewers of the Nazi atrocities in that ghetto,
particularly stressing that the Nazis had tortured and murdered Jews solely
because they *were* Jews.[38] This was undoubtedly an exceptional event in the
Soviet Union.

No less important was the publication of Anatolii Kuznetsov's documentary novel *Babi Yar* (Doc. 159), in the periodical *Yunost* in 1966, and
in book form in 1967.[39] Despite the strenuous work of censorship which

removed some passages from the book and changed others – as is proved by the uncensored version of the book published in the West after Kuznetsov's defection from the Soviet Union[40] – this book is one of the most important documents ever published in the Soviet Union on the Jewish Holocaust and on the attitude of the local population towards the Nazi extermination of the Jews.

'As Long as the Murderers Walk the Face of the Earth' by Evgeny Evtushenko (see, too, Doc. 39) was also published in 1965.[41] Equally significant in this respect was the public speech of the Ukrainian author Ivan Dzyuba on 29 September 1966, the day of remembrance marking the extermination of the Jews at Babi Yar twenty-five years previously. But Soviet authorities criticised Dzyuba's act and did not permit press publication of his statement.[42]

In 1966, a pamphlet in Yiddish, Polish, Russian and English was published on the museum in Paneriai, a site of Jewish extermination, and it, too, contained details on the Jewish Holocaust.[43] In 1965–7, the Soviet press reported on nine trials of Nazi henchmen in the Russian, Belorussian, Ukrainian, Lithuanian, Latvian and Estonian republics. All these reports mentioned the extermination of the Jewish population.[44]

However, as stated above, there was no change in the way in which the Holocaust and Jewish resistance were portrayed in comparison with the Khrushchev period. While certain concessions were undoubtedly made after Stalin's death, and particularly after 1957, the Soviet authorities refused to respond to the demands of the Jewish population and of a part of the Soviet intelligentsia to perpetuate the memory of the Holocaust victims or to provide extensive information on these subjects.

Documents to Chapter 12

Soviet Jews under Nazi occupation: destruction and resistance

Document 154* Jewish partisans in the struggle against Fascism (1948)[45]

Editor's note

The book *The Brotherhood of the Partisans*, now being put before the reader, is one of the books which tell of the heroic fight of the Soviet people in the days of the Great Patriotic War of our socialist motherland against Fascist Germany, and of the struggle behind the German forces, in Soviet territories temporarily occupied by the Hitlerites.

The Brotherhood of the Partisans is designed as a collection. It is based on materials on the struggle of Jewish partisans collected by the Jewish Anti-Fascist Committee in the USSR. The collection includes the reminiscences of former commanders and commissars of partisan units and detachments, of rank-and-file partisans, as well as essays written by Soviet writers depicting episodes of partisan warfare, individual portrayals of its heroes. At the same time, *The Brotherhood of the Partisans* is a book with a single and integral purpose. All the materials in it deal with one subject.

This subject is the brotherly friendship of the Soviet peoples. The friendship fostered by the leaders of genius, Lenin and Stalin; the friendship which was established from the first days of the Great October Socialist Revolution, tempered in the stormy days of the Civil War, became the monolithic alloy of the union of Soviet peoples in the years of their heroic struggle to fulfil Stalin's Five-Year Plans, which was vividly expressed in the Great Patriotic War against the Hitlerite invaders. [...]

Soviet people of widely differing nationalities fought in the partisan units and detachments as well as in the Red Army. Soviet patriots who for some reason had remained on territory temporarily occupied by the enemy and who could fight became partisans. They fought bravely and selflessly for the honour, freedom and independence of their motherland, the mother of all the peoples inhabiting it. Among the 'people's avengers', together with Russians, there were also Ukrainians, Belorussians, Georgians, Armenians, Latvians,

---

* *Source*: *Partizanskaya druzhba* (The Brotherhood of the Partisans), Moscow, OGIZ State Publishing House/Der emes, 1948, pp. 3-5.

Uzbeks, Kazakhs, Jews, and the sons of other Soviet peoples. All of them felt they belonged to one fighting partisan family.

The 'people's avengers' who fought the hated enemy, deep in the rear, displayed remarkable examples of the indivisible fraternity, inviolable friendship, ideological and spiritual closeness of people who felt equally native to their socialist motherland.

The struggle of the Jewish partisans against the Fascist cannibals is shown in the book *The Brotherhood of the Partisans* as part of the common struggle of all the fraternal peoples who stood up as one man to defend their motherland.

Side by side with the partisans of all other nationalities, the Jewish partisans fought the German invaders. They exploded bridges in the enemy's rear, burned military trains, destroyed the reserves of the Fascist army, killed their generals, officers and soldiers; filled with hatred they wiped out the Hitlerite scum, the brutal nation-killers.

The collection *The Brotherhood of the Partisans* reveals only a few pages of the heroic partisan struggle of the Soviet peoples in whose fraternal family, headed by the great Russian people, the Soviet Jews also defended the achievements of the Socialist Revolution. But in those few pages, like the sun in a drop of water, the greatness of the universally historic victory of the Soviet people is reflected, the victory of the state and social system of the great country of socialism.

Document 155* Heroism in the Kaunas ghetto (1958)

On 14 July 1941, the Hitlerite Commissar of the Kaunas District, Lentzen, decreed that all surviving Jews were to be deported to the Vilijampol concentration camp – to the ghetto. The Kaunas suburb was surrounded with barbed wire which cut off from the world workers, doctors, lawyers, shoemakers, tailors, their wives and children.

But the fighting spirit penetrated here, too. A group of Communists – Mere Lanaite,[46] Moiseyus Rofas, Moiseyus Shermanas, Elya Shmuilovas – organised an underground cell and enlisted the cooperation of the Young Communists E. Pyanko, M. Rubinsonas,[47] Z. Goltsbergas,[48] Z. Zilberis. Shmuilovas was especially active. With the help of the Young Communist Yanina Chizhinauskaite, he managed to contact the Kaunas underground organisation. Quite a strong anti-Fascist group took shape in the ghetto.

Zalmanas Goltsbergas, secretary of the Komsomol cell of the ghetto, managed to make his way to the village of Murava, to Romualdas Kulvinskas, whom he knew from the days of their underground activity in bourgeois Lithuania.

The youngsters in the ghetto were often sent to load and unload railway carriages. They were eager to get this work. Once, during an air raid, the Young Communist, Kapelmanas, seeing that the overseer had taken cover, set the train on fire.

Every day the Gestapo sent one brigade from the ghetto to work in the Third

* *Source*: 'Komsomoltsy getto' (Komsomol Youth in the Ghetto), *Druzhba narodov*, 1958, no. 10, p. 167.

Fort where arms were stored. The underground sent as many of their people there as they could.

In July 1943, the Young Communist Meeris Lurye[49] organised an explosion of the ammunition stored in the Fort in which many Fascists were killed. The whole town knew of the feat of this fearless Young Communist. But Meeris Lurye was killed while fulfilling his patriotic duty; he was posthumously awarded the Order of the Red Banner.

The experienced and brave underground fighter Elya Shmuilovas fell by chance into the hands of the Gestapo and also perished. The Fascists could not find out his real name. They tortured him for eight months, using red-hot irons, harnessing him to a plough and driving him on with a whip. Shmuilovas did not inform on anyone. He managed to pass a letter from prison to his wife Vera, who was living in the ghetto and expecting a child. Exhausted from his torments, Elya Shmuilovas found strength in himself to write uplifting letters to her. 'I believe', he wrote, 'that we shall meet. And if I die, I beg you one thing only, take care of our child and tell him about his father.'

Eight months later Elya Shmuilovas was shot. He was posthumously awarded the Order of the Patriotic War, First Class.

Having contacted Kostas Radionovas, the future leader of the detachment 'Death to the Invaders!' through the partisan Albinna Glezerite, many of the Young Communists left the ghetto and made their way to the partisans in Rudnitskaya Pushcha.

Document 156* Partisans in Lithuania (1962)

Each member of the Pozhely underground organisation wore a red ribbon on which there were three white letters: CPL [Communist Party of Lithuania]. This red ribbon symbolised their loyalty to the Party, to the people, to the idea of friendship between peoples, proletarian internationalism. This ribbon was worn by the Lithuanian Povilas Vaichyunas, by the Russian Martyan Rybakov, by the Jew Haim Zilber and by the Ukrainian Peter Savchenko. [...][50]

The Hero of the Soviet Union Bronyus Urbanovichyus has to his credit seventeen enemy troop trains out of the forty-three that had been derailed by the partisan detachment 'Vilnius'. The Russian Vasily Vasilyev, the Ukrainian Efim Pronchenko, the Pole Yan Vrublevsky, the Belorussian Ippolit Shaban, the Jew Yankel Maitkovich and others blew up enemy troop trains with him. [...]

Here on Antakalnis there stands a marble plaque – a memorial to the fallen: Yuozas Vitas, Yan Pshevalsky, Itsik Vitenberg,[51] Makar Korablikov, Vintsas Labanauskas, Aleksandr Mazhuts, Sonya Madeisker,[52] and others. [...]

Itsikas Meskupas-Adomas,[53] the Secretary of the Central Committee of the Communist Party of Lithuania was buried in the common grave next to the memorial. [...]

Socialist internationalism, and deep faith in one another among partisans of different nationalities, were also reflected in the national composition of

* *Source*: P. Shtaras, 'Partizanskaya druzhba' (The Brotherhood of the Partisans), *Sovetskaya Litva*, 25 November 1962.

commanders of the partisan detachments. Out of the ninety-two commanders of the partisan detachments there were sixty-nine Lithuanians, twelve Russians, four Ukrainians, four Jews, one Belorussian, one Pole and one Georgian.

Document 157* Commemoration of the Warsaw ghetto uprising (1963)

It was in the year 1943. The ominous shadow of the swastika hung over Poland. Millions of Poles and prisoners from other countries were languishing in Fascist concentration camps. Seventy thousand Jews were awaiting their doom behind the barbed wire of the Warsaw ghetto. A hundred thousand of the ghetto inhabitants had already been done away with, three hundred thousand had been sent to extermination camps. [...] It seemed that the spirit of the people, isolated from the world, humiliated, hungry and exhausted, must be broken. The Hitlerites were preparing the final bloody orgy with sadistic glee. Motorised detachments of Hitlerite cut-throats, armed to the teeth, were moved to the Warsaw ghetto for the final destruction of its population.

And here the people said 'No!' to the executioners. On 19 April 1943, an uprising flared up in the Warsaw ghetto. The dumbfounded Hitlerites had to withdraw their detachments from Zamenhof Street and Nalevki, from Gensia Street and Shchensliva Street. And by morning fighting had broken out in Muranuv Square.

The leaders of the Jewish fighting organisation – the Communist Jozef Lewartowski,[54] M. Anieliewicz[55] and others – had contacts with the Polish Resistance. There were possibilities, though they were minimal, of getting arms.

The inhabitants of Warsaw, all the anti-Fascist forces, came to the assistance of the insurgent ghetto prisoners at once. It was not only moral help, but also direct combat support. The very next day several groups of the *Gwardia Ludowa* (a secret military organisation created by the Polish Workers' Party) went into action in the enemy rear, shooting at Fascist batteries which were firing at the ghetto.

For five days, from 19 to 24 April 1943, the rebels fought heroically in the ghetto streets. And only when the Fascists threw in their artillery and planes, when the whole ghetto was ablaze, could the Hitlerite general Jürgen Stroop report to his commanders on the suppression of the uprising. A group of rebels assisted by the fighters of the *Gwardia Ludowa* managed to make their way through the sewers into other districts of Warsaw and from there to the partisans.

The uprising in the ghetto was not just an act of desperation. The rebels were trying to make their contribution to the struggle against Hitlerism. On 23 April, the rebels addressed the Warsaw population with the ardent words: 'From the smoke of the charred ruins and the sea of blood of the martyred Warsaw ghetto, we send you our heart-felt brotherly greetings. You must

* *Source*: A. Panfilov, 'Pepel stuchit v serdtse' (The Ashes Knock at the Heart), *Izvestiya*, 19 April 1963.

know that every threshold in the ghetto will be a fortress, that we may all die fighting, but we shall not surrender. Like you, we are eager to have our revenge on our common enemy for all their crimes. This is a fight for our freedom and yours. For your human, social, national honour and dignity and for ours.'

The dream of freedom of the ghetto prisoners was realised thanks to the heroic deeds of the Soviet Army which routed the Hitlerite hordes and saved mankind from Fascism. [...]

On the twentieth anniversary of the tragedy of the Warsaw ghetto, the fighters for peace appeal again to honest people in the West: do not forget that those who passed the racial laws in Nuremberg, who burned people in the incinerators of Auschwitz and Maidanek, who posed for the cameras against a background of gibbets and the charred ruins of the ghetto, are donning their Hitlerite orders again today. West Germany is again ruled by those who brought Hitler to power. Revanchism and militarism are reborn west of the Lower Elbe. It should be mentioned that reactionary forces are trying to activate Zionist elements. These attempts are directed at undermining the unity of the peoples' movement for peace, despite the threat of a nuclear missile catastrophe and the restoration of revanchism and militarism in West Germany.

Document 158* Diary from the Vilnius ghetto (1965)

The diary of the girl who described how her family hid in someone else's attic during the German occupation of Holland in order to escape the annihilation to which the Hitlerites doomed the Jewish population has been translated into many languages and has spread across the whole world. The girl kept the diary about what she saw and heard there, and *The Diary of Anne Frank* has become a record of Fascism's bestial crimes and a testimony to man's heroism because it describes unaffectedly and naively the beauty of the human spirit overcoming the fear of death.

Masha Rolnikaite[56] was not yet fourteen when the Hitlerites entered Vilnius. They established a ghetto there, moved the entire Jewish population of the city into it, and from time to time culled human material from it. Those selected were sent to the suburb of Ponary, where blood-thirsty acts were carried out – the mass murder of the Jewish population. The aims of the ruthless extermination was to be able to display on the city gates the pretentiously vile sign: *Judenfrei* – 'no more Jews'.

The girl feels the tragedy of her people with all her heart. One of the entries in her diary was filled with ineffable despair: 'What have I done? What did Mummy do, what have the others done? How is it possible to kill a person only because of his nationality? Where does this savage hatred of us come from? Why?'

Masha Rolnikaite lived in the ghetto almost until the end of 1943. All that time she stood on the brink of the grave, for each day the family might be dispatched to sinister Ponary. Day after day she witnessed heart-rending

* *Source*: Yury Poletika, 'Nikogda!' (Never!), *Novy mir*, 1965, no. 8, pp. 249–50.

scenes of children taking leave of parents, husbands of wives, old people of young. There were instances of courage of the highest order and selfless love. And side by side with this, there was an abyss of baseness and viciousness. [...]

One hundred thousand persons were massacred in Ponary at that time.

It is impossible to remain calm while reading some of Masha's descriptions of life after she left the ghetto. For another year and a half she suffered in camps which were deliberately arranged to exhaust the inmates, who were then sent to the crematorium. She was senselessly tormented and beaten, starved in service to a Fascist kulak. Her notes during this period are sterner and drier, more 'kaleidoscopic'; they are no longer alive with description; they merely record and register events. There was no paper, no time, no strength – hardly strength to live, much less to write.

She was rescued by Soviet soldiers. They opened the gates of the crowded shed and dragged out the 'write-offs' whom the Fascists had planned to burn alive when they liquidated the camp.

A remarkable feature of Rolnikaite's diary is the girl's mature awareness, despite her youth, of the identity of her own fate with that of her people, with the other victims of Fascism. She regards not only the German Fascists as the concrete source of the evil but their underlings as well, those who sought to save themselves at the price of the destruction of others. These include the *Judenrat*, the ghetto council, made up of the wealthy Jews of Vilnius, and the police who helped the Hitlerites destroy their people in order to save themselves, and the unbridled dictator of the ghetto, its commandant Gensas with his sycophantic clique of relatives and wealthy people. With unchildlike perspicacity the girl foresaw their end; with purely childlike directness she describes the inglorious end of the *Judenrat*, the police and, finally, of Gensas himself. Their betrayal did not help them; money did not save them – one after another they were all dispatched to Ponary.

On the other hand, with what deep respect the girl writes about a secret partisan organisation in the ghetto, about leaflets that appeared. She is proud of the cases of armed resistance to the Fascists, of how the young partisan Asya Big spat in the face of the hangman. With unconcealed pain she tells how the head of the underground partisan organisation, Vitenberg, a Communist, turned himself over to the Fascists in order that the ghetto might not be exterminated. 'Today he saved me. Not only me – Mummy, Mira, the children, thousands of mothers and children', she wrote with sorrow and gratitude.

'I Must Tell the Story' is the title Rolnikaite has given her diary. She wrote it in a school copy-book, then on scraps of cement sacks, and at the end she memorised the entries. Hers was an act of heroism, committed without regard for the possibility of death, under circumstances in which she could easily have been caught – at a time of hopelessness and despair. Not all of her entries are of equal value, as we have said, but even as they have come down to us twenty years later it is impossible to read them unmoved. 'Her diary is one of the terrible pages of the history of the twentieth century, written in blood', the Lithuanian poet Eduardas

Meželaitis says in the preface to the diary. Her notes and memoirs portray the tragedy of an entire people. Great love and great hatred wrote her book.

Literature does not always address itself to the human conscience. Far from it. But when it does, it acquires special value, calls together the living, awakens the sleeping, warns the unthinking and the indifferent.

Can anyone believe that Rolnikaite will ever consent to forgive and forget what she saw? That we, her readers, will forgive and forget? Never!

The Babi Yar affair

Document 159* The Babi Yar massacre (1966)[57]

'I've got great news for you!... From tomorrow there won't be a single Yid left in Kiev. It seems it's true what they said about them setting fire to the Kreshchatyk. Thank the Lord for that! That'll put paid to them getting rich at our expense, the bastards. Now they can go off to their blessed Palestine, or at any rate the Germans'll deal with 'em. They're being deported! There's an order posted up.'

We all dashed outside. A notice printed on cheap grey wrapping-paper, with no heading and no signature, had been stuck on the fence:

All Yids living in the city of Kiev and its vicinity are to report by 8 o'clock on the morning of Monday, 29 September 1941, at the corner of Melnikovsky and Dokhturov Streets (near the cemetery). They are to take with them documents, money, valuables, as well as warm clothes, underwear, etc.
Any Yid not carrying out this instruction and who is found elsewhere will be shot.
Any civilian entering flats evacuated by Yids and stealing property will be shot.[....]†

At this point I myself took fright. I was tired, my head was buzzing from everything that was going on, and I was scared lest I should be unable to get back and they would cart me off. So I began to force my way back in the opposite direction to the crowd, worked my way out of it and then wandered for a long time through the deserted streets, along which a few latecomers were practically running, to the accompaniment of whistles and shouts from the doorways.

When I got home I found my grandfather standing in the middle of the courtyard, straining to hear some shooting that was going on somewhere. He raised his finger.

'Do you know what?' he said with horror in his voice. 'They're not deporting 'em. They're *shooting* 'em.'

Then, for the first time, I realised what was happening.

From Babi Yar came distinctly the sound of regular bursts of machine-gun fire: ta-ta-ta, ta-ta ...

It was the sort of rather quiet, unexcited, measured firing you hear during training. Our Babi Yar lies between Kurenevka and Lukyanovka: you have to

* *Source*: A. Anatoli (Kuznetsov), *Babi Yar*, pp. 66–72.
† Central State Archives of the October Revolution, Moscow, Collection 7021, inventory 65, storage unit 5.

cross it to get to the cemetery. They had driven them from there, from Lukyanovka, it seemed, into our ravine.

Grandpa looked puzzled and frightened.

'Maybe it's fighting?' I suggested.

'That's not fighting!' Gramp shouted plaintively. 'The whole of Kurenevka is already talking about it. Some folk have climbed trees and seen what's going on. Viktor Makedon ran all the way back; he went down with his wife, she's a Jewess, and he only just escaped being taken himself. Oh, Mother of God, Queen of Heaven, what is this, why do they do that to them?'

We moved indoors. But it was impossible just to sit there. The firing went on and on.

Document 160* Demand for monument in Babi Yar (1959) (I)[58]

On the outskirts of Kiev, in Lukyanovka, beyond the ancient Jewish cemetery, there is a huge ravine the name of which is now known to all the world. This is Babi Yar. It was precisely here, in this ravine, that one of the most heinous crimes in the whole history of mankind was committed eighteen years ago. On 29 September 1941, the Hitlerites drove here some tens of thousands of peaceful people who were guilty of no crime and shot them mercilessly. The exact number of those shot cannot be ascertained. In the note of the People's Commissar of Foreign Affairs of the USSR dated 6 January 1942 the figure of 52,000 people is mentioned. Further investigations showed the number to be much greater.

At the Nuremberg trial the report was made public of the Extraordinary State Commission on the destructions and atrocities of the German Fascist invaders in the city of Kiev (document USSR–9). It states that a Special Commission headed by N. S. Khrushchev established that, according to incomplete data, more than 195,000 Soviet citizens were killed (tortured, shot, poisoned in mobile gas-chambers), including:

1. More than 100,000 men, women, children and old people in Babi Yar.
2. More than 68,000 Soviet prisoners of war and peaceful citizens in Darnitsa.
3. More than 25,000 peaceful Soviet citizens and prisoners-of-war in the anti-tank ditch, near the Syretsky camp and on the territory of the camp proper.
4. Eight hundred mentally ill people in the territory of the Kirillov Hospital.
5. About five hundred peaceful citizens in the territory of the Kiev-Pechersk Monastery.
6. Four hundred peaceful citizens in the Lukyanovka Cemetery.

Eighteen years have passed.

And here I stand in the same place where in September 1941 thousands of Soviet people were brutally killed. I am standing over Babi Yar. Silence. A wasteland. Houses are being built on the other side of the ravine. There is water at the bottom of the ravine. From where? [...]

And while standing over deserted, inundated Babi Yar, I remembered that a monument was to have been erected here. There was even a project of the

* *Source*: V. Nekrasov, 'Pochemu eto ne sdelano?' (Why is it Left Undone?), *Literaturnaya gazeta*, 10 October 1959.

monument by the well-known architect A. V. Vlasov, severe, simple, prism-shaped. The artist V. Ovchinnikov worked on sketches for the pictorial presentation of the tragedy of Babi Yar. Where are those projects now? Why have they been forgotten?

Now I have been told at the Architecture Administration of Kiev that Babi Yar is to be 'flooded' (hence the water!), in other words, filled in, levelled out for a park and a stadium is to be built there.

Is that possible? Who could think of that. To fill a ravine 30m deep, and to make merry and play football where the greatest tragedy took place.

No, it is impermissible!

When a man dies, he is buried, and a monument is placed on his grave. Can it be that such a token of respect is not deserved by the 195,000 people of Kiev brutally shot in Babi Yar, Syrets, Darnitsa, the Kirillov Hospital, the Monastery, the Lukyanovka Cemetery?!

Document 161* Demand for monument in Babi Yar (1959) (II)

The Soviet people revere the memory of their sons and daughters who perished at the hands of the German Fascists in the Great Patriotic War. Their graves are cared for with love, and the best sculptors of the country create monuments to the eternal glory of the heroes.

There is no need to stress how important and meaningful this is both for the memory of the dead and for the education of the rising generation in a spirit of deep veneration for those who gave their lives at the front or fell victim to Fascism. It seems to us that the graves of the victims of the past war, in towns and villages, or wherever they are, ought to be adorned with flowers, that monuments should be erected, and public gardens placed around the graves.

That is the deep meaning of V. Nekrasov's article published in *Literaturnaya gazeta* on 10 October 1959, in the column 'The Writer Proposes'. This article, touching upon the well-known tragedy of Babi Yar, naturally attracted the particular attention of the people of Kiev. V. Nekrasov proposes to erect a monument at the place of the mass shooting.

We also consider that this must be done as soon as possible. But we feel that V. Nekrasov's proposal needs some corrections.

Near Babi Yar a new residential district of Kiev is under construction, modern multi-storied residential blocks with all conveniences are being built there. This outlying district will soon be connected with the centre of the city by trolley-bus. The territory of Babi Yar will be cared for; there are plans for laying out a park there, and in the park a monument will be erected to the victims of Fascism.

Should the ravine be kept as it is? We, the authors of the present letter, all of us veterans of the Great Patriotic War, residents of Shevchenko District, have discussed the problem and have come to the firm conclusion that it should not. In Lidice the ashes and the site of the shooting have not been kept as they were after the Fascists were driven out. Instead, a rose garden was planted there.

* *Source*: 'Pismo v redaktsiyu. Eto neobkhodimo sdelat' (Letter to the Editor. This Must Be Done), *Literaturnaya gazeta*, 22 December 1959.

We think that in Babi Yar, too, a park should be laid out with a monument in the centre.

> V. Yarkhunov, Deputy of the Shevchenko District Soviet of Workers' Deputies, N. Vlasov, A. Ermakov, V. Esipov, A. Konchits, P. Kurochkin, A. Mikhailov, V. Saraev.

> Kiev.

The Eichmann trial

Document 162* Report on Eichmann's capture (1960)

At the end of May, thousands of kilometres from the borders of West Germany, an event occurred which found an echo in many countries and brought confusion to the ruling circles of Bonn.

The Israeli police announced the arrest of the former SS-Sturmbann-führer, Adolf Eichmann. In this connection, the papers recalled that Eichmann had been one of the bloodiest henchmen of Fascist Germany. On his conscience lie six million people shot, burned in gas chambers or tortured in concentration camps.

The office held under Himmler by this Gestapo bandit was officially called 'head of the bureau for the solution of the Jewish question'. What this 'solution' meant is told in the thousands of pages of the protocol of the sessions of the International Military Tribunal in Nuremberg. It is told by Mauthausen, Auschwitz, Babi Yar – and there are those who miraculously escaped death and tell the terrible testimony of the crimes of Hitlerism.

With a feeling of anxiety and profound indignation they watch, together with all decent men and women, how the former myrmidons of Hitler, Himmler and Kaltenbrunner are once again flourishing in Adenauer's land, occupying key posts in the Bundeswehr, the State apparatus and the Government of the Federal German Republic.

One of the first cables from Jerusalem said that Eichmann proposes to compromise the highest West German officials at his trial if he gets no help and support from Bonn.

The SS-man's friends and acquaintances hastened to respond. The Minister of Justice of the Federal German Republic, Scheffer, shed some crocodile tears because Eichmann would not be tried by a West German Court. A similar statement was made by Eckhardt, head of the Information and Press Bureau attached to the Federal Government.

* *Source*: B. Irinin, 'Konets "karery"' (The End of a 'Career'), *Vechernyaya Moskva*, 7 June 1960.

PART VI

A separate development

13

The Oriental Jews of the Soviet Union

Although the non-Ashkenazi or Oriental Jews constitute only a small minority of some 5% – 7% of the total Jewish population in the Soviet Union, there is every justification not only for including them in this book but also for devoting a separate chapter to them. These communities, their history and way of life are of interest in themselves, but it is in the context of the study of Soviet Jewry as a whole that the struggle of the Oriental Jews against the waves of assimilation and for independent national and religious existence is of particular significance.

The Oriental Jews of the Soviet Union are divided into four separate communities: the Georgians, the Mountain Jews, the Bukharans and the Krymchaks.[1] While they share a certain common past and characteristics they differ in several respects.

The Georgian Jews

The origins of the Jewish community in Georgia, one of the fifteen republics of the Soviet Union, situated in the south-western Caucasus, are shrouded in the mists of ancient history. According to one tradition current among the Georgian Jews themselves, they are descendants of the ten tribes carried off into exile by Shalmaneser in 724 BC. Another tradition connects the arrival of the Jews in the Caucasus with Nebuchadnezzar's exiles. Be that as it may, it is generally accepted today that there were Jews settled in the Caucasus by the early centuries of the Christian era. From the sixth century onwards there seems to have been a wave of Jewish migration into the Caucasus not only from the east, but also from the Byzantine Empire lying to the west.

Over the centuries, the Georgian Jews knew periods of toleration and prosperity as well as times of persecution and material and spiritual impoverishment (Doc. 163).[2] The conquest of Georgia by the Soviets in 1921, and the changes it brought about in the economic and social spheres of the environment, opened a new chapter in the history of this community. Soviet policy could not but leave its mark on the Jews of Georgia, who had previously maintained a clearly separate way of life, with their own quarters, patriarchal family structure and distinctive approach towards religion.

These transformations can be examined in the spheres of demography and economy; religion; and culture and national identity.

Demography and economy

The Oriental Jews of Georgia numbered an estimated 24,000 in 1917. But, according to the 1926 census, their number in all areas of the Caucasus was only 21,471,[3] of whom 95% lived in nineteen communities numbering between 1,000 and 5,000 people. The most important communities in terms of size were Kutaisi – 4,738 (about 7,000 according to one estimate); Tbilisi – 3,160; Kulashi – 2,407; Tskhinvali – 1,739; and Oni – 1,176. It can be assumed that the true number of Georgian Jews in the Caucasus (a certain percentage of them lived outside the Caucasian republics) was higher than that shown by the official statistics. This was the result of the way in which nationality was defined in 1926 as well as the problem of applying this definition to Georgian Jewry. M. Plisetsky, a leading specialist on Georgian Jewry, estimates that, despite the 'many misunderstandings' during the census, there were some 30,000 Georgian Jews at the end of the 1920s.[4] In a number of towns and townsteads they even constituted a sizeable percentage of the total population.

At the end of the 1930s, 18.6% of all Georgian Jews were still living in rural areas, as compared with 13% of the total Jewish population of the Soviet Union and despite the powerful process of migration from the villages and small townsteads which had begun in the early 1920s. However, despite this predilection for an agrarian life – part of the urban population, too, engaged in the cultivation of fruit and vegetables on plots next to their homes – the attempts to settle the Georgian Jews on kolkhozes were mostly unsuccessful. Only those Jews who had previously resided in the most backward villages agreed to move to the eight Jewish kolkhozes which according to *Ozet* had been established by 1930.

The nineteen such kolkhozes functioning in 1936 had a total population of 1,376.[5] Most of the Jewish population continued in the 1920s to be engaged as petty traders and artisans. Their poverty-stricken lives were slightly improved at the beginning of the 1930s, when the authorities helped establish cooperative workshops in which some of this stratum found employment.

No statistics were published on the Oriental Jews in the 1939 census. In the 1959 census the Georgian Jewish community numbered 36,000 persons. That is an increase of 64% in thirty-three years. This increase, which comes close to 2% per annum, was even higher than the natural growth rate of the Georgian population (less than 1.5%). If the natural growth rate between the years 1959 and 1970 was on the average equal to that of the proceeding period, the Georgian Jewish population would have numbered 44,000 in 1970. It may indeed be assumed that the natural growth rate of the family, insofar as there was a drop, was evened out by a drop in the mortality rate since the 1920s.[6] Of equal importance, unlike the Ashkenazi Jews, the Mountain Jews and the Krymchaks, the Georgian Jews did not suffer major losses during the Holocaust.

There can be little doubt that from the 1930s onwards, and especially after World War II, changes occurred in the employment and professional stratification of Georgian Jewry. Some went into government offices and public services, and there was an ever-growing stratum of educated people, although a significant percentage continued to work in agriculture. However, a considerable section of Georgian Jewry remained engaged in commerce and in the 'grey' market (or 'second economy'), which is still important in Soviet economic life even today.

Any discussion of Georgian Jewry cannot neglect the role of the family. Despite the changing times and pressures of the regime, it still remains the basic cell of the community, and seven or eight children are not unusual even today.

Religion

Religion, too, continues to play a leading role in the life of the Georgian community. As one of the main forms of group identity, it has acted as a consolidating force enabling Georgian Jewry to withstand to a large extent the changes brought about by the Soviet regime. Moreover, as we shall see, it exercises considerable influence over the cultural and educational spheres as well.

The synagogue has been the pillar of support in the religious life of the Georgian Jews, acting not only as an ordinary prayer-house, but as the focus of social activities and meeting place for all members of the community. The large synagogues had buildings attached for the baking of *mazot* and taking of ritual baths. In fact, it serves as a kind of stronghold of the Jewish quarter in the Georgian towns and, as such, is supported financially by the worshippers.

In the late 1930s, some sixty synagogues were still operating in the important Jewish centres of Georgia, some of them housed in fine buildings, others in small and miserable-looking huts. While the fierce and relentless struggle conducted against all the religions (see Chapter 8) left its mark on the Georgian community, they were affected to a lesser degree than their Ashkenazi co-religionists. This was in part due to the special situation prevailing in the Georgian Republic and in part to the stubborn resistance of the Georgian Jews. Nevertheless, some forty synagogues were closed during the 1950s and 1960s, leaving less than twenty 'official' synagogues in the second half of the 1960s.[7] To these must be added a number of prayer-houses in rented apartments.

The isolated cases of synagogues being set on fire – as, for example, in the townstead of Tskhakaya when unknown persons threw a drum of petrol into the wooden building and set it ablaze on the Passover Sabbath of 1962[8] – seem to have been individual acts of hooliganism quite unconnected with official state policies.

The synagogues were headed by *ḥakhamim* (rabbis), only some of whom were ordained for the rabbinate and not all of whom possess a comprehensive and profound knowledge of the Jewish sources. This, it seems, is one of the reasons for the absence of any written rabbinical literature in the Georgian community. It should be noted that the Georgian *ḥakham* plays primarily a pastoral role and fulfils the varied tasks of teacher, cantor, ritual slaughterer and synagogue caretaker. As such, his status and authority differ from those of the Ashkenazi rabbi in the Soviet Union; his authority is almost unquestioned and his impact on the whole life of the community very great.

Religious observances and customs have always been maintained to a high degree in the Georgian community, and great efforts are made to observe the Sabbath and festivals and to perform ritual slaughter, circumcision, traditional marriage and *Bar-mizvah* ceremonies. Even Jewish members of the Communist Party who hold various posts in the administrative apparatus maintain some of the religious ordinances, although without too much show.

Culture and national identity

In contrast to the other Soviet Jewish communities, both Ashkenazi and Oriental, the Georgian Jews adopted the Georgian language. What is still more unusual, they even use the Georgian script, which is written from left to right, among themselves.[9] There is no doubt that this has had repercussions on the development of an independent Georgian Jewish culture.

The *ḥeder* was the focal point of education for children of the Georgian community until the 1930s and even later. Attempts to run *ḥadarim* in secret continued into the 1950s and 1960s, despite the Soviet authorities' decree closing them and their prolonged struggle against them.

Illiteracy among the Georgian Jews, which reached 67.1% in 1926 (only 27.7% among the Ashkenazi Jews in the same year), was gradually reduced in the 1930s and seems to have disappeared almost entirely by the 1940s. But the flow of Georgian Jewish youth into general schools and educational establishments encouraged integration into Georgian society and had a deleterious effect on the creation of an autonomous Jewish culture.

An important place in the creation and preservation of Georgian Jewish culture belongs to the Historical Ethnographic Museum (see Docs. 164–5), which was founded on 23 November 1933 on the initiative of the *Evkombed* (Jewish Committee of the Poor) under the direction of A. Linetsky. Among the active organisers of the museum were A. Krikheli, M. Danielov, M. Mamistvalov, Sh. Israelashvili and H. Baazov. With departments of ethnography, history, folklore, scientific archive, manuscripts and a library, the museum's main functions were to train local research students in the history of Georgian Jewry, to collect and publish written material and to organise exhibitions on various aspects of Georgian Jewish culture.[10]

A. Krikheli, permanent director of the museum from the time of its foundation, was an active Communist who was arrested and charged with Jewish nationalism in 1949, when the campaign against Jewish cultural activists reached its peak. The museum itself was not closed until 1952, and was in fact the only Jewish establishment of its kind to remain open so long. When the order to close it was issued by the Georgian Ministry of Culture, most of the material was transferred to Georgian museums, rare books were moved to the library of the Georgian Academy of Sciences and some of the material was destroyed by the liquidation committee.

A second form of secular cultural expression was literature in the Georgian language on Jewish themes. One of the most outstanding figures in this sphere was without doubt the writer and dramatist Herzl Baazov, son of the Zionist Rabbi David Baazov. In such works as *The Dumb Opened Their Mouths*, *The House of Hayin* and the well-known historical drama *Itska Rizhinashvili*, he portrays Georgian Jews against the background of their ancient historical or more recent past. He also depicts the changes which took place after the establishment of the new regime with special emphasis on the class and revolutionary struggles and socialist construction.[11]

Haim Yashvili is one of the Georgian Jewish writers whose works were issued in *samizdat*. This is not surprising, as he was against assimilation and for the preservation of the Jewish spiritual heritage. Poems on Jewish themes were written by Avraham Mamistvalov and Georgy Koboshvili. While Boris Gaponov was not of Georgian Jewish origin, his most important work was related to Georgia. His great undertaking, the translation of the Georgian national epic *The Knight in the Panther's Skin* by Rustaveli into Hebrew, was a noted event in Georgia and earned him high praise even from the local administration.[12]

In the sphere of art, it should be noted that Jewish themes permeate the paintings of Shalom Koboshvili. Again, historical research on Georgian Jewry was undertaken by Shalom Mikhalashvili and Aharon Krikheli.

The subject of the Zionist national awakening of the Jews of Georgia in the wake of the Six-Day War is beyond the scope of this book.[13] However, their strong Jewish national identity, which was undoubtedly a decisive factor behind this awakening, ought to be briefly mentioned here. As pointed out, religion was the primary factor in the preservation of this identity. An important question which is difficult to answer with any certainty is the degree to which the emissaries of Ḥabad (a Hasidic sect) who went to Georgia in the 1920s succeeded in broadening the scope and deepening the understanding of religious observance; it is nevertheless reasonable to assume that they did exert a considerable influence.

The strong family bonds and virtual absence of intermarriage among members of this community also guarded against the processes of assimilation, as did the relatively limited influence of Communist ideology on a sizeable section of Georgian Jewry. Moreover, in contrast to the situation of the Ashkenazi Jews, the Jews of Georgia were less affected by anti-Semitism.

The links with Israel were not only religious and emotional, but also practical. There is no doubt that visits from Israel's Embassy staff and tourists, the programmes broadcast by Israel's *Kol ziyon la-golah*, the study of the Hebrew language and correspondence with Israeli citizens were important factors in the increasing development of the national identity of Georgian Jewry. The connections, which undoubtedly existed, between the Georgian and Ashkenazi Jews of the Soviet Union must also have influenced the sense of national identity (although such contacts may have worked as a stimulus to assimilation).

The Mountain Jews

The early historical origins of the Mountain Jews, like that of their neighbours the Georgian Jews, are by no means clear.[14] While the community itself has a number of traditions concerning its origins, it is almost certain that their colonisation of the eastern Caucasus is to be dated to the second half of the fifth century, when the Jews of Babylon and northern Persia were compelled to seek a new place of refuge. The Jewish population increased steadily in the sixth and seventh centuries. The relations between the Mountain Jews and the Khazar rulers in the area, who by all accounts adopted the Jewish religion, remain largely wrapped in mystery.[15]

The fact that many Mountain Jews were sympathetic to the Zionist idea is due in large part to the efforts of Rabbi Yaakov Yitskhaki, rabbi of the Dagestan Jews, who did much to inculcate it.[16] Scores of families emigrated to Palestine from Dagestan during the Second *Aliyah* (in the years prior to 1914) settling in Beer Yaakov and participating actively in the *Ha-shomer* organisation. During and after World War I, Gershon Muradov took over the task of spreading the Zionist idea among the Mountain Jews, and four of the twenty-eight delegates to the Congress of Caucasian Zionists held in Baku on 21 August 1917 were Mountain Jews. In 1919 a Zionist newspaper, *Tubushi Sabukhi*, was even printed in the Tat language.

During the Civil War, in the years 1918–21, when the struggle of the Muslim peoples of the Caucasus against the Soviet regime took an extreme anti-Jewish turn, the Jews reacted by enlisting in the Bolshevik forces by the thousand.[17] Influenced by Communist ideas, these recruits believed that the establishment of the Soviet regime there would bring far-reaching improvements in their economic and cultural situation. However, the hatred of much of the local population for the Mountain Jews only increased, and in the second half of the 1920s, when the Soviet regime was already firmly entrenched, blood libels were still heard of from time to time; they brought about waves of disturbances that could only be stopped by the firm intervention of the central authorities.[18] This hostility emerged once again during World War II, encouraged as it was by the Nazis who overran part of the northern Caucasus.

Demography and economy

In the 1926 census, when the Mountain Jews were registered as a separate ethnic group, they numbered 25,974.[19] However, as in the case of Georgia, it may be assumed that their actual number was greater. An American sociologist who visited the Caucasus in 1933 was told that they numbered 40,000.[20] In contrast to the Georgian Jewish community, the Mountain Jews did sustain losses during the war, when a section of the population was put into temporary concentration camps and slaughtered *en masse*.

According to the 1959 census, the Mountain Jews totalled only 30,000 (21,427 of whom, minus an unknown but probably small number of Ashkenazi Jews, resided in the Dagestan Autonomous Republic).[21] Although the Mountain Jews were not listed as such in the 1970 census, if we estimate that their natural growth rate was no less than half that of the other Dagestan peoples, then their number would have reached 37,000 in 1970.[22] From another figure from the 1970 census, which shows a huge increase in the Tat population (from 11,963 in 1959 to 17,109 in 1970)[23] despite information that this population is in advanced stages of assimilation, we deduce that the authorities apparently encouraged the Mountain Jews to register as Tats. (The Mountain Jews speak the Tat language, but have not normally regarded themselves as part of the Tat nationality which is composed of both Muslims and Christians.) New immigrants to Israel from Dagestan have confirmed that many Jews did so register in 1970. It is therefore reasonable to assume that the Mountain Jews could have numbered as many as 45,000 in 1970.[24] It seems that more than half of the community was concentrated in the Dagestan Autonomous Republic, about a third in the Azerbaidzhan Republic and the remainder in the Kabardino-Balkar and Chechen-Ingush Autonomous Republics in the northern Caucasus.

By 1926, 85.4% of the Mountain Jews in Dagestan were already classed as urban.[25] And, by 1970, the percentage of Jewish agricultural workers had apparently dropped below 10% (still a high percentage in comparison with other Jewish communities). The agricultural workers were concentrated on a number of kolkhozes in Dagestan and Azerbaidzhan which engaged chiefly in tobacco-growing, viticulture and fruit-tree orchards.[26] A small number of Mountain Jews have been working in fishing cooperatives since the 1930s.

The towns where the Mountain Jews were concentrated were Makhachkala, Buinaksk and Derbent in Dagestan; Kuba, Kirovobad and Baku in Azerbaidzhan; and Nalchik and Grozny in the northern Caucasus. The most popular occupations were those of carpenter, locksmith, and driver, although commerce and entrepreneurship (mainly in sheep's wool) also occupied an important place.

From the 1930s onwards, an intelligentsia also began to form, and by the late 1960s academic professions such as pharmacy, medicine, and engineering were quite common among the Mountain Jews, much more so than among Georgian Jews. However, such professionals undoubtedly formed a very thin layer in comparison with the comparable stratum among the Ashkenazi Jews of the Soviet Union. An interesting phenomenon was the high percentage of Jews in the field of entertainment in the Dagestan Autonomous Republic.[27] A number of Mountain Jews still occupied a prominent place in the government administration and Party in the 1960s (see Docs. 167 and 170).

Despite the processes of disintegration to which the family structure of the Mountain Jews has been subjected ever since the 1920s,[28] it still represents the strongest single factor of cohesion in this community, preserving it from assimilation through intermarriage. The older generation has retained much of its influence and authority, and the head of the family has the last word in all family matters, that word being law for all his children, both married and unmarried. Another consolidating factor in the social sphere was the fact that the Mountain Jews lived in their own quarters, thus reinforcing the family and community frameworks and thereby also the authority of the traditional leadership.

Religion

The religious factor, which was of central importance among the Mountain Jews before the October Revolution and in the first years of the new Soviet regime, apparently weakened significantly from the 1930s (to a much greater extent than in the Georgian Jewish Community).

At the beginning of the 1950s, the Mountain Jews had synagogues in Nalchik, Baku, Derbent, Makhachkala and Kuba.[29] There were also synagogues in such places as Buinaksk. However, the extreme anti-religious campaign launched in the Khrushchev period (see Chapters 3 and 8) did not leave Dagestan untouched. In 1960, a local Buinaksk newspaper published a virulently anti-Semitic article by a certain Daya Magmudov, who claimed that the Jews use Muslim blood once a year (Doc. 53).[30] A few weeks earlier, the same newspaper had published an article demanding the closure of the only synagogue in the town on the grounds that its existence caused great damage to the population by encouraging the performance of harmful religious precepts and hindering the education of the youth in a Communist spirit (Doc. 169).

By 1966, the number of synagogues serving the Mountain Jews in all the towns of the Caucasus was estimated at only six, of which a mere two remained in Dagestan, in the towns of Makhachkala and Derbent, while the synagogue in Buinaksk was closed in 1965. The synagogues were usually in small private apartments into which the worshippers crowded on Sabbaths and festivals.[31] In addition, religious services were held regularly in private homes. The most basic religious precepts, such as circumcision, marriage and burial, were scrupulously observed, but other precepts were kept far less punctiliously, if at all, by the younger generation.

Culture and national identity

The language of the Mountain Jews is Tat, which belongs to the western group of the Iranian linguistic family, enhanced by a substratum of Hebrew words, the majority of which are linked to religion. Until 1928, it was written in the Hebrew alphabet, but the process of Latinisation which began in the early 1920s in Azerbaidzhan and after 1926 in the northern Caucasus did not leave the Tat language unaffected. The Hebrew alphabet was officially replaced by the Latin in 1928, but the change-over was not completed until 1930 due to resistance on the part of the Jews. In 1938, the Tat language, like many others, underwent another 'linguistic revolution', and the Latin script was replaced by the Cyrillic. The change-over took until 1941 and the Cyrillic script remains in force today.

The percentage of Jews who were able to read and write in their own language or in any other language was only 19.7% in 1926,[32] the lowest literacy rate among all the Soviet Jewish communities. In the same year, 97% declared Tat to be their mother tongue; in 1959 this dropped to 83%. This is a small drop in view of the fact that the Tat-language schools had been liquidated; that the number of publications in the language were reduced (see below); and that the small nationalities in the USSR were generally subject to very marked linguistic assimilation.

The Mountain Jews, like other Caucasian nationalities, were largely bilingual, speaking both Tat and Russian, although the extent of this bilinguality differed from region to region. In settlements where the Jewish community has been established for a longer period, and the Jews continued to reside in their own quarter, Jewish Tat was the language spoken in the home by the older and middle generations. However, in those areas where Jews have settled relatively recently and did not live compactly, the Tat language is gradually disappearing as the spoken language. Even when Tat was still spoken at home, Russian was used almost exclusively at work and elsewhere.[33]

In the 1920s, a network of Tat-language schools was set up, in which during the first four classes all subjects were taught in Jewish Tat. However, even this limited system was found only in Dagestan. A gradual reduction seems to have begun at the end of the 1930s and, after World War II (in 1948), instruction in the Tat language ceased to exist in the elementary classes of Dagestan schools. Years later this step was justified by the Tat Jewish scholar, M. Ikhilov, known for his assimilatory tendencies, who argued that the Mountain Jews were tending to adopt Russian culture (Doc. 167). As M. Zand has rightly pointed out, 'this measure, which was undoubtedly intended to speed up the process of enforced Russification, was taken only as regards the Mountain Jews, whereas regarding the other six peoples [in the area] the instruction in their mother tongues in elementary schools was not discontinued'.[34] In this way, as with the Ashkenazi and Bukharan Jews, the fundamental pillar of the existence of independent national culture in the Soviet system was removed.

In the 1920s, cultural clubs were opened and amateur ensembles founded which operated in the Tat language. On 3 June 1928, a Tat-language newspaper, *Zakhmetkesh* (The Workers), began appearing in Makhachkala. Other newspapers also appeared for short periods. A group of writers and poets emerged from among the Mountain Jews, among them Sh. Rubinov and Y. Borukhov. In 1934, a Tat literary circle was founded in Derbent and, in 1936, the Tat Department of the Writers' Union was set up. However, those active in the cultural life of the Mountain Jews were among the victims of the great Stalinist purges of 1936–8. But the liquidation of the Jewish Tat culture began only after the war, when, together with the closure of the schools, the newspaper *Zakhmetkesh* was shut down, and books in the Jewish Tat language ceased being published during 1948–53.

In the 1950s and 1960s, the average number of Tat books published each year was only two. The most important writer of this period was Khizgil Avshalumov, whose works dealt with the events of World War II. The only remaining forum for Jewish Tat literature was the almanac entitled *Vatan Svetinu* (Our Soviet Motherland), which was supposed to appear annually, but did not in fact always do so. Interestingly, part of the material in the almanac was written by the Mountain Jews in Russian and translated back into Tat, demonstrating the extent to which linguistic assimilation had grown.

In 1959, after continuing efforts, an ensemble whose repertoire was based on the folklore of the Mountain Jews was founded in Nalchik. Its activities were financed by the synagogue with the help of the more prosperous Jews,[35] and its performances were attended by between 300 and 500 people. In 1966, the ensemble ceased its activities, but these were renewed as a result of a demonstration organised by the Jews (after a young Jewish member of the ensemble had been murdered in June 1967) to demand a Jewish cultural centre, schools and *kosher* meat.

Thus, the national identity of the Mountain Jews has found expression in the considerable preservation of their language and to a lesser extent of their culture, in spite of the difficulties and pressures to which they have been subjected. Additional factors have helped retard the process of assimilation among Mountain Jews, among them the continued observance of religious precepts, the practice of which has largely been due to the family cohesiveness mentioned above. And to this must be added another force, likewise of great importance: the Zionist idea, which apparently did not die out even during and after World War II.[36]

The establishment of the State of Israel brought about a great awakening among the Mountain Jews; their rejoicing knew no bounds in those days. Despite the fact that those who began listing candidates for emigration to Israel paid dearly for it (Doc. 168), the study of Hebrew, sporadic contacts with members of the Israeli Embassy and individual tourists, and the influence of Israel's overseas broadcasts kept the ashes glowing.

While the effect of the Six-Day War only added to the general Zionist exhilaration, the broad Zionist awakening did not come about until the early 1970s. It was probably held back by the special situation of the Mountain Jews – the threats and pressure from the authorities combined with their relative isolation from the centres of the Soviet Union.

The Bukharan Jews

The distant historical past of the Bukharan Jews is also shrouded in mystery. According to various traditions, the Jews began to arrive in Central Asia at the time of the first exile. But, even if there were some Jews in this area in this early period, the Arab and later the Mongol conquests led to their almost total annihilation. The Bukharan Jews, who call themselves *Ivri, Isroel* or *Yahudi*, are termed as they are because the majority settled in the Emirate of Bukhara from the fourteenth century onwards. The name *Yahudihoi Mahalli* took root after the Revolution (Docs. 171–2).[37]

At the 3rd Congress of Russian Zionists in June 1917, Avraham Pinhasov from Samarkand was the Bukharan delegate. Zionist organisations, such as *Poalei ziyon, Zeirei ziyon* and the General Zionist Organisation, continued to function in Bukhara and Samarkand for a number of years during the transitional period of the Bukharan Emirate (1917–20) and even at the beginning of the Soviet period. The Sovietisation of the autonomous Jewish communities ended only in 1927.[38] It must be emphasised that the position of the Bukharan Jews during this ten-year period greatly deteriorated.

Demography and economy

According to the 1926 census, the Jews of Bukhara numbered 18,698 (Doc. 172). However, Soviet authors themselves suggest that this figure was not accurate and considerably underestimated the total Bukharan Jewish population. From figures compiled by the organisation for Jewish agricultural settlement, *Komzet*, it appears that in 1929 there were some 45,000 Bukharan Jews on the territory of the Uzbek Republic alone,[39] but this same organisation gave the number of Bukharan Jews as 24,000 in 1934, most of whom lived in the cities of Samarkand, Tashkent, Bukhara and Kokand (Doc. 172).

In the 1959 census, the number of Bukharan Jews was given as 28,000, but this, too, was an underestimate, since their region had not been overrun during World War II and their natural growth rate was much higher than that of the Ashkenazi community in the Soviet Union. Estimates of the actual Jewish population vary from 30,000 to 60,000.

Today, the Bukharan Jews are concentrated in the cities of Samarkand, Tashkent, Bukhara, Kokand, Andizhan and Margelan in the Uzbek Republic, and in Dushanbe, the capital of the Tadzhik Republic. Although some of them have left their quarters and moved to other parts of town, in the 1960s a sizeable number were still to be found in the old quarters. This was especially true of towns like Samarkand, Bukhara and Kokand.

Before Soviet power was properly established, and even during the New Economic Policy era until the late 1920s, most Bukharan Jews were engaged in commerce. Prior to the Revolution, the number so employed, chiefly in small-scale trade, was about 60%, while the remaining 40% included artisans, agricultural workers, blue and white collar workers and the unemployed (who totalled 8%).[40] From the second half of the 1920s, the authorities sought to bring the Bukharan Jews into urban and rural cooperatives. In 1929, 65% were still small-time independent artisans or organised into artels, and only 10% were agricultural workers; the remaining 25% were petty traders or without regular employment. It was in that year that the first Bukharan Jewish kolkhozes were set up, with about 1,000 families. In 1933, there were fifteen Jewish kolkhozes, with a population of 3,150 persons.[41]

Despite intensified processes of industrialisation in Uzbekistan from the 1930s onwards, many Bukharan Jews continued to work in the service sector, playing a major role as entrepreneurs and in commerce (legal and semi-legal).[42] We possess no figures for the percentage of Jews working in heavy industry. It is even more difficult to estimate the size of the Bukharan Jewish intelligentsia which developed from the 1930s;[43] however, the number of Bukharan Jews in key positions was small.

The family structure, in which the father was all-powerful, weakened with time, but certainly did not disintegrate during the period of this book, and the extended family still remains largely intact.

Religion

As in the case of the Georgian Jews, religion continues throughout to play a far more important role among the Bukharan Jews than it does in the Ashkenazi community of the Soviet Union. In the 1920s, there was still a large number of synagogues in all the towns where Jewish communities existed. There were thirty-two synagogues in Samarkand, for example, at the end of the 1920s.[44] The number gradually dwindled from the 1930s onwards. And by the 1960s there were only eleven synagogues left in Central Asia.[45]

Jewish religious establishments and the religious practices conducted in them were attacked by the local authorities, who conducted a fierce propaganda campaign against them in the press, especially from the end of the 1950s. (Circumcision and ritual bathing were attacked in particular for 'sanitary and health' reasons.) The rabbis of the Bukharan Jews were compelled – like their Georgian and Mountain Jewish co-religionists – to state in the press that discrimination and anti-Semitism were non-existent in the

Soviet Union and to take part in bitter attacks on the State of Israel and Zionism (see Doc. 117 and Chapter 8, n. 64). There were blood libels in the early 1960s, sparked off by religious enmity, which in a number of cases turned into pogroms (Docs. 54–5). The growing contacts between Uzbekistan and various Arab states undoubtedly contributed in some part to the exacerbation of relations between the local Muslim population and the Jews.

Nonetheless, the main religious injunctions seem to have been observed by the Bukharan Jewish population up to and beyond 1967. This was, no doubt, partly due to the activities of the *Ḥabad* emissaries among the Bukharan Jews, which began at the end of the nineteenth century. However, it should be pointed out that, although the Jewish religion has been preserved to some extent in this community, even here religious attachment has steadily and severely eroded among the younger generation.

Culture and national identity

The language of the Bukharan Jews is a distinctive dialect of Tadzhik, which belongs to the western group of the Iranian family of languages. What distinguishes it mainly is its lexical elements and special features of phonology and morphology. From the end of the nineteenth century, the intelligentsia of the community began to elevate this dialect to an independent literary language. In 1928, it was decided to replace the Hebrew alphabet of the Bukharan Jews by the Latin alphabet, but this was only finally accomplished in the years 1931–2, and then only after stormy debates.[46] The second 'linguistic revolution' which took place in the Soviet Union in 1935 failed to overtake the Bukharan Jewish language. The question of replacing the Latin by the Cyrillic alphabet was debated in 1938; and the decision to refrain from doing so proved to be a negative omen, as the last Bukharan Jewish publications appeared in 1940.

Although the percentage of Bukharan Jews who were able to read and write in their own language or any other language was 24.2% in 1926 (the second lowest among the Jewish communities of the Soviet Union), illiteracy dropped rapidly from the 1930s. Again, in 1926, 93.8% declared the Bukharan Jewish language to be their mother tongue. While this percentage dropped to 75% in 1959, it was very high considering that the network of Bukharan Jewish educational and cultural institutions had already been liquidated.

Until the beginning of the 1920s, Bukharan Jewish children were educated mainly in the *ḥeder* and *yeshivah* by the old methods, the most important subject being the commentary on the week's portion from the Pentateuch. In Samarkand, Tashkent and Kokand there were state Russian–Hebrew schools for the local Jews, where general Russian studies were taught together with Jewish subjects. But, once the Soviet government was firmly established, a fierce struggle was waged between the local authorities and the founders and directors of the Jewish schools over the use of Hebrew as a language of instruction. After the intervention of Commissar of Education A. Lunacharsky, Hebrew was approved as a language of instruction, but this decision held sway only until the academic year 1922–3.

At the end of the 1920s, there were twenty-four Bukharan Jewish schools in the towns of Uzbekistan with 2,760 pupils,[47] but the network of Soviet state schools in the Bukharan Jewish language had disappeared by the end of the 1930s. Although the number of *ḥadarim* also gradually decreased, they continued to exist in secret or semi-secrecy for a long time.

The first newspapers in the Bukharan Jewish language appeared in Samarkand. From 1921 to 1923, there was a wall-newspaper called *Rosta* (Russian Telegraphic Agency). From 19 September 1925, a newspaper called *Rushnoi* (Light), which published original works by Bukharan Jewish writers,[48] began appearing regularly under the editorship of A. Pinkhasov. This was the organ of the *Evsektsiya* in Uzbekistan and of the Committee for National Minorities attached to the Central Executive Committee of Uzbekistan. In the 1920s and 1930s, many books of prose, verse and drama were printed in the Bukharan Jewish language (37 in 1930 and 177 in 1933). The most important writers were Muhib (Mordekhai Bachaev), Gavriel Samandarov, Yunotan Kuraev, Yaakov Haimov, M. Aminov, Y. Mordekhaev and P. Abramov. Among the other cultural institutions which existed in the 1920s and 1930s were a theatre (which functioned only from 1921 to 1925), cultural clubs and a Historical–Ethnographic Museum in Samarkand, which was founded in 1922 and functioned until the second half of the 1930s.

The Great Purge of the 1930s dealt a heavy blow to Bukharan Jewish culture; the writer Abramov and the poet Muhib were among those arrested at that time, and the last three books to be published in the Bukharan Jewish language appeared in 1940. Thus, Bukharan Jewish culture was liquidated even before the cultures of the other Soviet Jewish communities. From the 1940s onwards, the only survivals of independent Bukharan Jewish culture were to be found in literary works on Jewish themes, written in the Tadzhik or Uzbek languages, and in the performances of Jewish-born singers which very occasionally included Jewish folk-songs.[49]

The factors contributing to the preservation of the national identity of the Bukharan Jews are much the same as those effecting Georgian and Mountain Jews. Religion continued to play a dominant role for the older and middle generations and for many of the younger people as well, the influence of the *Ḥabad* emissaries being of particular importance here.[50] Also of significance in this respect is the fact that intermarriage does not seem to have constituted a serious threat in this community, and that here too family bonds have remained strong. Finally, the long-standing interest in the land of Israel, and the desire to emigrate there, was strengthened after the State of Israel was established. (The large emigration of Bukharan Jews to Israel began with a trickle in 1971 and greatly increased after 1973.)

The Krymchak Jews

The Krymchak Jews, who constitute the smallest of all the Oriental Jewish communities in the Soviet Union, differ from the others in many respects. According to tradition and historical research, the first Jews reached the Crimea two thousand years ago (Doc. 173).[51] The name Krymchak was given to them in 1597, prior to which they were called simply 'Jews' or 'Talmudic Jews'.

In the 1926 census the Krymchaks numbered 6,383, as compared to some 8,000 during World War I, many of them having fled during the Civil War. Although the 1939 census lists the number of Krymchaks as only 3,000, other estimates suggest that there were as many as 8,000 at that time, the differences arising from the changed definition of nationality between the census of 1926 and that of 1939 and the different methods of registration in the two censuses. The killing of about 70% of all Krymchaks by the Nazis during World War II reduced their number to some 2,500, and there were no figures on them in the 1959 and 1970 censuses. However, since they were in advanced stages of assimilation, it is reasonable to assume that they numbered between 2,000 and 2,500 by 1970.

The percentage of Krymchak Jews who knew how to read and write their own Jewish dialect – Crimean-Tatar – was 58.2% in 1926, a much higher percentage than in the case of the other Oriental Jewish communities.[52] In that same year, 74.1% of all Krymchak Jews declared this dialect to be their mother tongue, while only 9% did so in 1959, rendering the process of linguistic assimilation among the Krymchak Jews more rapid than that prevailing in any other Jewish community.

Nothing remains of the cultural enterprises of the Krymchak Jews from the 1920s and 1930s, and very little is known about their religious life. In contrast to all the other Jewish communities of the USSR, there is no indication that they have shared in the Jewish national awakening.

Documents to Chapter 13

The Georgian Jews

Document 163* The Georgian Jews: a Soviet characterisation (1958)[53]

Georgian Jews do not differ in their culture from the surrounding population, and they speak Georgian. The only thing that distinguishes them is their religion, owing to which they keep themselves in isolation. This seclusion is a result of the persecution from which they suffered under different religious sects. Therefore, in former times, the religious leaders used to occupy an important role in their social life. Corresponding to the rabbis of Western Jews, here there was the *Ḥakham*, who exercised considerable authority over the Jewish population.

By descent, Caucasian Jews, such as the 'Mountain Jews' and Georgian Jews, have very little in common with European and Russian Jews. They are the descendants of ancient Jewish settlers of the Caucasus, possibly of the pre-Christian epoch.

Document 164† Jewish culture in Georgia (1948)

A Historical-Ethnographic Museum of Georgian Jews[54] has been in existence for more than fifteen years in the capital of the Georgian Republic, Tbilisi.

In a talk with our correspondent, the Director of the Museum, Comrade Aron Krikheli,[55] said: 'The Historical-Ethnographic Museum is one of the most respected scientific-research and cultural-educational institutions in the Georgian Republic. The task of the museum is to study the history and ethnography of Georgian Jews. In addition, we study the history of the Transcaucasian Jews. We also carry out regular cultural and educational activities among the Jewish population.

'The museum has a serious scientific basis which allows us to develop a wide range of research work. We have a great number of valuable historical documents, monuments, archive materials and exhibits. Since 1939, the

---

* *Source*: S. A. Tokarev, *Etnografiya narodov SSSR* (Ethnography of the Peoples of the USSR), Moscow, Izdatelstvo Moskovskogo universiteta, 1958, pp. 305–6.
† *Source*: 'Naye arbeten in geshikhtlekh-etnografishn muzey fun di gruzishe yidn' (New Works in the Historical-Ethnographic Museum of Georgian Jews), *Eynikeyt*, 2 March 1948.

museum has published three volumes of scientific research, including twenty-two monographs, as well as a number of separate publications.

'The museum has a large regular exhibition on the following subjects: History and Ethnography, Socialist Construction, The Great Patriotic War, Folk Handicrafts, The Fourth Stalin Five-Year Plan, Shalom Aleikhem's Works, Mendele Mokher Seforim, and others. It possesses archives of historical documents, a department of unique manuscripts, a scientific library, a department of folklore and music and a department of photographic collections. Its collections amount now to seventeen thousand different exhibits.

'This year we are publishing an illustrated guide to the museum, a book on the activities of the revolutionary, Itska Rizhinashvili (1885–1906),[56] the fourth volume of research works of the museum and a book, *Classics of Georgian Literature on the Jews*.

'Last year the museum did some good work in Kutaisi. We discovered and studied a number of materials illuminating the past of the Georgian Jews – their way of life, their former legal status, their economy, their participation in the revolutionary movement, etc. Altogether we studied about four hundred documents there (twenty-seven printed sheets).

'Last summer the museum organised an expedition to South Ossetia, where interesting monuments and tombstones from the eleventh and twelfth centuries were discovered. This year the museum is organising a great exhibition devoted to Soviet Jewish literature and art.

'Thanks to the everyday care of the Georgian government the museum has achieved good results in its activities.'

Document 165* Beria and the Georgian Jews (1955)[57]

Beria's treatment of his Georgian countrymen is cited as one support for this argument but, as I have noted, unless a man is deserving of praise for corruption and favoritism it is doubtful that Beria should win any plaudits on this account.

The other argument cited in Beria's behalf is that he was more humane toward the Jews than the Soviet regime as a whole. Since Beria, as police chief, actually carried out a series of highly anti-Semitic measures, involving the arrest of some thousands or tens of thousands of Jews and their forcible deportation to some of the worst forced residence areas of the Soviet state, I find little grounds in his actual conduct to support this argument, either.

The only possible substantiation for portraying Beria as less anti-Semitic than some of the other chief Soviet leaders lies in certain things Beria did down in Georgia. It also has been said that Beria, who was born in Mingrelia, a tiny mountain area close to the Turkish frontier, was half Jewish and that his mother was a member of the extremely ancient and tiny sect of Mingrelian Jews. While I have been told this both in Tiflis [Tbilisi] and Moscow by both Georgians and Russians, other Georgians indignantly deny that Beria was of Jewish descent and contend that he was pure Georgian.

Regardless of Beria's ancestry, I made one discovery in Georgia which

* *Source*: H. E. Salisbury, *American in Russia*, New York, Harper and Brothers, 1955, pp. 89–91.

supports the picture of Beria as a liberal. In a narrow twisting sidestreet of Tiflis I found a curious and interesting sight. It was a Jewish ethnological museum which was founded at Beria's instigation. The curious thing was that while one of Tiflis's most ancient synagogues was closed in order to provide quarters for this museum, the exhibit itself was most comprehensive and bore neither an anti-religious nor an anti-Jewish character.

Instead, the museum was clearly designed to enhance among the Jews their knowledge of the cultural and traditional history of the Jewish people. Here there were paintings and models, depicting the ancient rites and customs of the Jewish Church, scenes from the Bible, reconstructions of early Jewish churches in Georgia, representations of the oppression of Jews by the Turks and the Mongols, pictures of beautiful Jewish women being sold as harem slaves or traded for great Caucasus sheep dogs at the rate of three women for one dog.

The Director of this museum,[58] a scholarly Jew of middle age, had nothing but kind words for Beria. He told me that by the time of the Revolution the Jews in Georgia had fallen to almost unbelievable depths of poverty and ignorance. [...]

In the twenties, the Director told me, Beria helped start a programme for rehabilitating the Jews. Special schools, trade and handicraft centers were opened. Special Jewish farms were set up. A Jewish charitable society was organised under Beria's sponsorship to help the people help themselves. This sounded very strange to my ears because the Soviet, theoretically, frowns on any kind of charity.

And, as part of this programme, the Jewish museum was founded.

The Director took me about the building. Here were photographs of the life and times of Shalom Aleikhem, including a picture of his funeral in New York. Here was a special layout on Albert Einstein, telling about his achievements in the field of physical theory and his struggle against oppression of the Jews. Here was a large section devoted to Nazi persecution of the Jews, to the anti-Semitic outrages in Germany and the horrors of the Nazi cremation chambers. And beside it was a layout of Jewish generals in the Soviet Army and Jewish heroes in the Red Army during the Second World War.

So far as I could see there was nothing wrong with the museum. It was just what it purported to be, strange as this seemed against the background of open and notorious anti-Semitism in Moscow. Still, there was the curious bit about the synagogue being closed to provide a building for this institution. Perhaps, in fact, an effort was being made to discourage church-going. I asked the Director whether there were any synagogues in Tiflis.

Yes, indeed, he replied. There are two. A big one for Georgian Jews and a smaller one for Russian Jews.

I asked him where the synagogues were located and went around to check up on whether he was telling the truth. He was. On a Friday evening both synagogues were busy and active, and seemingly, operating without interference.

So, perhaps, Beria had some feeling of tolerance and consideration for the Jews of Georgia – natural enough, if he himself were half Jewish.

The Mountain Jews

Document 166* Research on the Mountain Jews (1950)

On 13 December 1949, a graduate student of the Institute, M. M. Ikhilov,[59] defended his candidate dissertation on the subject of 'The Mountain Jews (a research monograph)'. His official examiners were Doctor of Historical Sciences P. I. Kushner and Candidate of Historical Sciences E. S. Zevakin. The dissertation discusses the main problems of the origins and history of the small mountain people living in the Dagestan ASSR and partly in the Azerbaidzhan SSR, and gives basic information on their life before the Great October Socialist Revolution and under Soviet rule and on the flourishing of their economy and culture at present. The dissertation is mainly based on the author's field materials collected during his expeditions in 1944–8, with much literary and archive material added.

As pointed out by P. I. Kushner, M. M. Ikhilov's argument is permeated by the fundamental idea of the closeness of the culture of the Mountain Jews to the culture of the other peoples in Dagestan because of their common historical fate. The author analyses different agricultural implements of the Mountain Jews and their methods of tilling the soil and growing plants, and comes to the conclusion that they are similar to those used by the surrounding population and that therefore it is impossible to speak of having special ethnic customs of husbandry. If there are some differences between the economic activities of the Mountain Jews and the neighbouring national groups in Dagestan, they are caused not by the special ethnic features of the people, but by socio-economic factors and partly by the difference in religious precepts. An analysis and description of the housing and clothing of the Mountain Jews lead to the same conclusions.

The examiner stressed that (as distinct from many pre-Revolutionary authors) M. M. Ikhilov considers the Mountain Jews to be mainly tillers of the soil and vine-growers. Handicrafts and retail trade he regards as secondary in the economy of this people, and he explains their development only by the fact that the Mountain Jews were deprived of the right to own land. They were compelled to rent the land at a high cost. To justify the expense they tried to grow those food and industrial crops which were most valuable – from the commercial point of view – even though they were labour intensive. As distinct from the national economy of the other mountain people, that of the Mountain Jews was more of a commodity economy, from where the notion of their being a commercial people may have arisen. The data supplied by the author lead to the conclusion that the Mountain Jews really were an agricultural people and that their main source of existence was productive agricultural labour and not commerce. Commerce was of considerable importance to the Mountain Jews living in the towns. But this was mainly retail peddling. There were no more than ten large-scale merchants who possessed much capital and real estate.

In his study of the social structure and family relations of the Mountain Jews in the past, M. M. Ikhilov demonstrates from his original materials the

* *Source*: 'Zashchita dissertatsii v institute etnografii' (Defence of Dissertation in the Institute of Ethnography), *Sovetskaya etnografiya*, 1950, no. 2, pp. 201–2.

existence (in some places up until the October Revolution) of large families, their disintegration and the changes in the family way of life of this people. In his chapter on religion and beliefs the author expresses clearly, and proves by facts, arguments on the reactionary role of Judaism and its links with the chauvinist ideology of Zionism.

Document 167* The Mountain Jews: tradition and change (1960)

A large part of the Mountain Jews lives in Dagestan; individual groups of them also live in the Northern Caucasus and Azerbaidzhan. In the past they were mountain dwellers, whence their name – the Mountain Jews – but in the eighteenth and nineteenth centuries they were already beginning to leave the mountains for the lowland. At present they live in the settlements of Madzhalis (Kaitag District), Mamrach, Zhanzhal-Kala (Magaramkent District) and in the cities of Derbent, Makhachkala and Buinaksk in the Dagestan ASSR; in the settlements of Krasnaya Sloboda, Vartashen and a number of cities of the Azerbaidzhan SSR. The majority of Mountain Jews are scattered among the other inhabitants of these republics. A small number of Mountain Jews live in the cities of Grozny, Nalchik, etc. According to the 1959 census, there were more than 15,000 Mountain Jews in Dagestan and more than 10,000 in Azerbaidzhan. The language of the Mountain Jews is Tat (a distinctive dialect of Modern Persian). [...]†

In day-to-day life, however, some old traditions have been preserved. For example, some peasant families have the habit of taking their meals on the floor – on a carpet or a *palas* [double-sided carpet with no pile], spread like a table-cloth, despite the fact that the room has a table and chairs. Another custom which continues to exist is eating while sitting on pillows and mattresses and serving the food on tiny low tables. [...]

There are almost no compulsory marriages in the contemporary family of the Mountain Jews. Nowadays a marriage is concluded on the basis of the couple's mutual love, and the parents readily meet their wishes. Sons and daughters are not married off at a young age. Such customs as levirate marriages have disappeared from the conjugal system of the Mountain Jews, though in very rare cases sororate marriages are encountered. The practice of taking two wives has ceased. The number of marriages to relatives has decreased. Mixed marriages have become more frequent. As a result of the decline of religion in recent years, the customs of officially registering a marriage and celebrating a wedding in the presence of a rabbi are no longer observed by the majority of families. Only a small part of the older generation still clings to religious traditions.

Medical services for the population have been organised; quack medicine has been eliminated. In the towns and villages there are maternity homes,

---

* *Source*: M. M. Ikhilov, 'Gornye evrei' (The Mountain Jews), *Narody Kavkaza*, vol. 1, Moscow, Izdatelstvo Akademii Nauk SSR, 1960, pp. 554, 557, 558, 559–60, 560–1.

† Because they have established their writing and culture in the Tat language, they are known both as Mountain Jews and as Tats. However, the Tats are, properly speaking, the population using the same language as the Mountain Jews, but differing from them in origins and, in the past, in religion (the Mountain Jews profess Judaism, and the Tats proper – Islam).

hospitals, polyclinics, medical centres, kindergartens, *crèches*, etc. Magical birth rites have ceased to exist.

Tremendous changes have taken place in the culture of the Mountain Jews during the years of Soviet power. Illiteracy has been totally eliminated. Considerable cadres of the intelligentsia have emerged from among the Mountain Jews. Writing in the Tat language has been established, literary works are published. Before the Great Patriotic War, instruction in the youngest classes was given in the Tat language. From 1928 the Tat-language newspaper *Zakhmetkesh* [The Workers] appeared and played a significant role in the reshaping of the life of the Mountain Jews and in their education. After the war, because of the Mountain Jews' gravitation towards Russian culture, instruction in the schools was given in Russian. In view of this, the publication of the newspaper also ceased.

The Mountain Jews are active in the cultural and scientific life of the country. Among the intelligentsia of the Mountain Jews there are scientific workers, artists, etc., including the philologist Professor I. Anisimov, the Honoured Art Worker of the RSFSR T. Izrailov, the People's Artist of the Dagestan ASSR M. Shcherbatova, the Honoured Art Worker of the Dagestan ASSR Kh. Khanukaev, the composer D. Ashurov, etc. Amateur artistic activities are widely developed. The cultural aspect of the village population is approximating more and more to that of the urban population. Theatrical collectives from the towns frequently perform in the settlements, and films are shown. The reading of books has become a permanent feature in the life of both town-dwellers and villagers.

Currently one of the most developed spheres of the Mountain Jews' popular creativity is folklore, rich in works on themes from contemporary life. Folk poetry has reflected the deeds of Soviet soldiers who fought against the German invaders and images of heroes of socialist labour.

The poets and writers who have emerged from the people include M. Bakhshiev,[60] M. Dadashev,[61] D. Atnilov, Kh. Avshalumov,[62] S. Izgiyaev.[63] In their works they tell of the people's difficult past and of the great changes which have taken place in Dagestan, as everywhere in the USSR, under Soviet rule.

Document 168* National fervour among the Mountain Jews (1969)[64]

Most of the inhabitants of this unique Jewish colony are steeped in a Jewish national spirit and observe the Jewish traditions according to the strict letter of the law. The Soviet authorities had not prevented them, just as they had not prevented all the other peoples and tribes in the Caucasus, from remaining true to their old way of life and beliefs. In 1938 I saw in a photographer's display window photographs of an October demonstration in which the Secretary of the Republic Communist Party, Batal Kalmykov, a Kabardinian, and the Chairman of the Council of Commissars, Cherkasov, a Balkar, were marching together with the tall, patriarchal *Ḥakham* of the 'Jewish colony', and next to him the *gabai* of the synagogue. The Jewish

* *Source*: Nisan Rozental (A. Ben-Dov), 'Bein yehudim harariim' (Among the Mountain Jews), *He-avar*, May 1969, vol. XIV, pp. 230, 231–2.

representatives were wearing the same costume as the rest of the Caucasian peoples. Only the silver handles of their daggers were conspicuous on account of the small 'Stars of David', which were engraved on them among all the other designs. [...]

In the latter half of the month of May 1948, there was rejoicing in all the houses of the Mountain Jews: the good tidings had reached them that the two-thousand-year-old dream of the people of Israel had come true. The Jewish 'colony' is celebrating: they blow the *shofar* and invite the congregation into the large courtyard of the synagogue. There *Hallel*[65] is said by the whole community. Their unique national artistic troupe plays and dances, and they sing songs in the Tat language. All the Jews sing prayers and melodies and weep for joy. In the courtyards of the houses long tables are erected and set with all kinds of drinks – homemade wine and other beverages – as well as spicy national dishes. Great is the rejoicing. Old and young take part, and even inquisitive non-Jews from the neighbouring streets.

The *Hakham*, an old man, but still as erect as a cypress and as agile as a deer, sets off on an exultant mountain dance in the middle of the street. The crowd stands around him and claps. Opposite him dances the old man, Ben-Ziyon Shabti, who in days gone by had been a teacher of *Torah*. The skirts of his festive Caucasian coat flap to the sides and he soars as if in winged flight.

Shabti organises the festivities. He commands great respect in the Jewish 'colony', and the Jews love him. He has an excellent command of the Tat language and speaks Hebrew fluently. In the first days of the Soviet regime, he still taught the children of the Mountain Jews Hebrew. For years now he has not worked. He is nearly eighty but is still filled with Jewish fervour, believes in the Redemption and is happy to have lived to see the liberation of the land of his forefathers. He heads the festivities. His close helpers are Avinoam the shoemaker, Zekhariah the tanner, Mizrahi the young blacksmith, and his son-in-law Ahitov, a dental technician. They go from house to house and proclaim 'Long live the people of Israel' and immediately make a list of the Jews who want to emigrate to Israel. We must make haste to emigrate, they say, the War of Independence is not yet over. We must help defeat the enemy. Old Shabti drafted a proclamation, made a number of copies and posted them up in the synagogue courtyard and on some telegraph-poles. The proclamation was written in the Tat language and contained many passages from the Pentateuch and the Prophets.

The local NKVD had from the very beginning looked on tolerantly at all the goings-on in the Jewish 'colony'. They did not understand the significance of the festivities, the lists and the proclamations. The local Communist Party committee was of the opinion that for the time being no pressure was to be brought to bear on the Mountain Jews. Their nationalistic temper springs from political backwardness. Propagandists ought to be sent here to explain to the Mountain Jews that their only true homeland is the Soviet Union.

The Mountain Jews received the propagandists very coldly. They stood by their views, and a large number of them were ready to emigrate to Israel. Shabti did not cease to encourage them to be ready to leave in order to help in the liberation of the land.

Representatives came to Nalchik from other places where Mountain Jews were living, and wanted to know whether it was possible to emigrate to the land of Israel. With the consent of the rabbis and the *gabaim* the large assembly went into the synagogue. Once again they said *Hallel*, blew the *shofar* and swore next to the open Holy Ark: 'If I forget Thee, O Jerusalem, let my right hand forget its cunning.' Ben-Ziyon declared from the dais that as soon as the Israeli Ambassador arrived in Moscow he would go to him and find out all that was necessary for the Mountain Jews to be able to emigrate at the earliest opportunity.

A few days later the NKVD carried out a thorough search of Ben-Ziyon Shabti's house. They took away the proclamations, the books, the money which had been collected to assist Jews to leave for Israel. At night they would haul him off for cross-examination, they threatened him, tortured him and demanded the names of his helpers. But he told them nothing and resolutely refused to tell them. It was made clear to him now that it was forbidden even to conceive of putting in requests for exit visas.

Ben-Ziyon fell ill from the excitement and died a few weeks later. The whole of the Jewish 'colony' and some European Jews who lived in the city attended his funeral. They stood in silence around his open grave and no funeral orations were said.

Document 169* Need for synagogue for Tat Jews denied (1960)

Assisted by the great Russian nation and the brotherly Dagestan peoples, the small eleven-thousand-strong Tat people have, in the years of the Soviet regime, made an enormous step forward in their economic and cultural evolution.

The vine-growers of the Tat kolkhozes around Derbent are far-famed in Dagestan. Several leading workers from these kolkhozes were the first in Dagestan to receive the honoured title of Hero of Socialist Labour. There are also quite a few Tats in the front rank of Buinaksk enterprises.

The Tats have representatives among the Dagestan scientists, instructors in higher educational institutions, engineers, physicians and teachers. Though few in number, the Tat people have their own literature, writers and poets. In other words, the Tat people make their modest contribution to the building of Communism and are full of gratitude to their own Communist Party and their elder brothers in the family of Soviet nations.

At the same time, we still find in the small family of the Tat people backward elements, carriers of harmful survivals of the past, who hamper our progress. One of these factors is the existence of a synagogue in Buinaksk. Though it is frequented only by a few dozen aged people, the mere fact of its existence brings great harm.

All harmful survivals and rites such as circumcision, traditional marriage ceremonies and many other things are inspired and supported by the synagogue, which contributes to their preservation and revival. The same situation prevails with the mosque and Moslem Spiritual Board in Buinaksk. It may

* *Source*: Y. Nasimov, 'Nuzhna li v Buinakske sinagoga?' (Is a Synagogue Needed in Buinaksk?), *Kommunist* (Buinaksk), 30 July 1960.

consequently be said with certainty and without exaggeration that the synagogue is harmful to the subsequent Communist education of the Tat youth, the building of Communism and the subsequent spiritual evolution of the Tats.

The time has therefore come for Tat public opinion to raise the question of closing the synagogue. This does not mean, of course, that we ignore the religious feelings of the believers. They can perform their necessary religious rituals without hindrance in their homes, without a synagogue, just like believers in the Lower Dzhengutai and other villages do.

Document 170* Letter of Dagestan Jews to the *New York Herald Tribune* (1961)

Khizgil Avshalumov,
6a, Sovetskaya St, apt 23,
Makhachkala,
USSR.

To the Editor
of the *New York Herald Tribune*:

A group of Dagestan Mountain Jews, inhabitants of the Dagestan Autonomous Soviet Socialist Republic, is addressing this open letter to you. We were prompted to write it by an article by Joseph Newman, published in the *New York Herald Tribune* on 4 November, in which he deals with the conditions of the Mountain Jews in our republic.[66]

The subject of the article was a reader's letter published in a local newspaper of the Buinaksk District of the republic, which Mr Newman sought to interpret as a manifestation of national hostility.

Is that correct? Of course not! The appearance of such a letter was an extremely rare and exceptional case, the like of which has never before occurred in our country and, we are sure, will never be repeated. It was a pure accident, a mistake of irresponsible journalists, made without any ill intent. In keeping with the Constitution of the USSR and the Constitution of all the Union and Autonomous Republics, such mistakes are severely punished by the Soviet power, irrespective of whether they were intentional or not.

On the day following the publication of this letter, the newspaper made its excuse to the readers for having printed material which, owing to the author's ignorance, contained an absurd falsehood. The government and Party organisations, the entire public of the Dagestan ASSR sharply condemned the mistake made by the newspaper, and those responsible for it were punished accordingly. Therefore, to assert on the basis of this incident that 'Jews are persecuted' in the Dagestan Republic means to distort crudely the true state of affairs, to mislead readers intentionally.

The subscribers to this letter belong to different sections of the Dagestan Mountain Jewish people: collective farmers, workers, and writers. And we know better than anyone else that in our country there is no hostility between the peoples, that the relations between them are based on brotherly friendship

* *Source*: 'Daghestan Jews Answer the N.Y. Herald Tribune', *Morgn frayheyt*, 22 January 1961.

and mutual esteem. The equality of nations is solemnly proclaimed both in the Constitution of the USSR and in the Constitution of our republic. [...]

Before the Revolution our people, like all others too, were oppressed by poverty and lack of rights. More than 95% of the Dagestan Mountain Jews were illiterate.

And now? The sons and daughters of our people are engineers, scientists, writers and composers. Each of us can choose any profession, any trade for which he has a leaning. Our people is a very small one, yet many of our Mountain Jews hold high posts in Party and government organs of the republic, head industrial enterprises, construction sites, collective farms.

For instance, the names of the prominent Party leaders of the republic Hanun Abramov and Anatoly Danilov, those of Isai Nakhshunov, Master of Economics, who is the Vice-Chairman of the Economic Council of the Republic, and Yakov Izmailov, Deputy Minister of Local Industry of Dagestan, are widely known in our republic.

Professors, teachers, scientists, from the midst of the Dagestan Mountain Jews are working in higher educational establishments, research institutes, and the local branch of the All-Union Academy of Sciences. The Derbent collective farms, the members of which are Dagestan Mountain Jews, are famous throughout the republic for their labour exploits. Recently, seven of our collective farmers merited the title of Hero of Socialist Labour – the highest labour award in the Soviet Union.

We also enjoy broad opportunities of developing our language and our culture. According to the Constitution of the Dagestan ASSR, nine languages are considered state languages in the republic, including the Tat language, i.e. the language of the Mountain Jews. Works by writers, poets and playwrights are published in our language. Radio broadcasts are given in it. The Tat professional theatre recently organised in Derbent has already won popularity with the inhabitants of the republic.

As for the Jewish religion, it enjoys the same rights as all other religions in our country. The religious Jews, just like the Muslims, have every opportunity of performing their religious rites. Synagogues function normally in the capital of the republic, Makhachkala, in the cities of Derbent and Buinaksk. The Soviet Constitution grants every citizen freedom of religious worship, as well as freedom of anti-religious propaganda. But there is no need to prove that anti-religious propaganda is the propaganda of a scientific world outlook, the propaganda of natural science. And it is not, of course, conducted in our country in the way that Mr Newman tries to present it.

In conclusion, we declare once again: the statements contained in Mr Newman's article on the situation of the Mountain Jews, on the relations of the other Dagestan peoples to them do not conform to the truth. The relations between them are built on sound principles, on the principles of the Leninist friendship of the peoples.

> Yours respectfully,
>
> GYULBOOR DAVYDOVA, collective farmer. Hero of Socialist Labour, Deputy to the Supreme Soviet of the DASSR
>
> KHIZGIL AVSHALUMOV, writer, member of the Union of Soviet Writers of the USSR

KHANUKO GADILOV, locomotive engineer of the Derbent railway depot, head of a Communist Work Team

GIRSUN BABAEV, doctor in the Buinaksk city hospital

MISHI BAKHSHIEV, writer, member of the Union of Soviet Writers of the USSR

The Bukharan Jews

Document 171* The Bukharan Jews: a Soviet characterisation (1958)

National minorities of Central Asia

Central Asian Jews (about 18,000–19,000 in 1926) who call themselves *Ivri*, or *Yahudi* as they are called by neighbouring peoples, live mainly in the towns of Bukhara, Tashkent, Samarkand and other towns. They are not related by origin to Western, Ukrainian, Belorussian and Polish Jews. They have been living for many years on the territory of Central Asia; by tradition from the Assyrian epoch; in any case, they settled here before the beginning of our era.

In their manner of living the Jews assimilated to a significant degree to the surrounding population. They did not keep their own language; they speak Tadzhik and Uzbek. By way of occupation they hardly differ from the urban population of other nationalities. They differ only in their religion. In the epoch of Muslim Khans, Jews were oppressed and without rights. They had no right to buy land and could not engage in agriculture. They lived in special quarters (*makhallya*) of the towns, wore special dress tied with rope belts, had no right to ride horses in town and were subject to many other humiliating decrees and limitations, and to heavy extortions.

Document 172† Bukharan Jews in the Soviet period (1963)

The Jews living in the Central Asian republics and speaking one of the dialects of the Tadzhik language are called Central Asian Jews. The Central Asian Jews call themselves *yahudi*, representatives of the older generation – *isroel* or *bane isroel* (the children, descendants of Israel). After the October Revolution the term *yahudihoi mahalli* (local Jews) was widely employed. In the literature on the subject, the Central Asian Jews are known also by the name of 'Bukharan', 'Native', 'local' Jews.

According to the data of the All-Union census of 1926, the Central Asian Jews in the USSR numbered 18,698, of whom 9,364 were males and 9,334 were females. The majority of them – 17,172 – lived in Uzbekistan.

---

* *Source*: S. A. Tokarev, *Etnografiya narodov SSSR* (Ethnography of the Peoples of the USSR), Moscow, Izdatelstvo Moskovskogo universiteta, 1958, p. 400.

† *Source*: Ya. I. Kalontarov, 'Sredneaziatskie evrei' (Central Asian Jews), in *Narody srednei Azii i Kazakhastana* (The Peoples of Central Asia and Kazakhstan), Moscow, Izdatelstvo Akademii nauk SSSR, 1963, vol. 2, pp. 610, 615–16, 617–18, 619, 628, 629, 630.

According to the data of the Uzbekistan Committee for the Settlement of Jewish Toilers on the Land (*Komzet*), there were about 24,000 Jews registered in 1934 in the Uzbek SSR, the overwhelming majority of whom lived in the cities: Samarkand (5,750), Tashkent (3,340), Bukhara (1,850), Kokand (2,000), Khatyrchi (980), Shakhrisyabz (970), Andizhan (900), Margelan (860), and a few others. About 4,500 persons were registered in rural localities.

During the last twenty-five to thirty years, around 5,000 Central Asian Jews have moved to the Tadzhik SSR, the overwhelming majority coming from Samarkand, Bukhara and Shakhrisyabz, and to a lesser degree from Tashkent and the cities of the Fergana, where the local Jews were bilingual, i.e. with a good command of both the Tadzhik and the Uzbek languages. [...]

In the Soviet period the Central Asian Jews produced their own poets, prose writers and dramatists; a literature was born devoted to the contemporary life of the Central Asian Jews, to the themes of the new way of life, work and the struggle against religious stagnation and survivals of the past. Among contemporary poets there are Yakhiel Akilov, Yunotan Kuraev, Mordukhai Bachaev, Yakub Khakhamov, Pinkhos Abramov, etc. Also well known are the dramatist Yakub Khaimov and the prose writers Gavriel Samandarov and Moshe Yagudaev.

The folklore of the Central Asian Jews is to a large extent borrowed from their neighbours, the Tadzhiks of the plains and the Uzbeks. The specifically national element is present in folk-tales and parables on Biblical themes, and there are also folk sayings and riddles in which certain differences between the Jewish way of life and that of their neighbours are reflected. [...]

The October Revolution facilitated the development and growth of many talents in the sphere of the vocal arts. The traditions of musical and vocal art are widely developed. The art of the folk-singers enjoys great popularity. The most popular folk-singers are the People's Artists of the Uzbek SSR, the brothers Mikhoel and Gavriel Mulakandov, and Mikhoel Tolmasov. Many gifted singers with special conservatory education appear on the stages of the opera theatres and philharmonic halls.

The Krymchaks

Document 173* Research on the Krymchaks (1974)[67]

They [the Krymchaks] are a small people numbering today a little over 2,500 and living mainly in the Crimea. [...]

In the opinion of a number of scholars (S. Dubnow,[68] A. Harkavy,[69] Sh. Weissenberg,[70] P. Lyakov, and others) the Krymchaks have been living in the Crimea for over 2,000 years. As far as we know, the Krymchaks were mentioned for the first time in official Tsarist documents in 1841. [...]

Until then, the Krymchaks were called *yehudim* or 'Talmudic Jews', both in the Khanite documents that were given to a few Krymchak families in 1597 and 1742, and in official Russian documents. The term 'Krymchak' was also

* Source: Evsei Peisakh, 'Krimtshakes' (The Krymchaks), *Sovetish heymland*, 1974, no. 7, pp. 171–2, 173, 175–7; no. 9, pp. 138–41.

mentioned in a 'Decree of a Ministerial Committee of 18 August 1859', concerning the transfer of Krymchak agricultural workers from the colony at Rogatlikoi to the status of urban dwellers of the city of Karasubazar, and in order to allocate them concessions in connection with taxation and recruitment. [...]*

As can be seen from old statistics, the number of Krymchaks reached 2,466 in 1897. According to the census which was carried out in 1913 in nineteen population centres of the Crimea and the Caucasus, 5,282 Krymchaks were living in these areas. Beside these, about 2,700 were living in fourteen population centres not included in the count. In 1926, the number of Krymchaks in the Crimea was a little over 6,000, and there were about 500 who had left for Leningrad, Moscow, the Caucasus and elsewhere. At the beginning of the Great Patriotic War the number of the population had already reached about 8,000. During the temporary occupation of the Crimea by the Fascist murderers, more than 70% of the Krymchaks were killed, and in 1945, 2,500 were registered there. This figure has remained almost unchanged till today. [...]

In 1910, Isaak Samoilovich Kaya, a graduate of the Vilnius Teachers' Training College and the first Krymchak with higher education, was appointed head of the Karasubazar school. He set about his work with great enthusiasm, introducing a four-year programme and organising musical, dramatic and sports circles. Kaya directed this school until 1921, and many Krymchaks not only received four years' education, but also went on to study further.

I. S. Kaya would give lectures to the adult population on Saturdays and also read newspapers and books aloud. He wrote more than ten works on the history of the Krymchaks, six of which appeared in the journals *Vestnik evreiskogo prosveshcheniya*, *Evreiskaya starina*, *Oku Ishleri*, etc. He was one of the organisers behind the implementation of the census among the Krymchaks in 1913. [...]

The revolutionary Krymchak youth were particularly active in fighting during the White Terror in the Crimea in the years 1918–20. They distributed Bolshevik leaflets and supplied the partisans with food. Vrangel's men took cruel revenge on the brave young fighters. For carrying out revolutionary agitation among the soldiers of the White Army, the Krymchak Yakov Valit was shot in 1918 in Sevastopol. An interesting historical document was later found in his secret abode, the original copy of a leaflet 'To All Soldiers', which had been issued by the Sevastopol Committee of the Crimean organisation of the RSDRP in 1905.

After the October Revolution, the life of the Krymchaks took a new direction. Centres for the liquidation of illiteracy and clubs for the adult population were opened. In Simferopol a seven-year school was set up under the direction of Haya Isaakovna Trevgoda with instruction in Russian and Krymchak. Former pupils of this and other schools later became well-known doctors, pedagogues, engineers, musicians and artists. The Leningrad

* See: V. O. Levanda, *Polny khronologichesky sbornik zakonov i polozhenii kasayushchikhsya evreev ot 1649–1873 gg.* (Complete Chronological Collection of Laws and Statutes Concerning the Jews from the Years 1649–1873), St Petersburg, 1874, pp. 920–2.

engineer M. A. Trevgoda was awarded a State Prize. The poet Ya. Yu. Chapichev was made a Hero of the Soviet Union for bravery at the front in the Great Patriotic War.

Before the war the centre of Krymchak life was Karasubazar [now Belogorsk], where half the population lived; they were mainly engaged in shoemaking. The centre has now shifted to Simferopol, where the Krymchaks work in factories and plants, and in various institutions and organisations. In the period of total collectivisation of agriculture, two Krymchak collective farms were established in the vicinity of the village of Tabuldi: 'Krymchak' and 'Yengi Krymchak'. They were destroyed together with the clubs, schools and other institutions during the Fascist occupation.

In the years of the Great Patriotic War, many sons and daughters of the Krymchak people fought side by side with the other peoples of the Soviet Union against the common enemy. In the Crimea, the partisans Yasha Manto and Sara Bakshi are well-known. Some of the Krymchaks were evacuated to the rear at the beginning of the war, but the majority, left behind in the Crimea, were murdered by the Fascists. [...]

The Krymchaks speak a language which has not yet been properly studied. Most of the words in the language sound like Tatar, Azerbaidzhani, Karachaevo-Balkar, Kumyk. The archaisms in their vocabulary prove that the language arose before the Tatar period in the history of the Crimea. During the latter period (about 500 years) the Krymchaks took over most of the Tatar concepts. However, quite a large number of words from their earlier language remained. Thus, for example, the names of the majority of Krymchak dishes are for the most part in the original language. A number of words have been taken over from Persian, Arabic and Hebrew.

The Krymchaks had no written alphabet of their own. Before the Revolution they used at different times, the Aramaic (Hebrew), Arabic, Latin and Russian alphabets. In 1936, they, like the majority of Turkic-speaking peoples, changed to the Russian alphabet.

Krymchak literature contains a large number of interesting historical documents, ancient manuscripts, Khanite documents, etc. Many travellers and scholars who visited the Crimea in the last century wrote that the Krymchaks possessed prayer-books produced 1,200 years ago. It is known that, in 1839, A. Firkovich[71] brought to light many ancient Krymchak manuscripts which were in the *genizot* of Karasubazar and Feodosia, and had them transferred to the Petersburg Public Library as Karaite works. Firkovich himself writes about this in his book *Avnei Zikaron* (Stones of Memory, in Hebrew, Vilnius, 1872): 'I arrived in Karasubazar and in the morning went to the synagogue. The Krymchaks greeted me on my arrival. I showed them the letter from the authorities requesting permission to look through their ancient manuscripts. The community's representatives answered that they could not give me permission since it would be sacrilegious even to touch whatever there was in the hide-out. Seeing that there was nothing to be done, I was compelled to call on the police to help. When the officer saw the letter from the Governor-General, Count Vorontsov, he took two Tatar policemen and we left for the Krymchak synagogue ... I myself took a shovel, began to dig at the wall of the hide-out and had soon dug a hole through the wall the size of a window ... And what did I see? The hide-out was packed with books and manuscripts which would require several wagons to cart them away! With the help of my co-religionists [i.e. the Karaites – E.P.] I emptied the hide-out, taking everything of value ... packed it into sacks, sealed it and sent it to Simferopol.'

Firkovich's collection is supposed to contain very important information on the Krymchaks of the sixth to the eighth centuries and, it is thought, even of the fourth century.

Among the greatest Krymchak scholars one must mention first of all Moshe Ha-Goleh (fifteenth century), whose works have come down to us. The Crimean Tatars, during their attack on Kiev, captured and carried off his sons to the Crimea. Some time later, he went there to redeem them. He lived at first in Solkhat (Old Crimea) and later in Kaffa (Feodosia). The Krymchaks elected him as their rabbi, and he was the intermediary between the descendants of all kinds of communities – Askhenazi, Babylonian and Roman Jews – for whom he drew up a common *mahzor* [Festival prayer-book]. In the Saltykov-Shchedrin Public Library in Leningrad one can find his works *Shoshan edut* [The Testimony of the Rose], *Sefer Yezirah* [The Book of Creation], *Ozer Nehmad* [The Dear Treasure], etc., which are of great value for the investigation of the Krymchaks' social life in the fifteenth and sixteenth centuries...

Almost no study has been made of the folklore of the Krymchaks, and this is really a shame because today few people are left who remember the wonderful melodies and the texts of hundreds of songs which were handed down from generation to generation. The majority of old songs have a religious subject matter which they share in common with the songs and prayers of other Jews, but they differ in performance from the Sefaradi, Roman and also from the Karaite tunes. The Krymchak tunes are closer to the Indian, Arabian and Persian melodies.

Notes

1. The Jewish national question in the Soviet Union

1 Marx's work 'On the Jewish Question', printed in 1844, 'The Holy Family', written jointly with Engels in 1845, and a great number of their other writings are interspersed with extreme anti-Jewish remarks. As E. Silberner rightly points out, Marx was determined to avoid the term 'the Jewish people', because for him the Jew did not belong to a real people, but to an imaginary one. See E. Silberner, *Ha-sozialism ha-maaravi u-sheelat ha-yehudim* (Western Socialism and the Jewish Question), Jerusalem, Mosad Bialik, 1955, p. 146.

2 Lenin, *Collected Works*, vol. 7, p. 63; vol. 8, p. 496.

3 *Ibid.*, vol. 7, pp. 99–100.

4 *Ibid.*

5 *Ibid.*, vol. 7, p. 102.

6 *Ibid.*, vol. 23, p. 313.

7 Stalin, *Works*, Moscow, Foreign Languages Publishing House, 1953, vol. 2, pp. 345–6.

8 For example, constitutions, declarations of independence, laws, decrees and resolutions of the Communist Party. All of them solemnly and explicitly decreed that 'equal rights for all citizens regardless of their racial and national origins' were to be guaranteed; that 'the unimpeded development of the national minorities and the ethnic groups inhabiting Russian territory' was to be allowed; that every citizen had the right to use his mother tongue in his contacts with government institutions and public organisations. See *Istoriya sovetskoi konstitutsii, Sbornik dokumentov, 1917–1957* (A History of the Soviet Constitution. A Collection of Documents, 1917–1957), Moscow, Akademiya nauk, 1957, pp. 20, 111, 117.

9 See Y. Kantor, *Natsionalnoe stroitelstvo sredi evreev SSSR* (National Construction Among the Jews of the USSR), Moscow, Vlast Sovetov, 1934; S. Schwarz, *The Jews in the Soviet Union*; B. Pinkus, 'Yiddish-Language Courts and the Nationalities Policy in the Soviet Union', *Soviet Jewish Affairs*, 1971, no. 2, pp. 40–60.

10 A. Chemerisky, one of the heads of the *Evsektsiya*, wrote in 1926, 'not only from a political point of view but also from a practical standpoint it is possible to create Jewish autonomy in our country, but is it desirable? Yes, *it is desirable* because Jewish territorial autonomy in the Soviet Union, which is possible from a political and practical point of view, is desirable and necessary and therefore we can see it as a real prospect, as a possible, practical goal of our work, as a goal which we shall aspire to realise.' See *Di alfarband-komunistishe partey un di yidishe masn* (The All-Union Communist Party and the Jewish Masses), Moscow, Shul un bukh, 1926, p. 72.

    In the same year the economist, Yury Larin, declared: 'Our line is to give a national republic to every nation living in our State.' See *Ershter alfarbandisher tsuzamenfor fun 'Gezerd'* (First All-Union Convention of Gezerd), Moscow, Gezerd, 1927, p. 94. And in 1931, Dimanshtein, one of the heads of the *Evsektsiya*, once again claimed that only on acquiring territorial autonomy would the Jews become a nation. See S. Dimanshtein, 'Evreiskaya Avtonomnaya Respublika v Birobidzhane', *Tribuna*, 1931, no. 32–3, p. 4

11 On the reasons for this failure, and for further developments in the Birobidzhan affair, see Chapter 10.

12 Stalin, *Works*, vol. 2, p. 307.

13 I. P. Tsameryan, 'Aktualnye voprosy marksistsko-leninskoi teorii natsii' (Current Problems of Marxist–Leninist Nationality Theory), *Voprosy istorii*, 1967, no. 6, p. 109.

14 V. Kozlov, 'Sovremennye etnicheskie protsessy v SSSR' (Contemporary Ethnic Processes in the USSR), *Sovetskaya etnografiya*, 1969, no. 2, p. 72.

15 An important point in connection with national rights, and particularly with regard to the development of national culture, is that there is a significant difference – perhaps not fully and clearly expressed in the constitution and other constitutional documents – between the Union republic (the highest national unit) and units lower in the hierarchy such as the autonomous republic, autonomous region or national territory. When it comes to the practical possibilities of maintaining and nurturing a national culture, the autonomous region is at the bottom of the pyramid.

16 On all the problems connected with the subject of the passport in the Soviet Union, see R. Beermann, 'Russian and Soviet Passport Laws', *Bulletin on Soviet Jewish Affairs*, 1968, no. 2, pp. VI/1–11.

17 T. M. Volgin, 'The "Friendship of Peoples" . . . Pages from a Notebook', *Problems of Communism*, 1967, no. 5, pp. 105–7.

18 The felicitous term 'negative nationality' is used by Prof. Ettinger in his review of S. Schwarz's book in *Slavic Review*, 1968, no. 3, p. 496.

19 'Aus Schicksalsgemeinschaft erwachsende Charaktergemeinschaft', in O. Bauer, *Die Nationalitätenfrage und die Sozialdemokratie* (The National Question and Social Democracy), Vienna, Verlag der Volksbuchhandlung, 1924, p. 113.

20 E. Renan, *Discours et Conférences* (Speeches and Lectures), pp. 306–7, as quoted in Sidney Herbert, *Nationality and Its Problems*, London, Methuen, 1920, p. 40.

21 In Belorussia only 9.6% made such a declaration; in the Ukraine 22.6%; and in the RSFSR approximately 40%. See *Evrei v SSSR. Materialy i issledovaniya. Vypusk IV* (Jews in the USSR. Materials and Research. 4th Issue), Moscow, ORT, 1929, p. 62.

22 A. Yusupov, *Natsionalny sostav naseleniya SSSR* (National Composition of the Population of the USSR), Moscow, Gosstatizdat, 1964, p. 34.

23 See Zvi Gitelman, 'The Jews', *Problems of Communism*, 1967, no. 5, p. 99.

24 See V. Naulko, *Etnichny sklad naseleniya ukrainskoi SSR* (Ethnic Composition of the Population of the Ukrainian SSR), Kiev, Naukova dumka, 1965, p. 109.

25 M. Altshuler, 'Some Statistics of Mixed Marriages among Soviet Jews', *Bulletin on Soviet and East European Jewish Affairs*, 1970, no. 6, p. 31.

26 We refer here to the publications of Jewish *samizdat*, the organised study of Hebrew, the signing of petitions to Soviet leaders and foreign heads of state, sit-in demonstrations, hunger strikes, etc. True, there were similar manifestations before the Six-Day War, too, but these were sporadic and exceptional in contrast to the years 1969–71, when these phenomena became numerous and widespread.

27 This group includes all those who concealed their Jewishness in the censuses, usually the children of mixed marriages who have forgone, at least for the time being, any kind of allegiance to the Jewish nation, its past, its political and cultural present, and its future.

28 Ilya Erenburg was of course the most outstanding representative of assimilated Soviet Jewry, particularly if one considers the profound and varied expression which he gave it; but there is no lack of other examples. It is enough to name the following: Vasily Grossman (see Doc. 11), Pavel Antokolsky, Margarita Aliger, Yakov Khelemsky, Lev Ozerov, Leonid Pervomaisky, Mikhail Svetlov, Eduard Bagritsky, and many others among Russia's leading writers after the October Revolution. On the assimilated group, see also Doc. 10. On Ilya Erenburg's life and works, see Chapter 11, n. 151.

29 Ilya Erenburg's attitude to the phenomenon of anti-Semitism and its close association with his national consciousness were clearly expressed on 24 August 1941, in his speech at the inaugural session of the Jewish anti-Fascist Committee, where he stated: 'I am a Russian and a Russian writer, but Hitler has reminded me of something additional. My mother's name was Hannah. I am a Jew. I say this with pride!' *Pravda*, 25 August 1941. Twenty years later, on his seventieth birthday (21 January 1961), Erenburg declared on Radio Moscow: 'I am a Russian writer. And as long as there exists in the world even one anti-Semite I shall proudly reply to the question as to my nationality: a Jew.'

30 However, it is important to point out that Yiddish literature attained its proudest, most profound and national expression during the war, for example, in the following excerpt from I. Fefer's poem 'I Am a Jew':

Rabbi Akivah's sagacity,
And wise Isaiah's word,
Kept alive my love in me,
Till my hatred stirred,
And I felt the blood of the Maccabees,
I cried from all the gallow-trees,
Though the tyrants flay and slay me,
'I am a Jew'.

The Russian Jews in the War, p. 9. See also Chapter 7.

31 See Chapters 5 and 7.

32 The fact that leading Yiddish writers and poets such as Yosef Kerler, Zyama Telesin, Rahel Baumvol, Hirsh Oserovich and Meir Kharats have arrived in Israel in recent years proves, if any further evidence is needed, that Yiddish culture has no future in the Soviet Union.

33 See Wiesel, *The Jews of Silence*, pp. 61–7.

34 The results of the January 1939 census were published only in part. Figures from the 1926 and 1939 censuses were published in Lorimer, *The Population of the Soviet Union*. For figures on the Jewish national minority, see Zinger, *Dos banayte folk*. For figures from the population censuses for the years 1939–70, see Tables 1–2.

35 Y. Larin, *Evrei i antisemitizm v SSSR* (Jews and Anti-Semitism in the USSR), Moscow, Gosizdat, 1929, p. 304, as quoted in M. Altshuler, 'Kavim li-demuto ha-demografit shel ha-kibuz ha-yehudi bi-vrit ha-moazot' (On the Demographic Structure of Soviet Jewry), *Gesher*, 1966, no. 2–3, p. 13.

36 J. Lestchinsky, 'Yidn in sovetnfarband' (Jews in the Soviet Union), *Yidisher kemfer*, 1946, no. 669, p. 95, as quoted in Altshuler, 'Kavim li-demuto ha-demografit . . .', p. 13.

37 J. Lestchinsky, *Tfuzot yisrael le-ahar ha-milhamah* (The Jewish Diaspora after the War), Tel Aviv, Be-terem, 1948, p. 134.

38 Y. Tenenbaum, *Race and Reich: The Story of an Epoch*, New York, Twayne Publishers, 1956, p. 339.

39 Y. Kantor, 'Yidn af dem grestn un vikhtikstn front', *Folks-shtime*, 18 April 1963.

40 The Soviet Union did not publish the number of its losses after the war. In 1965, the Soviet demographer, D. Valentei, wrote that they numbered twenty million. See D. Valentei, 'Naselenie i voina', *Nedelya*, 1965, no. 19, p. 17.

41 For an analysis of the results of the 1959 census, see: Altshuler, 'Kavim li-demuto ha-demografit ...'; M. Abramovich, 'Ha-yehudim ba-mifkad ha-sovieti, 1959' (The Jews in the Soviet Census, 1959), *Molad*, 1960, no. 144–5, pp. 320–9; J. Rothenberg. 'How Many Jews Are In the Soviet Union', *Jewish Social Studies*, 1967, no. 4, pp. 234–40; A. Nove & J. Newth, 'The Jewish Population: Demographic Trends and Occupational Patterns', in Kochan (ed.), *The Jews in Soviet Russia Since 1917*, pp. 125–58.

42 The reason for estimating that more Jews concealed their Jewishness in the 1959 census than in the 1926 and 1939 censuses is that a number of Jews, having already concealed their origins during the war in order to escape extermination, did not resume their identity after the war. Stalin's anti-Semitic policy, and the anti-Jewish discrimination which continued in various spheres during the Khrushchev era, undoubtedly influenced these people to continue to conceal their Jewish nationality.

43 *Naselenie zemnogo shara* (Population of the Globe), Moscow, Nauka, 1965, p. 33.

44 The main figures from this census are adduced in Tables 1–2. For an analysis of the census, see Altshuler, 'Ha-yehudim be-mifkad ha-ukhlusin ha-sovyeti' (The Jews in the Soviet Census), *Behinot*, 1972, no. 2–3, pp. 9–23; I. Milman, 'Major Centres of Jewish Population in the USSR and a Note on the 1970 Census', *Soviet Jewish Affairs*, 1971, no. 1, pp. 13–18.

45 Perhaps even more if we take into account that the Jewish national awakening might have led more persons who were previously registered as Russians, Belorussians and Ukrainians to declare themselves to be Jewish.

46 For details, see Altshuler, 'Kavim li-demuto ha-demografit ...'.

47 According to Ivor Milman, the urban Jewish population amounted to 96% of all the Jews in the Soviet Union who declared themselves to be Jewish. See Milman, 'Major Centres of Jewish Population', p. 17.

48 For 1970 figures, see Y. Kapeliush, 'Yidn in sovetnfarband' (Jews in the Soviet Union), *Sovetish heymland*, 1974, no. 9, p. 175. Other large Jewish concentrations were: Kishinev, 49,900 (14%); Minsk, 47,100 (5.13%); Riga, 30,600 (4.18%); Baku, 29,700 (2.35%); Tbilisi, 19,600 (2.2%); and Vilnius, 16,500 (4.43%).

49 For further details, see Nove & Newth, 'The Jewish Population', p. 155.

50 The figures which John Armstrong adduced for the early 1950s, estimating the Jews at 10% of the total number of Soviet students, seem to be incorrect and more suited to the late 1930s. In any case, we have not traced a Soviet source for these figures. See J. Armstrong, *The Politics of Totalitarianism*, New York, Random House, 1961, p. 242. Armstrong quotes as his source Choseed, who was in turn relying on the American journalist, Harry Schwarz. See B. Choseed, 'Jews in Soviet Literature', in Simmons (ed.), *Through the Glass of Soviet Literature*, p. 111.

51 There was also a further drop in the overall numbers as well as in the percentage of Jewish students for the academic year 1970/1. See Table 3.

52 See, for example, Rabinovich, *Jews in the Soviet Union*, pp. 56–7.

53 See Zinger, *Dos banayte folk*, p. 106. However, according to S. Schwarz, Zinger's figures belong to 1937 and not 1939. See Schwarz, *The Jews in the Soviet Union*, p. 300.

54 *Soviet Weekly*, 4 June 1966, as quoted in Nove & Newth, 'The Jewish Population', p. 150. Similar details had already appeared in 1962: 'Fifteen percent of the Soviet doctors, nearly ten percent of the writers and journalists and over ten percent of the lawyers are Jews' ('Jews – Equal Nationality', *Moscow News*, 24 November 1962).

55 See Chapter 6.

56 This sentence, which in effect represents Stalin's definition of a nation (see Stalin, *Works*, vol. 2, p. 307), is omitted from the definition of 'Jews' in the 1972 edition of the *Large Soviet Encyclopaedia*.

57 We were unable to discover a Russian original of this article. It is reasonable to assume that the article was never published in the Soviet Union, but written with the specific purpose of being published abroad. Its importance lies, first and foremost, in its having been written by a leading Soviet philosopher who has also occupied various Party and government posts. It is also of interest that Kammari tries to analyse the Jewish question in the Soviet Union not only on the basis of rigid, official Marxist–Leninist theory, but also from a 'personal point of view', as a Soviet citizen of Finnish origin who actually encounters some of the same problems as those facing Soviet Jews.

58 The Karaites settled in Russia in the twelfth and thirteenth centuries. They were concentrated for the most part in the Crimea, Lithuania and the Ukraine. According to the census of 1897, there were 14,000 Karaites living in Russia; according to the 1926 census, their number had declined to 9,000. The reason behind this decline is the establishment of the independent Lithuanian State after World War I which had a large concentration of Karaites. According to the census of 1959, there were only 5,727 Karaites living in the Soviet Union, despite the fact that Lithuania had since been re-annexed. The two main factors contributing to this decline, apart from the low natural growth rate, are: (1) the extermination of a portion of the Karaite population during World War II, despite attempts on the part of the Karaites to prove that they were not part of the Jewish nation; and (2) acceleration of the process of assimilation.

It should be pointed out that Soviet publications vary greatly in their descriptions of the connection between the Karaites and Judaism. Under the entry 'Karaites' in the 1936 *Small Soviet Encyclopaedia*, the Jewish origins of the Karaites were specifically discussed; but at the end of the 1940s, the influence of Muslim as well as Jewish culture on the Karaites was indicated. In the *Large Soviet Encyclopaedia* of 1953, the unity of Karaite with Tatar culture in the past and with Russian culture today was specifically mentioned, whilst the connection between the Karaites and Judaism was not recalled at all.

59 Maskhud Sadykovich Dzhunusov (1919–), an important Soviet specialist on the subject of the national question. In 1951, he was appointed head of the philosophy department of the University of Frunze. Dzhunusov is a corresponding member of the Academy of Sciences.

60 See Doc. 3.

61 The anonymous Soviet Jew was the late Barukh Mordekhai Vaisman, an active member of the *Evsektsia*, who worked at the Kiev Institute of Jewish Culture; he died in 1963. Vaisman's manuscript, *To My Brothers in the State of Israel*, a kind of diary in letter form, reached Israel at the end of 1955. From the manuscript it emerges that the work was begun in early November 1952. A selection of the letters, edited by Dr B. Eliav, was first published in 1957 by 'Kiryat Sefer' in Jerusalem. It was printed in a limited edition of 500 copies and only distributed privately. Only ten years later, after the author's death, did his name become known publicly. An enlarged edition, including an autobiographical sketch which reached Israel later, was published in 1973 under the title *Yoman maḥteret ivri mi-vrit ha-moaẓot* (A Hebrew Diary from the Underground in the Soviet Union), Ramat-Gan, Massadah.

62 On David Hofshteyn, see Docs. 99–100.

63 Vladimir Aleksandrovich Belitser (1906–), biochemist, has worked at the Ukrainian Academy of Sciences, of which he is also a member, since 1944.

64 Eliyahu Spivak (1890–1952), philologist and Yiddish literary scholar, was born into a religious Jewish family in the Ukraine. He was a teacher in Jewish schools. At the beginning of the 1920s, he worked at the Kiev Yiddish Technical High School. He held important posts in Jewish cultural life in the Soviet Union and wrote a number of works on Yiddish philological and literary subjects. From 1937 he was director of the Jewish Institute attached to the Ukrainian Academy of Sciences. He

was also a member of the Jewish Anti-Fascist Committee. He was arrested at the beginning of 1949 together with other Jewish writers and cultural workers, and was sentenced to death in July 1952. He was executed on 12 August 1952.

65 This paragraph was omitted from the 1973 edition of Vaisman's letters.

66 We publish here the translation of Erenburg's article which appeared in *Jewish Life*, June 1949, pp. 25–7.

67 Julian Tuwim (1894–1953), Polish poet and translator, was born in Lodz into a Jewish family. His first poems were published in 1913. In the 1920s, he ran literary clubs in Warsaw. During World War II he lived in Romania, France, Portugal and the USA. He returned to Poland in 1946. He expressed his view on the Jewish question, which closely resembled that of Erenburg, during the war. Jewish subjects also find expression in some of the poems. Erenburg returns to Tuwim's article again and quotes extensively from it in his memoirs. See *Novy mir*, 1961, no. 9, pp. 102–3; I. Erenburg, *Memoirs 1921–1941*, New York, 1963, pp. 32–4.

68 See Doc. 7.

69 On Grossman, see n. 75.

70 This paragraph appeared in the first edition of Erenburg's memoirs, published in *Novy mir*, but was deleted from the edition included in the author's *Collected Works*.

71 Maimonides (Rabbi Moshe ben Maimon) (1135–1204), rabbinic authority, codifier, philosopher and court physician.

72 Yehudah Ha-levi (before 1075–1141), Hebrew poet and philosopher.

73 Aron Vergelis (1918–), since 1961 editor of the journal *Sovetish heymland* and a quasi-official Soviet spokesman on Soviet Jewish affairs. Vergelis was born in Lyubar in the Ukraine. He began publishing his verse in 1935. In 1940, he graduated from the literature faculty of the Lenin Pedagogic Institute in Moscow. Vergelis was resident for a while in Birobidzhan. He fought in the ranks of the Red Army during World War II.

74 See Doc. 26.

75 Vasily Semenovich Grossman (1905–64), Soviet writer, was born in Berdichev into a Jewish engineer's family. His mother was employed as a teacher. He graduated from the physics and mathematics faculty of Moscow University in 1929. One of his early works, *V gorode Berdichev* (In the Town of Berdichev, 1934), describes the life of the Jews in this town during the stormy period of the Civil War. Jewish subjects occupy an important place in other works of Grossman, e.g. *Stepan Kolchugin* (1937–40); *Stary uchitel* (The Old Teacher, 1942); *Narod bessmerten* (The People are Immortal, 1942); and *Vse techet* (Forever Flowing, which was published posthumously in the West, see Doc. 216). Grossman was an active member of the Jewish Anti-Fascist Committee and, together with Ilya Erenburg, edited 'The Black Book'. In December 1943, after the liberation of the eastern provinces of the Ukraine, Grossman described the tragedy of Ukrainian Jewry in *Eynikeyt*, in his essay 'The Ukraine Without Jews'. The article, it seems, was to be the first of a series; however, no further articles were published, because this one contained severe criticism not only of the Nazis but also of the local population.

This extract from Grossman's travelogue, 'Good Luck to You', is taken from the slightly abridged version which appeared in *Soviet Literature*, 1969, no. 6. The full Russian text was first published in the collection *Dobro vam!* (Good Luck to You), Moscow, Sovetsky pisatel, 1967, which also included some of Grossman's early works and previously unpublished material. *Dobro vam!* was one of his last works.

2. Official Soviet statements on the Jewish question

1 Stalin's remarks were made during the course of a speech delivered to the Moscow Soviet on 8 November 1941. See Stalin, *Sochineniya* (Works), vol. 2 (15), p. 22.

2 *Morgn frayheyt*, 30 September 1955, as quoted in Schwarz, *Evrei v Sovetskom Soyuze*, pp. 234–5.
3 See Khrushchev's secret speech in *The Anti-Stalin Campaign and International Communism*, New York, Columbia University Press, 1956.
4 Dr Henry Shoshkes, in an interview with Kaganovich, asked the then Deputy Premier of the Soviet Union what he thought about the plans to revive Yiddish literature. 'Kaganovich said that he is convinced that the Jews of the Soviet Union want to become partners in the great Russian culture. He explained that there is generally no need for a separate Jewish culture ... He agreed that if there is a demand among Jews for Jewish culture, this demand should be fulfilled. However, he did not believe that there is such a demand even from a minority of the Jews.'
   On the liquidation of the leading Yiddish writers and the 'Doctors' Plot', 'Kaganovich blamed this on a bad, short period in the history of Russian Communism. In general, however, he said, he cannot imagine anti-Semitism under a Communist order.' See *Tog-morgn zhurnal*, 20 August 1956.
5 See 'Soviet–Australian Letters on the Jews of the USSR', *Jewish Life*, September 1957, pp. 24–6.
6 See his talks with Salsberg, one of the leaders of the Canadian Progressive Party, whose first visit to the Soviet Union in the post-Stalin period took place in August 1955 (Doc. 96); see also his meeting with the American clergyman, Dr Jerome Davis, *The Times*, 8 September 1959. There was also a meeting with businessmen, jurists and teachers who visited the Soviet Union in summer 1957; see S. Margoshes, 'Khrushchev's New Interview', *Der Tog*, 13 June 1958.
7 See *Pravda*, 19 November 1957.
8 See *Izvestiya*, 27 March 1958, and the translation of the passage in n. 50 below.
9 See the *Herald Tribune*, 22 April 1958; *Le Monde*, 23 April 1958.
10 See Tatu, *Le Pouvoir en URSS de Krouchtchev à la direction collective*, p. 23.
11 See *Le Monde*, 16 September 1959.
12 See *Pravda*, 15 January 1960.
13 See for example, *Le Monde*, 19 February 1959.
14 See *Izvestiya*, 21 February 1959; see also Radio Moscow broadcasts in Arabic on 19 and 26 February 1959, as quoted by Y. Ro'i, 'Emdat brit ha-moaẓot le-gabei ha-aliyah ke-gorem bi-mdiniutah klapei ha-sikhsukh ha-yisraeli-aravi (1954–1967)', *Beḥinot*, 1974, no. 5, pp. 38–9.
15 On the economic trials, see Chapter 5.
16 See also the discussion of Khrushchev's remarks in Chapter 3.
17 For a detailed discussion of this point, see Chapter 6.
18 This statement of the Soviet Foreign Minister, Andrei Vyshinsky, came in reply to the Israeli representative's demand for a debate on the anti-Jewish policy of the Soviet Union, which reached its peak in January 1953 when the discovery of the 'Doctors' Plot' was published. On the 'Doctors' Plot', see Chapter 5.
   Andrei Yanuarevich Vyshinsky (1883–1954) first emerged into prominence as procurator at the important economic trials which were held against the 'saboteur' engineers from 1928 to 1930. However, he reached the summit of his career in the mid-1930s when, as Procurator General of the USSR, he was made responsible for the conduct of the great show trials against the Trotskyites and the Bukharinites (which took place in 1936–8). Vyshinsky's diplomatic career began in 1940 with his appointment as Deputy Foreign Minister. From 4 March 1949, until the day of his death, Vyshinsky was Foreign Minister of the Soviet Union. According to reports the authenticity of which is difficult to prove, Vyshinsky expressed his negative attitude towards the Jews with anti-Semitic venom.
19 There is no doubt that this is one of the most important documents with regard to top-level official Soviet statements on Soviet Jewry, and, as far as we know, the

Soviets have not denied the accuracy of the protocol. The topics discussed by the Soviet leaders and the French delegation at the second session included religion, anti-Semitism, freedom of thought and opinion, Israel and the Middle East, and the Muslims in the USSR.

20 An article entitled 'On Errors in Conducting Scientific-Atheist Propaganda Among the Public', containing the text of the Central Committee's decree, appeared in *Pravda* on 11 November 1954. The article complained of insulting attacks on the clergy and believers and of administrative interference by local organisations and individuals in the activity of religious associations and groups. This, the article claimed, was a violation of the Soviet approach to the struggle against religion. Consequently the Central Committee decreed:

That Province and Territory Party committees, Party central committees of the Union republics and all Party organisations be required resolutely to eliminate errors in atheist propaganda and in no event to permit future offence to the feelings of believers or clergymen or administrative interference in the activity of the church. It must be borne in mind that actions insulting the church, clergy and citizens who are believers are incompatible with the policy of the Party and state in the conduct of scientific-atheist propaganda and are contrary to the USSR constitution, which grants freedom of conscience to Soviet citizens.

N. Khrushchev, Secretary of the Central Committee of the Communist Party of the Soviet Union.

10 November 1954

21 There is, of course, no foundation to these various claims with regard to the Jewish religion. See Chapter 8.

22 On the preparations for the Doctors' Trial, see Chapter 5.

23 Lavrenty Pavlovich Beria (1899–1953), Party and government official. Until 1938, he held senior Party and government posts in Georgia and Transcaucasia. In 1938, he replaced Ezhov as the USSR Commissar of Internal Affairs. In July 1953, he was relieved of his posts, expelled from the CC CPSU and tried for espionage. He was executed in December 1953. Beria's attitude to the Jewish question has still not been fully clarified. However, there can be no doubt that during the war and after, he exercised considerable influence in this sphere. See also Chapter 3.

24 On General Kreizer, see Chapter 9, n. 38 and Doc. 139.

25 On Raizer, see Docs. 136, 140.

26 On Vannikov, see Doc. 141.

27 We have not been able to clarify the Lifshits that Khrushchev had in mind. It seems, however, that the reference here is to a deputy minister or senior civil servant in the Soviet apparatus, and not to a minister.

28 In 1955, at his meeting with J. Salsberg (see Doc. 96), Khrushchev, quoting identical arguments in his denial of official anti-Semitism in the USSR, specified that numerous Jews held key positions in the Soviet administration; that his daughter-in-law was Jewish; that Jewish children would have more opportunities by attending Russian schools and that many Ukrainians preferred to send their children to Russian schools; that in Lvov, for example, the Russian theatre (manned almost exclusively by Jews) competed with the Ukrainian theatre.

29 A transcript of Khrushchev's and Bulganin's press conference, held in London on 27 April 1956, appeared in *Pravda* the following day. On the subject of the Middle East, Bulganin stated:

There was an exchange of opinions between ourselves and representatives of the English government on the situation in the Near and Middle East. We expressed our point of view on the main reason for the aggravation of the situation in this area, explaining it to be that, in the opinion of the Soviet government, the chief source of international conflicts and tension in the Near and Middle East, the cause of the deterioration of relations between the Arab states and Israel, and also other countries, is the creation of military blocs such as the Baghdad Pact.

On peace efforts, the Soviet leaders stated:

We also agreed that, with this aim in mind, effective measures must be taken in the nearest future in accordance with the national aspirations of the peoples concerned and the necessity of guaranteeing their independence, and in full accord with the principles of the UNO Charter.

30 The Baghdad Pact, signed in February 1955, created an alliance of four countries (Turkey, Iran, Iraq and Pakistan) under British leadership.

31 In the 27 April 1956 press conference in London, reported in *The Times* on the following day, the Soviet leaders answered questions on a variety of topics, including the Middle East and the Baghdad Pact.

32 On Kaganovich, see Doc. 138; see also Chapter 9, n. 37. Kaganovich's statement comes in reply to Philip, a member of the delegation, who defined socialist humanism as giving paramount importance to individual freedom. The French socialists, Jaurès and Sembat, had taken up the cause of Dreyfus for this reason, ignoring the latter's bourgeois origins. Philip rejects Khrushchev's justification of violence by the dictatorship of the proletariat as a reaction to the inhumanity of the bourgeoisie. In Philip's view, the working class must not borrow the methods of the bourgeoisie but should create its own socialist and humanist culture. Philip's statement came in reply to a long discourse given by Kaganovich on the dictatorship of the proletariat according to the orthodox Leninist view, which was not recorded by Lochak.

33 Alfred Dreyfus (1859–1935), the officer (a Jew) employed in the French general staff who was arrested in 1894 on charges, later proved false, of spying for Germany.

34 Menakhem-Mendl Beilis, a factory worker in Kiev, was arrested in 1911 (not in 1909 as Khrushchev says) on the charge of murdering the boy Andrei Yushchinsky for ritual purposes. The charge came from the extreme anti-Semitic circles centred around the 'Union of the Russian People'. When Beilis came to trial, in 1913, some of the most famous lawyers in Russia defended him, and he was acquitted for lack of evidence. Liberal and progressive circles in Russia, among them the writers Korolenko and Gorky, came out with a fierce attack on the anti-Semitic policy of the Tsar and his government which had resulted in the accusation against Beilis.

35 Mark Borisovich Mitin (1901–), philosopher and Party activist, was born in Zhitomir into a family of Jewish workers. He joined the Communist Party in 1919. In 1929, he graduated from the philosophy department of the Institute of Red Professors. Mitin held important posts at the Institute of Philosophy of the Academy of Sciences. He edited the journal *Pod znamenem marksizma* from 1930 to 1944, and was a member of the editorial board of the journal *Bolshevik* from 1944 to 1956. From 1956 to 1960, Mitin was Chairman of the Board of the Society for the Dissemination of Political and Scientific Knowledge. He has been a member of the Academy of Sciences since 1939. He was elected a member of the Central Committee from 1939 to 1961 and a delegate to the Supreme Soviet from 1950 to 1962.

36 In the informal conversation that followed the discussion, Kaganovich was heard to exclaim: 'I was a simple shoemaker. I rose up with my Party. And now I'm a statesman of international stature.'

37 Ekaterina Furtseva (1910–74) joined the Communist Party in 1930. In 1950, she was elected Second Secretary to the Moscow Soviet of the Party, and in 1954 she was made First Secretary. She was a member of the Supreme Soviet. From 1956 she became a candidate member and from 1957 to 1961 a full member of the Presidium. Furtseva held the post of Minister of Culture of the Soviet Union from 1960 till her death.

38 See Doc. 74.

39 Aleksandr Mikhailovich Arsenyev (1906–), pedagogue. Arsenyev joined the Communist Party in 1927. From 1949 to 1958, he was Deputy Minister of

Education of the RSFSR. In 1959, he was elected Chairman of the Organising Committee of the Society of Pedagogues.

40 Abraham Isaac Katsh (1908–), university professor, was born in Poland and moved to the USA in 1925. His father was rabbi of Petah Tikvah in Israel. Katsh has visited the Soviet Union frequently. On his first trip, in 1956, he visited the Deputy Minister of Education of the RSFSR, A. Arsenyev. When Katsh raised the question with Arsenyev of facilities for the study of Hebrew, Arsenyev's first reaction was to suggest that the Hebrew language and culture be fostered in Birobidzhan. It was only after Katsh pointed out that the vast distance from Moscow and Leningrad to Birobidzhan would mean that Jews wanting to study Hebrew would have to settle there that Arsenyev quoted the law on instruction in the national languages, saying that this applied to Hebrew as well as Yiddish. Katsh asked for this statement in writing and, on the following day, he received the letter reproduced here. See: A. Katsh, 'The Soviet Anomaly', *Jewish Spectator*, March 1972.

41 Leonid Fedorovich Ilyichev (1906–). Since 1938, Ilyichev has been at different times a member of the editorial board of the journal *Bolshevik* and editor-in-chief of the newspapers *Pravda* and *Izvestiya*. He has held various posts in the Party apparatus. In the years 1953 to 1958, he was Director of the Press Section of the Soviet Foreign Ministry, and from 1958, he was Director of the Department for Information and Propaganda of the Central Committee. Ilyichev was elected a member, and later Secretary, of the Central Committee at the 22nd Party Congress (1961).

42 See Doc. 74.

43 Petran then quotes Rabbi Shlifer of Moscow, who had made a similar statement in an earlier interview with the *National Guardian*, 25 June 1956: 'Together with Jewish leaders, Russian professional and cultural leaders were also arrested. Therefore, we didn't regard the arrest of Jewish leaders as having an anti-Semitic character.' Shlifer added: 'All the Jewish people are building the Soviet State. There is no Jewish question in any part of Soviet life. During Beria's regime there were isolated manifestations of anti-Semitism in different places. But even under Beria there was never any state anti-Semitic doctrine.'

44 A sentence has been omitted here due to the illegibility of the text. However, it seems almost certain that what Ilyichev said was that, although the cases were being reviewed and the good names of the victims were being rehabilitated, it was not Soviet policy to issue statements on past miscarriages of justice. See *Hearings Before the Committee on Internal Security, House of Representatives, Ninety-Third Congress, First Session, 20 February, 1973 (The Theory and Practice of Communism*, Part 2), Washington, US Government Printing Office, 1973, p. 1984.

45 The Polish Communist Party suffered more from Stalin's purge than did any other foreign Communist party. Polish Communists in the USSR had been arrested throughout the 1930s, but from 1937 to 1939 the Party was almost totally annihilated. Among those who were executed or who disappeared were Warski, Budzynski, Ring, Henrykowski, Walecki and Kostrzewa. All twelve members of the Central Committee then in Russia perished, along with several hundred others, including all the Party's representatives on the Executive Committee and the Control Commission of the Comintern. See Conquest, *The Great Terror*, pp. 433–5.

46 Bela Kun (1886–1939), leader of the Hungarian Communist Party, who headed the Revolutionary Government for a short time in 1919. Kun held various posts in the Comintern in the Soviet Union, Hungary and Germany. He was accused of Trotskyism and executed in 1939. Of Jewish birth, he never maintained any ties with Judaism.

47 Ilyichev is referring to Khrushchev's statements at the 20th Party Congress in 1956, on the victims of Stalin's purges.

48 Petran refers here to the article 'Khrushchev Talk on Jews Related' (*The New York Times*, 10 June 1956), in which Khrushchev admitted that the number of Jews in professional positions is restricted to the relative proportion of Jews in the Soviet Union, i.e. between 1% and 1.5%.

It seems that Khrushchev also met with Dr Jerome Davis, an American Christian sociologist, sometime in 1957. Davis quotes Khrushchev as saying that he and other members ot the Politburo had opposed and prevented Stalin's move to exile all the Jews to Siberia. See *The Times*, 8 September 1959.

49 Serge Groussard was one of the leading journalists of the French newspaper *Le Figaro*. There is no doubt as to the authenticity of the interview with Khrushchev, which was held on 19 March 1958. Hence the great importance of this interview, in which Khrushchev expressed in the most frank manner his views on the basic questions of Jewish existence in the Soviet Union and in the State of Israel.

50 The exchanges on Soviet Jewry and the State of Israel were omitted from S. Groussard's long interview with Khrushchev on questions of Soviet domestic and foreign policy, published in *Izvestiya*, 27 March 1958; only the following isolated lines touching upon the Jewish question were included:

National barriers disappear only in a socialist society. The national question is correctly solved only under socialism. In old, Tsarist Russia, for example, there were frequent pogroms of Jews, massacres of Armenians and Tatars and other bloody manifestations of national enmity inflamed by the capitalists. All this has disappeared under Soviet rule. Children, Soviet youth, learn about these loathsome events of the past only from stories of the older generation and from literature.

After the interview had been published in its entirety in the newspaper *Le Figaro*, no official denials appeared in the Soviet press; however, in radio broadcasts to foreign countries on 24 and 26 April and on 5 May, protests were voiced against the 'fabrications' of Serge Groussard. But it was not specifically denied that Khrushchev had touched on the Jewish question in the Soviet Union in their interview. See Schwarz, *Evrei v Sovetskom Soyuze*, pp. 270–1.

51 The Jewish delegation from France that arrived in Moscow at the beginning of March 1958 included M. Vilner, one of the editors of the pro-Communist Yiddish newspaper *Naye prese* which appeared in Paris; Dr Haim Sloves, for many years a legal adviser to the Soviet Embassy in France and a Jewish cultural worker; and Albert Yudin. All three were members of the French Communist Party. The delegation was invited by leading 'state political bodies' in the Soviet Union. Since the Minister of Culture was away on a visit to the Far East at the time, the delegation was received by the Deputy Minister, A. Danilov. The Director of the Ministry of Culture and representatives of the CC CPSU also participated in the talks. On their return to France, Dr Sloves presented a detailed report on the conditions of the Jews in the Soviet Union to the leader of the French Communist Party, M. Thorez.

Aleksandr Ivanovich Danilov (1916–), who received the delegation, is a historian and is active in the field of education. Vilner is mistaken in calling Danilov Minister of Culture.

52 On the Yiddish Theatre in Moscow, see Docs. 104–8, and the notes to these documents.

53 Zinovy Shulman (1908–77), Yiddish singer. Shulman, who graduated from the Railways Institute in Odessa, began his singing career (in Yiddish) in 1925. In 1935, he began appearing at the Stanislavsky Musical Theatre in Moscow and giving concerts all over the country. His repertoire included works by Kompaneets, Kogan and Shostakovich. Shulman was arrested in 1949. From 1956, he lived in

Moscow and once again gave programmes of Yiddish songs. Starting in 1963, he appeared with V. Shvartser's Moscow Yiddish Drama Ensemble.

54 Emil Gorovets (1926–), actor and singer, was born in Vinnitsa and studied at the Moscow State Yiddish Theatre School. He began appearing as a soloist of Yiddish songs in the second half of 1955. He emigrated to Israel in 1974.

55 On Shaul Lyubimov's performance of Yiddish songs in August 1955, one of the first appearances after an interval of a number of years, see Chapter 7. Lyubimov suffered a stroke in the second half of the 1950s and ceased to appear. He died in 1970 in Moscow.

56 Nehama Lifshits (1927–), born in Vilnius, was one of the most popular Yiddish singers in the Soviet Union in the 1950s and 1960s. In 1945, she joined the Communist Party. She graduated from the Vilnius Conservatory in 1951. Until she emigrated to Israel in 1969, she appeared in numerous concerts in Yiddish throughout the Soviet Union. See Doc. 114.

57 Anna Guzik (1909–), Yiddish actress, was born into a family of actors. Her father, Yaakov Guzik, was the founder of the Yiddish Travelling Folk Ensemble of Musical Comedy. Anna Guzik began her professional stage activity in 1924 in her father's troupe. She acted in the comedies and operettas of Goldfaden, in stage versions of the works of Shalom Aleikhem, and so on. In the middle 1930s, she appeared in Yiddish operetta and in variety. In the 1950s and 1960s, she toured the cities of the Soviet Union with a variety ensemble whose programme included performances of Shalom Aleikhem's *Wandering Stars*. Anna Guzik emigrated to Israel in 1973.

58 Sidi Tal (pseudonym of Birkental; 1912–83), Yiddish actress, born into a baker's family in Romania. She began her stage career in 1928. Before 1940, she played in theatres in Chernovtsy, Jasi and Bucharest. After 1940, she played in the Yiddish Theatre in Kishinev. From 1946, Tal acted in the Yiddish ensemble of the Chernovtsy Philharmonic Society. From 1956, she appeared as a soloist in various Yiddish ensembles. She was made an Honoured Artist of the Ukrainian SSR in 1965. She emigrated to Israel.

59 Emmanuel Isaakovich Kaminka (1902–), actor and recitalist, was born in Kharkov and studied at Savelnikov's studio there. From 1930, he began giving solo readings. His repertoire included the works of Gogol, Tolstoy, Mark Twain and Shalom Aleikhem.

60 See Tables 11–18. The list of twenty-two writers given by Danilov included D. Bergelson, A. Vergelis, M. Gartsman, L. Kvitko and P. Markish.

61 The *Birobidzhaner shtern* was founded in 1930 as a Yiddish-language provincial daily of the Jewish Autonomous Region. From 1 October 1970, it appeared in a four-page instead of a two-page edition, and in 1971 it began appearing five times a week instead of three. Until 1970, it was printed in 12,000 copies. Its editor was then Nahum Korchminsky, who held that post for many years. Most of the newspaper is taken up with translations of news about the Soviet Union in general, with little space devoted to local news. Once a week, there is a literary section, and considerable space is given to anti-Zionist and anti-Israel articles which, moreover, comprise the only material of Jewish content to appear in the newspaper. See J. Lvavi (Babitsky), 'Ha-maḥoz ha-yehudi ha-otonomi (Birobidzhan) al saf shnot ha-shivim' (The Jewish Autonomous Region (Birobidzhan) on the Threshold of the Seventies), *Beḥinot*, 1974, no. 5, p. 63. See also Lvavi, *Ha-hityashvut ha-yehudit be-birobidzhan*, pp. 325–6.

62 Lina Solomonovna Shtern (1878–1968), biologist and physiologist, was an active member of the Jewish Anti-Fascist Committee during the war. She was arrested at the end of 1948, together with the heads of the Jewish Anti-Fascist Committee, and was sentenced in July 1952 to life imprisonment. She was released, it seems, in 1955, and was rehabilitated, but she never returned to her scientific work.

63 According to the Soviet census of 15 January 1970, the Jewish population of Birobidzhan totalled 11,452 persons or 6.6% of the total population, as opposed to 14,269 or 8.8% in the 1959 census. See Lvavi, 'Ha-maḥoz ha-yehudi', *Beḥinot*, 1974, no. 5, pp. 56–8.

64 Frol Romanovich Kozlov (1908–65), who visited the USA in 1959, was then at the summit of his political career, as a member of the Praesidium of the Communist Party and one of N. Khrushchev's first deputies. Hence the importance of his statements.

   While visiting the USA, Kozlov repeatedly denied charges that synagogues in the Soviet Union had been forcibly closed. At Sacramento he said 'Those charges are slander', claiming that Soviet Jews 'live a much better life' than the Jews in Israel. *En route* to San Francisco he called attention to Soviet 'ministers and deputy ministers who are of the Jewish nationality' and denied that the Jewish religion was being suppressed in the Soviet Union. See *The New York Times*, 4 July 1959 and 5 July 1959.

65 The Australian delegate was Mr White; he had raised the question of the treatment of the Jews in the Soviet Union. White spoke of attacks on the Jews in the press and on the radio, and of restrictions placed on religious observance. At the same time he added: 'If the USSR had difficulty in giving Jews full freedom to practise their religion, it had a moral obligation, under article 13, paragraph 2, of the Universal Declaration of Human Rights, to permit them to leave the country.'

66 This letter appeared in English in the Sunday English-language supplement of the Yiddish daily newspaper *Morgn frayheyt*, 6 May 1962. The signatories to the letter were the writer, Z. Vendrof; the jurist, Professor Boris Eidelman; the composer, Lev Pulver; the editor-in-chief of the journal *Narody Azii i Afriki*, Professor Iosif Braginsky; and Professor Ilya Strashun, a member of the USSR Academy of Medical Sciences.

67 On the economic trials in the Soviet Union, see Chapter 5.

68 See Doc. 26.

69 On the Babi Yar affair, see Chapters 3 and 12.

70 The situation was not as simple as Khrushchev described it. On the rights of Jewish merchants in the Russian Empire, see *Evreiskaya entsiklopediya* (Jewish Encyclopaedia), vol. 9, pp. 916–22.

71 Zinovy Timofeevich Serdyuk (1903–), senior Party activist in the Ukrainian Communist Party and close to Khrushchev. During the war, Serdyuk fought at Stalingrad, and there were rumours about his extreme anti-Semitism. It is quite likely that it was not coincidence that the reports on the traitor Kogan, who was supposed to have been von Paulus's interpreter, were an invention of General Serdyuk.

72 On the Kogan affair, see Chapter 3.

73 Evno Fishelevich Azef (1869–1918), one of the leaders of the Russian Socialist-Revolutionary Party and Tsarist secret police agent at the same time.

74 Yakov Abramovich Zhitomirsky, member of the Social-Democratic Party and the Bolshevik Party. Zhitomirsky, an agent of the Tsarist secret police, passed on information about the revolutionary movement which led to the arrest of many Bolsheviks.

75 Sergei Vasilyevich Zubatov (1866–1917), colonel in the Tsarist *okhrana*; inspired the idea of bringing the Jewish labour movement in the Pale of Settlement under police protection and control (1901–3).

76 In an article published in *The Observer*, 13 January 1963, Edward Crankshaw discussed the argument over anti-Semitism in the Soviet Union which developed between Khrushchev and a gathering of writers and artists held on 17 December 1962. The only speech that has been published from this meeting is that of Leonid

Ilyichev, chairman of the then recently formed Ideological Commission of the Central Committee. A version of Ilyichev's speech appeared in *Pravda*, 22 December 1962, but he is said to have spoken for ten hours. Crankshaw claimed that Ilyichev's attack on Shostakovich, for having used the text of Evtushenko's 'Babi Yar' in his symphony, occasioned a debate on anti-Semitism in which Khrushchev contended that it was better for Jews not to hold top government posts because then they would not arouse popular resentment. Khrushchev also maintained that 'the nationalities question had been solved' and only 'individual anti-Semitism' remained. Crankshaw went on to say that Khrushchev's remarks were not published because the latter had been warned by leaders of Soviet bloc countries that the arrest of Jews on currency charges and the closure of synagogues at that time was already creating a bad impression in the outside world.

77 On 18 July 1965, Kosygin addressed an audience in Riga at a celebration to mark twenty-five years of Latvia's incorporation into the Soviet Union. The opening speech was made by V. P. Ruben, Chairman of the Council of Ministers of the Latvian SSR; he was followed by A. Ya. Pelshe, Secretary of the Central Committee of the Communist Party of Latvia. Speaking next, Kosygin referred to Latvia's revolutionary past and the close cooperation between Latvian and Russian revolutionaries. He went on to mention Latvia's economic success and the country's progress in general, a result of its close cooperation with all Soviet peoples. The ideological core of Kosygin's speech is given in the extract reproduced here.

78 Kosygin paid an official visit to France from 1 to 9 December 1966. He held talks with President de Gaulle on 1, 2 and 8 December, and, on 3 December, met journalists of the Diplomatic Press Association. A joint Franco-Soviet statement was published on 10 December.

79 Kosygin arrived in New York to address the extraordinary session of the General Assembly of the UN which took place in the wake of the Arab–Israel war in June 1967. During his stay in the USA, he held talks with the representatives of many states, including President Johnson. Kosygin's statements at a press conference held on 25 June 1967 were published in *The New York Times* on 26 June 1967 and in *Izvestiya* on 27 June 1967. *Izvestiya*'s version of Kosygin's reply to N. Silberberg is slightly different: '*Answer*: There has never been anti-Semitism in the Soviet Union, nor is there now – neither an "old" nor a "new" wave. The Jews of the Soviet Union enjoy the same rights as other citizens. They occupy responsible posts in the government. For example, one of the Deputies of the Chairman of the Council of Ministers of the USSR is a Jew. The author of this question has invented "the problem of anti-Semitism" in the Soviet Union.'

Kosygin also answered questions on the Middle East, NATO and the Warsaw Pact.

3. Anti-Semitism in the Soviet Union

1 In his article on anti-Semitism in the Soviet Union, Weinryb adduces thirty different definitions of anti-Semitism and no doubt this list can easily be extended. See B. Weinryb, 'Anti-Semitism in Soviet Russia', in Kochan (ed.), *The Jews in Soviet Russia Since 1917*, pp. 288–91.

2 See, for example, Lenin's numerous diatribes against anti-Semitism and the pogroms: V. I. Lenin, *Sobranie sochinenii* (Collected Works), 5th edition, vol. 9, p. 333; vol. 10, p. 83, 266–9, 373; vol. 12, pp. 38, 76–7; vol. 13, pp. 198–203, 209, 223, 280; vol. 14, pp. 3–5, 38; vol. 16, p. 17; vol. 20, pp. 22, 326; vol. 21, pp. 17, 177–8, 278, 280; vol. 24, pp. 135, 183–5, 324; vol. 25, pp. 10, 14–18, 64–6, 85–6; vol. 30, p. 324; vol. 31, p. 12; vol. 34, p. 8.

3 _Izvestiya_, 27 July 1918.

4 Lenin, _Sobranie sochinenii_, vol. 38, pp. 242–3. Interestingly, this speech was one of the few that were not included on the record of Lenin's collected speeches issued to mark the ninetieth anniversary of his birth.

5 Thus, out of the total of 100 books and pamphlets on anti-Semitism published in Russian in the Soviet state since its establishment, 46 came out in the years 1917–21 alone. In fact, apart from two pamphlets written during World War II, 1933 can be taken as the last year for the publication of literature attacking anti-Semitism in the USSR. See Pinkus, Greenbaum & Altshuler (eds.), _Pirsumim rusiim al yehudim_, pp. 51–66.

6 See, for example, paragraph 83 of the RSFSR Criminal Code of 1922, _Ugolovny kodeks RSFRS_, Moscow, 1922, as quoted in Schwarz, _The Jews in the Soviet Union_, p. 275.

7 It is sufficient to recall such prominent members of the 'United Opposition' as Trotsky, Zinovyev, Kamenev, Sokolnikov, Radek and Ioffe.

8 Trotsky's evidence on this point strikes us as very significant. In his biography of Stalin he writes: 'He [Stalin] and his henchmen even stopped to fish in the muddied waters of anti-Semitism. I particularly recall a cartoon in the _Rabochaya gazeta_ entitled "Comrades Trotsky and Zinovyev". There were any numbers of such caricatures and doggerels of anti-Semitic character in the Party press'; L. Trotsky, _Stalin. The Revolutionary in Power_, London, Panther History, 1969, vol. 2, p. 224; and see also Trotsky's letter to Bukharin, Trotsky Archives, T 4106, as quoted in J. Nedava, _Trotsky and the Jews_, Philadelphia, JPS, 1974, p. 176.

9 In the years 1927–31, thirty-two books and pamphlets on Soviet anti-Semitism were published in Russian alone. See Pinkus, Greenbaum & Altshuler (eds.), _Pirsumim rusiim al yehudim_. After examining the contents of files containing a complete collection of newspaper extracts on Jewish topics from the years 1928–9, in the Centre for Documentation of Soviet and East European Jewry at the Hebrew University, we can state that in this period almost all the newspapers (central and local) printed articles, reports and items on manifestations of anti-Semitism and on the need to combat them.

10 _KPSS v rezolyutsiyakh_ (The CPSU in Resolutions), Moscow, Gospolitizdat, 1953, vol. 2, p. 614.

11 Stalin, _Sochineniya_ (Works), Moscow, Gosudarstvennoe izdatelstvo politicheskoi literatury, 1951, vol. 13, p. 28.

12 Stalin's words were cited in Molotov's speech on the new constitution. See following note.

13 The best example of such a condemnation can be seen in Molotov's speech at the 8th Congress of the Soviets on the new constitution, where he said, among other things: 'Whatever may be said by present-day cannibals in the ranks of the Fascist anti-Semites, our fraternal feeling towards the Jewish people springs from the fact that it gave birth to the creator of genius of the ideas of the Communist liberation of mankind, Karl Marx ...; that the Jewish people along with the most advanced nations has produced a great number of outstanding men of science, technology and art; that it provided many heroes in the revolutionary struggle against the oppressors of the working people ... All this determines our attitude to anti-Semitic bestiality wherever it may arise'; _Pravda_, 30 November 1936, as quoted in Schwarz, _The Jews in the Soviet Union_, p. 296.

14 'There had been a substantial vein of anti-Semitism underlying the purges of the 1930s. The joke: You're not a Trotskyite and you're not a Jew, so why were you arrested? had a good deal of validity.' Salisbury, _To Moscow and Beyond_, p. 68.

15 I. Deutscher, _The Prophet Outcast, Trotsky 1929–1940_, London, Oxford University Press, 1970, pp. 368–9.

16 In one of his celebrated table talks Hitler revealed that Stalin did not hide from Ribbentrop the fact that he was waiting only for the emergence of a sufficiently large indigenous intelligentsia to make short shrift of the Jews as a leadership stratum which he then still needed. Hitler's *Tischgespräche* (Table-Talks), Bonn, Athenaeum, 1951, p. 119.

17 Anti-Semitism found its most serious expression in the occupied territories (e.g. cases of collaboration with the Nazis in destroying the Jewish people). The anti-Semitism in the Red Army and the rear took on less extreme forms and found expression mainly in the charges that Jews do not like to work, live from black-marketeering and above all do not want to fight, preferring to seek refuge in the rear. This latter accusation was first propagated by the Nazis and readily accepted throughout the Soviet Union. The Soviet Jews found it particularly offensive, and it received forceful treatment in Russian and Yiddish literature. For example, Perets Markish, in the poem 'Milkhome' (War) which he began writing early in 1943, describes a soldiers' conversation, putting the following declaration in the mouth of one of them:

> War: but Jews you don't see them on any of the fronts!
> People say the Jews are hiding out somewhere,
> They say that Jews loaded with sacks crowd all the trains,
> They say the Jewish sacks are so stuffed they can't be budged,
> They say that everywhere the roads are jammed with Jews and Jews,
> And you – you have to fight and give your life for them.

As quoted in J. Kunitz, 'The Jewish Problem in the USSR', *Monthly Review*, 1953, no. 11, p. 403. And, in answer to the Russian poetess of Jewish origin, Margarita Aliger, an anonymous Jewish poet wrote:

> Only to be told: 'Where were the Jews?
> They fought their battles in Tashkent!'
> We are not loved because we are Jews,
> Because our faith is the source of many faiths.

As quoted in Kochan (ed.), *The Jews in Soviet Russia Since 1917*, p. 287.

18 Throughout the war only one pamphlet was published dealing with Nazi anti-Semitism, and even this appeared at the beginning of the war: V. V. Struve, *Fashistsky antisemitizm* (Fascist Anti-Semitism), Moscow–Leningrad, Akademiya nauk SSSR, 1941. Even the number of articles on the subject was minimal: see Schwarz, *The Jews in the Soviet Union*, pp. 168–87.

19 See his speech on 8 November 1941, at the Moscow Soviet: I. V. Stalin, *Sochineniya* (Works), Stanford, Hoover Institute of War, Revolution and Peace, 1967, vol. 2 (15), p. 22.

20 There is evidence of the anti-Jewish feelings of a number of senior functionaries at the head of the Soviet government, e.g. Shcherbakov, member of the Politburo, head of the Sovinformburo and of the Political Administration of the army; General Shtemenko, who held senior posts in the army; Ponomarenko, one of the heads of the Belorussian Republic and in the 1950s Soviet Ambassador to Poland; and Ignatyev, who was responsible for the security services at the time of the Doctors' Plot. See Salisbury, *Russia on the Way*, pp. 290–3; P. F. de Villemarest, *La Marche au pouvoir en URSS*, pp. 60–2; Schwarz, *The Jews in the Soviet Union*, pp. 196–7; Embree, *The Soviet Union Between the 19th and 20th Party Congresses 1952–1956*, pp. 14–17.

21 According to Stanislaw Kot, Stalin even repeated this insulting phrase twice – 'bad and miserable soldiers'. See S. Kot, *Listy z Rosji do Generala Sikorskiego* (Letters from Russia to General Sikorski), London, 1956, p. 204; Kot, *Rozmowy z Kremlem* (Conversations with the Kremlin), London, 1959, pp. 167–88 (English translation: *Conversations with the Kremlin and Dispatches from Russia*, Oxford University Press, 1963, p. 153). For General Anders's version, see W. Anders, *Bez ostatniego rozdzialu*.

Wspomnenia z lat 1939–1946 (Without a Final Chapter. Memoirs of the Years 1939–1946), 3rd edition, London, Gryf Publishers, 1959, p. 99.

22 See the evidence of Stettinius, the American Foreign Minister at the time, who wrote: 'Stalin observed that the Jewish problem was extremely difficult. The Soviet Union had tried to establish a national home for the Jews, but they had stayed only two or three years before returning to the cities. The Jews were natural traders, he added, but much had been accomplished by putting small groups of them in agricultural areas.' E. R. Stettinius Jr, *Roosevelt and the Russians: The Yalta Conference*, New York, Doubleday and Co., 1949, p. 278.

23 On the policy of Khrushchev (then head of the Ukrainian administration) on the Jewish question, see pp. 90–5 below.

24 See Docs. 32–4. Also important are the testimonies of V. Grossman and A. Kuznetsov; see V. Grossman, *Vse techet* (Forever Flowing), Frankfurt am Main, Posev, 1970; A. Anatoli (Kuznetsov), *Babi Yar*, New York, Pocket Books, 1971. To these can be added numerous accounts by new emigrants from the Soviet Union to the West.

25 R. Loewenstein, *Psychanalyse de l'antisémitisme* (Psychoanalysis of Anti-Semitism), Paris, PUF, 1952, p. 7.

26 See R. V. Daniels, *The Conscience of the Revolution*, Cambridge, Massachusetts, Harvard University Press, 1960, pp. 104–7; L. Schapiro, *The Origin of the Communist Autocracy*, London, Bell and Sons, 1956, pp. 245–52. See also M. Djilas's pronouncements, Doc. 31.

27 As well as the extracts in Docs. 33–34, Allilueva's two books (*Twenty Letters to a Friend* and *Only One Year*) provide further insight into Soviet anti-Semitism.

28 For example: Stalin's personal grudge against Molotov's wife, Polina Zhemchuzhina, because of her allegedly 'fatal influence' over his own wife which led to her suicide in 1932; or his bitter opposition to the marriage of his children to Jews. Allilueva, *Twenty Letters to a Friend*, pp. 109–11.

29 See, for example, Docs. 31 and 33; see also *Khrushchev Remembers*, pp. 259–69.

30 Stalin's exiling of different peoples during the war, even when victory over Germany was assured, is well known. Reports of a plan for the mass exile of the Jews began to reach the West after his death; see Embree, *The Soviet Union Between the 19th and 20th Party Congresses*, p. 285; Schechtman, *Star in Eclipse*, pp. 42–3; Goldberg, *The Jewish Problem in the Soviet Union*, pp. 148–9. Reports of Jews being exiled from various regions (mainly the Ukraine and Belorussia) had appeared in the West even earlier, but it seems that they were exaggerated: see *Jewish Chronicle*, 29 July 1949, 23 November 1951, 9 May 1952.

31 The claim made by Khrushchev (insofar as his memoirs are authentic) that Kaganovich's position was thoroughly anti-Semitic is unconvincing; it suggests instead an attempt to settle accounts with a political rival who had become his sworn enemy. See *Khrushchev Remembers*, p. 243.

32 If reports are accurate, it is clear that Molotov and Voroshilov, together with Kaganovich and Mikoyan, openly and vehemently opposed the plan to exile the Jews discussed by the Politburo at the end of February 1953; see Schechtman, *Star in Eclipse*, pp. 42–3; Goldberg, *The Jewish Problem in the Soviet Union*, pp. 148–9; *Jewish Chronicle*, 14 June 1957. Particularly interesting in this context are Voroshilov's memoirs, which shed light on his sympathetic attitude towards the Jews and on his strong desire to demonstrate that his Bolshevik education helped immunise him from this contagion; see K. E. Voroshilov, 'Rasskazy o zhizni', *Oktyabr*, 1967, no. 9, pp. 37, 46; no. 10, pp. 148–90.

33 Franz Borkenau was one of the first to emphasise Zhdanov's positive stand on the Jewish question, in contrast to Malenkov's; see F. Borkenau, 'Was Malenkov Behind the Anti-Semitic Plot?', *Commentary*, May 1953, pp. 438–46. Against this, Djilas claimed that the purge of Jews from Party and government apparatus was inspired by Zhdanov; see Doc. 31.

34 See n. 35 below; see also Conquest, *Power and Policy in the USSR*, pp. 79–80.

35 See M. Ebon, *Malenkov, Stalin's Successor*, New York, McGraw-Hill, 1953, pp. 10–12, 100.

36 See Doc. 165; see also Salisbury, *To Moscow and Beyond*, pp. 70–1. How far this assumption is true it is difficult to judge. However, there can be no doubt that various Jewish cultural establishments in Georgia (e.g. the Jewish Museum) remained open long after similar establishments in other republics had been liquidated. It is equally certain that the attitude towards the Jewish religion in Georgia was better than in the other republics. It is, however, likely that this was due more to the special situation prevailing in the Georgian Republic than to any assistance Beria may have rendered to Georgian Jewry.

37 *The Anti-Stalin Campaign and International Communism*, pp. 63–4; and Doc. 81.

38 Schechtman, *Star in Eclipse*, p. 81; *Jewish Chronicle*, 17 May 1957. This statement was authenticated by Jewish immigrants to Israel who had held important posts in the Polish Party and government. See also Anon., 'USSR and the Politics of Polish Anti-Semitism, 1956–1968', *Soviet Jewish Affairs*, 1971, no. 1, p. 20. For Khrushchev's apology to Zambrowski, see *Jewish Chronicle*, 10 January 1958.

39 Leneman, *La Tragédie des juifs en URSS*, p. 167.

40 *Pravda*, 19 November 1957.

41 Werth, *Russia: Hopes and Fears*, p. 200. On Khrushchev's anti-Semitism, see also E. Crankshaw, *Khrushchev: A Career*, New York, Avon Books, 1966, pp. 78, 160–2.

42 This whole discussion centres on Khrushchev's anti-Semitism, but, since their social and political background resembles that of Khrushchev himself, there can be no doubt that the majority of high- and low-echelon Party leaders took a similar approach.

43 In that interesting and valuable document, Nadezhda Mandelstam's autobiography, the author argues that she and her husband never concealed their Jewishness, never encountered anti-Semitism from the popular strata (workers and peasants) and that if anti-Semitism existed in the Soviet Union it stemmed from the authorities and the bureaucracy. Mrs Mandelstam's approach is, of course, that of an assimilated Jewess endeavouring to justify her 'philosophy of life'; further, it deals more with the 1930s than with the 1950s and 1960s. See N. Mandelstam, *Vospominaniya* (Memoirs), New York, Izdatelstvo imeni Chekhova, 1970, p. 362 (English translation: N. Mandelstam, *Hope Against Hope*, New York, Atheneum, 1970, p. 342).

A somewhat similar approach, though less insistent and less well known, is sometimes heard from new Soviet immigrants to the West. In their view, anti-Semitism does indeed exist in the Soviet Union, but they never encountered it personally. Without wishing to doubt the reliability of their testimony, this claim could be based on a rationalisation of the desire to show that the reasons for their emigration were positive (the longing for political liberty or Jewish national consciousness, as the case might be), and not negative (discrimination and hostility against them as Jews).

44 Professor L. Feuer suggested doing research of this nature during his meeting with the heads of the Philosophy Institute of the Academy of Sciences, but he was met by a blank refusal. See L. Feuer, 'Meeting the Philosophers', *Survey*, 1964, no. 41, pp. 21–2.

45 While the Harvard project of the years 1950–1, on the 'Soviet social system', did question 329 people (Soviet *emigrés* in the USA, Germany and Austria) on their attitude towards Jews, in our opinion this cross-section did not represent the Soviet population at that time and is certainly unsuitable for drawing conclusions about the situation during the Khrushchev era; it can, however, serve as a limited source of evidence. See W. Korey, 'The Origins and Development of Soviet Anti-Semitism: An Analysis', *Slavic Review*, 1972, no. 1, pp. 111–35.

46 One example of strained relations between Jewish and non-Jewish neighbours, and of the anti-Semitism exemplified in the deliberate mispronunciation of a Jew's name, can be seen in Valtseva's story; see Doc. 153. André Blumel, then chairman of the Soviet–French Friendship League, cited the case of a Russian woman who tormented her religious Jewish neighbour by throwing pork into the latter's cooking-pot; see *Undzer vort*, 24 October 1960.

47 See, for example, the anti-Semitic leaflet posted on the walls at Malakhovka (Doc. 51) and Vasily Grossman's story, *Dobro vam!* (Doc. 11).

48 See also Fejtö, *Les Juifs et l'antisémitisme dans les pays communistes*, pp. 170–4; Schechtman, *Star in Eclipse*, pp. 46–9.

49 Schwarz, *Evrei v Sovetskom Soyuze*, pp. 356–7.

50 *Ibid.*, p. 358.

51 Even the Jewish general, David Dragunsky, who was in Paris at the time, was enrolled for this purpose. In an interview with the journalist Skornik, Dragunsky stated that the publications on Malakhovka were anti-Soviet provocations. And the Soviet Embassy in Paris approved this statement in order to lend it more weight. See *Undzer vort*, 7 December 1959.

52 See the statement of André Blumel, who investigated the affair during his visit to the Soviet Union, *Undzer vort*, 2 October 1960. On the Malakhovka affair, see also Markish, *Le Long Retour*, p. 284.

53 For further details, see Schwarz, *Evrei v Sovetskom Soyuze*, pp. 352–3.

54 M. Gorsky, *Nesvoevremennye mysli: Zametki o revolyutsii i kulture* (Untimely Thoughts: Notes on Revolution and Culture), Petrograd, Kultura i Svoboda, 1917, p. 109.

55 *Ibid.*, p. 114.

56 The mass murder of the Jews of Kiev at Babi Yar in September 1941, and the reactions of Soviet Jewry (which also found expression in Soviet literature), are discussed in Chapters 11 and 12.

57 In this context we are concerned only with the liberal intelligentsia as a whole. However, it is important to point out that Jews played a very prominent role in this group's struggle against the revival of Stalinism and on behalf of freedom of expression. It is sufficient to mention names like Erenburg, Kaverin, Antokolsky, Aliger, Grossman, Romm, Slutsky, Daniel, Yakir, Litvinov.

58 *Literaturnaya gazeta*, 22 December 1959.

59 It is worth noting here that, despite this and many other promises, the plan was not carried out. On the chain of developments in the affair of the Babi Yar memorial, see Schechtman, *Star in Eclipse*, pp. 98–104; W. Korey, 'The Forgotten Martyrs of Babi Yar', in Rubin (ed.), *The Unredeemed: Anti-Semitism in the Soviet Union*, p. 134; P. Grose, 'The Kremlin and the Jews', in Salisbury (ed.), *The Soviet Union: The Fifty Years*, pp. 421–3; Schwarz, *Evrei v Sovetskom Soyuze*, pp. 359–60.

60 See Gribachev's speech at the Congress, *Pravda*, 28 October 1961.

61 The first performance of the symphony took place on 18 December 1962. However, the Soviet press gave it only a single-line mention. On 25 December, the journal *Sovetskaya kultura* carried a leading article which criticised Shostakovich's work without mentioning the composer himself. See B. Schwarz, 'Soviet Music Since Stalin', *Saturday Review*, 30 March 1963, and 'Soviet Music Since the Second World War', *Musical Quarterly*, January 1965, p. 274.

62 Evtushenko himself flatly denied that he was pressured by Khrushchev during the debate in December 1962. He claimed that he had received 20,000 letters, only thirty of which were written in an anti-Semitic spirit, and that after reading many of the letters he was convinced of the need to introduce the changes without thereby altering the content of the poem. See *Le Monde*, 12 and 14 February 1963. According to another version, it was Shostakovich who asked Evtushenko to make the changes; see Johnson & Labedz (eds.), *Khrushchev and the Arts*, p. 13. See also Doc. 43.

63 The attacks became more severe after the publication of Evtushenko's auto-biography in France. See *Pravda*, 29 March 1963; *Komsomolskaya pravda*, 30 March 1963; A. Solodanov in *Mezhdunarodnaya zhizn*, 1963, no. 6, pp. 73–9.

64 See *Ha-arez*, 21 December 1966.

65 The examination was made on the basis of materials in the almost-complete collection of articles from the Soviet press in *Evrei i evreisky narod*, 1960–7.

66 M. Rolnikaite, *Ya dolzhna rasskazat* (I Must Tell), Moscow, Politizdat, 1965.

67 Although the book was rigorously censored – as Kuznetsov revealed after his defection from the Soviet Union and the publication of the original version in the West – the fact that this documentary novel appeared in the journal *Yunost* was of great significance.

68 Milovan Djilas (1911–), Yugoslav political leader and writer, joined the Communist Party in 1932. Djilas served as a partisan in World War II and was a friend of Marshal Tito. He became Vice-President of Yugoslavia, but was expelled from the Yugoslav Communist Party in January 1954, after he appealed for 'democratis-ation'. In 1956, he was sentenced to a ten-year term for expressing the ideas contained in *The New Class* (New York, Frederick A. Praeger, 1957). Djilas was released in 1961, only to be imprisoned again in 1962 after the announcement of the American publication of his *Conversations with Stalin*. He was released again in 1966.

69 Moshe Pijade (1890–1957), Yugoslav Communist Party and government leader. Pijade was born in Belgrade into a Sephardi family. He joined the Communist Party in 1920. In 1923, he founded the Independent Labour Party, and he was arrested a number of times between 1925 and 1939. During the war, he was President of the Anti-Fascist Council for National Liberation. From 1948 to 1952, he was a member of the Politburo. Pijade was a Deputy President and Chairman of the Parliament (from 1954). He died in Paris while on an official mission. Pijade was not interested in Jewish affairs, but he was a fervent supporter of the State of Israel. The fierce attacks on him in the Soviet and Czechoslovak press, during and after the Slansky trial, were marked by clearly anti-Semitic overtones.

70 Aleksei Innokentyevich Antonov (1896–1962), Soviet general. Antonov was Chief-of-Staff from February 1945 till March 1946 and held other senior posts in the army. He was not Jewish himself, but there were rumours that his wife was a Jewess.

71 Matyas Rakosi (1892–1982), Hungarian Communist Party leader. He was First Secretary of the Central Committee of the Hungarian Workers' Party and Chair-man of the Council of Ministers until 1956. In 1962 he was expelled.

72 Cf. M. Djilas, *Conversations with Stalin*, New York, Harcourt, Brace and World, 1962, pp. 154, 170–1, where the author repeats some of the claims made in the *Borba* article.

73 Evtushenko's 'Autobiography', from which Docs. 32 and 39 are drawn, was published first in the French journal *L'Express* on 21 February 1963 and the three following issues. The editors announced that, in the event that denials should come from either the author or the Soviet authorities, they possessed the author's manuscripts proving that he had indeed written the work. The only editorial additions were the sub-headings. After he had been severely upbraided by Khrush-chev himself, Evtushenko announced that he had acted irresponsibly and made a serious mistake in publishing his 'Autobiography'. See *Le Monde*, 29 March 1963.

74 Lev Davidovich Trotsky (pseudonym of Bronshtein; 1897–1940), Bolshevik leader. Trotsky was born in Yanovka, in the Kherson Region, the son of a Jewish settler. Little interested in the Jewish question despite the fact that he was born into a Yiddish-speaking family, Trotsky was convinced that it would be solved by means of total integration under a socialist regime. From the time of the 2nd Congress of the Russian Social Democrat Workers' Party, he attacked the position of the Bund.

In 1904, in an article published in *Iskra*, he envisaged the swift disappearance of the Zionist movement. In 1914, he published an article on the situation of the Jews in Romania. In the 1930s, Trotsky warned against Stalin's use of anti-Semitism for achieving political ends. His opposition to Zionism in the 1930s was less extreme than in the preceding period. In an interview which he gave to a Jewish journalist on 24 January 1937, he even declared that he recognised the existence of the Jewish question and that the Jews needed to have a country of their own. He expressed a similar approach before his death in 1940. However, in his opinion, Zionism was incapable of solving the Jewish question by means of immigration to Palestine. The only real solution, according to Trotsky, was the destruction of the capitalist order.

75 On the 'Doctors' Plot', see Chapter 5.

76 Vladimir Vladimirovich Mayakovsky (1893–1930), Russian poet, was a leading representative of the experimental school of Futurist poets and editor-in-chief of the journal *LEF* from 1922 to 1928. Mayakovsky's influence on his contemporaries went far beyond Futurist circles to embrace all the leading creative artists of the time. In 1928, he published his poem 'Zhid', attacking anti-Semitism. In 1930, Mayakovsky committed suicide following a growing sense of isolation in his personal and professional life.

77 Boris Abramovich Slutsky (1919–), Russian poet of Jewish origin, was born in Slavyansk in the Ukraine. He graduated from the Gorky Institute of Literature in Moscow in 1941. With the outbreak of war, he was enlisted in the army. His first poems were published in 1941, and he joined the Communist Party in 1943. From the end of the 1940s until 1953, his works ceased to be published although he was not publicly attacked during the anti-cosmopolitan campaign. Among Slutsky's works are short verses and long narrative poems on Jewish subjects, especially on the Holocaust.

78 For how Khrushchev's memoirs reached the West and an assessment of their probable authenticity, see J. L. Schechter in *Khrushchev Remembers. The Last Testament*, pp. xi–xix

79 On S. Lozovsky, see Chapter 9, n. 39 and Doc. 142.

80 On S. Mikhoels, see Chapter 7, n. 150 and Docs. 104–6.

81 Jakub Berman (1901–); member of the Politburo of the Communist party in Poland 1944–56, responsible for security and secret police affairs.

82 Hilary Minc (1905–74), member of the Polish Communist Party from 1921 and the Politburo from 1944 to 1956.

83 Boleslaw Bierut (1892–1956) held the post of General Secretary of the Central Committee of the Polish Communist party from 1948 until his death.

84 Josef Cyrankiewicz (1911–). Prime Minister of the Polish government 1947–52.

85 Wladyslaw Gomulka (1905–82), replaced as Party leader in 1948; arrested in 1951; released 1954; First Secretary of the Polish United Workers' Party 1956–70.

86 Roman Zambrowski (1909–77), member of the Politburo of the Polish Communist party from 1945–63; removed from all political offices in 1967.

87 Grigory Konstantinovich Ordzhonikidze (1886–1937), leading Soviet Party and government leader. He fought in the Civil War, and later helped organise Soviet power in the Caucasus and Transcaucasia.

88 The twenty-six Bolshevik commissars who were operating in the Caucasus were executed on 20 September 1918 by the British and local authorities. It is known that among these commissars were also the Jews Y. Zevin, M. Basin, S. Bogdanov, A. Bogdanov, M. Koganov and I. Mitin.

89 The extracts from the Evtushenko–Khrushchev exchanges and Romm's speech were first published in *Commentary*. In his introduction to these two documents, Moshe Decter discussed their authenticity, since the documents were not published in the Soviet Union but were circulated in typescript form and smuggled out to the

West in a number of versions. Having examined the various versions, Decter vouches for the authenticity of the texts. Evtushenko's statements on anti-Semitism were probably made at the gathering of artists and Party leaders held on 17 December 1962, while Romm's speech was delivered at a meeting of film and theatrical workers held in the autumn of 1962. For the poem 'Babi Yar', see Doc. 39. For a slightly different version of Romm's speech, see *Jewish Frontier*, 1968, vol. 35, pp. 9–10.

90 At this point, Evtushenko read out the last lines of his poem 'Babi Yar':

> There is no Jewish blood in mine,
> But I am hated by every anti-Semite as a Jew,
> And for this reason,
> I am a true Russian.

91 The Black Hundreds were armed gangs, recruited mainly among urban and rural roughs and the lower middle classes, who initiated pogroms against Jews and members of the Russian radical intelligentsia. They were in fact an arm of the Union of the Russian People, a right-wing, fanatically anti-Semitic movement, founded in 1905 and enjoying the patronage of Tsar Nicholas II. Among its leaders were A. Dubrovin and V. M. Purishkevich; in 1907, Purishkevich broke away and founded the equally anti-Semitic Union of the Archangel Michael.

92 This cartoon appeared on the front cover of *Krokodil* on 20 March 1949. In Russian, the word *zhid* (dirty Jew) and the name 'Gide' are spelt and pronounced alike.

93 Sergei Iosifovich Yutkevich (1904–), professor and stage and film director.

94 Leonid Zakharovich Trauberg (1902–), playwright and film director. He was fiercely attacked during the anti-cosmopolitan campaign.

95 Sutyrki is apparently a mistake for V. Sutyrin (1902–), film director and critic. Sutyrin was one of the leaders of RAPP (Russian Association of Proletarian Writers). Although it seems that he is not Jewish, he was fiercely attacked during the anti-cosmopolitan campaign.

96 Nikolai Arkadyevich Kovarsky (1904–), script writer and film critic.

97 Mikhail Yuryevich Bleiman (1904–73), script writer and film critic.

98 Vsevolod Anisimovich Kochetov (1912–74), Russian novelist. Kochetov was editor-in-chief of *Oktyabr* from 1961. He was often singled out as the unofficial leader of the conservative camp in Soviet literary life. On Jewish themes in his works, see Chapter 11.

99 Romm refers here to the article by V. Lynkov and Yu. Panov ('Kto li gorizonty?', *Oktyabr*, 1962, no. 5, pp. 182–7), which criticises his film 'Nine Days of One Year'.

100 Lenin, *Sobranie sochinenii*, vol. 7, p. 245.

101 Igor Semenovich Kon (1928–), philosopher, graduated in 1947 from the history faculty of the Herzen Pedagogic Institute in Leningrad. Since 1956, he has been teaching at the University of Leningrad. In 1955, he became a member of the Communist Party; in 1960, he received his doctor's degree; and in 1963, was made a professor.

102 The poem 'Babi Yar' was published in the organ of the Soviet Writers' Union, *Literaturnaya gazeta*, on 19 September 1961, and was read publicly for the first time by Evtushenko at a Moscow poetry reading on 16 September. A number of changes are said to have been introduced into the text, the most significant of which was the transfer of the passage beginning 'O my Russian people' and ending '"The Union of the Russian People"' to immediately after the line 'I am every boy who was shot here'. The English version used here, by Max Hayward, appeared in *Jews in Eastern Europe*, May 1963, pp. 40–1, with lines 6 and 54 omitted.

103 V. Kosolapov was the chief editor of *Literaturnaya gazeta* who sanctioned the publication of 'Babi Yar'. According to Evtushenko, the decision was taken without the approval of the secretariat of the Writers' Union or the Ideological

Section of the Central Committee of the Communist Party. Kosolapov was dismissed from his post on 25 December 1962, and the conservative Russian writer of Jewish origin, A. Chakovsky, was appointed in his place. See Johnson & Labedz (eds.), *Khrushchev and the Arts*, p. 15; *Le Monde*, 13–14 January 1963.

104 Aleksei Yakovlevich Markov (1920–), Russian poet, one of the leading conservative writers in the Soviet Union. After Khrushchev's speech in March 1963, Markov was appointed Chairman of the Moscow Writers' Union. See M. Tatu in *Le Monde*, 17–18 March 1963.

105 On the use of the word 'cosmopolitan', see Chapter 4.

106 Dmitry Viktorovich Starikov (1931–), literary critic, was born in Moscow and is apparently of Jewish origin. He graduated from the literature faculty of Moscow University in 1955 and joined the Communist Party in 1962. From 1964 to 1968, he was deputy editor of the conservative literary journal *Oktyabr*, and since 1969 has been on the editorial board of the journal *Znamya*.

107 For the full text of Erenburg's poem, 'Babi Yar', see Erenburg, *Sobranie sochinenii*, vol. 3, p. 455.

108 Evtushenko's poem 'Babi Yar' was also subjected to criticism by speakers at an All-Russian Conference of Young Poets. The poet was accused of 'confusing many different kinds of conceptions and creating a stir around a question long since solved by our way of life', and the poem itself, considered in the light of lofty Party principles, was declared 'a serious creative error'. See A. Elkin, 'Talant – eto otvetstvennost', *Komsomolskaya pravda*, 4 October 1961.

109 Dmitry Dmitrievich Shostakovich (1906–75), leading Soviet composer and member of the Supreme Soviet of the RSFSR. Shostakovich was born in St Petersburg into an engineer's family. He graduated from the Leningrad Conservatory of Music in 1923. His many works include some on Jewish themes (e.g. the cycle of songs 'From Jewish Folk Poetry', 1948). The Thirteenth Symphony was first performed in Moscow on 18 December 1962. Ilyichev criticised the work for its undesirable theme in his address at the meeting between Soviet artists and intellectuals and Party leaders on 17 December, prior to the work's first performance in Moscow. No reviews appeared in the major organs of the press, and performances were temporarily stopped. Only after Evtushenko introduced some minor changes into his poem were performances renewed and reviews published. See also *Testimony: The Memoirs of Dmitri Shostakovich as Related to and Edited by Solomon Volkov*, New York, Harper and Row, 1979, pp. 156–9, 185.

110 Anatoly Vasilyevich Kuznetsov (1929–79), writer, was born in Kiev. In 1960, he graduated from the Gorky Institute of Literature in Moscow. He began writing when still very young (1946) under the influence of the war. In 1955, he joined the Communist Party. His first book appeared in 1957. In August 1966, he began publishing chapters from his documentary novel *Babi Yar* in the journal *Yunost*. The first reviews, by G. Radov in *Literaturnaya Rossiya* (18 November 1966) and A. Borshchagovsky in *Literaturnaya gazeta* (22 November 1966), welcomed the book enthusiastically. A more official and not altogether unfavourable review appeared in *Izvestiya* on 22 January 1967. Part of a letter by Dina Mironovna Pronicheva, a survivor of the Babi Yar massacre, published in *Literaturnaya gazeta* (22 February 1967) emphasised the Jewish aspect of the tragedy. Ariadna Gromova then published a favourable review in *Novy mir*, 1967, no. 2. The reviews of Borshchagovsky and Gromova were eventually attacked, along with the book itself, by A. Egorov in *Sovetsky voin*, 1967, no. 8. The uncensored version of Kuznetsov's *Babi Yar* appeared in the West after the author fled the Soviet Union. In the West, he employed the *nom de plume* A. Anatoli.

111 Porfiry Porfirovich Gavrutto, writer, was born in Riga. In 1951, he graduated from the Gorky Institute of Literature of the Soviet Writers' Union. Gavrutto's fir

book, which relates the deeds of a unit of Soviet paratroop-saboteurs commanded by the Jewish officer, A. A. Bluvshtein, appeared in 1945 in a Yiddish translation (*Sovetisher desantler* (Soviet Parachutist), Moscow, Der emes, 1945). Since the 1950s, Gavrutto has published a number of books on World War II. The first edition of *Tuchi nad gorodom* appeared in 1963 (Moscow, Molodaya gvardiya) in an edition of 65,000 copies. The second edition, in 75,000 copies, appeared in 1965 (see Doc. 45), and a third edition appeared in 1968. Gavrutto's attitude towards the Jews underwent a metamorphosis between 1945 and 1963; his attitude of complete admiration for the Jews changed to one of extreme anti-Semitism, as expressed in his portrayal of the 'traitor' Kogan. This novel carries an editorial note stating that there are no fictitious characters in the book.

112 Moisei Grigoryevich Kogan (1919–), mentioned in Gavrutto's book as a traitor, who served the Nazis as an interpreter at General von Paulus's headquarters, was captured by the Germans on the Kiev front in 1941. In December 1942, he succeeded in escaping and returning to the Russian front, near Stalingrad. He was arrested by the security organs on 25 February 1943 and was sentenced to ten years' forced labour on the charge of having worked as an interpreter in the German Army. The charge sheet did not claim that Kogan delivered Soviet citizens in Kiev into the hands of the Nazis. An engineer by profession, Kogan arrived in Israel in 1972. He brought with him many documents contradicting Khrushchev's 1963 charges against him as well as those levelled by Gavrutto in his book published that same year. In fact, Kogan pretended to be an Armenian while he worked as a driver for the Germans (see Doc. 48).

113 The 1968 edition of Gavrutto's novel differs at this point; it reads as follows: 'They sent him to work as an interpreter at the military commandant's office in Poltava, and later, *by way of promotion* [our emphasis], with the Sixth Army of the well-known German General, Paulus. There Kogan has been quietly occupied until now. In short, the degenerate is helping the Hitlerites to smash us.' It is not known whether these changes in the 1968 edition represent additions or whether they are the same as the text of the original 1963 edition of the book, which we have been unable to acquire.

114 The 1968 edition of Gavrutto's book omits the words 'who had betrayed to the Germans all the Kiev underground', as well as 'cleaned his boots'.

115 Ariadna Gromova is a journalist and writer resident in Kiev. While she is not Jewish herself, her husband, who was killed at Babi Yar, was. This letter provoked numerous replies to the newspaper *Literaturnaya gazeta*. But these were not published by the editors, except for that of Fedyai (Doc. 47), which supports Gavrutto's version. Gromova refers to A. G. Kogan instead of M. G. Kogan in her letter. This is either her mistake or a printing error.

116 Many immigrants to Israel from the USSR recalled this particular *feuilleton* as evidence of official anti-Semitism in the USSR.

117 Aleksandr Ivanovich Kuprin (1870–1938), Russian writer.

118 Ilya Ilf (pseudonym of Ilya Arnoldovich Fainzilberg; 1897–1937) and Evgeny Petrov (pseudonym of Evgeny Petrovich Kataev; 1903–42), Russian writers, famous for their satirical novels, stories, essays and *feuilletons*, written together. Lieutenant Schmidt was a revolutionary hero of ethnic German origin.

119 *The Lay of Igor's Campaign* (*Slovo o polku Igoreve*) is considered the greatest literary work of the Russian medieval period.

120 The *feuilletons* reproduced here represent only a small selection. It should be noted that the publication of such articles continued after 1958, in both the central and local press.

121 The texts of the two leaflets reproduced here were reportedly put out in Malakhovka and Lyubertsy, two small towns near Moscow, on 3 October 1959,

the eve of the Jewish New Year. The first was titled 'An Appeal', and was signed 'Beat the Jews Committee' (*Komitet bei zhidov*). The distribution of the anti-Semitic leaflets occurred a few hours before the synagogue and the house of its caretaker in Malakhovka were burnt down. The caretaker was saved, but his wife was found strangled. These events seem to have been the climax of a number of anti-Semitic outrages in Malakhovka (which has a population of some 3,000 Jews) during the previous few months. See *Jews in Eastern Europe*, November 1959, pp. 9–13; *The New York Times*, 13 October 1959; *Maariv*, 16 October 1959.

122 Among those who denied the truth of reports on the Malakhovka affair was the American Rabbi, Abraham Bick; see *Kol ha-am*, 15 November 1959. In a later article in *Naye prese* (23 November 1959), Bick admitted that the synagogue had been set on fire. 'It is believed that this was done by a young hooligan. The fire was soon put out and services were not interrupted.'

123 Label Katz, then President of the American Jewish organisation, B'nai B'rith, delivered his report at a press conference in Washington held on 23 January 1963.

124 On Rabbi Levin, see Chapter 8.

125 Vladimir Shvartser (i.e. Binyamin Shvartser; 1892–1978), a veteran Jewish actor in the Soviet Union, who headed the Moscow Jewish Ensemble since the beginning of the 1960s. For further details, see Chapter 7.

4. The campaigns against 'Jewish nationalism' and 'cosmopolitanism'

1 'Great Russian nationalism' as defined by Lenin and by Soviet theory generally manifests itself in one or more of the following ways: (1) the occupation of all or most of the positions in the autonomous republics of the Union by Russians and at the expense of local national cadres; (2) the determination of policies from above by the predominantly Russian central leadership, without taking into consideration the particular interests of the local nationality; (3) an attitude of contempt for the languages and cultures of the minority nationalities and the desire to neutralise them by melding them with – or even replacing them by – the Russian language and culture.

2 According to the Soviet definition, 'local nationalism' is characterised by the desire to withdraw into narrow national frameworks; by the over-exaggeration of particular national traditions or claims; by the neglect of proletarian internationalism; and by the reluctance to identify national interests with those of the state as a whole.

3 The period from the October Revolution until the outbreak of World War II can be divided into three main sub-periods: (1) the years 1917–23, which were distinguished by fierce struggles against non-Communist national movements (even though, at the same time, certain strongly nationalist groups were to be found temporarily within the ranks of the Communist Party); (2) the years 1923–9, in which the struggle against local nationalism was the least severe in the whole history of the Soviet Union, although from 1926 onwards the first signs of an imminent change in this policy could be detected; (3) the years 1930–9, in which, especially from 1934 onwards, a full-scale and bloody campaign against local nationalism was conducted.

4 *O partiinoi i sovetskoi pechati, Sbornik dokumentov* (On the Party and the Soviet Press, Collection of Documents), Moscow, Izdatelstvo Pravda, 1954, pp. 528–9; *KPSS v rezolyutsiyakh i resheniyakh syezdov, konferentsii i plenumov Ts. K.* (CPSU in the Resolutions and Decisions of the Congresses, Conferences and Plenary Sessions of the Central Committee), 8th edition, Moscow, Politizdat, 1971, vol. 6, pp. 130–4.

5 See M. Morozov, 'Ob istorii Kazakhskoi SSR', *Bolshevik*, 1945, no. 6, pp. 74–8.

6 F. Barghoorn, 'Stalinism and the Russian Cultural Heritage', *Review of Politics*, 1952, vol. XIV, no. 2, pp. 178–203.

7 See *Pravda Ukrainy*, 30 June 1947; K. Litvin, 'Ob istorii ukrainskogo naroda', *Bolshevik*, 1947, no. 7, pp. 41–54; 'Rezolyutsiya Prezidiuma pravleniya soyuza sovetskikh pisatelei', *Oktyabr*, 1946, no. 9, p. 185; R. Sullivant, *Soviet Politics and the Ukraine 1917–1957*, New York, Columbia University Press, 1962, pp. 252–62.

8 It included the Armenians, Uzbeks, Kirgiz, Buryat-Mongols, Moldavians, and Azerbaidzhans. See Tillet, *The Great Friendship*, pp. 84–109; Barghoorn, *Soviet Russian Nationalism*, pp. 61–6.

9 See S. Rabinovich, 'In krumen shpigl', *Eynikeyt*, 10 October 1946.

10 Y. Dobrushin, 'Vos darfn mir bahandlen', *Eynikeyt*, 12 October 1946.

11 'Dekn dem khoyv farn land un folk', *Eynikeyt*, 14 October 1946.

12 'Far a hoykhn kinstlerishn ideish ongezetiktn estrade repetuar', *Eynikeyt*, 5 April, 1947; G. Bloshteyn, 'Di yidishe estrade-kunst in chernovits', *Eynikeyt*, 5 April 1946; M. Notovich & Sh. Roytman, 'Oktyabr un di yidishe sovetishe literatur', *Heymland*, 1947, no. 1, p. 141.

13 The story by Kipnis was published in *Eynikeyt* on 26 July 1945, with the 'nationalistic' sections omitted. The unabridged version appeared in the 19 May 1947 issue of the Lodz Yiddish newspaper, *Dos naye lebn*, the organ of the Central Committee of Polish Jews. It describes a noble Ukrainian woman who, during the Nazi conquest, saved a Jewish boy and girl who became part of her family. Kipnis, of course, expressed deep-felt gratitude to this woman, who endangered her life to save the Jewish children; however, he greatly regrets that the children will probably never return to the world of their Jewish origins. 'I have become', writes Kipnis, 'most jealous in recent years. I am greatly concerned for what has remained whole. Whenever I see a Jewish student, a beautiful young girl, a bold and sturdy-looking soldier, a learned old man, an academician and a plain, simple Jew, I long for them to address me in Yiddish.'

14 'Natsionalizm untern shlever fun felker frayntshaft', *Eynikeyt*, 3 July 1947.

15 Kvitko also arraigned the literary critics Dobrushin and Nusinov, who had, he maintained, contributed to the disorientation of Yiddish literature. See L. Kvitko, 'Tsu naye ideish kinstlerishe hoykhn', *Eynikeyt*, 5 July 1947.

16 *Ibid.*; see also Itsik Fefer's strong criticism of Kipnis, 'Mitn kop arop', *Eynikeyt*, 9 August 1947.

17 *Literaturnaya gazeta*, 25 September 1947.

18 G. Polyanker & M. Talalaevsky, 'Pro odne shkidlyve opovidannya', *Literaturna gazeta*, 18 September 1947, as quoted in B. J. Choseed, Reflections on the Soviet Nationalities Policy in Literature: The Jews, 1938–1948', unpublished PhD thesis, New York, Columbia University, 1968, p. 333.

19 'Za ideinu chistotu ukrainskoi radyanskoi literatury', *Literaturnaya gazeta*, 23 October 1947. As stated in the conference's minutes, the meeting did not accept Itsik Kipnis's self-criticism.

20 M. Notovich, 'Di sovetishe yidishe literatur oyfn nayem etap', *Eynikeyt*, 28 October 1947. This is the third part of the article; the first two parts appeared on 23 and 25 October.

21 In addition to those previously referred to, the following articles may also be mentioned: A. Miral, 'Shafn a hoykh-ideishn un kinstlerish fulvertikn repertuar ...', *Eynikeyt*, 17 February 1948; D. Bendas, 'Farzamlung fun di kiever sovetishe yidishe shrayber', *Eynikeyt*, 20 March 1948; 'Tifer derkenen un shildern di sovetishe virklichkayt', *Eynikeyt*, 14 August 1948.

22 Loytsker does not weary of counting the many times Osherovich or Grubian have recourse to the word 'Jew'. In one of the stories, Loytsker exclaims, this word appears thirteen times. See Doc. 56.

23 For example: *sekilah, metame, metaher, eglah arufah, gezar zavaah* (Doc. 56).

24 For example: the vision of the dry bones; Naomi and Ruth; the burning bush; Noah's Ark (Doc. 56).

25 Doc. 56. How can it be, thunders Loytsker, that Kipnis wants the symbol of the struggle against the Nazis and the symbol of militant Zionism to be worn side by side on the breast of the Soviet soldier?

26 On the liquidation of Jewish culture and its leading representatives, see Chapters 5 and 7.

27 'Vysoko nesty prapor radyanskogo patriotyzma', *Vitchyzna*, 1949, no. 3, p. 16, as quoted in B. Choseed, 'Jews in Soviet Literature', in Simmons (ed.), *Through the Glass of Soviet Literature*, p. 148.

28 'Vysshe znamya sovetskogo patriotizma', *Literaturnaya gazeta*, 12 March 1949; V. Seduro, *The Belorussian Theatre and Drama*, New York, Research Programme on the USSR, 1955, p. 225. Similar accusations were voiced by the secretary of the Belorussian Communist Party, N. Gusarev, who, as has recently come to light, was involved in the murder of Mikhoels in January 1948. See *Sovetskaya Belorussiya*, 17 February 1949, as quoted in Namir, *Shlihut be-moskvah*, p. 281.

29 The single exception was the newspaper, *Birobidzhaner shtern*, the very existence of which was known to only a few people in the Soviet Union itself, and the Jewish content of which was minimal since it was, after all, no more than a news-sheet translated from Russian.

30 It is interesting to point out that, in the eyes of Soviet leaders and theoreticians, the idea of patriotism was a fundamentally negative one until the end of the 1920s. 'Patriotism', it is stated in the *Encyclopaedia of State and Law* of 1929, 'plays the part of the most reactionary ideology in our age, seeking to establish imperialistic exploitation and to silence the class consciousness of the proletariat by setting up insuperable barriers along the path of its struggle for liberation.' See *Entsiklopediya gosudarstva i prava*, Moscow, Kommunisticheskaya akademiya, 1927–9, vol. 3, p. 252.

31 This tendency reached its peak in Stalin's famous speech to Red Army officers. See *Pravda*, 25 May 1945.

32 N. Baltiisky, 'O patriotizme', *Novoe vremya*, 1945, no. 1 (11), p. 6. The term 'cosmopolitanism' was by no means negative in the USSR in the 1920s, and was at times identical with the term 'internationalism'. However, from the second half of the 1930s, it was increasingly emphasised that cosmopolitanism was an ideology alien to Marxism–Leninism. During the war, the novelist A. Fadeev wrote: 'The German invaders were deliberately encouraging rootless cosmopolitanism, which stems from the so-called idea that everybody is a "citizen of the world", that nation and homeland are actually outlived concepts.' A. Fadeev, 'O sovetskom patriotizme i natsionalnoi gordosti narodov SSSR', *Pod znamenem marksizma*, 1943, no. 11, p. 34, as quoted in Choseed, 'Reflections on the Soviet Nationalities Policy in Literature', p. 373.

33 *Pravda*, 10 February 1946.

34 'Doklad t. Zhdanova o zhurnalakh Zvezda i Leningrad', *Zvezda*, 1946, no. 7–8, pp. 7–22.

35 See *Decisions of the Central Committee, CPSU (Bolsheviks) on Literature and Art (1946–1948)*, Moscow, Foreign Languages Publishing House, 1951.

36 'Vospitanie sovetskogo patriotizma – vazhneishaya zadacha ideologicheskoi raboty', *Bolshevik*, 1947, no. 14, p. 5.

37 *Bolshevik*, 1947, no. 16, pp. 7–23.

38 *Oktyabr*, 1947, no. 7, pp. 148–63. The only person who dared to criticise Fadeev, in particular, for his stand on Veselovsky's theory of literature was V. Shishmarev. See his article in *Oktyabr*, 1947, no. 12.

39 Fadeev, *Oktyabr*, 1947, no. 7, pp. 154–5.

40 R. Hankin, 'Post-War Soviet Ideology and Literary Scholarship', in Simmons (ed.), *Through the Glass of Soviet Literature*, p. 265. The sharp attacks against Nusinov

in particular were published from 1948 until his arrest in 1949. See *Literaturnaya gazeta*, 24 January 1948; Kirpotin in *Oktyabr*, 1948, no. 1; A. Tarasenkov in *Novy mir*, 1948, no. 8; *Voprosy filosofii*, 1948, no. 1; V. Ermilov in *Literaturnaya gazeta*, 29 August 1949.

41 P. Vyshinsky, 'Sovetsky patriotizm i ego velikaya sila', *Bolshevik*, 1947, no. 18, p. 33.

42 A. Zhdanov, 'O mezhdunarodnom polozhenii', *Bolshevik*, 1947, no. 20, pp. 10–39.

43 *Bolshevik*, 1947, no. 21, p. 16.

44 See, for example, L. Plotkin, 'Propovednik bezydeinosti – M. Zoshchenko', *Zvezda*, 1946, no. 7–8, pp. 212–17; A. Isbakh, 'Vladimir Mayakovsky i zapad', *Novy mir*, 1947, no. 4, pp. 162–80; A. Shtein, 'Nechisty dukh slepogo podrazhaniya', *Novy mir*, 1947, no. 9, pp. 190–208.

45 I. Erenburg, 'Zashchitniki kultury', *Novoe vremya*, 1947, no. 46, pp. 5–10.

46 See, for example, the attack on the historian Solomon Y. Lurye, *Vestnik drevnei istorii*, 1948, no. 1.

47 *Novy mir*, 1948, no. 2. This was an article by the literary critic A. Tarasenkov, who had himself been attacked earlier; thus, he presumably felt compelled to attack Nusinov in the most vehement terms.

48 Z. Paperny, 'Perechityvaya Belinskogo, Protiv bezrodnykh kosmopolitov', *Literaturnaya gazeta*, 5 June 1948. Paperny is the nephew of Nakhman Mayzel, one of the editors of the Jewish journal, *Yidishe kultur*, which appears in New York, and a well-known critic of Yiddish literature.

49 It is interesting that in nineteenth-century Russia, cosmopolitanism was condemned not only by members of the radical wing, such as Belinsky, but also – and mainly – by the right, which placed the Jews in the forefront of their attacks. For example, to quote from a book which appeared in 1889: 'The Jews are the cosmopolitans. They do not live on their own land nor in an environment which favours them but wherever it suits them, according to the theory: *ubi bene, ibi patria.*' 'Therefore', the author added ironically, 'the best thing is to surrender our surplus of this talented tribe to the West.' *Sovremennaya Rossiya. Ocherki nashei gosudarstvennoi obshchestvennoi zhizni* (Contemporary Russia. Essays on the Life of Our State and Society), St Petersburg, 1889, p. 323.

50 For example, spy, traitor, enemy of the people. See the article of Georgy Aleksandrov, who had himself been attacked earlier by Zhdanov, in *Voprosy filosofii*, 1948, no. 3.

51 *Literaturnaya gazeta*, 21 July 1948.

52 Among those attacked were many Jews, e.g. Shmalgauzen, Rapoport and Zhebrak. See R.S., 'The Biology Discussion: A Commentary', *Soviet Studies*, 1949, vol. 1, no. 2, pp. 106–18; Medvedev, *The Rise and Fall of T. D. Lysenko*.

53 A detailed but 'processed' report appeared in the journal *Oktyabr*. See 'Voprosy dramaturgii na XII plenume SSP', *Oktyabr*, 1949, no. 2.

54 Stalin's personal interest in the anti-cosmopolitan campaign and his demand for its intensification were reported by the writers K. Simonov (see Doc. 70) and A. Fadeev, Chairman of the Writers' Union and one of the leading spokesmen of this policy. See Erenburg, *Sobranie sochinenii*, vol. 9, p. 574.

55 'Proiski antipatrioticheskoi gruppy teatralnykh kritikov', *Kultura i zhizn*, 30 January 1949.

56 The reader will find this material in a collection of Russian-language documents, Pinkus (ed.), *Evrei i evreisky narod 1948–1953*.

57 As is pointed out in the note to the table, this number does not represent all the articles on the subject of cosmopolitanism in the Soviet press, but the total number of 'different articles'.

58 On the special meeting of newspaper editors at which the editors were told by representatives of the Central Committee to restrain the campaign, see Salisbury,

Moscow Journal, p. 29 (Salisbury was *The New York Times* reporter in Moscow in 1949). See also the evidence of Ilya Erenburg, *Sobranie sochinenii*, vol. 9, p. 574.

59 Even if there are some errors in the table – unavoidable because of the lack of information on the nationality of those attacked – these would operate both ways (i.e. non-Jews would be included in the list of Jews and *vice versa*), and therefore cancel out to a great extent. It is worth noting that this table represents only the 'leading cosmopolitans' and discounts the long list of their aides, close supporters and even sympathisers.

60 The art and sculpture sector, as is pointed out in the note to Table 7, does not provide a complete picture of all those accused of cosmopolitanism. However, if we add to these data experts and critics in the plastic arts who were condemned as cosmopolitans, then it will be seen that here too the Jews were in a clear majority.

61 These arguments ceased when the Marr school was liquidated in 1950, after Stalin's personal intervention.

62 There were, however, a number of exceptions, for example, the sharp attacks on the Russian philosopher Kedrov. See Aleksandrov, 'Kosmopolitizm – ideologiya imperialisticheskoi burzhuazii', *Voprosy filosofii*, 1948, no. 3, pp. 186–91; or the particularly strong attacks on the Russian writer of Polish origins, A. Grin; see V. Vazhdaev, 'Propovednik kosmopolitizma', *Novy mir*, 1950, no. 1, pp. 257–72.

63 For example, the theatre and literary critics Gurvich, Levin, Altman, Borshchagovsky, Yuzovsky, Danin, Varshavsky, and Subotsky.

64 A list of articles from twenty-one newspapers and journals is given in Table 6. To this must be added articles which appeared in other newspapers and journals, of which complete sets are not at our disposal and are therefore not included in the table.

65 Erenburg, for example, relates in his memoirs that he wrote a letter to Stalin in which he complained that for two months his articles were no longer being published; see Erenburg, *Sobranie sochinenii*, vol. 9, p. 573. On the interruption in publication of economist E. Varga's book, as early as 1948, see *Planovoe khozyaistvo*, 1948, no. 5, pp. 82–9.

66 A partial examination of the literary journals of these years shows that a number of the writers and literary critics were prevented from publishing their works for only a short period in the years 1949–50; these included Vaisfeld, Gofenshefer, Meilakh, Gurvich, Golovanivsky, Grosman and Inber. Others were able to publish their works only from 1955 onwards; these included Borshchagovsky, Gozenpud, Varshavsky, Kogan, Shklovsky and many others.

67 From the sum of definitions of cosmopolitanism which appeared in the Soviet press during 1948–53, it is worth quoting in particular this one by Yu. Pavlov: 'Cosmopolitanism is the gospel of so-called "world citizenship", the abandonment of allegiance to any nation whatsoever, the liquidation of national traditions and culture under the screen of creating a "world" culture. Cosmopolitanism is the denial of the historically evolved singularities in the development of peoples, the denial of the national interest, national independence and state sovereignty of the peoples.' *Pravda*, 7 April 1949.

68 It is interesting that among the first to disclose pseudonyms was the ideological organ of the Central Committee, *Bolshevik*; see the article of Golovchenko, *Bolshevik*, 1949, no. 3. At about the same time, the name of another cosmopolitan was disclosed in the organ of the Writers' Union; see the article of Y. Kovalchik in *Literaturnaya gazeta*, 12 February 1949.

69 I.e. Melnikov (Melman); see 'Peredovaya sovetskaya literatura na novom podyeme', *Bolshevik*, 1951, no. 14.

70 See, for example, the coverage of the plenum of the Ukrainian Writers' Union, *Pravda Ukrainy*, 6 March 1949.

71 See, for example, H. Swayze, *Political Control of Literature in the USSR 1946–1959*, Cambridge, Mass., Harvard University Press, 1962, p. 63; A. Yarmolinsky, *Literature Under Communism*, Bloomington, Indiana University Press, 1960, p. 81.

72 G. Struve, *Soviet Russian Literature 1917–1950*, Norman, University of Oklahoma Press, 1951, p. 344; W. Vickery, 'Zhdanovism: 1946–1953', in *Conference on Soviet Literature 1917–1962*, Oxford, 1962, pp. 17–18.

73 The Soviet 'theory of the dialectical amalgam' apparently succeeded, in this case, in misleading a number of Western scholars.

74 Mirzo Fursan-Zade, 'Protiv kosmopolitizma i paniranizma', *Literaturnaya gazeta*, 19 February 1949; Kh. Rasulev, 'Reaktsionnaya sushchnost panislamizma i panturkizma', *Pravda Vostoka*, 14 August 1952.

75 Among those who attacked cosmopolitanism in the Ukraine were the poets Rylsky and Tychyna, who were known to be personal friends of many Yiddish writers and sympathetic to the Jewish people. While it is likely that they were compelled to do so, the sharpness of Tychyna's attack. for example (see Doc. 67), leads one to believe that the chance to settle accounts with Jewish literary critics whom he personally loathed also played an important role.

76 On the importance of Stalin's anti-Semitism in regard to this question, see Chapter 3.

77 'Protiv retsidivov antipatrioticheskikh vzglyadov v literaturnoi kritike', *Pravda*, 28 October 1951. It is interesting that in this year a historian submitted a doctoral thesis to the University of Moscow on the subject of cosmopolitanism: S. Rokhlin, 'Perezhitki nizkopoklontsva pered inostranshchinoi i ikh preodolenie v sovetskom obshchestve' (The Survivals of the Sycophantic Attitude towards the Foreign and their Elimination in Soviet Society), PhD thesis, Moscow State University, 12 February 1951.

78 See, for example, A. Dementyev, 'Partiya i voprosy literaturnogo yazyka', *Novy mir*, 1954, no. 6, p. 232, and the article 'Internatsionalizm – nashe znamya', *Komsomolskaya pravda*, 18 August 1955.

79 This tendency was clearly enunciated by the Ukrainian writers; see 4th Plenary Session of the Board of the Ukrainian Writers' Union, *Literaturnaya gazeta*, 15 January 1957, as quoted in the *Current Digest of the Soviet Press*, 1957, vol. IX, no. 19, p. 13.

80 See the pronouncements of the writer, K. Simonov, who was very active in the anti-cosmopolitan campaign in 1949, in Doc. 70.

81 See the interview which Khrushchev granted to the American journalist, Henry Shapiro, *Pravda*, 19 November 1957.

82 See, for example, the story 'Tishina' by Yu. Bondarev, *Novy mir*, 1962, nos. 3–5.

83 A. Tertz, *The Trial Begins*, New York, Vintage Books. 1960, pp. 7–128; A. Solzhenitsyn, *The First Circle*, New York, Bantam Edition, 1969, pp. 487–94.

84 Haim Loytsker (1898–1970), Yiddish literary critic, was born into an artisan's family in Kanev. He graduated from the pedagogic faculty of the 2nd Moscow State University in 1930. Loytsker's first works appeared in 1925. He published a number of works on Yiddish literature and language, including studies of D. Bergelson (1948), Shalom Aleikhem (1959), and David Hofshteyn (1962–4).

85 See above, pp. 152–3.

86 Maksym Tadeyovych Rylsky (1895–1964), Ukrainian poet, member of the Soviet Academy of Sciences and delegate to the USSR Supreme Soviet. Rylsky wrote on Jewish themes and was in close contact with Yiddish writers in the Ukraine (see Chapter 7).

87 Yuriy Ivanovych Yanovsky (1902–54), Ukrainian prose writer and poet.

88 Ivan Yukhmymovych Senchenko (1901–?), Ukrainian prose writer and poet.

89 Itsik Kipnis (1894–1974), Yiddish writer. Born in Slovechno in Volyn Province.

He studied at a *ḥeder*, worked as a leather-worker and took part in the Civil War and World War II. His first works appeared in 1922. His book *Khadoshim ve-yomim* (Months and Days), which appeared in 1926 and describes the pogroms against the Jews, was attacked by the literary critics. During 1947–8, Kipnis was accused of nationalism and was attacked in the most severe fashion. He was arrested and tried at the beginning of 1949. Kipnis was rehabilitated and lived in Kiev. See also E. Rozental, 'Itsik Kipnis, aza, vi ikh ken im', *Di goldene keyt*, 1967, no. 61, pp. 123–68; H. Loytsker, 'Itsik Kipnis', *Sovetish heymland*, 1966, no. 2, pp. 136–42.

90 The Bund (abbreviation of *Algemeyner yidisher arbeter bund in [lite], poyln un rusland*) (General Jewish Workers' Union in Lithuania, Poland and Russia), Jewish socialist party founded in Russia in 1897 which came to be associated with devotion to Yiddish, autonomism, and secular Jewish nationalism. Advocating the development of a full-fledged Jewish proletarian culture in Eastern Europe, it sharply opposed Zionism.

91 David Eynhorn (1886–?), Yiddish poet, was born in Korelichi, Novogrudok Region, Grodno Province, in Belorussia, into a well-connected family. His father was a military doctor. Eynhorn had a religious upbringing, studying first in a *ḥeder* and later in a Vilnius *yeshivah*. He wrote his first poems in Hebrew, but he turned to Yiddish later as a result of his Bundist sympathies. Eynhorn's first Yiddish works appeared in 1904. Forced to leave Russia in 1912 due to his revolutionary activity, he settled first in Europe and later in the USA, where he became a bitter opponent of Communism and advocated a return to the traditional Jewish way of life.

92 Hersh-David Nomberg (1876–1927), Yiddish writer and publicist. Nomberg was born in Amshinov, Warsaw Region, Poland, into a Hasidic family and was brought up in a strict Hasidic spirit. His wealthy background enabled him to devote himself to independent study, and his first works appeared in 1900. Nomberg exhibited Bundist sympathies. In 1908, he went with Perets, Shalom Ash and A. Reyzen to the Yiddish Language Conference in Chernovtsy, where he formulated and carried through the famous 'Chernovtsy Resolution' on Yiddish as a national language. In 1916, Nomberg was one of the founders of the *Yidishe Folkspartey* (Jewish People's Party) in Poland. He lived in Argentina from 1922 to 1923, and visited Palestine (1924), America (in 1912 and 1926), and the Soviet Union (1926). He remained active in Jewish life until his death.

93 A. Vayter (pseudonym of Ayzik-Meyer Devenishsky; 1878(9?)–1919), Yiddish writer, was born in Benyakoni, Vilnius Region, into a rabbinical family. Vayter was taught Bible, Gemara and grammar and, later in Smorgon, secular studies including Yiddish and Hebrew literature. Later still he learnt Russian and Polish, became acquainted with European thought, and joined the Bund. In 1905, at the height of the revolutionary activity, Vayter underwent a spiritual crisis after the wave of pogroms which swept the Pale at that time; he gradually abandoned politics for literature. Vayter was living in Vilnius and occupied an important post in the Commissariat of Education, when in 1919 the city was occupied by the Polish legionnaires. The Polish soldiers carried out a pogrom in which he was murdered.

94 In a context where Jewishness is irrelevant, the Yiddish word 'Yid' means 'somebody', a 'man' or 'person' – hence, also, 'you' or 'he', e.g. 'Vos vil der yid?' – 'What do you [does he] want?'

95 Hirsh Osherovich (1908–), Yiddish poet, was born in Panevežys, Lithuania. He graduated from the faculty of jurisprudence at the University of Kaunas in 1933, and his first works began to be published in 1934. Osherovich was fiercely attacked at the end of the 1940s during the campaign against Jewish nationalism. He was one of the contributors to the journal *Sovetish heymland*. He emigrated to Israel in 1972.

96 See Ezekiel 37.

97 Ayzik Platner (1885–1961), Yiddish poet, was born into a tailor's family in Sokolov-Podleskov, in the former Sedletsk Province. He studied in *ḥeder* and *yeshivah*. In 1921, he emigrated to the USA where he graduated from a Jewish teachers' training college. In 1932, he returned to the USSR. He was arrested at the end of 1948 and rehabilitated in 1956. Platner's book, *With Love and Faith*, was published in Moscow in 1947. 'Two Sisters' was written in 1945; 'The Bridge' in 1944; and 'Ballad of a Tailor' in 1943.

98 Motl Saktsier (1907–), Yiddish poet, was born into a tailor's family in Leovo in Moldavia, where his father was deputy mayor. Saktsier studied at the Vienna Teachers' Seminary and then worked in a Paris factory. From 1934, he was editorial secretary of the Bucharest progressive journal, *Di vokh*. His first works appeared in 1928, and his first collection of verse, *Derfar* (In Return), in 1936. In 1936, he went to the Soviet Union where he worked on the construction of the Moscow underground railway. He was arrested during the purges, sent to Siberia and released in 1941. In 1948, he was again arrested and sent to Siberia. Released for the second time after Stalin's death in 1953, he returned to Bessarabia. He contributed to *Sovetish heymland*.

99 Motl Grubian (1909–), Yiddish poet, was born in the small town of Sokolovka in the present Kiev Province. He graduated from the faculty of literature in the Minsk Pedagogic Institute in 1938. His first works appeared in 1930.

100 *Ḥalah*; here, the portion of dough set aside and given to the priest; see Numbers 15:19–20. The laws dealing with *ḥalah* and its separation are treated in the Talmudic tractate *Ḥalah*.

101 'I am the man who has seen affliction under the rod of his wrath'; Lamentations 3:1.

102 Avraham Velednitsky (1897–1959), Yiddish prose writer and poet, was born in Radomyshl in the Ukraine. He taught at a technical college and at a Party high school from 1925 to 1935. In 1932–5, he worked at the Institute of Jewish Culture in Kiev. His first works were published in 1922. Velednitsky served as an officer in World War II. He died in Kiev.

103 Hirsh Dobin (1905–), Yiddish writer, was born in Zhlobin in Belorussia. The subject of Birobidzhan occupies an important place in his works, which began to appear in 1929. He fought in the ranks of the partisans during World War II. He was arrested at the end of 1948. Dobin contributed to the journal *Sovetish heymland*.

104 *Der shtern*, literary almanac of the Soviet Jewish writers of the Ukraine. Beginning with the second issue, the sub-title was changed to 'Almanac for Literature and the Arts, Organ of the Soviet Writers' Union of the Ukraine'. The almanac's editor (from the second issue) was H. Polyanker. In the years 1947–8, seven issues were produced in all, although apparently the last issue (no. 7) was not distributed.

105 Evgeniya Ivanovna Kovalchik (1907–53), Russian literary critic.

106 Lyubomyr Dmytrovych Dmyterko (1911–), Ukrainian writer. Dmyterko was Deputy Chairman of the Ukrainian Writers' Union and editor of the journal *Vit-chyzna*. During the campaign against bourgeois nationalism and cosmopolitanism, he was one of the most vehement critics of Jewish writers and literary critics in the Ukraine. The object of his attack here was Yakov Gordon, a literary critic.

107 Savva Evseevich Golovanivsky (1910–), poet and playwright writing in Ukrainian, was born in the small town of Elisavetgradka, in the present Kirovo-grad Province in the Ukraine, into the family of a Jewish clerk. He studied at the Agricultural Institutes of Kharkov and Odessa. His first works began to be published in 1927. During World War II, he served as a war correspondent. Golovanivsky joined the Communist Party in 1942. Jewish topics occupy little place in his works.

108 Leonid Solomonovich Pervomaisky (pseudonym of Ilya Shlemovich Gurevich; 1908–73), prose writer and poet in Ukrainian. Pervomaisky was born in Krasnograd in the Ukraine into a Jewish bookbinder's family. He began publishing his poems in 1924. During World War II, he served as a war correspondent. He joined the Communist Party in 1943. After the Six-Day War, he lent his name to the campaign of the Soviet 'public' against Zionism and the State of Israel. Jewish topics occupy considerable space in his works, for example: the short stories of *Parasolka Pinkhusa-Moti* (Pinkhus-Motya's Umbrella, 1926) about a Jewish carpenter murdered by the White Guards; *Odna nich z dytynstva Illyushi* (One Night in the Childhood of Illyusha, 1937), on a pogrom in a Ukrainian small town; 'The History Teacher' (1937); the poems, 'Maidanek', 'V Babynim Yaru' (In Babi Yar, not dated), *Pid nebon chuzhym* (Under Foreign Skies, 1944), *Mistechko Ladenyu* (The Small Town of Ladenyu, 1928–31); and the novel *Diky med* (Wild Honey, 1963).

109 Taras Grygorovych Shevchenko (1814–61), one of the greatest of Ukrainian poets and thinkers. He expressed his nationalist ideas in his works, which possessed an anti-Russian and anti-Jewish bias.

110 Ivan Yakovych Franko (1856–1916), Ukrainian writer and philosopher.

111 Lesya Ukrainka (pseudonym of Larysa Petrivna Kosach; 1871–1913), Ukrainian prose writer and poetess.

112 On the journal, *Der shtern*, see Doc. 57 and n. 104 above. See also Chapter 7.

113 On Beregovsky, see Chapter 7, n. 107 and Doc. 93.

114 Dmitry Lvovich Klebanov (1907–), composer, was born into a Jewish family in Kharkov. In 1927, he graduated from the S. Bogatyrev Institute of Music and Drama. He was a violinist and conductor of a Leningrad orchestra. In 1948–9, he was a member of the administration of the Ukrainian Composers' Union, but was dismissed during the anti-cosmopolitan campaign. Klebanov was one of the composers of the Ukrainian Republic anthem and has composed numerous other works. He has been a signatory to anti-Israel and anti-Zionist letters and statements.

115 Valerian Danylovych Dovzhenko (1905–), Ukrainian musicologist and composer.

116 Valentyn Oleksandrovych Ponomarenko (1928–), composer. Since 1961, he has been teaching at a Kharkov music school.

117 Abram Akimovich Gozenpud (1908–), literary and musical scholar of Jewish origin writing in Ukrainian and Russian, was born in Kiev. He graduated from the literature faculty of the Kiev Institute of People's Education in 1930. His first works appeared in 1930. He taught in Kiev institutes of higher education. In 1952, he moved to Leningrad, apparently on account of the numerous attacks against him during the anti-cosmopolitan campaign.

118 Mariana Fedorovna Geilig (1909–), musicologist, now resident in Saratov.

119 Liya Yakovlevna Khinchin (1914–), musicologist, now resident in Novosibirsk.

120 Mykola Maksymovych Gordeichuk (1919–), Ukrainian musicologist.

121 Andriy Samiylovych Malyshko (1912–), Ukrainian poet.

122 Aleksandr Isbakh (pseudonym of Isaak Abramovich Bakhrakh; 1904–77), writer and journalist of Jewish origin, writing in Russian. Isbakh was born in Dvinsk, in the former Vitebsk Province. He graduated from the faculty of literature of Moscow University in 1924 and from the Institute of Red Professors in 1934. His first works were published in 1920. He joined the Communist Party in 1926. Isbakh helped organise the groups of proletarian writers *Rabochaya vesna* (Workers' Spring), *Oktyabr* (October) and MAPP (Moscow Association of Proletarian Writers). He was a member of the secretariat of VAPP (All-Russian Association of Proletarian Writers) and worked on the editorial boards of the journals *Oktyabr* and *Znamya*. During World War II, he served as a war correspondent. Jewish

themes occupy an important place in his work. Especially important is his autobiographical volume, *Years of Life*, published in 1948.

123 The stories published in *Years of Life* were reissued in two later and revised editions of Isbakh's short stories: *Povesti i rasskazi* (Stories and Tales), Moscow, Sovetsky pisatel, 1957; and *Yunost moya, komsomol moi* (My Youth, My Komsomol), Moscow, Sovetsky pisatel, 1966.

124 Fedor Markovich Levin (1901–), Soviet literary critic and scholar. Levin was dismissed from the A. M. Gorky Literary Institute of the Soviet Writers' Union by the Institute's Party Bureau following a discussion of the letter, 'On Cosmopolitans and Formalists in the Literary Institute', printed in *Kultura i zhizn*, 20 February 1949. See *Kultura i zhizn*, 10 March 1949.

125 Mikhail Kuzmich Lukonin (1918–), Russian poet. The present extract from Lukonin's article is noteworthy for the way it associates Zionism and Jewish bourgeois nationalism.

126 Pavel Grigoryevich Antokolsky (1896–), Soviet poet and literary scholar. Antokolsky was born into an assimilated Jewish family in St Petersburg. He studied at a private *gymnasium* and at the faculty of jurisprudence of Moscow University. He worked at the drama school of the stage director Vakhtangov and in other theatres. In 1943, he joined the Communist Party. During World War II, he served as a war correspondent. From 1944, he taught at the Gorky Institute of Literature. Antokolsky was one of the most frequently attacked poets during the anti-cosmopolitan campaign. Like many other Soviet Jewish writers, Antokolsky came to write on Jewish topics only under the profound impact of the Holocaust. For this, as can be seen from Lukonin's article, he was later charged with Zionism and bourgeois nationalism. His works on Jewish themes are 'Son', written in 1943 (in memory of his son who fell in battle); 'The Uprising in the Camp at Sobibor', written jointly with V. Kaverin in 1945; in the same year he wrote the poems 'Death Camp' and 'No Eternal Memory', published in 1946. See P. Antokolsky, *Izbrannoe* (Selected Works), Moscow, 1947, pp. 281–2. During the anti-cosmopolitan campaign, P. Antokolsky was dismissed by the Party Bureau of the Gorky Literary Institute of the Soviet Writers' Union, together with G. Brovman and F. Levin; see *Kultura i zhizn*, 10 March 1949.

127 Grigory (Hirsh) Bloshtein (1895–1979), Yiddish poet, was born in Kedainiai, Lithuania, the son of an itinerant tailor. He first studied at a religious school and then graduated from a *gymnasium* as an external student. He taught in Lithuania and the Ukraine. Bloshtein's first verses appeared in 1912. In 1925, he emigrated to Argentina, where he taught in left-wing oriented Jewish schools and also worked in the Communist press. From 1926 to 1931 he edited the progressive Yiddish journal, *Naye velt*. Following his arrest in 1931, he returned to the Soviet Union. In 1932, he took Ukrainian citizenship. During World War II, he was evacuated to Kazakhstan. Since the war, he has lived and worked in Chernovtsy. On Haim Malamud, see Chapter 7, n. 110.

128 Meir Kharats (1912–), Yiddish poet, was born in Markuleshty in Bessarabia. He moved to Chernovtsy, where he studied and worked at various trades. His first works were published in 1934. During the war he lived in Central Asia, and in 1946–8 he was again resident in Chernovtsy. He was arrested at the end of 1948, during the campaign against Jewish nationalism. After his release from the camps, he returned to Chernovtsy. He contributed to *Sovetish heymland*. Meir Kharats, generally considered the most gifted of the contemporary generation of the Chernovtsy Yiddish poets, emigrated to Israel in 1972.

129 Leon Feuchtwanger (1884–1958), German writer, was born into a religious Jewish family in Munich. He studied philosophy at the Universities of Berlin and Munich. He published numerous historical novels on Jewish themes (e.g. *Jew Süss*

and the trilogy on the Jewish Wars). After Hitler came to power, Feuchtwanger moved to France and then to the USA. He visited the Soviet Union in 1937, and published a book justifying the show trials staged by Stalin against his political rivals. A key figure in the trilogy is Josephus Flavius, the Jewish historian, who lived in the first century, and during the Jewish Revolt went over to Rome.

130 It seems Feuchtwanger's remarks are taken from his address, 'On Sense and Nonsense in the Historical Novel', delivered at the Paris International Congress of Writers in 1935. The speech was published first in the Soviet journal, *Mezhdunarodnaya literatura*, 1935, no. 9, and subsequently in *Centum Opuscula*, Rudolstadt, Greifenverlag, 1956.

131 This article also appeared in *Kultura i zhizn* on 30 January 1949.

132 Yu. (Iosif Ilyich) Yuzovsky (1902–64), Soviet literary and theatre critic of Jewish origin. Yuzovsky graduated from the faculty of sociology of the University of Rostov-on-Don in 1924. From 1930, he lived in Moscow. His first articles began to appear in 1925. In 1946–8, he was a research associate at the Institute of World Literature, but he was dismissed during the anti-cosmopolitan campaign. Yuzovsky began to publish again only in the second half of the 1950s.

133 Abram Solomonovich Gurvich (1897–1962), literary and theatre critic of Jewish origin.

134 Grigory Nersesovich Boyadzhiev (1909–74), Russian critic and theatre scholar.

135 Aleksandr Aleksandrovich Kron (Krein) (1909–), dramatist writing in Russian, was born in Moscow into a Jewish musician's family. Kron published his first works in 1928. He graduated from the historical and philosophical faculty of Moscow University in 1930. He joined the Communist Party in 1939. During World War II, he worked as a journalist attached to the navy.

136 Aleksandr Mikhailovich Borshchagovsky (1913–), writer and literary critic, was born in Belaya Tserkov, Kiev Province, into the family of a Jewish journalist. He began his literary activity in 1933. He graduated from the Kiev Institute of Theatre in 1935. In 1940, he joined the Communist Party. Borshchagovsky has published numerous articles on literary and theatrical topics, as well as a number of historical novels.

137 Leonid Antonovich Malyugin (1909–68), Russian dramatist.

138 Boris Sergeevich Romashov (1895–1958), Russian dramatist and theatre critic.

139 Nikolai Evgenyevich Virta (1906–76), Russian writer. Virta's play *Khleb nash nasushchny* (Our Daily Bread), written in 1947, was awarded a Stalin prize in 1948.

140 Ilya Isaakovich Stebun (pseudonym of Katsnelson; 1911–), Jewish literary critic and scholar who writes in Ukrainian. Stebun was born in Gorodnya in the Ukraine. He graduated from the Chernigov Institute of People's Education in 1929. He began publishing in the first half of the 1930s. Stebun has published numerous studies of Ukrainian writers of the pre-Revolutionary and Soviet periods. He joined the Communist Party in 1940 and took part in World War II. Since 1965, he has been a professor at the University of Donetsk.

141 Evgeny Grigoryevich Adelgeim (1907–), Jewish literary critic and scholar, who writes in Ukrainian. Adelgeim was born into a lawyer's family in Kiev. He began publishing his works in 1929 and has edited literary journals. He fought in World War II.

142 Lazar Samoilovich Sanov (pseudonym of Smulson; 1912–), Jewish poet and literary critic who writes in Ukrainian, was born into a clerk's family in Kiev. In 1930, he graduated from a technical college, and from 1930 to 1933, he worked as a locksmith. His first works began to appear in 1934. In 1938, he completed his studies at the philology faculty of Kiev University. During the war, Sanov served as a war correspondent.

143 Elyzaveta Ivanivna Starinkevich (1890–1966), Ukrainian literary critic.

144 Abram Isaakovich Katsnelson (1913–), Jewish poet and literary critic who writes in Ukrainian. The brother of Stebun-Katsnelson, Katsnelson was born in Gorodnya. He graduated from the philology faculty of the University of Kiev in 1939, and served as a war correspondent in World War II. His first book of poems appeared in 1935. Katsnelson joined the Communist Party in 1945.

145 Mykyta Mykheyovych Shumylo (1903–72), Ukrainian writer. In the post-war years Shumylo worked as deputy editor of *Literaturna gazeta*.

146 Viktor Platonovich Nekrasov (1911–), Russian writer. Nekrasov fought in World War II. He joined the Communist Party in 1944. His novel *V okopakh Stalingrada* (In the Trenches of Stalingrad), written in 1945, was awarded a Stalin Prize in 1947. Nekrasov was one of the most prominent members of the liberal intelligentsia of the 1950s and 1960s. In 1959, he published a letter in connection with the Babi Yar affair (see Doc. 160). Nekrasov left the Soviet Union in 1974.

147 On Pervomaisky being accused of nationalism, see Doc. 59.

148 Grigory Mikhailovych Gelfandbein (1908–), Jewish literary and theatre critic, who writes in Ukrainian. Gelfandbein was born in Kherson into a Jewish worker's family. He studied at the Kharkov Institute of People's Education, and has published many works on Ukrainian literature and theatre.

149 Leonid Aronovich Yukhvid (1909–), writer, the son of a Jewish lawyer, who writes in Ukrainian. Yukhvid was born in the village of Gulyai-Pole, Zaporozhy Province. His first book appeared in 1931. He joined the Communist Party in 1931. During World War II, he was on the editorial staff of Radio 'Dnipro' and he served as a war correspondent.

150 Oleksandr Evdokymovych Korneichuk (Korniychuk) (1905–78), Ukrainian dramatist and political activist.

151 Natan Samoilovich Rybak (1912–78), writer in Ukrainian, was born into a Jewish family in the village of Ivanovka, Cherkassy Province. In 1940, he joined the Communist Party. Rybak served as a war correspondent in World War II. His novel, *Pereyaslavska Rada* (The Diet of Pereyaslavl), appeared in two volumes between 1948 and 1953 and was awarded a State Prize in 1950. The novel describes the Ukrainian leader Bohdan Khmelnytsky, who was responsible for the decimation of the Jewish population in the seventeenth century, in laudatory terms.

152 Naum Dmitryevich Melnikov (pseudonym of Melman; 1918–), literary critic and playwright.

153 On the 'Doctors' Plot', see also Chapter 5.

154 Meer (Miron) Semenovich Vovsi (1897–1960), professor of medicine, Major-General in the Army Medical Corps. Vovsi, a cousin of the actor Mikhoels, was born into a well-to-do family in Kraslava in Latvia. He graduated from the medical faculty of Moscow University and taught there. From 1941 to 1949, Vovsi was head of the army therapy section. He was a member of the Jewish Anti-Fascist Committee. From 1948, he was a member of the USSR Academy of Medical Sciences. He was, it seems, arrested in November 1952 in connection with the 'Doctors' Plot'.

155 Konstantin Mikhailovich Simonov (1919–79), Russian writer. Simonov was a candidate member of the Central Committee of the Communist Party from 1952 to 1956. He was a delegate to the Supreme Soviet from 1946 to 1954 and occupied senior posts in the Soviet Writers' Union. During the anti-cosmopolitan campaign, Simonov was among those writers most active in vilifying their fellow writers and critics.

156 Simonov is referring to the 'theory' of 'order of priority' according to which critics writing from hostile positions must be exposed and removed before criticism can be levelled against Soviet works.

157 I.e., the plenum of the Soviet Writers' Union at the end of 1948.
158 See Doc. 66.
159 Valentin Vladimirovich Ovechkin (1904–68), Russian writer.
160 Mikhail Semenovich Bubennov (1909–), Russian writer. Part 1 of his novel *Belaya bereza* (White Birch), written in 1947, was awarded a Stalin prize in 1948. Part 2, which appeared in 1952, was criticised as varnishing reality. See also Chapter 11.
161 Vasily Nikolaevich Azhaev (1915–68), Russian writer. His novel *Daleko ot Moskvy* (Far From Moscow), which appeared in 1948, was awarded a Stalin prize in 1949. See also Chapter 11.
162 That attacks on cosmopolitans did not cease with Stalin's death is evidenced by A. Dementyev's article, 'Partiya i voprosy literaturnogo yazyka', *Novy mir*, 1954, no. 6. The author attacked the Jewish writer, I. Selvinsky, for reprinting an extract from his *Pushtorg* where the poet mocks at 'pretty Russianisms', states that he is in favour of 'pulling out roots and mixing French and provincial Russian', and calls on writers to 'strive for a new language of Latinised diversity'. For such admissions Dementyev linked Selvinsky's name with that of the Futurist poet Tretyakov, who was shot in 1939 as an enemy of the people.

5. Jews on trial in the Soviet Union

1 On the tragic episode of Erlich and Alter, who were to have headed the new Jewish Anti-Fascist Committee about to be established by the Soviet authorities, see *The Case of Henryk Erlich and Victor Alter*, New York, American Representation of the General Jewish Workers Union in Poland, 1943; *Henryk Erlikh un Viktor Alter*, New York, Undzer tsayt, 1951; S. Redlich, 'The Erlich–Alter Affair'.
2 This period in general and the wave of arrests in particular have not yet been seriously researched. This is principally due to the paucity of available sources. Today, given the large number of emigrants from the USSR to the West, an oral history study would be possible. On the rumours about the arrests and the exile of Jews to Siberia, see *Jewish Telegraphic Agency Bulletin* (hereafter *JTA*), 4 January 1945, p. 4; 26 April 1946, p. 2.
3 We do not include here arrests for smuggling, which was categorised differently and which indeed occurred. It, too, was considered a very grave offence against state security and was punished accordingly.
4 See Erenburg's article in *Pravda* (Doc. 7); see also Chapter 6. This was undoubtedly the first sign that the Soviet authorities had decided to sever the contacts between Soviet Jewry and Zionism and Israel.
5 In the information received from a Soviet Jew by the Israel legation in Moscow in 1949, it was stated: 'The law courts pervert judgement and maliciously stiffen penalties against Jews. This year, many have been thrown into prison and sent to camps for sympathising with Israel or showing a desire to emigrate to Israel or for taking part in street demonstrations last year in honour of our legation'; Namir, *Shlihut be-moskvah*, pp. 307–8. Among those imprisoned he named Mordekhai Dubin, one of the leaders of *Agudat Yisrael* in Latvia. Many immigrants who arrived in Israel in recent years were imprisoned for Zionism in this period, for example, Meir Gelfond, Vitaly Svechinsky, Mikhail Margolis.
6 An important document in this connection refers to the case of a Jew who, at the beginning of 1953, was sentenced by the Military Collegium of the Supreme Court of the Soviet Union to twenty-five years' imprisonment in labour camps. Upon appeal, the sentence was mitigated to ten years. Among other things, the judgement stated that the defendant 'has been found guilty in that, out of anti-Soviet motivations and nationalistic attitudes and a hostile attitude towards the Soviet regime, he came into

criminal contact with — of the Diplomatic Representation of the State of Israel in Moscow in autumn 1949, to whom he gave oral consent to collect and submit information of a classified nature on the condition of the Jews in the USSR'; Namir, *Shliḥut be-moskvah*, p. 331.

7 The death penalty, which had been abolished in 1947, was reintroduced in January 1950. The almost standard sentence handed down by the Special Boards of the MGB in this period was ten years of forced labour under harsh conditions, with the possibility of a further five-year extension.

8 See, for example, the case of the Jewish workers in the 'Serp i Molot' factory in the city of Kharkov, twelve of whom were dismissed from their jobs in February 1952 and who were tried and exiled to Siberia immediately after.

9 This report appeared in the Yiddish newspaper *Morgn zhurnal*, 17 July 1949, as quoted in the *American Jewish Yearbook*, 1951, p. 533. Among those arrested were Colonel Grisha Feldman (who served as editor of the newspaper *Tägliche Rundschau*), Colonel David Noidorf and Major Vladimir Blokh.

10 Among the Yiddish-language writers and literary critics who were arrested and executed or who died in prison in the late 1930s were Izi Kharik, Moshe Kulbak, Max Erik, Yashe Bronshteyn, Israel Tsinberg and Haim Dunits. Among the most prominent *Evsektsiya* functionaries to be purged were Shimon Dimanshteyn, Mariya Frumkin (Esther), Avraham Merezhin, Aleksandr Chemerisky, Avraham Beylin, Hershl Bril, Aharon Veynshteyn (Rahmiel), Moshe Litvakov and Mikhail Levitan.

11 On the liquidation of the institutions of Jewish culture, see Chapter 7.

12 Most of the writers and cultural functionaries (such as Zhits, editor of the journal *Eynikeyt*, and Y. Strongin, director of the publishing house 'Der emes'), were arrested in December 1948 and January 1949. Also arrested then were Leyb Kvitko, David Bergelson, Der Nister, Itsik Fefer, Perets Markish, Itsik Kipnis, Haim Loytsker and many others. See Pomerants, *Di sovetishe harugey malkhes*.

13 The following picture emerges from material which began to be published in 1956 and appeared in greater quantity at the beginning of the sixties. The poet David Hofshteyn and literary critics Yitskhak Nusinov and Yehezkel Dobrushin were among the first to be arrested. In this period – apparently the beginning of December (see Leneman, *La Tragédie des juifs en URSS*, pp. 68–72) – a special meeting of the Yiddish writers in Moscow was convened by the Soviet Writers' Union to condemn the nationalist writers. The main speaker was to have been the poet A. Kushnirov, but because of illness aggravated by the emotional crisis of the moment, he lost his voice and was incapable of uttering a sound (he died in hospital of throat cancer in September 1949), and the writer Eli Gordon took his place. The wave of mass arrests began after this gathering, which was intended to provide a kind of authorisation for the police operations.

14 Broderzon, *Mayn laydn-veg mit Moyshe Broderzon*, pp. 55, 65.

15 Among those arrested were Itsik Fefer's wife (in 1949) and sister; the wives of Leyb Kvitko, Binyamin Zuskin, David Bergelson, Perets Markish and Aharon Kushnirov (Kushnirov himself was not arrested because of his illness). The arrests and exiles occurred, in the main, at the end of 1952 and the beginning of 1953, that is after the trial and execution of their husbands; see Pomerants, *Die Sovetish harugey malkhes*; Markish, *Le Long Retour*, pp. 209–18.

16 See Leneman, *La Tragédie des juifs en URSS*, p. 67; *Folks mishpat* (The People's Trial), New York, Jewish Labor Committee, 1956, pp. 54–62; Gilboa, *The Black Years of Soviet Jewry*.

17 Cang, *The Silent Millions*, p. 103 (list on pp. 225–8).

18 For example, among those included who were arrested in the thirties were Abchuk, Bukhbinder, Kiper, Kirzhnits, Levin, Merezhin, Sudarsky and Viner. Among those listed by Cang who do not seem to have been arrested were Baumvol,

Borokhovich, Holdes, Pervomaisky (it is not clear why Pervomaisky is listed among the Yiddish-language writers), Volkshteyn, Telesin.

19 While we have no conclusive proof that such a trial was indeed planned, it is a reasonable assumption based on the following facts: (a) the history of the thirties and forties indicates that there was no need for prolonged investigations for conviction by secret trial (for example, the trials of the heads of the army and of the Communist Party leadership in Leningrad); (b) a number of defendants, unable to endure the lengthy interrogations undertaken to extract confessions, died; (c) some charges from this trial were transferred to the one which was to take place on 18 March 1953 (see below, on the 'Doctors' Plot').

20 See the rehabilitation letter sent to a relative of one of those executed (Doc. 73); Khrushchev's remarks to the head of the Canadian Communist Party delegation (Doc. 96); the report in the Communist journal, *Folks-shtime* (Doc. 74). Many official Soviet publications give 12 August 1952 as the day of execution. A trial prior to this date was undoubtedly necessary, since, even in the Stalinist regime of terror, judicial procedures and customs were adhered to. According to Esther Markish, this was a re-trial, the first trial having taken place in May 1952; see Markish, *Le Long Retour*, pp. 291–2.

21 S. Broderzon writes that twenty-four persons were tried; see Broderzon, *Mayn laydn-veg mit Moyshe Broderzon*, p. 165. This is also the number specified by Dr Haim Shoshkes after his return from the Soviet Union; see Leneman, *La Tragédie des juifs en URSS*, p. 89.

22 There were rumours that the defendants included a group of Jewish engineers from the Stalin Factory in Moscow. Khrushchev's memoirs, insofar as they are authentic, speak of a special trial of the Jewish workers of this factory. See *Khrushchev Remembers*, p. 278.

23 A relatively large amount has been written about the 'Crimea Affair' which served as grounds for this accusation, but we still do not have a full picture of its origin and evolution. What is clear is that, as soon as they learned of the region's liberation in April 1944 and of the expulsion of its Tatar population, circles in the Jewish Anti-Fascist Committee raised the idea of renewed Jewish settlement in the Crimea, with an eventual Jewish republic there. Members of the Committee attempted to clarify the positions of three senior members of the Soviet leadership – Kaganovich, Molotov and Litvinov – as well as that of Lozovsky, who was the Committee's direct superior. According to one testimony, Kaganovich and Molotov supported the idea, while Litvinov opposed it, claiming that insofar as the Jews actually needed any territory, Palestine, supported by the Jews of the world, was preferable; see A. Sutskever in *Di goldene keyt*, 1967, no. 61, p. 32. Another testimony has Litvinov among this idea's enthusiastic supporters (remarks of the writer and journalist Herts Kahn in conversation with the author). According to the journalist Harrison Salisbury, Lozovsky supported the plan for Jewish settlement in the Crimea, and the proposal was transferred to the Politburo for discussion, but Stalin opposed it; see Salisbury, *To Moscow and Beyond*, p. 72. It is also known that Khrushchev opposed the plan; see *Khrushchev Remembers*, pp. 259–63. On the Crimea Affair in general, see Vaynroykh, *Blut oyf der zun*, pp. 10–11; I. Emiot, *Der birobidzhaner inyen* (The Birobidzhan Affair), New York, Bogorad, 1960, p. 8; Yanasovich, *Mit yidishe shrayber in rusland*, pp. 255–8; Leneman, *La Tragédie des juifs en URSS*, pp. 88–98. According to Esther Markish, her husband opposed the Crimea plan and supported the establishment of a Jewish republic in the Volga region, from which the Germans had been expelled. She also claims, apparently incorrectly, that the Crimea Affair occurred in 1947 and that the proposal came from Kaganovich and Molotov, who suggested to the heads of the

Jewish Anti-Fascist Committee that they apply to Stalin on the matter; see Markish, *Le Long Retour*, p. 178.

24 According to other information, Yitskhak Nusinov also received twenty-five years' imprisonment. Apparently, the poet David Hofshteyn was not executed, but died in a mental hospital.

25 The most prominent examples are to be found in the documents to this chapter, but see also *Pravda Ukrainy*, 11 January, 21 October, 19 November and 3 December 1948, and 3 February 1949; *Pravda Vostoka*, 10 July and 1 and 15 September 1948; *Sotsialisticheskaya zakonnost*, 1948, no. 10; *Vechernyaya Moskva*, 5 September 1949, 7 June 1950; *Izvestiya*, 24 June 1951.

26 See *Vechernyaya Moskva*, 7 June 1950, 24 December 1952; *Pravda Ukrainy*, 28 December 1952; *Izvestiya*, 30 January 1953; *Pravda*, 1 and 6 February 1953.

27 See *Pravda Ukrainy*, 29 November 1952. Reports also reached the Israeli Embassy that at the beginning of 1952 Jews accused of economic crimes had been exiled from Ukrainian cities (Poltava, Kharkov, Lvov and Dneproderzhinsk) to labour camps in Birobidzhan.

28 The competency of the military courts extended to offences involving military personnel (espionage, sabotage, treason, acts of terror, disclosure of state secrets, theft of arms, the sale and purchase of arms). See D. Karev, *Organizatsiya suda i prokuratury v SSSR* (Court and Prosecution Organisation in the USSR), Moscow, Gosyurizdat, 1954, pp. 146–7.

29 On this, see the example given in Doc. 49.

30 The Jews sentenced to death were Rudolf Slansky, Bedrich Reicin, Ludwig Freyka, Bedrich Geminder, Rudolf Margolius, Otto Fishel, Otto Šling and Andre Simon. Three non-Jews were so sentenced: Vladimir Klementis, Yosef Frank and Karl Švab. The three Jews sentenced to life imprisonment were Artur London, Vavro Hajdu and Evzen Loebel. See the official transcript of the trial, *Procès des dirigeants du centre de conspiration contre l'Etat dirigé par Rudolf Slansky* (Trial of the Leaders of the Centre of Conspiracy Against the State Headed by Rudolf Slansky), Prague, Ministère de la Justice, 1953, p. 644; see also Jiri Pelikan (ed.), *The Czechoslovak Political Trials*.

31 In addition to a daily report on the trial in all the Soviet media, commentaries also appeared. See *Pravda*, 21–3 and 25–8 November 1952; *Literaturnaya gazeta*, 22 and 27 November 1952; *Novoe vremya*, 1952, no. 49, pp. 22–5.

32 For example, the testimony of the Israeli witness, Mordechai Oren, at the Slansky trial, where the Czechoslovak interrogator told Oren: 'We have all the proof that you, as a central envoy of international Zionism, responsible for the organisation of Zionist activity in the Socialist countries, are among the chief organisers of the Zionist-nationalist underground operating in the Soviet Union ... Your vital interest demands that you reveal to us the full truth of this matter. Otherwise we will be compelled to transport you to another place – very far from here – and you will be interrogated by someone else. There the truth will certainly be obtained from you.' Oren, *Reshimot asir prag*, p. 287. Israeli citizens such as Oren were particularly suitable as witnesses in a trial centred on Zionist conspiracy and on the link between Jewish institutions and Western espionage services.

33 It will suffice here to mention the Writers' Trial, the economic trials and the particularly acrimonious anti-Zionist campaign. On Stalin's general policy during this period, see Conquest, *Power and Policy in the USSR*, pp. 95–153.

34 Clearly there was no need to wait for Khrushchev's revelations at the 20th Party Congress in February 1956 to realise that this was indeed Stalin's programme. In addition to the removal, beginning at the end of 1951 and in early 1952, of Beria and his closest associates from the head of the security services and the imprisonment of

his supporters in Georgia, there was a clear hint in a *Pravda* article published on the day the 'Doctors' Plot' was publicly announced that Beria and his close associates would be the principal defendants in the forthcoming trials. 'The security services', stated *Pravda*, 'failed to expose in good time the terrorist sabotage organisation which operated among the doctors'; *Pravda*, 13 January 1953.

35 E.g. the necessity to prepare a show trial down to the minutest detail, with the attendant risk (which materialised in the case of Traichko Kostov in Bulgaria in 1949) that one of the defendants might refuse to play his allotted role at the last moment. Trials of this kind can also have a negative effect on citizens who suddenly see their most admired leaders reviled as abject traitors who have been serving the enemy for many years.

36 While Khrushchev did note in his secret speech that Dr Lidiya Timashuk – whose letter to Stalin was the direct cause of the doctors' being arrested – worked in the security services, he did not explain under whose orders she was acting when she sent the letter. Since it is hardly conceivable that she acted on her own responsibility, two other possibilities exist: (1) Stalin himself initiated the entire episode through the security services, with Ignatyev leading them; (2) the initiative came from a group of leaders in the Party who thereby sought to liquidate their political rivals. In this case, it would appear that only Malenkov and his associates could have been behind the plan.

37 In a story published in *Novy mir* ('Povest nepogashennoi luny' (Story of the Unextinguished Moon), *Novy mir*, 1926, no. 5), Boris Pilnyak wrote about the death of one of the heads of the Red Army who died following an unnecessary operation in 1925. He was later compelled to deny that there was any connection between his story and the rumours about Frunze's death. See G. Katkov, *The Trial of Bukharin*, London, Batsford, 1969, p. 171. Before his suicide, Ioffe, one of the most important diplomats of the twenties, wrote to his close associate, Trotsky, that he had no faith in Professors Davidenko and Levin (the same Dr Levin who, in the Bukharin trial of 1938, was charged with having participated in the murder of the Communist leaders). See *Ibid.*

38 Among the doctors accused in 1938 were Levin, Pletnev and Kazakov; see *Anti-Soviet Bloc of Rightists and Trotskyites*, Moscow, People's Commissariat of Justice, 1938, pp. 530–614.

39 In the trial Slanksy 'admitted' having delegated Dr Haskovec, who belonged to the Freemasons, as Gottwald's personal physician in order to cut short the life of the President of the Czechoslovak Republic; see *Procès des dirigeants*, p. 102.

40 The extent to which this consideration was correct may be seen from the declaration of French doctors (among them four Jews), expressing full support for the Soviet authorities in their war against the criminal acts of the accused doctors; see *Humanité*, 27 January 1953, as quoted in *Commission pour la vérité sur les crimes de Staline*, 1963, no. 2, p. 10.

41 Erenburg, *Sobranie sochinenii*, vol. 9, p. 729.

42 Vinogradov was the medical expert in the trial of 21 March 1938, which confirmed the charges against doctors Levin, Pletnev and Kazakov; Vovsi and Kogan took part in the condemnation of that 'sadistic doctor' and 'enemy of the people', Pletnev, in June 1937. (In the campaign conducted against him in this period Pletnev was, among other things, accused of having bitten a woman's breasts so hard as to draw blood, and of having thus made her seriously ill.) See *Pravda*, 8–11 June 1937.

43 Only a small number of these articles are cited in this chapter. Particularly prominent in this denunciatory work were the satirical journal, *Krokodil*, the trade-union organ, *Trud*, and the organ of the Communist Youth Organisation, *Komsomolskaya pravda*. A *Krokodil* lead article of 30 January 1953, headed 'Poisoners',

stated, among other things: 'Black hate of our great country has united in one camp the American and British bankers, the estate owners, the armaments kings, the defeated generals of Hitler dreaming of revenge, Vatican representatives, those loyal to the Zionist *kahal*' (*Krokodil*, 1953, no. 3, p. 2). Besides the 'good company' in which the Zionist movement was placed, this was the first time the term 'Zionist *kahal*', taken straight out of the *Protocols of the Elders of Zion* of the Tsarist period, was mentioned.

44 Erenburg relates in his memoirs that, shortly before he was to receive a prize on 27 January, he was called in by Grigoryan, who told him: 'It will be a good thing if you mention [during the ceremony] the criminal doctors'; Erenburg, *Sobranie sochinenii*, vol. 9, p. 729.

45 See Erenburg's novella, *The Thaw* (Doc. 80); Terts, *The Trial Begins*; E. Feldman, *Kele le-lo sugar* (Prison Without Bars), Tel Aviv, Am ha-sefer, 1964, pp. 150–1.

46 Vasily Grossman, *Forever Flowing*, pp. 21–2.

47 This document makes it clear that more than fifteen doctors had been arrested, of whom six or seven were Jews, even though the *Tass communiqué* of 13 January mentioned only nine doctors, six of whom were Jews.

48 See *Pravda*, 6 April 1953.

49 For one such reference, see below, n. 101, where the 'Doctors' Plot' is mentioned as a negative phenomenon in the life of Soviet society.

50 V. Gsovsky, 'The Soviet Amnesty', *Problems of Communism*, 1953, vol. II, no. 2, pp. 9–14.

51 For example, in a report in the Soviet journal *Sovetskaya torgovlya*, dated 20 August 1955, the names and patronymics of the Jewish defendants were noted in order to remove any doubt that they were Jews. See also *Jewish Chronicle*, 9 December 1955; 22 February 1957.

52 The first Criminal Code based on the new legislation was pased by the Uzbek Republic on 21 May 1959. The Criminal Code of the Russian Republic was passed on 27 October 1960, and the last republic to follow suit was the Turkmen Republic, on 22 December 1961. See *Ugolovnoe zakonodatelstvo Soyuza SSR i Soyuzynkh Respublik* (The Criminal Code of the USSR and the Union Republics), Moscow, Gosyurizdat, 1963, vol. I, p. 6.

53 On this shift and its causes, see H. Berman, *Justice in the USSR*, Cambridge, Mass., Harvard University Press, 1966, pp. 84–8. On the economic trials in general, see G. Kline, 'Economic Crime and Punishment', *Survey*, 1965, no. 57, pp. 67–72.

54 *Vedomosti Verkhovnogo Soveta SSSR*, 1961, no. 13/137, as quoted in 'Economic Crimes in the Soviet Union', *Journal of the International Commission of Jurists*, 1964, vol. V, no. I, pp. 5–6.

55 *Vedomosti Verkhovnogo Soveta*, 1961, no. 19/207; 1961, no. 27/291; 1962, no. 8/85, as quoted in *ibid.*, p. 6.

56 See Tables 8–10.

57 For example, in a Leningrad trial of eleven defendants, the names of only five were mentioned, three of whom were Jews; *Komsomolskaya pravda*, 30 May 1962. In a Moscow trial of nine defendants, the names of seven were mentioned, five of whom were Jews; *ibid.*, 6 June 1962.

58 Not only illegal transactions in foreign currency, but also cases involving large-scale theft or fraud are brought to court by the KGB rather than by the police. See 'Economic Crimes in the Soviet Union', p. 13.

59 It must be stressed that this is only the number of trials reported in the Soviet central and republican press.

60 See the remarks of Genady Terekhov, member of the Collegium of the Procuracy of the Soviet Union, who was the chief prosecutor in a number of economic trials; *Sovetish heymland*, 1963, no. 6, p. 83.

61 The justification given for mentioning Jewish names is of great interest here. Paupanov, for example, wrote: 'We mention the Jewish names of those who belonged to this gang because we attach no importance whatever to the defamations occasionally appearing in the Western press'; *Izvestiya*, 20 October 1963.

62 Between 1955 and 1967, such trials took place in Moscow, Kiev, Leningrad, Minsk, Riga and other cities.

63 On the reasons for these trials and the objectives in holding them, see Chapter 6.

64 V. Dyachenko, 'Padenie', *Izvestiya*, 24 February 1967.

65 *Jewish Life* was published monthly from 1937 by the New York State Jewish Bureau of the Communist Party. Z. Blitz's article is an attack on S. Dorfson, a correspondent of *Morgn zhurnal*, for his account of Ilya Erenburg's press conference in London. Dorfson claimed that Erenburg was unwilling to answer questions on Soviet Jewry, including the fate of the Yiddish writers. Blitz quotes Jacob Leon's account of the press conference, which appeared in the Tel Aviv *Al ha-mishmar*, and which not only shows Erenburg willing to talk about Soviet Jewry, but as confident in his answers.

66 Leon (Aryeh) Leneman (1909–), journalist, was born in Warsaw. Leneman began his journalistic activity in Warsaw in 1931. From 1944 to 1946, he was the Moscow correspondent of the New York Jewish Telegraphic Agency. He has lived in France since 1947. In 1950, he was made an executive member of the French General Zionist Party, and, in 1953, Vice-President of the Association of Jewish Writers and Journalists in France. Since 1948, he has been Paris correspondent of some eight Jewish newspapers throughout the world. In 1953, he became editor-in-chief of *Tsienistishe bleter*. Leneman is the author of *La Tragédie des juifs en URSS*.

67 This document is reproduced in Markish, *Le Long Retour*, pp. 192–3.

68 This standard certificate of rehabilitation, sent to the families of the writers, is particularly important because it is the first official Soviet document testifying that Jewish writers and cultural figures had been tried in July 1952. Since we know from other Soviet sources that 12 August 1952 was the date on which a number of Jewish writers and artists were executed, there is now no longer any doubt that this secret trial took place. The 'rehabilitation' was brought to Israel by Tamar Plat-Zuskin, daughter of Binyamin Zuskin, an actor of the State Yiddish Theatre in Moscow and its director after the murder of Mikhoels, who was sentenced at this trial. See Y. A. Gilboa, *Ha-shanim ha-sheḥorot shel yahadut brit ha-moaẓot* (The Black Years of Soviet Jewry), Tel Aviv, Am ha-sefer, 1972, pp. 273–5.

69 Hersh Smolar, author of this article, has written a note, 'The Consolation Did Not Come' (*Sheut*, 1974, no. 2, p. 184), in which he gives the background to the publication of his article.

As editor-in-chief of the Polish Yiddish-language newspaper *Folks-shtime*, Smolar received a numbered copy of Khrushchev's secret speech to the 20th Party Congress in 1956. He was shocked to find no mention in it of the destruction of Jewish social and cultural life in the USSR. He then wrote his article and read it to fellow members of the editorial board, Shimon Zakhariash and Mikhael Mirski, after which he revised it in the light of their suggestions. Smolar submitted the final version to the Secretary of the Central Committee of the Polish Workers' Party, Yezi Murawski, who was one of the first to reject the explanation of the 'cult of personality' and to see the root and cause of Stalin's crimes in the system. Murawski's reaction to the article was indifferent, and he passed it on to Tadeusz Glinski, head of the press section of the Central Committee. Glinski said (on 2 April 1956) that he saw no reason not to publish the article. The first official Soviet reaction came from L. Ilyichev, who defined the article as anti-Soviet in his interview with T. Petran (Doc. 16). As a result, the editorial board sent a letter to

Ilyichev demanding clarification of his statement within one month, after which they would publish an open letter in the newspaper. Smolar claims that both senior military circles in the USSR and A. Mikoyan expressed the view that there was nothing wrong with the article. However, writes the author, it seems that certain Soviet and Polish circles never forgave him for his 'amplification' of Khrushchev's secret speech with public 'additions' of specifically Jewish content; see n. 77.

70 The 20th Congress of the Communist Party of the Soviet Union was held in Moscow from 10 to 25 February 1956. Stalin's policies were subjected to devastating criticism at this Congress in the secret speech delivered by N. Khrushchev. In the West, the speech was published for the first time in 1956; see *The Anti-Stalin Campaign and International Communism*.

71 In June 1919 the First Kiev Reserve Communist Regiment, which included a special Komsomol unit, and the Shulyavka Workers' Battalion were sent to fight Ataman Zeleny's bands operating in Denikin's service in the area around the small town of Tripolye, 50 km from Kiev. Zeleny was defeated after a three-day battle, after which the Red Army unit took up holding positions. Betrayed by a Red Army commander, the unit was suddenly attacked by Zeleny's forces and all but six were killed. The Communists' last stand was led by M. Sheinin and M. Rotmansky.

The 'Tripolye Tragedy' was the subject of L. Pervomaisky's poem 'Trypilska tragediya' (1929); see L. Pervomaisky, *Tvory* (Works), Kiev, Dnipro, 1969, vol. 2, pp. 151–64.

72 On Petlyura, see Chapter 6, n. 74.

73 Stanislav Nikodimovich Bulak-Balakhovich (1883–1940), Russian general. Bulak-Balakhovich volunteered to serve in the Russian army in World War I. In 1918, he joined the Red Army, but in the same year went over to the White forces which were fighting against the Soviet regime. From 1919 to 1920, he headed army units grouped in Poland to fight the Red Army in Belorussia and the Ukraine. These units also carried out pogroms against the Jewish population. In 1940, Bulak-Balakhovich was assassinated in Poland by an unknown assailant.

74 Binyamin Zuskin (1899–1952), Yiddish actor, was born in Panevežys in Lithuania. In 1921, he entered the studio of the State Yiddish Chamber Theatre (later the State Yiddish Theatre) and, within three months, was incorporated into the theatre troupe. Zuskin's most famous roles were Senderl in *The Travels of Benjamin the Third* (1927); the Fool in *King Lear* (1935); Hotsmakh in *Wandering Stars* (1940); the *batkhn* in *Freylekhs* (1945); and the partisan Lyakhovich in *The Sighing of the Forests* (1947). Zuskin also acted in a number of films on Jewish themes. From 1948 he was artistic director of the State Yiddish Theatre. He was arrested in 1949 and executed together with the Yiddish writers on 12 August 1952.

75 Yitskhak Nusinov (1889–1950), Yiddish and Russian literary critic.

76 Shmuel Persov (1889–1952), Yiddish writer, was born in the small town of Pochep in the present Bryansk Province, RSFSR.

77 Leonid Ilyichev's remark to Tabitha Petran, that the *Folks-shtime* article was 'slanderous and anti-Soviet' (see Doc. 16), prompted a reply in the form of an open letter from the editors of *Folks-shtime* in the issue of 3 November 1956. This letter appeared after the editorial board had written to Ilyichev privately, asking him to clarify his statement to the *National Guardian* reporter. Among other things, the editors challenged Ilyichev to disprove their assertions that administrative steps were taken to close down Soviet Jewish schools in the years 1937–8; that, in 1948–9, all Jewish communal and cultural institutions were destroyed without exception; and that there was open aggravation of anti-Semitic feelings with the publication of such *feuilletons* as 'Pinya from Zhmerinka' (see Doc. 49).

78 On Solomon Mikhoels, see Docs. 104–6.

79 Fefer's and Mikhoels's journey to the USA is discussed in the first part of Chapter 7.

80 Vladimir Georgievich Dekanozov (1898–1953), senior official at the Soviet Ministries of Internal and Foreign Affairs. Dekanozov was one of Beria's close
collaborators. During the period of Soviet–German friendship, he served as special
envoy in Berlin. He was a member of the Central Committee from 1941.
Dekanozov was dismissed from his post of Minister of the Interior of the Georgian
Republic in June 1953 and was sentenced to death together with Beria on 23
December 1953.

81 On Solomon Lozovsky see Chapter 9, n. 39 and Doc. 141.

82 This is a mistake on the part of the author. The reference, it seems, is to the Soviet
diplomat of Jewish origin Boris Efimovich Shtein (1892–1961), the Soviet ambassador to Italy from 1934 to 1939. Shtein was one of the few senior members of the
diplomatic corps who remained in the service after World War II and up to 1952.
He served with the Soviet delegation to the UN, where he took part in the debates on
the Palestine issue.

83 Wanda Wasilewska (1905–64), writer and political activist, was born in Cracow.
She was active in the Polish Socialist Party. She lived in the Soviet Union from 1939.
During World War II, she was a member of the Polish Patriots' Union. In 1945, she
married the Ukrainian writer Korneichuk and moved to Kiev.

84 Henryk Erlich (1882–1941), journalist and Bundist leader in Poland, was born into
a well-to-do family in Lublin. He received a Jewish education at home. Erlich joined
the Bund in 1903, when he was a student at the University of Warsaw. He
graduated from the law faculty of St Petersburg University. He was arrested several
times. During the 1917 October Revolution, Erlich played an important role in the
Petrograd Soviet. He returned to Poland in 1918, where he became active in the
Bund. Erlich edited the central organ of the Polish Bund, *Di folkstsaytung*. Following
the German invasion of Poland in September 1939, he made his way to the Soviet
Union, where he was arrested and sentenced to death for subversive activity and
spying. The sentence, however, was commuted to ten years' imprisonment. He was
released in September 1941, following the amnesty which was declared for Polish
citizens in the same month. The Soviet authorities suggested to Erlich and Victor
Alter that they set up a Jewish Anti-Fascist Committee; they agreed and set about
implementing the programme, but they were re-arrested on 4 December 1941 in
Kuibyshev and executed.

85 Victor Alter (1890–1941), Bundist leader in Poland, was born into a well-to-do
Hasidic family in Mlawa. He graduated from a technical college in Lodz in 1910,
began working as an engineer, and joined the Bund in Warsaw in 1912. Between the
two world wars, Alter was one of the leaders of the Bund and the trade-union
movement. He was also a delegate to the Warsaw City Council. He fled from Poland
to the Soviet Union in September 1939, where he was arrested with Erlich, released,
re-arrested and executed on 4 December 1941.

86 Ilya Erenburg's letter to the editors of the reputable French newspaper *Le Monde*, in
reply to Bernard Turner's accusations, is an interesting and an important document. This was apparently one of the few occasions that a Soviet citizen addressed
himself to a Western newspaper on a personal matter without official
encouragement.

87 Erenburg has in mind here the Yiddish journal *Di goldene keyt*.

88 Erenburg denies Turner's claim again in his memoirs, where he writes: 'Several
years later, a journalist in Israel came out with some sensational disclosures. He
said that while in prison he had met the poet Fefer who, he alleged, told him that I
was responsible for the arrest of the Jewish writers. This calumny was taken up by
several Western papers. Their single-minded line of reason was: "He has survived,
so he must be a traitor."' See I. Erenburg, *Post-War Years 1945–1954*, Cleveland–
New York, The World Publishing Company, 1967, p. 133.

89 Howard Melvin Fast (pseudonym of Walter Ericson, 1914–), American writer of historical novels, was born of Jewish parents in New York. From 1943 to 1956, he was an active Communist, and in 1953, he was awarded a Stalin Peace Prize. After Khrushchev's revelations at the 20th Party Congress, Fast left the Party. Until he took this step his works had been well received in the Soviet Union.

Fast wrote a number of works on Jewish themes: *Haym Salomon: Son of Liberty* (1941), *Romance of a People* (1941), *Picture-Book History of the Jews* (1942), *My Glorious Brothers* (1948), *Moses, Prince of Egypt* (1958). *Romance of a People*, written during the war, and *My Glorious Brothers*, written at the time of the establishment of the State of Israel and dealing with the Maccabean struggle for independence, were not published or commented upon in the USSR. See also H. Fast, 'A Matter of Validity', *Midstream*, 1958, no. 2, a reply to Gribachev's attack on Fast in *Literaturnaya gazeta* (February 1958).

90 Boris Nikolaevich Polevoi (pseudonym of Kampov; 1908–), Soviet Russian (non-Jewish) writer who was closely involved in his various positions in Soviet Jewish affairs. As editor of the liberal journal, *Yunost*, Polevoi published works on Jewish themes, in particular A. Kuznetsov's documentary novel, *Babi Yar*. Polevoi himself wrote about the Holocaust in *We Are Soviet People* (see the extract in Doc. 151) as well as in his novel, *Doctor Vera*.

91 The reference is to the novel by Vladimir Dudintsev (1918–), *Ne khlebom edinym* (Not By Bread Alone), which created a furor when it was published in the Soviet Union in 1956 because of the author's harsh criticism of the period of Stalin's rule.

92 Frol Kozlov, who was one of the most prominent leaders of the Communist Party during the Khrushchev era, was at this time Second Party Secretary of Leningrad City. In his article, published in the central ideological organ of the Party, *Kommunist*, one can discern the first sign of the direction that the arrests and trials being prepared by Stalin were to take in the next few months.

93 Laszlo Rajk (1909–49), Hungarian Communist Party leader, sentenced to death in a show trial and executed in 1949. In contrast to the trial in Bulgaria, Zionism was implicated at this trial, in which three of the leading figures among the accused were of Jewish origin. Rajk was rehabilitated in 1956.

94 Traichko Dzhunev Kostov (1897–1949), Bulgarian Communist Party leader sentenced to death for Titoism in 1949 in one of the first show trials in Eastern Europe. Kostov was rehabilitated posthumously in 1956.

95 Rudolf Slansky (1901–52), Czechoslovak Communist Party leader, of Jewish birth, sentenced to death in 1952.

96 V. I. Lenin, *Collected Works*, vol. 31, p. 46.

97 On Vovsi, see Chapter 4, n. 154. The Jews among the accused were M. S. Vovsi, M. B. Kogan, B. B. Kogan, A. I. Feldman. Ya. G. Etinger and A. M. Grinshtein.

98 Boris Shimelovich was the Director of the large Botkin Hospital in Moscow for many years. He was an active member of the Jewish Anti-Fascist Committee during and after the war.

99 Of the six doctors who did not appear in the Tass announcement of 13 January 1953, it seems that only one – N. A. Shereshevsky – was Jewish. It is worth pointing out that only nine doctors were named in the January list of whom six were Jewish.

100 Article 4, Paragraph 5 of the RSFSR Criminal Procedure Code states: '(5) In the absence, in the actions ascribed to the accused, of the elements of a crime ... criminal proceedings may not be initiated, and, if initiated, shall not be continued, but shall be terminated whatever the stage of the trial ...'

101 Khrushchev discusses the 'Doctors' Plot' in his memoirs, *Khrushchev Remembers*, pp. 283–7. A note appeared in *Pravda* on 1 August 1962, in which reference was made to a discussion in the Central Committee of the Communist Party on the

advisability of using or banning a particular medical preparation. The Central Committee's stand was that: 'The Party Central Committee does not consider it possible to assume the role of arbiter in the approval of methods of treatment. Only medical scientists can determine whether the use of one or another method of treating illness is correct. Attempts to administer science by injunction can come to no good, and it is common knowledge that in the not too distant past such attempts led to undeserved accusations against, and the discrediting of, certain prominent scientists and doctors in our country (the "Doctors' Plot").' This was one of the very few occasions when the subject of the 'Doctors' Plot' was officially recalled in later years.

102 The Jew accused in this trial was A. Shtulman.
103 The Jews accused in this trial were B. Oizerman, A. Kaplun, L. Levit, Ya. Dolgopolsky, S. Shapiro, S. Markovich and B. Khaikin.
104 All the accused in this trial were Jewish.
105 Gedaliyahu Pechersky (1901–75), was born into a tanner's family in the small town of Babinovichi, Vitebsk Province. He attended a *ḥeder*. After the Revolution, he tried to join a *hakhsharah* (training) farm near Vitebsk and the *Tiferet baḥurim* Society founded by the *Ḥabad* (Hasidic) movement. At the end of the NEP period, he was arrested for avoiding payment of taxes. He studied to be a dental technician and worked in this profession. Pechersky began to take an interest in public affairs during World War II. Even during Stalin's lifetime, he sent unsigned letters to the authorities concerning the religious community of Leningrad. He was appointed *gabai* (synagogue official) in 1954, a post which he decided to leave in 1956 as a result of pressure from those in charge of religious matters in the city. Pechersky emigrated to Israel in 1972.

6. The Soviet regime and Zionism

1 To date, three doctoral dissertations have been written on the subject of Soviet–Israeli relations: Allen, 'The Policy of the USSR towards the State of Israel'; Ro'i, 'Yaḥasei brit ha-moaẓot-yisrael, 1947–1954' (see, too, his *Soviet Decision Making in Practice*); Krammer, *The Forgotten Friendship*. See also P. Brod, *Die Antizionismus und Israel politik der UdSSR: Voraussetzungen und Entwicklung bis 1956*, Baden-Baden, Nomos, 1980; Laqueur, *The Struggle for the Middle East*, pp. 43–63; Dagan, *Moscow and Jerusalem*; Namir, *Shliḥut be-moskvah*. On the situation of Zionism in the USSR in the 1920s, see Goldman, *Zionism Under Soviet Rule*; A. Tsentsiper, *Eser shnot redifot* (Ten Years of Persecution), Tel Aviv, 1930; J. B. Schechtman, 'The USSR, Zionism and Israel' in Kochan (ed.), *The Jews in Soviet Russia Since 1917*, pp. 99–124.
2 The territorial expansion of the years 1939–40 brought with it the addition of about 23 million persons of various nationalities, among them some two million Jews, to the population of the Soviet Union. According to one estimate, 1,692,000 persons out of a total of 12.5 million – i.e. over 13% – were exiled from regions formerly belonging to Poland. To the extent that the rate of exile among Jews was similar to that among the population as a whole, some 163,000 Jews (13% of 1,250,000) would have been exiled from Poland to forced labour camps or to particularly harsh areas of the USSR, and another 70,000 from the other territories – a total of some 233,000. The exiled Jews included, in addition to Zionists and Bundists, also members of the 'bourgeoisie' and the intelligentsia who were not always members of parties; see P. Barton, *L'Institution concentrationnaire en Russie 1930–1957* (The Institution of Concentration Camps in Russia 1930–1957), Paris, Plon, 1959, pp. 108–9. According to Schechtman's estimate, some 400,000 Jews were exiled in the years 1939–41; see Schechtman, *Zionism and Zionists in Soviet Russia*, p. 113.

3 Reports on the various meetings are to be found in the following Israeli archives: the Zionist Archive in Jerusalem, the Weizmann Archive in Rehovot, the *Avodah* Archive in Tel Aviv, the *Iḥud ha-kvuẓot ve-ha-kibbuẓim* Archive; and in private collections of persons who actively participated in these meetings. See also *Yediyot, alon liga 'V'* ('V' League News Bulletin); *Sbornik* (Collection), Jerusalem, 1943; A. Kohen, *Im ambulansim le-Teheran* (With Ambulances to Teheran), Merhaviah, Ha-kibuẓ ha-arẓi ha-shomer ha-ẓair, 1943.

4 See Ro'i, 'Yaḥasei brit ha-moaẓot-yisrael', p. 43.

5 Roosevelt told Stephen Wise in March 1945 that 'The Big Three agreed on handing over Palestine to the Jews. As far as the immediate future is concerned Jewish immigration will be continued' (see Weizmann Archive, 18 March 1945).

6 *Jewish Chronicle*, 23 February 1945, as quoted in Ro'i, 'Yaḥasei brit ha-moaẓot-yisrael', p. 46. On a meeting of members of the *Histadrut* delegation with the Soviet delegation member M. Tarasov, see *Palkor*, 1945, no. 51, pp. 2–3.

7 Although the consent of the Soviet authorities was apparently necessary here, one cannot ignore the influence which the governments of Poland, Czechoslovakia and Romania still had in this period in everything concerning their internal affairs. And, because of the material difficulties and the political and social complications involved in absorbing the refugees, these governments were undoubtedly interested in permitting displaced persons to leave.

8 K. Serezhin, 'Problemy arabskogo vostoka', *Novoe vremya*, 1946, no. 3, p. 15.

9 In another article written two months later, Serezhin stressed again that the solution was to be found not in emigration to Palestine but in restoring the uprooted Jews to normal lives. See Serezhin, *Novoe vremya*, 1946, no. 11, pp. 14–17.

10 K. Serezhin, 'Sovremennaya Palestina', *Novoe vremya*, 1946, no. 15, p. 21. It is interesting that Serezhin employed a phrase which was habitual during much of the fifties and sixties when he noted that Tel Aviv was a product of capitalist Jewish emigration and was therefore pictured by the Zionists as their 'paradise'; *ibid.*, p. 19.

11 V. Lutsky, *Palestinskaya problema* (The Palestinian Problem), Moscow, Pravda, 1946.

12 *Ibid.*, p. 29.

13 Ro'i, 'Yaḥasei brit ha-moaẓot-yisrael', p. 86.

14 A. Gromyko (14 May 1947): 'During the last war, the Jewish people underwent exceptional sorrow and suffering. Without any exaggeration, this sorrow and suffering are indescribable. It is difficult to express them in dry statistics on the Jewish victims of the Fascist aggressors. The Jews in territories where the Hitlerites held sway were subjected to almost complete physical annihilation. The total number of members of the Jewish population who perished at the hands of the Nazi executioners is estimated at approximately six million. Only about a million and a half Jews in Western Europe survived the war.

'But these figures, although they give an idea of the number of victims of the Fascist aggressors among the Jewish people, give no idea of the difficulties in which large numbers of Jewish people found themselves after the war.

'Large numbers of the surviving Jews of Europe were deprived of their countries, their homes and their means of existence. Hundreds of thousands of Jews are wandering about in various countries of Europe in search of means of existence and in search of shelter. A large number of them are in camps for displaced persons and are still continuing to undergo great privations. To these privations our attention was drawn in particular by the representative of the Jewish Agency, whom we heard in the First Committee.' (General Assembly, 1st Special Session, 77 Plenary Meeting, vol. 1, p. 132.)

S. Tsarapkin (13 October 1947): 'The essence of the question was the right of self-determination of hundreds of thousands of Jews and Arabs living in Palestine; the right of the Arabs as well as of the Jews of Palestine to live in freedom and peace in a state of their own. It was necessary to take into consideration all the sufferings and needs of the Jewish people whom none of the states of Western Europe had been able to help during their struggle against the Hitlerites and the allies of the Hitlerites for the defence of their rights and their existence.

'The Jewish people were therefore striving to create a state of their own and it would be unjust to deny them that right. The problem was urgent and could not be avoided by plunging back into the darkness of the ages.

'Every people – and that included the Jewish people – had full right to demand that their fate should not depend on the mercy or the good will of a particular state. The Members of the United Nations could help the Jewish people by acting in accordance with the principles of the Charter, which called for the guaranteeing to every people of their right to independence and self-determination.' (General Assembly, 2nd Session, Ad Hoc Committee on the Palestine Question, pp. 69–70.)

15 These apprehensions increased sharply following Harry Truman's speech of 11 March 1947.

16 For example, the vote in favour of partition on 29 November 1947, the opposition to the trusteeship plan proposed by the United States in March 1948, the *de jure* recognition of Israel immediately upon its establishment, the opposition to the Bernadotte programme and the opposition to the Arab states' annexation of territories in Palestine.

17 The terms employed by the Soviet representatives at the UN and by the Soviet press were: the legitimate aspiration of the Jewish people to establish an independent state in Palestine, to which it has been tied since ancient times (Gromyko's speech in the Political Committee of the General Assembly, *Izvestiya*, 23 April 1948), the legitimate right of the Jewish and Arab populations to establish their own states (*Pravda*, 29 May 1948), the right of all nations to self-determination, and the like.

18 V. Lutsky, *Angliisky i amerikansky imperializm na blizhnem vostoke* (Anglo-American Imperialism in the Middle East), Moscow, Pravda, 1948, pp. 24, 26.

19 A. Kanunnikov, 'Kto vinovat v palestinskoi tragedii', *Novoe vremya*, 1948, no. 37, pp. 29–31. It is interesting to note that, four months previously, the same commentator had written in quite a different manner; see *Novoe vremya*, 1948, no. 22, pp. 8–10.

20 See the pamphlet by I. Genin, *Palestinskaya problema* (The Palestinian Problem), Moscow, Pravda, 1948. And see also other attacks on Zionism at the end of 1948: *New Times*, 1948, no. 51, p. 16; P. Osipova in *Voprosy istorii*, 1948, no. 12.

21 See *Eynikeyt*, 20 May 1948.

22 See Fefer in *Eynikeyt*, 19 June 1947; 26 February, 19 June and 16 November 1948; Bergelson, *ibid.*, 11 December 1947; Hindes, *ibid.*, 1 November 1947, 30 March 1948; Mindlin, *ibid.*, 18 November 1948.

23 'The current reactionary position of the Joint', wrote Fefer, 'is no novelty for us. We still remember how the Joint supported the reactionary organisations during the war ... The match between the Joint and the angels of Marshall is not accidental'; see *Eynikeyt*, 26 February 1948. It is worth recalling that in the period of the campaign against Zionism in the Soviet Union and Eastern Europe the Joint was to become the target of virulent vituperations.

24 See G. Mindlin's article, referred to in n. 22, and that by the editor of *Eynikeyt*, G. Zhitz, in *Eynikeyt*, 19 October 1948.

25 For a detailed description of these demonstrations, see Namir, *Shlihut be-moskvah*, and *Jewish Chronicle*, 8 and 28 October 1948.

26 See his speech in the symposium, held in Moscow at the Institutes for Economics and Pacific Ocean Studies attached to the Academy of Sciences of the Soviet Union, on the subject of the struggle for national liberation in the colonies and

semi-colonies; *Voprosy ekonomiki*, 1949, no. 10, pp. 83–7. Two of the participants in the symposium published very sharp articles against Zionism in early 1953: Mark Mitin, a member of the Academy of Sciences, a Jew (Doc. 89), and V. Minaev, 'Sionistskaya agentura amerikanskoi razvedki', *Novoe vremya*, 1953, no. 4, pp. 13–16. Articles harshly attacking the Joint are to be found in *Pravda Ukrainy*, 11 February 1953; *Trud*, 15 February 1953; *Literaturnaya gazeta*, 24 February 1953; *Meditsinsky rabotnik*, 3 March 1953.

27 'Panislamskie plany vsemirnogo khalifata', *Novoe vremya*, 1949, no. 44, pp. 30–2.

28 'Ocherednie zadachi istorikov vostokovedov', *Voprosy istorii*, 1950, no. 12, p. 5. On the Comintern's resolutions on this matter, see Jane Degras (ed.), *The Communist International 1919–1943*, London, Oxford University Press, 1956, vol. 1, pp. 143–4, 365–6, 385; vol. 2, p. 183; vol. 3, pp. 76–84.

29 On the 'chauvinistic ideology of Zionism', see Doc. 89. For a sharp attack on *Mapai*, and particularly on the editor of *Be-terem*, Levenstein (Livne), for his criticism of the USSR, see *Novoe vremya*, 1950, no. 17, pp. 29–30.

30 See Chapter 5. On the declaration that the diplomat Kubovi was *persona non grata* in Czechoslovakia and Poland, see *Pravda*, 9 December 1952; *Novoe vremya*, 1952, no. 51, p. 32.

31 See especially Anna Lungu, 'V Izraile', *Literaturnaya gazeta*, 22 July 1951; P. Khazov, 'Poezdka v Izrail', *Novoe vremya*, 1951, no. 35, pp. 22–5; A. Leonidov, 'Anglo-amerikansky duel v Izraile', *Novoe vremya*, 1951, no. 47, pp. 22–7.

32 For a description of these negotiations, which were conducted in Bulgaria between the Israeli envoy, Dr Ben Zion Razin, and the Soviet Ambassador to Bulgaria, M. Bodrov, see *Ma'ariv*, 10 March 1972, pp. 21–2.

33 Ro'i, 'Yaḥasei brit ha-moaẓot-yisrael', p. 521.

34 E. Palmor, 'Yaḥasei brit ha-moaẓot-yisrael', *Beḥinot*, 1970, no. 1, p. 98; *Jewish Chronicle*, 18 September, 2 October, 6 and 20 November 1953.

35 In 1955, the Western press (including *The New York Times*) reported that the Soviet Union would demand a ransom of $3,000 for every emigrant, but the USSR denied this; see *Ha'arez*, 2 March 1955. Later on, of course, this idea was implemented.

36 On 22 January 1954. On the Soviet pro-Arab positions in UN institutions during this period, see *Izvestiya*, 24 January 1954.

37 On the announcement of the president of Egypt regarding this deal, and on official Soviet support for it, see *Pravda*, 2 October 1955.

38 *Pravda*, 30 December 1955. See also Khrushchev's view on Israeli–Arab relations and on the place of the Western powers in this issue in the talks he and other Soviet leaders held with the leaders of the delegation of the French Socialist Party in 1956; see Doc. 13.

39 Articles dealing with the State of Israel generally made almost no mention of Zionism; see, for example, the descriptions of visits to Israel of representatives of Soviet delegations: *Novoe vremya*, 1954, no. 23, pp. 27–9; *ibid.*, 1956, no. 30, pp. 24–6. Exceptional in this regard is the article in the same periodical – in reply to a question on the reasons for the Arab–Israeli conflict – which spoke of the close ties between the United States and the reactionary Zionist leaders ever since the establishment of the State of Israel; see *Novoe vremya*, 1956, no. 5, pp. 30–2.

40 *Pravda*, 6 November 1956.

41 *Pravda*, 8 and 11 November 1956.

42 See *Novoe vremya*, 1956, no. 45, pp. 15–16; 1956, no. 46, pp. 5, 8; *Mezhdunarodnaya zhizn*, 1956, no. 12, pp. 3–11; E. Lebedev and G. Mirsky, *Suetsky kanal* (The Suez Canal), Moscow, Znanie, 1956, pp. 30–3; E. Lebedev, *Iordaniya v borbe za nezavisimost* (Jordan in the Struggle for Independence), Moscow, Gospolitizdat, 1956, pp. 118–23.

43 B. Strelnikov, *Pravda*, 4 March 1957.

44 See, for example, *Jewish Chronicle*, 5 and 19 April 1957.
45 On the festival and the excitement it aroused among Soviet Jews who had long been virtually cut off from Israel and world Jewry, see Doc. 90 and *Jewish Chronicle*, 2 and 16 August 1957; 13 September 1957. See also the letter from a Soviet Jew to the Yiddish newspaper in New York, *Forverts*, 20 September 1957, as quoted in Fejtö, *Les Juifs et l'antisémitisme dans les pays communistes*, pp. 224–9.
46 The Soviet security services coaxed and threatened Hazan in order to persuade him to cooperate with them. Following this episode, he was compelled to return immediately to Israel. See *Jewish Chronicle*, 20 and 27 September 1957.
47 *Pravda*, 22 September 1957.
48 See K. Ivanov, *Mezhdunarodnaya zhizn*, 1957, no. 12, pp. 52–62.
49 See Khrushchev's remarks to French journalist Serge Groussard in 1958 (Doc. 17) and those made at his appearance in Vienna in July 1960 (Doc. 24).
50 See, for example, Doc. 22, and *Pravda*, 2 March 1959.
51 The first book on the State of Israel, by Ivanov and Sheinis, was published in 100,000 copies in 1958. After it had been favourably received – though it was also criticised for its 'moderation' – a second edition with 'corrections and additions' appeared in 50,000 copies in 1959; see K. Ivanov and Z. Sheinis, *Gosudarstvo Izrail i ego polozhenie i politika*. During the years 1959–64, seven books were published on Israel and Zionism alone. A number of additonal books, which dealt with the Jewish religion, devoted considerable space to attacks on Zionism and Israel; see Pinkus, Greenbaum & Altshuler (eds.), *Pirsumim rusiim al yehudim*, nos. 77, 99, 352, 406, 418, 419.
52 Ivanov and Sheinis, *Gosudarstvo Izrail*, p. 21; A. Leonidev in *Sovremenny vostok*, 1957, no. 5, pp. 17–19.
53 G. Drambiants in *Novy mir*, 1958, no. 5, pp. 267–9.
54 See, for example, A. Gorev, 'Mif ob izrailskom sotsializme', *Sovremenny vostok*, 1959, no. 8, pp. 11–14; B. Prakhye, *Pravda o 'zemle obetovannoi'* (The Truth About the 'Promised Land'), Odessa, Odesskoe Knizhnoe izdatelstvo, 1961, p. 6.
55 For the cooperation between Zionism, the heads of the Gestapo and the SS, the authority is the Kasztner–Gruenwald trial, and later the Eichmann trial. Kasztner himself was allegedly murdered by Israeli intelligence agents to prevent the crimes committed by Zionist leaders from being revealed; see Ivanov and Sheinis, *Gosudarstvo Izrail*, p. 134, and Doc. 92. Another book, by Zyskin, stated that Israel knew Eichmann's hiding place as early as 1953, but did nothing to arrest the executioner of the Jews. Again, he alleged, the Zionist, Arlosoroff, in the 1930s had brought about the termination of the Jewish boycott against Nazi Germany; see G. Zyskin, *Yudaizm i sionizm komu i kak oni sluzhat* (Judaism and Zionism: Whom Do They Serve and How), Kuibyshev, Kuibyshevskoe Knizhnoe izdatelstvo, 1963, pp. 44–5.
56 *Ibid.*, p. 43.
57 See F. Mayatsky, *Sovremenny yudaizm i sionizm* (Contemporary Judaism and Zionism), Kishinev, Karta Moldovenyaske, 1964, pp. 53–4.
58 *Trud* published especially virulent articles by N. Erlikh, a Jew; see *Trud*, 16 March 1961; 9 June 1963; 11 March 1964. And see also Pakhman's article in *Trud*, 30 August 1964.
59 For example, *Znamya kommunizma*, 15 April 1960; 14 April 1963; 7 July 1964; *Vecherny Rostov*, 19 June 1964; and *Sovetskaya Latviya*, 24 March 1961.
60 See *Trud*, 26 May 1959.
61 Various press reports lead us to conclude that emigration to Israel was minimal between 1957 and 1964, not exceeding an average of two hundred persons annually. We should, however, stress that the Khrushchev–Gomulka agreement on the emigration of Polish citizens from the Soviet Union resulted in over thirty thousand

persons reaching Israel in the years 1957–60. While there is no doubt that the Soviet authorities knew Polish citizens of Jewish origin would go on from Poland to Israel, the agreement with Gomulka was not based on the question of Soviet Jews. In fact, Khrushchev announced in Vienna (see Doc. 24) that they were definitely not applying for emigration permits. On emigration from the Soviet Union in this period, see Pinkus, 'The Emigration of National Minorities'.

62 Even the article with the extreme heading 'A Gathering of Bankrupts' (on the 26th Zionist Congress) was bare of the anti-Zionist pronouncements and vituperations common in the Stalin and Khrushchev periods; see N. Sorin, 'Sborishche bankrotov', *Literaturnaya gazeta*, 25 February 1965. The emphasis was focused on Zionist leaders being compelled to admit that the Zionist movement was undergoing a severe crisis and even a slow death; see *Vecherny Leningrad*, 13 July 1966, and Doc. 91.

63 Palmor, 'Yaḥasei brit ha-moaẓot-yisrael', p. 106.

64 There is no doubt that the KGB chiefs and extreme anti-Zionist and anti-Israel circles among the leadership attempted to create all manner of provocations in order to cause tension between the Jewish population and the embassy personnel. The most prominent example of this is what happened in Odessa in April 1965; see *Jews in Eastern Europe*, 1965, vol. III, no. 3, pp. 67–71.

65 In early 1967, almost immediately after Kosygin's declaration, anti-Israel and anti-Zionist articles began to appear in which life in Israel was painted in sombre colours in an attempt to frighten off potential emigrants; see, for example, *Sovetskaya Moldaviya*, 18 January 1967; *Sovetskaya Latviya*, 1 February 1967; *Dagestanskaya pravda*, 9 February 1967. Far graver in this respect was Dolnik's trial in February 1967 for Zionism, collaboration with the Israeli Embassy and espionage; see *Izvestiya*, 24 February 1967, and Chapter 5 of this work.

66 One of the best examples of this propaganda campaign is Ivanov's article in *Komsomolskaya pravda*, 26 December 1967; from 1967 until the present, this writer has been distinguished by the exceptional severity of his attacks on Israel and Zionism. On the campaign after 1967, see J. Frankel, 'The Anti-Zionist Press Campaigns in the USSR, 1969–1971: An Internal Dialogue?', *Soviet Jewish Affairs*, 1972, no. 3, pp. 3–26.

67 Evgeny Mikhailovich Zhukov (1907–), historian and expert on Japanese affairs. From 1943 to 1950, he was Director of the Pacific Institute. Since 1957, he has been a member of the USSR Academy of Sciences.

68 Vladimir Borisovich Lutsky (1906–62), orientalist and expert on the Arab countries, lived in Palestine in the 1920s. He graduated from the Oriental Institute of Moscow University in 1930. From 1932, he was a senior research worker in the institutes of the Soviet Academy of Sciences. In his works on Lebanon, Syria and Egypt Lutsky maintained a negative attitude towards Israel and Zionism. A stenographic report of his public lecture on the Palestine problem was published in 1946; *Palestinskaya problema* (The Palestinian Problem), Moscow, Pravda, 1946.

69 On M. Mitin, see Chapter 2, n. 35. This article also appeared in *Komsomolskaya pravda*, 24 February 1953.

70 Theodor Herzl (1860–1904), writer and journalist; the founder of political Zionism and of the World Zionist movement.

71 The first meeting between Herzl and Kaiser Wilhelm II took place in Constantinople on 18 October 1898; the second official meeting took place in Jerusalem on 2 November 1898. However, both these meetings were disappointing to Herzl as they failed to yield any practical results.

72 The meeting between Herzl and the Sultan of Turkey took place on 17 May 1901. In 1902, Herzl was again invited to the Turkish capital, but he did not meet with the Sultan.

73 The meeting between Herzl and Joseph Chamberlain, the British Colonial Secretary, took place on 22 October 1902. The question of Jewish settlement in Cyprus was discussed in these talks; however, the British Colonial Secretary rejected Herzl's proposal and expressed his positive attitude to Jewish colonisation of the Sinai Peninsula.

74 Simon Petlyura (1879–1926), leader of the Ukrainian national movement, was active in the Ukrainian Social-Democratic Workers' Party. In 1919, he was the Ukrainian Prime Minister and supreme commander of the armed forces. His armies were responsible for the pogroms against the Jews occurring in the Ukraine in the years 1919–20. The agreement between Jabotinsky and Petlyura on the setting up of Jewish defence forces, in the event that an independent Ukrainian state be established again, was concluded in the summer of 1921. Petlyura was shot in Paris by the Ukrainian Jew Shalom Schwarzbard on 26 May 1926.

75 Josef Pilsudski (1867–1935) was one of the founders of independent Poland after World War I and its first head of state.

76 Benito Mussolini (1883–1945), founder of Italian Fascism and Italian leader from 1922 to 1945. Mussolini, who met Chaim Weizmann a number of times, maintained an ambivalent attitude towards the Zionist movement.

77 Franz von Papen (1879–1969), German statesman, Deputy Prime Minister from 1934 to 1938 and Nazi Germany's ambassador to Turkey from 1939 to 1944. He was tried at Nuremberg and acquitted.

78 Dr Chaim Weizmann (1874–1952), research chemist, Zionist leader and first president of Israel.

79 Robert Szold (1889–1977), American jurist and life-long active Zionist.

80 Tibor Szönyi, leader of the war-time Communist exiles in Switzerland, was sentenced to death together with Rajk, after 'admitting' that he had spied 'together with Zionist agents' for American intelligence in Switzerland.

81 Henry Morgenthau Jr (1891–1967), agricultural expert and US Secretary of the Treasury.

82 A bomb exploded in the courtyard of the Soviet Legation in Tel Aviv on 19 February 1953 (at the time of the 'Doctors' Plot') wounding four of the staff. Despite prompt apologies from the Israeli government, the Soviet Union immediately broke off diplomatic relations with Israel.

83 On the 'Doctors' Plot', see Chapter 5.

84 Andrei Aleksandrovich Zhdanov (1896–1948), member of the Soviet Communist Party's Politburo and one of Stalin's closest associates.

85 Aleksandr Sergeevich Shcherbakov (1901–45), Soviet political activist.

86 M. Sneh, 'Ḥaslanei ha-raayon mul ḥaslanei ha-irgun' (Negators of the Idea Versus Negators of the Organisation), *Kol ha-am*, 23 December 1960. The quotation in full reads as follows: 'The roots of the crisis do not lie in passing external circumstances, nor in a certain amount of distortion committed by this or that person or some institution or other, whether unintentionally or wilfully, but in the very essence of Zionism; *the idea has disappointed, thus the movement is paralysed, and the organisation has become emptied of meaning.*'

87 Nahum Goldmann (1895–1982), Zionist leader. In 1960, Goldmann was Chairman of the first international conference for Soviet Jewry in Paris. His words here, taken from a 'Kol Israel' broadcast marking the centenary of Herzl's birth, are quoted in Sneh's article, *ibid.*

88 Aleksandr Vasilyevich Kolchak (1873–1920), admiral in the Tsarist navy, and one of the leading commanders of the White forces during the Civil War.

89 Anton Ivanovich Denikin (1872–1947), general in the Tsarist army. During the Russian Civil War, 1918–20, Denikin commanded the White Russian forces in Southern Russia.

90 Israel Kasztner (1906–57), journalist, jurist and Zionist leader in Romania and Hungary. In the years 1943–5, Kasztner was Vice-Chairman of the Hungarian Zionist movement. He conducted negotiations with the Germans in the effort to rescue Hungarian Jewry in exchange for goods (*Blut für Ware*). In 1953, Kasztner, now an active member of Mapai and occupying a senior government post in Israel, was accused by Malkiel Gruenwald of having cooperated with the Nazis and of having been instrumental in the extermination of Hungarian Jewry by saving the Nazi officer, Kurt Becher, with his evidence at the Nuremberg trials. The 'Gruenwald–Kasztner' trial, which created a public furore and government crisis, went on throughout the years 1955–8. The High Court acquitted Kasztner posthumously: he had been assassinated on 3 March 1957.

91 Alfred Nossig (1864–1943), writer, sculptor and musician. Nossig was born in Lvov. He was a supporter of Zionism. During World War II, he tried to get Jews out of areas conquered by the Nazis and have them conveyed to Israel. The Germans appointed him a member of the *Judenrat* in the Warsaw Ghetto and the Jewish underground in the ghetto condemned him to death for cooperating with the Nazis.

92 This is a mistake of the author. The reference is not to Moshe Shapira but to Yaakov Shimshon Shapiro, the Minister of Justice in the Eshkol government, while Haim Moshe Shapira, a leader of the National Religious Party, was Minister of the Interior in Eshkol's government.

93 Moshe Kol (1911–), Zionist leader and Israeli politician.

94 Pinhas Lavon (Lubianiker, 1904–76), was Minister of Defence in Moshe Sharett's government from 1954 to 1955. He was compelled to resign from office because of a major scandal involving security operations.

95 Jacob Koppel Javits (1904–) and Abraham A. Ribicoff (1910–), US senators at the time.

96 The organisation of the Jewish War Veterans of the United States of America was founded in 1896 with the aims of maintaining true allegiance to the USA, combating bigotry and fostering the education of ex-servicemen and ex-servicewomen in the ideals and principles of Americanism. Its publication is the *Jewish Veteran*.

97 The writer is presumably referring here to the National Conference on Soviet Jewry (formerly the American Jewish Conference on Soviet Jewry), which was established in 1964 and reorganised in 1971. The National Conference, a coordinating agency for major national Jewish organisations and local community groups in the USA, acts on behalf of Soviet Jewry through public education and social action; it publishes a newsletter and reports, sponsors special programmes and projects and organises public meetings and forums. Its organ is *Outlook*.

7. Jewish culture in the Soviet Union

1 See Shmeruk, 'Ha-tarbut ha-yehudit bi-vrit-ha-moaẓot'.

2 On Soviet policy towards the Hebrew language and Hebrew literature, see Y. Slutsky, 'Pirsumim ivriim bi-vrit ha-moaẓot', in Cohen & Shmeruk (eds.), *Pirsumim yehudiim bi-vrit ha-moaẓot*, pp. 19–54; A. Greenbaum, 'Hebrew Literature in Soviet Russia', *Jewish Social Studies*, 1968, vol. xxx, no. 3, pp. 136–48; Y. A. Gilboa, *Oktobraim ivriim: toldoteha shel ashlayah* (Hebrew Octobrists: The History of an Illusion), Tel Aviv, Tel Aviv University, 1974.

3 See Schulman, *A History of Jewish Education in the Soviet Union*, p. 9. See also H. Lipset, 'Jewish Schools in the Soviet Union, 1917–1941: An Aspect of Soviet Minorities Policy', EdD Thesis, Teachers' College, New York, Columbia University, 1965. Published as *Jewish Schools under Czarism and Communism: A Struggle for Cultural Identity*, New York, Springer, 1976.

4 *Bolshaya sovetskaya entsiklopediya*, vol. SSSR, 1948, p. 1821. In the same period there were no less than thirteen Uzbek schools in the Ukraine, even though that region had a very small Uzbek population.

5 Schulman, *A History of Jewish Education in the Soviet Union*, p. 163.

6 *Jewish Chronicle*, 15 December 1939, as quoted in Redlich, 'The Jews under Soviet Rule During World War II', p. 32.

7 *Ibid.*, p. 35.

8 Schulman, *A History of Jewish Education in the Soviet Union*, p. 163; Lvavi, *Ha-hityashvut ha-yehudit be-birobidzhan*, pp. 264–73; Emiot, *Der birobidzhaner inyen*, pp. 9–10; *Eynikeyt*, 20 March 1948.

9 Lvavi, *Ha-hityashvut ha-yehudit be-birobidzhan*, pp. 270, 272, 277.

10 *Eynikeyt*, 24 April 1945.

11 H. Osherovich in *Eynikeyt*, 18 March 1948.

12 The last report on the opening of a new academic year at this school appeared in *Eynikeyt*, 7 September 1948. According to information received from a former principal of this school who emigrated to Israel, it still existed in 1950.

13 *Eynikeyt*, 31 January 1948.

14 For example, Polish schools in Lithuania, Polish and Hungarian schools in the Ukraine, German schools in Kazakhstan and in other republics, etc.

15 This Institute had only twenty-one graduates until 1933. See Lipset, in *Beḥinot*, 1970, no. 1, p. 65.

16 On the central place of the *Evsektsiya* in the fostering of the Jewish educational network in the Soviet Union, see Gitelman, *Jewish Nationality and Soviet Politics*, pp. 335–55; Altshuler, *Ha-yevsektsiah bi-vrit ha-moazot*.

17 An additional factor affecting the possible renewal of Yiddish-language education in the USSR is the opposition of some Jewish Zionist youth to this language. They opposed, on principle and not merely for tactical reasons, the renewal of Jewish culture in its Yiddish and *Evsektsiya* format. See Doc. 15.

18 On the development of Yiddish literature in the Soviet Union, see Ch. Shmeruk, 'Yiddish Literature in the USSR', in Kochan (ed.), *The Jews in Soviet Russia Since 1917*, pp. 232–68; N. Mayzel, *Dos yidishe shafn un der yidisher shrayber in sovetnfarband* (Jewish Creative Activity and the Jewish Writer in the Soviet Union), New York, YKUF Farlag, 1959; Yanasovich, *Mit yidishe shrayber in rusland*.

19 Ch. Shmeruk, 'Introduction', in Cohen & Shmeruk (eds.), *Pirsumim yehudiim bi-vrit ha-moazot*, p. 66. A further factor which reduced Yiddish publications in this period was the authorities' tendency to support translation of Yiddish works into Russian, Ukrainian and Belorussian, rather than publishing the original; *ibid.*, p. 90.

20 On the Jewish Anti-Fascist Committee, see Redlich, 'The Jewish Anti-Fascist Committee in the Soviet Union', *Jewish Social Studies*, 1969, no. 1, pp. 25–36; Y. Litvak, 'Ha-vaad ha-yehudi ha-antifashisti', *Gesher*, 1966, no. 2–3, pp. 218–32; Gilboa, *The Black Years of Soviet Jewry*, pp. 42–86.

21 The Slavic Committee occupied an important place among the various committees set up in this year. Established on 10 August 1941, it listed among its ranks not only the Communist refugees and those close to them in the Soviet Union, but wide circles outside the USSR as well. In 1944, an international conference of representatives of the Slavic peoples was convened in London. See E. Pavlovski, 'Pan-Slavism During World War II', unpublished PhD Thesis, Georgetown University, 1968.

22 Shmeruk, 'Introduction', in Cohen & Shmeruk (eds.), *Pirsumim yehudiim bi-vrit ha-moazot*, pp. 97–9.

23 Several books of *belles-lettres* were published in editions of 10,000 to 25,000 copies.

24 About 64% of all the books in Yiddish in these years were *belles-lettres*.

25 The total circulation of these three periodicals was 12,000–15,000; Shmeruk, 'Yiddish Literature in the USSR', p. 123; Altshuler, 'Introduction' in Pinkus, Greenbaum & Altshuler (eds.), *Pirsumim rusiim al yehudim*, pp. 73–4.

26 In 1949, a Lithuanian translation of Shalom Aleikhem's *Tevye the Milkman* appeared in Vilnius. In the same year, a Russian translation of a children's book by the poet Yosef Kotlyar was published. In 1951, a pamphlet of children's poems by Z. Telesin appeared, followed in 1952 by two books by Yosef Kotlyar. Thus the entire harvest of translated Russian literature totalled five books in five years. See Altshuler, 'Introduction' in Pinkus, Greenbaum & Altshuler (eds.), *Persumim rusiim al yehudim*, p. 72.

27 See the speech by the literary critic Nahum Oyslender at a meeting of Yiddish writers in Moscow, in which he told of a 'memorandum' on the situation of Jewish culture sent to the Union of Soviet Writers at its demand. See A. Kvaterko in *Folks-shtime*, 27 August 1957.

28 The Yiddish Communist newspaper published in New York; see *Morgn frayheyt*, 20 July 1956, as quoted in the *Institute Annual, 1956*, New York, Institute of Jewish Affairs, 1956, p. 375.

29 In August it was announced in Moscow that the periodical *Heymland* would appear in October; *Naye prese*, 20 August 1956. And see, for example, Doc. 111 and the articles by G. Kenig following his return from a visit to the USSR; *Naye prese*, October 1956. There was also a report that a Jewish periodical was going to appear in Kiev in January 1957; *Morgn frayheyt*, 8 September 1956.

30 See the letter which writer and journalist Boris Polevoi (one of the heads of the Union of Soviet Writers) sent to newspaper editors and writers in 1957; 'Notes on the Political Diary RRS 10002/6', *Radio Free Europe, Research Bulletin*, 1971, no. 35 (2616); *Politichesky dnevnik* (Political Diary), Amsterdam, Fond imeni Gertsena, 1972, pp. 102–5.

31 Literary critic Israel Serebryany said this in his introduction to the bibliographic list prepared in Moscow in November 1956 and published in a Yiddish periodical in France; *Parizer tsaytshrift*, 1956–7, no. 15–16, p. 101.

32 The Yiddish book published in 1959 was *Selected Writings of Shalom Aleikhem*, with an introduction by A. Vergelis.

33 The first issue of the periodical *Sovetish heymland* was published in September 1961 in 25,000 copies; between 1966 and 1967, it appeared in editions of 16,000 copies; from 1968 on, of only 12,000 copies.

34 The seven books included three by classic writers (Shalom Aleikhem, Mendele, Perets) and two by Soviet Yiddish writers. The two socio-political books were (1) a collection devoted to the twenty-fifth anniversary of the declaration of Birobidzhan as an autonomous national region, and (2) a collection of reportage and documentary stories called *This Is How We Live*, which appeared in 1964.

35 There was a decline in the publication of Yiddish books in 1968, when only two books were published, but in 1969, the peak year for such publication in the post-Stalin period, nine books appeared. See the bibliographies by B. Pinkus in *Behinot*, 1970, no. 1, pp. 205–6; 1972, no. 2–3, pp. 190–2.

36 Even if a number of front-ranking writers and poets (such as Shmuel Halkin, Itsik Kipnis, Z. Vendrof) have remained alive, the trauma they underwent during the liquidation of Yiddish culture and the horrors of the Stalinist prisons have prevented them from producing literary works which contribute to the advancement of Yiddish culture in the Soviet Union.

37 Shmeruk, 'Yiddish Literature in the USSR', p.267.

38 On Yiddish publication in the 1960s, see Altshuler, 'Introduction', in Pinkus, Greenbaum & Altshuler (eds.), *Pirsumim rusiim al yehudim*, pp. 79–83.

39 The book *Poets of Israel* appeared in 1963; a volume of the best poems of Alexander Pen and a collection of stories by Israeli writers in 1965; a collection of novellas in 1966; and the best poems of Avi Shaul in 1967.

40 Two German newspapers appeared in 1960, and three in 1967. In 1960, six Polish and five Hungarian newspapers appeared, and in 1967, four Polish and six Hungarian newspapers. Data according to *Pechat SSSR* (Publications of the USSR), Moscow, Vsesoyuznaya knizhnaya palata, 1960, 1967.

Between 1946 and 1959 2,417 German, 1,287 Polish and 719 Hungarian books were published; *Pechat SSSR*, 1960, pp. 46–53. It is true that these books were intended not only for Germans, Poles and Hungarians residing within the USSR, but also for the people of these nations living outside it, while for Yiddish publications this factor of externally directed propaganda is virtually non-existent. But other peoples in the USSR who share the same situation as the Jews do publish a fairly large number of books; for example, the Osetins, who published 1,418 books in this period, the Avars with 548 books and the Khakas with 274.

41 Geographically, these theatres were divided as follows: four in the Russian Republic (in Moscow, the Crimea and Birobidzhan); twelve in the Ukrainian Republic (in the cities of Odessa, Kharkov, Kiev, Vinnitsa, Dnepropetrovsk, Kremenchug, Nikolaev and Kalinindorf); and two in the Belorussian Republic (in Minsk).

42 According to Zinger, there were only ten Jewish theatres in the USSR on 1 January 1939; see Zinger, *Dos banayte folk*, p. 109. According to Mikhoels, there were twenty such theatres before the outbreak of the war; see *Yidishe kultur*, 1943, no. 6–7, p. 66. Still another source lists fourteen Jewish theatres in 1941; see Nusinov in *Eynikeyt*, 8 November 1944; *Yidishe kultur*, 1947, no. 1, p. 31. These differences may derive from the way a permanent theatre is defined (as opposed to a theatre company), or from the desire to underline the existence of Jewish culture in the Soviet Union.

43 The Moscow and Odessa theatres were transferred to Tashkent, the Minsk Theatre to Novosibirsk and the Kiev Theatre to Dzhambul (Kazakhstan). See *Eynikeyt*, 28 October 1947; *Sovetish heymland*, 1966, no. 12, p. 110; *Folks-shtime*, 20 February 1947.

44 The Minsk Theatre returned to its former site in February 1945 by decision of the Council of Ministers of the Belorussian Republic; see *JTA*, 26 February 1945. The Moscow Theatre had already returned to Moscow in September 1943; Macleod, *Actors Cross the Volga*, p. 155. The Kiev Theatre, while it returned to the Ukraine, was now based in Chernovtsy; *Sovetish heymland*, 1966, no. 12, p. 110. The Odessa Theatre was the last to return to its former site by decision of the republic's Council of Ministers; *Eynikeyt*, 28 October 1947.

45 The play, in two acts, presents a Jewish wedding. Direction was by Mikhoels, music by L. Pulver and décor by the painter A. Tishler. See *Eynikeyt*, 30 August 1945.

46 Markish's play, written during the war but never published in the Soviet Union, was performed in Brazil in 1956. Direction was by P. Kaverin, music by L. Pulver and décor by A. Tishler; see *Eynikeyt*, 25 September 1947. Fefer's play, written during the war, had its première in 1947 under the direction of Mikhoels and Hersht; music was by Milner and décor by Rabinovich; see *Eynikeyt*, 11 March 1948.

47 *Zoriah Bilinkovich* tells of a Hero of the Soviet Union, submarine captain Israel Fisanovich, who was killed in battle in 1944. The play was translated and adapted by the poet Aharon Kushnirov. Direction was by P. Veisbrem, music by L. Pulver and décor by A. Tishler. Fisanovich's commanding officer, Admiral I. Kulishin, attended the première performance. See *Yidishe kultur*, 1948, no. 8, p. 58. *The Sighing of the Forests*, based on the book *The War Behind Enemy Lines* (on the partisan war in Belorussia), is by the Hero of the Soviet Union G. Linkov ('Batya'). One of its main protagonists is the Jewish Commissar, David Kemakh, who fell in battle against the

Nazis. Direction was by S. Mikhoels, music by L. Pulver, and the leading parts were played by Zuskin and Shvartser. The première was on 12 November 1947. See *Eynikeyt*, 27 November and 18 December 1947; *Folks-shtime*, 10 January 1948.

48 *Bar Kokhba* was performed by the State Yiddish Theatre in Moscow in 1938 (*Pravda*, 26 March 1938), by the Minsk Theatre then located in Novosibirsk during the war (Macleod, *Actors Cross the Volga*, p. 118) and in Riga in 1946 (*Yidishe kultur*, 1947, no. 1, p. 33). *Shpilfoygl* was staged in the Kaganovich Yiddish Theatre in Birobidzhan (Lvavi, *Ha-hityashvut ha-yehudit be-birobidzhan*, p. 392).

49 Pinchevsky's play, staged by the Ukrainian Yiddish Theatre in Chernovtsy, was attacked for its nationalistic content. See *Eynikeyt*, 24 September 1946 and 26 August 1947.

50 Staged during the war by the Belorussian Yiddish Theatre of Minsk; interview with Mrs Rodensky-Fridman, The Institute of Contemporary Jewry, Department of Oral Documentation, Tape no. 52/22.

51 There is lack of adequate information with regard to the staging of three plays; see Table 15.

52 One of the first confirmations of this new policy to reach Israel was provided in 1957, by a former actor in the Yiddish Theatres of Moscow and Chernovtsy. Many more testimonies were provided after 1967, when other former actors of the Yiddish theatres in the USSR arrived in Israel.

53 For example, 20,000 spectators at the appearances of the Minsk Theatre in Latvia (*Eynikeyt*, 16 September 1948); 140,000 spectators for the play *Freylekhs* (*Eynikeyt*, 7 September 1948); 166 performances and 60,000 spectators during three months of appearances of the Yiddish theatre company from the Ukraine (*Eynikeyt*, 30 October 1948).

54 The final report of its appearances appeared on 19 October 1948. See *Eynikeyt* of that date.

55 According to J. Emiot's testimony. See Lvavi. *Ha-hityashvut ha-yehudit be-birobidzhan*, p. 299.

56 According to Mrs Rodensky-Fridman, in March 1949 the theatre received a directive from the Committee for Art Affairs in Minsk stating: 'As the theatre is unprofitable it has no right to exist and must be dissolved.' (Interview as in n. 50.)

57 On this, see Chapter 4.

58 The final report on its performances is of 11 September 1949; see *Pravda Ukrainy* of that date. According to the director, M. Goldblat, the theatre was closed early in January 1950.

59 The final report in the USSR of the theatre's performances is of 16 November 1949 (*Izvestiya*), while a further report appeared in Poland in the Yiddish newspaper *Folks-shtime* on 15 December 1949.

60 We have found no confirmation for Yaakov Mestel's reports in the pro-Communist periodical, *Yidishe kultur* (1952, no. 3, p. 54) that there were Yiddish companies in Lvov and Birobidzhan in 1952.

61 According to a Canadian Yiddish newspaper, Yiddish performances began again in 1954. See *Vokhenblat*, 5 July 1956, as quoted in the *Institute Annual 1956*, New York, Institute of Jewish Affairs, 1956, p. 373.

62 *Pravda Vostoka*, 19 February 1955, as quoted in *Jewish Life*, August 1955, p. 18.

63 Of course, not all of them operated continuously throughout the entire period covered by Table 18. Many closed down for various periods and then re-opened; others underwent changes of personnel and of permanent location, etc.

64 Mikhael Aleksandrovich, Mikhael Apelbaum, Begam, Mark Broida, Chizhina, Flam, Rosalya Golubyova, Marina Gordon, Berl Gutikov, Anna Guzik, Tamara Hanoym, Emil Harkavi, Emil Horovets, Surim Kadzhar, Emanuel Kaminka, Zinovy Kaminsky, Binyamin Khayatuskas, Elya Khalif, Yaakov Klebanov, Y.

Klein, Lea Kolina, Lam, Leyb Levin, Nehamah Lifshits, Shaul Lyubimov, Mikhael Magid, Roza Plotkina, Margarita Polanskaya, Dina Polevskaya, Shmuel Rakitin, Yitskhak Rakitin, Mark Razumny, Mark Reznik, Dina Roytkop, Esther Roytman, Sofia Sayten, Anna Shablyova, Klementina Shermel, Zinovy Shulman, Binyamin Shvartser, Sidi Tal, Klara Vago.

65 Reports to this effect appeared in the Western press. See, for example. *Naye prese*, 11–12 January and 28–9 June 1958.

66 *Tevye the Milkman* was staged in Moscow in June 1960 (*Folks-shtime*, 4 June 1960); *200,000* in the cities of Dvinsk, Odessa, Kiev and Minsk in 1961–4 (*Folks-shtime*, 4 November 1961; 26 July 1962; 21 January 1964); and *Wandering Star* in Chernovtsy (*Folks-shtime*, 20 June 1967).

67 *Folks-shtime*, 5 September 1967.

68 *Folks-shtime*, 20 February 1967.

69 On Jews in Soviet literature, see Chapter 11.

70 Staged by a student company in 1960 (*Folks-shtime*, 30 November 1960) and in Tbilisi in 1965. The Shvartser Company in Moscow also intended to perform *The Diary of Anne Frank*, but as far as is known they never did stage the play.

71 In Moscow; *Folks-shtime*, 29 March 1966.

72 This play, on the extermination of the Jews in Babi Yar, was staged in Moscow; *Folks-shtime*, 19 March 1966.

73 Staged in Moscow; *Folks-shtime*, 5 October 1961.

74 This film, which had its premiere in 1936, was directed by V. Korsh with music by Isaak Dunaevsky. The actor Binyamin Zuskin portrayed a Jew named Pinya Gofman, the son of an emigrant family from America, who loathed physical labour and aspired to become wealthy without working. It ends with Pinya being caught trying to escape across the border with a bottle of sand which he believes is gold. On this film, and on attempts to film Jewish life in Birobidzhan, see Lvavi, *Ha-hityashvut ha-yehudit be-birobidzhan*, pp. 306–7.

75 M. Kalik, the director, now living in Israel, recounted the attempt by Jewish director Leonid Trauberg to make a film based on Shalom Aleikhem's *Tevye the Milkman*. See Kalik's lecture at the symposium held in Jerusalem in January 1971 on Jewish Culture in the Soviet Union, Tel Aviv, Cultural Department of the World Jewish Congress, 1973, pp. 148–53. Kalik himself had proposed adapting Shalom Aleikhem's *Wandering Stars* and Yitskhak Meras's *Stalemate with Death* for the screen, but his efforts, too, were to no avail.

76 For example, in 1948 plays (such as *Freylekhs*), concerts of Yiddish songs, readings of stories and passages from Yiddish novels, lectures on Jewish literature and culture. See *Eynikeyt*, 16 March; 14, 19, 21, 30 October; and 6 November 1948.

77 They were received by the British Broadcasting Service for the last time on 14 February 1949. See *Summary of World Broadcasts* (*SWB*), Part 1, 22 February 1949.

78 On 1 January 1949, only a short time before his arrest, Perets Markish broadcast a report on the contented life of the Jews of the Soviet Union; see *SWB*, Part 1, 10 January 1949. The first Radio Moscow broadcast in 1956, of Jewish folk-songs in Yiddish, apparently took place on 16 April; see *Naye prese*, 17 April 1956.

79 Such as the appearance of the singer Shaul Lyubimov (*Yidishe shriftn*, 5 May 1956); that of the Jewish choir in Riga (*Naye prese*, 22–3 August 1959); of the singer Rivkin on Belorussian television (*Sovetish heymland*, 1965, no. 8, p. 158); and of a Jewish company on Vilnius television (*Folks-shtime*, 25 January 1962).

80 Krein composed the music for Perets's *A Night in the Old Market* (1924), Shalom Aleikhem's *The Doctor* (1925) and *Uriel Akosta* (1932); see *Sovetskie kompozitory* (Soviet Composers), Moscow, Sovetsky kompozitor, 1957, pp. 302–7; *Kniga o russkom evreistve, 1917–1967* (A Book on Russian Jewry), New York, Soyuz russkikh evreev, 1968, pp. 260–1. Pulver composed the music for most of the plays staged by the

Yiddish theatre in the Soviet Union during and after the war; among them, *The Witch*, *Tevye the Milkman*, *Zoriah Bilinkovich*, *Freylekhs* and *Revolt in the Ghetto*.

81 On the composer Shaul Senderie (1905–67), see *Folks-shtime*, 10 June 1965; 9 August 1967.

82 Kompaneets's five songs to words of the poets Vergelis, Katsovich and Kerler appeared in Moscow in 1960; see Z. Kompaneets, *Pyat pesen* (Five Songs), Moscow, Muzgiz, 1960.

83 A book of Boyarskaya's music to words of Yiddish poets appeared in 1966; see R. Boyarskaya, *Pesni na stikhi evreiskikh poetov* (Songs to Words of Jewish Poets), Moscow, Muzgiz, 1966.

84 A book of Kogan's music to Jewish folk-songs appeared in 1958; see L. Kogan, *Evreiskie narodnye pesni* (Jewish Folk Songs), Moscow, Sovetsky kompozitor, 1958.

85 M. Beregovsky, *Evreiskie narodnye pesni* (Jewish Folk-Songs), Moscow, Muzgiz, 1962.

86 On the attack on this work during the anti-cosmopolitan campaign, see Chapter 4 and Doc. 60.

87 The works of Moshe Veinberg (a relative of Solomon Mikhoels) on Jewish subjects include: Six Songs to Words of Y. L. Perets (1942), the Second Symphony (1961), the Sixth Symphony with a Boys' Choir (1963), and the Eighth Symphony to Words of Julian Tuwim (1964).

88 On the Jewish painters in the Soviet Union, see *Yidishe kultur*, 1949, no. 1, pp. 51–2; *Folks-shtime*, 7 March 1961; 14 April and 16 June 1962.

89 Kaplan's illustrations for the Jewish folk-tale *The She-Goat* and for Jewish folk-songs appeared in 1961, but in an edition of only 125 copies intended for export. During the years 1958–66, Kaplan prepared lithographs for Shalom Aleikhem's *The Enchanted Tailor*, *Tevye the Milkman* and *Stempenyu*; see Pinkus, Greenbaum & Altshuler (eds.), *Pirsumim rusiim al yehudim*, pp. 106–7. On Kaplan's work, see *Folks-shtime*, 19 July 1958; 20 February 1960; 26 April 1961; 24 January 1963; 8 August 1970.

90 On one exhibition, held in April 1948 in Minsk, in which G. Azgur, H. Kodervich and K. Izirginer exhibited some of their works, see *Eynikeyt*, 1 April 1948.

91 For example, the show in Leningrad in 1959 (*Folks-shtime*, 7 April 1959), and that in Moscow in 1960, in which the works of L. Krivitsky, Y. Khanon, M. Klainsky and N. Altman were exhibited (*Folks-shtime*, 11 October 1960).

92 Outstanding among such institutes were the Historical-Ethnographic Society in Leningrad, which functioned from 1918 to 1929; the Historical-Economic Commission attached to the All-Russian Directorship of *Ort*, which operated in Moscow between 1925 and 1930; and the *Oze* Society, which functioned in Leningrad from 1926 to 1930 and published several collections of essays on the biology and pathology of the Jews. No comprehensive study has yet appeared on these institutes. The sole related study is that of A. Greenbaum, *Jewish Scholarship in the Soviet Union*, Boston, n.p., 1959. See also the new edition, *Jewish Scholarship and Scholarly Institutions in Soviet Russia 1918–1953*.

93 The Institute underwent several stages of development: Jewish department, Jewish sector, Jewish branch, and finally scientific institute. It was closed in late 1935 or early 1936.

94 This Institute, too, went through various stages of development: university chair, institute, bureau.

95 Such as Y. Dobrushin, N. Oyslender, Y. Nusinov, Margolis and Heilikman from Moscow; Holdes from Kharkov; and Borovoi from Odessa. See the conversation with the Bureau Director Spivak in *Eynikeyt*, 2 April 1946.

96 See *Eynikeyt*, 7 October 1947.

97 Arrested in early 1949, he was condemned to death in the Writers' Trial of July 1952.

98 *Eynikeyt*, 28 March 1946.

99 *Eynikeyt*, 29 June 1944.

100 *Eynikeyt*, 8 and 24 July 1948.
101 Salisbury, *Moscow Journal*, p. 201; on the museum, see Doc. 164.
102 See Lvavi, *Ha-hityashvut ha-yehudit be-birobidzhan*, pp. 290–2.
103 See *Eynikeyt*, 28 March 1946; 17 August 1948; S. Kacherginsky, *Tsvishn hamer un serp* (Between Hammer and Sickle), Paris, Grohar, 1949.
104 The Lenin Library in Moscow, which contains many books in Yiddish, organised an exhibition in honour of the 100th anniversary of Shalom Aleikhem's birth; *Naye prese*, 28–9 June 1958.
105 *Folks-shtime*, 14 July 1956.
106 Researchers in the field of Hebraica include the non-Jews, Professors Starkova and Sharbatov, and B. Grande, Isaak Vinikov, Iosif Amusin and Avraam Rubinshtein – all of whom are Jews.
107 Moisei Yakovlevich Beregovsky (1892–1961), Jewish musicologist and folklorist, was born in the village of Tarmakhovka, Kiev Province. His father was a teacher. He studied in a *ḥeder* till the age of thirteen. From 1905 Beregovsky lived in Kiev, where he studied at the *gymnasium* as an external student. From 1910, he studied music in Kiev and later in Leningrad. He also played the cello in a Kiev orchestra. From 1915 to 1936, he was a choirmaster and teacher at Jewish schools in Kiev and Leningrad. From 1930 to 1948, he was Director of the Centre for Musical Folklore at the Institute of Jewish Proletarian Culture of the All-Ukrainian Academy of Sciences. In 1944, he was awarded the degree of Candidate of Musical Sciences. Arrested at the beginning of 1949 together with other writers and activists of Jewish Culture in Kiev, he was rehabilitated after Stalin's death and returned to Kiev.
108 This document emphasises the many hopes which the Jewish cultural leaders of the USSR still had, even in 1948, regarding Jewish artistic development. As is known, however, nothing came of these plans.
109 Shire Gorshman (1902–), Yiddish poetess, born into a poor family in the small town of Krok in Kaunas Province. In 1923, she emigrated to Palestine, where she worked at the home of the poet Haim Nahman Bialik. She returned to the Soviet Union in 1929. Her first works were published in 1939. Gorshman contributed to the journal *Sovetish heymland*.
110 Haim Malamud (1907–), Yiddish writer, was born in the small town of Khash-chevatoe in the Ukraine. His first works were published in 1932. He joined the Communist Party in 1936, and fought in World War II.
111 Haim Zilberman (1907–), Yiddish writer, was born into a family of poor workers in Odessa. His first works appeared in 1935. He fought in World War II. He was arrested at the end of 1948 and released from prison in 1955.
112 Yitskhak Lyumkis (1908–), Yiddish writer, was born in a small town in the Ukraine, where he worked as a labourer. He began publishing his works in 1925. He lived in Central Asia during the war and, later, in Moscow and Birobidzhan. Lyumkis was arrested at the end of 1948. Released in 1956, he now lives in Riga.
113 Shmuel Rosin (1890–1941), Yiddish poet, was born into a coachman's family in Shumyachi in the former Mogilev Province. He studied at a *ḥeder* and in a *yeshivah*. He began writing poems at the age of fourteen, and his first poems were published in 1918. Rosin fell in battle in October 1941.
114 Yosef Kotlyar (1908–62), Yiddish poet, was born in Berdichev. He graduated from an institute in Kharkov. His first poems were published in the late 1920s.
115 Moshe Teyf (1904–66), Yiddish poet, was born in Minsk. He studied in the Yiddish department of the University of Minsk. He began publishing his works in 1923, and took part in World War II. His family was killed in the Minsk ghetto. Teyf was on the editorial board of the journal *Sovetish heymland*.

116 Zyame Telesin (1912–), Yiddish poet, was born in Kalinkovich, in the Polesye area, Belorussia. His first works appeared in 1931. Telesin translated Russian and Soviet classics into Yiddish. During World War II, he was an officer in the Red Army and a correspondent of the Moscow *Eynikeyt*. In 1971, he emigrated to Israel, together with his wife, the Yiddish poetess Rahel Baumvol.

117 Shmuel Godiner (1892–1941), Yiddish writer, was born in the small town of Telekhany in Minsk (now Brest) Province, where he received a traditional Jewish education. In 1907, he moved to Warsaw where he was active in the Bund. His first works appeared in 1921. Godiner fell in the battle for Moscow in 1941.

118 M. Daniel (pseudonym of Mark Meerovich; 1900–40), Yiddish writer, was born into a poor family in Dvinsk. He studied in a *ḥeder* and *talmud torah*. In 1921, he moved to Moscow, where he took an active part in Jewish cultural life. Daniel's first works were published in 1924.

119 The reference here is to the resolutions of the Central Committee of the Communist Party taken during the years 1946–8 on matters of literature and art, in which writers and artists who had diverged from the official line during the war years were attacked. See Chapter 4.

120 Meir Viner (1893–1941), writer and student of Yiddish literature, was born in Cracow. He studied philosophy at the University of Zurich. From 1922 to 1925, he lived in Berlin where he joined the Communist Party. Viner came to the Soviet Union in 1927, where he edited literary journals. In 1941, he was captured by the Germans and killed. The most important of his many research works is his *Yidishe literatur in 19. yorhundert* (History of Yiddish Literature in the Nineteenth Century).

121 Moshe Notovich (1912–68), critic of Yiddish literature, was born in Berdichev and finished pedagogic institutes in Odessa and Moscow. He published books and articles on Yiddish literature in the Soviet Union and the rest of the world. He studied in the Moscow State Yiddish Theatre School. Notovich was a member of the Jewish Anti-Fascist Committee. He contributed to the journal *Sovetish heymland*.

122 Shlomo Roytman (1913–), Yiddish poet, was born into an artisan's family in Mogilev Podolsky in Vinnitsa Province. He studied at the Moscow Pedagogic Institute. His first poems appeared in 1931. He contributes to the journal *Sovetish heymland*.

123 Uri Finkel (1896–1957), critic of Yiddish literature, was born in Rakov in the former Minsk (now Molodechno) Province, into the family of a *shoḥet* (ritual slaughterer). He attended a *ḥeder* and studied general secular subjects as well. In 1916, he studied at a technical college in Kharkov, and later at the University of Minsk. Finkel's first articles appeared in 1917. He worked on Yiddish newspapers, taught at the University of Minsk, and took part in World War II.

124 Evsei Lyubomirsky (1884–1977), Yiddish theatre critic, finished his studies at the Kiev Institute of Commerce in 1914 and began his theatrical and literary work in 1924.

125 Eliyahu Falkovich (1898–1979), linguist, was born in Gomel. He graduated from the linguistics faculty of Moscow University and began publishing works on Yiddish linguistics in 1927. In the 1930s, he was reader in the Yiddish language in the faculty of Yiddish linguistics at the 2nd Moscow University. He took part in the language convention in Moscow on 15 December 1936, in which the question of according Yiddish the status of an official language was discussed in connection with the Soviet government's decision to establish a Jewish Autonomous Region. During World War II, he was a member of the Jewish Anti-Fascist Committee. Later, he volunteered for the Red Army and was taken prisoner, but he escaped.

126 Moshe Altshuler (1887–1969), Soviet Jewish linguist, writer and translator, studied at a *ḥeder*. Until 1918, he was a member of the Bund. In 1923, he was

elected secretary of the head office of the *Evsektsiya* in the Ukraine, but he was dismissed in 1924. In 1924, he was one of the editors of the *Evsektsiya*'s Komsomol organ in the Ukraine, *Yunge gvardie* (Young Guard). In 1925, he was transferred to Moscow and appointed editor at 'Tsenterfarlag', the central publishing house for Yiddish books. He was co-opted onto the Central Bureau of the *Evsektsiya*, probably in 1926. From 1931 to 1935, he edited the Yiddish edition of the organ of the Association of Militant Atheists. During and after World War II, he worked with the Jewish Anti-Fascist Committee. After Stalin's death, he was active in anti-religious propaganda. In 1948, he published *Guf un neshome* (Body and Soul).

127 Grigory Polyanker (1911–), Yiddish writer, was born into an artisan's family in Uman. He joined the Communist Party in 1930. His first works were published in 1932. Polyanker fought in World War II. He was arrested in 1949 and released in 1955. He contributes to the journal *Sovetish heymland*, and was a signatory to anti-Israel declarations in 1970.

128 Matvei Talalaevsky (1908–78), Yiddish poet, was born in the village of Mokhnachka in Kiev (now Zhitomir) Province. He graduated from an institute in Kiev in 1934. His first poems were published in 1926, and he joined the Communist Party in 1942. Talalaevsky was an officer in the Red Army during World War II. After the war, he was secretary of the Bureau of Yiddish Writers in the Ukraine. He was arrested at the height of the campaign against Jewish writers in 1949. He lives in Kiev and contributes to the journal *Sovetish heymland*.

129 Hanah Levina (1900–69), Yiddish poetess. Levina worked as a seamstress and saleswoman. Her first works were published in 1917. She published numerous works, including children's literature. After the war she lived in Kharkov and was an active contributor to the journal *Sovetish heymland*.

130 Perets Markish (1895–1952), one of the most outstanding Soviet Yiddish poets, was born into a poor family in the small town of Polonnoe in Volyn. Until the age of ten, he studied in a *ḥeder*. He left home at the age of eleven and then lived in Berdichev, Odessa, and other towns in Moldavia, where he worked as an assistant cantor and private tutor. In 1915, he was enlisted into the army, wounded and released in 1917. His first works were published in 1917. In 1921, Markish left the Soviet Union and lived in Warsaw, Berlin, Paris and London. In 1923, he visited Palestine and returned to the Soviet Union in 1926. Markish was occasionally criticised for his nationalist leanings. During World War II, he was an active member of the Jewish Anti-Fascist Committee and joined the Communist Party in 1942. Markish was arrested in 1949 and executed on 12 August 1952.

131 Vladimir Mikhailovich Kirshon (1902–38), playwright, was one of the leaders of the Russian Association of Proletarian Writers (RAPP) and on the editorial boards of a number of literary journals. He joined the Communist Party in 1920 and fought in the Civil War. He was arrested at the time of the great purges and died in prison on 28 July 1938.

132 Yury Nikolaevich Libedinsky (1898–1959), writer, was born into a doctor's family in Odessa. He lived in the Urals, fought in the Civil War and joined the Communist Party in 1920. Libedinsky was one of the leaders of RAPP. During World War II, he served as a war correspondent. Jewish themes occupy a considerable place in his works, for example, in the novels *Nedelya* (One Week), *Zavtra* (Tomorrow), *Komissary* (Commissars); in the short story *Gvardeitsy* (The Guardsmen); in the drama *Vysoty* (The Heights); and in the essay on Shalom Aleikhem published a year before his death.

133 Avraham Sutskever (1913–), Yiddish poet, was born into a family of rabbis in Smorgon, Belorussia. He is a relative of Yitskhak Ben-Zvi, the second President of Israel. His family became refugees during World War I and moved to Siberia, where Kirgiz almost became his mother tongue. Sutskever returned to Smorgon

in 1920, but soon moved to Vilnius. He studied at a *ḥeder* and *talmud torah*, and then at a Polish Jewish high school. He wrote his first poems in 1927 in Hebrew. In 1932, he moved to Warsaw and his poems were published for the first time there in 1933. The outbreak of war found him in Vilnius, and Sutskever helped save some of the most valuable items from the Vilnius ghetto, now in the YIVO collection. In 1943, he escaped from the ghetto to join the partisans. He was given a hero's welcome in Moscow, and met the leading Russian Yiddish poets. An active member of the Jewish Anti-Fascist Committee, Sutskever gave evidence on Nazi crimes at the Nuremberg trials. In 1946, he left the Soviet Union for Poland, which he left in 1947 with his wife and daughter for Palestine. In 1949, he became editor of the quarterly *Di goldene keyt*.

134 *Kabalah* is the most commonly used term for the esoteric teachings of Judaism and Jewish mysticism. The *Zohar* is the central book of the *Kabalah*.

135 David Hofshteyn (1889–1952), one of the greatest Yiddish poets of the Soviet Union, was born in Korostyshev in the former Kiev (now Zhitomir) Province. His father was a chief forester. Hofshteyn received a traditional Jewish education in a *ḥeder* and at home. He learnt Hebrew and Russian with a private tutor. Anti-Jewish quotas prevented him from being accepted at university, but he studied at the Institute for Psychology in St Petersburg and at the Institute of Commerce in Kiev. At the age of nineteen, he began writing poems in Hebrew, and later he wrote in Russian and Ukrainian. He began writing in Yiddish in 1914. After the Revolution, he lived in Kiev where he was active in Jewish cultural life. In 1924, Hofshteyn signed a petition condemning the persecution of Hebrew writers in the Soviet Union. As a result he was forced to leave the editorial board of the journal *Shtrom* and went to Berlin. Hofshteyn visited Palestine in 1925, where he published his Hebrew poems; however, he returned to the Soviet Union in 1926 where he was compelled to criticise his past mistakes. He contributed to various journals and played a role in the Writers' Union. During the war, he was an active member of the Jewish Anti-Fascist Committee. At the beginning of 1948, he was elected a member of the Jewish Section of the Writers' Union of the Ukrainian SSR. Hofshteyn was arrested at the end of 1948 and executed on 12 August 1952.

136 Oles Dosvitny (pseudonym of Oleksandr Fedorovych Skrypal; 1891–1934), Ukrainian writer, was one of the victims of Stalin's purges.

137 Petro Panch (pseudonym of Petro Yosypovych Panchenko; 1891–1978), Ukrainian writer, held posts in the Soviet Writers' Union and the Ukrainian Writers' Union.

138 Nikolai Ivanovich Tereshchenko (1898–1966), Ukrainian poet, is considered one of the founders of Ukrainian Soviet poetry.

139 Bohdan Khmelnytsky (1595–1657), was leader of the Cossack and peasant uprising against Polish rule in the Ukraine in 1648 which resulted in the destruction of hundreds of Jewish communities. The troops under the command of Khmelnytsky ('the Wicked', as he is known in Jewish history) were responsible for the massacres of 1648–9.

140 Itsik Fefer (1900–52), Yiddish poet, was born into a teacher's family in Shpola. At the age of twelve, he began to work in a printer's shop. A member of the Bund, Fefer joined the Communist Party in 1919. In the 1930s he was accused of Trotskyism. During the war he was an active member of the Jewish Anti-Fascist Committee. Together with the actor Mikhoels, Fefer went to the USA and elsewhere on behalf of the Committee. He was deputy editor of the newspaper *Eynikeyt*. Arrested at the beginning of 1949, Fefer was executed on 12 August 1952.

141 Ivan Mikhailovich Bespalov (1900–37), Russian literary critic.

142 Artem Vesely (pseudonym of Nikolai Ivanovich Kochkurov, 1899–1939), Russian writer, was a victim of Stalin's purges.

143 Ivan Ivanovich Kataev (1902–39), Russian writer, was a victim of Stalin's purges.

144 Similar rehabilitation notices appeared in *Literaturnaya gazeta* on Y. Nusinov and S. Persov on 29 March 1956, and on Y. Dobrushin, 30 October 1956.

145 David Bergelson (1884–1952), one of the most important of Soviet Yiddish writers, was born in Okhrimovo, near Uman in the Ukraine, into a wealthy Jewish family. He learnt Yiddish, Hebrew and Russian and began writing in 1902. His first work was published in 1909. In 1921, he left Soviet Russia for Germany and was active in the Jewish cultural life of Europe. In 1934, he returned to the Soviet Union, where he was very active in the Jewish Anti-Fascist Committee during the war years. Bergelson was arrested at the beginning of 1949 and sentenced to death in July 1952.

146 Leyb Kvitko (1890–1952), Yiddish poet and children's writer, was born into a teacher's family in the village of Goloskovo in the Ukraine. He studied at a *ḥeder* for a short while and left home at the age of ten to work as a painter's assistant. His first works were published in 1918. In 1921, he left the Soviet Union and lived in Berlin and Hamburg, where he joined the German Communist Party. In 1925, he returned to the Soviet Union. At the end of the 1920s, Kvitko was charged with Jewish nationalism. He was a delegate at the First USSR Writers' Congress in 1934. He was an active member of the Jewish Anti-Fascist Committee during the war and, afterwards, was secretary to the Moscow Yiddish Writers' Bureau and on the editorial board of *Heymland*. Kvitko was arrested at the beginning of 1949 and was executed on 12 August 1952.

147 Lev Abramovich Kassil (1905–70), children's writer and journalist, was born into an assimilated Jewish family in Pokrovsk (now Engels). His father was a doctor and his mother a music teacher, and Kassil himself studied at the faculty of physics and mathematics of Moscow University. He began his literary activity in 1925. His two autobiographical works, *Konduit* (Conduit) (1930) and *Shvambraniya* (1933), deal with Jewish topics, while his short story, 'Fedya of P—' (1942), has the Hero of the Soviet Union Isaak Arkadyevich Palkovsky as one of its central heroes. In 1970, Kassil was a signatory to an anti-Israel declaration.

148 Bruno Yasensky (1901–41), Polish and Russian writer, emigrated to France from Poland in 1925. In 1931, he was deported from France and moved to Russia. He was arrested in 1937 on a charge of spying, and died in prison.

149 Vladimir Germanovich Lidin (1894–1979), Russian writer.

150 Solomon Mikhailovich Mikhoels (pseudonym of Vovsi; 1890–1948), Yiddish actor and Chairman of the Jewish Anti-Fascist Committee, was born into a tradesman's family in Dvinsk. He attended a *ḥeder* and studied with a private teacher before going on to a *gymnasium* in Riga and the Kiev Institute of Commerce. In 1915, he began to study law at the University of St Petersburg where he completed his studies in 1918. Mikhoels's theatrical career began in 1919 when he joined the director Granovsky's studio. In the 1920s, he appeared in leading roles at the State Yiddish Theatre in Moscow. He was appointed the theatre's artistic director in 1929. In 1939, Mikhoels was elected to the Arts Council of the Committee for Art Affairs of the Council of Ministers of the USSR and was awarded the Lenin Prize. In 1941, he was made a professor. In April 1942, Mikhoels was elected Chairman of the Jewish Anti-Fascist Committee, which had just been established, and he was sent abroad in the name of the Committee. At this time the State Yiddish Theatre was located in Tashkent, and Mikhoels worked as director at the Uzbek Theatre. On 13 January 1948, while on a mission in Minsk, he was murdered by agents of the secret police, apparently on the direct orders of Stalin.

151 'To S. Mikhoels – An Eternal Light at the Bier'. Parts 1 and 7 appeared for the first time in *Eynikeyt*, 17 January 1948; Parts 1–6 appeared in *Tog-morgn zhurnal*, 31 March 1957, with the following note by Haim Shoshkes: 'I am now making public

the full text of a poem by Perets Markish in which he describes for the first time in Soviet Russia the death of [...] S. Mikhoels as "murder" [...] I possess the original text typed by Perets himself – with corrections in his own hand. After his arrest on 27 February 1949, the original text fell into the hands of a very close friend who found refuge in a town in South Russia. It was there that we met and that I received the poem.' It seems that the copy which H. Shoshkes received breaks off at Part 6. In the only Russian translation (P. Markish, *Izbrannoe* (Selected Works), Moscow, Sovetsky pisatel, 1957, pp. 108–12) there are seven parts, of which Parts 1–6 are given according to the text in *Tog-morgn zhurnal* (also reprinted in *Yidishe kultur*, 1957, no. 5 and in *Di goldene keyt*, 1962, no. 43), and Part 7 according to *Eynikeyt*. See also Markish, *Le Long Retour*, pp. 294–5.

152 The Gur (*Ger* in Yiddish) Hasidic dynasty, one of the most celebrated dynasties, existed in Poland from 1859 to 1939. The founder was Isaac Meir Rothenberg Alter (1789–1866), whose father was a disciple of Levi Yitskhak of Berdichev.

153 Levi Yitskhak Ben Meir of Berdichev (*c.* 1740–1810), Hasidic *zadik* and rabbi, was the founder of Hasidism in Central Poland, consolidated it in Lithuania and furthered it in the Ukraine; but he did not found a dynasty. He became a popular hero in both Hebrew and Yiddish fiction and poetry.

154 Georges Pitoëff (1884–1939), French actor and stage director, was born in Tbilisi and acted in Russia before leaving the country in 1915.

155 Vladimir Ilyich Golubov (pseudonyms: N. P. Potapov, V. Glinsky; 1908–48), theatre scholar, critic, ballet script writer.

156 See *Sovetskaya Litva*, 13 January 1963.

157 This document, together with a similar notice on the closure of the school of the State Yiddish Theatre in Moscow, are the only official Soviet publications on the liquidation of the State Yiddish Theatre in November 1949. Among the Theatre School's effects were stenographic reports of Mikhoels's conversations and lectures, and the manuscripts of Y. Dobrushin's 'Outline of B. Zuskin's Creative Art' and of Y. Nusinov's 'Basic Stages in the Development of Yiddish Drama'.

158 Aleksei Mikhailovich Granovsky (pseudonym of Abraham Azarkh; 1890–1937), Soviet theatrical director and founder of the Moscow State Yiddish Theatre, was born in Moscow and educated in St Petersburg and Munich. In 1919, he organised an amateur Yiddish drama group, and he was authorised to open a studio in Petrograd in 1919. Granovsky's studio grew into a repertory theatre which moved to Moscow and was renamed the State Yiddish Theatre of Moscow. The theatre presented works mainly by Jewish authors.

159 On Rabbi Levin, see Doc. 128.

160 Perets Hirshbeyn (1880–1948), Yiddish dramatist and novelist, was born in Kleszczele, Eastern Poland (now Belorussia). He studied at *yeshivot* and, at the age of eighteen, began writing stories in Yiddish and poems in Hebrew. In 1900, he moved to Vilnius and in 1904, to Warsaw. In 1908, he organised a dramatic group in Odessa which presented a serious repertoire. Hirshbeyn moved to the USA in 1911. In the 1920s, he travelled round the world. His works show a distaste for city life and a yearning for nature, as in his famous trilogy, *Grine Felder* (Green Fields, 1923). (Note that Hirshbeyn's initial is mistakenly given as 'B' in the Prokopowicz article.)

161 Moshe Kulbak (1896–1940), Yiddish poet, novelist and dramatist, was born at Smorgon near Vilnius. Apart from a three-year period in Berlin, he lived and worked in Vilnius, until he moved to the Soviet Union in 1928 and settled in Minsk. He was arrested in 1937 and died in a labour camp in 1940.

162 Mordekhai Gebirtig (1877–1942), a joiner by profession, received no formal schooling. He wrote his songs only for himself and his family – his wife and three daughters, although he would sometimes sing them in his joiner's workshop. He

perished in the Cracow ghetto. A third, expanded edition of his songs, *My Songs*, was published in New York in 1948. The first edition appeared in 1936, and the second in 1942.

8. The Jewish religion in the Soviet Union

1 *Istoriya sovetskoi konstitutsii* (History of the Soviet Constitution), Moscow, Akademiya nauk, 1957, pp. 50–1. The most important collection of documents on religious affairs until 1926 is P. Gidulianov (ed.), *Otdelenie tserkvi ot gosudarstva* (The Separation of Church and State), Moscow, Yurizdat RSFSR, 1926.

2 *Antireligioznik*, November 1938, p. 58, quoted in Conquest (ed.), *Religion in the USSR*, pp. 112–13. See also Kolarz, *Religion in the Soviet Union*. As was stated in the rehabilitation announcement of April 1964, Rabbi Medalia was executed 'in the period of the personality cult'. His son, a mathematics professor, was also arrested in 1951; see *Jews in Eastern Europe*, 1967, vol. III, no. 5, p. 22.

3 See, for example, the 1943 appeal of the synagogue committee of the city of Sverdlovsk to English Jewry, *The Russian Jews in the War*, pp. 60–1.

4 Contacts with the Israeli legation, which were in any case very limited, became even more so during the final years of Stalin's life. An exception was, perhaps, the appeal of a number of rabbis from the Soviet Union to the Ministry for Religious Affairs in Jerusalem requesting that *etrogim* for the festival of *Sukot* be sent them. On the relations between Rabbi Shlifer and the personnel of the Israeli legation in Moscow, see Namir, *Shliḥut be-moskvah*, pp. 46–50, 63, 67, 254, 315–21.

5 *Naye prese*, 28 January 1953.

6 The Society for the Dissemination of Atheistic Information, established in 1947, was a kind of revised and less extreme version of the anti-religious organisation that operated in the Soviet Union during the twenties and thirties. From 1947 to 1954, this new organisation distributed 172 million pamphlets on 4,000 different aspects of atheism. See D. E. Powell, 'Antireligious Propaganda in the Soviet Union, 1959–1963', PhD Thesis, Yale University, 1967, p. 164, published in book form in 1975.

7 Just how important it was for the Soviet Union to appear in the guise of the preserver of religious freedom – including that of the Jewish religion – may be seen from *Pravda*'s report of the visit of a trade-union delegation from the United States: upon its return home the delegation declared that Jewish synagogues were operating freely throughout the USSR. See *Pravda*, 13 August 1951.

8 It is true that in the Stalin period, too, Rabbi Shlifer 'sent greetings' to Jews living abroad, but these were generally delivered by a Communist or 'progressive' emissary who visited the Moscow synagogue and was requested by Rabbi Shlifer to declare that religious freedom existed in the Soviet Union. See, for example, the letter of H. Fagan, secretary of the Association for British–Soviet Friendship, to the *Jewish Chronicle* in *Jewish Life*, October 1951, p. 26.

9 *Voprosy ideologicheskoi raboty* (Problems of Ideological Work), Moscow, Gospolitizdat, 1961, pp. 61–5. See also B. Bociurkiw, 'Church–State Relations in the USSR', in Hayward & Fletcher (eds.), *Religion and the Soviet State*, p. 96.

10 One of the notable examples of the unrestrained attack on religion (this time on Islam) is Prof. Klimovich's article in the newspaper *Zarya Vostoka*, 10 October 1954.

11 *Pravda*, 11 November 1954.

12 *Naye prese*, 2 September 1954.

13 *Naye prese*, 30 June 1954.

14 *Jewish Chronicle*, 6 July 1956, and *Ha-arez*, 29 May 1956.

15 *Jewish Observer and Middle East Review*, 1 June 1956, p. 1.

16 *Ibid.*, 29 June 1956, p. 3.

17 *Jewish Chronicle*, 24 August 1956.

18 *Jewish Chronicle*, 12 October and 2 November 1956.

19 The first report that a *yeshivah* was about to be opened in Moscow reached the West in 1955 from J. B. Salsberg, one of the heads of the Canadian Progressive Labour Party; see *Naye prese*, 19 August 1955. Further reports to this effect appeared in the West throughout 1956; see *Jewish Chronicle*, 9 March and 8 August 1956.

20 According to Rothenberg (*The Jewish Religion in the Soviet Union*, p. 185), the *yeshivah* had thirty-five pupils upon its establishment.

21 Rabbi Shimon Trebnik (b. 1891) graduated from the Radin *yeshivah*. He arrived in Moscow in 1957 and served as principal of the *yeshivah*'s school until his death on 28 April 1961. He was a sympathiser of the State of Israel.

22 First reports of the *sidur*'s appearance had reached the West in 1955; see *Naye prese*, 19 August 1955. Publication of another new *sidur*, in Leningrad, to be based on the Hasidic tradition, was announced in 1957, but it never appeared; see *Jewish Chronicle*, 14 June 1957.

23 See the stenographic transcripts of this seminar in the collection *Nauka i religiya*, Moscow, Znanie, 1957.

24 For a complete list of these books and of all the other anti-religious publications during the years 1958–67, see Pinkus, Greenbaum & Altshuler (eds.), *Pirsumim rusiim al yehudim*, pp. 21–36.

25 See Bociurkiw, 'Church–State Relations in the USSR', pp. 96–7.

26 Our calculations are based on the data in *Evrei i evreisky narod*, 1960–4. As the information in this collection was gathered from some 150 Soviet newspapers and periodicals that appeared in these years, it provides a reliable sample of the total number of publications on the question of the Jewish religion. The number of anti-religious articles in periodicals and the local press was: 1960 – 460; 1961 – 345; 1962 – 447; 1963 – 449; 1964 – 429.

27 See 'Kirovorad (in Ukrainian) Text of Talk "Swindles Under the Mask of God's Servants"', *BBC Monitoring Service Section: Soviet Union, no. 205/A4*, 12 September 1959, pp. 3–5.

28 See Powell, 'Antireligious Propaganda', p. 105.

29 For example, the seminar organised by the Regional Committee of the Party in the city of Zhitomir; see *Agitator*, 1960, no. 8, p. 63.

30 These periodicals and year-books are: *Nauka i religiya* (Moscow, 1959); *Voiovnychyi ateist* (Kiev, 1960); *Ludinai svit* (Kiev, 1961); *Voprosy istorii religii i ateizma* (Moscow, 1950); *Ezhegodnik Muzeya istorii religii i ateisma* (1957).

31 Yu. Aleksandrov, 'Mestnye sovety i zakonodatelstvo o kultakh', *Agitator*, 1966, no. 13, pp. 57–9.

32 See J. Rothenberg, 'Jewish Religion in the Soviet Union', in Kochan (ed.), *The Jews in Soviet Russia Since 1917*, pp. 180–1.

33 See Yodfat, 'Jewish Religious Communities in the USSR', p. 66.

34 *Ibid.*

35 *American Jewish Yearbook*, 1961, p. 287.

36 *Ibid.*, 1962, p. 367.

37 *Ibid.*, 1964, p. 269.

38 Conquest (ed.), *Religion in the USSR*, p. 116.

39 Rothenberg, 'Jewish Religion in the Soviet Union', p. 180, and Yodfat, 'Jewish Religious Communities in the USSR', p. 66. Rothenberg's book, *The Jewish Religion in the Soviet Union* (p. 47), cites the following figures: Caucasian Republics – 19 synagogues; RSFSR – 17; Central Asian Republics – 11; Ukrainian Republic – 8; Latvian and Lithuanian Republics – 2 each; and Belorussian, Moldavian and Estonian Republics – 1 each. On the situation in Birobidzhan, see Doc. 148.

40 Aleksandrov, 'Mestnye sovety i zakonodatelstvo o kultakh', p. 59.
41 *Jews in Eastern Europe*, 1963, vol. II, no. 2, p. 61.
42 On this, see Chapter 13.
43 According to Moscow Rabbi Levin's remarks in 1965, several hundred worshippers attended Sabbath services in the synagogue, while on weekdays their number was between 100 and 150. See Rothenberg, *The Jewish Religion in the Soviet Union*, p. 74.
44 As early as 1961, the number of worshippers on this festival in Leningrad was estimated at about 12,000; see *Daily Mail*, 9 November 1961. According to a 1964 estimate, a crowd of some 50,000 persons gathered around the Great Synagogue in Moscow on *Simḥat Torah*; Rothenberg, *The Jewish Religion in the Soviet Union*, p. 80.
45 The cities in which *mazot*-baking was permitted were Moscow, Leningrad, Tbilisi, Tashkent and Sukhumi, in all of which the Jewish community had its own bakeries. See *The New York Times*, 17 March 1964.
46 *Jews in Eastern Europe*, 1963, vol. II, no. 3, p. 26.
47 The Soviet press was full of such letters. See, for example, *Izvestiya*, 21 March 1964; *Pravda Vostoka*, 17 March 1964; *Vecherny Leningrad*, 24 March 1964; *Sovetskaya Moldaviya*, 26 March 1964.
48 For further details, see 'Passover and Matzoth: A Case History of Soviet Policy', *Congress Bi-Weekly*, 1966, vol. XXXIII, no. 16, pp. 13–19.
49 This information derives from the manuscript of a Soviet Jew who has not yet emigrated to Israel, so that his name cannot be made public.
50 See Rothenberg, *The Jewish Religion in the Soviet Union*, p. 96.
51 A description of these services is to be found in the archives of the Centre for Documentation and Research of Eastern European Jewry at the Hebrew University in Jerusalem, File no. 393.
52 *Ibid.*
53 A. Gershuni, 'Korot ha-redifot shel ha-dat ha-yehudit bi-vrit ha-moaẓot' (On the Persecution of Judaism in the Soviet Union), *Gesher*, 1966, no. 2–3, pp. 168–9.
54 See G. Gerodnik, 'Razdumya o Parkakh dobrykh vospominanii', *Nauka i Religiya*, 1964, no. 4, p. 48; no. 6, pp. 33–7.
55 See, for example, a description of the destruction of the Moscow cemetery; *Jewish Chronicle*, 13 November 1959, p. 17.
56 Embassy personnel were occasionally warned by the rabbi and the *gabaim* to refrain from any contact with the worshippers. They were particularly forbidden to give the worshippers *sidurim* or *talitot* (prayer-shawls).
57 Calculations based on *Evrei i evreisky narod*, 1965–7.
58 For example, the books by Iosif Krivelin, and Zenon Kosidowski's *Bibleiskie skazaniya* (Biblical Tales), which was translated from the Polish.
59 'Passover in the USSR', *Jews in Eastern Europe*, 1966, vol. III, no. 4, pp. 29–30.
60 S. Loory, 'A Soviet Pledge on Jewish Privileges', *Herald Tribune*, 27 July 1965.
61 Conquest (ed.), *Religion in the USSR*, p. 117. The *yeshivah* had, in fact, ceased to function in 1963, although it had not closed officially.
62 Solomon Shlifer (1889–1957) was born in Aleksandrovka, a small town in the Ukraine. Until the outbreak of World War I, he was Rabbi of Aleksandrovka. During the war, he moved to Moscow, where he worked as secretary to the rabbinate. At the beginning of the 1930s, in the period of religious persecutions, Rabbis Shlifer and Medalia were both charged with heading a band of speculators and thieves. An announcement was even published of Rabbi Shlifer's impending trial, which, as far as is known, never took place. In the second half of the 1930s, Rabbi Shlifer worked as a book-keeper in a Soviet establishment. As a result of the sharp change in the government's policy towards religion at the beginning of World War II, he was appointed Rabbi of Moscow. Later he was evacuated to Tashkent with the Moscow religious community.

Rabbi Shlifer took part in the work of the Congress of the Jewish Anti-Fascist Committee (2 April 1944), at which he delivered a speech. In April 1946, he was appointed Chairman of the Jewish Religious Community of Moscow, replacing Samuil Chubrotsky he retained this post until his death on 31 March 1957.

Rabbi Shlifer carried on a constant correspondence, mainly on questions of religion, with well-known rabbis abroad. He sometimes dealt with political subjects on the initiative of the Soviet authorities, who were interested in acquiring the signatures of public figures, including rabbis, for their calls against arming Germany with atomic weapons and against war (including the Sinai Campaign of 1956). As a member of the Soviet delegation of Jews, Shlifer took part in the unveiling of the memorial in Paris to victims of the Nazis. In the last years of his life, he functioned as Chairman of the Moscow Jewish Religious Community, of the Choral Synagogue and of the Moscow Jewish Theological Seminary 'Kol Yaakov'.

On 9–12 May 1952, a Conference in Defence of Peace of all Churches and Religious Associations in the USSR was held in Zagorsk. Rabbi Shlifer and Rabbi Itsko Shekhtman of the Kiev Jewish Religious Community represented the Jewish religion. All the churches in the Soviet Union recognised by the authorities took part in this Conference, viz., the Armenian Church; the Evangelical Lutheran Church (only the Churches of Latvia and Estonia were represented); the Catholic Church (only its Latvian and Lithuanian dioceses were represented); the All-Union Council of Evangelical Christians – Baptists, Old Believers; the All-Union Council of Seventh Day Adventists; the Reformed (Calvinist) Church of the Transcarpathian Province; the Methodist Church of Estonia; the Community of Spiritual Christians (Molokans) of Baku and Tbilisi; the Muslims; the Central Buddhist Council; the Jewish Communities of Moscow and Kiev.

It is obvious from this list that the Jewish religion is one of the few in the Soviet Union that have no general national organisational framework. See the protocols of the Conference: *Conference in Defence of Peace of All Churches and Religious Associations in the USSR*, Moscow, Moscow Patriarchate, 1952.

63 The use of rabbis for political purposes, as reflected in this document, is not an innovation of the post-Stalin period, but was one of the means regularly employed by Stalin in World War II. See also Docs. 118–20.

Vorkul, Rabbi of Kaunas, fought in the Lithuanian Brigade of the Red Army against the Nazis. He is now living in Israel.

64 This document and Doc. 119 show the Soviet authorities' interest in displaying the supposedly negative attitude of the Soviet Union's non-Ashkenazi Jewish communities towards the Sinai Campaign; hence the special announcements of the Bukharan and Georgian Jewish communities, instead of a joint *communiqué* of all Soviet rabbis as was the case in 1955; see Doc. 116. Unlike the beginning of the 1940s, no announcements were published on behalf of the non-religious Jewish public. The procedure for publishing *communiqués* in the name of various bodies in the Soviet Union is well known; either a previously prepared text is brought to the signatories or, at best, the signatories are requested to formulate a statement along the lines dictated to them, the final text requiring the approval of the authorities.

65 From the list of signatories to this statement, we can see the distribution of synagogues in the Soviet Union in 1956 as well as of the rabbis and heads of Jewish communities at this time. Unfortunately we have no biographical data on the signatories (except for Vorkul; see n. 63 above).

66 Rabbi David B. Hollander, the Honorary President of the Rabbinical Council of America, headed their delegation to Russia. He is a leader of the *Mizrahi* movement in America and head of the Mount Eden Jewish Center, Bronx, New York.

67 On Gedaliyahu Pechersky, see Chapter 5, n. 105 and Docs. 86–7. In the Stalin period, Pechersky did not venture to lodge open complaints with government

institutions, contenting himself with sending anonymous ones. It is interesting that the Commissioner of the Leningrad Police promised to take disciplinary measures against those to blame, one indication of the important change in the conduct of the forces of authority in the post-Stalin period with regard to citizens' complaints.

68 The Council for the Affairs of Religious Cults, which was established in 1944, functions under the auspices of the USSR Council of Ministers. Its main tasks are to supervise the introduction of laws and resolutions designed to implement the separation of church from state and of schooling from the church; to adopt the necessary measures to guarantee freedom of conscience for Soviet citizens; to assist religious organisations in their dealings with various state bodies. It covers all the recognised religions except the Russian Orthodox Church. The Council has representatives in the governments of the Union and of the autonomous republics, and also in the executive committees of territorial and provincial Soviets of workers' deputies.

69 The question of baking *mazot* in the Soviet Union is discussed at the beginning of this chapter. This request from the Leningrad Jewish community, dated 7 March 1955, was acknowledged by the Party Secretary and then forwarded, it seems, to the Ministry of the Provisions Industry.

70 For this decree see Chapter 2, n. 20.

71 Pechersky's complaint to the Procurator General about the unseemly behaviour of a number of worshippers at the synagogue followed previous complaints to the Leningrad police and to the Committee for the Affairs of Religious Cults. The negative reply of the Procurator General of Leningrad was due to the fact that the worshippers in question were tools of the authorities.

72 Rabbi Zalman Natan Kiselgof, Deputy Chief Rabbi of Moscow, was born in the small town of Novo-Vitebsk, Kherson Province. His father, Shlomo, was killed when he was two, and he was brought up by his grandfather, Zvi, son of Asher Antshil Ha-Kohen. Kiselgof studied at a *yeshivah* in Kremenchug with Rabbi Yitskhak Tsukerman. He learnt to be a ritual slaughterer with his father-in-law, and was ordained as a rabbi by Rabbi Yaakov Makavetsky of Kharkov and the Rabbi of Novy Rog. Kiselgof was rabbi and ritual slaughterer in Novo-Podolsk, Novo-Zhitomir, and elsewhere. He wrote four books: *Birkat ha-ZaN* (The Blessing of Zalman Natan), on the Gemara; *Even Shlomo* (Solomon's Stone), on the Mishnah; *Haderat Zevi* (The Glory of Zvi), on the Torah; and *Konteres derashot ha-ZaN* (Booklet of Zalman Natan's Sermons), a short version of his first book.

73 Song of Songs 6:11.

74 II Samuel 3:38.

75 Mishnah – early codification of Oral Law (as distinct from Written Law, the Bible); *Ein Yaakov* – a collection of legends and homilies from the Talmud by Rabbi Yaakov, son of Shlomo Ibn Haviv (sixteenth–seventeenth centuries).

76 This extract is taken from Mitin's speech at the Seminar on Problems of Scientific-Atheist Propaganda of the All-Union Society for the Dissemination of Political and Scientific Knowledge, which took place in Moscow from 20 to 30 May 1957. On the author, M. B. Mitin, see Chapter 2, n. 35.

77 After a lull of about two years (1955–6), the term 'cosmopolitanism', which had been central to the campaign against Jewish intellectuals in the Soviet Union during the Stalinist era, began to be used again. See Chapter 4.

78 Yehudah Leyb Levin (1894–1972), rabbi, was born in Ekaterinoslav (now Dne-propetrovsk), where his father was rabbi. During World War I, he became rabbi of the Ukrainian town of Grishino (now Krasnoarmeisk), and later of Ekaterinoslav. Because of difficulties imposed on the clergy and conflicts with his congregations, he returned to Krasnoarmeisk to be a religious scribe for various Jewish communities, particularly those in Georgia. In 1957, when Rabbi Shlifer inaugurated the *yeshivah*

in the Moscow Great Synagogue, Levin was appointed rabbi of the synagogue and head of the *yeshivah*. He travelled abroad with official delegations. Levin's family emigrated to Israel after his death.

79 Refutations on the subject of synagogue closures in the Soviet Union were heard in particular from the Soviet leader Frol Kozlov during his visit to the USA. See Chapter 2, n. 64 and Doc. 21.

80 This certificate was shown to us by Zilber, who is now in Israel. It reads:

Respected Comrade *Zilber*,
The seven-year School No. 65 of the Lenin District of Kazan expresses its gratitude to you for the good upbringing of your daughter.
Your daughter, *Zilber Sara*, always receives 'excellent' and exhibits excellent discipline.
Director
7-year School No. 65
Lukoyanova (Lukoyanova)

On Zilber, see also Doc. 83.

81 See M. Shvartsman, 'Erusalymski yarmulky', *Radyanska Bukovyna*, 26 August 1960.

82 Yakiv Davydovych Kirshenblat (1912–), biologist, was born in Tbilisi. He finished Leningrad University in 1932 and the Leningrad Medical Institute in 1948. Kirshenblat, who has been a member of the Communist Party since 1944, has held the Chair of Physiology at the Chernovtsy Medical Institute since 1954.

83 Semen Abramovych Kats (1907–), surgeon, was born in Chervonoarmeiskoe. He finished the Rostov Medical Institute in 1932 and worked there till 1942. From 1945 to 1955, he was a senior lecturer at the Kharkov Medical Institute. Since 1955, he has held the Chair of Surgery at the Chernovtsy Medical Institute. Kats joined the Communist Party in 1928.

84 Valentyn Lvovych Khenkin (1901–), surgeon, was born in Rostov-on-Don. He finished the medical faculty of the Pivnichno-Kavkaz University in 1926. From 1938, he worked at the Rostov Medical Institute, and, from 1950, at the University of Uzhgorod. Since 1955, he has held chairs at the Chernovtsy Medical Institute. Khenkin joined the Communist Party in 1943.

85 Trofym Kornilovych Kychko, research student of Judaism. His first book, *Iudeiska religiya, pokhodzhennya, sut* (The Jewish Religion, Origins and Nature), was published in Kiev in 1957. He was awarded the degree of Candidate of Philosophical Sciences for his research work *Suchasny iudaizm i iogo reaktsyina rol* (Contemporary Judaism and Its Reactionary Role).

Kychko, a member of the Communist Party, spent the war under German occupation. In D. Medvedev's documentary story *Na beregakh yuzhnogo Buga* (On the Banks of the Southern Bug), which appeared in the journal *Zhovten*, 1952, nos. 7–9, Kychko is mentioned (under the fictitious name of Samsonov) as one of the heroes of the Soviet underground in Vinnitsa. Medvedev's story was subjected to sharp criticism in an article by L. Ozyabkina and N. Zarudny, published in the Ukrainian language in *Vinnitska pravda* and reprinted in the *Literaturnaya gazeta* of 10 February 1953. The authors of the article criticised Medvedev for the distortion of facts. They affirmed that Kychko and his friends were never members of the Vinnitsa underground and that in the story they overshadow the real fighters against Fascism; that Kychko in fact compromised himself by his behaviour during the occupation. As a result of an investigation carried out by local Party organs, Kychko was excluded from the ranks of the Communist Party. In 1961, Medvedev's story came out in book form, published by the Ministry of Defence of the USSR, following a verification – as is noted in the editor's remarks – of the controversial facts with regard to the activities of the members of the underground. At this time Kychko was reinstated into the Party.

In 1963, Kychko's book *Iudaizm bez prykras* (Judaism Without Embellishment), published in Kiev, provoked an angry outcry in the West for its blatant anti-Semitic tendency. The book was also subjected to criticism in the Soviet Union.

Due to the severe criticism, Kychko's works did not appear in print for a long time. Since 1967, his articles – anti-Zionist and anti-Israel in content – have begun to appear again.

86 It is not clear to which edition of the translation by N. Pereferkovich (1871–1940) of the Mishnah, *Tosefta*, *Mekhilta* and *Sifra* Kychko's footnote refers. The work appeared in at least two editions, and Kychko's note is inaccurate in both cases. His footnote should read: Tractate *Avot*, Chs. 1-v, in N. Pereferkovich (trans. and ed.), *Talmud, Mishnah and Tosefta*, vols. 1–7, St Petersburg, Izdanie P.P. Soikina, 1899–1904, vol. 4, pp. 478–99.

87 For the various rabbinical homiletic explanations of Moses's smashing of the tablets of stone, see *Midrash Rabbah: Exodus* (trans. by Rabbi Dr S. M. Lehrman), London, Soncino Press, 1939, pp. 528–9; *Pentateuch with Targum Onkelos and Rashi's Commentary* (trans. and annotated by Rev. M. Rosenbaum and Dr A. M. Silbermann), vol. 2, *Exodus*, London, Shapiro and Vallentine, 1930, p. 191; *The Babylonian Talmud, Seder Nashim*, vol. 5, *Nedarim* (trans. and annotated by Rabbi Dr H. Freedman), London, Soncino Press, 1936, p. 118.

88 Kychko seems to be referring to a passage in *Pesaḥim* 49b (not 19b), which reads:

Rabbi Eleazar said: An *am ha-arez*, it is permitted to stab him [even] on the Day of Atonement which falls on the Sabbath.

Said his disciples to him, Master, say to slaughter [ritually]?

He replied: This [ritual slaughter] requires a benediction, whereas that [stabbing] does not require a benediction.

While this extract undoubtedly reflects the strong antipathy that existed between scholars and the *am ha-arez*, it is of course only to be understood as a witticism.

89 See K. Marx & F. Engels, *Werke*, Berlin, Dietz Verlag, 1958, vol. 1, pp. 372, 374. For an English version of Marx's 'Zur Judenfrage' (On the Jewish Question), see *Writings of the Young Marx on Philosophy and Society* (ed. L. D. Easton and K. H. Guddat), New York, Doubleday, 1967, pp. 216–48.

90 Cf. A. Alekseev, *Besedy pravoslavnogo khristianina iz evreev s novoobrashchennymi iz svoikh sobratii ob istinakh svyatoi very i zabluzhdeniyakh talmudicheskikh* (Conversations of an Orthodox Christian from the Jews with the Newly Converted of his Brethren on the Truths of the Holy Faith and the Errors of the Talmud), Novgorod, n.p., 1875, p. 93. (See following note.)

91 A. A. Alekseev (baptised name of Vulf Nakhlas), the author of this book, was born in 1826 in the small town of Nezaritsy in the former Podolsk Province. His father was a poor but well-known talmudic scholar. Alekseev was converted to the Orthodox faith while serving in the Tsar's army and wrote many books on the life of the Russian Jews from the point of view of a convert.

92 The Ideological Committee of the Central Committee of the Communist Party, which is the central body responsible for handling ideological and cultural questions in the Soviet Union, met to discuss T. Kychko's book only after it had aroused a wave of protests in the West, including protests from Communist parties and Leftist circles. See B. Lobovik & K. Yampolsky, 'Knyga pro reaktsiiu sut iudaizmu', *Radyanska kultura*, 26 March 1964.

9. Jews in Soviet government

1 The term 'Soviet government' refers to the supreme institutions of the Communist Party (the Central Committee, the Politburo, the Orgburo and the Secretariat); representative institutions of the state such as the Supreme Soviet; and the

government (all its branches, and the senior administration at the level of directors and deputy directors of offices and departments in the various ministries) – all these at the central and republican level. (The information given herein reflects the extent to which we possess the relevant data.)

2 Another factor was that many Jews were expelled from the Party leadership as a result of the fierce internal struggles within the Communist Party in the first half of the twenties, in the course of which both the left and right factions were defeated by Stalin. Trotsky, Zinovyev, Radek and Sokolnikov were among those affected.

3 Among the many central figures of Jewish origin who were accused in the show trials and the many other secret trials of 1936–9 were Zinovyev, Kamenev, Draitser, Sokolnikov, Rozengolts, Radek, Lifshits, Drobnis, Boguslavsky, Norkin, Turok, Yagoda, Yakir and Khataevich. Some of them were condemned to death and executed; others died in prisons or concentration camps.

4 *Sotsialny i natsionalny sostav VKP (b)* (Social and National Composition of the All-Russian Communist Party (Bolsheviks)), Moscow–Leningrad, Gosizdat, 1928, p. 114. For additional data, see also Rigby, *Communist Party Membership in the USSR 1917–1967*, pp. 366–88; J. A. Newth & Z. Katz, 'Proportion of Jews in the Communist Party of the Soviet Union', *Bulletin on Soviet and East European Jewish Affairs*, 1969, no. 4, pp. 37–8.

5 The annexation of the Western Ukraine to the Soviet Union in 1939 presents a special problem from the point of view of statistical data. But it is evident that in that brief period of only five months (Rigby's data for the Ukraine are from May 1940; *Communist Party Membership in the USSR*) not many Jews were accepted into the Communist Party.

6 This estimate of half a million Jews in the Red Army is cited by the Soviet Jewish demographer, Y. Kantor. See his article, 'Yidn oyf dem gresten un vikhtikstn front', *Folks-shtime*, 18 April 1963, pp. 8, 11.

7 With the annexation of the territories from Poland, Romania and the Baltic States, the Soviet Union's population stood at 193 million (not taking into account the natural increase of 1939–40). If we accept the estimate of five million Jews in the USSR prior to the outbreak of the Soviet–German war in June 1941, then the Jews constituted 2.5% of the entire population. See *Bolshaya sovetskaya entsiklopediya* (Large Soviet Encyclopedia), 1st edition, volume devoted wholly to 'The Soviet Union', Moscow, Ogiz, 1948, p. 50.

8 'Apparently', because the plethora of reports in the West on discrimination against Jews in the Soviet Union in various spheres – such as admittance to institutions of higher education, to certain positions and to various ruling institutions – has not, to the best of our knowledge, mentioned the question of Party admittance; further research is required here.

9 See above, n. 4.

10 'KPSS v tsifrakh', *Partiinaya zhizn*, 1976, no. 10, p.16; Altshuler, *Ha-kibuz ha-yehudi*, pp. 242–3.

11 Iona Emmanuilovich Yakir (1896–1937), military commander.

12 According to Seweryn Bialer, there were fifteen Jewish members and candidates on the Central Committee, and not fourteen, as we have determined (Tables 21–3). But, as he does not provide a list of names of the Central Committee members, it is unclear whom he regards as the fifteenth member of Jewish origin. See S. Bialer, 'How Russians Rule Russia', *Problems of Communism*, 1964, vol. XIII, no. 5, p. 46.

13 Jews constituted 10.1% of the 16th Congress in 1930 and about 12.2% of the 17th Congress in 1934 (calculation according to a list of Central Committee members).

14 See *Rezolutsyes fun der XVIII alfarbandisher konferents fun der ALKP (B)* (Resolutions of the 18th All-Union Conference of the All-Union Communist Party (Bolshevik)), Moscow, Der emes, 1941, pp. 27–8.

15 Allilueva, *Only One Year*, p. 155.
16 We find no authority for Newth and Katz's opinion (see n. 4) that Shkolnikov, a member of the Central Committee and Party Secretary of the Voronezh Region, is a Jew. This name does not appear in any of the many lists of all the 'who's who' of Jewish origin published in recent years by the Soviet authorities.
17 See *Izvestiya*, 16 March 1949.
18 *Vestnik statistiki*, 1967, no. 3, pp. 91–2.
19 *Itogi vyborov i sostav deputatov verkhovnykh sovetov soyuznykh i avtonomnykh respublik* (Results of the Elections and of the Composition of the Delegates to the Supreme Soviets of the Union and Autonomous Republics), Moscow, Izvestiya, 1971, pp. 18, 20. For 1963, see *Itogi vyborov*, 1963.
20 In the 1938 elections, 92 Jews out of 3,594 delegates, or 2.5%, were elected in the eleven republics, whereas Jews constituted only 0.26% of these delegates in 1959 – an astonishing decrease; see sources for Table 23, *Vybory v Verkhovny Sovet*, pp. 14–17.
21 See above, n. 19.
22 For 1971, we have data only for the Russian Republic: 3,127 Jewish delegates were elected out of a total of 1,092,750. See *Itogi vyborov i sostav deputatov mestnykh sovetov RSFSR, 1971* (Results of the Elections and of the Composition of the Delegates to the Local Soviets of the RSFSR, 1971), Moscow, Sovetskaya Rossiya, 1972, pp. 22–3; see also E. M. Jacobs, 'Jewish Representation in Local Soviets, 1959–1973', *Soviet Jewish Affairs*, 1976, no. 1, pp. 18–26.
23 In early 1946, a number of Jews (in addition to those listed in Table 27) held the post of deputy minister, but we do not know whether they continued in their positions after that year. They were V. V. Burgman, Yu. S. Kogan, V. B. Haisin, M. D. Shapiro, S. N. Borobosin, S. M. Sandler. See *Eynikeyt*, 23 and 26 March 1946.
24 See Docs. 13–14 and 17.
25 The report by the correspondent of the *Rakaḥ* (Israel Communist Party) periodical *Zo ha-derekh*, to the effect that Savar Azimov, Deputy Premier of Uzbekistan and its Minister of Education, was a Jew (and was even preparing a screenplay called 'I Am a Jew'), was not confirmed by any other source. Indeed, the fact that Azimov served as Soviet Ambasador to Syria indicates that the report was unfounded.
26 *Evrei i evreisky narod*, 1960, no. 2/48; *Mažoji Lietuviškoji Tarybine Enciklopedija*, Vilnius, Mintis, vol. 1, p. 228.
27 *Pravda Ukrainy*, 24 February 1949.
28 *Evrei i evreisky narod*, 1960, no. 1/74.
29 See *Sovetskaya Moldaviya*, 19 July 1967.
30 There were some extremely interesting data in Ordzhonikidze's speech at the 15th Congress of the Communist Party in December 1927: Jews constituted 22.6% of the governmental machinery in the Ukraine, and 30.3% in the city of Kiev; 30.6% in Belorussia, and 38.6% in the city of Minsk; 6% in Uzbekistan; 5.8% in Birobidzhan, and 10% in the city of Baku. One may confidently assert that the proportion of Jews in the senior administration was not much lower. See *XV syezd Vsesoyuznoi kommunisticheskoi partii (bolshevikov), stenograficheskiy otchet* (The 15th Congress of the All-Union Communist Party (Bolsheviks), Stenographic Report), 2nd edition, Moscow–Leningrad, Gosizdat, 1928, pp. 399–401.
31 Of interest here is Col. Oleg Penkovsky's testimony claiming that the Jews had already been expelled from all the security services in the Stalin period and that this process culminated in 1954–5. See *The Penkovsky Papers*, New York, Doubleday, 1965, p. 358.
32 See Rabinovich, *Jews in the Soviet Union*, p. 52.
33 Grigory Yakovlevich Zeldin served as a member of the Supreme Court as late as 1949 (see *Izvestiya*, 16 March 1949), and Yan Mikhailovich Grinberg was a senior official there until 1956 (see *Ezhegodnik BSE*, 1959, pp. 582–3).

34 Semi-official data published during the war spoke of about one hundred generals of Jewish origin in Red Army service (so Mikhoels and Fefer, members of the Jewish Anti-Fascist Committee, declared during their 1943 visit to the United States). From 1940 to 1946, the number of Jewish generals was 206; see *Evreisky samazdat*, vol. 9, pp. 60–85. While we do not know how many of them continued in active service following the war, from the list of Jewish generals we have drawn up on the basis of their being mentioned in the Soviet press during 1948–68, it turns out that at least forty-three (from the rank of major-general upwards) maintained contacts with the army. The two most famous Jewish generals, Kreizer and Dragunsky, even filled posts in the army during the late 1960s. Other generals who have held posts in the army in recent years are A. Tsirlin, M. Milshtein, Isaak Rabinovich, Isaak Rogozin and Aleksandr Shatsky.

35 Semen Zakharovich Ginzburg (1897–?), leading Soviet technocrat, was born into a poor family in Minsk. He joined the Communist Party in 1917, taking part in the Civil War. In 1927, he graduated from the Advanced Technical School in Moscow. From 1930, he occupied various posts in the Sovnarkhoz (Soviet of People's Economy) and the ministries. From 1947 to 1950, he held the post of Minister of the Building Materials Industry. From 1951 to 1957, he was deputy minister in various ministries. He became Deputy Director, and later Director of the Stroibank (Construction Bank) in 1958. Ginzburg took part in conferences against 'Israeli aggression in the Middle East' and signed an anti-Israel statement together with other representatives of the 'Jewish community' of the Soviet Union.

36 On David Yakovlevich Raizer, see Doc. 140.

37 Lazar Moiseevich Kaganovich (1893–?), leading Communist Party activist. Kaganovich was appointed First Deputy Chairman of the Soviet of Ministers of the USSR in March 1953. At the plenary meeting of the CC CPSU in October 1952, after the 19th Party Congress, Kaganovich was elected a member of the Presidium of the CC CPSU. Together with other members of the 'Anti-Party Group', he was dismissed from all Party and government posts in June 1957.

There is much convincing data testifying to Kaganovich's genuine interest in Jewish affairs. There is also no doubt that he fought against Zionism and the Bund. In the 1920s and 1930s, when holding responsible government and Party posts in the Ukraine, Kaganovich must have met with the problem of the position of the Jews, and it is quite possible that he received individual and collective appeals from Jews and Jewish communities. Kaganovich was one of the supporters of the establishment of the Jewish Autonomous Region in Birobidzhan. Like all Bolsheviks – Jews and non-Jews alike – he saw assimilation as the only genuine, and desirable, solution to the Jewish question. The 'Crimean Affair' and Kaganovich's role in it has never been fully clarified. It is thought that he was one of the initiators of the idea of founding a Jewish republic in the Crimea after the victory over Germany, or, at least, that he approved the idea. There is also evidence of a visit by Kaganovich to the State Yiddish Theatre at the end of the 1930s and of his criticising the theatre for not including genuine Jewish heroes, such as the Maccabees and Bar-Kokhba, in its repertoire.

38 Yakov Grigoryevich Kreizer (1905–69), military commander, was born in Voronezh, the son of a Cantonist. In 1923 he graduated from the Voronezh Infantry School, in 1942 from the General Staff Academy, and in 1949 he completed advanced courses at the same Academy. During World War II he commanded various armies, and after the war he was made commander of various military districts. In 1962 he was made army general, and in 1963 Commandant of the 'Vystrel' Higher Officers Courses. In 1954 he was elected a member of the CC CP of the Ukrainian SSR. Kreizer was a deputy to a number of Supreme Soviet convocations, and a delegate to CPSU Congresses. From 1961 to 1966 he was a

member of the CPSU Central Auditing Committee. In 1941 he was made a Hero of the Soviet Union. Kreizer was a member of the Jewish Anti-Fascist Committee. At the time of the Suez Crisis, he signed a public protest against the actions of Israel.

39 Solomon Abramovich Lozovsky (pseudonym of Dridzo, 1878–1952), Soviet statesman and trade-union leader. Lozovsky was born into a poor family in Danilovka in the former Ekaterinoslav Province. He went to work at the age of eleven and completed his studies on his own. He joined the Russian Social-Democratic Workers' Party in 1901, and in 1905 attached himself to the Bolshevik wing. Lozovsky participated in the 1905 Revolution. From 1909 to 1917 he resided in France where he was active in the socialist movement. He returned to Russia after the February Revolution and was immediately appointed Secretary of the Trade Union Council. His opposition to Lenin's policies during and after the October Revolution led to his expulsion from the Party between March 1918 and December 1919, when he rejoined the Bolsheviks. From 1920 on he was appointed to a number of important posts, serving as head of the Communist Trade Union International from 1921 to 1937, Director of the State Publishing House from 1937 to 1939, Deputy Commissar of Foreign Affairs from 1939 to 1947, Deputy Director and later Director of the Soviet Information Bureau. From 1939 to 1949 he was a member of the CC CPSU.

As Director of the Information Bureau, Lozovsky was responsible for the work of the Jewish Anti-Fascist Committee and was concerned with world Jewish affairs. It is believed that in 1944 he supported the plan to set up a Jewish autonomous settlement in the Crimea, which led to his arrest in 1949. Lozovsky was sentenced with other Jewish intellectuals in July 1952 and was executed on 12 August 1952.

40 Veniamin Emmanuilovich Dymshits (1910–), Soviet economist and engineer, a Deputy Premier of the Soviet Union since 1959. Dymshits was born in Feodosiya, now Crimea Province, the son of the Hebrew writer Avraham Rakovsky. In 1962 he was made Chairman of the USSR State Planning Committee.

10. The Jewish Autonomous Region of Birobidzhan

1 While it found public expression only in 1926, at the first all-Soviet conference of *Ozet*, there is no doubt that the idea of establishing a Jewish republic was engendered long before that date. The decisive factor in the rejection of the demand to set up a Jewish republic was the *Evsektsiya* leaders' apprehension that its establishment at too early a stage was more likely to hurt than help.

2 On the historical background to the creation of the Jewish Autonomous Region and the history of the Jewish settlement there, see Lvavi, *Ha-hityashvut ha-yehudit be-birobidzhan*; Ch. Abramsky, 'The Biro-Bidzhan Project, 1927–1959', in Kochan (ed.), *The Jews in Soviet Russia Since 1917*, pp. 62–75.

3 Lvavi, *Ha-hityashvut ha-yehudit be-birobidzhan*, pp. 107, 115.

4 On the aftermath of this obscure and tragic episode, which was one of the pretexts for the arrest of the leaders of the Jewish Anti-Fascist Committee and their trial for treason, see Chapter 5.

5 It may be assumed that among them were M. Kalinin (who died in 1946), one of the programme's initiators, and L. Kaganovich, who was a kind of guardian of the Jewish Autonomous Region in the thirties. Even though Stalin admitted the failure of the Birobidzhan project in his discussion with Roosevelt at Yalta on 10 February 1945, he certainly had no objections to the renewed attempts to settle the region with Jewish immigrants after World War II.

6 As was said on Radio Moscow: 'There is no basis for the claims that the Jewish people in the Soviet Union is doomed to extinction, for the name of the Jewish

Autonomous Region is engraved in letters of gold in the Stalin constitution.' See I. Fefer's remarks: *Summary of World Broadcasts*, Part I, 24 June 1947.

7 This notion – that in 1945, under the influence of the Jewish Anti-Fascist Committee, the Soviet government attempted to influence the Polish Committee for National Liberation (which was being groomed by the USSR as the future Provisional Polish Government) to consent to the former Jewish citizens of Poland being directed to Birobidzhan – is cited in Leneman, *La Tragédie des juifs en URSS*, pp. 30–1.

8 According to reports in *Eynikeyt*, the registration began in the Ukrainian city of Vinnitsa. See *Eynikeyt*, 19 October 1946.

9 Lvavi, *Ha-hityashvut ha-yehudit be-birobidzhan*, pp. 103–5.

10 The overall number of Jews in the region was estimated by specialists at between thirty and thirty-five thousand.

11 For further details, see Chapter 7, especially Tables 14, 15 and 17.

12 Among the prominent personages arrested were: Mikhail Levitin, former Chairman of the Regional Executive Committee, and the authors Yisrael Emiot, Dov-Ber Slutsky, Buzi Miler, Hershl Rabinkov, Leva Vaserman, Haim Maltinsky and others.

13 See, for example, *Jewish Chronicle*, 12 January and 2 February 1951. The extent to which even the Israeli legation in Moscow lacked information on what was happening in Birobidzhan may be seen in Namir, *Shlihut be-moskvah*, pp. 310–12.

14 See *The New York Times*, 21 and 22 June 1954, and Doc. 146, which contains a summary of Salisbury's visit.

15 *Jewish Chronicle*, 3 September 1954.

16 *Jewish Chronicle*, 22 and 25 November and 9 December 1955. It was predominantly the Warsaw Yiddish newspaper *Folks-shtime* and the Paris Yiddish newspaper *Naye prese* that began to publish these reports.

17 *Naye prese*, 24 April 1958.

18 *Evreiskaya avtonomnaya oblast* (The Jewish Autonomous Region), Khabarovsk, Khabarovskoe knizhnoe izdatelstvo, 1959.

19 See *Sovetskaya Rossiya*, 7 May 1959. On the same day there was a fifteen-minute programme on Radio Moscow which included some sections in Yiddish.

20 *Itogi vsesoyuznoi perepisi naseleniya 1959 goda* (Results of the 1959 All-Union Population Census), vol. RSFSR, pp. 334–5, 360–1, 384–5.

21 This may be calculated from the ratio of women to men in the region: there were 1,260 women to every 1,000 men, as compared with a ratio of 1,169 women to every 1,000 men in the Jewish population of the RSFSR (the life-span of the women being higher than that of the men). See Z. Katz, 'The Anomaly of the Jewish Autonomous Region in Birobidzhan: Recent Soviet Figures', *Bulletin on Soviet and East European Jewish Affairs*, 1968, no. 2, p. v/6

22 Since the fifties non-Jews have headed the region and its districts, and its governmental and Party institutions alike. About 10% of the seventy-five members of the Regional Party Committee elected in 1963 were Jews and 10%–12% of the ninety-nine delegates to the region's Council, elected on 3 March 1963. See Lvavi, *Ha-hityashvut ha-yehudit be-birobidzhan*, pp. 244–6.

23 See, for example, A. Mikoyan's 1959 statement in the United States, Doc. 20, and *Jewish Chronicle*, 30 January 1959.

24 See 'Oblast Loses Character', *Christian Science Monitor*, 21 June 1965.

25 One may add the publication of the pamphlet *Evreiskaya avtonomnaya oblast* (The Jewish Autonomous Region), Khabarovsk, Khabarovskoe knizhnoe izdatelstvo, 1965.

26 The claim heard in the West that the Jewish Autonomous Region was not abolished by the authorities because of constitutional difficulties is of course groundless, for even a Union republic, i.e. the supreme level in the Soviet federation –

the Karelo-Finnish Republic – was abolished with no difficulty in 1956. Thus, the abolition of an autonomous region would certainly present no problem if the authorities desired it.

27 Yaakov Lestchinsky (1876–1966), Russian-born pioneer in sociology, economics and demography of Jewish life, studied at Berne and Zurich universities. Lestchinsky helped found the Zionist Socialist Workers' Party. Although he abandoned party politics in 1906, he remained an active Zionist. In 1921, he left Russia for Berlin, where he helped establish the Institute for Research into Contemporary Jewry and Judaism in the early 1920s. He was expelled from Germany by the Nazis, and moved to Warsaw in 1934. He was expelled from Poland for publishing material on the plight of Polish Jewry. In 1938, he went to the USA, and in 1959, to Tel Aviv and later to Jerusalem. Throughout his life Lestchinsky wrote numerous works on the statistics and demography of the Jewish people; he was one of the first students of the Holocaust and he published a survey of Soviet Jewry.

28 Aleksandr Bakhmutsky was appointed to the post of First Secretary of the Regional Party Committee in Birobidzhan in 1943 and served in this capacity until his arrest at the end of 1948. He was sentenced to death but the sentence was commuted to twenty-five years' imprisonment.

29 See Chapter 7.

30 We did not find Lestchinsky's article in this issue of *Forward*.

31 Mikhail Levitin was the Chairman of the Regional Executive Committee of Birobidzhan from 1947 to 1948. He was arrested at the end of 1948 and sentenced to twenty-five years' imprisonment. It would appear that he died in prison.

32 Shmerke Kacherginsky (1908–54), Yiddish writer. Kacherginsky was born in Vilnius. During World War II he escaped from the Vilnius ghetto and joined the partisans. After the war, he went to Poland, Paris and finally in 1950 to Argentina. He was killed in an airplane crash.

33 This article by the Soviet Jewish demographer and statistician, L. Zinger, was published in the weekly publication of the Jewish Anti-Fascist Committee, *Eynikeyt*, in 1948 and in the pro-Communist English journal in March 1949, in other words after the great purge that was carried out in the Autonomous Region and after the cessation of cultural activity in Yiddish.

34 The journalist Harrison Salisbury visited Birobidzhan in June 1954 and, as he justly notes, he was without doubt the first foreign visitor to the Jewish Autonomous Region after the curtain had descended on it in 1949.

35 The reference is to Lev Benkovich, who was one of the heads of the region after the liquidation of the former Jewish leadership at the end of 1948. He was elected a delegate to the Supreme Soviet of the RSFSR on 18 February 1951.

36 According to the testimony of the actor Feybish Arones, the Birobidzhan Yiddish Theatre was closed on 5 October 1949.

37 The film *The Seekers of Happiness*, written by Kovach and Zeltser, directed by V. Korsh, with the actors Binyamin Zuskin, Blumental-Tamarina and Tsesarskaya, was made in Birobidzhan in the second half of 1935.

38 Iosif Romanovich Bumagin (1907–45), Hero of the Soviet Union, was born in Vitebsk. He was awarded the title of Hero of the Soviet Union posthumously, on 27 June 1945.

39 David Abramovich Kudryavitsky (1919–43), Hero of the Soviet Union. The title Hero of the Soviet Union was awarded to him posthumously, on 15 January 1944.

40 Iosif Lvovich Bokor was also Communist Party Secretary of the Birobidzhan Town Committee from 1961 to 1963.

41 Naum Abramovich Korchminsky worked in the Shalom Aleikhem Library in

Birobidzhan from 1946 to 1947. From the 1950s, he worked off and on as editor of the *Birobidzhaner shtern*.

42 Boris Izrailevich Miler (1913–), Yiddish writer, was born in the small town of Kopai in Vinnitsa Province. He graduated from the Moscow Pedagogic Institute in 1936. His first works were published in 1931. He joined the Communist Party in 1941. From 1937 to 1946, he was editor of the newspaper *Birobidzhaner shtern*. Miler was arrested at the beginning of 1949 and rehabilitated in 1956. He lives in Birobidzhan, and Jewish life in Birobidzhan occupies an important place in his works.

43 On the Jewish religion in the USSR, see Chapter 8.

11. Jews in Soviet literature

1 We shall refer to some 200 works of prose, poetry, drama and memoirs, published between 1948 and 1967, in which the Jewish theme is given some kind of expression, be it a portrayal of the Jewish experience and way of life, or the inclusion of protagonists of Jewish origin. We shall also refer to numerous works published before 1948, especially during the war period.

2 Y. Klaiman deals with this aspect of Soviet literature; see 'Evrei v noveishoi russkoi literature', *Evreisky vestnik* (Leningrad), 1928, pp. 155–8. On the Jewish subjects in Russian literature, see V. Lvov-Rogachevsky, *Russkaya evreiskaya literatura* (Russian Jewish Literature), Moscow, Gosizdat, 1922.

3 On the Jews in Soviet literature, see J. Kunitz, *Russian Literature and the Jew*, New York, Columbia University Press, 1929; B.J. Choseed, 'Jews in Soviet Literature', in Simmons (ed.), *Through the Glass of Soviet Literature*, pp. 110–58; M. Friedberg, 'Jewish Themes in Soviet Russian Literature', in Kochan (ed.), *The Jews in Soviet Russia Since 1917*, pp. 188–207.

4 Choseed, 'Jews in Soviet Literature', pp. 132–5.

5 Among these one may mention Fadeev, Surkov, Polevoi, Simonov, Korneichuk, Vasilevskaya, Kochura, Tychyna, Mavr and many others.

6 Erenburg, *Sobranie sochinenii*, vol. 3, p. 435.

7 See Erenburg, *Voina* (War), vols. 1–3, Moscow, 1942–4; 'Konets getto', *Novy mir*, 1944, no. 3.

8 We were unable to discover the source and date of publication of this work. In the course of a sharp attack on the author during the anti-cosmopolitan campaign, the writer Dmyterko quoted lengthy passages from it; *Literaturnaya gazeta*, 9 March 1949 (Doc. 59).

9 *Tzum zig* (To Victory), Moscow, 1944, pp. 62–9.

10 In the poems 'I Saw It' (1942), 'Kerch' and 'Kandava'. See *Znamya*, 1945, no. 1–2; *Sbornik stikhov* (Anthology of Poems), Moscow, 1947, p. 7.

11 In the poems 'Babi Yar', 'Maidanek'; see L. Pervomaisky, *Sochineniya* (Works), Kiev, vol. 1, pp. 480–1.

12 In his great poem 'My Son', Antokolsky wrote;

> For the hot ashes of all the burned Bibles
> Of all the Polish ghettos and concentration camps
> For all, for all who perished,
> Did he half-Russian and half-Jew
> Rise up for war.   (*Znamya*, 1943, no. 7–8, p. 8)

In his poem 'No Eternal Memory', published in 1946, the poet notes his connection to thousands of years of the history of the Jewish people and uses the words of the Hebrew prayer *Shema yisrael* (Hear, O Israel) (*Znamya*, 1946, no. 7, pp. 64–5).

13 In her autobiographical poem 'Your Victory' (*Znamya*, 1945, no. 9, pp. 1–28), Aliger expresses the grave crisis experienced by an entire generation of Soviet Jews

who believed that assimilation was the answer to the nationality problem: but the war put this faith to the test. Margarita Aliger is proud of being a descendant of the brave Maccabees, although she admits that it was only the Germans who reminded her of her links to her people.

14 Ozerov (Goldberg) wrote the poem 'Babi Yar' in 1944–5 (although it was only published in 1946; see *Oktybar*, 1946, no. 3–4, pp. 160–3). This is one of the most stirring works written in the USSR on the Jewish Holocaust. The poet is at one with all those who were put to death and buried at Babi Yar for him – relatives who cry out to him from beneath the ground and demand that he live their lives which were cut off, and take their revenge.

15 Before the war ended, Khelemsky wrote two poems devoted to the liberation of Riga (*Znamya*, 1945, no. 4, pp. 51–2), in which he expressed the feeling of the Jewish fighter who arrives at the liberated city and finds nothing but a desolate ghetto without a living being. 'Every house', says Khelemsky, 'heaves into sight here like the wall of tears, and there are no words in the language of the Torah able to express the final grief of those led to death, the grief which cries out in all the terror of muteness from within the pit, from the suffocation of the shadow of death.'

16 See especially V. Grossman, *Treblinsky ad* (The Hell of Treblinka), Moscow, 1944; P. Antokolsky and V. Kaverin, 'Vostanie v Sobibore', *Znamya*, 1945, no. 4–5; I. Erenburg (ed.), *Merder fun felker* (Nation-Killers), vols. 1–2, Moscow, 1944–5; B. Gorbatov, 'Lager Maidanek', *Pravda*, 11–12 August 1944. It is also important to mention *The Black Book*, edited by Erenburg and with an introduction by V. Grossman, which did not appear in the Soviet Union because of the Soviet policy of silence about the Jewish Holocaust; see Chapter 12.

17 Among the first Jewish fighters in Soviet literature of the war period is the Commissar Mirovich in Y. Libedinsky's novel *Men of the Guard* (1942). See also the story 'The Weapons Are With Us', by the Jewish-Ukrainian writer Natan Rybak, on Hero of the Soviet Union Laizer Papernik (in *Ukraina v ognyu* (The Ukraine on Fire), Ufa, 1942), and a story on Hero of the Soviet Union Isaak Palkovsky in a work by Lev Kasil ('Fedya iz podplava', *Znamya*, 1943, no. 1).

18 Among the authors who touched on the Jewish issue in the war period were K. Simonov, M. Sholokhov, A. Korneichuk, L. Uspensky, A. Kalinin and V. Gerasimova.

19 'Solntse s vostoka', *Oktyabr*, 1946, nos. 1–2.

20 *Lyudi chistoi sovesti* (People of Clear Conscience), Moscow, 1946.

21 *Voina v tylu vraga* (War in the Enemy's Rear), Moscow, 1947.

22 *V okopakh Stalingrada* (In the Trenches of Stalingrad), Moscow, 1947.

23 *V krymskom podpolye* (In the Crimean Underground), Moscow, 1947.

24 *Molodaya gvardiya* (The Young Guard), Moscow, 1946.

25 *V osade* (Under Siege), Moscow, 1947.

26 'Shchastia', *Radyansky Lviv*, 1947, no. 1.

27 *Podpolny obkom deistvuet* (The Underground Regional Committee Carries On), Moscow, 1947.

28 'Zelenava brama', *Oktyabr*, 1946, no. 12.

29 'Otche nash', *Soviet Short Stories*, Moscow, 1947.

30 A poem of his written in 1942 mentions the Maccabees:

> Weep not, lament not o'er thy loss
> Behold! The age-long griefs avenging,
> The son of love arises fierce
> Red Army soldier, Levi Hirsh,
> Scion of the mighty Maccabeans.

A. Surkov, 'Like Birds about their Ravaged Nest' in *The Road to the West*, as quoted in B. J. Choseed, 'Reflections on the Soviet Nationalities Policy in Literature: The

Jews, 1938–1948', unpublished PhD thesis, New York, Columbia University, 1968, p. 327.

31 Maksim Tank, writing of the ruins of the Minsk ghetto, says:
... even the lament of Jeremiah
Hath not the strength to resurrect the dust grown cold.

M. Tank, *Stikhotvoreniya* (Poems), Moscow, 1948, pp. 28–9, as quoted in Choseed, 'Reflections on the Soviet Nationalities Policy', p. 246.

32 In his poem 'To the Jewish People' (1942), M. Rylsky writes:
Upon us will beam great Marx and Heine ...
... boldly we march
With a sage sneer, like that of old Mokher Seforim
Like your Shvartsman with a sword.

M. Rylsky, *Stikhotvoreniya i poemy* (Lyrics and Poems), Moscow, 1945, p. 260, as quoted in Choseed, 'Reflections on the Soviet Nationalities Policy', p. 252.

33 On Tychyna's poem, see Choseed, 'Reflections on the Soviet Nationalities Policy', p. 252.

34 The authoress V. Panova uses the story of David and Goliath and mentions the Kings of Israel, in particular King David's words that the truth shall be your weapon. See V. Panova, *Sputniki* (Travelling Companions), Moscow, 1946, as quoted in Choseed, 'Reflections on the Soviet Nationalities Policy', p. 345.

35 Ilya Erenburg's *The Storm*, written and published in this period, is perhaps the best illustration of this. Erenburg, whose political sense was highly developed, was certainly aware of the changes occurring in Soviet policy. He therefore found it necessary – for 'balance' and to win over the authorities – to integrate sharp anti-Western elements in his book, in which the Jewish theme occupies an important place. However, it must be said to his credit that he succeeded, whether intentionally or not, in portraying the common Jewish destiny, which is not dependent upon borders or regimes.

36 A. Isbakh, *Gody zhizni* (Years of Life), Moscow, 1948.

37 For another attack on Isbakh, see the article by V. Kozhevnikov in *Novy mir*, 1949, no. 5. Isbakh himself disappeared for seven years, and it was only in 1956 that his name reappeared in the Soviet press.

38 K. Fedin, *Neobyknovennoe leto* (An Extraordinary Summer), Moscow, 1948. In the first part of his trilogy *Distant Joys*, the author also describes a terrifying scene of pogroms carried out by the Black Hundreds against the Jews in 1905.

39 L. Kabo, 'Za dnestrom', *Novy mir*, 1950, nos. 5, 9, 10.

40 We have not been able to obtain the 1953 edition of Leonov's novel *Russky les*, and are therefore basing ourselves on the 1967 edition. But, as M. Hayward notes, some passages dealing with Jewish subjects appeared only in editions up to 1965; see 'Some Observations on Jews in Post-Stalin Soviet Literature', *Bulletin on Soviet and East European Jewish Affairs*, 1969, no. 4, pp. 16, 18–19.
The other two works were I. Kremlov, 'Krepost na Volge', *Zvezda*, 1949, no. 2; V. Belaev, *Staraya Krepost* (The Ancient Fortress), Moscow, 1954.

41 Leonov, *Russky les* (The Russian Forest), Moscow, 1967, p. 285.

42 V. Popov, 'Stal i shlak', *Znamya*, 1949, no. 1.

43 Y. Galan, 'Lvivski narysy', *Vitchyzna*, 1950, no. 5. Interestingly, this reportage does not appear in the work's Russian translation. See Y. Galan, *Izbrannye* (Selected Writings), Moscow, 1951.

44 V. Kataev, *Za vlast Sovetov* (For Soviet Rule), Moscow, 1951.

45 V. Latsis, 'K novomu beregu', *Zvezda*, 1951, no. 9.

46 O. Maltsev, 'Yugoslavskaya tragediya', *Znamya*, 1951, no. 10.

47 Erenburg describes Osip Alper, one of the book's main protagonists, going to mourn over the grave of his mother Hanah and his sister Alya, who were murdered at Babi Yar.

48 Grossman mentions the murder of the mother of the scientist Shtrum, one of the main characters in his book, and of another five thousand Jews in a Ukrainian town; V. Grossman, 'Za pravoe delo', *Novy mir*, 1952, no. 7. The second part of Grossman's book has been published piecemeal in the West in recent years, e.g. in *Kontinent*, 1975, no. 4, pp. 179–216; no. 5, pp. 7–40; *Posev*, 1975, no. 7, pp. 53–5; *Grani*, 1975, no. 9, pp. 3–31.

49 *V strane poverzhennykh*, Moscow, 1951.

50 P. Vershigora, 'Karpatsky reid (Zapiski)', *Zvezda*, 1950, nos. 3, 5. Vershigora stresses that the partisan commanders were prepared to accept everyone into their ranks, without distinction of nationality.

51 D. Medvedev, *Silnye dukhom* (Strong in Spirit), Moscow, 1950.

52 V. Andreev, 'Narodnaya voina', *Novy mir*, 1948, no. 6.

53 O. Dzhigurda, 'Teplokhod, Kakhetiya', *Znamya*, 1948, no. 1.

54 A. Korovin, 'Zapiski voennogo khirurga', *Leningradsky almanakh*, 1948.

55 Y. German, 'Podpolkovnik meditsinskoi sluzhby', *Zvezda*, 1949, no. 1. Venomous criticism was nonetheless levelled at this book, of which only the first part was published. One critic wrote: 'I would like to see in this novel the true heroic life of the hospital, where everything takes place around the wounded, and not the Levins [a widely used term in the period of the anti-cosmopolitan campaign]. A Levin does not at all resemble an intelligent Soviet, an officer.' See A. Dementyev, 'O zadachakh Leningradskikh prozaikov', *Zvezda*, 1949, no. 5, p. 149.

56 M. Bubennov, *Belaya bereza*, Moscow, 1955.

57 V. Azhaev, 'Daleko ot Moskvy', *Novy mir*, 1948, nos. 7–8.

58 V. Vasilevskaya, 'Reki goryat', *Novy mir*, 1951, no. 7.

59 V. Dobrovolsky, 'Troe v serykh shinelyakh', *Novy mir*, 1948, no. 1; 'Zhenya Maslova', *Novy mir*, 1950, no. 1.

60 F. Panferov, *Bolshoe iskusstvo* (Great Art), Moscow, 1949. Immediately it appeared, this book was severely criticised; see *Literaturnaya gazeta*, 28 January and 1 February 1950.

61 E. Vorobev, 'Vysota', *Novy mir*, 1951, no. 11.

62 G. Mustafin, 'Karaganda', *Druzhba narodov*, 1952, no. 5.

63 See V. Sobko and B. Balaban, 'Moya pobeda', *Teatr*, 1953, no. 1, pp. 132–4.

64 V. Kochetov, 'Zhurbiny', *Zvezda*, 1952. no. 2.

65 On the changes in Soviet literature in the wake of the 20th Party Congress, see H. Swayze, *Political Control of Literature in the USSR 1946–1959*, Cambridge, Mass., Harvard University Pres, 1962; G. Gibian, *Interval of Freedom: Soviet Literature During the Thaw, 1954–1957*, Minneapolis, University of Minnesota Press, 1960; E. R. Frankel, *Novy Mir: A Case Study in the Politics of Literature*, Cambridge, Cambridge University Press, 1981.

There is no comprehensive study of the Jews in Soviet literature in the post-Stalin period. The studies that have been published (in addition to M. Hayward's article, mentioned in n. 40) are: Friedberg, *The Jew in Post-Stalin Soviet Literature*; A. Sergin, 'Jews in the October Revolution in Recent Soviet Literature', *Soviet Jewish Affairs*, 1971, no. 2, pp. 68–79.

66 There is also a Jewish theme in Paustovsky's memoirs; see K. Paustovsky, 'Kniga skitanii', *Novy mir*, 1963, nos. 10–11.

67 N. Brykin, 'Na vostochnom fronte peremeny', *Neva*, 1960, no. 10.

68 Y. Taits, *Negasimy svet* (The Eternal Flame), Moscow, 1963.

69 A. Brushtein, *Vesna* (Spring), Moscow, 1961.

70 S. Marshak, 'V nachale zhizni', *Novy mir*, 1960, no. 2.

71 Erenburg's memoirs appeared in the years 1960–5, in *Novy mir* and in book form.

72 L. Utesov, 'Moya Odessa', *Moskva*, 1964, no. 9.

73 I. Babel, 'Zabytye rasskazy', *Znamya*, 1964, no. 9.

74 E. Kazakevich, 'Vragi', *Izvestiya*, 20 April 1963.

75 *Voprosy istorii KPSS*, 1963, no. 4, pp. 94–7.

76 E. Kazakevich, *Sinyaya tetrad* (The Blue Notebook), Moscow, 1961.

77 A. Rutko, 'Plenitelnaya zvezda', *Nash sovremennik*, 1960, no. 3; V. Panova, 'Sentymentalny roman', *Novy mir*, 1958, no. 10.

78 Y. Kolesnikov, *Tma sgushchaetsya pered rassvetom*, Kishinev, 1959. Kolesnikov is apparently the author of one of the most anti-Semitic stories published in recent times in the USSR; see 'Zemlya obetovannaya', *Oktyabr*, 1972, nos. 9–10.

79 N. Chukovsky, 'Brodyaga', in *Literaturnaya Moskva* (Literary Moscow), 1956, vol. 2, pp. 418–35; 'Varya', in *Izbrannoe* (Selected Works), Moscow, 1963, pp. 215–91. Another work by Chukovsky, written in 1937 and republished in 1961, tells of Albert Belenky, a Jew, who aspires to enlist in cadet school, but is not accepted. In the end, he is active in the ranks of the Socialist Revolutionaries who are fighting against the Communists, despite the fact that the anti-Semitism among the Socialist-Revolutionaries extends to executing anyone even suspected of being a Jew. As against this, in a novel Chukovsky wrote in 1938, there is a Jewish commissar named Semen Nakhimson, who is murdered by the Whites.

80 N. Ilyina, 'Vozrashchenie', *Znamya*, 1957, nos. 1–4.

81 The trilogy appeared in the Ukraine between 1955 and 1960, and the first part appeared in Russian translation in Moscow in 1959. We were unable to obtain a copy of this book and are relying on the manuscript which a Soviet Jew smuggled out of the USSR. It is of interest that the book was re-published in Lvov in 1965 in a printing of 150,000 copies.

82 V. Tevekelyan, 'Granit ne plavitsya', *Moskva*, 1962, no. 3.

83 Y. Pilyar, 'Vse eto bylo', *Novy mir*, 1955, nos. 10–11; V. Bondarets, *Voennoplennye: Zapiski kapitana* (Prisoners of War: A Captain's Notes), Moscow, 1960; V. Larin and I. Nozarov, *V pamyati ostaetsya vse* (Memory Retains Everything), Alma-Ata, 1961. In 1968, Yury Pilyar, who was imprisoned in the Mathausen Camp, and afterwards in Soviet forced labour camps, was given a sharp warning by the authorities for having written a letter on behalf of the imprisoned writers; see *Posev*, 1969, no. 2, p. 7.

84 See M. Lev, *Partizanskie tropy* (Trials of Partisans), Moscow, 1958. In contrast, Paustovsky gave a far more realistic description of the death of the poet and soldier Ruskin, who had to poison himself after one of the soldiers informed the Germans of his Jewishness; see Paustovsky, 'Kniga skitanii', *Novy mir*, 1963, nos. 10–11.

85 A. Yoselevich, *Pobedili smert* (They Conquered Death), Kharkov, 1964.

86 M. Yatskiv, 'Pir v Karpatakh', in *V teskakh* (In the Clutches), Moscow, Sovetsky pisatel, 1960, pp. 426–35.

87 V. Vasilevskaya, 'Lyudi', *Znamya*, 1960, no. 7.

88 A. Batrov, 'Novelly stepnogo poberezhya', *Sovetskaya Ukraina*, 1961, no. 6.

89 A. Lupan, 'Gde tvoi pakhari zemlya', *Dnestr*, 1962, no. 10.

90 For example, L. Lateva, 'Irka', *Dnestr*, 1961, no. 9; A. Sharov, *V Polete* (In Flight), Moscow, 1961; Y. Mushketina, 'Otche nash', *Dnipro*, 1962, no. 2; B. Vlestrau, 'Kotomka', *Rasskazy* (Stories), Kishinev, 1959.

91 Among the few cases in which this is treated are in a work by Vershigora, one of the heads of the partisans in the Ukraine: Vershigora, 'Pereprava', *Dnipro*, 1961, no. 1; and Bela2's book describing the murder of Jews by Ukrainian Fascists as revenge for the murder of Petlyura; see the story of 'Svet v mrake', in V. Belaev, *Granitsa v ogne* (Border Afire), Moscow, 1962, pp. 139–249.

92 V. Ampilov and V. Smirnov, 'Doroga v geto', in *V malenkom gorode Lide* (In the Small Town of Lida), Moscow, 1962, pp. 67–70.

93 See n. 91.

94 I. Gursky, *V Ogne* (In the Fire), Minsk, 1961.

95 T. Gor, 'Dokuchlivy sobesednik', *Zvezda*, 1961, no. 7; L. Barsky, 'Nash fakultet', *Dnestr*, 1962, no. 3; V. Voinovich, 'Khochu byt chestnym', *Novy mir*, 1963, no. 2.

96 B. Polevoi, *Gluboky tyl* (Deep in the Rear), Moscow, 1959.

97 Written in 1960, the poem is dedicated to the Soviet Jewish poet B. Slutsky; see I. Selvinsky, *Lirika* (Lyrics), Moscow, 1964, pp. 427–30. Two other poems dealing with the Holocaust and the murder of the Jews are Semen Lipkin's 'Tyan Shan' (*Novy mir*, 1959, no. 6, p. 114) and B. Slutsky's 'How They Murdered My Grandmother' (B. Slutsky, *Rabota* (Work), Moscow, 1964, pp. 93–4).

98 Y. Meras, 'Nichya dlitsya mgnovenie' (Stalemate with Death), Moscow, Khudozhestvennaya literatura, 1966.

99 K. Simonov, 'Mertvye i zhivye', *Znamya*, 1959, nos. 4, 10, 11, 12; 'Novogodnyaya noch (Glavy iz romana)', *Izvestiya*, 14 April 1962; 'Soldatami ne rozhdayutsya', *Znamya*, 1964, nos. 1–3.

100 I. Gerasimov, 'Solovi', *Neva*, 1963, no. 10.

101 L. Pervomaisky, 'Diky med', *Oktyabr*, 1963. nos. 2–3.

102 A. Isbakh, *Oni borolis za Frantsiyu* (They Fought for France), Moscow, 1960.

103 See, for example, F. Grachev, 'V teni na Vasilyevskom', *Zvezda*, 1960, no. 2, on the Jewish journalist who refuses to leave besieged Leningrad; see also Paustovsky's *Dym otechestva* (The Smoke of the Homeland), Moscow, 1963, on the specialist Lepeshkin, who also lived in besieged Leningrad after he was saved from the occupied region.

104 G. Makhorkin, *I snova zhizn* (And Again Life), Moscow, 1964. The Sovetskaya Rossiya publishing house published the book in 50,000 copies.

105 M. Prelezhaeva, 'Pushkinsky vals', *Yunost*, 1961, no. 3; and see n. 95 above.

106 G. Kalinovsky, 'Zabytaya istoriya', *Nash sovremennik*, 1962, no. 4.

107 Y. German, 'Ya otvechayu za vse', *Zvezda*, 1964, nos. 11–12.

108 E. Evtushenko, 'Stantsiya Zima', *Oktyabr*, 1956, no. 10.

109 Y. Bondarev, 'Tishina', *Novy mir*, 1962, nos. 3–5; 'Dvoe', *Novy mir*, 1964, nos. 4–5.

110 G. Nikolaeva, *Bitva v puti*, Moscow, Sovetsky pisatel, 1959.

111 N. Shundruk, 'Rodnik u berezy', *Neva*, 1959, no. 2.

112 Y. Tynyanov, 'Iz zapisnykh knizhek', *Novy mir*, 1966, no. 8.

113 E. Gabrilovich, 'Pervaya chetvert', *Iskusstvo kino*, 1967.

114 I. Selvinsky, 'O yunost moya', *Oktyabr*, 1966, nos. 6–7.

115 N. Rybak, 'Takova zhizn', *Raduga*, 1966, no. 4.

116 D. Halkin, 'Tsimbalisty', *Oktyabr*, 1967, no. 12.

117 For example, A. Vasilyev, 'V chas dnya vashe prevoskhoditelstvo', *Moskva*, 1967, no. 9; Y. Gnat, 'Gody dalekie, gody blizkie', *Raduga*, 1967, no. 6; V. Tevekelyan, 'Reklamnoe byuro gospodina Kochega', *Moskva*, 1967, nos. 10–11.

118 S. Dongurov, 'Diplomaty', *Druzhba narodov*, 1966, no. 4.

119 V. Dmitrevsky, 'Bandera rossa', *Neva*, 1967, no. 2.

120 V. Zakrutkin, 'Sotvorenie mira', *Oktyabr*, 1967, no. 2.

121 V. Kochetov, 'Ugol padeniya', *Oktyabr*, 1967, no. 10.

122 Such as the Lithuanian Jewish writer Y. Meras, and M. Rolnikaite, who described the murder of the ghetto Jews in her diary. See M. Rolnikaite, *Ya dolzhna rasskazat* (I Must Tell), Moscow, 1965.

123 I. Marek, 'Za toboiu tin', *Vsesvit*, 1965, no. 8.

124 See T. Golovchenko & O. Musienko, 'Chorne sontse', *Vitchyzna*, 1965, no. 5, and A. Klenov, 'Poiski lyubvi', *Znamya*, 1966, no. 9.

125 I. Konstantinovsky, *Srok davnosti* (A Period Long Past), Moscow, 1966.

126 V. Taras, 'Evtanazia', *Neman*, 1967, no. 7.

127 B. Polevoi, 'Doktor Vera', *Znamya*, 1966, nos. 4–6; T. Migal, 'Shinok osielediets na lantsiuzi', *Zhivten*, 1965, no. 10; Y. Meras, 'Na chem derzhitsya mir', *Yunost*, 1966,

no. 4; V. Sobko, 'Tochno o desyatiy', *Dnipro*, 1967, no. 4. Of these works, the most important are those by Polevoi and Meras.

128 G. Baklanov, *Iyul 41 goda* (July of '41), Moscow, 1965; N. Dubov, 'U otdelno stoyaschego dereva', *Raduga*, 1966, no. 2. Baklanov's novel, which recounts the tragic retreat of the Red Army in the first days of the war, is a lethal criticism of Stalin and of his policy which caused this terrible defeat.

129 'Vo ves golos' (At the Top of One's Voice), *Soviet Poetry*, Moscow, 1965, pp. 304–5.

130 A. Voznesensky, *Akhillesovo serdtse* (The Heart of Achilles), Moscow, 1966. To these should be added E. Evtushenko's poem 'The Bratsk Power Station', which tells of the electrician Izya Kremer, who recalls his sweetheart in the ghetto; see E. Evtushenko, 'Bratskaya GES', *Yunost*, 1965, no. 4.

131 I. Grekova, 'Na ispytaniyakh', *Novy mir*, 1967, no. 4.

132 M. Roshchin, 'S utra do nochi', *Novy mir*, 1967, no. 8.

133 B. Kostyukovsky, 'Zemnye bratya', *Zvezda*, 1967, no. 5.

134 R. Zernova, 'Solnechnaya storona', *Zvezda*, 1967, no. 8.

135 L. Sheinin, 'Volki v gorode', *Oktyabr*, 1965, no. 1.

136 V. Tevekelyan, 'Za Moskovoyu-rekoyu', *Moskva*, 1966, no. 9.

137 One of the *samizdat* poems which has reached us is Solomon Mikhoels's 'I Wasn't Born a Slav'. See the Jewish *samizdat* edition of the mid-sixties: *Sbornik izbrannykh stikhotvorenii na evreiskie temy* (Anthology of Selected Poems on Jewish Subjects) (n.d., n.p.), p. 18.

138 Among the well-known writers of Jewish origin who wrote poems on Jewish subjects in the fifties and sixties are B. Slutsky, V. Inber, L. Ozerov, S. Marshak and E. Kazakevich. Lev Ozerov's poem 'Anew in Babi Yar', written in 1958, is a kind of continuation of his 1946 poem on the same subject (mentioned earlier), with one important difference: this time it was not published in a Soviet periodical; *ibid.*, p. 27.

139 For example, the reply to the poet Evtushenko by Jews of Lvov; S. Marshak's reply to Markov; Plotkin's reply to Starikov; E. Kazakevich's reply to Markov; Mikhelson's reply to Markov; A. Yakovlev's reply to Markov; Plotkin's letter to Yakovlev. *Ibid.*, pp. 29–33.

140 See Galich's songs on Jewish subjects: 'Train' (dedicated to the memory of S. Mikhoels), 'Warning', and others; A. Galich, *Pesni* (Songs), Frankfurt am Main, 1969. Other important songs by Galich are: 'In My Slumber and Upon My Awakening', 'Song on the Eternal Flame', 'Poem on Janus Korczak'. See also I. Brodsky's great poem 'Isaac and Abraham', as well as 'The Jewish Cemetery'; I. Brodsky, *Stikhotvoreniya i poemy* (Lyrics and Poems), New York, 1965; *Grani*, 1965, no. 58, pp. 167–70.

141 On Pasternak and Judaism, see J. Stora, 'Pasternak et le Judaïsme', *Cahiers du Monde russe et soviétique*, 1968, nos. 3–4, pp. 353–64. The central idea in *Doctor Zhivago*, as regards the Jewish issue, is that there is no longer any reason for the continued existence of the Jewish people.

142 V. Grossman, *Forever Flowing*, New York, Harper and Row, 1972. For Russian edition, see Chapter 3, n. 24.

143 N. Arzhak [Y. Daniel], *Govorit Moskva* (This is Moscow Speaking), Washington, 1962.

144 See A. Tertz [Sinyavsky], *The Trial Begins*, New York, Vintage Books, 1960; *The Makepeace Experiment (Liubimov)*, London, 1965.

145 I. Ivanov, *Est li zhizn na Marse?* (Is There Life on Mars?), Paris, 1961.

146 A. Korotova, 'Litso zhar-ptitsy', *Grani*, 1964, no. 56.

147 A. Solzhenitsyn, *The First Circle*, New York, Bantam Edition, 1969; *August 1914*, New York, 1972. On Solzhenitsyn and the Jews, see R. Rutman, 'Solzhenitsyn and the Jewish Question', *Soviet Jewish Affairs*, 1974, no. 2, pp. 3–16; E. Rogovin

Frankel, 'Russians, Jews and Solzhenitsyn', *Soviet Jewish Affairs*, 1975, no. 2, pp. 48–68.

148 Konstantin Georgievich Paustovsky (1892–1968), writer, was born in Moscow. He studied at the natural history faculty of Kiev University from 1911 to 1913, and at the faculty of jurisprudence of Moscow University. His first story was published in 1912. From 1913 to 1929, he worked at a variety of jobs.

This extract is taken from the second book of Paustovsky's autobiography, *Bespokoinaya yunost* (Restless Youth), which began to appear in 1955. The theme of the book as a whole is the development and maturing of the author as a man and writer. The action ranges from the beginning of World War I to the declaration of the setting up of the Provisional Government in February 1917. The incident at Kobrin, which comprises an episode in itself, is one of Paustovsky's lengthier pieces on the fate of the Jews in the Pale of Settlement during World War I. At this time – in the summer of 1915 – Paustovsky was a medical orderly attached to a certain Gronsky, commander of a field medical base.

149 Anatoliy Andriyovych Dimarov (1922–), Ukrainian writer, was born in Mirgorod, Poltava Province, into the family of a teacher. On finishing school in 1940, he was called up for military service. He fought in World War II both in the ranks of the Red Army and as a partisan. His first works were published in 1944. He has worked as editor-in-chief of the Lvov Province Publishing House and of the Radiansky Pismennyk Publishing House. Dimarov is a member of the Communist Party of the USSR.

Dimarov's novel is set in the Ukraine immediately after the Civil War. The story depicts two Jews: Grigory Ginzburg, a local Communist Party secretary, of whom we learn little other than that he is an exemplary Communist, and Solomon Lander, the local chief of the secret police. It is on this latter figure that Dimarov concentrates his attention. In the extract given here the author gives the history of the Lander family in the Ukraine, recounting this Jewish family's traditional hatred of the Ukrainian people.

150 On Boris Polevoi see Chapter 5, n. 90.

151 Ilya Grigoryevich Erenburg (1891–1967), writer, was born in Kiev. His mother was a deeply religious woman, while his father was an assimilationist. All the Jewish festivals were kept in his home, and the food was *kasher*. Erenburg also studied Hebrew and Talmud at home. In 1906, the family moved to Moscow. From the age of fourteen Erenburg became involved in revolutionary activity. He was arrested at the beginning of 1908 and spent a few months in prison. Released in December 1908, he went to Paris, where he became acquainted with Lenin. Once there, however, he abandoned politics, associating with artists and writers in the cafés of Montparnasse. The years preceding World War I were marked by spiritual searchings; he became interested in Catholicism and mysticism, even toying with the idea of entering a monastery.

During World War I, he volunteered for the French Foreign Legion but was rejected on grounds of health. Erenburg became the Paris correspondent of the Moscow paper *Utro Rossii* and later of the Petersburg paper *Birzhevye vedomosti*. He returned to Russia in July 1917. During the Civil War, he was imprisoned by both Vrangel's forces and the Bolsheviks. When finally released, he was allowed to leave the Soviet Union with a Soviet passport, and he arrived in Paris in 1921 as a Soviet citizen. He produced his best literary works in the 1920s, including *Neobychainye pokhozhdeniya Khulio Khurenito i ego uchenikov* (The Extraordinary Adventures of Julio Jurenito and his Disciples, 1922). In the 1920s and 1930s, he was foreign correspondent of the central Moscow newspapers. He returned to Russia for a short while at the beginning of the 1930s, leaving again to take part in the Spanish Civil War as a newspaper correspondent. In 1940, when the Germans entered France, he returned to Moscow.

During World War II, Erenburg was an active member of the Jewish Anti-Fascist Committee and a war correspondent of *Krasnaya zvezda* and other Soviet newspapers. His war-time newspaper articles played a decisive part in Soviet propaganda work against German Fascism. However, at the end of the war, with a change in the Party line, Erenburg was attacked for not making the distinction between 'good' and 'bad' Germans (see *Pravda*, 14 April 1945).

Erenburg's story *Ottepel* (The Thaw), published in 1954, the first echo in Soviet literature of the changes in Soviet society after Stalin's death, lent its name to the post-Stalin period. From 1956, Erenburg emerged as the most prominent representative of the liberal Soviet intelligentsia. His memoirs *Lyudi, gody, zhizn* (People, Years, Life), which began to appear in 1960, had an enormous historical and cultural impact.

The Jewish question occupies an imporant place in Erenburg's works and activity. In 1911, he published the poem 'Evreiskomu narodu' (To the Jewish People) in an early collection of verse in which he expresses the longing for Zion (see Erenburg, *Ya zhivu* (I Live), St Petersburg, 1911, p. 52). In 1915, he wrote the poem 'Gde-to v Polshe' (Somewhere in Poland), in which he talks of the harsh lot of the Jews (Erenburg, *Sobranie sochinenii*, vol. 3, p. 368).

The Jewish theme enters into the plot of the novel *Julio Jurenito*, in which one of the heroes is the author himself; Chapter 11, which is called 'The Prophecy of a Teacher of the Jewish Race', foretells the disasters of the Jews. In the collection of stories *The Thirteen Pipes*, 'The Third Pipe' is about Jews (see Erenburg, *Sobranie sochinenii*, vol. 1, pp. 414–22).

The novel *Rvach* (The Grabber, 1925) and the story 'V Protochnom pereulke' (In Protochny Lane, 1927) describe Jewish NEP-men. The novel *Burnaya zhizn Lazika Rotshvanetsa* (The Stormy Life of Lazik Rotshvanets, 1927) is wholly Jewish in both form and content. It is replete with the sayings of Hasidic *zadikim*, quotations from the Talmud, and Jewish folklore. The hero is a Jewish tailor from Gomel who has been compared to Hasek's Svejk.

In his novel *Den vtoroi* (The Second Day, 1933) Erenburg devotes considerable space to Jewish characters, including the old rabbi Shvartsberg, as well as to the Jewish question. He discusses Fascist anti-Semitism in his novel *Padenie Parizha* (The Fall of Paris, 1940).

Erenburg also devoted a number of poems from the war years to the theme of the suffering of the Jews; see, for example, *Sobranie sochinenii*, vol. 3, pp. 435, 455. During the war, he published many articles on the Nazis' bestialities, especially those perpetrated against the Jews. Together with V. Grossman, he edited *The Black Book* on the Nazi crimes against the Jews; never published in the USSR, it was published in part in Romania. In his post-war novel *Burya* (The Storm) he describes the fate of the two Alper brothers, sons of a Kiev tailor. One lives in the West in Paris and the other, Osip, lives in Kiev. Erenburg depicts the destruction of Kiev Jewry at Babi Yar, where Osip's wife, Raya, perishes together with his mother and his daughter Alya; his brother dies at Auschwitz. Osip visits the site of Babi Yar immediately after the liberation of Kiev.

The novel *Devyaty val* (The Ninth Wave) continues the story of Osip, the sole survivor of his family. In the present extract Major Osip Alper, now serving in the army in the Soviet zone of Germany, returns to Kiev on leave. He is impressed by the speed with which the city has been rebuilt. He once again visits the site of Babi Yar and then calls on a war-time friend. The anti-Israel remarks put in the mouth of Osip by Erenburg are in keeping with the book's virulent anti-American and anti-Western line.

152 Anna Valtseva's story 'Apartment No. 13', which first appeared in the literary magazine *Moskva* (1957, no. 1), is typical of works written by the liberal intelligentsia of the time. It is an account of life in a communal apartment as seen

through the eyes of a housewife who is also a writer. In this extract, which is an episode in itself, the latent anti-Semitism of the apartment's only unpleasant resident, Kovelev, is revealed.

12. The Holocaust and Jewish resistance as reflected in Soviet academic literature and the press

1 See *Dokumenty obvinyayut: Sbornik dokumentov* (The Documents Accuse: Collection of Documents), Moscow, Gospolitizdat, 1943, vol. 1. The second volume of the document collection appeared in 1945, and contained a number of documents dealing with the Nazi extermination of the Jews. See vol. 2, pp. 17, 23, 140–3, 151.

2 *Pravda*, 19 December 1942.

3 There were also exceptions to this policy, particularly at the end of 1944 when this Commission reported on Nazi atrocities against the Jews in the Lvov and Latvia regions. See Schwarz, *Evrei v Sovetskom Soyuze*, p. 148.

4 *Ibid.*, p. 146.

5 Of seventy-nine books that appeared during 1941–5, twenty-one were on Jews in the war; see Ch. Shmeruk, in *Sifrut yehudei brit ha-moazot bi-[ye]mei ha-shoah ve-ahareha* (The Literature of the Jews of the Soviet Union During and After the Holocaust), Jerusalem, Yad va-Shem, 1960, p. 28. Of particular importance were two collections of documents, edited by Ilya Erenburg, which presented material on the slaughter in the occupied areas of the Soviet Union; see Erenburg, *Merder fun felker* (Nation-Killers), Moscow, Der emes, 1944–5, vols. 1–2.

6 *Information Bulletin*, Embassy of the USSR, Washington DC, 2 June 1942, as quoted in Redlich, 'The Jews Under Soviet Rule During World War II', p. 203.

7 On the establishment and activity of the Commission, see the testimony of A. Sutskever, a Yiddish poet now residing in Israel, in his article 'Ilya Erenburg a kapitl zikhroynes fun di yorn 1944–1946', *Di goldene keyt*, 1967, no. 61, pp. 34–5. On *The Black Book* in general, see D. Litani, 'Sefer shahor al shoat yehudei brit-ha-moazot', *Yediot Yad va-Shem*, 1960, no. 23–4, pp. 24–6; M. Altshuler in Pinkus, Greenbaum & Altshuler (eds.), *Pirsumim rusiim al yehudim*, pp. lxv–lxvi; Gilboa, *The Black Years of Soviet Jewry*, pp. 72–7.

8 *Eynikeyt*, 21 May 1946. Parts of this collection were published in the two pamphlets edited by Erenburg (see n. 5).

9 Erenburg writes in his memoirs: 'They told us the book would appear at the end of 1948 ... At the end of 1948 they disbanded the Jewish Anti-Fascist Committee, [closed] the newspaper *Emes* [this, of course, should read *Eynikeyt*], dissolved *The Black Book*.' It is interesting that, in the reprinting of Erenburg's memoirs in his collected works, the passage on *The Black Book* was omitted (cf. *Novy mir*, 1965, no. 2, pp. 54–5, and Erenburg, *Sobranie sochinenii*, vol. 9, pp. 571–2).

10 *The Black Book: The Nazi Crime Against the Jewish People*; Ilya Erenburg, Vasily Grossman, Lev Ozerov and Vladimir Lidin, *Cartea Neagra*, Bucharest, Editura Institul Roman de Documentare, 1947. Full editions have recently been published in the West in Russian and English: *Chernaya kniga*, Jerusalem, Tarbut Publishers, 1980; *The Black Book*, New York, Holocaust Publications, 1981.

11 *Morgn frayheyt*, 3 December 1947, as quoted in Pinkus, Greenbaum & Altshuler (eds.), *Pirsumim rusiim al yehudim*, p. lxiv.

12 See Erenburg, *Sobranie sochinenii*, vol. 9, pp. 376–7. Erenburg adds that, following these remarks by Kondakov, he appealed to the latter's superior, Shcherbakov, who told him that his deputy had admittedly shown 'exaggerated diligence', but that the text must in any case be changed. Referring to Erenburg's articles, Shcherbakov added, *inter alia*: 'The soldiers want to hear about Suvorov, and you quote Heine'; *ibid.*, p. 377.

13 According to the editor of the Hebrew edition of this book, Binyamin Vest, it is not known whether the manuscript was printed and published; see B. Vest, 'Le-korot ha-shoah ve-ha-partizaniyut ha-yehudit bi-vrit hamoaẓot', *Gesher*, 1966, no. 2–3, p. 242. It does, however, appear that the book was printed but not circulated.

14 In 1952, the monument in Paneriai, which had been erected by the Jews in 1945, was even destroyed. See details in Schwarz, *Evrei v Sovetskom Soyuze*, p. 253.

15 M. Morozov, *Natsionalnye traditsii narodov SSSR*, Moscow, Gospolitizdat, 1955, as quoted in Leneman, *La Tragédie des juifs en URSS*, p. 220. The figure for the number of Jews awarded medals for heroism during World War II is given as 16,772 in Kychko's book, *Yudaizm bez prykras*, p. 179. According to the Soviet Army Museum's information on the number of decorations and heroes of 1 April 1947, published in *Folks-shtime*, 18 April 1963, the correct figures are as follows: the number of Jews decorated in World War II – 160,772; this number as a percentage of the total number of persons decorated – 1.74. According to the figures published in *Sovetish heymland*, 1970, no. 5, pp. 43–6 and no. 8, p. 140, the number of Jewish Heroes of the Soviet Union is 131.

16 S. Golikov, *Vydayushchiesya pobedy sovetskoi armii v velikoi otechestvennoi voine* (Outstanding Victories of the Soviet Army in the Second World War), Moscow, 1952, p. 187, as quoted in Leneman, *La Tragédie des juifs en URSS*, p. 222.

17 *Pravda*, 6 May 1965.

18 *Nyurnbergsky protses: Sbornik materialov* (The Nuremberg Trial: Collection of Materials), Moscow, Gosyurizdat, 1955 (2 vols.).

19 *Dnevnik Anny Frank* (The Diary of Anne Frank), Moscow, Inostrannaya literatura, 1960.

20 M. Rolnikaite, *Turiu papasakoti* (I Must Tell), Vilnius, Gospolitnauchizdat, 1963. A Russian translation of the book appeared in 1965.

21 Many books and articles mention the heroic deeds of the pilots Boris Lunts and Yitskhak Presaizen, the woman pilot Paulina Gelman, the submarine commander Israel Fisanovich and many others; see *Kniga o geroyakh* (A Book of Heroes), Moscow, Voennoe izdatelstvo, 1963, pp. 105–24; A. Verkhozin, *Samolety letyat k partizanam* (Airplanes Fly to the Partisans), Moscow, Politizdat, 1964. Many Jewish names also appear in the many war memoirs, though mainly without any note being taken of nationality.

22 *Geroi i podvigi 1941–1945* (Heroes and Heroic Acts), Moscow, Gospolitizdat, 1958, p. 62. For a similar description relating to the underground organisation in Lithuania, see Doc. 155.

23 See, for example, D. Genkina, 'Reid k moryu', *Sovetskaya Litva*, 30 July 1964; S. Aleshin, 'Zvezdy svetyat lyudyam', *Krasnaya zvezda*, 15 August 1964.

24 See also A. Virshulis, *Put geroev* (The Path of Heroes), Moscow, Molodaya gvardiya, 1959. In a few cases, the Zionist affiliation of the leaders of the uprising is noted, for instance, in reference to Mordekhai Anieliewicz, commander of the Warsaw ghetto revolt. But here, too, it is noted that the anti-Fascist bloc that was formed was headed by A. Shamdit (PPR) and M. Anielewicz (*Ha-shomer ha-ẓair*); see 'Vostanie v Varshavskom getto', *Voennoistorichesky zhurnal*, 1963, no. 4, pp. 122–6.

25 Often in books and articles a lengthy list of the nationalities that participated in the war effort is given, but the Jewish nation is absent from them. In one book of this kind we read: 'Together with the fighters of Russian nationality, there fought Ukrainians, Belorussians and Uzbeks, Lithuanians, Estonians and Kirgiz, Armenians and Georgians, Moldavians and Azerbaidzhans, Tadzhiks and Bashkirs'; see *V bolshom nastuplenii* (In the Great Attack), Moscow, Voennoe izdatelstvo oborony, 1964, p. 8.

26 M. Eglinis, *Mirties Fortuose* (The Death Fort), Vilnius, Gospolitnauchizdat, 1957.

On this book, see D. Levin, 'Al gvurat yehudim be-sifrut lita ha-sovyetit', *Yediot Yad va-Shem*, 1960, no. 23–4, pp. 22–4.

27 See especially S. Golubkov, *V fashistskom lagere smerti: vospominaniya byvshego voennoplennogo* (In the Fascist Death Camp: Memoirs of a Former War Prisoner), Smolensk, Smolenskoe knizhnoe izdatelstvo, 1963, which tells of the Buchenwald extermination camp. On the extermination of Jews and the anti-Semitic attitude of Russian prisoners (White, of course), see A. Iosilevich, *Pobedili smert* (They Conquered Death), Kharkov, Prapor, 1964. Of especial importance from this point of view is the book by the Czech Jew Yosef Gertner, which includes a chilling description of the transport of the Jews of Riga to their extermination in Rumbuli; see *V Salispalskom lagere smerti* (In the Salispalsk Death-Camp), Riga, Latviiskoe gosudarstvennoe izdatelstvo, 1964; A. Lebedev, *Soldaty maloi voiny* (Soliders of the Small War), Moscow, Gospolitizdat, 1961.

28 A. Bryukhanov, *Vot kak eto bylo* (That's The Way It Was), Moscow, Gospolitizdat, 1958, p. 145.

29 *V bolshom nastuplenii*, p. 173.

30 See Documents 21, 42, 46, 60 in *Prestupnye tseli – prestupnye sredstva* (Criminal Ends – Criminal Means), Moscow, Gospolitizdat, 1963.

31 See Dov Levin's article, cited in n. 26.

32 See D. Garber, 'Rumbuli ha-babi-yar shel riga', *Davar*, 4 May 1970; M. Perah, 'Ha-mitingim be-rumbuli', *Yalkut moreshet*, 1971, no. 13, pp. 5–16.

33 A systematic examination of the handling by the Soviet press of this question during the years 1954–9 has not yet been made; however, from those newspapers and periodicals we have seen, and from the books dealing with the war, this conclusion is apparently correct. This is also dealt with by Emanuel Brand, 'Al mishpatim neged poshim natsiim ve-ozrehem', *Yediot yad va-Shem*, 1966, no. 36, pp. 15–22. On the trial of Stasisi Tserkhnobitchius, who was condemned to death in 1959, see *Chervony shtandar*, 1 February 1961.

34 The calculations are those of E. Brand; see previous note. (Six trials were held in Lithuania, six in the RSFSR, four in Belorussia, three in the Ukraine, three in Estonia and two in Latvia. Most of the trials took place in the years 1961–3.)

35 See *Sovetskaya Litva*, 25 February 1961 and 19 October 1962; *Sovetskaya Estoniya*, 17 January and 28 February 1961; *Lyudi budte bditelny* (People, Be Vigilant), Tallin. Gosizdat Estonii, 1961; *Sovetskaya Latviya*, 9 March 1961; *Krasnaya zvezda*, 13 April 1963; *Sovetskaya Belorussiya*, 20 August 1963; *Leningradskaya pravda*, 25 October 1963.

36 See *Pravda Ukrainy*, 25 May 1960; *Pravda*, 24 June 1960; *Trud*, 25 May 1960.

37 See *Sovetskaya Belorussiya*, 2 April 1961; *Pravda*, 28 April 1961 (article headlined: 'Trial or Farce'); *Neva*, 1962, no. 3, pp. 159–66; *Sovetskaya yustitsiya*, 1962, no. 3, pp. 25–7; *Komsomolskaya pravda*, 15 May 1962; *Sovetskaya Moldaviya*, 22 May 1962; A. Poltorak, *Ot Myunkhena do Nyurnberga* (From Munich to Nuremberg), Moscow, Institut Mezhdunarodnykh Otnoshenii, 1961, p. 265–85; Lebedev, *Soldaty maloi voiny*, pp. 119–27.

38 See I. Guri, 'Mah kotvim bi-vrit ha-moaẓot al shoat yehudeha', *Yediot Yad va-Shem*, 1965, no. 35, pp. 2–8.

39 *Yunost*, 1966, nos. 8–10; A. Kuznetsov, *Babi Yar, Roman-dokument* (Babi Yar, A Documentary Novel), Moscow, Molodaya gvardiya, 1967; see also n. 57.

40 A. Anatoli (Kuznetsov), *Babi Yar*, Frankfurt am Main, Posev, 1970.

41 See *Krugozor*, 1965, no. 6; *Literaturnaya gazeta*, 10 April 1965.

42 The speech was published in the West in a collection of documents smuggled out of the Soviet Union; see *The Chornovil Papers*, New York, McGraw-Hill, 1968, pp. 222–6.

43 *The Paneriae Museum*, Vilnius, Minitis Publishing House, 1966, 22 pages plus illustrations.

44 *Sovetskaya Litva*, 21 August 1965; *Sovetskaya Latviya*, 12–17, 19–24, 26, 28 and 31 October 1965; *Pravda*, 1 February 1966; *Sovetskaya Estoniya*, 16 February 1966; *Pravda*, 12 March 1966; *Komsomolskoe znamya*, 19 October 1966; *Pravda Ukrainy*, 3 September 1967; *Izvestiya*, 16 November 1967.

45 As stated in the document, the book *Partisan Friendship* was among the last undertakings of the Jewish Anti-Fascist Committee. It includes twenty-three chapters of memoirs, reviews and eye-witness accounts describing the heroic deeds of Soviet Jewish fighters in World War II. The chapters are written mainly by the non-Jewish commanders of partisan units.

46 Mere Lanaite (1915–48), member of the revolutionary movement in Lithuania, was born in Ionava and was a dressmaker by profession. She joined the Komsomol in 1929 and the Communist Party in 1933. She was sentenced to four years' imprisonment for the dissemination of Communist literature. From 1940 to 1941 she worked on the committee of the Ionava administrative area. During the German occupation Mere Lanaite was a member of the underground anti-Fascist organisation of the Kaunas ghetto and was sent by this organisation to establish contact with the partisans. From September 1943, she fought in the partisan detachment 'Death to the Occupiers'. After the war she worked as an instructor of the Kaunas Province Committee. She was killed by members of the Lithuanian anti-Communist movement.

47 Mikhail Rubinsonas (1923–), journalist, was born in Kaunas. He joined the Komsomol in 1938. He finished the *gymnasium* in Kaunas in 1941 and a university of journalism department in 1956. From 1942 to 1943, he was a member of the staff of the anti-Fascist underground organisation in the Kaunas ghetto. From 1943 to 1944, he fought in the 'Death to the Occupiers' detachment. He became a member of the CPSU in 1949. After the war he worked on various republic newspapers, for example, *Rabotnik militsii*, *Komsomolskaya pravda*, *Tiesa*. Since 1959, he has been the managing editor of the newspaper *Vechernie novosti*.

48 Zalmanas Goltsbergas (1923–), member of the revolutionary movement and former partisan, was born in Kaunas, the son of an official. He joined the MOPR (International Organisation of Aid to Revolutionary Fighters) in Taurage in 1937, and the Komsomol in 1939. During the war he was a member of the underground organisation in the Kaunas ghetto, a member of the Komsomol Committee and maintained contacts with Komsomol groups in the city. From 1943, he fought in the partisan detachment 'Death to the Occupiers'. After the liberation of Lithuania he joined the Soviet Army, and, in 1947, became a member of the CPSU. From 1947, he worked on the *Krestyanskaya gazeta*. In 1954, he graduated from the faculty of jurisprudence at the university of Vilnius. Goltsbergas has emigrated to Israel.

49 Meeris Lurye (1923–43), member of the revolutionary movement, joined the Komsomol in 1940. He was a member of the underground organisation in the Kaunas ghetto and the leader of a group of Komsomol saboteurs in the ghetto. Lurye was killed while blowing up an ammunition dump.

50 The use of a phrase of this kind: 'by the Russian Martyan Rybakov, by the Jew Haim Zilber', which is intended to demonstrate the existence of Soviet internationalism, was quite widespread in *belles lettres* and scholarly literature from the second half of the 1950s; however, the designation of Jews in illustrations such as these was much more infrequent.

51 Yitkshak (Itsik) Vitenberg (1907–43), member of the revolutionary and partisan movements, was born in Vilnius into a worker's family. He took an active part in the underground work of the trade unions. He joined the Communist Party in 1938 and was Chairman of the tanners' union. At the end of 1941, he formed an underground Party organisation in the Vilnius ghetto and, at the beginning of 1941, an amalgamated underground organisation of which he was chief-of-staff. In 1943, he

became a member of the Vilnius Party Committee. On 15 July 1943, he was arrested by the Germans but managed to escape. On 16 July, the Germans issued an order that if Vitenberg did not appear in person at the police station, the whole ghetto would be destroyed. Vitenberg appointed another chief-of-staff in his place and then gave himself up; he was executed by the Germans.

52 Sheyne Madeiskerite (Sonya Madeisker; 1914–44), member of the revolutionary movement and a partisan in World War II, was born in Vilnius. Her father was a member of the intelligentsia. She joined the Komsomol when still a school girl and was twice sentenced for revolutionary activity. She became a member of the Communist Party in 1933. From 1940 to 1941, she studied at the Pedagogic Institute in Grodno. In 1941, she became a member of the Party organisation of the Vilnius ghetto and Secretary of the Vilnius Komsomol Committee. In 1942, she was made a member of the city Party Committee and led an illegal existence. In April 1944, when on a Party mission, she was involved in a fight with the Gestapo and was seriously wounded. Afterwards she was subjected to torture and finally shot.

53 Itsikas Meskupas (pseudonym of Adomas; 1907–42), member of the revolutionary movement and Party worker, was born in Ukmerge, the son of an artisan. He joined the Komsomol in 1924 when he was still a schoolboy. After finishing school in his home town, he entered Kaunas University in 1926. There he became actively involved in Communist underground activity, becoming Secretary of the Komsomol in Ukmerge and Kaunas. He was arrested in 1927 on a charge of revolutionary activity, and was sentenced in 1929 to eight years' imprisonment. At his trial he delivered a strongly worded speech exposing the Fascist government of Lithuania. Meskupas was released ahead of time by an amnesty. In 1931, he became a member of the Central Committee of the Lithuanian Komsomol and was sent by the Party to Berlin to organise the publication of Party literature and its dispatch to Lithuania. In 1933, he was arrested in Berlin, and, in 1934, extradited to Lithuania. From 1934 he was Secretary of the Lithuanian Komsomol and editor of its paper. He was also active in MOPR (International Organisation of Aid to Revolutionary Fighters) and was a delegate to the Comintern and the Congress of International Communist Youth.

Meskupas became a member of the Communist Party in 1935, and a member of the Secretariat of the Lithuanian Central Committee, and later of the Politburo and Secretariat of the Central Committee of the Lithuanian Communist Party. He also worked in the Communist press. He was occasionally subjected to administrative punishments and was imprisoned from 1938 to 1939. In December 1939, he was sent to Moscow to report on the activity of the Lithuanian CP to the Cominterm. From 1940 to 1941, he was Second Secretary of the Central Committee of the Lithuanian CP, a deputy of the People's Seim, in 1940 and in 1941, a deputy of the Supreme Soviet of the USSR.

At the beginning of World War II, Meskupas was evacuated deep into Russia. On 7 March 1942, he was in Lithuania as the head of an operational group for partisan work and partisan struggle. On 13 March 1942, he was killed in an unequal fight with the enemy who had surrounded his group.

54 Jozef Lewartowski (pseudonym of Josif Finkelszteyn; 1895–1942). Lewartowski was born in Bielsk Podlaski in Poland. He was active in Jewish and Polish Labour Movements. From 1918 to 1921, he was a member of *Poalei ziyon*. In 1921, he became a member of the Polish CP. From 1923 to 1926, he was Secretary of the Central Jewish Bureau of the Central Committee of the Polish CP, and from 1925 to 1927, a member of the Central Committee of the Polish CP. In 1934, he was sentenced to twelve years' imprisonment for revolutionary activity. In 1942, Lewartowski became the representative of the Central Committee of the Polish

Workers' Party in the Warsaw ghetto and one of the leaders of the anti-Fascist bloc in the ghetto.

55 Mordekhai Anieliewicz (1919–43), commander of the Warsaw ghetto uprising, was born in Wyszkow, Poland, into a working-class family. In his youth he was a member of Zionist movements. With the German advance on Warsaw he tried to escape to Palestine, but was caught at the Romanian border. He returned first to Vilnius and then to Warsaw where he was eventually named commander of the Zydowska Organizacja Krajowa (Jewish Fighting Organisation) and was in effective control of the whole ghetto. He led the Warsaw ghetto uprising and fell fighting the Germans on 8 May 1943.

56 Masha Rolnikaite (1927–), writer, was born in Klaipeda and went to school in Plunge and Vilnius. From 1941 to 1943 she was in the Vilnius ghetto, and from 1943 to 1945 in concentration camps. In 1955, she finished a correspondence course at the Gorky Literary Institute in Moscow. She joined the CPSU in 1961. Her book of memoirs, entitled *Ya dolzhna rasskazat* (I Must Tell the Story), which recounts the years spent in the ghetto and camps, appeared in 1963. This book was translated into many languages of the peoples of the USSR and of countries abroad (in 1965, the translation of the book into Yiddish and Hebrew was finished). In 1970, Rolnikaite's second book *Tri vstrechi* (Three Encounters) was published. She also works as a translator from Russian to Lithuanian.

57 Kuznetsov's book *Babi Yar, A Documentary Novel* first appeared in the Soviet Union in the journal *Yunost* in 1966. It was published in book form by 'Molodaya gvardiya' in 1967. The document reproduced here is from the English translation of the uncensored Russian text.

The following extract, which was not included in the Soviet editions of the book, is an example of the Soviet censor's work; 'It seems it's true what they said about them setting fire to the Kreshchatyk. Thank the Lord for that! That'll put paid to them getting rich at our expense, the bastards. Now they can go off to their blessed Palestine, or at any rate the Germans'll deal with 'em.' *Yunost*, 1966, no. 8. pp. 7–8, and A. Kuznetsov, *Babi Yar, Roman-Dokument*, Moscow, Molodaya gvardiya, 1967, p. 48.

58 This very important document is the first of its kind to be published in the Soviet Union after World War II. On the Babi Yar affair generally, see Chapter 3, and for an answer to Nekrasov's appeal, see Doc. 161.

13. The Oriental Jews of the Soviet Union

1 The Karaite community or sect is not discussed in this book because the sensitive question of whether they are part of the Jewish people has not yet been resolved. As an example, one can quote Rabbi Zvi Harkavi, speaking at a symposium in Jerusalem on 30 January 1972: 'The late Phillip Friedman, a Holocaust researcher, compiled a great bibliography about the Karaites during the Holocaust. I myself contributed an article summarising this in *Gesher* [1969, no. 4, pp. 107–9]. Not only were the Karaites – in the Crimea as well as in Poland – not categorised as Jews by the Nazis, they even collaborated with them in actions against the Jews. As a result they were exiled by the Soviet authorities along with the Tatar collaborators.' Professor Zand stated in reply, 'I only want to point out that there is now a young generation of Karaites in the Soviet Union and this generation, or part of it, identifies itself with the Jews. They came to us and asked for assistance in their *aliyah*, they consider themselves an inseparable part of the Jewish people. Now how are we to react? Shall we spurn their outstretched hand? Will our Jewish conscience permit us to do so? Generations come and generations go; this is a new generation.' See *Jewish Culture in the Soviet Union*, pp. 41, 48. See also Chapter 1, n. 58.

2 See Plisetsky, *Religiya i byt gruzinskikh evreev*; Magid, *Evrei na Kavkaze*; I. Pulner, 'Itogi i zadachi izucheniya kavkazskikh evreev', *Sovetskaya etnografiya*, 1936, nos. 4–5, pp. 106–20; Neishtat, *Yehudei gruzia. Maavak al ha-shivah le-ziyon.*

3 See Neishtat, *ibid.*, p. 33; for 1926 census data, see Lorimer, *The Population of the Soviet Union*, p. 55.

4 See M. Plisetsky in *Religioznye verovaniya narodov SSR* (Religious Beliefs of the Peoples of the USSR), Moscow–Leningrad, Moskovsky rabochy, 1931, vol. 2, p. 334.

5 See Neishtat, *Yehudei gruzia*, pp. 60–1.

6 Estimates of the Georgian Jewish population in 1970 range between 60,000 and 95,000, some 15,000 of whom live outside the Georgian Republic. The large-scale emigration of Georgian Jews to Israel began after the last census was held.

7 According to Rothenberg (*The Jewish Religion in the Soviet Union*, p. 47), there were no more than thirteen synagogues in 1966.

8 Neishtat, *Yehudei gruzia*, p. 90.

9 This, as well as the use of genuinely Georgian surnames, is evidence of a continuing process of cultural and linguistic assimilation. See Ben Zvi, *The Exiled and the Redeemed*, p. 50.

10 See also 'Gosudarstvenny istoriko-etnografichesky muzei evreev Gruzii', *Sovetskaya etnografiya*, 1946, no. 4, pp. 219–20.

11 See B. Yakobishvili, 'Georgian Jewish Culture', in *Jewish Culture in the Soviet Union*, p. 129.

12 On Boris Gaponov see A. B. Yafeh, 'Parshat boris dov gaponov', *Behinot*, 1973, no. 4, pp. 119–25.

13 In the years 1970–4, about 27,000 Jews emigrated to Israel from Georgia, i.e. more than a quarter of all emigrants from the Soviet Union in this period. There is evidence that the Jews of Georgia thought of emigrating to Israel as early as 1948, but were well aware that there was no chance of realising this desire. At the end of 1956, when the Mikhalashvili family of Kulashi received an exit visa for Israel, great excitement spread among the Georgian Jews. However, the Zionist awakening, in the full sense of the word, and the concomitant struggle to emigrate, began only in the late 1960s (information received from G. Tsitsuashvili in an interview in Jerusalem, 7 June 1975); see also A. Tirosh in *Maariv*, 18 March 1974.

14 On the Mountain Jews, see V. Miller, *Materialy dlya izucheniya evreiskogo-tatskogo yazyka* (Materials for the Study of the Jewish Tat Language), St Petersburg, n.p., 1892; Magid, *Evrei na Kavkaze*; B. Miller, *Taty, ikh rasselenie i govory* (The Tats, Their Dispersion and Dialects), Baku, Obshchestvo obsledovaniya i izucheniya Azerbaidzhana, 1929; M. Altshuler, in Altshuler, Pinhasi & Zand (eds.), *Yehudei bukharah ve-ha-yehudim ha-harariim*, pp. 21–35; M. Neishtat, 'Ha-yehudim ha-harariim be-mizraḥ kavkaz', *Shvut*, 1973, no. 1, pp. 74–86; M. Zand in *Jewish Culture in the Soviet Union*, pp. 119–25.

15 Eliav, *Between Hammer and Sickle*, pp. 215–19.

16 See M. Altshuler (ed.), *Igrot u-teudot; me-arkhion ha-rav yaakov yizḥaki* (Correspondence and Documents from the Archive of Rabbi Yaakov Yitskhaki), Jerusalem, Ha-arkhion ha-merkazi le-toldot ha-am ha-yehudi, 1974, p. 3.

17 According to a Soviet source, the Mountain Jews constituted 70% of all Red Guard fighters in Dagestan. See Larin, *Evrei i antisemitizm v SSSR*, p. 128.

18 On the blood libels of 1926 and 1929, see *ibid.*, pp. 127–30; Larin in *Pravda*, 23 June 1928.

19 Lorimer, *The Population of the Soviet Union*, p. 55.

20 F. Halle, 'The Caucasian Mountain Jews', *Commentary*, 1946, no. 4, p. 355.

21 *Itogi vsesoyuznoi perepisi naseleniya 1970 goda*, vol. 4, p. 16.

22 See Altshuler, in Altshuler, Pinhasi & Zand (eds.), *Yehudei bukharah ve-ha-yehudim ha-harariim*, p. 25.

23 *Itogi vseesoyuznoi perepisi naseleniya 1970 goda*, vol. 4, p. 11.
24 According to Neishtat's estimate, it may even have reached 50,000 to 60,000. See Neishtat, 'Ha-yehudim ha-harariim be-mizraḥ kavkaz', p. 84. Professor Zand, on the other hand, thinks that their number is little more than 30,000; see *Jewish Culture in the Soviet Union*, p. 119.
25 Lorimer, *The Population of the Soviet Union*, p. 55.
26 The existence of Jewish agricultural workers is explicitly mentioned in the letter to the *New York Herald Tribune*; see Doc. 170.
27 The best example is the famous 'Lezginka' ensemble, half of whose members are Mountain Jews.
28 Important, if somewhat tendentious, research on the family structure of the Mountain Jews was carried out during 1947–8 by M. Ikhilov. See 'Bolshaya semya i patronimiya u gorskikh evreev', *Sovetskaya etnografiya*, 1950, no. 1, pp. 188–92.
29 Namir, *Shliḥut be-moskvah*, pp. 385–6.
30 After the contents of this article had become known and aroused indignation in the West, the authorities were obliged to reply in the traditional manner: they appointed a number of local Jews to handle the matter; see Doc. 170.
31 According to Mrs Rubin, who was interviewed by M. Altshuler, the synagogue in Makhachkala was situated in a single room, in which about forty men would gather on the Sabbath eve during the years 1967–8. See the Institute of Contemporary Jewry, tape 556/K.
32 Lorimer, *The Population of the Soviet Union*, p. 55.
33 Altshuler in Altshuler, Pinhasi & Zand (eds.), *Yehudei bukharah ve-ha-yehudim ha-harariim*, p. 29; see also the evidence of Dina Kuvent in her interview with Altshuler, Institute of Contemporary Jewry, tape 228/1, January 1973. Professor Zand, who visited Dagestan before emigrating to Israel, states: 'I was able to discern that in many families mostly members of the older generation spoke the language; the intermediate generation was bi-lingual, preferring Russian to Tat, whereas the younger generation, which, it is true, still understood Tat, did not use it as a language of communication, and the children scarcely understand the language.' See *Jewish Culture in the Soviet Union*, p. 141.
34 See *Jewish Culture in the Soviet Union*, p. 140.
35 For details, see the evidence of Valery Kuvent, the founder and director of the ensemble, in Altshuler, Pinhasi & Zand (eds.), *Yehudei bukharah ve-ha-yehudim ha-harariim*, pp. 41–2; see also the interview of M. Altshuler with Valery Kuvent on 1 January 1973, Institute of Contemporary Jewry, tape 224/A.
36 Evidence of this is given by a young Polish Jew who lived in Derbent during the war. When the Mountain Jews parted from him they said 'Shalom yerushalayim! Nizkeh lirotah!' (Jerusalem, Greetings! We shall live to see Jerusalem!); B. Yaakov, 'Im yehudei he-harim', *Davar*, 1 July 1946, as quoted by M. Altshuler in Altshuler, Pinhasi & Zand (eds.), *Yehudei bukharah ve-ha-yehudim ha-harariim*, p. 33.
    Another example of the Mountain Jews' longing for the Holy Land is found in a Soviet source. The Yiddish poet, Moshe Helmond, lived in Makhachkala during the war, and, it would appear, recorded a collection of folk poems from the mouth of a folk narrator, which appeared in *Eynikeyt* on 14 February 1946 under the title 'Shiroho'. For details, see M. Altshuler, 'Le-virur amamiut ha-epos shel ha-yehudim ha-harariim', *Beḥinot*, 1973, no. 4, pp. 108–17.
37 On the Bukharan Jews in general, see Y. Pinkasi, 'Yehudei bukharah' in Altshuler, Pinhasi & Zand (eds.), *Yehudei bukharah ve-ha-yehudim ha-harariim*, pp. 11–20; M. Zand, 'The Culture of the Mountain Jews of the Caucasus and the Culture of the Jews of Bukhara', in *Jewish Culture in the Soviet Union*, pp. 134–7; M. Zand, 'Bukharan Jewish Culture under Soviet Rule', *Soviet Jewish Affairs*, 1979, no. 2, pp. 15–23; Z. Amitin-Shapiro, *Ocherk pravovogo byta sredneaziatskikh evreev* (Essay on the Legal

Customs of Central Asian Jews), Tashkent–Samarkand, Uzbekgiz, 1931; L. Kantor, *Tuzemnye evrei v Uzbekistane* (The Indigenous Jews of Uzbekistan), Tashkent–Samarkand, Uzbekgiz, 1929.

38 According to Amitin-Shapiro, it was only in 1927 that Soviet institutions such as the courts (in the Bukharan Jewish language) and police stations begin functioning properly in place of the former autonomous institutions; see *Ocherk pravovogo byta sredneaziatskikh evreev*, p. 10.

39 Kantor, *Tuzemnye evrei v Uzbekistane*, p. 10. To this figure can be added about 2,000–3,000 Bukharan Jews who were living at this time outside Uzbekistan. Amitin-Shapiro claims that the figures adduced by Kantor are totally unreliable; *Ocherk pravovogo byta sredneaziatskikh evreev*, p. 40.

40 See Kantor, *Tuzemnye evrei v Uzbekistane*, p. 13.

41 See Z. Amitin-Shapiro, 'Sredneaziatskie evrei posle Oktyabrskoi revolyutsii', *Sovetskaya etnografiya*, 1938, no. 1, p. 54.

42 E.g. Eliav, *Between Hammer and Sickle*, pp. 222–30.

43 The assertion that 20% of the specialists in the Uzbek Republic are Jews, in spite of their constituting only 2% of the population of the republic (see Doc. 55), does not help us since both Bukharan and Ashkenazi Jews are included in this figure.

44 See Kantor, *Tuzemnye evrei v Uzbekistane*, p. 28.

45 An official Soviet source gives details on the existence of synagogues in Tashkent, Samarkand, Andizhan, Kokand and Bukhara. See Chapter 8, n. 39.

46 Zand in *Jewish Culture in the Soviet Union*, p. 145.

47 Kantor, *Tuzemnye evrei v Uzbekistane*, p. 22.

48 From 1929, the name of the newspaper, which appeared twice weekly, was *Bairoki mikhnat*. From 1933, it appeared daily in 7,000 copies. In the second half of the 1930s, the newspapers *Roi Lenini* and *Oktyabr* began appearing. See Amitin-Shapiro, *Ocherk pravovogo byta sredneaziatskikh evreev*, and 'Iz otcheta o komandirovke 1936 goda v natsionalnye raiony sredneaziatskikh respublik', *Sovetskaya etnografiya*, 1937, no. 4, p. 144.

49 The emphasis in the Soviet academic press and literature on the contribution of the Bukharan Jews to the Tadzhik and Uzbek cultures sometimes deludes the inexperienced reader into thinking that an independent, rich and comprehensive Bukharan Jewish culture exists to this very day. However, the reference is only to artists and writers of Jewish birth, who work within the framework of the cultures of the nationalities among whom they live. See, for example, Doc. 172.

50 See Shulamit Tylayov in Altshuler, Pinhasi & Zand (eds.), *Yehudei bukharah ve-ha-yehudim ha-harariim*, p. 40.

51 See also R. Loewenthal, 'The Extinction of the Krimchaks in World War II', *The American Slavic and East European Review*, 1951, no. 2, pp. 130–6.

52 Lorimer, *The Population of the Soviet Union*, p. 55.

53 This is one of few books appearing in the USSR in the 1950s to contain a fairly extensive demographic analysis of Soviet Jewry. The author, S. A. Tokarev, a leading Soviet ethnographer, has expressed his anti-assimilationist attitude and, to a certain extent, his positive attitude to Jewish national existence in the Soviet Union as well; see also Doc. 3.

54 The Historical-Ethnographic Museum of the Georgian Jews was established on 23 November 1933 with the aim of training young cadres of research workers from among the Jews of Georgia to undertake research in the history and ethnography of the Caucasian Jews in general and the Georgian Jews in particular. The museum began its practical work in 1935.

　　After the war the important work of collecting material on the Jews of Kutaisi was carried out. In 1948, an exhibition dedicated to the culture and art of the Georgian Jews was organised. Despite the liquidation of Jewish institutions in the Soviet

Union in the years 1948–9, and the arrest of the museum's Director, A. Krikheli, in 1949, the museum continued to exist for a number of years. In 1952, it was liquidated by order of the Georgian SSR's Ministry of Culture. Some of the exhibits were transferred to other museums, unique books to the Scientific Library of the Georgian Academy of Sciences, and a considerable amount of material was burnt on the orders of the liquidation commission.

55 Aron Meirovich Krikheli (1906–74), historian and ethnographer, was born in Tskhinvali (Georgia). He studied in Tbilisi. From 1928 to 1943, he was Director of the Literature Section at the People's Commissariat of Education of the Georgian SSR. From 1934 to 1949 he was Director of the Historical-Ethnographic Museum of the Georgian Jews. In 1949, he was arrested, and later rehabilitated.

56 Itska Rizhinashvili (1885–1906), Georgian revolutionary. An outstanding historical personality in the Georgian revolutionary movement, Rizhinashvili was born into a poor Jewish family in Kutaisi. Endowed with great ability, he secured an education at the Kutaisi *gymnasium*. Rizhinashvili saw in the revolutionary movement a way of liberating the Jews from the Tsarist regime. He escaped to Germany with a price on his head and continued his studies in Leipzig. In 1906, despite the pleas of his relatives, he returned to Kutaisi. He was shot while trying to avoid arrest.

Rizhinashvili's life was the subject of a play by Herzl Baazov, which was translated from Georgian into Yiddish and Russian. The play reached a final dress rehearsal before being withdrawn. See B. Yakobishvili, 'Kultura evreistva Gruzii', *Sion*, 1972, no. 1, p. 51.

57 Harrison Evans Salisbury (1908–), journalist. Salisbury was born in Minneapolis. He studied at the University of Minnesota, and worked for United Press International from 1930 to 1948. From 1949 to 1954, he served as the Moscow correspondent of *The New York Times*.

58 It would seem that this is not Aron Krikheli, who was Director of the museum from its establishment until the day of his arrest in 1949.

59 Ikhilov is himself one of the Mountain Jews. In the 1950s and 1960s he published a number of works on the national question in the Soviet Union, but he did not deal with the question of Soviet Jewry in general or the Mountain Jews in particular in these articles. Ikhilov voices the assimilationist trend which supports the idea of the mingling of nationalities, the main expression of which is their linguistic and cultural Russification. See also Doc. 167.

60 Mishi Bakhshiev (1910–72), Tat poet and dramatist, was one of the founders of Tat literature in the late 1920s and early 1930s.

61 Manuvakh Dadashev (1913–43), Tat poet, was born in Derbent into a poor family. He worked on the Tat newspaper *Zakhmatkesh* where his first verses appeared. His narrative poem 'Two Letters' (1934), on the granting of equal rights to women, is well known. Dadashev fought and died in World War II.

62 Khizgil Avshalumov (1913–), Tat prose writer, began writing just before World War II. In 1967, he was awarded the S. Stalsky Republic Prize for his novel *The Bride With the Surprise* (1966).

63 Sergei Izgiyaev (1924–), Tat poet, took part in World War II. His publications include the anthology *Pesni molodosti* (Songs of Youth, 1959), *Dumy poeta* (A Poet's Thoughts, 1966), *Razgovor s serdtsem* (Conversation With the Heart, 1970).

64 Rozental lived for more than ten years (1938–48) among the Mountain Jews of the Caucasus, in the Kabardino-Balkar Autonomous Republic. He worked as a teacher in Nalchik in a school where the majority of the children of the Mountain Jews studied. Living in the midst of the Mountain Jews, he made many friends among them and had the opportunity to observe their way of life, customs, national predispositions and feelings. 'Among the Mountain Jews' is a chapter from the

author's book *Yidish lebn in ratfnarband* (Jewish Life in the Soviet Union), Tel Aviv, Perets Farlag, 1971.

65 *Hallel*, Psalms 113–18, recited as a unit in the liturgy on *Sukot, Ḥanukah*, Passover, *Shavuot*, the New Moon and in many communities on Israel's Independence Day.

66 On 4 November 1960, J. Newman published an article in the *New York Herald Tribune* on an alleged blood libel in Dagestan. The letter of the Dagestan Jews denying this allegation was sent to the Moscow correspondent of the New York Yiddish daily *Morgn frayheyt*, S. Rabinovich, who sent copies to *Morgn frayheyt* and the *New York Herald Tribune*. But only the former published the letter.

67 Evsei Isaakovich Peisakh, the author of the two articles on the Krymchaks which appeared in *Sovetish heymland*, is himself a Krymchak and lives in Leningrad. He devoted all his efforts to studying the history and culture of his people. He is the author of the entry 'Krymchaks' in the 3rd edition of the *Large Soviet Encyclopaedia* and the organiser of Krymchak exhibits at the Leningrad Ethnographic Museum.

68 Simon Dubnow (1860–1941), historian and political ideologist.

69 Albert (Avraham Eliyahu) Harkavy (1835–1919), Russian orientalist, scholar of Jewish history and literature, was born in Novogrudok, Belorussia. He studied at *yeshivot* and at the Universities of St Petersburg, Berlin and Paris. He began his literary and scientific work in 1861. In a series of essays and articles, Harkavy attempted to prove that many of the manuscripts and tombstone epitaphs which Firkovich claimed to have found in the Crimea were forgeries and were intended by him to obtain equality for the Karaites (but not for all the Jews) within the empire. (On Firkovich, see n. 71).

70 Shmuel Weissenberg (1867–1928), Russian physician and anthropologist, was born in Elizavetgrad in the Ukraine. He specialised in Jewish ethnic and physical characteristics, travelling widely, amassing material for anthropological studies of the Jews of Palestine, Syria, Iraq, North Africa and Yemen, and also of various Karaite communities.

71 Abraham Firkovich (1786–1874), Karaite leader and bibliographer, was born in Luck, Poland. He was concerned in establishing the independence of the Karaites from talmudic Judaism; in pursuit of this end he searched for old manuscripts and books that would prove that the Karaites had entered the Crimea from Byzantium and that it was the Karaites who had converted the Khazars to Judaism.

Glossary

ABWEHR (Ger.), military intelligence; counter-espionage service.

AGUDAT YISRAEL (Heb., 'Union of Israel), world Jewish movement and political party in Israel seeking to preserve orthodoxy.

ALIYAH LE-TORAH (Heb.), being called to Reading of the Law (Torah) in synagogue.

AM HA-AREẒ (Heb., 'people of the land'), in biblical Hebrew, generally denotes 'population' whether Israelite or non-Israelite; in Second Temple and Mishnaic Hebrew, a social concept used in a pejorative sense; in later times, a person ignorant of the Scriptures and Jewish ritual; ignoramus or boor.

ASHKENAZI (Heb., pl. *Ashkenazim*), Jews whose forefathers lived originally in Central or Eastern Europe and/or spoke Yiddish, as contrasted with Sephardi(m).

AVOT, see *Pirkei Avot*.

BAR-MIẒVAH (Heb., 'son of the commandment'), ceremony marking the initiation of a boy at the age of thirteen into the Jewish religious community.

BATKHN (Yid., 'entertainer'), jester, particularly at traditional Jewish weddings in Eastern Europe.

BLACK HUNDREDS, Russian nationalist, reactionary and anti-Semitic gangs, established in 1905, that perpetrated and encouraged pogroms.

BLOOD LIBEL, the allegation that Jews murder non-Jews, in order to obtain blood for the Passover or other rituals.

B'NAI B'RITH (Heb., 'sons of the Covenant'), the world's oldest Jewish service organisation, founded in New York in 1843.

BUND (Yid. abbr. of *Algemeyner yidisher arbeter bund in lite, polyn un rusland*, General Jewish Workers' Union in Lithuania, Poland and Russia), Jewish socialist movement founded in Vilna in 1897; supported Jewish national rights; Yiddishist and anti-Zionist.

CHEKA (Russ. abbr. of *Chrezvychainaya Komissiya po borbe s kontrrevolyutsiei, sabotazhem i spekulyatsiei*, the Special Commission for the Struggle against Counter-Revolution, Sabotage and Speculation), 1918–22; hence *Chekist* as a general term for member of the secret police in the USSR.

COMINFORM (Russ. abbr. of *Kommunisticheskoe informatsionnoe byuro*, Communist Information Bureau), international organisation of Communist parties, 1947–56.

CPSU, Communist Party of the Soviet Union.

DAFN (Yid.), pages of the Talmud.

EGLAH ARUFAH (Heb., 'the decapitated heifer'), an expiatory ceremonial for an untraceable murder prescribed in Deut. 21:1–9.

EIN YAAKOV, a collection of legends and homilies from the Talmud by Yaakov ben Shlomo ibn Habib (?1445–1515/16).

EL MALE RAḤAMIM (Heb., 'God full of compassion'), requiem prayer.

ESTRADA (Russ., 'variety, vaudeville'), institution embracing all the stage activities of variety artists in the Soviet Union.

ETROG (Heb., 'citron'), one of the 'four species' used on the festival of Sukot.

EVKOMBED (Russ. abbr. of *Evreisky komitet bednoty*, Jewish Committee of the Poor), established in Georgia, 1928, in order to initiate cultural and economic transformation (clubs, producer cooperatives etc.).

EVSEKTSIYA (Russ. abbr. of *evreiskaya sektsiya*, Jewish section), Jewish Section of the Communist Party of the Soviet Union, 1918–30.

GABAI (Heb.), official of a Jewish congregation.

GEMARA (Aram., 'completion', 'tradition'), traditions, discussions and rulings of Jewish scholars, commenting on and supplementing the Mishnah and forming part of the Babylonian and Palestinian Talmuds.

GESHEFT (Yid.), business.

GESTAPO (Ger. abbr. of *Geheime Staatspolizei*, Secret State Police), secret police in Nazi Germany.

GORDONIA, pioneering Zionist youth movement founded in Galicia in 1923 (named after A. D. Gordon).

GOY (Heb., 'people, nation'), gentile.

GYMNASIUM (Ger.); *gimnaziya* (Russ.), secondary or high school.

ḤABAD (Heb. abbr. of *ḥokhmah, binah, daat*, 'wisdom, understanding, knowledge'), Hasidic movement founded in Belorussia (also known as the Lubavich movement).

HAIDAMAKS, paramilitary bands that disrupted the social order in Polish Ukraine during the eighteenth century, and perpetrated massacres among the Jewish population.

ḤAKHAM (Heb., 'wise, sage'), title given to rabbinic scholars.

ḤALAH (Heb., 'loaf'), loaf of white bread used for the Sabbath and festivals.

HALLEL (Heb.), term denoting Psalms 113–118, when they form a unit in the liturgy. *Hallel* is recited as an expression of thanksgiving on festivals.

ḤALUZ (Heb.), pioneer, especially in agriculture, in Israel.

ḤANUKAH (Heb., 'dedication'), an annual eight-day festival celebrating the victory of the Maccabees over the Syrian king Antiochus Epiphanes and the subsequent re-dedication of the Temple.

HA-POEL HA-MIZRAḤI (Heb., 'The Worker of the East'), religious pioneering and labour movement in Israel, founded in 1922.

HA-SHOMER (Heb., 'The Watchman'), association of Jewish watchmen in Israel, founded in 1909 to protect Jewish settlements.

HA-SHOMER HA-ẒAIR (Heb., 'The Young Guard'), Zionist youth movement formed in 1913.

ḤASIDUT (Heb., 'Hasidism'), a popular religious movement that emerged in the second half of the eighteenth century, characterised by mass enthusiasm, close-knit group cohesion and charismatic leadership, hence, Hasidim.

HA-TIKVAH (Heb., 'The Hope'), anthem of the Zionist movement and national anthem of the State of Israel.

ḤAVER (Heb., 'member'), the name for those belonging to a group that undertook to observe meticulously such laws as 'leave-offering' and 'tithing' (as opposed to the *am ha-arez*).

HEBRAISM, use of Hebrew words in Yiddish.

ḤEDER (Heb., pl. *ḥadarim*, 'room'), school for teaching children Jewish religious observance.

HISTADRUT (Heb. abbr. of *Ha-histadrut ha-klalit shel ha-ovdim ha-ivrim be-erez yisrael*, General Jewish Federation of Labour in Palestine), founded in 1920.

ḤOSEN MISHPAT (Heb.), fourth part of Joseph Caro's Code of Jewish Law, *Shulḥan Arukh*, dealing with civil, criminal law, court procedure, etc.

JARGON, unflattering term for Yiddish.

JEWISH ANTI-FASCIST COMMITTEE, 1941-48. A group of Soviet Jewish public figures organised to mobilise world Jewish support for the Soviet war effort.

JOINT DISTRIBUTION COMMITTEE (commonly known as JDC or the Joint), Jewish relief organisation founded in the USA in 1914.

JTA, Jewish Telegraphic Agency, founded 1919.

JUDENFREI (Ger., also *Judenrein*, 'cleansed of Jews'), Nazi term, referring to towns and regions after their entire Jewish population had been deported or killed.

JUDENRAT (Ger., 'Jewish Council'), Council set up in Jewish communities and ghettos under the Nazis to execute their instructions.

KABALAH (Heb.), most commonly used term for esoteric teachings of Judaism and Jewish mysticism.

KADISH (Aram.), prayer for the dead.

KARAITE (Heb., *karaim*), member of Jewish sect originating in the eighth century which rejected rabbinic Judaism, accepting only Scripture as authoritative.

KASHER (Heb., also *kosher*, 'fit, proper'), ritually permissible food.

KGB (Russ., *Komitet gosudarstvennoi bezopasnosti*, Committee for State Security), official name of secret police, since 1954.

KHOKHOL (Russ., pl. *khokhly*, 'tuft of hair'), pejorative term for Ukrainians (from their custom of shaving the head except for a single tuft of hair).

KOL NIDREI (Aram.), prayer with which evening service of Day of Atonement commences.

KOL ẒIYON LA-GOLAH (Heb., 'Voice of Zion to the Diaspora'), Israel Radio foreign broadcasting service.

KOMITET BEI ZHIDOV (Russ., 'Beat the Jews Committee'), anti-Semitic group taking name from popular slogan of Tsarist times, 'Beat the Jews: Save Russia!'

KOMZET (Russ., *Komitet po zemelnomu ustroistvu trudyashchikhsya evreev*, 'Committee for the Settlement of Jewish Toilers on the Land'), founded in 1924.

KRISTALLNACHT (Ger., 'crystal night' meaning 'night of broken glass'), organised destruction of synagogues, Jewish houses and shops, which took place in Germany and Austria on the night of 9–10 November 1938.

LADINO, Judeo-Spanish, the spoken and written Hispanic language of Jews of Spanish origin.

LEBENSRAUM (Ger., 'living space'), Nazi term for territory believed to be necessary for national existence.

LEF (Russ. abbr. of *Levy front iskusstv*, Left Front of the Arts), a group of writers and critics associated with the journals *Lef* (1923–5) and *Novy Lef* (1927–8).

LUBYANKA, central prison in Moscow.

LUFTMENTSH (Yid.), term describing the many poverty-stricken Jews of Eastern Europe who had no fixed occupation.

LULAV (Heb., 'palm branch'), one of the 'four species' used on the festival of *sukot*.

MAARIV (Heb.), evening prayer.

MACCABEE, additional name given to Judah, son of Mattathias, military leader of revolt against Syria in 168 B.C.E.; also applied to his family as well as to the Hasmonean dynasty as a whole.

MAME-LOSHN (Yid.), mother tongue, esp. the Yiddish language.

MAPP (Russ. abbr. of *Moskovskaya assotsiatsiya proletarskikh pisatelei*, Moscow Association of Proletarian Writers).

MAQUIS, French resistance movement during World War II.

MARRANO, descendant of Jews in Spain and Portugal whose ancestors had been converted to Christianity under pressure but who secretly observed Jewish rituals.

MAẒAH (Heb., pl. *mazot* 'unleavend bread'), the only bread permitted for use during Passover.

MEKHILTA (Aram., 'measure'), collection of materials dealing with rabbinic law.

MENORAH (Heb.), candelabrum; seven-branched oil lamps used in the Tabernacle and Temple; also eight-branched candelabrum used on Ḥanukah.

MESHULAḤ (Heb.), emissary sent to raise funds for rabbinical academies or charitable institutions.

MIKVEH (Heb.), ritual bath.

MINḤAH (Heb.), afternoon prayer.

MINYAN (Heb.), group of ten male adult Jews, the minimum required for communal prayer.

MISHNAH (Heb.), earliest codification of Jewish Oral Law.

MOHEL (Heb.), official performing circumcisions.

MOPR (Russ. abbr. of *Mezhdunarodnaya organizatsiya pomoshchi bortsam revolutsii*, International Organisation of Aid to Revolutionary Fighters), founded in 1922.

NARKOMNATS (Russ. abbr. of *Narodny komissariat po delam natsionalnostei*, People's Commissariat for Nationality Affairs), 1917–24.

NAROD (Russ.), people.

NARODNOST (Russ.), small nationality, ethnic group, in the Soviet Union.

NATSIONALNOST (Russ.), nationality.

NEDARIM (Heb. 'vows'), third tractate of the order *Nashim* of the Mishnah.

NEP (Russ. abbr. of *Novaya ekonomicheskaya politika*, New Economic Policy), 1921–8. Measures taken to restore the Soviet economy after the Civil War and termed 'state capitalism' by Lenin. The *Nepmen* (a generally pejorative term): traders and manufacturers benefiting from the relatively free market.

NKVD (Russ. abbr. of *Narodny komissariat vnutrennikh del*, People's Commissariat for Internal Affairs), name for secret police.

NOMENKLATURA (Russ.), Soviet system by which the appointment to specified posts in government and administration are made by organs of the Communist Party.

OBLAST (Russ., province), an administrative division of the USSR.

OKHRANA (Russ., coll.), Secret Police Department in Tsarist Russia.

OPERATION KADESH (Heb., *Mivza Kadesh*), Sinai Campaign, the 1956 Egypt–Israel War.

ORGBURO (Russ. abbr. of *Organizatsionnoe byuro*, Organisational Bureau), one of the top committees of the Soviet Communist Party in the 1920s and 1930s.

ORT (Russ. abbr. of *Obshchestvo remeslennogo i zemledelcheskogo truda sredi evreev v Rossii*, The Society for Craft and Agricultural Labour among the Jews in Russia), founded in 1880.

OSOBOE SOVESHCHANIE (Russ.), special committee of the NKVD (secret police).

OVIR (Russ. abbr. of *Otdel viz i registratsii*, Department of Visas and Registration); handles the applications for emigration.

OZE (Russ. abbr. of *Obshchestvo okhranenii zdorovya evreiskogo naseleniya*, The Society for the Health Protection of the Jewish Population), founded in 1912.

OZET (Russ. abbr. of *Obshchestvo zemleusroistva evreiskikh trudyashchikhsya v SSSR*, Society for the Settlement of Jewish Toilers on the Land), founded in 1925.

PALE OF SETTLEMENT, twenty-five provinces of Tsarist Russia where Jews were permitted permanent residence.

PASSOVER (Heb., *Pesaḥ*), a spring festival, commemorates the Exodus from Egypt.

PESAḤIM (Heb., 'paschal lambs'), a tractate in the Mishnah.

PIRKEI AVOT (Heb., 'Ethics of the Fathers'), ninth tractate of the order 'Damages' in the Mishnah; a collection of ethical maxims of the sages.

POALEI ẒIYON (Heb., 'Workers of Zion'), a labour Zionist movement which came into existence in Russia at the turn of the century.

POLITBURO (Russ.), the Politbureau (Political Bureau of the Central Committee of the Communist Party), highest policy-making body in the Soviet Union.

PPR (Pol., *Polska Partia Robotnicza*), Polish Workers' Party.

PURIM, festival held in commemoration of the delivery of the Jews of Persia in the time of Esther.

RAION (Russ.), district; administrative division of USSR, one level lower than the *oblast*.

RAPP (Russ. abbr. of *Russkaya assotsiatsiya proletarskikh pisatelei*, Russian Association of Proletarian Writers), an organisation of militantly Communist writers, founded 1925, disbanded by the regime in 1932.

ROSH HA-SHANAH, two-day holiday at the beginning of the month of Tishri (September–October), the Jewish New Year.

SAMIZDAT (Russ., coll.), unauthorised reproduction in the USSR of works lacking official approval.

SD (Ger. abbr. of *Sicherheitsdienst*, 'security service'), security service of the SS formed in 1932 as the intelligence organisation of the Nazi party.

SEDER NASHIM (Heb., 'Order of Women'), an order of the Mishnah.

SEKILAH (Heb.), death by stoning.

SEPHARDI (Heb., pl. *sephardim*), Jew(s) of Spain and Portugal and their descendants, wherever resident, as contrasted with Ashkenazi(m).

SHAHARIT (Heb.), morning service.

SHAMASH (Heb.), synagogue beadle.

SHEMA YISRAEL (Heb., 'Hear, O Israel', Deut. 6:4), Judaism's confession of faith, proclaiming the absolute unity of God.

SHOHET (Heb.), person qualified to perform ritual slaughtering of animals.

SHTETL (Yid.), Jewish small-town community in Eastern Europe.

SIDUR HA-SHALOM (Heb., 'Prayer-book of Peace'), the authorised Jewish daily prayer book in the Soviet Union. (*Sidurim*, prayer books.)

SIFRA (Aram., 'Book'), collection of rabbinic statements expounding the Book of Leviticus.

SIMHAT TORAH (Heb., 'Rejoicing of the Law'), holiday marking the completion in the synagogue of the annual cycle of reading the Pentateuch; the last day of Sukot.

SOVINFORMBURO (Russ. abbr. of *Sovetskoe informatsionnoe byuro*, Soviet Information Bureau), department of the Soviet Foreign Ministry responsible for propaganda during and after World War II.

SR (Russ. abbr. of *Sotsialisty-revolyutsionery*, Socialist Revolutionaries), the Party of Socialist Revolutionaries, founded in 1902.

SUKOT (Heb.), feast of Tabernacles.

TALMUD (Heb., 'teaching'), compendium of discussions on the Mishnah by generations of scholars and jurists in many academies over a period of several centuries.

TALMUD TORAH (Heb.), term generally applied to Jewish religious study; also to traditional Jewish religious public schools.

TAMIZDAT (Russ., coll.), the publication abroad of unauthorised manuscripts written in the USSR.

TASS (Russ. abbr. of *Telegraficheskoe agentsvo sovetskogo soyuza*, Telegraphic Agency of the Soviet Union), founded 1925, the official press agency of the USSR.

TEVAH (Heb., 'ark'), Noah's ark.

TEVET (Heb.), tenth month of Jewish religious year, fourth of the civil, approximating to December–January.

TORAH (Heb.), Pentateuch or the pentateuchal scroll for reading in synagogue; or the entire body of traditional Jewish teaching and literature.

TOSEFTA (Aram.), collection of teachings and traditions of rabbinic teachers, closely related to the Mishnah.

UBI BENE, IBI PATRIA (Lat., 'Wherever convenient, there is my fatherland'); phrase often used to condemn lack of patriotism.

ULPAN (Heb.), centre for intensive study of Hebrew by adults.

UNION OF THE ARCHANGEL MICHAEL, Russian anti-Semitic movement founded in 1907.

UNION OF THE RUSSIAN PEOPLE, right-wing, anti-Semitic political movement founded in Russia in 1905.

UPI, abbr. of United Press International.

VAPP (Russ., abbr. of *Vsesoyuznaya assotsiatsiya proletarskikh pisatelei*, All-Union Association of Proletarian Writers).

VYGOVOR (Russ.), reprimand; *strogy vygover*, severe reprimand.

WMCA, radio station in New York.

YESHIVAH (Heb., pl. *yeshivot*), Jewish traditional academy devoted to study of rabbinic literature.

YIDISHKEYT (Yid.), Jewishness, Judaism.

YISHUV (Heb.), the Jewish community of Palestine in the pre-State period.

YIVO (abbr. of *Yidisher visenshaftlekher institut*, Institute for Jewish Research), the principal world organisation conducting research in Yiddish, founded in 1925.

YIZKOR (Heb., 'He shall remember'), opening word of memorial prayer for close relatives, popularly applied to the whole memorial service.

YUDUSHKA (Russ. pejorative), Judas, traitor.

ZADIK (Heb.), person outstanding for his faith or piety; especially a Hasidic rabbi or leader.

ZEIREI ZIYON (Heb., 'Young Men of Zion'), Zionist movement (founded by and for young people), active mainly in Russia, dating from approximately the period of the 1905 revolution.

ZHDANOVSHCHINA (Russ.), draconian restrictions on Soviet literature and cultural life (as justified in the pronouncements of A. A. Zhdanov, 1946–8).

ZHID (Russ., pejorative), Jew.

ZHIDOVSKAYA MORDA (Russ., pejorative), Jew face.

ZOHAR, mystical commentary on the Pentateuch; central book of the *Kabalah*.

Select bibliography

Bibliographies

Altshuler, M. *Yahadut brit ha-moazot be-aspaklariah shel itonut yidish be-polin; Bibliografia, 1945–70* (Soviet Jewry in the Mirror of the Yiddish Press in Poland; Bibliography 1945–70), Jerusalem, Hebrew University, 1975.

Braham, R. L. *Jews in the Communist World*, New York, Twayne Publishers, 1961

Cohen, I. & Shmeruk, Ch. (eds.). *Pirsumim yehudiim bi-vrit ha-moazot 1917–1960* (Jewish Publications in the Soviet Union 1917–1960), Jerusalem, Historical Society of Israel, 1961

Dombrowska, D. & Pinkus, B. (eds.). *Yahadut brit ha-moazot be-aspaklariah shel ha-periodikah ha-maaravit* (Soviet Jewry in the Mirror of Western Periodicals), Jerusalem, Centre for Research and Documentation of East European Jewry, 1972

Fluk, L. R. *Jews in the Soviet Union*, New York, The American Jewish Committee, 1975

Orenstein, S. *Source Book on Soviet Jewry, An Annotated Bibliography*, New York, The American Jewish Committee, 1981

Pinkus, B. *Yahadut brit ha-moazot, 1917–1973* (Soviet Jewry, 1917–1973), Jersualem, The Zalman Shazar Center, 1974

Pinkus, B., Greenhaum, A. & Altshuler, M. (eds.). *Pirsumim rusiim al yehudim ve-yahadut bi-vrit ha-moazot* (Russian Publications on Jews and Judaism in the Soviet Union), Jerusalem, Society for Research on Jewish Communities, The Historical Society of Israel, 1970

Rosenberg, L. R. *Jews in the Soviet Union: An Annotated Bibliography, 1967–1971*, New York, The American Jewish Committee, 1971

Rothenberg, J. *An Annotated Bibliography of Writings on Judaism in the Soviet Union, 1960–1965*, Waltham, Mass., Brandeis University, 1969

Soviet Jewry: A Selected Bibliography, London, The Institute of Jewish Affairs, 1971

Periodicals

Alon yediot shel Maoz, Tel Aviv, 1964–

Behinot, Tel Aviv–Jerusalem, 1970–9

Bulletin on Soviet and East European Jewish Affairs, London, Institute of Jewish Affairs, 1968–1970

Focus on Soviet Jewry, London. Published irregularly, 1968–72

Gesher, Tel Aviv, 1953–

He-avar, Tel Aviv, 1952–75

Jewish Observer Newsletter, London, 1958–9

Jews in Eastern Europe, London, 1959–75

Shvut, Tel Aviv, 1973–

Soviet Jewish Affairs, London, Institute of Jewish Affairs, 1971–

Yalkut Magen, Tel Aviv, 1957

Yediot yisrael–S.S.S.R., Tel Aviv, 1947–59

Documents and statistics

The Anti-Stalin Campaign and International Communism, New York, Columbia University Press, 1956

Ben Arie, A. & Redlich, S. (eds.). *Evrei i evreiskii narod. Petitsii, pisma i obrashcheniya evreev SSSR* (Jews and Jewish People, Petitions, Letters and Appeals from Soviet Jews), Jerusalem, Centre for Research and Documentation of East European Jewry, 1973–82, 10 vols.

The Black Book: The Nazi Crime Against the Jewish People, New York, Jewish Black Book Committee, 1946

Brit ha-moazot u-tkumat yisrael. Divrei shliḥeihem shel amei s.s.s.r. ba-um uv-moezet ha-bitaḥon (The USSR and the Establishment of Israel. Speeches by Delegates of the Peoples of the USSR in the UN and Security Council), Tel Aviv, Sifriat poalim, 1950

Itogi vsesoyuznoi perepisi naseleniya 1959 goda (Results of the 1959 All-Union Population Census), Moscow, Gosstatizdat, 1962

Itogi vsesoyuznoi perepisi naseleniya 1970 goda (Results of the 1970 All-Union Population Census), Moscow, Statistika, 1973, vol. 4

Evrei i evreisky narod (Jews and the Jewish People), London Contemporary Library, 1960–

Evreisky samizdat (Jewish Samizdat), Jerusalem, Centre for Research and Documentation of East European Jewry, 1974–1982, 25 vols.

Narodnoe khozyaistvo SSSR v 1959–1970 (USSR Economy in 1959–1970), Moscow, Gosstatizdat, 1959–61; Moscow, Statistika, 1962–70

The Paneriai Museum, Vilnius, Minitis Publishing House, 1966

Pinkus, B. (compiler and editor). *Evrei i evreisky narod 1948–1953* (Jews and the Jewish People 1948–1953), Jerusalem, Centre for Research and Documentation of East European Jewry, 1973, 7 vols.

The Russian Jews in the War, London, 1943

The Second Soviet Jewish Anti-Fascist Meeting, Moscow, May 24, 1942, Moscow, Foreign Language Publishing House, 1942

Vysshee obrazovanie v SSSR (Higher Education in the USSR), Moscow, Gosstatizdat, 1961.

Monographs, memoirs and theses

Abosch, H. *Antisemitismus in Russland: Eine Analyse und Dokumentation zum Sowietischen Antisemitismus*, Darmstadt, Melzer, 1972

Admiration is not Enough: The Russian Jews in the War, London, Jewish Fund for Soviet Russia, n.d.

Agar, H. *The Saving Remnant: An Account of Jewish Survival*, New York, Viking, 1960

Allen, M. W. 'The Policy of the USSR towards the State of Israel', unpublished PhD, London University, 1961

Allilueva, S. *Only One Year*, New York–Evanston, Harper and Row, 1969

Allilueva, S. *Twenty Letters to a Friend*, New York–Evanston, Harper and Row, 1967

Allworth, E. *Nationality Group Survival in Multi-Ethnic States: Shifting Support Patterns in the Soviet Baltic Region*, New York, Praeger, 1977

Altshuler, M. *Ha-yevsektsiah bi-vrit ha-moazot (1918–1930). Bein leumiut le-komunizm* (The Jewish Section of the Communist Party of the USSR. Between Nationalism and Communism), Tel-Aviv. Sifriat poalim, 1980

Altshuler, M. *Ha-kibuz ha-yehudi bi-vrit ha-moazot be-yameinu, nituaḥ sozio-demografi* (Soviet Jewry Today. A Socio-Demographic Analysis), Jerusalem, Magnes Press, 1979

Altshuler, M., Pinhasi, B. & Zand, M. (eds.). *Yehudei bukharah ve-ha-yehudim ha-harariim: shnei kibuzim be-drom brit ha-moazot* (The Jews of Bukharah and the Mountain Jews,

Two Communities in the South of the Soviet Union), Jerusalem, The Institute of Contemporary Jewry, 1973

Anatoli, A. (Kuznetsov). *Babi Yar*, New York, Pocket Books, 1971

Anti-Semitism in the Soviet Union: Its Roots and Consequences, Jerusalem, Centre for Research and Documentation of East European Jewry, 1979–84 3 volumess.

Azbel, M. Y. *Refusenik, Trapped in the Soviet Union*, Boston, Houghton Mifflin, 1981

Barghoorn, F. *Soviet Russian Nationalism*, New York, Oxford University Press, 1956

Baron, S. *The Russian Jew under Tsars and Soviets*, New York, Macmillan, 1964; 2nd edition 1976

Belayev, I., Kolesnichenko, T. & Primakov, E. *The Dove has been Released (Soviet Review of Israel–Arab June 1967 Conflict)*, Washington, Joint Publications Research Service, 1968

Ben Horin. *Ma kore sham: sipuro shel yehudi mi-vrit ha-moazot* (What is Happening There: The Story of a Soviet Jew), Tel Aviv, Am oved, 1971

Ben Zvi, I. *The Exiled and the Redeemed*, Philadelphia, Jewish Publication Society, 1961

Berger, I. *Shipwreck of a Generation*, London, Harvill Press, 1971

Bland-Spitz, D. *Die Lage der Juden und die jüdische Opposition in der Sowjetunion 1967–1977* (The Situation of the Jews and the Jewish Opposition in the Soviet Union), Diessenhafen, Rügger Verlag, 1980

Blattberg, W. *The Story of the Hebrew and Yiddish Writers in the Soviet Union*, New York, Institute of Jewish Affairs, 1953

Brafman, M. & Schimel, D. *Trade for Freedom: Détente, Trade and Soviet Jews*, New York, Shengold Publishers, 1975

Braun, J. *Jews in Soviet Music* (Research Paper no. 34), Jerusalem, The Soviet and East European Research Centre, 1978

Brod, P. *Die Antizionismus- und Israelpolitik der UdSSR: Voraussetzung und Entwicklung bis 1956*, Baden-Baden, Nomos, 1980

Broderzon, S. M. *Mayn laydn-veg mit Moyshe Broderzon* (My Path of Suffering with Moshe Broderzon), Buenos Aires, Union Central Israelita Polaca en la Argentina, 1960

Brumberg, J. & Brumberg, A. *Sowyetish Heymland: an Analysis*, New York, Anti-Defamation League of B'nai B'rith, 1966

Bugaenko, E. *People I Know in Birobijan*, Moscow, Novosti Press, 1975

Cang, J. *The Silent Millions, A History of the Jews in the Soviet Union*, London, Rapp and Whiting, 1969

Carrère d'Encausse, H. *La Politique soviétique au Moyen-Orient*, Paris, Presses de la Fondation nationale des Sciences politiques, 1975

Carrère d'Encausse, H. *Decline of an Empire: Soviet Socialist Republics in Revolt*, London, Newsweek, 1980

Chossed, B. 'Reflections of the Soviet Nationalities Policy in Literature: The Jews 1938–1948', unpublished PhD, Columbia University, 1968

Cohen, E. *The New Red Anti-Semitism: A Symposium*, Boston, Beacon Press, n.d.

Cohen, R. (ed.) *Let My People Go*, New York, Popular Library, 1971

Conférence internationale sur la situation des Juifs en Union Soviétique, Paris, 1960

Conquest, R. *The Great Terror*, London, Macmillan, 1968

Conquest, R. *Power and Policy in the USSR*, New York, St Martin Press, 1961

Conquest, R. (ed.). *Religion in the USSR*, London, The Bodley Head, 1968

Dagan, A. *Moscow and Jerusalem*, New York, Abelard-Shuman, 1970

A Decade of Destruction: Jewish Culture 1948–1958, New York, Congress for Jewish Culture, 1958

De Witt, N. *Education and Professional Employment in the USSR*, Washington, National Science Foundation, 1961

Djilas, M. *Conversations with Stalin*, New York, Harcourt, Brace and World, 1962

Domalsky, I. *Russkie evrei vchera i segodnya* (Russian Jews Yesterday and Today), Jerusalem, Aliya, 1975

Don Ogen. *The Leningrad Branch of the RSFSR Union of Composers* (in Russian), Jerusalem, The Soviet and East European Research Centre, 1975

Dragunsky, D. *A Soldier's Life*, Moscow, Progress, 1977

Eckman, L. S. *Soviet Policy Towards Jews and Israel 1917–1974*, New York, Shengold Publishers, 1974

Economic Crimes in the Soviet Union, Geneva, Journal of the International Commission of Jurists, 1964 (vol. v, no. 47)

Eliashiv, S. *Ha-sifrut ha-sovietit ha-ḥadashah* (Modern Soviet Literature), Tel Aviv, Tverski, 1960

Eliashiv, S. *Rishmei masa* (Travel Notes), Tel Aviv, Am oved, 1951

Eliav, A. [Ben Ami]. *Between Hammer and Sickle*, Philadelphia, Jewish Publication Society of America, 1967

Embree, G. D. *The Soviet Union Between the 19th and 20th Party Congresses 1952–1956*, The Hague, Nijhoff, 1959

Emiot, E. *The Birobidzhan Affair: A Yiddish Writer in Siberia*, Philadelphia, The Jewish Publication Society of America, 1981

E[h]renburg, I. & Grossman, V. (eds.). *The Black Book. The Ruthless Murder of Jews by German-Fascist Invaders Throughout the Temporarily Occupied Regions of the Soviet Union and in the Death Camps of Poland During the War of 1941–1945*, New York, Holocaust Publications, 1981

E[h]renburg, I. *Men, Years, Life*, London, Macgibbon and Kee, 1962–6, 6 vols.

Erenburg,· I. *Sobranie sochinenii* (Collected Works), Moscow, Khudozhestvennaya literatura, 1964, 9 volumes

Even-Shoshan, S. *Sipuro shel masa esrim yom bi-vrit ha-moazot* (The Story of a Twenty-Day Journey to the USSR), Tel Aviv, Ha-kibuẓ ha-meuḥad, 1964

Evreiskaya avtonomnaya oblast (The Jewish Autonomous Oblast), Khabarovsk, khabarovskoe knizhnoe izdatelstvo, 1959

Fejtö, F. *Les Juifs et l'antisémitisme dans les pays communistes*, Paris, Plon, 1960

Feldman, E. *Kele le-lo sugar* (Prison Without Bars), Tel Aviv, Am ha-sefer, 1964

Frey, S. *The Truth about Jews in the Soviet Union*, New York, New Century Publishers, 1960

Friedberg, M. *The Jew in Post-Stalin Soviet Literature*, New York, B'nai B'rith International Council, 1970

Genin, I. *Palestinskaya problema* (The Palestine Problem), Moscow, Pravda, 1948

Gershtein, I. *Leksikon ha-gvurah* (Lexicon of Heroism), Jerusalem, Yad va-Shem, 1968

Gershuni, A. *Yahadut be-rusia-ha-sovietit: le-korot redifot ha-dat* (Judaism in Soviet Russia: The History of Religious Persecution), Jerusalem, Mosad ha-rav Kuk, 1961

Gilboa, Y. A. *The Black Years of Soviet Jewry, 1939–1953*, Boston, Little, Brown and Company, 1971

Gilboa, Y. A. *Lashon omedet al nafsha: tarbut ivrit bi-vrit ha-moazot* (A Language Will Survive: The Hebrew Culture in the Soviet Union), Tel-Aviv, Sifriat poalim, 1977

Gitelman, A. *The Jewish Religion in the USSR*, New York, Institute for Jewish Policy Planning and Research, Synagogue Council of America, 1971

Gitelman, Z. Y. *Assimilation, Acculturation and National Consciousness Among Soviet Jews*, Ann Arbor, University of Michigan (mimeo), 1972

Gitelman, Z. Y. *Jewish Nationality and Soviet Politics: The Jewish Sections of the CPSU, 1917–1930*, New Jersey, Princeton University Press, 1972

Glazer, N. *Perspectives of Soviet Jewry*, New York, B'nai B'rith, 1971

Gli Ebrei nell' URSS: a cura di 'Nuovi Argomenti', Milan, Garzanti editore, 1966

Gliksman, J. *Tell the West*, New York, The Gresham Press, 1948

Goldberg, B. Z. *The Jewish Problem in the Soviet Union*, New York, Crown Publishers, 1961

Goldhagen, E. (ed.). *Ethnic Minorities in the Soviet Union*, New York, Praeger, 1968

Goldman, G. *Zionism Under Soviet Rule (1917–1928)*, New York, Herzl Press, 1960

Goldstein, A. *The Soviet Attitudes Towards Territorial Minorities and the Jews*, New York, Institute of Jewish Affairs [1953?]

Govrin, Y. *Israel-Soviet Relations 1964–1966* (Research Paper no. 29), Jerusalem, The Soviet and East European Research Centre, 1978

Greenbaum, A. A. *Jewish Scholarship and Scholarly Institutions in Soviet Russia 1918–1953*, Jerusalem, Centre for Research and Documentation of East European Jewry, 1978

Grossman, M. *In the Enchanted Land*, Tel Aviv, Rachel, 1961

Grossman, V. *Forever Flowing*, trans. from the Russian by Thomas P. Whitney, New York, Harper and Row, 1972

Gurland, A. R. *Glimpses of Soviet Jewry*, New York, American Jewish Committee, 1948

Halevy, Z. *Jewish Schools under Czarism and Communism. A Struggle for Cultural Identity*, New York, Springer, 1976

Halevy, Z. *Jewish University Students and Professionals in Tsarist and Soviet Russia*, Tel Aviv, Diaspora Research Institute, 1976

Hayward, M. & Fletcher, W. (eds.). *Religion and the Soviet State*, New York, Praeger, 1969

Heller, M. *Le Monde concentrationnaire et la littérature soviétique*, Lausanne, l'Age d'Homme, 1974

Israel, G. *Les Juifs en URSS*, Paris, Edition spéciale, 1971

Israel, G. *The Jews in Russia*, New York, St Martin, 1975

Istoriya sovetskoi mnogonatsionalnoi literatury (The History of Soviet Multinational Literature), Moscow, Nauka, 1970, vol. 1, pp. 511–25; vol. 3, pp. 585–93

Ivanov, K. & Sheinis, Z. *Gosudarstvo Izrail: ego polozhenie i politika* (The State of Israel and its Situation and Policy), Moscow, Gospolitizdat, 1959

Ivanov, Y. *Ostorozhno sionizm. Ocherki po ideologii, organizatsii i praktike sionizma* (Beware Zionism. Essays on the Ideology, Organisation and Practice of Zionism), Moscow, Politizdat, 1969

Jewish Culture in the Soviet Union, Jerusalem, The Cultural Department of the World Jewish Congress, 1973

Johnson, P. & Labedz, L. (eds.). *Khrushchev and the Arts. The Politics of Soviet Culture, 1962–1964*, Cambridge Mass., MIT Press, 1965

Kahanovich, M. *Milḥemet ha-partizanim ha-yehudiim be-mizraḥ eiropah* (The War of the Jewish Partisans in Eastern Europe), Tel Aviv, Ayanot, 1954

Kaminska, I. *My Life, My Theatre*, New York, Macmillan, 1973

Kaminska-Turkow, R. *I Don't Want to be Brave Anymore*, Washington DC, New Republic Books, 1978

Katz, K. *Budapest, varshah, moskvah. Shagrir el medinot mitnakrot* (Budapest, Warsaw, Moscow. Ambassador to Alien States), Tel Aviv, Sifriat poalim, 1976

Katz, Z. (ed.). *Handbook of Major Soviet Nationalities*, New York, Free Press, 1975

Keren, I. *Ha-hityashvut ha-ḥaklait ha-yehudit ba-ḥatsi ha-i krim (1922–1947)* (Jewish Agricultural Settlement in the Crimean Peninsula, 1922–1947), Jerusalem, Z. Zak, 1973

Khrushchev Remembers, Boston, Little, Brown and Company, 1970

Khrushchev Remembers. The Last Testament, Boston, Little, Brown and Company, 1974

Klauzner, M. *Duaḥ al yahadut rusiah* (Report on Russian Jewry), Tel Aviv, Ha-igud li-kishrei tarbut hadadiim yisrael-brit ha-moaẓot, 1965

Kochan, L. (ed.). *The Jews in Soviet Russia Since 1917*, London, Oxford University Press, 1970; 2nd edition, 1972; 3rd edition 1978

Kolarz, W. *Religion in the Soviet Union*, New York, Macmillan, 1961

Korey, W. *The Soviet Cage; Anti-semitism in Russia*, New York, Viking Press, 1973

Krammer, A. *The Forgotten Friendship: Israel and the Soviet Bloc, 1947–1953*, University of Illinois Press, 1974

Kychko, T. *Yudaizm bez prykras* (Judaism Without Embellishment), Kiev, Vydav-
nytstvo Akademii Nauk URSS, 1963
Kychko, T. *Judaism and Zionism*, Kiev, Society 'Znanie', 1968 (stencil)
Laqueur, W. *The Struggle for the Middle East*, London, Routledge, 1969
Larin, Y. *Evrei i antisemitizm v SSSR* (Jews and Anti-Semitism in the USSR), Moscow,
Gosizdat, 1929
Lawrence, G. *Three Millions More*, New York, Doubleday & Company, 1970
Leftwich, I. *Abraham Sutskever: Partisan, Poet*, New York, T. Yoseloff, 1971
Leneman, L. *La Tragédie des juifs en URSS*. Paris, Desclée de Brouwer, 1959
Lenin, V. I. *Collected Works*, Moscow Foreign Languages Publishing House, 4th edition,
1961–70, 45 volumes
Lenin, V. I. *Sobranie sochinenii* (Collected Works), 5th edition, Moscow, Gospolitizdat,
1967–70, 55 vols.
Levin, D. *Lohamim ve-omdim al nafsham. Milhemet yehudei lita ba-nazim 1941–1945* (They
Fought Back: Lithuanian Jewry's Armed Resistance to the Nazis, 1941–1945),
Jerusalem, Institute of Contemporary Jewry, 1974
Levy, H. *Jews and the National Question*, London, Hillway, 1958
Lifshits, Y. & Altshuler, M. (eds.). *Briv fun yidishe sovetishe shreibers* (Letters of Soviet
Yiddish Writers), Jerusalem, Centre for Research and Documentation of East
European Jewry, 1979
Lorimer, F. *The Population of the Soviet Union: History and Prospects*, Geneva, The League of
Nations, 1946
Lvavi, I. *Ha-hityashvut ha-yehudit be-birobidzhan* (The Jewish Colonisation in
Birobidzhan), Jerusalem, The Historical Society of Israel, 1965
Macleod, J. *Actors Cross the Volga*, London, Allen and Unwin, 1946
Magid, D. *Evrei na Kavkaze* (Jews in the Caucasus), Petrograd, 1918
Maltinsky, K. *Der moskver mishpet iber di birobidzhaner* (The Moscow Trial on the
Birobidzhanians), Tel-Aviv, Naye lebn, 1981
Mandelstam, N. *Hope Abandoned*, New York, Atheneum, 1974
Mandelstam, N. *Hope Against Hope*, Harmondsworth, Penguin, 1975
Marki[ch], E. *Le Long Retour*, Paris, Laffont, 1974; English edition *The Long Return*,
New York, Ballantine, 1978
Marshall, R., Bird, T. E. & Blane, A. (eds.). *Aspects of Religion in the Soviet Union,
1917–1967*. Chicago–London, University of Chicago Press, 1971
Mayatsky, F. *Sovremenny yudaizm i sionizm* (Modern Judaism and Zionism), Kishinev,
Karta Moldovenyaske, 1961
Medvedev, Z. A. *The Rise and Fall of T. D. Lysenko*, New York–London, Columbia
University Press, 1969
Mikhoels. Stati, besedy, rechi. Stati i vospominaniya o Mikhoelse (Mikhoels. Articles, Talks,
Speeches, Articles and Reminiscences on Mikhoels), Moscow, Iskusstvo, 1981, 3rd
revised edition
Mushkat, M. (ed.). *Lohamim yehudiim be-milkhamah neged ha-nazim* (Jewish Fighters in
the War Against the Nazis), Tel Aviv, Sifrait poalim, 1961
Namir, M. *Shlihut be-moskvah* (Israeli Mission to Moscow), Tel Aviv, Am oved, 1971
Neishtat, M. *Yehudei gruzia. Maavak al ha-shivah le-ziyon* (The Jews of Georgia. A
Struggle for the Return to Zion), Tel Aviv, Am oved, 1970
Nekrich, A. *The Punished Peoples*, New York, W. W. Norton, 1978
Nikitina, G. *The State of Israel, A Historical, Economic and Political Study*, Moscow, Progress
Publishers, 1973
Nir, Ye. *The Israeli-Arab Conflict in Soviet Caricatures 1967–1973*, Tel Aviv, Tcherikover
Publishers, 1976
Orbach, W. *The American Movement to Aid Soviet Jews*, Amherst, University of Massa-
chusetts Press, 1979

Oren, M. *Reshimot asir prag* (Notes of a Prague Prisoner), Merḥavia, Ha-kibuẓ ha-arẓi shel ha-shomer ha-ẓair, 1958

Pelikan, J. (ed.). *The Czechoslovak Political Trials, 1950–1954*, London, Macdonald, 1970

Perspectives on Soviet Jewry, New York, Academic Committee on Soviet Jewry, 1971

Plisetsky, M. *Religiya i byt gruzinskikh evreev* (Religion and Way of Life of the Georgian Jews), Moscow, Moskovsky rabochy, 1931

Pnimi, P. *Ha-yehudim ha-sovietiim ve-goralam* (Soviet Jews and Their Fate), Tel Aviv, Am oved, 1959

Poliakov, L. *De l'antisionism à l'antisémitisme*, Paris, Calman-Levy, 1969

Pomerants, A. *Di sovetishe harugey malkhes* (The Jewish Writers Martyred by the Soviets), Buenos Aires, Yiddish Scientific Institute in Argentina, 1962

Pommer, H. I. *Antisemitismus in der UdSSR und in den Satellienstaaten*, Bern, Schweizerisches Ost-Institute, 1963

Powell, D. E. *Antireligious Propaganda in the Soviet Union. A Study of Mass Persuasion*, Cambridge, Mass., MIT Press, 1975

Prital, D. (ed.). *In Search of Self: The Soviet Jewish Intelligentsia and the Exodus*, Jerusalem, Mount Scopus Publications, 1982

Rabinovich, S. *Jews in the Soviet Union*, Moscow, Novosti Press, 1967

Rass, R. with Brafman, M. *From Moscow to Jerusalem*, New York, Shengold Publishers, 1976

Redlich, Sh. *Propaganda and Nationalism in Wartime Russia, The Jewish Antifascist Committee in the USSR, 1941–1948*, Boulder, Colorado, East European Monographs, 1982

Redlich, S. 'The Jews under Soviet Rule During World War II', unpublished PhD, New York University, 1968

Remenik, G. *Ocherki i portrety. Statyi o evreiskikh pisatelyakh* (Essays and Portraits. Articles on Jewish Writers), Moscow, Sovetsky pisatel, 1975

Rigby, T. H. *Communist Party Membership in the USSR 1917–1967*, New Jersey, Princeton University Press, 1968

Ro'i, Y. 'Yaḥasei brit ha-moaẓot-yisrael, 1947–1954g', (Soviet–Israel Relations), PhD, Jerusalem, Hebrew University, 1972

Ro'i, Y. *Soviet Decision Making in Practice. The USSR and Israel, 1947–1954*, New Brunswick, Transaction Books, 1980

Rosenberg, S. A. *Rabbi Reports on Russia*, Toronto, Toronto Star, 1961

Rosental, N. *Yidish lebn in ratnfarband* (Jewish Life in the Soviet Union), Tel Aviv, Perez Publishing House, 1971

Rosental-Shneyderman, E. *Naftulei drakhim* (Winding Paths), Tel Aviv, Ha-kibuẓ ha-meuḥad, 1970 and 1972, 2 vols.

Rothenberg, J. *The Jewish Religion in the Soviet Union*, New York, Ktav Publishing House, 1971

Rubin, R. (ed.). *The Unredeemed: Anti-Semitism in the Soviet Union*, Chicago, Quadrangle Press, 1968

Rudy, H. *Die Juden in der Sowjetunion: Schicksal und Nationalitätenpolitik*, Vienna, Europa-Verlag, 1966

Rukhadze, A. *Jews in the USSR: Figures, Facts, Comment*, Moscow, Novosti Press, 1978

Rusinek, A. *Like a Song, Like a Dream. A Soviet Girl's Quest for Freedom*, New York, Charles Scribner's Sons, 1973

Russian Jewry 1917–1967, New York, Yoseloff, 1969

Salisbury, H. *Moscow Journal: The End of Stalin*, Chicago, University of Chicago Press, 1961

Salisbury, H. *Russia on the Way*, New York, Macmillan, 1946

Salisbury, H. (ed.). *The Soviet Union: The Fifty Years*, New York, Harcourt Brace and World, 1967

Salisbury, H. *To Moscow and Beyond*, New York, Harper Brothers, 1960

Sasar, M. *Yisraeli be-moskvah, rishmei siyur bi-vrit ha-moazot* (An Israeli in Moscow, Impressions of a Trip to the USSR), Jerusalem, Kiriat sefer, 1961

Sawyer, T. *The Jewish Minority in the Soviet Union*, Boulder, Colorado, Westview Press, 1979

Schechtman, J. B. *Star in Eclipse: Russian Jewry Revisited*, New York. Yoseloff, 1961

Schechtman, J. B. *Zionism and Zionists in Soviet Russia, Greatness and Drama*, New York, Zionist Organisation of America, 1966

Schloss, R. *Lass mein Volk ziehem, Eine Dokumentation* (Let My People Go. Documents), Munich, Gunter Verlag, 1971

Schroeter, L. *The Last Exodus*, New York, Universal Books, 1974

Schulman, E. *A History of Jewish Education in the Soviet Union*, New York, Ktav Publishing House, 1971

Schulman, E. *Sovetish-yidishe literatur etyudn* (Soviet-Jewish Literary Studies), New York, Ziko, 1971

Schwarz, S. *The Jews in the Soviet Union*, New York, Syracuse University Press, 1951

Schwarz, S. *Evrei v Sovetskom Soyuze s nachala vtoroi mirovoi voiny (1939–1965)* (Jews in the Soviet Union from the Beginning of World War II, 1939–1965), New York, Amerikanisky evreisky rabochy komitet, 1966

Sefer ha-partizanim ha-yehudiim (Book of the Jewish Partisans), Merḥavia, Sifriat poalim, 1958, 2 vols.

Shafer, H. *The Soviet Treatment of Jews*, New York–London–Washington, Praeger, 1974

Shaham, N. *Pegishot be-moskvah 1957* (Meetings in Moscow 1957), Merḥavia, Sifriat poalim, 1957

Shindler, C. *Exit Visa, Détente, Human Rights and the Jewish Emigration Movement in the USSR*, London, Bachman and Turner, 1978

Shalev, M. *A Study of Soviet–Israel Relations*, Washington, 1954

Shein, J. *Arum moskver yidishn teater* (Around the Moscow Yiddish Theatre), Paris, 1964

Shneiderman, S. L. *Ilya Erenburg*, New York, Yiddisher kemfer, 1968

Shurer, Kh. *Arbaim yom bi-vrit ha-moazot* (Forty Days in the USSR), Tel Aviv, Am oved, 1961

Simmons, E. J. (ed.). *Through the Glass of Soviet Literature: Views of Russian Society*, New York, Columbia University Press, 1953

Skoizylas, E. *The Realities of Soviet Antisemitism*, Philadelphia, University of Pennsylvania, 1964

Sloves, H. *La Culture juive en URSS*, Paris, La Vie Juive, 1959

Sloves, H. *Mamlaḥtiut yehudit bi-vrit ha-moazot: yovla shel birobidzhan* (Jewish Statehood in the USSR: Fifty years of Birobidzhan), Tel Aviv, Am oved, 1980

Smolar, B. *Soviet Jewry: Today and Tomorrow*, New York, Macmillan Company, 1971

Smoliar, H. *Heikhan ata haver sidorov?* (Where Are You, Comrade Sidorov?), Tel Aviv, Am oved, 1973

Smoliar, H. *Oyf der letster pozitsye, mit der letster hofenung* (On the Last Position, With the Last Hope), Tel Aviv, Perez Publishing House, 1982

Soifer, P. E. *Soviet Jewish Folkloristics and Ethnography: An Institutional History, 1918–1948*, New York, Yivo Institute, 1978

Stalin, I. V. *Sochineniya* (Works), Moscow, Gospolitizdat, 1949–54, 13 vols.

Stalin, I. V. *Sochineniya* (Works), Stanford, Hoover Institute of War, Revolution and Peace, 1967, 1–3 (14–16) competing vols. Soviet edition.

Stalin, I. V. *Works*, Moscow, Foreign Languages Publishing House, 1953

Svirsky, G. *Zalozhniki* (The Hostages), Paris, Editeurs Réunis, 1974

Svirsky, G. *Hostages: The Personal Testimony of a Soviet Jew*, New York, Knopf, 1976

Szajkowski, Z. *Jews, Wars and Communism*, New York, Ktav Publishing House, 1972–4, 2 vols.

Szajkowski, Z. *An Illustrated Sourcebook of Russian Antisemitism, 1881–1978*, New York, Ktav Publishing House, 1980

Tatu, M. *Le Pouvoir en URSS de Khroushtchev à la direction collective*, Paris, Grasset, 1967

Tatu, M. *Power in the Kremlin: from Khrushchev's Decline to Collective Leadership*, London, Collins, 1969

Teller, J. L. *The Kremlin, the Jews and the Middle East*, New York, Yoseloff, 1957

Tiktina, D. *A Rural Secondary School in the Ukraine, 1948–1952* (in Russian), Jerusalem, Soviet and East European Research Centre, 1978

Tillet, L. *The Great Friendship*, Chapel Hill, University of North Carolina Press, 1969

Timor, A. *Haverai la-krav: yehudim loḥamim ba-ẓava ha-sovieti* (My Battle Comrades, Jewish Fighters in the Soviet Army), Tel Aviv, Maarakhot, 1971

Ukrainians and Jews: A Symposium, New York, Ukrainian Committee of America, 1966

Vago, B. & Mosse, L. (eds.). *Jews and Non-Jews in Eastern Europe, 1918–1945*, New York, Wiley, 1974

Vaynroykh, N. *Blut oyf der zun* (Blood on the Sun), New York, Mensh un Yid, 1950

Villemarest, P. F. de, *La Marche au pouvoir en URSS*, Paris, Fayard, 1969

Vergelis, A. *On the Jewish Street. Travel Notes*, Moscow, Novosti Press, 1971

Volkov, S. (ed.). *Testimony: The Memoirs of Dmitri Shostakovich*, New York, Harper Colophon Books, 1979

Voronel, A. & Yakhot, V. (eds.). *Jewishness Rediscovered: Jewish Identity in the Soviet Union*, New York, Academic Committee on Soviet Jewry, 1974

Vovsi-Mikhoels, N. *Ani shlomo mikhoels* (I, Shlomo Mikhoels), Tel Aviv, Ha-kibuẓ ha-meuḥad, 1982

Weisberg, A. *Conspiracy of Silence*, London, Hamilton, 1952

Werth, A. *Russia: Hopes and Fears*, London, Penguin Books, 1969

West, B. *Ba-derekh le-geulah* (On the Road to Redemption), Tel Aviv, Tarbut ve-hinukh–Masadah, 1971

West, B. *Struggles of a Generation: The Jews under Soviet Rule*, Tel Aviv, Masadah, 1959

Weisel, E. *The Jews of Silence*, Philadelphia, Jewish Publication Society, 1967

Yahadut brit ha-moaẓot: maamarim u-reshimot (Soviet Jewry: Articles and Notes), Tel Aviv, Tarbut ve-ḥinukh, 1967

Yanasovich, Y. *Mit yidishe shrayber in rusland* (With Jewish Writers in Russia), Buenos Aires, Kiyum Farlag, 1959

Yehudi Sovieti Almoni (Anonymous Soviet Jew), *El aḥai bi-medinat yisrael* (To My Brothers in the State of Israel), Jerusalem, Kiryat sefer, 1957

Zerubabel, Y. *Bikur bi-vrit ha-moaẓot, reshamim u-fgishot* (A Visit to the USSR, Impressions and Encounters), Tel Aviv, Perez Publishing House, 1964

Zinger, L. *Dos banayte folk* (A People Reborn), Moscow, Der emes, 1948

Zinger, L. *Dos ofgerikhte folk* (A People Restored), Moscow, Der emes, 1948

Zohari, M,. Tartakover, A. & Zand, M. (eds.), *Hagut ivrit bi-vrit ha-moaẓot* (Studies on Jewish Themes), Jerusalem, World Hebrew Union and the Jewish Congress, 1976

Selected articles

Abramovich, M. 'Ktav ha-et ha-sovieti he-ḥadash be-yidish', *Molad*, 1962, no. 163, pp. 11–17

Abramsky, C. 'Russian Jews: a Bird's Eye View', *Midstream*, 1978, vol. XXIV, no. 10, pp. 34–43

Ainsztein, M. 'Jewish Tragedy and Heroism in Soviet Literature', *Jewish Social Studies*, 1961, vol. XXIII, pp. 67–84

Alexander, Z. 'Immigration to Israel from the USSR', *Israel Yearbook on Human Rights*, 1977, vol. VII, pp. 268–335

Altshuler, M. 'Georgian Jewish Culture under the Soviet Regime', *Soviet Jewish Affairs*, 1975, no. 2, pp. 21–38

Altshuler, M. 'Some Statistical Data on the Jews among the Scientific Elite of the Soviet Union', *Jewish Journal of Sociology*, 1973, no. 1, pp. 45–55

Beermann, R. 'Russian and Soviet Passport Laws', *Bulletin on Soviet Jewish Affairs*, 1968, no. 2, pp. vi/1–11

Ben-Shlomo, J. 'Khrushchev Apocrypha', *Soviet Jewish Affairs*, 1971, no. 1, pp. 52–75

Boim, L. 'The Passport System in the USSR and its Effect upon the Status of Jews', *Israel Yearbook on Human Rights*, 1975, vol. v, pp. 141–68

Brumberg, A. 'Sovyetish Heymland and the Dilemmas of Jewish Life in the USSR', *Soviet Jewish Affairs*, 1972, no. 3, pp. 27–41

Checinski, M. 'Soviet Jews and Higher Education', *Soviet Jewish Affairs*, 1973, no. 2. pp. 3–16

Choseed, B. 'Categorizing Soviet Yiddish Writers', *Slavic Review*, 1965, vol. xxvii, no. 1, pp. 102–8

Decter, M. 'The Status of the Jews in the Soviet Union', *Foreign Affairs*, 1963, vol. xli, pp. 420–30

Dinstein, Y. 'The International Human Rights of Soviet Jewry'. *Israel Yearbook on Human Rights*, 1972, vol. ii, pp. 194–210

Ettinger, S. 'The National Revival of Soviet Jewry', *Forum*, 1975, no. 23, pp. 124–44

Fish, D. 'The Jews in Syllabuses of World and Russian History: What Soviet School Children Read about Jewish History', *Soviet Jewish Affairs*, 1978, no. 1, pp. 3–25

Frankel, E. Rogovin. 'Russians, Jews and Solzhenitsyn', *Soviet Jewish Affairs*, 1975, no. 2, pp. 48–68

Frankel, J. 'The Anti-Zionist Press Campaigns in the USSR 1969–1971: An Internal Dialogue?', *Soviet Jewish Affairs*, 1972, no. 3, pp. 3–26

Gitelman, Z. 'The Jews', *Problems of Communism*, 1967, no. 5, pp. 92–101

Hen-tov, J. 'Contacts Between Soviet Ambassador Maisky and Zionist Leaders During World War II', *Soviet Jewish Affairs*, 1978, no. 2, pp. 46–55

Hirszowicz, L. 'Birobidzhan after Forty Years', *Soviet Jewish Affairs*, 1974, no. 2, pp. 38–47

Hirszowicz, L. 'Jewish Cultural Life in the USSR', *Soviet Jewish Affairs*, 1977, no. 2, pp. 3–21

Jacobs, E. M. 'Further Considerations on Jewish Representation in Local Soviets and in the CPSU', *Soviet Jewish Affairs*, 1978, no. 1, pp. 26–34

Jacobs, E. M. 'Jewish Representation in Local Soviets, 1959–1973', *Soviet Jewish Affairs*, 1976, no. 1, pp. 18–26

Litvak, I. 'Yehudim be-maarkhei ha-mada ve-hamehkar bi-vrit ha-moazot', *Shvut*, 1978, no. 6, pp. 7–16

Loewental, R. 'The Extinction of the Krimchaks in World War II', *American and East European Review*, 1951, no. 2, pp. 130–6

Loewental, R. 'The Judeo-Tats in the Caucasus', *Historia Judaica*, 1952, vol. xiv, pp. 61–82

Loewental, R. 'The Jews of Bukhara', *Revue des Etudes Juives*, 1961, vol. iii, no. 120, pp. 345–51

London, I. 'Days of Anxiety. A Chapter in the History of Soviet Jewry', *Jewish Social Studies*, 1953, vol. xv, no. 3–4, pp. 275–87

Lvavi, I. 'Ha-mahoz ha-yehudi ha-otonomi (birobidzhan) al saf shnot ha-shivim'. *Behinot*, 1974, no. 5, pp. 55–69

Minz, M. 'Mistifikatsiah sovietit shel ha-yehudi', *Shvut*, 1973, no. 1, pp. 28–34

Mowshowitz, J. 'Finding Babi Yar', *Worldview*, 1977 (January–February), pp. 29–36

Nove, A. 'Jews in the Soviet Union', *Jewish Journal of Sociology*, 1961, vol. iii, pp. 108–19

Palmor, E. 'Yahasei brit ha-moazot-yisrael (1947–1967)', *Behinot*, 1970, no. 1, pp. 97–111

Pinkus, B. 'Hitpathut ha-teoriah ba-beayah ha-leumit bi-vrit ha-moazot bi-tkufah sheleahar stalin (1953–1969)', *Behinot*, 1970, no. 1, pp. 35–55

Pinkus, B. 'Sefer haiav shel vasili grosman', *Molad*, 1971, no. 22, pp. 444–55

Pinkus, B. 'Soviet Campaigns Against Jewish Nationalism and Cosmopolitism, 1946–1953', *Soviet Jewish Affairs*, 1974, no. 2, pp. 53–72

Pinkus, B. 'The Emigration of National Minorities from the USSR in the Post-Stalin Era', *Soviet Jewish Affairs*, 1983, no. 1, pp. 3–36

Redlich, S. 'The Erlich–Alter Affair', *Soviet Jewish Affairs*, 1979, no. 2, pp. 24–45

Ro'i, Y. 'Emdat brit ha-moazot le-gabei ha-aliyah ke-gorem bi-mediniut klapei ha-sikhsukh ha-yisraeli-aravi (1954–1967)', *Behinot*, 1974, no. 5, pp. 28–41

Rothenberg, J. 'How Many Jews Are in the Soviet Union', *Jewish Social Studies*, 1967, no. 4, pp. 234–40

Rutman, R. 'Solzhenitsyn and the Jewish Question', *Soviet Jewish Affairs*, 1974, no. 2, pp. 3–16

Schapiro, L. B. 'Anti-Semitism in the Communist World', *Soviet Jewish Affairs*, 1979, no. 1, pp. 42–52

Schmelz, U. O. 'Al baayot yesod ba-demografiah shel yehudei brit ha-moazot', *Behinot*, 1974, no. 5. pp. 42–58

Schmelz, U. O. 'New Evidence on Basic Issues in the Demography of Soviet Jews', *Jewish Journal of Sociology*, 1974 (December), pp. 209–29

Sergin, A. 'Jews and the October Revolution in Recent Soviet Literature', *Soviet Jewish Affairs*, 1971, no. 2, pp. 68–79

Shmeruk, Ch. 'Ha-tarbut ha-yehudit bi-vrit ha-moazot', *Gesher*, 1966, no. 2–3, pp. 58–64

Shmeruk, Ch. 'Sifrut yidish bi-vrit ha-moazot', *Behinot*, 1970, no. 1, pp. 5–26

Shneiderman, S. L. 'Ilya Ehrenburg Reconsidered', *Midstream*, 1968, vol. XIV, no. 8, pp. 47–67

Shneiderman, S. L. '*Sovietish Heimland* and its Editor, Aron Vergelis', *Midstream*, 1971, vol. XVII, no. 8, pp. 28–42

Silver, B. 'The Status of National Minority Languages in Soviet Education: An Assessment of Recent Changes', *Soviet Studies*, 1974, vol. XXVI, no. 1, pp. 28–40

Smolar, B. 'Discovering the Jews of Bukhara', *Jewish Affairs*, 1974 (April), pp. 51–7

Sonntag, I. 'Yiddish Writers and Jewish Culture in the USSR: Twenty Years After', *Soviet Jewish Affairs*, 1972, no. 2, pp. 31–8

Yodfat, A. 'Yahasei brit ha-moazot-yisrael (1953–1967)', *Shvut*, 1973, no. 1, pp. 110–18

Yodfat, A. 'Jewish Religious Communities in the USSR', *Soviet Jewish Affairs*, 1971, no. 2, pp. 61–7

Yodfat, A. 'Rabbis and Jewish Clergy in the USSR, 1917–1974', *Judaism*, 1972, vol. XXI, no. 2, pp. 184–94

Zand, M. 'Bukharan Jewish Culture under Soviet Rule', *Soviet Jewish Affairs*, 1979, no. 2, pp. 15–23

Zivanovic, J. 'Little-Known Theatre of Widely Known Influence', *Education Theatre Journal*, 1973, no. 27, pp. 231–44

Index

Foreign journals, newspapers etc. are indexed under the first word in the title, including definite or indefinite article.